CASS LIBRARY OF AFRICAN STUDIES

GENERAL STUDIES

No. 87

Editorial Adviser: JOHN RALPH WILLIS

Centre of West African Studies, University of Birmingham

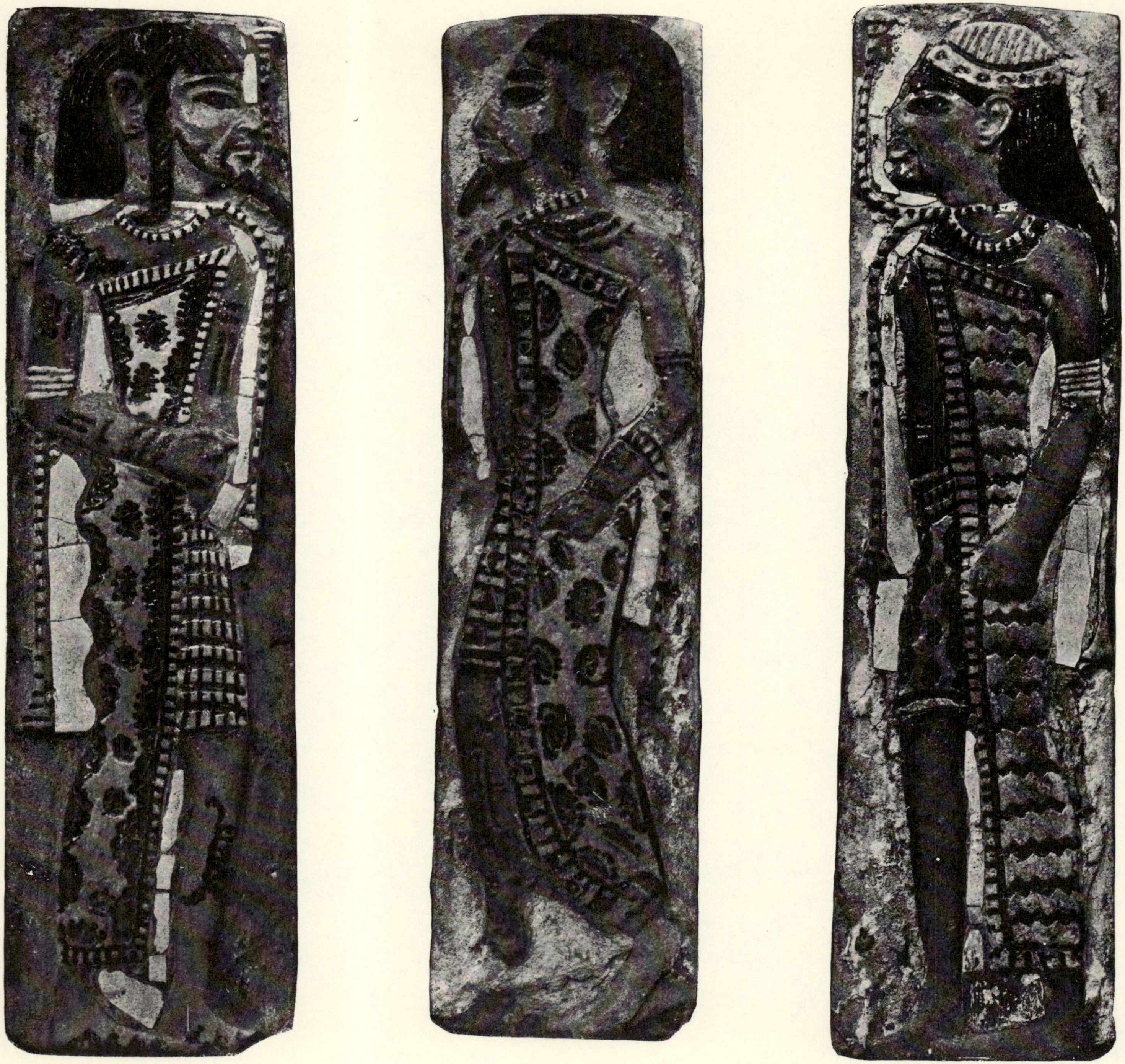

A B C

THREE LIBYANS (TILES FROM MEDÎNET HABU).

Frontispiece.

THE
EASTERN LIBYANS

AN ESSAY

BY

ORIC BATES

FRANK CASS & CO. LTD

1970

Published by
FRANK CASS AND COMPANY LIMITED
67 Great Russell Street, London WC1

First edition 1914
New impression 1970

SBN 7146 1634 6

Printed in Great Britain by Clarke, Doble & Brendon Ltd.
Plymouth and London

TO

GEORGE ANDREW REISNER, Ph.D.

AN ARCHAEOLOGIST WHOSE UNSWERVING DEVOTION TO SCIENCE

IS BOTH AN EXAMPLE AND AN INSPIRATION

THIS ESSAY IS DEDICATED

WITH AFFECTION AND RESPECT

PREFACE

The present volume needs but few words by way of preface. The materials here presented were first collected as part of the evidence relating to the history of Cyrenaica, to the study of which I have devoted already a number of years, and to which I hope to give more. As my Libyan notes grew in volume, and suggested the various questions which are discussed in the following pages, it became clear that in mere mass alone they would be a feature disproportionately large if introduced without abridgment into the work I hope ultimately to publish. Such an abridgment would, unless the way were first prepared by a series of articles in the journals, necessitate my making in many parts of my treatment of Cyrenaic history a number of statements which, without explanation, would appear dogmatic. That I have chosen to set forth the Libyan material in the present form instead of in the journals, is due to a conviction that the subject is of such importance as to warrant its treatment in book form ; to a desire to have the evidence easily accessible to others ; and to a wish to provide, as far as I may, a scientific basis for further study of the Libyans east of Africa Minor.

The importance of the Hamites in the eastern Mediterranean in Minoan times will not be underrated to-day by any thoughtful student of that sphere and period. Equally, to the Egyptologist, any systematic treatment of the people whose contribution to the civilization of the Nile Valley has, for over a decade, been the source of so much and such reckless controversy, should be welcome.

This essay both suffers and derives advantages from the fact that it has been written in the field. The disadvantages of being often cut off from all libraries are too obvious to be dwelt upon ; I am much to be blamed, however, if there do not appear in the following pages some traces of the opportunities of which, by being in the Levant, I have been able to avail myself. For I have had and used exceptional opportunities to collate the monumental and textual evidence to be found in Egypt, relating to the Libyans ; I have travelled in the Libyan Desert and Marmarica ; and, in regard to the Nubian question, treated in the first Appendix, I was actively engaged in the Nubian Archaeological Survey during the year in which the great "C Group" cemetery at Dakkah was excavated, and I personally examined every grave and its contents. These opportunities, if I shall seem to the reader to have made good use of them, I beg him to accept as an offset to such errors and omissions as would have been avoided had I been working with the aid of a European library.

A word may here be said about the spelling of foreign names. As the historical Egyptian names have been given English forms by Breasted, either in his *History*,[1] or in his *Ancient Records*,[2] his spellings have here been for the most part preserved, with this exception, that those which appear only in the *Records*, and which are there reproduced with the aid of diacritical signs, have been simplified by the method employed by Breasted himself in his *History*.

Arabic words have been transcribed according to the system tabulated below, although in the case of some of the more familiar names the usual European forms have been preferred to a literal transcription. Berber words have been transcribed by the same signs as Arabic ones.

ا A as in "father," or omitted in transcriptions.
ب B as in "bolt."
ت T as in "melt."
ث Ṯ or TH as in "thus."
ج G as in "get," or Ǵ as in "agitate."
ح Ḥ strong aspirate.
خ Ḫ like *ch* in the Scotch "loch."
د D as in "dalliance."
ذ Ḏ sometimes like *th* in "misanthrope," sometimes as *z* in "zany."
ر R as in "rat."
ز Z as in "zeal."
ژ Ǧ (Berber) as in "edge" (French *dj*).
س S as in "single."
ش Š or SH as in "shatter."
ص Ṣ like *ce* in "menace."
ض Ḍ hard palatal *d* as in "brigade."
ط Ṭ hard palatal *t* as in "tower."
ظ Ẓ as in "zoology."
ع ʿ or ʿ, somewhat like the pause in "co-operative."

[1] J. H. Breasted, *A History of Egypt*, 2nd ed., New York, 1911.

[2] Idem, *Ancient Records of Egypt*, Chicago, 1906. Hereafter cited as BAR, with volume (Roman numeral) and section numbers.

ڠ غ or GH, strong guttural resembling the *g* in *sagen*.
ف F as in "fowl."
ق Ḳ like *c* in "caisson."
ك K as in "keep."
ڭ Ġ (Berber) slight nasal quality, somewhat as in "banged."
ل L as in "long."
م M as in "mat."
ن N as in "note."
ه H as in "hurry."
و W or U as in "well" or "crude" respectively.
ى Y or I as in "yellow" or "machine" respectively.

The full titles of the modern works cited in the notes, and of the editions of the ancient sources used, will be found in the bibliography at the end of the work. In the notes, writers have been cited usually by brief titles.

In conclusion, among those whom I have to thank for helping me during the course of this work, I wish especially to mention the following :—

Dr. G. A. Reisner, with whom I served on four expeditions in Syria, Nubia, and Egypt, for continual help and criticism, especially in the parts relating to philological questions and religion ; Dr. R. Basset, of Algiers, for several valuable miscellaneous notes on religion, and Dr. J. Toutain, of Paris, for similar help ; Dr. A. Erman, for a notice of the god Ash ; Dr. L. Borchardt, for most generously and hospitably extending to me the privileges of the Imperial and Royal German Archaeological Institute in Cairo, where I was free at all hours to use the excellent Egyptological library there collected ; Dr. D. E. Derry, for an outline of his theory of the Egyptian race, and for the friendly enthusiasm he manifested toward this work while we were together in the Khedivial service, and later in the Egyptian Sudan ; Dr. G. Roeder, for continued sympathy and advice, and for bibliographic material ; Mr. E. M. Dowson, Director-General of H.H. Survey Department, and the officers of H.H. Coast Guards for the aid given me in connection with an expedition made in the Libyan Desert in the autumn of 1910, and especially, in this connection, Bînbashî L. V. Royle, whose guest I had the pleasure of being during part of that journey ; Dr. P. A. A. Boeser, of Leyden, for photographs ; Mr. C. M. Firth, for allowing me to use, after I had left the Government service in order to write this essay, unpublished material obtained by the Nubian Archaeological Survey then under his charge ; Professor G. F. Moore, of Harvard University, for his kindness in reading and criticizing the first draft of the chapter on Libyan religion ; Dr. G. H. Chase, of the same University, for generously reading the entire work, and making a number of valuable suggestions and corrections ; and finally, my father, Dr. Arlo Bates, for his untiring patience in correcting proofs. To those whose names are not mentioned in the above list, but who have given me their help in this work, I here wish to acknowledge my gratitude. As was necessarily the case in dealing with a subject of this sort, I have incurred a number of obligations which lack of space forbids me to specify.

ORIC BATES.

THE PYRAMIDS, GÎZAH, 1911.
GEBEL MOYAH, SENNAR, 1912.

CONTENTS

CHAPTER IX

APPENDIX I

APPENDIX II

APPENDIX III

APPENDIX IV

APPENDIX V

LIST OF ILLUSTRATIONS

[Except in the few instances specified below, the illustrations have been drawn or redrawn by the author.]

MAPS

PLATES

FIGURES IN THE TEXT

INTRODUCTION

THE name "Libya" has passed into our nomenclature from that of the Greeks and Romans.[1] The former of these people derived it from an Egyptian,[2] a Semitic,[3] or the original African source. The name was in classical times used to denote a region to which various other names were, with varying propriety, applied,[4] and which was more or less extended according to the writer's knowledge or geographical theories. Among Greek writers it therefore happens that *Libya* may denote all Africa,[5] or Africa west of Lower and Middle Egypt,[6] or Africa west of the Red Sea and of the Isthmus of Suez, exclusive of Egypt.[7] This vagueness regarding even the true eastern boundary of Libya—at best merely an academic question—persisted until Roman times. At that period the current significance of the term was generally restricted to Africa north of Aethiopia, west of Egypt, inclusive or exclusive of Africa Propria and the Mauretanias. But as long as it was employed, the word was often used very carelessly—much as we employ the word "India" in its stricter meaning, or to include Baluchistan, Kashmîr, Nepaul, Ceylon, and even Burmaḥ.

Under these circumstances, the reader is quite justified in asking, What, then, is "Eastern Libya"? In reply, it may at once be said that on the maps no such name is applied to any portion of Africa. Its significance is not geographical so much as ethnical; and even here it refers to a difference in culture rather than in race. The region which is throughout this essay to be understood by this name is bounded on the north by the Mediterranean, on the south by the deserts just north of the Anglo-Egyptian Sudan, on the east by the Nile Valley, and on the west by a line running

[1] Ἡ Λιβύη; Libya.

[2] From the ethnic 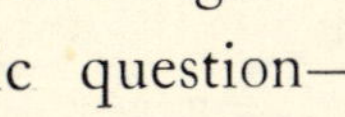, *r'bw*.

[3] The ethnic form exists as לובים *Lubîm*, in the O.T., as in 2 Chron. xii. 3; xvi. 8, etc.; or as להבים *Lehabîm*, as in Gen. x. 13.

[4] Steph. Byz. *in verb.* Λιβύη, where Libya is called χώρα πολυώνυμος, after Alexander Polyhistor.

[5] Herodotus iv. 42.

[6] Homer, *Odyss.* iv. 85, xiv. 295; Hesiod, *Theog.* 739. According to Scylax, *Periplus*, § 107, and Marcianus Heracleensis, *Periplus Maris Externi*, i. § 4, Libya began at the Canopic mouth of the Nile.

[7] Herodotus ii. 17, 18, iv. 167 *sqq.*; cf. Strabo i. pp. 86, 174; Ptolemy, ii. 1 § 5.

south-easterly from what was the Lake Tritonis of the ancients. The position of this last point has given rise to some controversy, but may be taken as either represented by the system of salt ponds and lakes south-west of the Gulf of Kabes, or by some one of these,[1] though Herodotus seems to have fallen into the error of mistaking the whole Syrtis Minor for the Lake.[2]

While the reader will at once understand that the occupation of the Nile Valley by the Egyptian race in the east delimited "Eastern Libya" upon that side by an ethnical as well as by a geographical boundary, it may not be equally clear just why Lake Tritonis has been chosen to mark the western confines of this area. As intimated above, the point in question marked a division not between two different races, but between two groups of the same race, who, on broad lines, were characterized by two different states of civilization. From Egypt to Lake Tritonis the ancient populations were mainly nomadic;[3] to the west of the lake the people were sedentaries, who differed from the nomads in their customs,[4] and who for the most part lived in permanent dwellings, and tilled the ground.[5]

The line between the two populations was, of course, not a hard and fast one. Large bodies of nomads were to be found on the Atlas slopes;[6] and in Eastern Libya permanent or semi-permanent communities existed, as for example at Augila[7] and Ammonium.[8] That the well-watered plateaux and enfilades of the Atlas System, west of Tritonis, should have been occupied by a people following a habit of life different from that of those scattered over the barren steppes of Tripolitana and Fezzan, or living in such fertile areas as were to be found in those regions, is not to be wondered at. The richness of the soil, the difficulties of moving about in large bodies in a region of high mountains and narrow defiles, and the knowledge that to the south and west of them lay less desirable lands,—all these factors contributed to inspire the western branches of the Libyan race to remain firmly seated in their country. Periodic droughts, a region for the most part open, and to be traversed, even though painfully, throughout its habitable length and breadth, and the rapidity with which the water or grazing in any one locality was exhausted, tended to keep the Eastern Libyans in that state of nomadism in which they entered their country. The Lake Tritonis was therefore a boundary not merely arbitrary, but with some real significance, and it is

[1] H. Barth, *Wanderungen*, vol. i. p. 252; Tissot, *De Tritonide Lacu*, passim; C. Perroud, *De Syrticis emporiis*, p. 19 *sq.* The last-named writer seems to have established finally (*a*) that the site of the old Tritonis Lacus is to-day marked by the Shott el-Gerîd and Shott el-Hameymet, and (*b*) that the Τρίτων ποταμός of Ptolemy iv. 3 § 3, Scylax § 110, etc., is not marked by the Wady Akarît, but by the lesser Ṭarf el-Ma.

[2] Herodotus iv. 179 *et alibi*.

[3] *Ibid.* iv. 186.

[4] *Ibid.* iv. 187.

[5] *Ibid.* iv. 191.

[6] Cf. Strabo ii. p. 131.

[7] Mela i. 8; Procopius, *De aedificiis* vi. 2.

[8] Herodotus ii. 32, 42 *et alibi*.

with the indigenous North African peoples who anciently dwelt between it and Egypt that this essay will deal, treating of their race, their history down to the time of the invasions of the Moslemîn in the seventh century A.D., their language, their religion, and their customs.

Analogies offered by modern conditions will be employed not infrequently, since desert environment has, despite hundreds of years, preserved among the modern indigenes of Eastern Libya many of the customs and usages of their forefathers.

The meanings of a few words that are of common occurrence in this and other works relating to North Africa, and on the maps, may here be fittingly introduced, with a view to obviating later comment. For the same reason, a table of the main outlines of Egyptian Chronology, which is that used in referring to the earlier historic periods in Libya, follows the glossary.

Africa.—In the modern continental sense, and not in the Roman, unless specified. *Africa Minor* = *Moghreb*, *q.v.*, and not, as sometimes, all North Africa.

'Ayn.—Spring of sweet water.

Berber.—Strictly, a word having only a glossological meaning : the modern language of the Libyan race, in all its dialects. Here, and in many other books, used in an ethnic sense to mean "modern Libyan," *e.g.* "Berber superstitions" = the superstitions, not of all Berber-speaking peoples, which would include some negroids, etc., but of those directly descended from the ancient Libyans.

Bîr.—Well, water-hole.

Birkah —A pond, or small lake.

Darb.—Route, road, trail.

Duffah.—Flat, desert, plateau of limestone.

Eastern Libya.—The region mentioned above, and in more detail in Chapter I.

Egypt.—The Nile Valley from the sea to Aṣwan (First Cataract).

Erg.—Desert of sand-dunes.

Garah.—Isolated bluff, or *mesa* of limestone.

Gebel.—A general term for all desert or mountainous tracts.

Hamadah.—Stony, burnt up, desert.

Hamitic.—Of, or pertaining to the Hamitic race. This race comprises the Berbers or Western Hamites, and the Aethiopian, or Eastern, Hamites. See *Libyan.*

Ḥaṭṭîah.—Desert halting-place where some grazing is to be had, and, rarely, water.

Historic.—After the IIIrd dynasty of Egypt.

Ḳafilah.—Camel-train, caravan.

Ḳerbah.—Water-skin (pl. *ḳerabah*).

Ḳaṣr.—Stronghold, fort. Applied by the modern Arabs to many ancient buildings regardless of their original purpose.

Libya.—North Africa west of Egypt, and north of the region of tropical rains.

Libyan.—Of or belonging to the indigenous population of Libya as a whole ; generally used in reference to the ancient population, and not synonymous with Hamitic, which has a wider meaning, including as it does such people, pure or mixed, as the Beǵah, Masai, Danakil, some Abyssinians, etc.

Marsa.—Port, harbour. *E.g.* in the Italian corruption Marsalla = مرسى الله Marsa-Allah = "God's Haven."

Moghreb or *el-Moghreb.*—North-west Africa—the whole Atlas region.

Mongar.—Spur of limestone cliff; isolated peak of limestone.

North Africa.—Mediterranean, Ṣaharan, and Atlantic Africa west of Egypt. Libya in its broader sense.

Nubia.—Nile Valley from Aṣwan (First Cataract) to Wady Ḥalfa (Second Cataract).

Pre-historic.—Before the IVth Egyptian dynasty.

Pre-dynastic.—Before the Ist Egyptian dynasty.

Proto-Berber.—Ancient Libyan language.

Proto-dynastic.—The Ist, IInd, and IIIrd Egyptian dynasties.

Rîf.—Fertile strip of cultivation, *e.g.* along the Nile; in a special sense, the African littoral along the north slopes of the Maroccan Atlas.

Sahel.—Plain-district at the foot of mountains or plateaux.

Sebḫah.—Salt-covered marsh, depression caked with salt.

Shott.—A wide, shallow pond of salt water.

Tell.—Table-land, heights, *e.g.* the Algerian Tell; a hill.

Wady.—Ravine, stream-bed (generally dry), valley.

The outline of Egyptian Chronology which now follows is that adopted with certain slight modifications by G. A. Reisner from the system of the Berlin School:—

Pre-dynastic period	B.C.	4500	to	3300
Old Empire	,,	3300	,,	2400
[Dynasties I. and II.	,,	3300	,,	3000]
Middle Empire	,,	2400	,,	1600
New Empire	,,	1600	,,	663
Saite period[1]	,,	663	,,	331
Ptolemaic period	,,	331	,,	30
Roman and Byzantine period	,,	30	,,	A.D. 650

[1] The latter part of this period, from about 500 to 331 B.C., may be conveniently styled the Late New Empire.

CHAPTER I

PHYSIOGRAPHY OF EASTERN LIBYA [1]

MAN'S relations to his physical environment are of such vital importance that it is essential at the outset of this essay for the reader to be acquainted with the physiography and climatology of those regions over which the Eastern Libyans were anciently distributed. This is the more necessary because, on the one hand, the characteristics of Africa between Egypt and Tunisia are such as profoundly to influence the lives and habits of those dwelling in that area, and because, upon the other, the existing general descriptions of this region as a whole are unsatisfactory.

Eastern Libya may be defined as that area bounded on the north by the Mediterranean Sea, on the east by the Nile Valley, and on the south by the twenty-second parallel of north latitude. To the west, it is bordered by a line running S. from the Shott el-Gerîd on the eighth meridian (E. Greenwich) to lat. 28° N.; thence on S.E. to lat. 22° N. In the most general terms, the region thus defined may be described as a central rectangle of desert, with a fertile coastal belt on the north; a still more fertile strip, the Nile Valley, on the east; the fertile mountains of Tibesti on the southwest, and a chain of small oases along the western border. South of the northern fertile zone runs another chain of oases; yet a third lies in the eastern section, parallel to the Nile. Such, in its broadest outlines, is the region which is discussed in the present chapter:[2] for convenience it will be treated under the following eight headings:—

I. The Littoral Zone—the Syrtes; Cyrenaica; Marmarica.
II. The Libyan Desert—Northern and Eastern Oases; Nile Valley; Kufra.
III. The West—the Chad Route Oases; Hamadah el-Ḥomrah; Hamadah Murzuk.
IV. Internal Geography—Roads; Rates of Travel.
V. Geographic position with regard to outlying regions—the West; South; East; North.
VI. Climatology.

[1] Throughout this and the following chapters the reader is referred for the general geography and physiography of Eastern Libya to the large scale map in the cover-pocket.

[2] Cf. P. Langhans, *Wandkarte*. An excellent physical map showing the whole area.

VII. Flora ; Fauna.

VIII. Man—Present Numbers ; Distribution ; Relations of Man to his Environment in Eastern Libya.

I. The Littoral Zone

The East Libyan littoral is about 1100 miles in length, measured from long. 10° E. in the Gulf of Kabes to long. 29° 30′ E. in the el-Arabs Gulf, near Alexandria. The general trend of the shore line, from its western extremity, is S.E. to the bottom of the Syrtis Major, a distance of about 500 miles ; thence N. by E. about 100 miles, following the western coast of Cyrenaica, thence to the el-Arabs Gulf, about 550 miles in a mean E.S.E. direction. The above courses define the main bends of the coast : they are, as it were, the simplest terms short of a right line to which the coastal traverse can be reduced. By examination of the littoral somewhat more in detail, though again without regard for its minor irregularities, it will be seen to proceed thus, from west to east :—

Gulf of Kabes to Cape Mizratah, about 275 miles S.E. by E.
Thence to Zerîd (S.W. part of the Syrtis Major), about 50 miles S.
,, Marsa Braygah (S.E. part of the Syrtis Major), about 180 miles S.E. by E.
,, Benghazî (W. extremity of Cyrenaica), about 100 miles N. by E.
,, Ras et-Tîn (E. extremity of Cyrenaica), about 175 miles E. by N.
,, Ras el-Mudawr (S.E. extremity of Cyrenaica), about 30 miles S.S.E.
,, Ras el-Milḥ (beginning of Gulf of Sollum), about 90 miles E. by S.
,, Sollum (S.W. point of Gulf of Sollum), about 30 miles S.
,, Long. 29° 30′ in the el-Arabs Gulf, about 250 miles E. by S.

In all this extent of coast, the most northerly points touched are lat. 33° 55′ N. (northern point Gerbah Island) in the west, and lat. 32° 57′ N. (Ras el-Hillil in Cyrenaica) in the east. The lowest latitude on the coast is 30° 17′ N. (Muḫtar, at the bottom of the Syrtis Major), and the whole coast lies therefore between the thirtieth and the thirty-fourth parallels.[1]

The physiography of the littoral zone may best be followed from west to east. Beginning at the Shott el-Gerîd,[2] a shallow salt lake interposed between the eastern extremity of the Atlas system and the lower and smaller mountains of the Syrtica Regio, the reader will, even from a glance at the map, note that the Shott has every appearance of having at one time been connected with the Gulf of Kabes. Such, in fact, seems once to have been the case, for although the level of the Shott is now different from that of the sea, the connecting channel between the two is still marked by the Wady Akarît. Immediately east of the Shott el-Gerîd, the Gebel Dahar recedes southward to meet the Gebel Nafusa in lat. 32° N. This latter range has a general E. trend, running, as the Gebel Gharyan, into the fertile zone from N.W.

[1] British Admiralty Chart No. 664-449, *Mediterranean Sea*, for the general position of the coast.

[2] T.S.G.S. maps, No. 1539-7, *Tripoli*, No. 1539-14, *Sella*, and No. 1539-15, *Aujila*, for the Syrtic region. The place-names are often incorrect, and other minor errors occur.

corner of the great Hamadah el-Ḥomrah in a direction roughly parallel with the coast. From the point of contact between the Gebel Nafusa and the Hamadah, the boundary of the fertile littoral district trends away S.E., following a direction approximately parallel to the coast, at a never greatly varying distance of about 125 miles from the Mediterranean. The line is marked by the northern declivities of the Hamadah, the edge of which, under the names of el-Mudar mta el-Hamadah, Gebel es-Sodah, Gebel Sharḳîah, and the Ḥarug es-Sod, is fairly well defined as far east as the Oasis of Wagîlah (Augila), where the Hamadah itself begins to give place to the sand dunes of the Libyan Desert. The shore line of the district just outlined is, excepting that of Marmarica, the most desolate and forbidding in the whole Mediterranean. After leaving Gerbah, the only inhabited island[1] on the East Libyan coast, the voyager sees only a monotonous succession of sand dunes, with an occasional cluster of palms at a seaside well. In the immediate neighbourhood of Tripoli town, the monotony is varied by the rich gardens that there stand by the sea, but these once passed, the coast again takes on a desolate character which it maintains throughout the rest of the Syrtic region. In some places, as along the west shore of the Gulf of Kebrît (Syrtis Major) in the vicinity of Melfah, the low dunes are backed by *sebḫas*, some of which are rendered dangerous to travellers by treacherous quicksands. Occasionally, shallow boat-coves occur, as at Marsa Zaffran and el-Hammah, but these interruptions are not sufficient to break the mournful monotony of the coast.

Between the sea and the Hamadah el-Ḥomrah (to return to the western part of this district) the interior country is diversified by numerous low hills and ridges, presenting for the most part a barren and stony appearance, which is, however, often relieved by the verdure of the wadys they contain. These latter are in some cases perennially fertile, at least in spots, and throughout the lower parts of their courses water may be had by excavation. The general trend of these wadys, and so of the ranges that form them, is E. or N.E., those in the vicinity of the Syrtis Major being less inclined from the meridian than those farther west. East of the Syrtis Major, lacking the mass of the Hamadah as a watershed, the wadys are fewer and drier; the Wady Farag, which, as its name implies, is without water, and runs S.W. and then W. to the coast near Marsa Braygah, is the only one of any considerable size. A few of the western wadys unite several smaller branches at points not far north of the edge of the Hamadah, and reach the coastal sands bearing a little water, which is increased in winter by the rains. Unlike the great water-bearing wadys of Algeria and Marocco, those of Tripolitana hardly ever carry water to the sea itself, except when in full spate from the winter rains.

On leaving the Syrtica Regio, with its sandy coast, its hills, and the Hamadah el-Ḥomrah, one passes at once into Cyrenaica,[2] which constitutes, together with the

[1] Moḥammad Abu Ras Aḥmed en-Naṣîr, *Description de . . . Djerba*, for this island.

[2] Applying this term in its fullest extent.

Gebel el-ʿAḳabah which lies next it on the east, the central portion of the East Libyan littoral. In shape, this district rudely resembles the segment of a circle thrust out into the Mediterranean, the chord of this segment being about 170 miles in length, and running E.N.E. from Bueb Bay in the Gulf of Kebrît, to Ras el-Mudawr in the Gulf of Bombah.[1] The area thus defined consists, in its northern part, of a mountainous limestone gebel, the N.W. end of the great Libyan Coastal Plateau which runs east and west behind the shore line, nearly to the Egyptian Delta. In Cyrenaica, the heights are separated from the sea by a very fertile *sahel* or ribbon of coastal plain, descending in steep terraces, which are broken by numerous short ravines and wadys, to the sea.

The height of the plateau, which from the fertility of its valleys is called the Gebel el-Aḫḍar ("Green Mountain"), is in its more elevated parts as much as 2200 feet above sea-level; its mean elevation is about 2000 feet. The depth of the fertile zone in Cyrenaica is at its greatest only about 70 miles, at which distance from the sea the plateau, which declines toward the south, takes on the appearance of a barren grass steppe. Still farther south, where the underground moisture from the north is dissipated by the sand and the heat, the grasses disappear, the limestone ends, and the dunes of the Libyan Desert, which have already been seen meeting the eastern extremity of the Hamadah el-Ḥomrah near Wagîlah, again appear.

Taking up the topography of Cyrenaica in greater detail, one finds that the western district, just north of Bueb Bay, and known as Barḳah el-Ḥomrah ("Barḳah the Red"), is a plain, roughly triangular, having its apex at the north where the mountains of the limestone plateau approach the sea. Its name is due to the hue of the soil, which is here a peculiar sandy loam, the colour of old tan-bark.[2] At Ras Teyones, a little south of Benghazî, the mountains approach the coast to within about 12 miles, and at about half this distance north of Benghazî, come almost to the sea, which they may be said to meet at a point yet farther north, near Ṭolmeyṭah.

In proceeding easterly from Ṭolmeyṭah, the traveller crosses a succession of ridges and ravines all the way to Ras et-Tîn, where the coast turns sharply to the southwards, and the high part of the plateau, dipping toward the S.W., recedes from the shore line. Many of the ravines just mentioned contain a little water permanently—all of them do so in the rains, some being at that time unfordable. South of Ras et-Tîn, at a distance of about 15 miles from that place, the Gulf of Bombah is entered.[3] This remarkable break in the coast line occurs between the two masses of the Gebel el-Aḫḍar on the west and the Gebel el-ʿAḳabah on the east. It may be said to consist of two small harbours, lying both on a N.W. by W.–S.E. by E. axis, facing each other, and separated by a small gulf, and a slight projection in the coast line at Ras er-Ramil. The northern

[1] T.S.G.S. maps: No. 1539-15, *Aujila*, No. 1539-8, *Ben-Ghazi*. G. Hildebrand, *Cyrenaïka*, Taff. iii., iv. British Admiralty Charts, No. 1031-241, *Benghazi to Derna*, and No. 1029-244, *Derna to Ras Bulau*.

[2] El-Idrîsî, *Clima* iii. 3, mentions this earth.

[3] British Admiralty Charts: No. 1030-245, *Bombah*, and No. 1029-244, *Derna to Ras Bulau*.

harbour is but a cove, sheltered from the sea on the E. by a narrow point ("Tank Point"), and ending in a salt marsh; the southern is a narrow inlet ("Enharit Kurzala"), formed by Ras el-Mudawr and "Seal Island," and running south from the gulf. Both, especially the latter, afford good anchorage for small craft, and are a favourite resort of the Greek sponge-fishermen at the present day. Of the islands in the gulf, Bombah or Burdah is an uninhabitable steep mass of granular limestone, while "Seal Island," which is low and flat, is suitable, to some extent, for human occupation.

From four points in the stretch of coast which has just been surveyed, natural passes give access from the sea to the interior. The most westerly of these is at Benghazî, east of which one may pass through a break in the high, coastwise barrier which (together with a number of semi-isolated peaks) terminates the Gebel el-Aḫḍar on the N.W. From this pass, going in a N.E. direction, one travels through a series of valleys to Merg, one of the more considerable towns of the interior, occupying the site of the ancient Barca. If, on entering the gebel at the same place, the traveller takes an E.N.E. route, he will come to the head of the greatest of the Cyrenaic wadys, the Wady Dernah, by which he may descend to the town of that name on the sea. The second important break in the gebel occurs at Ṭolmeyṯah, at the end of the coastwise barrier mentioned above. Having entered the Gebel el-Aḫḍar by this pass, and crossed a high N.-S. range behind the barrier, the traveller falls in upon the valley of Merg, at a point somewhat to the north of that place. Between Benghazî and Tolmeyṯah a minor pass leads from the coast at Tuḳrah to Merg, a fact mainly of note since the former place, anciently Taucheira, was at one time the port of Barca, which lay 27 miles from its harbour town. From Marsa Suzah, a port about half-way between Ṭolmeyṯah and Dernah, another of these secondary passes—in this case short and ill-defined—runs back to the modern Grennah. Marsa Suzah, anciently Sozusa (later Apollonia), was the port of the latter place, which marks the site, and preserves the name, of the old metropolis Cyrene. The third primary pass from the sea into the Gebel el-Aḫḍar, and the most important of them, is the Wady Dernah mentioned above. This valley, which in its lower course is perennially water-bearing, begins to assume an important size at a point about 30 miles southeast of Grennah. It runs from this point in an easterly direction for 25 miles, then turns N.N.E. toward the sea, and finally debouches at Dernah, coming to an end just behind the town, between two conspicuous shoulders of the plateau, which are clearly visible from the sea at a distance of some miles. The fourth wady leading into the interior is not one of great importance, since it passes through a desert country, and is only a little below the level of the plateau through which it runs. The wady in question is that called on the maps, though with doubtful authority, the Wady Gharrah. It enters the Gulf of Bombah from the south, and is formed by the junction of two smaller depressions, which run into the low plateau for about 35 miles in a S. and S.W. direction respectively.

Cyrenaica is, as a whole, better supplied with water than any equally large area in Eastern Libya. The occurrence of water-courses in the wadys has been noted: the Gebel el-Aḫḏar is furnished with numerous good springs, some of which are remarkably powerful. Along the coast, sites such as Marsa Suzah and Ṭolmeyṭah, which were formerly watered by aqueducts from the hills, are now but poorly supplied from *bîrs* and water-holes. In the region about the Gulf of Bombah, which is desert in character, the water obtained from these sources was formerly supplemented by that stored in cisterns. In some localities, away from the coast, as at Merg and Wady Ḳerayb, ponds of sweet water stand in the bottoms of the wadys. These after a long drought sometimes go dry, but, even in the cases when this occurs, the vegetation is sustained by the subterraneous moisture.

Good natural harbours, as has been mentioned, do not exist in Cyrenaica. The best are Benghazî, which can accommodate small coasters, and the coves of the Gulf of Bombah, mentioned above. At Tuḳrah, Ṭolmeyṭah, Ras el-Hamadah, Marsa Suzah, and Ras el-Hillil are boat-landings, but they are all exposed to raking winds from one or more quarters. It is barely possible that the subsidence of the Cyrenaic coast line[1] may have lowered ledges which formerly served as breakwaters, but as no vestiges of these appear on the charts, it is safe to suppose that until the Greek colonists in this region improved such anchorages as they found, the coast was anciently as inhospitable as it is to-day.

The Gebel el-ʿAḳabah, which forms the eastern half of the central section of the East Libyan littoral, is an elongated mass of limestone capping the northern side of the great Libyan Coastal Plateau, from Ras el-Mudawr to the Gulf of Sollum, a distance of about 90 miles. The depth of the ʿAḳabah plateau is only about 25 miles; its highest point, so far as known, is not much over 1800 feet. Like the Gebel el-Aḫḏar, it is separated from the shore by a narrow ribbon of plain, and its seaward face is cut by numerous little ravines. The coast, which is rocky, is at Marsa Ṭobruk broken by the best harbour of Eastern Libya, the port offering good anchorage even to large vessels, and being well protected by a high ridge running out easterly from the land. The Gebel el-ʿAḳabah has been passed by numerous travellers along the coast road, but its interior has yet to be explored. At present, little more can be added to what has been said of it than that it appears to be well watered, and the region to the south of the mountains becomes rapidly mere barren table-land. At the east end of the Gebel el-ʿAḳabah, the mountains cease abruptly, the Gulf of Sollum lying immediately to the east of the range. In this locality are three small boat-coves: "Port Bardia," Limreyg, and Sollum itself in the S.W. angle of the gulf which bears its name.

In passing eastwards from the Gulf of Bombah to the Gulf of Sollum, this survey

[1] Which is proved to have sunk slightly, even within the past 2000 years, as there are buildings of the Ptolemaic and Roman periods which may now be seen standing in the water at Marsa Suzah. It may here be remarked that the ruins marked on English charts as standing in the water at Ras el-Mudawr ("Ras allem Dawr") cannot be adduced as evidence of coastal subsidence, since they do not exist.

has already crossed the vaguely defined western boundaries of what, in Hellenistic and Roman times, was known as Marmarica. From Sollum to the Egyptian Delta, this district measures, roughly, 250 miles along an E. by S. trending coast; its southern limit is that of the S.E. edge of the Libyan Coastal Plateau which, from the vicinity of the Delta, runs away W.S.W. toward the Oasis of Sîwah. For the most part, this district consists of an extremely flat expanse of desert limestone, 300 to 500 feet above sea-level, here and there broken down into small, barren depressions of irregular shape, and in places diversified with isolated peaks or *mongars*. Near the edges of the plateau, especially in the north, occur occasional *ḥaṭṭîas*, which in this region are merely scant patches of camel-thorn and gazelle-grass, watered by the winter rains and heavy dews. Along the coast itself runs a narrow strip of clayey loam, which is now and then interrupted by tongues of sand making in from the sea dunes, or by limestone spurs projecting from the low gebel. The loamy strips, however, when watered by the winter rains, well repay the crude tillage they receive from the Bedawîn, and in the spring are covered with grasses and wild flowers. At some points, as in the neighbourhood of Marsa Matru, this arable land is of considerable extent, and would, with a little care, produce good crops.[1] The scarcity of water during much of the year, however, greatly interferes with cultivation. Along the coast it is obtained from water-holes which are fed by seepage, but which, when left open for a short period, become too salty for use. Wells, generally of ancient construction, also occur in considerable numbers, as do also cisterns of the Roman period.[2]

The Marmaric coast offers several harbours suitable for small craft, though none are capacious enough for modern commerce. Marsa Matru, for example, is admirably sheltered from all winds, though, owing to the difficult entrance, it cannot be half as good a refuge as was the ancient Paraetonium, the harbour of which is now a deep, land-locked lagoon immediately west of the modern port. Boat-coves also occur, as at el-Guttah and Ras eḍ-Ḍabbah, but they are all poor and ill-sheltered.

The Libyan Coastal Plateau from Ras el-Kanays eastward, where it is high and steep, is a little withdrawn from the sea, so as to give place between that point and the bottom of el-Arabs Gulf for a gently undulating stretch of land about 20 miles deep and 70 miles long—an area which, if cared for sufficiently, would support a considerable population. The plateau is in Marmarica penetrated at only two points by wadys of any size, but is itself so flat and low that it may easily be traversed in any direction with no other difficulties than those arising from the scarcity of water and forage. The former of these difficulties, even, may be obviated in winter, for rain-water collects in the "clean-ups" on the plateau, and for some time stands in pools and puddles. At a point S. of Marsa Matru, a slight depression leads toward the oases of Garah and

[1] Egyptian Government: *District of Mersa Matru*; *District of Ras allem Rum*. The arable areas are clearly shown on these maps.

[2] G. Maspero in T. B. Hohler: *Oasis of Siva*, p. 49 *sqq.*, discusses these wells and cisterns, and arrives at the conclusion that they date mainly from the second century A.D., and were used until the end of the fourth century.

Sîwah, from the former of which places a similar but less marked valley, the Wady et-Talat, runs northward some 40 miles. In the east, a little before the plateau is terminated by the Nile Valley and the Delta, it is crossed in a W.N.W. and E.S.E. direction by the Wady Naṭrun, which runs from near the bottom of el-Arabs Gulf to the apex of the Delta at Gîzah. Near the middle of its course occur a number of *sebḫas* in a locality where drinkable water is to be obtained from wells, and which is known in the annals of Christianism as the seat of numerous Coptic monasteries.

II. The Libyan Desert

Bordered on the north by the southern edge of the Libyan Coastal Plateau and the oases lying along its southern declivities, the Libyan Desert stretches away some 800 miles to the northern confines of Darfur and Kordofan in the south, and the Tibesti and Borku ranges on the southwest. On the east, the desert is diversified by the Egyptian oases, and bordered by the Nile Valley ; on the west, it is less definitely delimited by the Hamadas of Fezzan ; and on the northwest by the Ḥarug es-Sod and the "fertile" Syrtic zone which runs thence to the Oasis of Wagîlah. The southern portion of this region need not here be discussed, since it lies outside the Libyan ethnic sphere, which may be regarded, as has been said, as practically terminated on the south by lat. 22° N. In a fashion rough, but sufficiently accurate for present purposes, the boundaries and oases of the Libyan Desert may thus be traversed, beginning at Wagîlah, and moving thence easterly, southerly, westerly, and northerly.

Wagîlah (Augila) to Garabub	about	175 miles	E.N.E.
Thence to Sîwah (Ammonium)	,,	80 ,,	S.E. by E.
,, Garah (Umm eṣ-Ṣoghayr)	,,	65 ,,	N.E. by E.
,, apex of Egyptian Delta	,,	270 ,,	N. by E.

The last course follows along the south edge of the Libyan Coastal Plateau. Returning to Sîwah :

Thence to Baḥarîah	about	200 miles	E.S.E.
,, Fayum	,,	130 ,,	N.E. by E.

The area south of the Libyan Coastal Plateau and west of the Sîwah-Baḥarîah-Fayum line is, as far as known, a confused waste of dunes. Immediately south of the Sîwah-Baḥarîah-Fayum line, however, a harder gebel of sand and stone begins, extending S.S.W. from Sîwah to the Nile Valley in Nubia.

Baḥarîah to Farafrah	about	100 miles	S.S.W.
Thence to Iddaylah	,,	30 ,,	W.N.W.
,, Abu ʿUngar	,,	60 ,,	S. by W.
Baḥarîah to Daḫlah	,,	110 ,,	S.S.W.
Thence to Ḥargah	,,	100 ,,	E. by S.
,, Berîs	,,	55 ,,	S.
,, Kurkur (in direct line)	,,	120 ,,	S.E. by E.
,, Nile at Aṣwan	,,	35 ,,	E.N.E.

The traverses given above pass through the Egyptian Oases, the eastern ones of which —Ḫargah, Berîs, Kurkur—may be said to be in a segment of gebel, bounded on the east by a great deflection of the Nile toward the Red Sea. The courses of the Nile itself, the river being the true eastern boundary of the Libyan Desert, from the apex of the Delta (Cairo) to lat. 22° N. are approximately as follows :—

Cairo to el-Wasṭah	about	50 miles	S.
(Thence to Medînet el-Fayum	,,	20 ,,	W.)
Wasṭah to Minyah	,,	85 ,,	S. by W.
(Thence to Baḥarîah (Ḳaṣr)	,,	110 ,,	W. by N.)
Minyah to es-Sîuṭ	,,	65 ,,	S.S.E.
(Thence to Farafrah	,,	185 ,,	W. in direct line.)
(es-Sîuṭ to Ḫargah	,,	125 ,,	S. by W.)
(es-Sîuṭ to Daḫlah	,,	150 ,,	S.W. in direct line.)
es-Sîuṭ to Farshut	,,	105 ,,	S.E.
Thence to Ḳenah	,,	30 ,,	E. by N.
,, Esnah	,,	60 ,,	S. (direct).
(Esnah to Ḫargah	,,	125 ,,	W.)
Esnah to Edfu	,,	30 ,,	S.E. by E.
Edfu to Aṣwan (1st Cataract)	,,	65 ,,	S.
(Aṣwan to Kurkur, *ut supra*	,,	35 ,,	W.S.W.)
Aṣwan to Gerf Husseyn (in Nubia) . .	,,	50 ,,	S.
Thence to Korosko	,,	60 ,,	S.E. by S.
,, Derr	,,	15 ,,	N.W.
,, Wady Ḥalfa (lat. 21°55′ N., 2nd Cataract)	,,	75 ,,	S.W.

(This completes the Nile traverse.)

From the Nile, lat. 22° N., to N.W. end Tibesti	about	950 miles	W.

(This course approximately bisects the Libyan Desert.)

From N.W. end Tibesti to W. end Ḥarug es-Sod	about	350 miles	N. by E.
Thence to Wagîlah	,,	220 ,,	E.N.E. (direct).
,, Tayserbo (N. Kufra Oases) . .	,,	180 ,,	S.
,, Kebabo (S. ,,) . . .	,,	120 ,,	S.E.
,, Sîghen (N.E. ,,) . . .	,,	100 ,,	N.
Kebabo to N.W. end Tibesti	,,	300 ,,	S.W. by W.

Of the wide extent just surveyed it may be well said *vasta est magis quam frequens.*[1] The greater portion of the whole area is sheer desert of a character as formidable as any in the entire Ṣaḥara. The sand dunes of the Libyan Desert, trending in great ranges in a S.S.W. direction from the north, lie as an impassable barrier between Fezzan, Kanem, and Borku on the west, and the Nile Valley and the Egyptian oases on the east.

An examination in more detail of the courses noted above, in the same direction and from the same starting-place, shows that Wagîlah is one of the several small oases lying in a depression situated about 120 miles S.E. from Muḫtar in the Syrtis Major. The town of Wagîlah itself stands in the middle of a demi-lune of palms, which

[1] Mela i. 8. Said of Libya in general. Cf. Lucian, *De dipsadibus*, 1 : "The southern parts of Libya are all deep sand and parched soil, a desert of wide extent which produces nothing," etc.

measures, from end to end, about 6 miles, and which contains, roughly, some 16,000 trees. As is almost invariable with the north Libyan oases, a *sebḫah* occurs not far from the fertile zone. Water is obtained from wells, most of which are brackish and some sulphurous.

Some 28 miles E.S.E. of Wagîlah is situated the oasis of Galu, with its two towns of Leb and el-Arḫ, and palm groves which contain nearly 100,000 trees. At Galu, the wells are all brackish, the nearest sweet water being six hours distant. N.E. of this oasis is another belonging to the same group, called Igherrî, 18 miles from Galu. The palms at Igherrî are fewer and less cared for than in the other oases of this group, and the resident Arabs live in palm-leaf huts instead of mud houses. It may be remarked that anciently the name Augila, which now survives only as the name of the westernmost of the towns, probably embraced the whole group.

In passing from Galu to Garabub, the traveller encounters a few *ḥaṭṭîas*, but for the most part the way leads through stony or sandy desert. At Garabub itself, palm-trees occur, and there are wells which in the last fifty years have been increased in number by the industry of the Senusî brotherhood, who hold this small oasis as a place of great sanctity, and among the most important of their possessions.

Between this place and Sîwah, several small *ḥaṭṭîas* occur, as at Faghedrah and Gaygab, and at the extreme western end of the Sîwan depression, one falls in upon the small salt lake of Umm esh-Shîattah,[1] near which there are water-holes, and grazing, and the *ḥaṭṭîas* of Gerbah, and Umm Ghazlan.

The Sîwan oases occupy sites in a depression measuring about 35 miles from Maraghî in the western end to Zeytun at the eastern ; and about 7 miles from the declivities of the limestone on the north to the ever-encroaching sand dunes on the south. There are to-day in the extreme western parts of Maraghî only comparatively few palms, growing in the neighbourhood of a small salt lake, in the vicinity of which are several good *'ayns*. Besides the palms there are also plots of good arable ground, which are visited by the Sîwans during the summer ; but anciently, as is proved by the great number of rock-chambered tombs of the Ptolemaic and Roman periods in the cliffs immediately north of the lake, this district must have been much better cultivated than at present.

As one approaches Sîwah itself, the gardens become more numerous, though interrupted with *sebḫas* of forbidding aspect and considerable extent. The town from which the whole locality is named is perched on a limestone outcrop or *garah*, as is also Aghurmî, a smaller town situated among the palms 2 miles to the N.E. of Sîwah. The oases contain at present about 163,000 adult palms. Water is plentifully supplied by the numerous wells, many of which are of Roman construction. Zeytun, at the eastern end of the oasis, consists of a *zawîah* belonging to the Senusî, and is surrounded by gardens similar to those at Sîwah itself.

[1] O. Bates, *Umm es Shiatta and Umm Ghurbi.*

Garah, so called from its situation on a conspicuous, isolated outcrop of limestone, stands in the middle of a *ḥaṭṭîah*, in which springs and palm groves occur, though less frequently than in the Sîwan depression to the southwestward.

On the way from Sîwah to Baḥarîah (the ancient *Oasis Parva*), one passes through the small and poor oases of Gary, ʿArag, and Baḥreyn, and thereafter through a desert of sand and limestone. The oasis of Baḥarîah [1] is a large natural excavation in the Libyan Plateau, entirely surrounded by escarpments, and having within its area a great number of isolated hills. The oasis is roughly 55 miles in length, and 30 miles across at its widest part. There are four principal villages in the depression, all in the northern part, where water is most abundant. The oasis contains nearly 100,000 palms,[2] about 5000 apricot trees, and above that number of olives. Despite its fertility, the general health of the oasis is far from good, chiefly because of the inferiority of the water supply.[3]

The oasis of Farafrah,[4] south of the preceding, is best described as a collection of some twenty springs, each of which is surrounded by a fertile area, and all of which lie in a depression in the plateau. The produce of the oasis is barely sufficient for its inhabitants, who are sometimes constrained to import corn and flour from the other oases, or from the Nile Valley.[5] The oasis of Iddaylah, near Farafrah, is at present a mere halting-place where water may be had in passing between Farafrah and Sîwah. Its position, however, warrants mention of this point, as one worthy of notice, since it lies at the northern end of a large depression which, now covered with drifting sand, may in ancient historic times have been capable of supporting life.

One of the unsubmerged points in the southern part of the depression in which Iddaylah lies is the unexplored oasis of Abu ʿUngar. This oasis contains four wells and a number of ancient remains, but its inaccessibility, and its position towards the Senusî centre of Kufra, are the causes for its being at present uninhabited.[6]

The next oasis to be considered, that of Daḫlah,[7] anciently included in the *Oasis Magna* of the Romans,[8] is from its size and population the most important of the Egyptian oases at present. This oasis lies along a portion of an E.–W. escarpment of eocene limestone which rises to the north of it, and numbers many wells and springs, and some fifteen villages or hamlets. There are, all told, 200,000 palms in the oasis,[9] and a good deal of land is under cultivation, apart from the palm groves.

Nearly due east of the preceding, and also anciently a part of the *Oasis Magna*, lies Ḫargah.[10] The oasis depression is hemmed in on the northwest, north, and east by

[1] J. Ball and H. J. L. Beadnell, *Baharia Oasis, passim.*

[2] About 15 *per capita*, as opposed to 7.5 and 8.0 *per capita* in Daḫlah and Ḫargah respectively. J. Ball and H. J. L. Beadnell, *op. cit.* p. 43 *sq.*

[3] *Ibid.* p. 44.

[4] H. J. L. Beadnell, *Farafra Oasis.* Farafrah is to be identified with the ancient *Oasis Trinitheos.*

[5] *Ibid.* p. 11.

[6] L. V. Royle, verbal communication. Bînbashî Royle, learning of the existence of Abu ʿUngar, visited the oasis some years ago, in company with another officer.

[7] H. J. L. Beadnell, *Dakhla Oasis.*

[8] The Greek Αὔασις Μεγάλη. For the classical division of the Egyptian oases, *Georgii Cyprii Descriptio Orbis Romani*, p. 139 *sqq.*

[9] H. J. L. Beadnell, *op. cit.* p. 14.

[10] J. Ball, *Kharga Oasis.*

scarpments of limestone ; on the west, a barrier of vast sand dunes runs parallel to the eastern scarpment. Within the oasis depression a large number of hills rise from the floor.[1] The cultivable areas, lying principally in the north and south of the depression, are well supplied with pools and *'ayns*, and are extremely fertile, the oasis containing in all 60,000 *adult* palm-trees.[2] There are four towns or large villages and half a dozen hamlets.

Berîs, which appears in the rough traverse of the oases given above, is really but the chief place in the southern part of Ḫargah Oasis, as its name implies.[3] It is the largest village in the oasis, and contains a remarkably large thermal well ('Ayn Hushî).[4]

Southeasterly from Berîs lies Kurkur,[5] the last of the Egyptian oases. This oasis is small and at present uninhabited, but is important as a station on the natural desert road connecting the Egyptian oases with the Nile Valley in Nubia. It contains two wells and a number of scrub-palms.

The halting-places to be found in the west Nubian desert from Kurkur to Selîmah need not be particularized : but beyond the south Libyan desert the chief features of the western boundary of Eastern Libya deserve brief notice.

III. West—Chad Route Oases : Hamadah el-Ḥomrah : Hamadah Murzuk

The western boundary of Eastern Libya is a more arbitrary one than the others, but is at least marked geologically, and in some degree orographically, by a great wedge of limestone penetrating between Kufra and Murzuk southward toward Tibesti. From the intersection of lat. 20° N. with long. 18° E., on the north slopes of the Tu or Tibesti range, it is about 250 miles N.W. to Tummo, or War, which lies on the west side of the *duffah*, on the Chad–Tripoli road. From War to the Ḥarug es-Sod, which has been mentioned above, it is about 375 miles N.E. by N., at first along the western edge of the limestone *duffah* over the Chad route and through Gatrun, and then across the western expansion of the *duffah* itself, which runs toward the sunset into the Hamadah el-Ḥomrah. Along the edge followed by the Chad road exist a number of small *ḥaṭṭîas* and oases. Nearly due north of War, 200 miles distant, lies Murzuk. It is situated on the Hamadah of that name, a formation running W.S.W. and E.N.E. some 250 miles, and in the latitude of Murzuk is separated from the *duffah* just mentioned by about 75 miles of sand desert. The latter contains between the town and the edge of the *duffah* a number of small grazing-places and some water.

On the north side of the Hamadah Murzuk, as along the south, lies a desert of sand dunes. The northern desert, the Erg el-Edeyen, is bounded on the north by the Hamadah el-Ḥomrah. In a line taken N.W. from Murzuk to the south edge of

[1] J. Ball, *Kharga Oasis*, p. 38.

[2] *Ibid.* p. 46.

[3] بريس is seemingly a corruption of the Egyptian 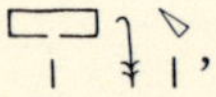, *pr-rs*, "the south mansion."

[4] J. Ball, *op. cit.* p. 59.

[5] Idem, *Jebel Garra and the Oasis of Kurkur.*

this Hamadah it is roughly 225 miles across the sands; prolonged across the Hamadah el-Ḥomrah some 150 miles farther in the same direction, the line would reach Ghadames. This last-named town is some 240 miles due south of the Shott el-Gerîd, the chief of the salt lakes which have been several times mentioned before, and which extend for about 120 miles westerly in from the Gulf of Kabes. Ghad̆ames, to return to that point, is located on the northern edge of the Hamadah el-Ḥomrah; the terrible desert of the Erg el-Kebîr lies between the town and the Red Hamadah on the one hand, and the oases of the territory of Tuggurt in the west, on the other. At its northern extremity the Erg el-Kebîr approaches the Shott el-Gerîd to within a very short distance.

The western boundary just defined is of a very desert character. The mountains of Tu or Tibesti, however, are high (Mount Tusidde, *circa* 6700 feet above sea-level) and fertile. The range is little known, only one European having crossed it and returned alive.[1] The *duffah* north from Tibesti has on it a good many sandy areas, and is for the most part sheer desert. A few *ḥaṭṭîas* do, however, occur, especially toward the west. The northwestern region, like the southern district, is mostly desert, *erg* and *hamadah* there succeeding each other until the fertile zone is reached in the vicinity of Southern Tunisia and Western Tripolitana.

IV. Internal Geography—Routes: Rates of Travel

The internal geography of Eastern Libya needs to be noticed, since both the population of the country and its culture have been greatly influenced by the position of the routes that run through it. The roads are of two sorts—primary and secondary. The former are the great *ḳafilah* tracks over which pass the caravans that undertake journeys a month or two in length; the latter are the shorter routes connecting one permanent centre with another. The former are the links between regions; the latter are the links between towns.

In the north, the first line to be noted is the great E.–W. route running parallel to the coast. This is the Darb el-Hag, so called because it is used by the Moslemîn of the Moghreb in making the pilgrimage to Mekkah. A glance at this road shows that, while the coast along which it runs is largely of a desert character, the shore line itself offers less obstacles to an E.–W. land-progress than do the opposite shores of the Mediterranean. The latter are diversified with capes and mountainous promontories; with the great peninsulas of Greece and Italy; with the seas into which these project—the Aegean, the Adriatic, and the Tyrrhenian. The African coast, on the other hand, runs west from Egypt to Tunisia without any abrupt break; only at one part the crescent of the Cyrenaic plateau pushes out into the Mediterranean, while to

[1] G. Nachtigal, *Săhără und Sûdân, passim*. More, it is hoped, will shortly be known of this obscure part of Africa. In 1911 an Austrian expedition purposed to carry out in this region a plan of penetration which, even in the annals of Ṣaḥaran exploration, deserved to be called bold. *Vide GJ*, vol. xxxvii. No. 1 (Jan. 1911), p. 95 *sq*. Unfortunately it failed.

the west of this the sea turns into the North African coast in the great bights of the Syrtes. The Darb el-Hag is really shorter by a little than the coast line itself, for having followed the curves of the shore from Kabes to Benghazî, it thence strikes across to the Gulf of Bombah, following the southern declivities of the Cyrenaic plateau. From Bombah it again runs easterly to Egypt, having the sea in sight upon the left for almost the whole of the way. The greatest obstacle offered by the Darb el-Hag to travellers moving in a large body is the lack of water, but it is nevertheless feasible even for armies. Thus, General Eaton, though not without great hardships, led his American forces over part of this route in 1805 from Alexandria to Bombah in about thirty days.[1] Cato succeeded in marching his 10,000 men from Cyrenaica to the western extremity of the Syrtes by dividing them into small bodies, for each of which a sufficient supply of water could be found.[2] Even without this device a very large body of nomadic people, inured to desert hardship and well supplied with animals to carry water and food, could probably traverse the Darb el-Hag from Kabes to Alexandria in from fifty to sixty days—at least, in the season of the rains. Cyrenaica, it may be observed in conclusion, being fertile and well watered, affords a recruiting station midway on this road.

Beside the Darb el-Hag, one other road crosses Eastern Libya running east and west. It lies in the interior, and is different in character from the coast route in this respect — that whereas the former serves chiefly to carry traffic from one of its extremities to the other, the latter is really a succession of secondary roads which may nevertheless be traversed in an easterly and westerly direction. By this route one marches from Tripoli in a S.E. direction to Soḫnah ; thence to Zellah and Abu Naym ; and on to Wagîlah and Sîwah ; from which last oasis the road may be taken either E.N.E. to the Egyptian Delta, or E. to the Nile *via* Baḥarîah. Except for reasons of trade, this road is seldom used in its entirety, though the eastern end of it, from Wagîlah to Egypt, is taken a good deal by the Arabs of Cyrenaica during the winter, to escape the rains and cold of the Darb el-Hag.

Except for this last-named route, all the primary roads of Eastern Libya are those which, having a N.–S. direction, connect the Mediterranean with the Sudan. The first and foremost of these links is the historic Chad to Tripoli road, which for over two thousand years has been the main channel through which the exportable products of Central Africa found their way to Europe. This famous line of march[3] passes from one small oasis to another,[4] in a direction almost due north from Lake Chad to

[1] Anonymous, *History of the War between the U.S. and Tripoli, etc.*, p. 121 *sqq.* ; R. Greenhow, *History and Present Condition of Tripoli, etc.*, p. 22 *sqq.* It is difficult to find how many marching hours were consumed in the journey, as the expedition was delayed by mutinies and other causes. The forces left Alexandria on March 6, 1805, and arrived at Bombah on April 16.

[2] Strabo xvii. p. 836 ; Plutarch, *Cato Minor*, § 56. It is Strabo who mentions the division of the army into small bodies. Plutarch says that Cato employed donkeys to carry his water-supply.

[3] Denham, Oudney, and Clapperton, *Narrative of Travels* ; H. Vischer, *Across the Sahara* ; H. Barth, *Reisen und Entdeckungen.* These works alone will suffice to give the reader a good idea of the Chad route.

[4] Small oases, when not too widely separated, have throughout the Ṣaḥara had something the same effect upon the

Murzuk, about 725 miles distant. Some of the oases which it threads are places capable of supporting permanent populations, as is the case at Teda and Kanuri. Towns also occur along the way. From mere halting-places some of these, as Bîlmah, Tummo, or War, and Gatrun, have grown to be of considerable size; War derives additional importance from being at that point on the Chad road where a divergent trail strikes off S.S.E. from the main line into the ranges of Tibesti or Tu. Similarly, from Gatrun a road between the north and east leads to Wagîlah, and so to Benghazî or to Egypt.

Murzuk is a centre, or *ganglion*, of the Ṣaḥaran body, and is of the greatest importance. Despite the unhealthfulness of its situation, the effects of which are clearly visible in the faces of the residents,[1] Murzuk is a large town. This is because it is at the focus of great roads. From Murzuk the caravans may pass E.N.E. to Wagîlah, and so to Benghazî and Egypt, or north to Soḫnah, a minor centre, from which they march N.W. to Tripoli town, about 475 miles from Murzuk, and thus 1300 from Lake Chad. Soḫnah, just mentioned, is united with the east by a road running to Zellah, Abu Naym, and Wagîlah.

Another great road to the south is that having its head at Ghat, and running into the Aïr and Niger Territories. With this, however, as it lies in Western rather than in Eastern Libya, this survey is not concerned. Ghat is situated at the western extremity of the Hamadah Murzuk, and is linked with the latter place by a short but difficult route. North of Ghat lies Ghadames, a centre of primary importance, situated at the junction of several great desert highways. It is not directly connected with Murzuk, from which it is separated by the Hamadah el-Ḥomrah and the Erg el-Edeyen. It is, however, connected with Ghat on the south, as has just been mentioned; with the Tedemait oases; and especially with In Salah, lying beyond the Hamadah et-Tinghert on the S.W.; with Wargla and Ghardayah in the W.N.W., and so with Laghwat at the foot of the Ṣaḥaran Atlas. In the marts of Ghadames, therefore, are exposed merchandise from the Sudan, the Atlas, Tripoli, and Europe, and the caravaneers of the north coast who do not know this oasis-town are not many.

To be included among the primary routes rather because of its length and directness than because of the amount of traffic it bears, is a line of march lying east of the Chad–Tripoli road. Within the last century it has come to have somewhat more importance than formerly, though the long stretches of waterless desert it traverses will prevent its ever being much used. The route in question is that running south from Wagîlah to Kufra, and thence on to Wanyanga (Wadyanga) and Borku. It is at present chiefly frequented by emissaries going to or from the Sîdî el-Mahdî es-Senusî, now resident at Kufra, rather than by merchant-caravaneers.

The last primary road which need be noticed is that penetrating the Sudan from

desert populations that the Aegean Islands have had on Greece. They tempt the adventurous, form half-way houses between distant points, and tend to produce small, hardy, and venturesome communities.

[1] Denham, Oudney, and Clapperton, *op. cit.* vol. i. p. xlviii.

Ḫargah, and called, from the number of days taken in traversing it, the Darb el-Arba'în, or "Forty Road." This road runs S. by W. to Selîmah, a small oasis where grazing and water are to be had, about 200 miles from Berîs, just south of Ḫargah. Thence the Darb el-Arba'în strikes off S.W. across the sands of the south Libyan Desert, passes through the wretched *ḥaṭṭîah* of Zaghawah, and goes on into Darfur, where it may be said to end at Masrub.

Of the secondary roads it need only be remarked that they form a network of convenient tracks between such inhabited places as are not far removed from each other, and which will be mentioned briefly later in this chapter in connection with the distribution of man in Eastern Libya.

A few words may here be added in regard to desert travel, since it is important for the reader to know something both of the means by which communication can be carried on in Eastern Libya, and of the rates of march.

The simplest and most primitive fashion of travelling in the desert is one which is only practicable for short distances, and which hardly exists on any extensive scale to-day—it is for the traveller to sling a *ḳerbah* across his shoulders and then trudge along on foot.[1] If a number of men share in carrying the water, journeys slightly longer than those of which a single man is capable may be undertaken. The rate of this sort of going depends largely on the ground and the time of year, but may be said to lie between 15 and 20 miles a day, according to season, footing, and number of men. To carry water by animals is, of course, immeasurably more convenient. The animals used for this purpose in Africa are the ass,[2] bullock, horse, and camel. The last is not native to Africa, but was known to the Libyans centuries before the irruptions of the Arabs. The ass and the bullock, under favourable conditions, can do 20 miles a day; the horse between 25 and 35.[3] All three of these animals are capable of adapting themselves to desert life to some degree, Bedawîn horses, for instance, learning to go frequently for two, or even three days without water. One difficulty, however, attends the use of all three, for even short journeys: on *hamadah* or *duffah*, or even where the sand is mixed with pebbles, their feet suffer terribly. A horse that has come north from Wadai to Wagîlah or Sîwah usually arrives, despite the fact that he is fairly well cared for on the way, with his hoofs split and tattered so badly that the wretched beast goes lame on all four feet. Between the camel and the other animals named above, there is, from the point of view of desert travel, no comparison for a moment. At a pinch, a good camel can go seven days without water; it can live off bitter thorns, or stiff *weshkah* (palm-scrub); it can carry a weight of two *ḳanṭars* (200 lbs.) for forty-eight hours at a stretch; and its eyes, nose

[1] C. M. Doughty, *Wanderings in Arabia*, vol. i. p. 24. A fatal instance of this sort of travel is there recorded.

[2] A single man goes readily enough from Garah to Sîwah with a donkey which carries its own and its driver's supplies of food and water for three days.

[3] For bullocks, cf. S. Augustinus, vol. xvi. p. 526, *Garamantum regibus tauri placuerunt* (*scil.* for travelling); Aymard, *Les Touareg*, p. 118 *sq*. Pls. 18, 19 for photographs of pack-bullocks, ringed through the nose, and in use in the S.W.

and ears are all wonderfully protected from the sand. In addition, the foot of the camel is a tough and elastic pad protected in front by the horny nails of the two toes. Even for kneeling on a stony desert ground, the camel is armed with thick callouses on his knees, and a callous pad on the breast. In short, this animal, so ungainly and unattractive at first sight, seems on further acquaintance a walking assemblage of desert "points." The rates of travel among camels vary. A *ḥamlah* camel plods over almost any road at about 2½ miles an hour, or 25 to 30 miles a day. A *hagîn* or trotting camel of good breed, on the other hand, can do 40 miles a day without difficulty, and over 50 if necessary. These paces the camel can maintain for a fairly long march, if only it be well fed; for whereas it can go far without drinking, it must be fed with as much regularity as possible.

V. Geographic Position with regard to Outlying Regions—The West: The South: The East: The North

The areas which have been outlined as constituting Eastern Libya present certain general characteristics which differentiate that region as a whole from those contiguous to it. With the great E.N.E.–W.S.W. ranges of the Atlas system on the north-west Eastern Libya has nothing to compare. To the west, the Ṣaḥara is diversified with larger habitable areas than are contained in the Libyan Desert, while to the south lie the fertile ranges of Tibesti and Borku, north of the Chad district, and the cultivable territories of Wadai and Darfur. To the east extends the Nile Valley, which is, of course, of extraordinary fertility, throughout its length.

In the north-west, Eastern Libya is the natural goal of peoples passing eastward through the long Atlas valleys; from the west it may be readily invaded by desert peoples from the Tassili-n-Asgar or Aïr. In the south it is only the present character of the Sudanese cattle-grazers that leads to the raids being from north to south, rather than the reverse; for the country is in that quarter guarded only partially by the Tibesti range. In the east, Eastern Libya has access to Egypt through the oases, which are themselves, however, so placed as to be debatable ground.

Broadly speaking, it may be said that it is mainly from the west and north-west that Eastern Libya, as a whole, is subject to incursions on a grand scale. For a population hemmed in by the Atlas mountains and moved eastwards along valleys by pressure exerted in the west is inevitably forced, as has just been said, into the East Libyan littoral zone. And from the west, nomadic tribesmen, there inured to desert life, may with ease expand in a direction toward the east and north-east. Only severe pressure from the south would force the pastoral Negro and negroid populations of the Chad region into the desert, as, once started on a migration, they would tend naturally to traverse the well-watered lands of the Sudan in a westerly or easterly direction.[1] The cultivator of the Nile Valley again, as is usually the case with peoples habitually

[1] As may be seen in the case of the Fulah or Fulbê peoples.

dependent on irrigation, has shown himself ready to submit to almost any degree of oppression rather than take his liberty with him into the desert. The one serious invasion which seems to have penetrated Eastern Libya from the east is that of the Moḥammadan Arabs. But not only was that invasion in itself attended with many circumstances which cannot be associated with racial migrations in general, but its main course was not, if one excepts the early raiding into Fezzan, deflected from the littoral zone, which it traversed to reach the richer regions of the west.

In the north, to turn now to those regions facing the Libyan coast across the eastern Mediterranean, at one point Cyrenaica is but a short day's sail removed from Crete, the distance between Cape Krio and Dernah being but 150 miles.[1] The position of the island with respect to the Libyan coast is indeed such as to attract attention in even a casual glance at the chart. For a distance of 135 miles it lies east and west, in a direction parallel to the trend of the Marmaric coast. Small craft passing from Crete to Egypt still generally run due south from the island 180 miles to Ras el-Milḥ, and thence easterly to Alexandria. It was the proximity of Crete to the African Pentapolis that led to the administrative union of the two as the single Roman province of *Creta-Cyrene* or *Creta et Cyrene*. Despite the scarcity of harbours on the African side, there are several small ports, such as Dernah, the Gulf of Bombah, Marsa Bahat, Marsa Ṭobruk, "Port Bardia," and Limreyg, which all lie under the island, and Crete itself has numerous small havens along its southern coast. As a "half-way house" between Crete and Egypt, the western portion of Marmarica must have been visited by ships at a very early period.

From the mainland of Greece itself the African coast is, of course, farther removed, the shortest distance being 207 miles, from Cape Matapan to Ras el-Hillil. As, however, early navigators preferred always to hold the land in sight, and so take their departure for the African coast from some point on the south coast of Crete, the relative positions of Libya and the Greek mainland are of only secondary importance. The same remark applies with even greater force to Asia Minor, distant some 300 miles.

The western part of the East Libyan littoral, it is evident at a glance, is farther removed from the European mainland, the Mediterranean widening in the Syrtic Gulfs toward the south, and in the Ionian Sea toward the north. From Ras Mizratah westward to the Gulf of Kabes, however, the African coast lies under the island of Sicily, which is 120 miles nearer this section of the Libyan coast than it is to Cyrenaica.[2] Malta and Gozzo lie in line with Sicily and the Libyan coast, it being about 190 miles from the former island due south to the African main. But it is not with the Tripolitan coast that Sicily and Malta come most closely into relations with Africa. For on coming from the east to Tunisia, the Libyan coast bends sharply northward for about three degrees of latitude, and so approaches not only the islands mentioned but

[1] From Ras et-Tîn to the island of Gaudo (Gaulis) is but 135 miles. A vessel making the passage between these two points would, in fair weather, be out of sight of land for only about 100 miles.

[2] Cape Passero to Benghazî, 365 miles; Tripoli Town to south coast of Sicily, about 245 miles.

Sardinia as well. As this bend lies northwards of the Shott el-Gerîd, it is outside the region which has been designated as Eastern Libya ; but as the connecting link between that region and Sardinia and Sicily it deserves at least passing notice. From Cape Bon (N.E. Tunisia) to Marsalla is under 80 miles ; from the same point on the coast it is under 159 miles to Cape Spartivento (S. Sardinia), a point which in direct (N.-S.) line is only 100 miles from the African coast. These distances are not such, at a favourable time of year, as to deter even the most timorous navigators from crossing in either direction. It is, therefore, not a matter for surprise to find the warlike Sardinian pirates acting in concert with the East Libyans at a very early period, since from Sardinia they could reach the African coast in a short day, and thereafter follow the littoral either to the west or the east.[1]

The chief features of the littoral having thus been touched on, it may be added that the region belongs to the eastern and central Mediterranean, being, as has just been pointed out, connected with the central islands and the west by the N.E. littoral of Tunisia. Except in Cyrenaica, the Libyan coast presents no great attraction to invaders from the north, and, in fact, the formation of the coast is such as to encourage the belief that such extraneous ethnological elements as directly entered Eastern Libya from the north came in by way of Tunisia or Cyrenaica.

VI. Climatology and Health

Eastern Libya lies under two climatic zones—the Mediterranean and the Ṣaḥaran.[2]

The district of the Mediterranean climate is that to which has already been applied the term "Littoral fertile zone." The region in question, not being at any point one of great width, and not presenting any barriers, toward the north, high enough to be of climatic importance, enjoys throughout its length the weather of the southern Mediterranean.

The prevailing winds along this coastal region, especially in summer, are northerly, while in winter and autumn there is a high percentage of southerlies. In the spring, the *ḳibly*, or hot southerly scirocco, is frequent,[3] its occurrence being unknown in summer, and its season, therefore, corresponding to that of the Egyptian *ḫamsîn*. The following table gives the percentages of the directions of the winds for the four seasons, based on the observations recorded at Benghazî, in the central part of the coast line, during the four years from 1891 to 1894 :—[4]

[1] H. R. Hall, *Oldest Civilization of Greece*, p. 181 *sq*., certainly, to my thinking, underrates the sailing qualities of early ships. This point cannot here be debated at length, but I have considered the evidence, and as one fairly familiar with sailing vessels of small tonnage, may say that I do not believe that there were any grave practical difficulties in navigating between Sicily, Sardinia, and Libya, or between Libya and Crete, even in the Old Empire.

[2] Oribasius, *Collect. medica*, ix. 7, correctly states that, owing to the influence of the sea, the littoral climate of Libya is more equable than that of the interior. [3] G. Hildebrand, *Cyrenaïka*, p. 206. [4] *Ibid.* p. 204.

	N.	N.E.	E.	S.E.	S.	S.W.	W.	N.W.	Prevalent Winds.
Winter . .	12.8	1.1	4.4	6.4	37.4	9.0	21.5	7.4	S., W.
Spring . .	32.7	2.7	2.9	3.5	24.5	5.2	13.9	14.6	N., S.
Summer . .	70.5	4.2	4.7	1.0	5.7	1.4	4.8	7.7	N.
Autumn . .	29.2	3.8	4.3	7.6	34.4	3.8	10.1	6.8	S., N.

The rainfall in the littoral zone occurs annually, the wet season generally extending from October to May, but the amount of rain is very irregular[1] from year to year. Droughts may occur owing to slightness of successive rainfalls and protracted summers, but they are not often severe. In its distribution, the rain falls more frequently near the shore, though extending so far south as almost to reach Sîwah in the east, and the Hamadah el-Ḥomrah in the west. The following is the mean of the rainfalls for four years at Benghazî :—

	Jan.	Feb.	Mar.	Apr.	May.	June.	July.	Aug.[2]	Sept.[2]	Oct.[2]	Nov.	Dec.
mm.	131	83	30	2	3	0	0	0	1	9	41	102

This gives the mean yearly total of 402 mm.—a mean of 81 mm. for the winter, of 1 mm. for the spring, of 0 mm. for the summer, and of 50 mm. for the autumn. The rainfall at Tripoli Town for three years was 547.6 mm., 662.8 mm., 224.0 mm., giving a mean of 478 mm.[3]

The temperature of the littoral zone is moderate, verging on the subtropical. In the highest parts of the Gebel Nafusa and the Cyrenaic Plateau the thermometer never rises as high as it does at some points which are actually on the sea coast, approximately 1° C. of temperature being lost with every 2000 feet of ascent. The average temperatures for four years at Benghazî were monthly as follows :—[4]

	Jan.	Feb.	Mar.	Apr.	May.	June.	July.	Aug.	Sept.	Oct.	Nov.	Dec.
Degrees C.	12.5°	13.3°	17.3°	18.5°	21.9°	24.4°	26.1°	26.3°	25.9°	24.4°	19.0°	15.3°

This gives a yearly average of 20.4° C., with a variation of 13.8° between the extremes 12.5° (January) and 26.3° (August). This yearly average of 20.4° C. is nearly equal to that of Kabes (19.6°) or of Tripoli Town (19.9°),[5] though below the annual mean of Southern Tunisia, away from the immediate vicinity of the coast (21.1°).[6]

[1] G. Hildebrand, *Cyrenaïka*, p. 210. As proof of this irregularity, see the table there given of the monthly rainfalls for 1891 to 1894, inclusive, at Benghazî.

[2] These months, being omitted during one year, are averaged on three instead of four records.

[3] G. Ayra, *Tripoli e il suo clima*, p. 63.

[4] G. Hildebrand, *op. cit.* p. 226. [5] *Ibid.* p. 222. [6] *Ibid.* p. 233.

The range of temperature at Benghazî (13.8°) is a good deal over that of Mogador (6.0°),[1] which, though practically under the same parallel, is more exposed to the equalizing action of a greater body of water than is Benghazî. It is, however, significant of much less violent seasonal change than the range of variation, for example, of Mesopotamia (26.0°),[2] situated to the eastwards on the same parallel. The seasonal averages for Benghazî are as follows: spring, 19.2°; summer, 25.6°; autumn, 23.1°; winter, 13.7°.[3] In the above figures, the intense heat which may for a short time prevail during a *ḳibly* does not appear as a factor. It is doubtful if the 132° F. (55.5° C.) recorded by one traveller as accompanying a *ḳibly*[4] was ever really recorded, but for the thermometer to stand at 50° C. for an hour or more during the height of these distressing winds is not unknown.

In conclusion of this short treatment of the littoral zone, it may be said that the region is one well adapted to man—especially for primitive man living largely in the open—from the climatic point of view. The seasons, as throughout the lower levels along the Mediterranean, are marked by the winter rains and the summer droughts, and while not as strikingly differentiated as in northern Europe, are nevertheless accompanied by appreciable changes of winds and temperature.

In leaving the littoral for the interior, one passes at once into a climatic region that extends from the Mediterranean zone on the north, to the region of tropical rainfall on the south. Deficient as are the data with regard to the littoral climate of Eastern Libya, the sources of knowledge for the interior are much more scanty. Owing to this lack of evidence, it is necessary to base most of the following remarks on observations taken a number of years ago, at the extreme north-western confines of Eastern Libya.

The following table of percentages is approximately indicative of the winds prevalent during the year in the interior western parts of Eastern Libya.[5]

	N.	N.E.	E.	S.E.	S.	S.W.	W.	N.W.	Prevalent Winds.
Winter . .	11.0	14.5	17.5	14.5	12.5	12.0	6.0	12.0	N.E., E., S.E.
Spring . .	13.0	14.4	30.6	13.6	10.1	3.7	6.3	8.3	E., N.E., S.E.
Summer . .	10.0	20.0	30.1	16.7	11.7	3.3	1.6	6.6	E., N.E., S.E.
Autumn . .	00.0	14.3	25.0	7.2	14.3	32.0	7.2	00.0	S.W., E.

In connection with this table, it should be observed that calms are common in August and December, while September, October, and November are almost perfectly windless, about 90 per cent of the days being quite so. From the table given above,

[1] G. Hildebrand, *op. cit.* p. 225. [2] *Ibid. loc. cit.* [3] *Ibid.* pp. 224, 225.

[4] H. Gorringe, *Coast of Africa*, in *JAGNY*, vol. xiii. p. 54.

[5] These percentages I have computed from the tables published by H. Duveyrier, *Les Touareg du Nord*, p. 91 *sqq.* and p. 124.

it is clear that the prevalent winds are E., veering towards the south during the summer heats, and towards the north in winter.

The hygrometry of the desert parts of Eastern Libya is exceedingly variable. A sudden drop in surface temperature owing to winds may, even in the most desolate districts, be followed by one or two nights of heavy dews.[1] Dew is also likely to fall on nights following showers of rain. Rain itself may not descend in certain parts of the desert for periods of ten, twenty, or even thirty years, but it is safe to assert that of no known region of the Libyan Desert may it be said that it is quite without rainfall. Rain may, even in very desert parts of the country, descend for a short period with a torrential violence which is almost tropical. Thus, in Nubia, which partakes largely of the desert climate, terrific local "cloud-bursts" are experienced at intervals varying in length from ten to twenty years. On these occasions, the rain descends in sheets for perhaps an hour, the flat, thatched roofs of the houses are beaten in, irrigated fields are turned to shallow pools of water, and the *ḫors*, or gullies, along the edge of the desert become the beds of raging streams which carry with them stones and small boulders to the lower levels. Beside these periodic deluges, rain may fall in slight showers in many parts of desert Libya—especially in the north and south-west—at any time of year. But years may go by without these rains, and they cannot therefore be depended upon for agriculture, or even for grazing.

The temperatures of Eastern Libya in the interior are generally higher than those in the littoral zone. This in itself is of less importance than the great range between maximum and minimum. The sands and rocks of the desert which during the day receive and reflect the heat, begin to cool rapidly shortly before the sun has gone down. By midnight the radiation has practically ceased, and the temperature of the gebel is approximately that of the cool night air. There is also great local variation away from the equalizing influence of the sea, altitude being in the desert a great factor in temperature. The following table, based on materials collected by Lieut. J. Ayer[2] in Tuggurt, contiguous to Eastern Libya on the west, is here presented as offering results based on more ample observations than any yet taken actually within the Ṣaḥaran portions of Eastern Libya itself.

	Jan.*	Feb.*	Mar.*	Apr.*	May.	June.	July.	Aug.	Sept.*	Oct.*	Nov.	Dec.
Degrees C.	15.4°	17.6°	22.5°	29.8°	34.9°	38.5°	43.6°	41.8°	40.8°	40.5°	22.3°	14.9°

The maximum temperature observed by Duveyrier in Eastern Libya was 44.6° (8th and 26th July) at Murzuk; the minimum −2.1° (18th December) at Timellulen,

[1] Personal observation.

[2] H. Duveyrier, *op. cit.* p. 114, where the table from which the mensual means have been calculated will be found. Those means marked with an asterisk (*) are based on four years' observations; the rest on three. The temperatures here used were taken at 2.30 P.M.

in the western part of the Hamadah el-Ḥomrah. This gives the range of 46.7° as compared to the variation of 13° to 14° in the littoral.

The annual mean, computed from the same source as the above mensual averages, is therefore rather misleading—it works out to 30.2°. The mensual averages clearly show the division into cold and hot periods which are the only "seasons" in the desert year. The cold lasts from December to March; the heat from June to September.[1]

For the Eastern portion of the interior zone, valuable data have been collected by the Egyptian Survey Department at Daḫlah. The prevalent winds, as calculated from the detailed report for 1908,[2] are as follows:—

	N.	N.E.	E.	S.E.	S.	S.W.	W.	N.W.	Prevalent Winds.
Winter . .	67.4	00.0	00.0	00.0	00.0	00.0	00.1	32.5	N., N.W.
Spring . .	48.0	2.3	0.7	00.0	00.0	0.3	3.0	45.7	N., N.W.
Summer . .	39.6	1.8	00.0	00.0	00.0	0.8	2.2	55.6	N.W., N.
Autumn . .	20.6	7.3	00.0	00.0	00.0	00.0	2.6	69.5	N.W., N.

The striking feature in the above table is the absence of south winds. For half the year, during winter and spring, the prevailing winds are northerly, hauling round to the north-west in summer and autumn. The shift at the beginning of winter is so striking in the above table that one is inclined to suspect that the observations from which the percentages have been compiled were taken during an exceptional year, but further records are needed before this can be proved.

The rainfalls at Daḫlah are so irregular and insignificant that they cannot be tabulated to advantage. The following list, kindly prepared by the director of the Ḥelwan Observatory,[3] will serve to show the nature of the rainfalls:—

Date.		Remarks.
1905	Feb. 2	Rain *circa* 5 mm.
	Oct. 16	" afternoon; slight.
	Nov. 12	" for 4 hours, beginning 8 P.M.
1906	Feb. 7	" in the morning; slight.
	" 9	" " " "
	" 11	" for 7 hours in the morning.
	" 14	" slight.
1908	May 18	" for 5 minutes at noon; slight.
1909	Jan. 17	" slight.
	" 27	" "
	" 28	" "
	May 16	" for 10 minutes at 3 P.M.; slight.
1911	Jan. 26	" *circa* 5 mm.

[1] H. Duveyrier, *op. cit.* p. 106.

[2] Egyptian Government, *Meteorological Report for 1908*, p. 182 *sqq.*

[3] Mr. B. F. E. Keeling, to whom I am greatly indebted also for valuable advice on several points connected with this chapter.

The monthly temperatures for 1908 at Dablah, as recorded for the Survey Department, are as follows :—

	Jan.	Feb.	Mar.	Apr.	May.	June.	July.	Aug.	Sept.	Oct.	Nov.	Dec.
Degrees C. at 2 P.M. .	17.4°	18.2°	23.4°	29.4°	32.7°	34.7°	35.1°	37.1°	35.4°	30.6°	25.2°	20.6°
Daily Means . .	13.0°	13.3°	18.6°	24.3°	27.3°	29.7°	30.1°	30.0°	28.2°	23.8°	17.0°	12.1°

This gives a yearly mean at 2 P.M. of 28.3°, and a yearly mean of daily means of 22.3°. The maximum recorded above is 37.1° (August). The lowest *absolute* minimum recorded in 1908 was 00.0° for February. This gives a range 37.1° for the 2 P.M. monthly means as opposed to 46.7° in the west, or 13° to 14° in the north.

These figures, relating to three widely separated portions of Eastern Libya, will suffice to give some idea of the climate of the country.

Even so short an account as the present one of the East Libyan climate would not be justified in passing over the atmospheric phenomena of the desert without comment. Solar halos and mock-suns are not infrequently seen, and lunar halos are common, especially where the desert approaches the littoral region. Rainbows may occur during a shower. Thunder and lightning are frequent accompaniments of the great periodic storms. The sunlight in the desert is intense, even to the point of being painful. In conjunction with the heat, it effects mirages, which are sometimes of extraordinary clearness. Usually, however, these take the simple form of a sheet of glittering water seen in a distant depression, the image being more clearly visible to one walking or close to the ground than to one mounted on a horse or camel.[1]

To conclude this notice on the present climatology of Libya, it may be said that the desert climate is so distinct from that of the Mediterranean zone on the north, or from that of the tropical zone on the south, that it may be properly regarded as Ṣaḥaran, and continental. It is marked by two seasons, the hot and the cold, which are independent of the rainfall, but vary greatly with altitude and remoteness from the sea. For long periods no rain may fall in any given locality ; it may then descend in a torrential storm, or in showers coming at any time of the year. Both the hot and the cold seasons are accompanied by the same minor phenomena, a fact which deserves to be noticed, since it tends to lessen the seasonal differentiation, the effects of which will be spoken of later in this chapter.

It has recently been maintained[2] that Eastern Libya has, within historic times, been subjected to a marked climatic change, but the evidence thus far brought forward to sustain this theory is not conclusive. It is indubitable that in many localities the

[1] Diodorus Siculus (iii. 1. 4) notices the occurrence of mirages as especially frequent in the Syrtica Regio.

[2] E. Huntington, *Kharga Oasis and Climatic Changes*, in *BAGS*, Sept. 1910, reviewed in *The Geographical Journal*, vol. xxxvi. No. 6 (Dec. 1910), p. 732 *sq.* See also H. J. L. Beadnell, *Mr. Huntington on Climatic Oscillations*, in *GJ*, vol. xxxvii. No. 1 (Jan. 1911), p. 108 *sq.*

population has declined, but this appears to be due to the advent of an ignorant and shiftless Arab population, rather than to any climatic oscillation. The almost if not entire absence of recent vegetable remains in places which supporters of the theory of desiccation maintain to have "gone dry" within the last two thousand years, the extraordinary preservation of the mud-brick tombs of the Christian necropolis at Ḫargah, the presence of cisterns along the Marmaric coast, where there is a heavy winter rainfall—this and similar evidence suggests that there has been no very great climatic change in Eastern Libya within recent times. In the Western Ṣaḥara, it is true, such changes seem to have taken place. Without going into the complicated question of the classical Nigir River, the fact seems to be sufficiently established by the finding of neolithic camp-sites along the borders of the now waterless Wady Igharghar, the dry bed of which runs through the West Libyan Desert to the Shott el-Gerîd. This cannot, however, be adduced as evidence for the desiccation of Eastern Libya, since, as the climate, the geology, and the orography of the Eastern and Western portions of Libya are now different in many respects, it is but fair to assume that they were as different anciently as to-day.

The healthfulness of Eastern Libya as a whole is exceptionally good. This is due to the dryness, to the fact that only in a few places humanity is crowded together, and to the intensity of the sunlight, which even in the towns has a deterrent effect upon infectious disease. Malaria and dysentery are rare, and hardly known outside the fertile areas. Some of these latter, however, have a bad name, owing to the prevalence of severe malarial fevers ("apricot fever," "Ḫargah fever") at certain times of year; many of the nomad Arabs will not enter Sîwah in the autumn for fear of this sickness, which is then rife. Ophthalmia and syphilis are the two most widespread diseases, the former being extremely common. Plague [1] and cholera have at intervals nearly depopulated the towns, but, owing to their mode of life, the nomadic population is protected from these epidemics. Wide, clean spaces, strong sunlight, simple food, hard physical work, and a climate which, while hot, is dry and bracing, have given to the greater portion of the modern inhabitants of Eastern Libya the same physique which excited the admiration of Herodotus. Having described the native practice of cautery, the Greek historian says that the practitioners themselves aver that "such is the reason why they are so much more healthy than other men. And indeed," he adds, "the Libyans are the halest men I know." [2] Of the same tenor are the remarks of Sallust, who described the Africans as "healthy, swift of foot, and able to endure fatigue. Most of them," he adds, "die by the gradual decay of age, except such as perish by the sword, or beasts of prey; for disease finds but few victims." [3]

[1] Thucydides (ii. 48) mentions an epidemic of plague in the extreme east of Libya.

[2] Herodotus iv. 187.

[3] Sallust, *Iugurtha*, xvii.

VII. Flora : Fauna

Of the Flora and Fauna of Eastern Libya, it is here sufficient to mention only such plants and animals as chiefly affect the habitability of the country.

The soil of the littoral zone produces most of the fruits and cereals found in Greece and the Levant, while even far in the interior,[1] the oases are wonderfully fruitful throughout the whole area. Wheat and barley are cultivated along the littoral; and the latter is even found in the oases, where, however, the more usual grain is that of the *ḏura*.

Lentils, peas, and beans of several varieties grow readily in all the fertile districts, as do also leeks, onions, and a small sort of the tomato. Numerous less important plants have also been found useful for food. Such, for example, are the leguminous *harra*,[2] the *left*,[3] which has an edible root, and the *'agul*,[4] of which the root is prepared as food by men, while its spinous leaves afford forage for camels and asses. Numerous varieties of gourds and melons are cultivated in all the fertile districts, and grapes are found not only cultivated, but wild. Lemons, figs, and oranges do not thrive, except in the northern oases and along the coast, though the prune, the apricot, and—more especially—the pomegranate are found in almost all the oases of the interior. Among the fructiferous trees which may be mentioned as especially belonging to this region—at least in its northwestern districts—should be noted the *Zizyphus lotus* (L.), the slightly acidulous fruit of which has by some enthusiasts been identified with the Homeric lotus. Another candidate for this distinction is the fruit of the *ghardek*,[5] which is small, pleasantly insipid, and which has a slightly stimulating effect. The olive is well suited to the climate of Eastern Libya, the trees now cultivated in the oases being, though of straggling growth, conspicuously good ones, and the old Greek trees in Cyrenaica having maintained themselves till the present practically without cultivation.

The most important of all Libyan vegetable products is the date-palm.[6] Its rôle in desert Flora is comparable to that of the camel in the animal kingdom, and like the camel, the date is of foreign origin, though now cultivated throughout the length and breadth of North Africa. A volume might be written on the uses of this extraordinary tree. Its fruit is eaten fresh, or dried, or cooked, or brayed; an intoxicant is made by fermenting the fruit, or from fermenting the sap of the tree itself; its leaves serve for fuel, thatching, camel forage, parts of camel-saddles, or, when the tender "head" is taken and boiled, for human consumption. The naturally reticulated fibre, which at first envelops the leaf, is used for stuffing pack-saddles, or for weaving good rope. The bark strippings serve as fuel, the logs, split lengthwise, as rafters or planks.

[1] For more detailed botanical notices for Eastern Libya, the reader is referred to H. Duveyrier, *op. cit.* p. 147 *sqq.*, for the west; to G. Hildebrand, *op. cit.* p. 240 *sqq.*; A. Rainaud, *Quid de natura Pentapolis monumenta . . . nobis tradiderint, passim*; D. Viviani, *Florae Libycae specimen . . .*; E. Cosson, *Descriptio plantarum novarum in Cyrenaica a G. Rohlfs detectarum*, p. 80 *sqq.*; *ibid. Plantae in Cyrenaica . . . notae*, p. 45 *sqq.*, for the north; J. G. Wilkinson, *Manners and Customs of the Ancient Egyptians*, vol. ii. p. 398 *sqq.*; F. Woenig, *Die Pflanzen im alten Ägypten*, for the east.

[2] *Diplotaxis duveyrierana.* The *D. pendula* and *Eruca sativa* are also called *harra*, and are both used for food.

[3] *Brassica napus.* [4] *Alhagi maurorum.* [5] *Nitraria tridentata* (Desf.).

[6] *Phoenix dactylifera* (L.); cf. G. Maspero, *Dawn of Civilization*, p. 27.

These are but some of the services rendered by the palm, but they are sufficient to show its importance. When it is added that a tree demands comparatively little care, bears after its fifth year, and, when mature, yields 200 to 300 lbs. of nourishing food which is excellently suitable for desert travel, the reader will realize the great difference its introduction and dissemination must have brought about in the economic condition of Africa.

Thus far, only that part of the flora has been glanced at which affords man his food. Before passing on to the question of timber, it should be remarked that many non-edible vegetables in Eastern Libya, a country wherein everything with valuable properties, either real or supposed, is sure to be used, are employed chemically or medicinally. Thus, the bark of the *gedarî* shrub,[1] and the fruit of the tamarisk,[2] are used in tanning leather ; *ḥalfa*[3] and esparto,[4] tough grasses, are used for making mats and ropes, both of fair quality ;[5] while many insignificant herbs serve the nomads for simples,[6] or savouries.[7]

The trees useful for timber in Eastern Libya are found chiefly in the north. It is a question of great interest but, at the present date, not to be solved, if the trees suitable for shipbuilding and the construction of houses were anciently to be found much farther south. It seems probable that the local desiccation of some places, as parts of the Syrtica Regio, for example, may be due to ancient deforestation ; and the habitability of a very considerable area may have been affected by reckless timbering in ancient times. In the south, the palm is the wood chiefly used for planks and beams. Thus, even at Sîwah, doors are made of palm-planks, houses are timbered with halved palm-logs, and graves are in some cases covered with quartered ones.

In the same oasis, the helves of mattocks and of bill-hooks are made from pomegranate branches or, more rarely, olive. Yet in some northern parts of Eastern Libya, good timber is to be found even plentifully. In Cyrenaica the cypress[8] occurs, as do also two varieties of pine,[9] and, frequently, the Levantine juniper.[10] Some of the wadys in the Gebel el-Aḫḍar and the Gebel el-ʿAḳabah have, from the thickness of the dark ranks of conifers standing along their sides, an aspect perfectly European. The sycamore, tamarisk, and carob occur, especially in the west, while the mimosa and acacia are more evenly distributed. All these trees yield wood suitable to a greater or less degree for building purposes, but only in a few localities are the trees found in enough numbers to make good timbering country.

Except, possibly, in extent of forestation, there is no reason to suppose that the Flora of Eastern Libya at the present day seriously differs from that of ancient historic times. The palm was undoubtedly introduced at a very early period, and the vine and

[1] *Rhus dioica* (Willd.).
[2] *Tamarix articulata*, *T. gallica*, *T. pauciovulata*, *T. laxiflora*.
[3] *Macrochloa tenacissima*.
[4] *Lygeum spartum*.
[5] It is chiefly for making paper that they are exported.
[6] E.g. *Lebbin* (*Euphorbia paralias*, L.), used against snake-bites.
[7] E.g. *Kaykut* (*Erythrostictus punctatus*, Schlecht.), which is put in "*kuskus*."
[8] *Cupressus sempervirens*.
[9] *Pinus halepensis*, *P. pinea ?*
[10] *Juniperus phoenicea*.

olive both flourished in the littoral zone in the days of Herodotus. But one interesting plant, the most famous in all the Flora Libyca, has become extinct—none of the numerous attempts which have been made to show that this or that modern plant represents the ancient silphium (σίλφιον) has been convincing.[1] This remarkable plant, which from its representations upon the Cyrenaic coins is known to have been a variety of umbellifer, deserves mention here for its historical importance and former economic consequence. Its ancient habitat lay in the barren steppe country south of the Cyrenaic plateau, from the vicinity of the Gulf of Bombah to that of Bueb Bay. It had a variety of uses: the stalks were valuable forage for cattle; it was introduced into food as a savouring; and from incisions made in its stalks was obtained the highly prized juice (ὀπὸς σιλφίου, *laserpitium*), by trading in which the Battiad kings of Cyrene attained to their great wealth.[2] Although both artificially cultivated, and existing naturally, it has now disappeared.

The Fauna of Eastern Libya numbers among the domesticated animals at the present day the camel, horse, ox, ass, sheep, goat, and dog. In communities composed of an Arab or Arabized population, the pigeon and cock are also found, though among the Berbers of East Libya neither these nor any other birds are eaten. Of the animals named above, the camel, as has been said, is not native to Africa. Of Asiatic origin, it is not found depicted on the Egyptian monuments before the Saitic period, and did not become common in Africa until the time of the Persian ascendancy in Egypt.[3] Once introduced, however, it rapidly usurped throughout all North Africa the place of the other animals used for desert travel. The horse is also of Asian origin, but found its way into Africa before the camel, suddenly appearing in Egypt at the beginning of the New Empire,[4] and finding its way to Crete, before this time, in the Early Minoan period.[5] The ox, though now rare in Eastern Libya, was nevertheless known anciently, as is shown by the representations of four of these animals at the plough, in the tomb of Pe-ṭut at Sîwah.[6]

[1] The following may be noted as the chief publications on this subject: J. P. Thrige, *Res Cyrenensium*, p. 304 *sqq.*, where the classical notices have been collected; R. M. Smith and E. A. Porcher, *History of the Discoveries at Cyrene*, p. 87 *sqq.*; S. Martin, *Aufsatz über das Silphium*; idem, *Note sur la prétendue Silphium Cyrenaicum* in the *Bull. Génér. Thérapeut. Médic. Chirurgic.* vol. xci. p. 23 *sqq.*; *ibid.*, *À propos du sÿlphium*, p. 222 *sq.*; P. Ascherson, *Drias e Sylphium*; G. Rohlfs, *Das Silphium*; A. Rainaud, *op. cit.* p. 118 *sqq.*

[2] It is possible that, as early as Minoan times, silphium formed an article of export from Libya to Crete. A. J. Evans, *Scripta Minoa*, vol. i. p. 215 *sq.*

[3] The camel (*C. dromedarius*) existed in Africa in quaternary times, but its historic introduction seems, as stated, to belong to Persian times. For a consideration of this question *vide* G.-B.-M. Flamand, *De l'introduction du chameau.*

[4] W. Ridgeway, *The Thoroughbred Horse*, p. 216 *sqq.* Ridgeway advocates the Libyan origin of the thoroughbred riding horse, and in support of his thesis has collected much material. But he has not explained (*a*) the absence of the horse in O.E. Egypt; or (*b*) why among the Libyans of the invasions horses were so scarce; or (*c*) how it happens that the horse was known in Crete before it appeared in Egypt.

[5] A. J. Evans adduced on this point a late Minoan seal-impression in which a horse is seen being carried in a one-masted vessel. This scene he interpreted as the first importation of the thoroughbred horse from Libya into Crete—a fourfold assumption for which there is no support. As a matter of fact, a seal of the Early Minoan Period, with a horse engraved on it, was afterwards noted by C. H. and H. Hawes, *Crete the Forerunner of Greece*, p. 43.

[6] G. Steindorff, *Durch die Libysche Wüste zur Amonsoase*, p. 100, fig. 75. A short time ago, there were no oxen in the oasis. They have recently been re-introduced by H.H. the Khedive.

The asses in Eastern Libya are of a very fine breed, and are more in harmony with their environment than any of the other animals in use, excepting only the camel. Of the wild animals useful to man for their skins or for food, the addax antelope, mohor antelope, orix, and moufflon (two varieties) occur, as do also the gazelle and, though but rarely, the wild ass.[1] Among the smaller quadrupeds may be mentioned the jerboa, hare, and rabbit. The commonest of the carnivorous animals are the hyena, a small wolf, jackal, fennec-fox, a variety of pard (*Felis jubata*), the wild-cat (*F. catus*), and, rarely, the panther. If the classical sources are to be believed, the interior of Eastern Libya shared with the ancient Moghreb a bad name on account of the number and ferocity of the wild animals it contained. Herodotus gives to a whole district of the interior the name ἡ Λιβύη Θηριώδης, or "Wild-Beast Libya."[2] Of birds, the ostrich may be mentioned as the largest and most useful. It has recently become extinct in the littoral zone,[3] though it once existed as far north as Marmarica, and its plumes, as will later appear, formed one of the distinctive features of Libyan dress. Bustard are found in the neighbourhood of the desert *ḥaṭṭiahs*, while in the summer and autumn the littoral zone is visited by vast migrations of quail. Wild doves occur in those districts having cliffs and ravines to shelter them, while water-hens, ducks, and flamingoes are found on the *shotts*.

Along the coast the fish are extremely numerous, and in many places sponges, which are to-day extensively fished for by the Greeks,[4] abound.

Of noxious animals, apart from the carnivorous beasts, snakes exist in all the habitable areas, and even in the *ḥaṭṭîahs*. The cobra is rare, but the almost equally deadly cerastes is in many places so common as to be a menace to grazing animals. Scorpions of several varieties are found in places not too far removed from damp soil, as are also centipedes. Poisonous tarantulas of large size live in most of the oases. Occasionally, flights of locusts ruin the grazing and the oasis-gardens,[5] and cause damage that is ill-atoned for by the fact that, on these occasions, these insects are eaten by both men and animals.

[1] The wild ass occurred till mediæval times as far north as near the Egyptian Oases. [2] Herodotus ii. 32.

[3] W. H. Browne, *Travels in Africa*, p. 16. Browne remarked that "near the few springs of water" on the way to Sîwah, "the tracks of the antelope and ostrich are frequently discoverable." G. E. Shelley, *Birds of Egypt*, p. 315 *sqq.*, has collected some evidence on this topic. Citing O. Finsch and G. Hartlaub, *Die Vögel Ost-Afrikas*, p. 597, Shelley notes the present extinction of the ostrich on the el-Moghrah plains between Cairo and Suez, where Burckhardt saw these birds in 1816. Prince Ḥalîm Basha testified that he had found freshly disturbed breeding-places of the ostrich a few days' journey from Cairo. In Pocock's time the ostrich was found in the hilly gebel S.W. of Alexandria; Sonini often saw fresh tracks in the desert about Baḥarîah; and General Minutoli, on his way from Alexandria to Sîwah, observed flocks of from ten to fifteen. It may be added that fragments of old ostrich-egg shells are found in the vicinity of Ḫargah Oasis. An English writer has therefore committed a serious blunder in adducing the southern (Sudanese) habitat of the ostrich as evidence in support of one of his hypotheses, as has been pointed out (O. Bates, *Dr. G. Elliot Smith and the Egyptian Race*).

[4] C. W. Furlong, *Gateway to the Sahara*, p. 120 *sqq.* A brief popular account of this industry will there be found—the only redeeming feature in an otherwise worthless book.

[5] Julius Obsequens, *De prodigiis*, 28, and Paulus Orosius v. 11, for an account of the devastations caused in Cyrenaica by locusts *anno* 125 B.C. Also *vide* Pliny xi. 29, where the methodical efforts taken by the Cyrenaeans to combat this pest are mentioned.

In conclusion, it may be said that the wild Fauna of Eastern Libya is not, at least at the present time, a very numerous one either in species or in number. It contains many animals, which, since they have adapted themselves to their environment by taking on desert colourings, etc., are of interest to naturalists ; but these wild animals cannot be said to form a very important factor in the life of the inhabitants, as is the case in tropical Africa, where the animals are much more numerous, or in Arctic countries, where the Flora is economically almost negligible.

VIII. Man—Distribution : Numbers : Relations of Man to his Environment in Eastern Libya

The modern population of Eastern Libya is divisible into two main classes which may be regarded as cultural rather than racial—the sedentary townsmen and the nomads.

The towns of Eastern Libya exist as centres of trade or as agricultural villages. The former are found at junctions of the caravan roads, or in small oases along the lines of march. The latter exist in the more extensive fertile areas, which in some cases have also the advantage of being well placed with regard to trade. Centres of the former class are those such as Murzuk on the great Chad–Tripoli route, at its junction with roads from Ghat in the west and Wagîlah in the east ; Ghat itself, on the road from Aïr and the Niger Territories, with Ghadames to the north and Murzuk to the east ; and Ghadames, with Ghat to the south, Tripoli Town to the N.E., and to the west, Wargla and Ghardayah. To this category of trade centres must also be added Soḫnah, between Tripoli Town, Wagîlah, and Murzuk. Towns that have grown up at the halting-places along the great desert roads are sometimes of considerable size, as Gatrun on the Chad–Tripoli route. The agricultural towns are as a rule much smaller than these harbours of the caravans. They lie chiefly in the Syrtic littoral zone, as Tatahuin, Misdah, " Bongem " (Bu Negem), Ẓellah, Abu Naym, etc., or in Cyrenaica, as Merg, Tuḳrah, Ṭolmeyṯah, etc. The latter pair, were they now practicable ports as in classical times, could be reckoned with Tripoli Town, Benghazî, or Dernah, as owing their importance partly to trade and partly to agriculture. This double source of prosperity is actually enjoyed to some extent by two of the larger oases, for Wagîlah, besides its palm groves, has the good fortune to be placed at the intersection of the Sudan-Kufra, Benghazî, Murzuk, and Sîwah roads, by the last of which one passes eastward into Egypt ; and Ḫargah is both rich in itself, and important as a station on the Darb el-Arbaʿîn. From Ḫargah it is but a short journey to Esnah in the east or es-Sîut in the north. In general the agricultural towns lie to the north, in littoral Tunisia and Tripolitana, and in the oases ; the trade towns are scattered about in a roughly N.-S. direction, west of the Libyan Desert.

To turn from the towns to the habitable portions of the desert, it must first be remarked that the nomads are not so independent of the permanent centres as is usually supposed. Throughout the Ṣaḥara, the material and moral existence of the nomads is only assured by the means of sedentary annexes in the centres, or at the peripheries, of their districts.[1] Therefore the area to which each tribe is limited almost always contains, or is within reach of, some permanent settlement. These latter not only serve as markets for indispensable articles as, for example, all such as are made from metal, or for dates, but are also the only places at which the nomad comes in contact with forms of life different from his own. They are the centres from which he derives most of the simple ideas he possesses, and are the sources of his religious enthusiasms. It is to the towns that he goes at certain seasons to meet other tribesmen, with whom he exchanges news, and whom he joins in planning raids, or discussing the rainfall and grazing. An example of these annual visitations may be seen at Delingat, in the western Delta, a town to which the Aulad ʿAlî repair in great numbers every autumn.

In the desert the nomad moves freely about within the tribal area, passing from one grazing ground to another with his camels and goats, in winter "following the rain," and in summer temporarily exhausting one *ḥaṭṭîah* after another.

Occasionally, if far enough removed from European influence, he joins his fellows on long raids into regions outside the tribal territory. The object of these raids is generally to obtain slaves or camels, or to plunder the homeward bound caravans from the south. These latter, if he but feel himself strong enough, he will rob without compunction, though in his own district he "protects" them for a substantial consideration against similar raids from without.

Of his visits to the towns, of his periodic foregatherings with his fellow tribesmen, of his camel and goat grazing, and, rarely, of the raids just mentioned, the life of the nomad is largely made up.[2]

The numbers of the present inhabitants of Eastern Libya, counting both sedentaries and nomads, cannot be stated without great reserve. Nor can one feel at all sure that, once an approximation has been made, one is provided with anything but a very rough indication as to the number of the ancient inhabitants ; for the Arab irruptions of the seventh and eleventh centuries, and the subsequent collapse of the Libyan predominance in the east, both tend to complicate this problem. It seems, however, certain that the changes to be reckoned with are all such as would tend to reduce rather than to increase the number of the population. The Arabs, with their genius for destruction, finished the work already begun by the nomadic Libyans, when they captured and sacked the now ruined cities of the sedentary Africans. The old centres have many of them remained uninhabited, or subsisted as mere hamlets, since the Moslem invaders clove their disastrous way through the most populous parts of

[1] H. Duveyrier, *Les Touareg du Nord*, p. 247. Duveyrier does not exaggerate the importance of the towns when he calls them *organes essentiels de la vie intérieure et des relations extérieures des tribus*.

[2] No more vivid account of nomadic life, which in its essentials varies little with time or place, can be read than that of C. M. Doughty, *op. cit.*

North Africa. Even in cases where a sequestered geographical position has favoured continuous occupation, one finds evidence of decline in the population, as in the now abandoned but fertile oasis of Abu 'Ungar, where the sole vestiges of man are the ruined walls and mounds of debris left by former occupants.[1] In the oasis of Ḫargah, evidence is to be seen of the decrease in population in the excellent preservation of the ancient masonry, which, had the number of the inhabitants increased, would have been quarried more extensively for building material. When these points are considered, and with them the questions of deforestation and the consequent encroachments of the desert sands, the number of the modern inhabitants may be accepted as a minimum below which, at least during the period of the Graeco-Roman occupation, the ancient population did not fall. The relation of the modern to the pre-classical total is more difficult to determine ; but as Graeco-Roman occupation tended to increase the population, the number of the East Libyans before the advent of the Greek colonists was probably nearer the modern figure.

The following approximation of the population of Eastern Libya at the present time is made without reckoning in the inhabitants of the Fayum ; for it is uncertain as to whether that district was, during full historic times, in the possession of the Libyans for any considerable period. Therefore this district may be dismissed with the remark that its present population is about 147,000.[2]

Eastern Tunisia (Shott el-Gerîd to Tripolitana)[3]	150,000
Tripolitana, Kufra and N. Fezzan[4]	1,000,000
Marmarica[5]	8,000
Sîwah and Garah[6]	6,000
Baḥarîah[7]	6,000
Farafrah[8]	550
Daḫlah[9]	1,700
Ḫargah[10]	7,850
Kurkur[11]	0
Total	1,180,100

Or, in round numbers, 1,180,000.

If this latter figure be taken to represent approximately the number of the Eastern Libyans, in the pre-classical period, or rather before the XXVIth Dynasty and the expansion of Egypt towards the west, it is possible to arrive at the number of fighting men they could have put in the field. If one-tenth of the total population was capable of bearing arms — a low percentage among a primitive people — the minimum fighting total would be 118,000. As it is not to be supposed that the Libyans were

[1] It is uncertain of what period. On intelligence (verbal) received from Bînbashî L. V. Royle, one of the two Europeans who have visited this oasis, I incline to believe the ruins to be Coptic.

[2] Egyptian Government, *Almanac*, 1911, p. 119. 147,324 is the number there given for 1907.

[3] Estimated on the basis of 10 per square mile.

[4] A. H. Keane, *Africa*, vol. i. p. 130.

[5] Egyptian Government, *op. cit.* p. 118, gives Mariut, etc., at 7805.

[6] After personal observations.

[7] J. Ball and H. J. L. Beadnell, *Baharia Oasis*, p. 42.

[8] H. J. L. Beadnell, *Farafra Oasis*, p. 13.

[9] H. J. L. Beadnell, *Dakhla Oasis*, p. 14.

[10] J. Ball, *Kharga Oasis*, p. 46.

[11] J. Ball, *Jebel Garra and the Oasis of Kurkur*, for this *ḥaṭṭîah*.

well enough united to draw at one time upon all these forces, they may be better exhibited according to areas of mobilization, thus :—

Region.		Population.	Fighting Men.
I. The Littoral	E. Tunisia	150,000	15,000
	Tripolitana	1,000,000	100,000
	Marmarica	8,000	800
		1,158,000	115,800
II. The Oases	Sîwah and Garah	6,000	600
	Baḥarîah	6,000	600
	Farafrah	550	55
	Daḫlah	1,700	170
	Ḫargah	7,850	785
		22,100	2,210
III. Western parts	E. Tunisia	150,000	15,000
	Tripolitana	1,000,000	100,000
		1,150,000	115,000
IV. North-Eastern parts	W. Tripolitana (half)	500,000	50,000
	Marmarica	8,000	800
	Sîwah and Garah	5,000	500
		513,000	51,300

From the above tables it is clear that the bulk of the Libyan strength-in-arms lay in the west; that the oases must have been always subordinated to the littoral, and that the Libyan invasions of Egypt must have derived their strength from as far west, at least, as Cyrenaica. Another point deserves mention: the smallness of the population of the oases, their fertility, and their position between the Egyptian power on the east and the chief seats of the Libyans on the west, must have made them, until late Egyptian times, a cause for contention and hostility between the two peoples.

It remains to speak of the effects of regional environment to which the modern inhabitants are subjected. As it is by the nomadic part of the population that these effects of climatic and physiographic factors are most clearly evinced, it need only be said of the town-dwelling traders or agriculturists, that they exhibit in varying, but lesser degrees, according to circumstances of race and geographical position, the physical and temperamental peculiarities of the nomads. Since, moreover, it is with the ancestors of the modern Berber-speaking indigenes, and not with the invading Arabs, that this essay deals, the following remarks are applicable to the former; especially as they have, for a longer period than the Arabs, been influenced by the nature of the country.

The physique of the nomad Berber clearly shows the effect of his environment.

As more will be said on this topic in discussing the ethnography of the ancient inhabitants, a very few brief remarks will here suffice. The typical North African nomad is tall, spare, and wiry. Like all spearmen he carries himself erect ; he is long-limbed, and in his movements dignified and grave. He walks with long, slow steps, as if suiting his pace to the stride of a camel. He is hardened alike to cold and heat, is nervously strong and indefatigably enduring. He eats and drinks sparely by necessity, though prone to over-indulgence when an opportunity presents itself. He displays, despite his present religion, a fondness for intoxicants when he can get them.[1] His face is either round or oval, with a broad forehead, clean-cut lips, high cheek-bones, and a firm round chin. If bearded, it is generally but slightly, and with straight, black hair. Bronzed by sun and wind in early life, he is, even by European standards, white at birth. The eyes are generally dark and piercing in the younger men, though sun-glare and ophthalmia almost invariably take the lustre from the eyes of the older ones. Blue eyes are rare, though not unknown. The women, noticeably smaller than the men, are often handsome, with a beauty which is European rather than Arab. Men and women alike have small hands and feet.[2] Like his forefathers in the days of Herodotus, the modern, indigenous nomad is conspicuously robust, having accommodated himself to an environment severe and desolate, but invigorating and healthful. In his mentality, the Berber-speaking nomad shows even more clearly than in his physique the effects of his environment. Centralized communal life on a large scale is an impossibility in most parts of Eastern Libya : the resources of any one locality suffice usually only for the needs of a few families. The nomads would therefore be by the nature of the country speedily reduced to a state of mere nihilism, had they not instinctively preserved themselves from this condition by maintaining their sense of tribal loyalty. The rights of each nomadic family are respected only because they are upheld by the tribe of which it forms a part, and which has its own places of resort, and its own rights of watering and grazing. The nomad has an appreciation of his interest in the tribe, and his loyalty to it is one which is not easily broken. This sense of tribal community he extends also to the confederation, by belonging to which the tribe itself is protected against foreign incursions on a large scale.

Other factors to be considered are the monotony and loneliness of the desert ; the difficulty of existing in it ; the great distance which often lies between one habitable point and another ; the absence of marked seasonal changes of climate, and the *personal* quality of what, in civilized communities, would be called public opinion.

The monotony of the desert is a thing not easily conceived by those who have not

[1] Thus, the Berber-speaking Wagîlans, Magabras, and Sîwans consume large quantities of *lakbî*, a mild intoxicant made from fermented dates or palm-sap. J. Hamilton, *Wanderings in North Africa*, pp. 189 *sqq.*, 195, *et alibi.* The Aghlebite rulers of Ḳayruan were notoriously hard drinkers. V. Piquet, *Les Civilisations de l'Afrique du Nord*, p. 86. Intemperance more than once cost the Libyans dear. Thus, the Carthaginian Imilco exterminated a body of them after they had consumed a quantity of wine, drugged with mandragore, which he had allowed to fall into their hands. Polyaenus, *Strategem.* v. 10, Ἰμίλκων . . . εἰδὼς τῶν Λιβύων τὸ φίλοινον, κτλ. Cf. *infra*, p. 234, for the loss, from a similar cause, of a victory by the Nasamones.

[2] H. Duveyrier, *op. cit.* p. 382.

experienced it. Its effect upon the nomadic peoples is seen chiefly in their extremely limited range of ideas, their minds not being stimulated by natural suggestion. The gravity of the Imushagh is almost as proverbial as their bravery, but is largely due to the fact that their minds are seldom stirred except under the stress of physical excitement. As a converse of this, the nomad, whose mind is so stiffened that he will regard his first locomotive engine with a dignified stolidity that masks nothing but an inability to grasp anything beyond the visualized fact, will display intense keenness and animation when tracking a gazelle. In the former case he passively accepts the presence of something outside his desert experience, and so a thing for which he cannot conceive any use : in the latter he is dealing with a matter with which he has been familiar from his childhood, and in tracking his food he displays a craftiness and skill born of intense and practised concentration many times before directed in this same channel.

The loneliness of desert life tends to increase the sense of liberty and personal freedom to which the nomad is born heir. For days he marches from one *ḥaṭṭîah* to another, without perhaps seeing another human being save his own immediate companions. Such as it is, he is master of the land : beyond the reach of government, a conformist to custom rather than to law, he yet has wit enough to understand the value of his freedom, and prizes it highly enough to fight for it—one of the few abstract possessions outside his religion for which he will give his life.

Despite the difficulty of his life, the Berber-speaking nomad has, according to his own code of honour, a regard for property. The Arab is his inferior in this respect, though living under much the same conditions. The Imushagh may collect together and launch themselves across five hundred miles of desert on a desperate camel-raid : this is war. On the road, they will pass and leave untouched a load of goods jettisoned against recovery by some unlucky cameleer : to take the forsaken bales would be disgraceful theft. To steal by trickery is, among the nomads, naturally a more serious offence than among a sedentary people. For the latter are surrounded by many superfluous things, the loss of which would be no more than annoying to the owner : the property of the average nomad, on the other hand, is of such vital sort that to deprive him of it is tantamount to threatening his existence. Yet to a nomad who starves perennially on milk and dates, the temptations to which he does not often yield are far greater than those before which the morals of a sedentary often give way. The very severity of his life has bred in him a rough code of honesty, which forbids him to plunder those with whom he lives.

The long marches to which the Libyan nomad must be accustomed have the effect of instilling in him an indifference to distance quite beyond the experience of sedentary peoples. A native of the desert thinks little of walking 60 miles in two days on a handful of dried dates, if he is reasonably certain of finding a puddle of water half-way on the road. With equal equanimity, he will face 500 miles with a camel, provided his road does not lead through hostile country.

This indifference to long journeys is partly due to a very vague conception of time. It is always with an effort that a desert people, in reply to the questions of a European, try to estimate the time required to reach a given point. Almost invariably they understate it ; but this is usually the result of mere ignorance, and not, as many travellers have unjustly said, of a deliberate wish to say the pleasing thing at the expense of truth. A caravaneer who may know every well, *ḥaṭṭîah*, waḍy, and *mongar* along a line of march, may quite honestly be several hours out in his reckoning each day. This uncertainty exists even in dealing with years : few tribesmen know their own ages, or, certainly, the ages of their children over six or seven. These peculiarities are due chiefly to the lack of incident in desert life, and to the absence of markedly differentiated seasons. The cold winds of winter cease, and summer comes in at a stride, to be again succeeded by the winter cold without any season of marked change intervening between the two.

The personal quality of public opinion mentioned above is due to the isolation of nomadic families. To the simple laws of his family, tribe, and confederacy the nomad is in most cases forced religiously to adhere. But, whereas, in civilized communities, it is mass-prejudice that enforces those regulations which make for the public good, with the nomad it is the opinion of the individuals of his family and acquaintance. Temperamentally nervous and sensitive, the nomad is always susceptible to ridicule and mockery, and he has the same hesitation to exposing himself to the sharp tongue of an old woman that a European would have to rendering himself contemptible to a city full of people with none of whom he was personally acquainted. Nomadic laws, to be effective, cannot be as complex as those governing a community in which every man is policed by his neighbour. This explains why public opinion among the East Libyan nomads does not censure the immorality of women until after marriage, when questions of paternity and inheritance are involved. The *lex talionis* obtains in all private quarrels ; but though opinion is not strong enough to prevail against protracted private feuds, it checks these indirectly through the remarkable institution of the *ṣoff*, or extra-tribal brotherhood.

Several of the factors just mentioned combine together to encourage in the North African nomad that highly-developed personal bravery which, did not the same factors deprive him of a spirit of discipline and of organization, would make him, even to-day, a most formidable element in modern African politics ; his lonely life makes him dependent upon himself and his own skill in arms—not to handle well his gun, lance, sword, and buckler means, in an encounter with an enemy in the desert, that he will be killed. He has lived for too many generations in an open country, where cover is scanty and trails are easily followed, to seek instinctively to hide from an enemy. It is not long since he spoke contemptuously of firearms as "weapons of treachery" ;[1] three thousand years ago his ancestors faced without flinching, for six hours, the deadly rain of arrows poured into their wild ranks by the well-trained Egyptian archers.[2]

To this bravery, it follows as a corollary that the Berber nomad is fairly truthful.

[1] H. Duveyrier, *op. cit.* p. 383.

[2] *Infra*, p. 217.

Even if he seeks to escape the consequences of some act of violence, and be taken by his pursuers, he may confess his guilt, though the admission cost him his life.[1] Once he has given his word, the chances are he will fulfil it, cost what it may : the Tripolitan merchant, who has no love for him, will yet entrust him with money or merchandise to be delivered to some trader in far-away Bornu.

Like almost all desert peoples the world over, the Berber nomad practises freely, when occasion presents itself and he has the means of dispensing it, an open-handed hospitality. The desert guest to-day enjoys the semi-sacred character, and suffers the same insecurity, as the Homeric traveller. Yet of that treachery which sometimes stained the annals of his sedentary kinsmen in classical times, as when Bocchus cold-bloodedly betrayed his son-in-law Jugurtha to the Romans,[2] the Libyan nomad is sometimes guilty ; he does not hesitate to use treachery toward an enemy, or towards one whom he considers as such. Hence it is that the Roman talked of "shifty" or "turncoat" Africans.[3] He is, however, loyal towards his guest ; nor will he, having harboured him, plunder him at a short distance from his tents, as can happen among the Arabs.

A conspicuous point of difference between the African and the Arab is also found in the former's almost European treatment of women. This may be due to the fact that the matriarchate seems to have been established among the Libyans at an early period, since other circumstances apparently traceable to that institution exist in Northern, as in Central, Africa.

The indigenous nomadic women enjoy a degree of freedom unknown among their Semitic sisters. A girl of the Imushagh refuses or accepts a suitor as she pleases : she may, before marriage, have a lover without suffering those penalties which, in most cases, would be visited upon an unmarried Arab woman under the same circumstances ; and she receives, after marriage, much of that consideration which among civilized people is paid to the mother of the family. Custom in Eastern Libya still pays more regard to maternal than to paternal filiation in dealing with questions of inheritance.[4]

While it is unnecessary to accept in all its enthusiastic details the somewhat rhetorical description of Berber character given by Ibn Ḫaldun, this topic may yet be concluded with his summary, which, even if it presents only the brighter side of the picture, has yet its basis in fact. And the reader is reminded that the little-changing conditions of desert life, which have preserved their main aspects for thousands of years, assure us that neither in character nor physique has the indigenous tribesman had reason greatly

[1] H. Duveyrier, *op. cit.* p. 385.

[2] Sallust, *Iugurtha*, 112 *sq.*

[3] Firmicus Maternus, *Mathes.* i. 4 : . . . *Galli stolidi, leves Graeci, Afri subdoli, avari Syri* . . . ; Servius *ad Verg. Aen.* iv. 724 : . . . *Afros versipelles.* But cf. *Junioris Philosophi Orbis Descriptio*, A § 62, where, speaking of Libya west of Egypt, the writer remarks : *inops est valde et viros paucissimos habet, sed bonos, prudentes, et pios.*

[4] H. Duveyrier, *op. cit.* p. 393 *sqq.* This question of matriarchal survival among the Libyan peoples is one of great complexity, and is far from being settled. *Vide infra*, p. 111 *sqq.*

to alter since prehistoric times.[1] "The virtues which do honour to man, and which have become for the Berbers a second nature," says the Arab historian, "are bravery and readiness in defending guests and dependants; faithfulness to promises, pacts, and treaties; patience in adversity; staunchness in great afflictions; gentleness of disposition; indulgence toward the faults of others; aversion to taking revenge; kindness toward the unfortunate; respect for the old and pious; eagerness to relieve the downcast; industry; hospitality; charity; great-heartedness; hatred of oppression; courage shown against the powers which threaten them . . . there," he concludes, "is a host of titles for the Berbers . . . —titles inherited from their fathers, and of which the exhibition in writing ought to serve as an example to the nations of future times." [2]

[1] T. Mommsen, *Römische Geschichte*, vol. v. p. 643: *Die civilisierten Fremdherrschaften wechselten; die Berbern blieben wie die Palmen der Oase und der Sand der Wuste.* Desert peoples are admittedly among the most conservative in the world.

[2] Ibn Ḫaldun, *Kitab el-'Ibar*, Trans. McG. de Slane, vol. i. p. 199 *sq.* It should be said that Ibn Ḫaldun is here speaking more especially of the Atlas tribesmen of the west. In addition, *vide* H. Duveyrier, *op. cit.* p. 383 *sqq.* In regard to Duveyrier's account of the character of the Imushagh, it must be said that he has deserved the censure which, for his *enthousiasme un peu juvénile pour les vertus touaregs*, he has received from E.-F. Gautier, *Sahara Algérien*, p. 137. The Imushagh are a fine people; but they are fine barbarians.

CHAPTER II

ETHNOLOGY AND ETHNOGEOGRAPHY

THE origin, whether European, Asiatic, or African, of the Hamitic race—which, with the Arabs, now shares that part of Africa which lies north of lat. 10° N.—yet awaits solution. A host of theories, a few of them plausible, none of them sufficiently supported, and most of them in direct contradiction to each other, have been launched as solutions to this problem, and have but rendered it more obscure. At present, and until a great mass of new and scientifically gathered evidence shall have been collected, only one main fact is indisputable—*viz.* that the so-called Hamitic race has absorbed a number of foreign ethnic elements,[1] which it has not succeeded in wholly assimilating physically, though it has imposed upon them this or that Hamitic dialect. The original pure Hamitic type seems to be that found among the Ṣaḥaran Berbers—a type tall, spare, long-limbed, and dark (*brun*) ;[2] hair black or dark brown, straight or wavy ; head dolichocephalic, orthognathous ; nose slightly aquiline or straight ; eyes dark and piercing, set rather widely apart ; mouth well-defined ; facial capillary system slightly developed ; movements generally slow and dignified. In the west, between the Wady Dra'ah ("Wed Draa") and the Senegal, this type has become fused with the Negro elements from the south, the resultant type sharing the physical peculiarities of both progenitors. The same thing appears to have happened in the case of the various Hamitic peoples of East Africa.

The most important extra-African elements among the Hamites are the brachycephalic Berbers and the blonds. Both, as one would *a priori* expect, are found in the north. The brachycephals[3] are, almost certainly, invaders, since they form but a small group near the northern seaboard of the dolichocephalic African continent. The blonds are much more numerous, but are even more clearly of extra-African origin. Various theories have been advanced to account for the presence of this xanthochroid element in Africa, it even having been asserted that the blonds owed their origin to the

[1] Cf. H. Weisgerber, *Les Blancs d'Afrique*, p. 82 *et alibi*.

[2] Cf. Lucan, iv. 678 *sq.*, *concolor Indo Maurus* ; Nemesian, *Cyneget.* 261, *coloratus Mazax* [*coloratus* here as in Martial x. 68, 3, *coloratis . . . Etruscis*] ; H. Schirmer, *De nomine populorum qui Berberi vulgo dicuntur*, p. 74.

[3] For this type, H. Weisgerber, *op. cit.* p. 53 *sqq.*

Vandals. This is, however, not only in itself incredible, owing to the number and distribution of the xanthochroids in the fastnesses of Morocco, but is even flatly contradicted by the ancient evidence. Whatever may be the true significance of the word Teḥenu, which some would have to mean "fair" or "bright" (*scil.* "people"),[1] evidence of a more satisfactory nature is to be found in the Egyptian monuments. For whereas the Libyan in earlier Egyptian art is regularly a *brun*, later representations exist showing Libyans not only blond, but even with red hair and blue eyes.[2] Classical notices of blond Africans also exist; and though they are few, they are explicit. The Greek colonists of Cyrene are mentioned by Callimachus as dancing with the blond Libyan women—μετὰ ξανθῇσι Λιβύσσῃς.[3] This passage may be compared with that of the *Pharsalia*, in which Lucan speaks of the blond Libyan and black Aethiopian serving-women of Cleopatra:—

Haec Libyces pars tam flavos gerit altera crines
Ut nullis Caesar Rheni se dicat in arvis
Tam rutilas vidisse comas; pars sanguinis usti
Torta caput, refugosque gerens a fronte capillos.[4]

The geographer Scylax says that the Libyans about Lake Tritonis are reported to be fair and finely built.[5] A passage in Pausanias might suggest the presence among the Libyans of blue or sea-coloured eyes (. . . γλαυκοὺς . . . ὀφθαλμούς . . .).[6] The presence of blond *natives* in the west is mentioned by Procopius,[7] and from these notices it is clear that, for nearly a thousand years before the advent of the Vandals, a xanthochroid element continuously existed in Africa. This blond element was not, probably, to be found far from the coast, the interior being occupied by the *brun* Hamitic type, and, as to-day, by mixed Hamites and negroes in the oases. The presence of the

[1] F. Chabas, *Études sur l'antiquité*, p. 181; P. le P. Renouf, *Who were the Libyans?* p. 602; G. H. Brugsch, *Geographie des alten Ägyptens*, vol. ii. p. 78.

[2] This is not, to be sure, always quite conclusive, since paintings do occur in which foreigners are represented with *red* eyes, *e.g.* W. M. Müller, *Egyptological Researches*, vol. ii. Plates xiv., xvi., xvii. *et alibi.* But *cf. ibid.* p. 135, note 2, where the author has justly observed that while the *brun* Libyan type is the only one portrayed in the Old Empire, the xanthochroids predominate in the New Empire representations.

[3] Callimachus, *Hymni* ii. (*Apolloni*) 85 (it will be remembered that Callimachus was himself a Cyrenean):—

Ἦ ῥ' ἐχάρη μέγα Φοῖβος
ὅστε ζωστῆρες Ἐννυοῦς
ἀνέρες ὠρχήσαντο μετὰ
ξανθῇσι Λιβύσσῃς.
Τέθμαι εὖτέ σφιν Καρ-
νειάδες ἤλυθον Ὧραι.

[4] Lucan, *Pharsalia*, x. 126 *sqq.*

[5] Scylax, *Periplus*, § 110, οὗτοι γὰρ Γύζαντες Λίβυες λέγονται ξανθοί, ἄπαστοι καὶ κάλλιστοι. On this passage *vide* C. Mehlis, *Die Berberfrage*, p. 37, and C. Müller, *ad Scyl. loc. cit.* (*Geogr. Graec. Min.* vol. i. p. 88 col. B).

[6] Pausanias i. 14.

[7] Procopius, *De bello Vandalico*, ii. 13. Procopius had this information from a native source, it being conveyed to him by a Moorish chief, "Orthaeas," who told him that beyond (west of) the desert were to be found a people who were not dark like the Moors, but who were of white countenance and fair-haired—οὐχ ὥσπερ οἱ Μαυρούσιοι μελανόχροοι, ἀλλὰ λευκαί τε λίαν τὰ σώματα καὶ τὰς κόμας ξανθοί.

last-named element explains how, in Greek argot, black hydrias came to be called "Libyans."[1]

That the xanthochroids were Nordic invaders, as was long ago supposed by Broca[2] and Faidherbe,[3] seems, despite the ingenious theory of Sergi to the contrary, indubitable. Sergi has advocated the African origin of the xanthochroids, claiming that, because the mass of them are found in the heights of the Atlas,[4] they are autochthonous indigenes whose pigmentation was modified by their mountain environment.[5] To sustain this theory, he cites an interesting piece of evidence from an Italian military anthropometrist,[6] who found in his examination of the recruits that the majority of those who were blond came from districts that were over 400 metres above sea-level. This, of course, is not evidence on the African xanthochroids; for it is not shown that the Italian blonds are not of Langobardic or of earlier Germanic stock, who, themselves Nordic invaders, found themselves most at home and survived better in the cooler mountain districts. And again, if mere altitude could make blonds, these would not be lacking in either the Rocky Mountains, or the Andes, where every altitude, and all conditions of climate and latitude, are to be found. As neither they nor the Himalayas and the Hindu Kush,[7] which reach by stages from hot moist plains to enormous altitudes; the Abyssinian highlands, well over a modest 400 metres; nor the orographic system about Victoria Nyanza, have yet produced a blond people, it may safely be said that no more so have either the Apennines or the Atlas. And since this is the case, and the African xanthochroids are found at the end of a road which was followed in historic times by another blond Nordic invasion,[8] it is only reasonable to suppose that the xanthochroids of the Egyptian monuments and classical notices were invaders in a country primarily peopled with "autochthonous" blacks and *bruns*. One may, as did de Quatrefages, say truly that the origin of the African blonds is as yet unknown,[9] but it is, for the reasons just given, safe to say they were immigrants.

The presence of the brachycephalic and of the xanthochroid elements in Africa naturally suggests that, since among the North Africans generally classed as Hamitic are a number of sub-types, some of these may have had their origin from yet other foreign immigrations. This is of course possible, though the differences between the sub-types are not such as to necessitate such an explanation. The prevalence among the Hamites of dolichocephaly, for example, and the great similarities of hair and of skin-colour seem to point to their common indigenous origin, various modifications having

[1] Hesychius, *in verb.* Λιβύας· τὰς μέλαινας ὑδρίας, ἐπὶ τοῖς τάφοις τιθεμένας. The true home of the Negro, anciently as to-day, was Central Africa and the Sudan. Cf. Firmicus Maternus, *Mathes*, i. 1 . . . *omnes in Aethiopia nigri* . . . and a host of other notices.

[2] P. Broca, *Les Peuples blonds et les monuments mégalithiques.*

[3] L. L. C. Faidherbe, *Instructions sur l'anthropologie de l'Algérie*, in the *Bull. Soc. Anthr.*, Paris, 2nd series, viii., 1873, p. 603 *sq.*

[4] C. Tissot, *Sur les monuments mégalithiques et les populations blondes du Maroc.* But, as the classical notices above cited show, they were distributed *littorally*, no matter where the bulk of the blond population was to be found.

[5] G. Sergi, *The Mediterranean Race*, p. 72 *sqq.*

[6] R. Livi, *Antropometria militare*, pt. i. p. 65 *sqq.*

[7] The one possible exception may be the Yeshkhuns of Dardistan, who have been reported to have red hair, etc.

[8] *I.e.* the Vandals.

[9] De Quatrefages, *Histoire générale des races humaines*, p. 486.

taken place owing to fusion with the negritians of the Sudan, or with the xanthochroids and brachycephals of the north. Such a modification is now well established in the case of the Trarza Moors, a people at first sight very different in aspect from the Ṣaḥaran Berbers who are known to be the result of a fusion between the latter and the Negroes of Senegambia.[1] Other evidence, of a linguistic nature, exists to prove that an ethnic sub-stratum of "autochthones" of a single race existed in North Africa. From the Mediterranean to the Sudan, and from the Atlantic to the Red Sea, dialects of the Hamitic family are yet to be found. In many places they have given place to Arabic, or, as in Abyssinia, to other Semitic tongues, but everywhere the linguistic survivals testify to the former prevalence of Hamitic. Among the western Hamites, again, can be found evidence of their having once been called by a common ethnic name.[2] This name may be radically represented as MZغ or MZGH,[3] and has at present the force of "*noble*" or "*free*"[4] (*scil.* "people"). It is seen as i-MuŠaGH among the Berbers west of Fezzan; in the Aïr district as i-MaǴiGH-en;[5] a feminine form is applied by the Auwelimiden of Adrar to their dialect, which they call ta-MaSeGH-t;[6] the Berbers of the Maroccan Rîf, Atlas, and South Atlas slopes call themselves i-MaZiGH-en,[7] while those of the Aures Mountains use the forms i-MaZiGH-en, i-MaZiR-en.[8] The same generic appears in classical times as MäZiC-es,[9] MaZaC-es or MaZaG-es,[10] MaZY-es,[11] or MaXY-es,[12] and is also seen in the Libyan inscriptions forming personal names.[13] It is not therefore surprising that the Berbers of mediaeval times should have thought themselves descended from a mythical eponymous ancestor named MaZîGH,[14] and the wide dissemination of the name as an ethnic, and its long employment,[15] is

[1] Collignon and Deniker, *Les Maures du Sénégal*; H. Weisgerber, *op. cit.* p. 181.

[2] It has been thought that such a name was to be seen in the word *Berber*, and until recently I personally inclined to this view, which I abandoned on reading Schirmer's brilliant study on this question. H. Schirmer, *op. cit.* The use of *Berber* as a generic name for the Hamites was supported by C. Tissot, *Géographie comparée*, vol. i. p. 395; V. de Saint-Martin, *Le Nord de l'Afrique dans l'antiquité*, p. 208. Against these, *vide* H. Schirmer, *op. cit.*, *passim*, and especially p. 26 *sqq.*

[3] Modified variously, but always in accordance with the equivalences noted *infra*, p. 75 *sq.*

[4] Leo Africanus, *Africae descriptio*, p. 18. The native African language is there called *Aquel Amarig*, *hoc est lingua nobilis*. The real reading should be *Kel Amazigh* = "tribe" or "race of the Amazigh," the name, not of the language, but of the Berbers themselves. *Vide* R. Brown, *Description of Africa . . . by . . . Leo Africanus*, vol. i. pp. 133, and 208, note 28.

[5] H. Duveyrier, *op. cit.* p. 317.

[6] Bissuel, *Les Touareg de l'Ouest*, p. 36.

[7] C. de Foucauld, *Reconnaissance au Maroc*, p. 10.

[8] Cf. E. Masqueray, *Le Djebel Chechar*, p. 260.

[9] Ptolemy iv. 2. § 5, Μάζικες; Aethicus, *Cosmographia*, p. 88, . . . *gentes Mazices multas* . . .; cf. Evagrius, *Hist. Eccles.* i. 7, p. 2440; Nicephorus Callistus, *Eccles. Hist.* xiv. 36, p. 1180; Philostorgius, *Hist. Eccles.* xi. 8, p. 603; Anonymus, *Expositio totius mundi*, p. 123; *CIL*, viii. 2786; Ammianus Marcellinus xxix. 5 § 17.

[10] Claudian, *Laus Stilichonis*, i. 357; Lucan iv. 681; and, doubtfully, Suetonius, *Nero*, 30.

[11] Hecataeus *ap.* Steph. Byz. *in verb.* Μάζυες.

[12] Herodotus iv. 191. Cf. the MaXY-tani of Justin xviii. 6. A form with X as the medial sibilant may perhaps be seen in the place-name *Maxula*, Μαξούλα, in Ptolemy iv. 3 § 7 (cf. *ibid.* iv. 3 § 34, M. Παλαιά) = *Maxula*, Pliny v. 4; cf. Victor Vitensis, *Historia persecutionis*, i. 5 § 6.

[13] *E.g.* MaSiK, MaSiR, MaSaK, etc. Halévy, *Études berbères*, i. pp. 75, 118, 151, 154, 158, 161, 179; L. L. C. Faidherbe, *Inscriptions numid.* p. 14 etc.

[14] Ibn Ḫaldun, *Kitab el-ʿIbar*, Translat. de Slane, i. p. 184.

[15] For its existence in Egyptian times, *vide infra*, p. 46 *sq.* I suggest with great reserve that the name of the "Mazoi" Aethiopians, of which the hieroglyphic form was , Copt. ⲘⲀⲦⲞⲒ, may be one more of these Hamitic MZGH names, and that the name of the Hamitic-Negro *Masai* also may be a survival of it.

PLATE I.

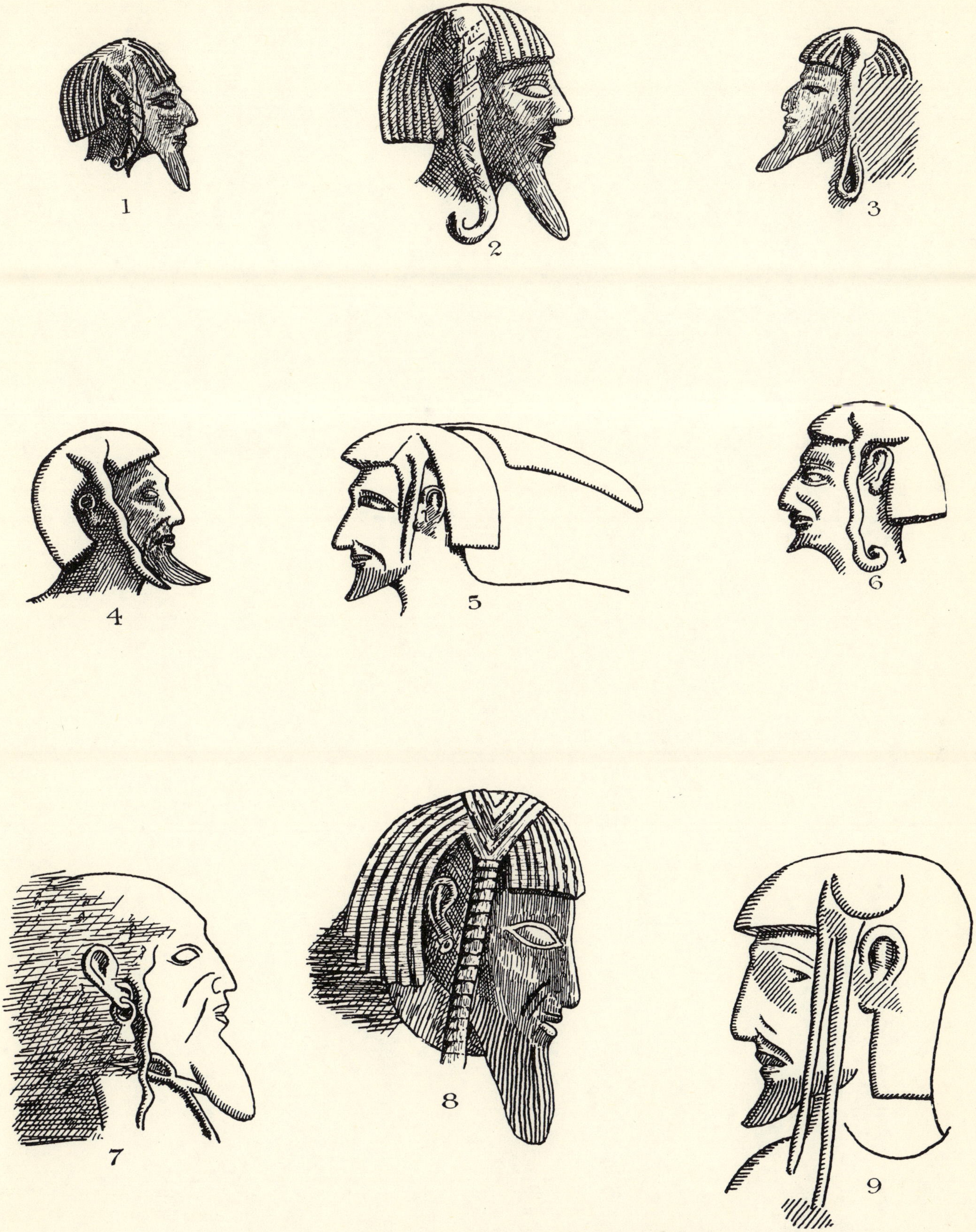

LIBYAN TYPES FROM THE EGYPTIAN MONUMENTS.

strong testimony of the underlying racial unity of the Berber-speaking peoples throughout North Africa. The name MZGH was undoubtedly employed as a generic term by the ancestors of the modern Imushagh and their various branches, and it is they who must be considered as the modern representatives of the old Hamitic stock which was invaded by the brachycephals and xanthochroids, and which in some cases has been modified so as to take on a negroid form.

In regard to this last point, the Egyptian monuments show that there already existed negroid Libyans by New Empire times. The pure western Hamitic type is seen in Plates I., II., and X., and is characterized by having an orthognathous profile, straight or slightly aquiline nose, and pilous system moderately developed. The eye is often represented as different from that of the Egyptians, the upper lid being longer than the lower, and having almost what classical archaeologists would term a "Scopadean roll" (cf. Fig. 1, *a*, Egyptian,[1] and *b*, Libyan). This peculiarity often exists to-day among the Berbers, as seen in Fig. 2, *a*, *b* (modern Kabyle; cf. *c*, *d*, modern Egyptian). The bodies are spare, well-knit, and long-limbed. Types of negroid Libyans are shown in Figs. 3 and 4. The degree of negrism is not high, but it is clearly marked by the platyrhinism and thick lips; the example shown might well be compared with the "Garamantic Type" of Duveyrier.[2] The fusion which produced this type probably took place in Nubia or in the Southern Egyptian Oases, as it will, before the conclusion of this chapter, be pointed out that the Temeḥu probably

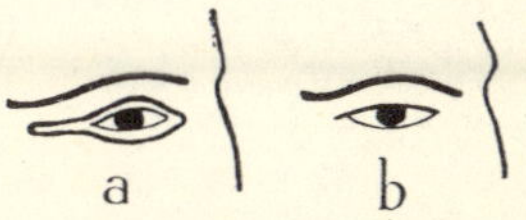

FIG. 1.

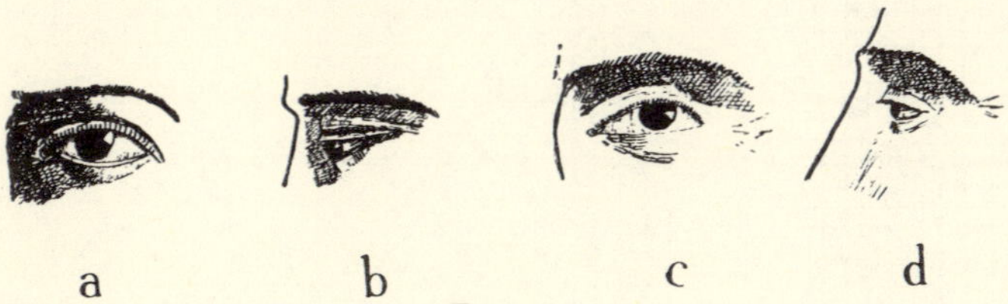

FIG. 2.

FIG. 3.

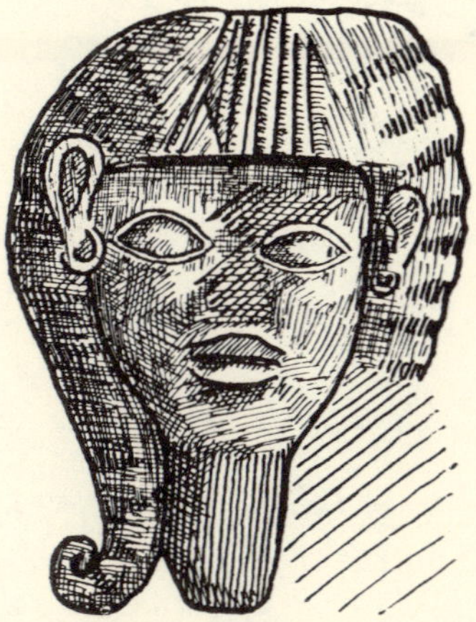
FIG. 4.

[1] In Fig. 1, *a*, the *koḥl*-stripe (collyrium) exaggerates the length of the eye.

[2] H. Duveyrier, *op. cit.* p. 288 *sq.*, pls. xvi., xvii. The "Gerîd type" of Collignon does not appear to be a fixed result of Negro admixture. H. Weisgerber, *op. cit.* p. 57.

occupied both these districts.[1] The intrusive xanthochroids are represented on the monuments, as already mentioned, but do not appear before the XIIth Dynasty.

The repartition of the Hamitic race in modern times is displayed in Map I. The great divisions, there noted by Roman numerals enclosed in circles, are as follows :—

I. *Guanches* of Canaria.—Extinct or fused with Europeans in recent historic times.

II. *Atlantic Hamites.*—More or less fused with Negro stocks, as in the case of the Haratîn Berbers and the Trarza Moors. In the north (Marocco) containing a marked xanthochroid element of foreign (Nordic) origin.[2]

III. *Mediterranean Hamites.*—Fused with various foreign elements—Nordic blond, brachycephalic *brun*, and (which applies also to II.) Semitic Arab.

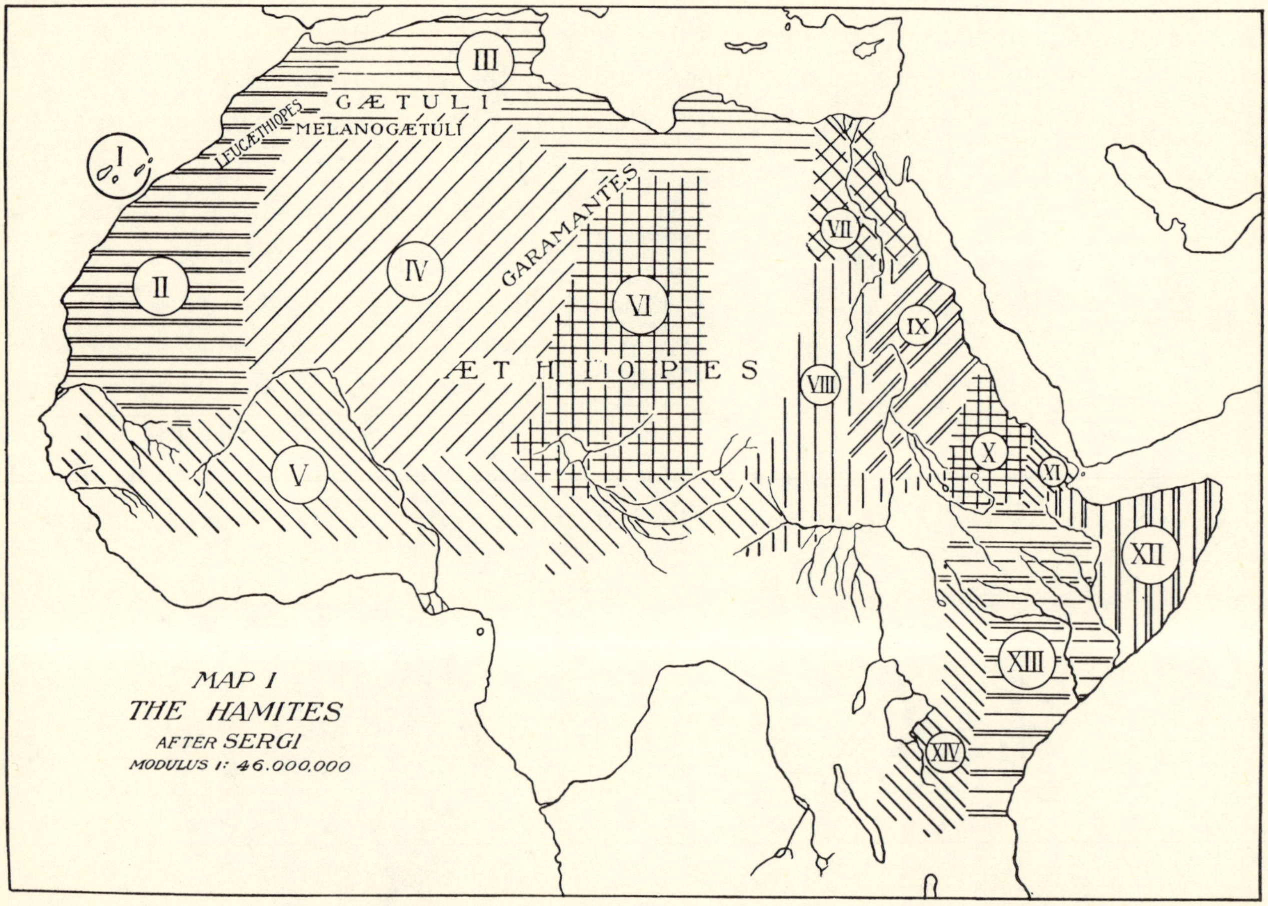

IV. *Ṣaḥaran Hamites.*—Slight Negro and Arab admixture, but purer and more typical than any other Hamitic people of the present time.

V. *Peulhs.*—A mixed race, containing Berber and Negro elements, and a Semitic infusion acquired in East Africa, their original home ; also a later Semitic strain due to contact with the Arabs.

[1] In this connection it is perhaps worth while to call attention to two passages in which the Libyan type is confused with the Aethiopic. Careful classical writers are explicit in distinguishing between the Berber and Negro types, but Adamantius (*Physiognom.* ii. 23) confuses them, . . . οἱ μὲν Λίβυες Αἰθίοψιν ὅμοιοι. Cf. Polemon, *Physiognom.* i. 3, . . . ἀλλ' οἱ μὲν Λίβυες, Αἰθίοψιν ὅμοιοι. . . . It is barely possible that a vague knowledge of the existence of negroid Libyans led to this confusion.

[2] Cf. the position, laid down on the authority of Ptolemy, of the "Leucaethiopes" and "Melanogaetuli" on Map I. These descriptives are good evidence of the ancient opposition of whites and blacks in the Ṣaḥara, and of their fusion. Cf. Orosius i. 2 § 88 . . . *gentes Libyoaethiopum* . . .

VI. *Tibbus.*—Dark Hamites (?) showing several puzzling ethnic peculiarities, but probably a fusion of IV. and Sudanese negroes.

VII. *Egyptians.*—A race mixed since very early times, having strains of IV., Nilotic Negroes, and Semites.

VIII. *Nubas.*—A people resembling VI., but, perhaps, with a greater degree of negrism.

IX. *Beǵas.*—A fusion of IV., VIII., and Semitic stocks.

X. *Abyssinians.*—The same, with Negro admixture.

XI. *Danakils.*—The same, with higher percentage of Semite.

XII. *Somalis.*—The same, with higher percentage of Negro.

XIII. *Gallas.*—The same, with small Semite admixture.

XIV. *Masai.*—A strongly negroid stock, perhaps containing a slight Hamitic, and an old Semitic strain—the ethnology of this people is doubtful.[1]

These fourteen groups may be thus subdivided :—

1. Western or Libyan Hamites.
   - Guanches.
   - Atlantic Hamites.
   - Mediterranean Hamites.
   - Ṣaḥaran Hamites.
   - Tibbus (?).
2. North-Eastern or Semito-Hamites.
   - Egyptians.
   - Beǵas.
   - Danakils.
3. Eastern or Aethiopian Hamites (Kushito-Hamites).
   - Abyssinians.
   - Somalis.
   - Gallas.
   - Nubas.
4. Mixed Southern Hamites.
   - Masai (?).
   - Peulhs.

It is with a portion of the Western Hamites that this essay deals. In antiquity, naturally, it was the Mediterranean Hamites who, owing to their geographical position, were best known to the Egyptians, Greeks, and Romans ; and whereas the western branch of this division of the Hamitic race assumed an importance in later times, it is the less known, but by no means insignificant, eastern portion that is here considered.

The Eastern Mediterranean Hamites—more conveniently, the Eastern Libyans—of the Egyptian period were known to the inhabitants of the Nile Valley under a variety of names. These names were in some cases those of tribes, in others they were those of regional groups of tribes. It is, unfortunately, on the given data, not always possible to distinguish between the tribes and the regional groups, but a provisional division has been made in the following list :—

[1] On the name, *vide supra*, p. 42, n. 15.

Groups	Tribes
Teḥenu.	Imukehek (?).
Temeḥu.	Ḳeheḳ.
Rebu.	Ḳeyḳesh.
Meshwesh.	Ṣeped.
	Eṣbet.
	Eḳbet.
	Shai.
	Heṣ.
	Beḳen.

The grounds on which the above division has been made are noted below.

Groups

Teḥenu, T̲ ḥ n w. (The country, T̲ ḥ n w).[1] Variants, T̲ ḥ n w,[2] etc. Both the ethnic and the geographical names were employed by the Egyptians until the time of the great invasions in a very loose manner to designate the people and the habitable countries to the west of the Nile Valley, north of the Negro zone. Therefore the Teḥenu are mentioned in a general way, together with other foreign nations, as with Nubians and Asiatics,[3] or in antithesis to "the four eastern countries."[4] They appear as the typical people of the west,[5] and the extent of their territories and the number of their divisions are attested by the frequency of such phrases as "the countries (*plur.*) of the Teḥenu,"[6] "the chiefs (*plur.*) of Teḥenu."[7]

Temeḥu, T̲ m ḥ w.[8] Variants (the country, T m ḥ); T̲ m ḥ, etc. The Temeḥu appear to have been a more clearly defined branch of the Teḥenu.[9] That they were themselves made up of more than one tribe is clear from the extent of their territories. That the Temeḥu appeared to the Egyptians to have been a well-defined group is shown by their being listed with such ethnic groups as the Irṯet, Mazoi, Yam, Wawat, and Kau Negroes of the south,[10] etc.

Rebu R'bw = Λίβυες.[11] This group, seated in the north, comprised a number of tribes, just as in classical times. This is borne out by the fact that the Rebu were so extensive a people that their importance led the Greeks into bestowing the generic term *Libyans* upon the indigenous North Africans as a whole. The Egyptian records, moreover, speak of the Rebu as of a powerful people at the time of the invasions. Furthermore, the name survives in Marmarica at the present time—*Ḥaṭṭîah el-Lebuk* (3 hours south of Sîwah); *Mongar Lebuk* (long. 29° E., lat. 30° N.; $k = u = w$). The Imukehek may have been a tribe of the Rebu, since they dwelt in the north,[12] and since the tribe called the Ḳeheḳ was associated with the Libyans at the time of the invasions.[13] The Eṣbet also, for the reasons given below, may have been a tribe of the Rebu.

Meshwesh. , M š w š.[14] The Meshwesh were a great and

[1] H. Brugsch, *Geographie d. altens Ägyptens*, vol. ii. p. 78, and Pl. xxii. 235. Cf. *ibid.* Pl. lxxxviii. 232.

[2] A. Erman, *Ägyptisches Glossar*, p. 148.

[3] BAR i. § 423 H.

[4] BAR i. § 675.

[5] BAR ii. § 892, and, plagiarized therefrom, iii. § 116, iv. § 37 *et alibi.*

[6] BAR ii. § 413, iii. § 464.

[7] BAR iii. § 132.

[8] H. Brugsch, *op. cit.* p. 79 and Pl. xxii. 240.

[9] *Ibid.* p. 79. The Temeḥu do occasionally appear to have been named in the general sense of "Westerners," *e.g.* BAR iv. § 42 . . . Rameses III. "protecting against Temeḥ," etc.; cf. iv. §§ 43, 49, 58 *et alibi.*

[10] BAR i. § 311.

[11] H. Brugsch, *op. cit.* p. 79, and Pl. xxii. 241, 242, 243.

[12] BAR ii. § 42.

[13] BAR iii. § 588 *et alibi.*

[14] H. Brugsch, *op. cit.* p. 80, Pl. xxii. 244.

PLATE II.

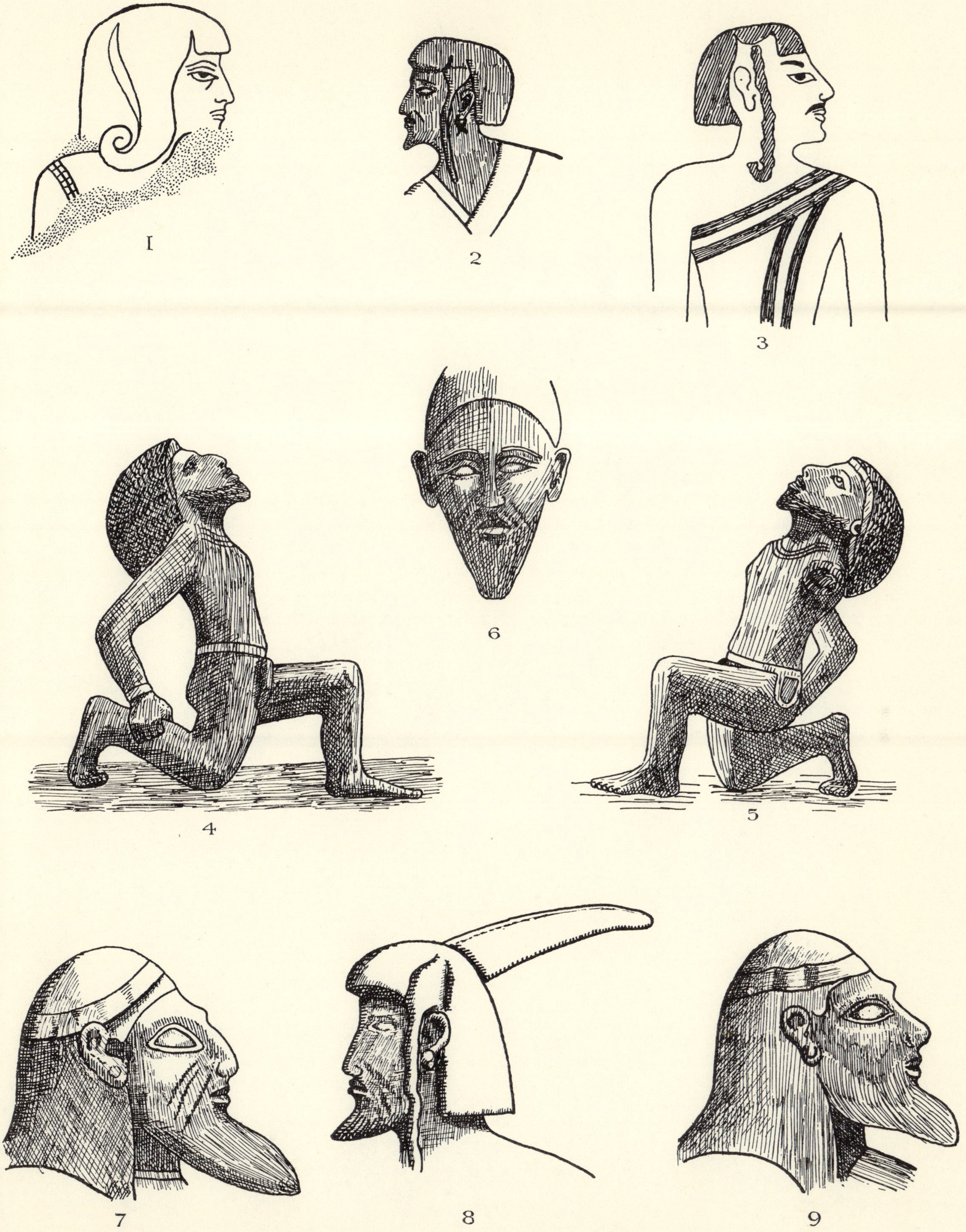

LIBYAN TYPES FROM THE EGYPTIAN MONUMENTS.

powerful group of allied tribes, who were able to overpower their eastern neighbours, and even eventually to obtain the Egyptian throne.[1] It is unreasonable to suppose that they were merely a single tribe, since their numbers and force point to a different conclusion. The name Meshwesh is but one form of the generic Berber appellative which has already been noticed above: MŠU- being the equivalent of M Z G H, as seen most clearly in such classical forms as MaXY-es, MaZY-es.[2] This does not necessarily mean that the Meshwesh were in very fact the ancestors of the Herodotean Maxyes, though such a statement is probable enough, and has recently been repeated by a scholar of high standing.[3] Rather, the identification means merely that the Meshwesh were of those who used the generic Hamitic designation which has been already noted as made on the radical √MZع.

Tribes

Imukehek. . The Imukehek appear but once in the Egyptian annals (XVIIIth Dynasty), but as they were a northern people,[4] and the Ḳeheḳ were Rebu, they were probably themselves a small Libyan tribe.

Ḳeheḳ. 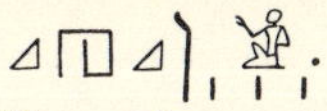. The Ḳeheḳ appear to have been a fairly numerous tribe, since they supplied the Egyptians with mercenaries.[5] They do not, however, appear as independent adversaries of Egypt, but as allies of the more powerful Rebu,[6] of whom they may be considered to have formed an important part.

Ḳeyḳesh. . This name is that either of a small tribe or is a misspelling of Ḳeheḳ.[7] It is found in the list of Rebu and Meshwesh forces defeated by Rameses III.[8]

Eṣbet. . A small tribe, only once mentioned. The name at once recalls that of the Asbystae, who are found in Pliny as the Hasbitae, and in Ptolemy as the 'Ασβῦται or 'Ασβῆται.[9] These lections might be due to the error of a copyist; but the occurrence of the second Σ in ἀΣΒύΣΤαι itself may be due to the change of one lingual mute before another (as ἴστε = ἴδ-τε), the original form of the name having been made on the radical consonants S-B-T-T. With this form S-B-T-T is to be compared the name Ṣeped, Ṣ-P-D, a tribe once mentioned in the records.[10]

Eḳbet. 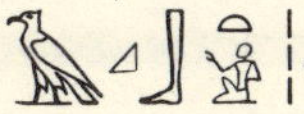. A tribe but once mentioned in the records.[11] Possibly a misspelling of Eṣbet.

Shai (perhaps *Shaitep*?). . The Shai appear but once,[12] in conjunction with the Eṣbet, Ḳeyḳesh, Heṣ, and the Beḳen, in the invasion of the Meshwesh and Rebu, defeated by Rameses III.

Heṣ. . Mentioned once,[13] with the Shai, etc. Cf. the هسّة *Hassah*, a modern Arabo-Berber tribe of Cyrenaica.[14]

Beḳen. . Mentioned once,[15] with the Shai, etc. This name may possibly

[1] *Vide infra*, p. 228.

[2] For the change of ع to H or U, *vide infra*, p. 75; and cf. the equivalences of Garth- = Hort-; Guillaume = William, etc.

[3] J. H. Breasted, *History*, p. 466. Previously, Petrie had, upon this identification, built a fabric which is only paralleled by his identifications of Syrian place-names. W. M. F. Petrie, *History*, vol. iii. p. 111 *sqq.*, and fig. 43, "Map of Tribes," etc. (The Syrian names are to be found, vol. ii. p. 325 *sqq.*)

[4] BAR ii. § 42.

[5] J. H. Breasted, *op. cit.* p. 477; BAR iv. § 410.

[6] BAR iii. § 588.

[7] BAR iv. §§ 402, 405.

[8] BAR iv. § 405.

[9] Pliny v. 5; Ptolemy iv. 4 § 6.

[10] BAR iv. § 91. Possibly again, iv. § 40, and note *d ad loc. cit.*

[11] BAR ii. § 70.

[12] BAR iv. § 405.

[13] BAR *loc. cit.*

[14] G. Haimann, *Cirenaica*, general map. This identification is made with the greatest reserve, for (*a*) the classical link is lacking, and (*b*) the Hassah may have come into Cyrenaica with the Soleym-Ben-Manṣur in the eleventh century. Cf. E. Mercier, *Histoire de l'établissement des Arabes*, etc., p. 148.

[15] BAR *loc. cit.*

be represented by the Greek ethnic Βάκαλες,[1] since L and N are dialectic equivalents in Berber that might warrant the identification of BeḲeN with Βάκαλ-ες.

The brief list of Libyan ethnic names to be found in the Egyptian texts being concluded, the question now arises: How were the owners of these names distributed geographically? The question can be answered only in the most general manner, and in the map (Map II.) illustrating the ethnogeography of the Libyans during the Egyptian period, the reader is asked to consider that the positions assigned to such ethnic groups as are given a place on the map at all are only approximative.

The whole of Africa west of the Nile was, to the Egyptian, a *terra incognita* which stretched away from the familiar haunts of men to the realms of the dead.[2] To this unknown country the vague general term , *imn-t*, "the West," was applied, either to signify the country itself, or the imagined soul-land that lay in or beyond it. Within it, as the Nile dwellers came eventually to know, lay the oases, and various tribes of foreign men. These men they designated by such terms as *Ḫestyw*, "barbarians,"[3] or by ethno-descriptives like Teḥenu, picked up from, or first applied to, near neighbours, and then gradually given a general significance. These "barbarians" in early historic times occupied not only the oases but also the Fayum, for by the position of the Libyan scenes in the Sa-hu-re temple, it is clear that the Libyans held country to the south of Memphis until the Vth dynasty.[4] And since the oases were not subjected by the Egyptians until the time of the New Empire, and were probably unconsidered[5] in the days of Sa-hu-re, the orientation of the Libyan reliefs in his temple must refer to the Libyan occupation of the Fayum.

The Libyans also held some stretches along the west bank of the Nile itself, above the First Cataract. The archaeological evidence on this point is reserved for treatment in an Appendix (I.) to this essay, but part of the textual evidence may be introduced here. Among the many offerings made by Rameses III. to the temples, we read in the Papyrus Harris of his having given two "Tymḥy stones of Wawat," each weighing

[1] Herodotus iv. 171, var. Κάβαλες.

[2] A. Erman, *Handbook of Egyptian Religion*, p. 87.

[3] BAR iv. § 106; cf. Herodotus ii. 158. Otherwise the Libyans were grouped with the *Nine Bows* or the *Ḥaunebu*. BAR *passim*.

[4] L. Borchardt, *Das Grabdenkmal des Königs S'aꜣḥu-Reʿ*, vol. i. p. 17 *sq*.

[5] Itendidi, as early as the XIIth Dynasty, visited "the land of the oasis dwellers," BAR i. § 527. From the Puemre inscription it is clear that the oases were under foreign chiefs, who sent their tribute to Egypt, BAR ii. §§ 385, 386. Later, in the XVIIIth Dynasty, we hear of a chief of "all the oasis country," BAR ii. §§ 763, 767. This title may have been an honorary one, for the "tribute" taken from Teḥenu by Hatshepsut was almost certainly, by its nature, exacted from the oasis dwellers, BAR ii. § 321. Under Rameses III. the oases were permanently colonized by the Egyptians, and planted with vineyards, BAR iv. § 213. The Mannier stela informs us that, as at present, the Oasis of Ḫargah was used as a place of banishment, BAR iv. § 650 *sqq*. Even in late times the inhabitants of Daḫlah were Liby-Egyptians, BAR iv. § 725; cf. Ptolemy, *Geogr.* iv. 5 § 12; and to this day Sîwan Berber is spoken at Manshîah el-ʿAguzah in Baḥarîah. The oases were, in later times, thus named: Ḫargah = , *Kenmet*, or , *Ut-reṣ*, "Oasis of the South;" Daḫlah = , *Desdeset*; Farafrah, perhaps = , *Ta-iḥet*; Sîwah, doubtfully = , *Seḳet-imit*, "Fields of Palm Trees." Cf. I. Dümichen, *Die Oasen der Libyschen Wüste*; G. Parthey, *Der Orakel und die Oase des Ammon*.

3 *kidet.*[1] The Wawat were a negro or negroid people[2] well to the south, but not probably much above the Second Cataract.[3] The name "Timḥy stone" at once suggests, as it did long ago to Brugsch,[4] Temeḥu. The stones would naturally be called Temeḥu stones if purveyed to the Egyptians by the people of that name, just as Carchedonian stones were so called because, though found in the interior of Libya, they reached the Greeks through the medium of the Carthaginians. And that the Temeḥu were in reality the northern neighbours of the Wawat is clear from the Harkhuf inscription (VIth Dynasty). Harkhuf, going for the third time on a trading journey into the Sudan, encountered "the chief of Yam going to the land of Temeh, to smite Temeh as far as the western corner of Heaven. I went after him," adds Harkhuf, "and I pacified him."[5] Since the Yam were close neighbours of the Wawat, and it is not probable that the negro chief designed to attack the Temeḥu in the distant Egyptian oases, it is plain that his enemies were either in Kurkur or Selîmah—both so small as to be very unlikely objectives for such an expedition—or else on the Nile. If it be supposed that from Berîs, the southernmost of the Egyptian oases, the Libyans followed the S.S.E. depression which leads thence to the Nile about Derr, and that, when they arrived at the river, and found no such strong opposition as they would have encountered below the First Cataract, they established themselves among the Nubians[6] in groups principally on the west bank, a simple hypothesis is arrived at which fulfils all the data, both archaeological and textual. This hypothesis becomes something more than theory when it is found that, in classical times, the Libyans were established, though still as intruders, farther to the South. Strabo, the best classical authority on the Sudan, who was himself as far south as Philae at a time when, because of the recent punitive expedition of Petronius,[7] much new information was to be had, makes the following remarkable statement: "Above Meroe is Psebo, a large lake, containing a well-inhabited island. As the Libyans occupy the western bank of the Nile, and the Aethiopians the country on the other side of the river, they thus dispute by turns the possession of the islands, and the banks of the river, one party repulsing the other, or yielding to the superiority of its opponent."[8]

It would thus appear that the Temeḥu of the time of Harkhuf, the traders in "Timḥy stones," had moved southwards, finding in that direction less resistance to their expansion than in the other, but still remaining an unabsorbed and foreign element

[1] BAR iv. §§ 373, 389.

[2] BAR i. § 311.

[3] Else we should not find Uni, in the time of Pepi I., recruiting mercenaries from them.

[4] H. Brugsch, *op. cit.* ii. p. 78; cf. LD iii. 229 *c*. Against Brugsch's view, *vide* BAR iv. § 373, note *ad loc. cit.* Breasted's objection is now, I believe, overruled by the new archaeological evidence.

[5] BAR i. § 335.

[6] Using the word in its geographical sense.

[7] J. G. Milne, *Egypt under Roman Rule*, p. 21 *sq.*, for this expedition.

[8] Strabo xvii. p. 822; cf. what is said by the same writer, xvii. p. 786, "On the left (west) of . . . the Nile live Nubae in Libya, a populous nation. They begin at Meroë and extend as far as the bends. They are not subject to the Aethiopians, but live independently, being distributed in several sovereignties." These "Nubae" were perhaps partly negroid Libyans. Ptolemy (iv. 6 § 5) gives the Libyan Garamantes a southeasterly extension to Lake Nuba (Psebo ?) . . . τό τε τῶν Γαραμάντων διῆκον ἀπὸ τῶν τοῦ Βαγράδα ποταμοῦ πηγῶν μέχρι τῆς Νούβα λίμνης.

among the older population. Under these circumstances, it is not strange that there should occasionally be found on the Egyptian monuments Libyans of slightly negroid aspect.

That the whole body of the Libyans of the Egyptian records lay properly in "Eastern Libya," and was not so remote from the Nile as some writers would place it,

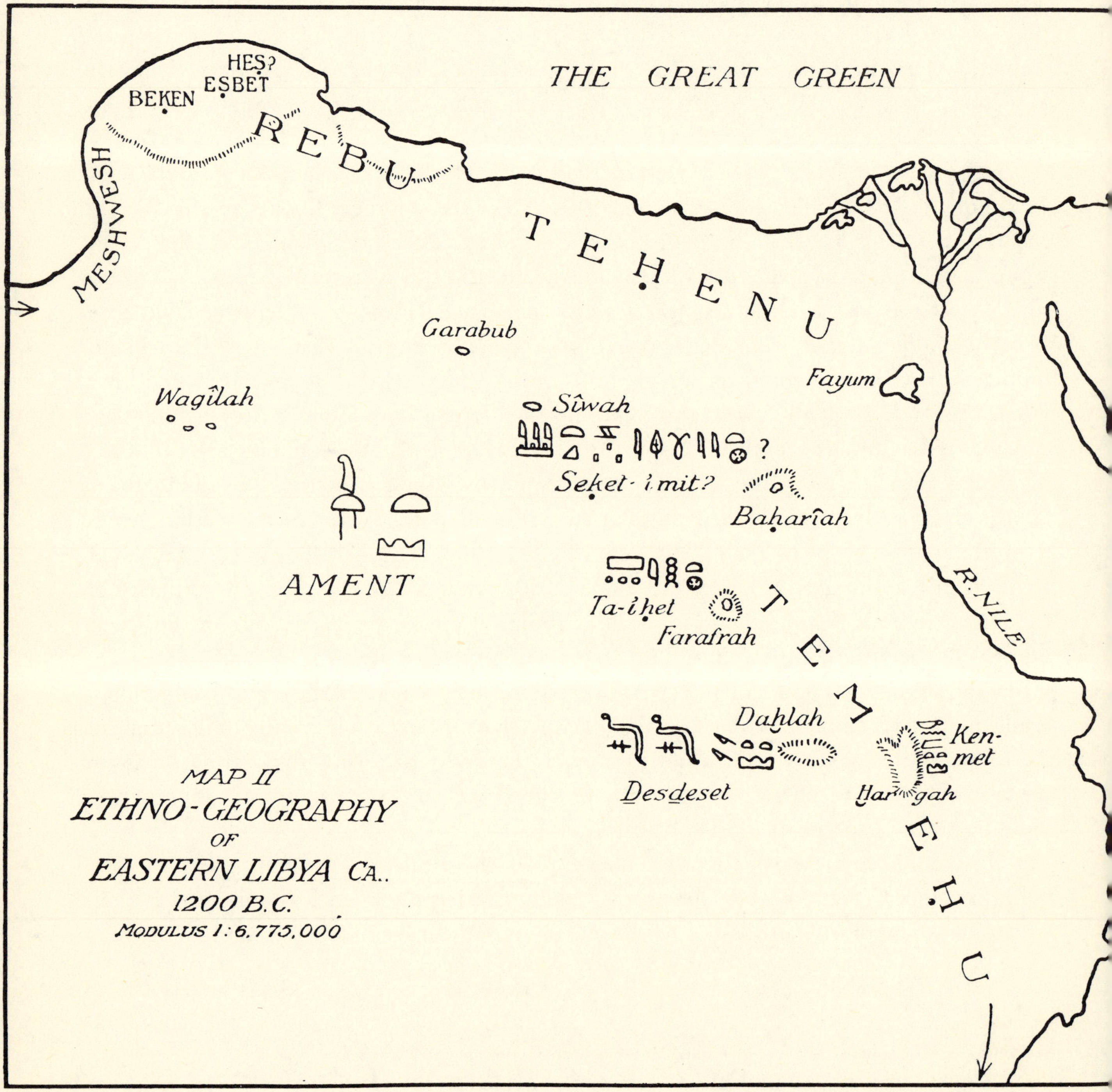

MAP II
ETHNO-GEOGRAPHY
OF
EASTERN LIBYA CA..
1200 B.C.
MODULUS 1:6,775,000

is clear from the fact that the Egyptians invaded the Rebu and their neighbours, and from the fact that the Merneptah invasion arrived in Egypt apparently about three weeks after starting. Twenty days at even twenty miles a day is only about 400 miles. With allowance for halts, etc., this gives roughly 300 miles, *i.e.* Cyrenaica to Egypt.

The ancient ethnic area of the Eastern Libyans in general having thus been sketched, the distribution of the various tribes, of which enough is known to place them on the map, may now be taken up in such detail as the data will allow (Map II.).

1. *Teḥenu.*—General designation for easternmost Libyans (*i.e.* immediately west of Egypt). By exclusion, probably in the (early) Fayum, and the northern oases, and between the Egyptians and the Rebu.[1]

2. *Temeḥu.*—As explained above, probably in the oasis of Ḫargah, and along the Nubian Nile.

3. *Rebu.*—Known after (1) and (2), and so west of them.[2] Probably in the Gebel el-ʿAḳabah and Cyrenaica. For they were attacked by the Meshwesh,[3] who came from well to the westward, and were historically associated with the Sea-Peoples from the west,[4] to whom Cyrenaica, from its fertility and northerly position, would be the part of Eastern Libya best known and most accessible. Also, the mention of the "Red Land" in connection with Libya suggests the famous *terra rossa* of Cyrenaica, mentioned by modern travellers and well known to the Arab geographers.[5]

4. *Meshwesh.*—West of the Rebu, and the last-mentioned Libyan people of importance in the Egyptian annals. In an unsettled state, moving from west to east from the time they first appear until they settled in Egypt. Their weapons and association with the Sea-Peoples suggest that they took a littoral road, as indicated by the arrow-line on the map.

5. *Eṣbet.*—For the reasons given above, introduced, with reserve, in the place later occupied by the Asbystae, as a part of (3).

6. *Beken.*—Introduced, with yet greater reserve, in the place later occupied by the Bacales.

7. *Ḳeheḳ.*—From their number and association with the Rebu, placed with reserve in the interior of the territories of the latter.

8. *Heṣ.*—Tentatively introduced in the place of the modern Hassah.[6]

Imukehek, *Shai.*—Omitted. So, too, with the *Ṣeped*, *Eḳbet*, and *Ḳeyḳesh*, if these are not forms of the *Eṣbet* and *Ḳeheḳ* mentioned above.

The Libyan ethnic names on the map are printed in Roman, the other names in italic, letters.

In classical times the earliest detailed account of the partition of the Libyan tribes is found in Herodotus. According to the historian, Libya began west of the Nile,[7] and ran to the Atlantic,[8] being bordered on the south by the land of the Aethiopians, who were black and woolly-haired.[9] Within Eastern Libya, which the Greek historian characterized as nomadic, lay the following tribes :—

1. *Adyrmachidae*, Ἀδυρμαχῖδαι.—From the Egyptian Delta westwards to the harbour called Port Plynus.[10]

2. *Giligamae*, Γιλιγάμαι.—From Plynus as far as the island of Aphrodisias.[11]

[1] Cf. BAR iii. § 579. The chief of the Rebu is there said to have attacked the Teḥenu, which he must have done from the west. Note that the name of the Teḥenu became early known to the Egyptians as a general term for Westerner, which testifies to their early geographic position as the Libyans nearest the Nile.

[2] Cf. BAR, *loc. cit.*

[3] BAR iv. § 83.

[4] BAR iii. § 588 *et alibi.*

[5] *E.g.* el-Idrîsî, *Clima* iii. 3. Cf. J. M. Hartmann, *Edrisii Africa*, p. 300 note *k*.

[6] See the caution *supra*, p. 47 *n.* 14.

[7] Herodotus ii. 17, iv. 191 ; cf. iv. 168.

[8] *Ibid.* ii. 32, iv. 196.

[9] *Ibid.* vii. 70.

[10] Herodotus iv. 168. Plynus is placed by Scylax two days west of Apis, *Periplus*, § 108 (="Port Bardia"?). Herodotus is explicit in stating that even as far east as Apis and Marea, the population was Libyan (ii. 18).

[11] Herodotus iv. 169. According to Scylax, *loc. cit.*, and Ptolemy, iv. 4 § 7, Aphrodisias would seem to be the Sharḳîah or Hammam Islands.

3. *Asbystae*, Ἀσβύσται.—West of (2), in the vicinity of Cyrene, but not reaching the coast, which was held by the Cyrenaeans.[1]

4. *Auschisae*, Αὐσχίσαι.—Just south of Barca, and reaching the sea at Euesperis (= Benghazî). On the east contiguous to the Asbystae.[2] The same people, apparently, as the Ausigdi, Αὔσιγδοι, mentioned by Callimachus[3] and Hecataeus.[4] The Ausigdi had a city called Ausigda.[5]

5. *Bacales*, Βάκαλες *var.* Κάβαλες.—A little tribe—ὀλίγον ἔθνος—enclaved by the Auschitae, touching the coast at Taucheira.[6]

6. *Nasamones*, Νασαμῶνες.—" A numerous people," according to Herodotus,[7] the (south-) western neighbours of the Auschisae, whose territories extended from the coast into the interior, where they dominated the oasis of Augila (= Wagîlah). Perhaps originally called *Mesamones*.[8] Western boundary at some undefined point in the Syrtis Major.

7. *Psylli*, Ψύλλοι.—This people had, in the days of Herodotus, withdrawn from their earlier seat on the Syrtic coast,[9] their lands there having passed into the hands of the Nasamones.[10] As, however, the Psylli still existed at a later period,[11] they are placed, with reserve, on the map illustrating Herodotus's repartition of the Libyan tribes (Map III.).

8. *Macae*, Μάκαι.—On the shores of the greater Syrtis, west of the Nasamones.[12]

9. *Gindanes*, Γινδᾶνες.—Adjoining (8) on the west. This name[13] appears to have been that of an important division of the Lotophagi. For the latter descriptive name was already, in the time of Herodotus, applied especially to a community living on a promontory in the territory of the Gindanes,[14] and tended to supplant, among the Greeks, to whom it had become traditionally familiar,[15] the indigenous name. The fact that besides the little group of Lotophagi mentioned by Herodotus, other tribes, like the Machlyes,[16] made use of the lotus fruit, would encourage the spread of the term.

10. *Machlyes*, Μάχλυες.—West of the Lotophagi, as far as the river Triton,[17] in the Lesser Syrtis.[18] Found later as the Μάχρυες in the same position.[19]

11. *Auseans*, Αὐσέες (*var.* Αὐσεῖς, as in Apollodorus[20]).—Like the Machlyes, from whom they were separated by the Triton river, the Auseans lived in the vicinity of the Lake Tritonis.[21] This is the last (westernmost) tribe of the *nomadic* Libyans of Herodotus,[22] but it is convenient to mention here the three following as well :—

[1] Herodotus iv. 170. Inland position of Asbystae, confirmed by Dionysius, *Perieg.* 211, Ἀσβύσται δ' ἐπὶ τοῖσι μεσήπειροι τελέθουσιν, κτλ. ; cf. Nonnus, *Dionysiaca* xiii. 370.

[2] Herodotus iv. 171.

[3] Callimachus *ap.* Steph. Byz. *in verb.* Αὔσιγδα.

[4] Hecataeus *ap. ibid. loc. cit.* = *Frag.* 300, in *FHG*.

[5] The intermediary form between ΑΥΣ-Χ-ιΣ-αι and ΑΥΣ-ι-Γ-Δ-οι is found as ΑΥΣ-Χ-ι-Τ-αι in Stephanus Byzantinus *in verb.* The permutation of S and T-D in Berber names is general.

[6] Herodotus, *loc. cit.*

[7] *Ibid.* iv. 172 ; cf. ii. 32. Cf. Scylax § 111 ; Strabo xvii. p. 836 ; Pliny v. 5.

[8] Pliny, *loc. cit.* Popular classical etymology related the name *Mesamones* to μέσος + ψάμμος, but the frequency of Mes- as a filiative prefix in Berber discredits this derivation. The name has in modern times been often analysed as קשי־אמן, " men of Amon " (first by S. Bochart, *Geogr. Sacra*, col. 284, l. 54 *sqq.*) ; and as 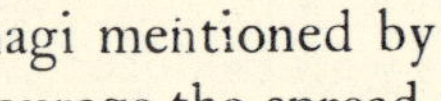, *nḥsy-ỉmn*, " the Southerners (or Negroes) of Amon " [!].

[9] Part of which was called in earlier times by Hecataeus the " Psyllic Gulf " ; Hecataeus, *Frag.* 303, in *FHG* = *Idem*, *ap.* Steph. Byz. *in verb.* Ψύλλοι . . . Ψυλλικὸς κόλπος, ἐν τῷ Λιβυκῷ κόλπῳ. . . .

[10] Herodotus iv. 173.

[11] Pliny v. 4 ; Ptolemy iv. 4 § 6 ; Strabo xvi. p. 838, etc.

[12] Herodotus iv. 175. Confirmed by Scylax, *loc. cit.* ; called by Ptolemy iv. 3 § 6 ; Μάκαι οἱ Συρτῖται, and misplaced inland.

[13] Herodotus iv. 176 ; Stephanus Byzantinus, *in verb.* Γινδᾶνες, ἔθνος Λιβυκὸν λωτοφαγον, κτλ.

[14] Herodotus iv. 177. The promontory, by a process of exhaustion, appears to have been Zarzis, or Zuchis, near the Syrtis Minor ; cf. Scylax, § 110 ; Strabo xvii. p. 835.

[15] From the time of Homer, *Odyss.* ix. 84. *sqq.*

[16] Herodotus iv. 178.

[17] *Ibid. loc. cit.*

[18] For the position of the lake and river Tritonis, *vide supra*, p. xiii.

[19] Ptolemy iv. 3 § 6. Miscalled Μάχμες in Stephanus Byzantinus *in verb.* Μάζυες. Cf. *infra*, p. 53 *n.* 1.

[20] Apollodorus, *Frag.* 109, in *FHG*.

[21] Herodotus iv. 180.

[22] *Ibid.* iv. 191.

12. *Maxyes*, Μάξυες.—Next to the Auseans.[1]

13. *Zaueces*, or *Zabyces*, Ζαύηκες *var.* Ζάβυκες.[2]—Next to the Maxyes.

14. *Gyzantes*, Γύζαντες *var.* Ζύγαντες.[3]—Next to the Zaueces.

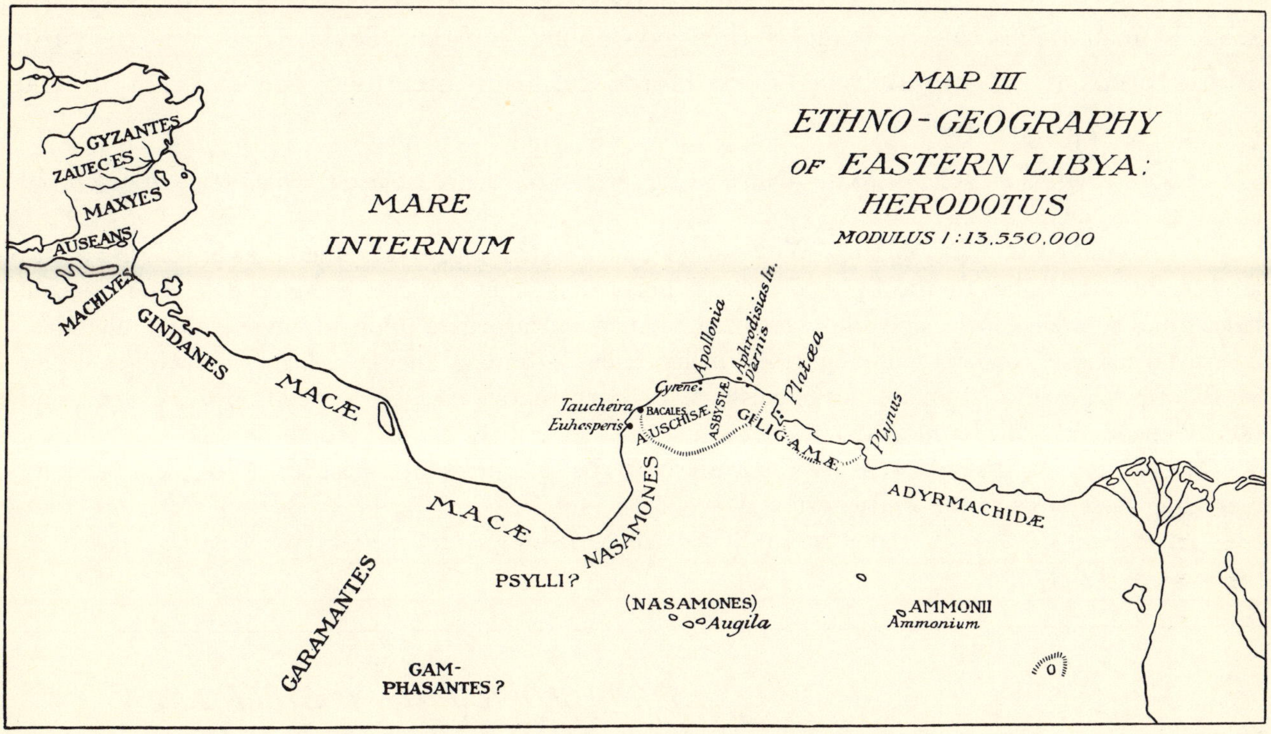

Thus far the coast has been followed in a direction from east to west. To turn to the interior, the positions may be noted of the following ethnic groups mentioned by Herodotus as being there situated :—

15. *Garamantes*, Γαράμαντες.—In the interior, ten days west of Augila, and so in northern Phazania (Fezzan), having a population of troglodytic Aethiopians as neighbours.[4]

16. *Gamphasantes* [*Γαμφάσαντες].—South of the Nasamones, in a wild-beast region. A powerless and degenerate tribe. Herodotus calls them Garamantes, but he describes them as feeble and ignorant of arms, and not knowing how to defend themselves.[5] This is flatly contradicted later,[6] where the Garamantes appear as a warlike nation of slave-hunters. In the second passage, moreover, the Garamantes are introduced as if for the first time. The text, therefore, is corrupt ; but the difficulty becomes clear from the later evidence. Mela and Pliny, closely following Herodotus, ascribe the weakness and ignorance of arms just mentioned, not to the Garamantes, but to a people called Gamphasantes,[7] by which the reading is to be restored.

[1] Herodotus, *loc. cit.* and iv. 193. Mentioned first by Hecataeus, *Frag.* 304, in *FHG*. The Μάζυες of Steph. Byz. *in verb.* Μάζυες, οἱ Λιβύης νομάδες· Ἑκαταῖος περιηγήσει. εἰσὶ δὲ καὶ ἕτεροι Μάξυες καὶ ἕτεροι Μάχμες. For Μάχμες one should almost certainly read Μάχλυες.

[2] Herodotus iv. 193 ; Hecataeus *ap.* Steph. Byz. *in verb.* The form Ζαβυ- may be a copyist's error for Βυζα-, seen in this region as *Byzacium*, etc., but cf. *var.* Gyz-antians, Zyg-antians, *infra*, p. 54.

[3] Herodotus iv. 194 ; Eudoxus Cnidius *ap.* Apollonium Dyscolum, xxxviii. For the variants cf. preceding note. The form Ζυγ- was that used by Hecataeus (*ap.* Steph. Byz. *in voc.* Ζυγαντίς) ; cf. *Zeug-itana*.

[4] Herodotus iv. 183 ; cf. Lucian, *De dipsadibus*, § 2. [5] Herod. iv. 174. [6] *Ibid.* iv. 183.

[7] Mela i. 8 ; Pliny v. 8. The name, it may be remarked, seems connected with that of Phazania—Gam-*phasan*-tes. The corruption of Herodotus is at least as early as Eustathius (*ad Dionysii Perieg.* 217), and Steph. Byz. (*in verb.*). Cf. Martianus Capella, *De nuptiis Philologiae*, etc., p. 232 *sq.* (lib. vi.). The name there appears as *Campasantes*. Capella is here following Pliny.

17. *Ammonians*, Ἀμμώνιοι.—Sedentaries of Sîwah Oasis.[1]

The above data are embodied in the map of fifth-century Libya (Map III.).

The next writer who contains information on which a satisfactory partition of the East Libyan tribes can be made is the geographer Scylax. Scylax does not treat the ethnic divisions as minutely as does Herodotus, but mentions the position of the following large groups :—

1. *Adyrmachidae*, Ἀδυρμαχῖδαι.—Next to Egypt, not on the coast itself, which was Egyptianized as far as the town of Apis.

2. *Marmaridae*, Μαρμαρῖδαι.—West of (1), and extending across the interior of Cyrenaica almost, but not quite, to the Syrtis Major. This is the first notice of this people who were in later times so well known, and who bestowed the name Marmarica upon the region they inhabited. The Marmaridae comprised undoubtedly many tribes[2]—among them, perhaps, the Giligamae of Herodotus, since the latter are not mentioned in later times (except by Steph. Byz. *in verb.*, and not independently of Herodotus).

3. *Nasamones*, Νασαμῶνες.—In the eastern Syrtis Major, south-west of Cyrenaica (2), and extending westwards to the Philaenorum Arae.

4. *Macae*, Μάκαι.—In the western Syrtis Major from (3) to the Cinyps river (*i.e.* nearly to the modern Tripoli).

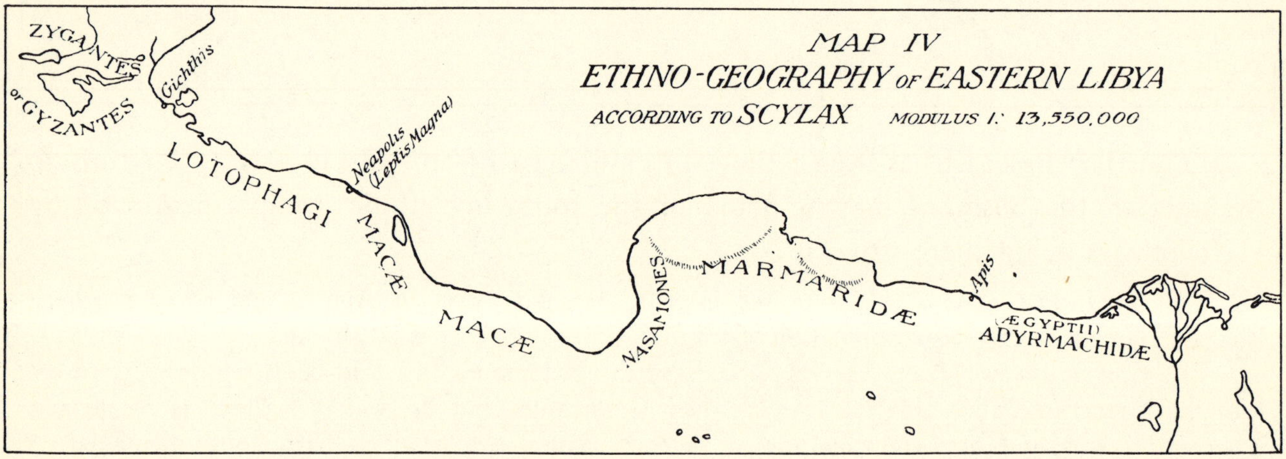

5. *Lotophagi*, Λωτοφάγοι.—Under this descriptive, Scylax designates those coastwise Libyans between the Cinyps on the east, and Gichthis (on the main opposite Gerbah Island) on the west. The name served to embrace a number of tribes, such, for example, as the Erebidae.[3]

6. *Zygantes*, Ζύγαντες.—About Lake Tritonis. This people would appear to be the Gyzantes of Herodotus, who are by the earlier writer given a place somewhat north of the position assigned them by Scylax. There is certainly some confusion as to this ethnic name. The simple metathesis of the Γυζ- of Herodotus to the Ζυγ- of Hecataeus[4] causes no difficulty in the Greek transcription of a barbarous name. When one considers the large body of evidence which indicates that the region inhabited by the people in question was called *Byzacenis*, *Byzacium*, or *Byzacitis*, the suspicion at once arises that the true form of the ethnic was neither Ζυγ- nor Γυζ- but Βυζ-.[5] Γ, it is hardly

[1] Herodotus iv. 181 ; cf. *Idem*, ii. 32.

[2] The later Marmaridae may have included some Semitic nomads from Sinai or Arabia. At all events, Agroetas, *Frag.* 1 in *FHG*, mentions an eponymous "Marmaris" son of "Arabs."

[3] Philistus, *Frag.* 33, in *FHG*. Ἐρεβίδαι, μέρος Λωτοφάγων.

[4] Hecataeus *ap.* Steph. Byz. *in verb.* Ζυγαντίς = *Frag.* 306 in *FHG*.

[5] Cf. Ptolemy iv. 3 § 6.

necessary to remark, is a dialect equivalent of B in Berber, and it may therefore be said with a fair degree of certainty that (*a*) the commonest form of the ethnic name was Βύζαντες; (*b*) a local variant was Γύζαντες; (*c*) while Ζύγαντες is another variant by metathesis.

The data drawn from Scylax are exhibited in Map IV. The date of Scylax has given rise to much discussion, but may be taken as *circa* 320 B.C.

The distribution of the Libyan tribes made by Strabo, some four and a half centuries after Herodotus, is, like that of Scylax, based on broader lines than that of the historian. Instead of treating the Libyans tribe by tribe, Strabo is content to deal with them in following ethnic groups:—

1. *Marmaridae*, Μαρμαρῖδαι.—West of Egypt along-shore to Cyrenaica,[1] *i.e.* as far as the Catabathmus Major[2] (= 'Aḳabah es-Sollum). It was in the west of this district that the bulk of the Marmaridae were to be found, and they extended south to Ammonium.[3]

2. *Nasamones*, Νασαμῶνες.—West of (1), across the south slope of the Cyrenaic plateau[3] to the Altars of the Philaeni (= approx. Muḫtar) in the bottom of the Syrtis Major.[4]

3. *Psylli*, Ψύλλοι.—Strabo mentions this people as sharing the Syrtis Major with (2).[5] As the latter came west, as just noted, to the Philaenorum Arae, it is to be supposed that the Psylli extended from that point to the Cephalae promontory (= Ras Mizratah), where the Libyphoenicians began.[6] It is therefore loosely that Strabo calls the Psylli Cyrenean.[7] In confirmation of the position just given the Psylli, is the order in which they are mentioned with other Libyans by Strabo.[8]

4. *Hesperitae Libyans*, Ἑσπηρῖται Λίβυες.—These are the only Libyans to whom Strabo gives a name, whom he places actually within fertile Cyrenaica.[9] They were, of course, called Hesperitae from Euhesperis (= Benghazî), near which, in the vicinity of the Lethalus (= Lethe) "river," they dwelt.

5. *Asbystae*, Ἀσβύσται.—Placed west of the Major Syrtis, between the Psylli and Byzacii, who extended to Carthage.[10] Strabo has here fallen into a serious confusion which it is not possible to untangle, and which, happily, is not usual to him. The position of the Asbystae is rectified on Map V., their position in Strabo being certainly wrong.

6. *Byzacii*, Βυζάκιοι.—See (5).

7. *Libyphoenices*, Λιβυφοίνικες.—Under this general descriptive, Strabo designates those tribes of the littoral which extended from the Cephalae Promontory (= Ras Mizratah) to Carthage.[11] The name is significant, and may be compared to such terms as Βλαστοφοίνικες, etc.

8. *Lotophagi*, Λωτοφάγοι.—This descriptive has been noted as applied by Herodotus to a group within the territories of the Gindanes. Strabo, on the authority of Artemidorus, mentions Lotophagi in Western Libya, in the interior, and adds that Lotophagi are reported to exist even as far east as Southern Cyrenaica.[12] Such an extension of a title merely derived from the practice of eating a fruit is of no significance; from Strabo himself it is clear that the Nasamones were the nation south of Cyrenaica. When this writer, however, specifically says that "there are others also called Lotophagi who inhabit Meninx, one of the islands opposite to the Lesser Syrtis,"[13] his statement warrants our placing "Lotophagi" on the map in the position named. The term Lotophagi belongs to that unsatisfactory class of descriptives of which Criophagi, Acridophagi, Ichthyophagi, Macrobii, etc., are examples.

1 Strabo ii. p. 131.
2 *Ibid.* xvii. p. 838.
3 *Ibid. loc. cit.*
4 *Ibid.* xvii. p. 836; cf. ii. p. 131.
5 *Ibid.* ii. p. 131.
6 *Ibid.* xvii. p. 835.
7 *Ibid.* xvii. p. 814.
8 *Ibid.* xvii. p. 838.
9 *Ibid.* xiv. p. 647.
10 *Ibid.* ii. p. 131.
11 *Ibid.* xvii. p. 835.
12 *Ibid.* iii. p. 157; cf. xvii. p. 829.
13 *Ibid.* iii. p. 157.

9. *Gaetulians*, Γαιτοῦλοι.—Beyond the Psylli, according to Strabo,[1] and, it may be added, away from the coast, lay the Gaetulians.[2] The Gaetulians covered a vast area, occupying the South Atlas slopes,[3] and the mountainous tracts south of the Libyphoenices.[4] Their eastern extremity was in the longitude of the Syrtis Major.[5]

10. *Garamantes*, Γαράμαντες.—South of the preceding,[6] with whose territories those of the Garamantes lay parallel, running as far to the east as to be 15 days' journey from Ammonium[7] (*i.e.* approximately to the longitude of the bottom of the Syrtis Major).

11. *Libyans*, name not otherwise specified.—Lastly must be noted the Libyans settled above Meroë, on the west bank of the Nile, already mentioned. (Not shown on the map.)

These data are summarized in Map V.

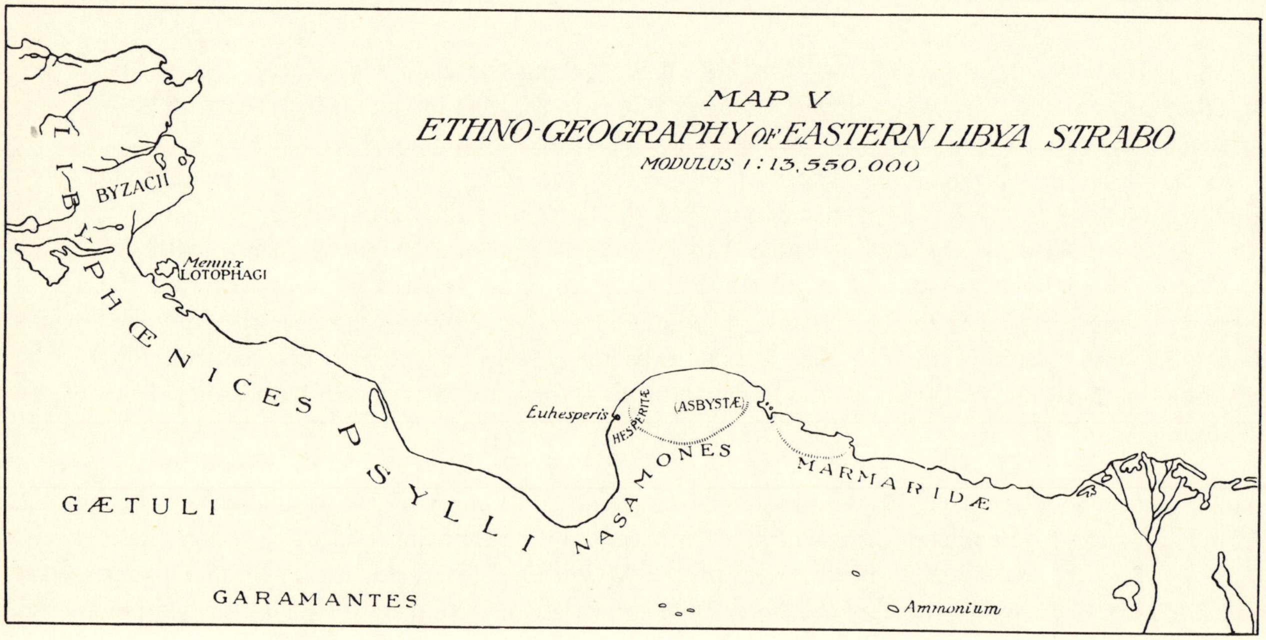

Another repartition of Libyan tribes made at about the same time as Strabo's, though with less care, is that of Diodorus Siculus. As one would expect, Diodorus, here, as usually, deficient in geographical sense, is content to outline the main masses of the Libyans in a very general manner. Of the divisions he makes, the following are to be noted :—

1. *Marmaridae.*—Egypt to Cyrenaica,[8] as in Strabo.
2. *Auschisae.*—South-western Cyrenaica.[8]
3. *Nasamones.*—Eastern part of Syrtica Regio,[8] below Auchisae.
4. *Macae.*—In the western part of the Syrtica Regio.[8]
5. *Libyphoenices.*—Held numerous towns along the coast,[9] extending, one may suppose, as far to the east as Carthage, as in the case of the Libyphoenices of Strabo.

[1] Strabo xvii. p. 838.
[2] Cf. *ibid.* ii. p. 131, and all other evidence on this people, which never established itself on the coast.
[3] *Ibid.* xvii. p. 826 ; cf. Eustathius, *ad Dionys. Perieg.* 215, where the Gaetuli are spoken of as the greatest of the Libyan peoples.
[4] Strabo xvii. p. 835.
[5] *Ibid.* ii. p. 131, xvii. p. 829.
[6] *Ibid.* ii. p. 131, xvii. p. 835.
[7] *Ibid.* xvii. p. 835.
[8] Diodorus Siculus iii. 49. 1.
[9] *Ibid.* xx. 55. 3.

These tribes, as signalized by Diodorus, are shown in Map VI.

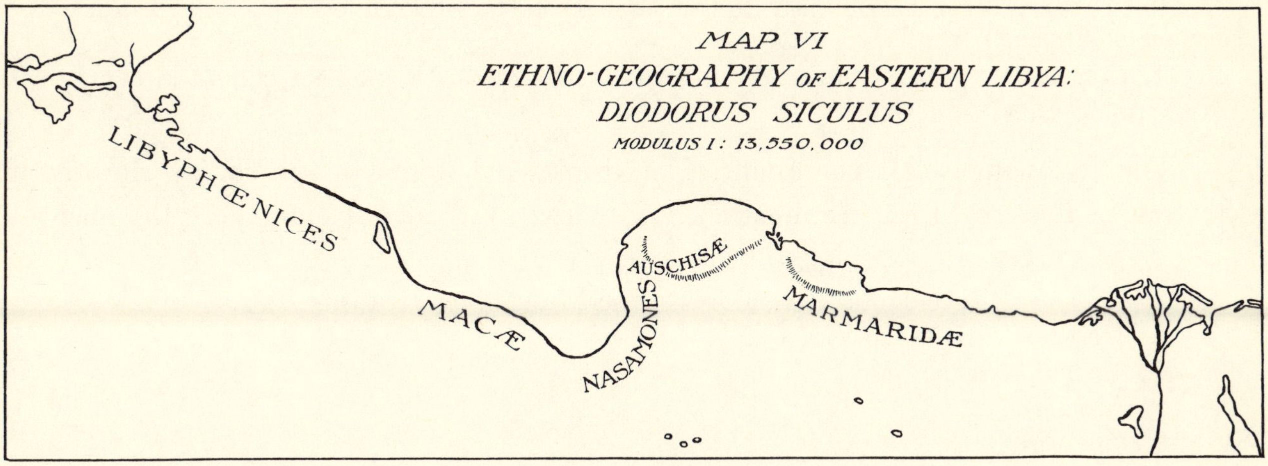

At a period a little after that of Strabo and Diodorus, but still in the first century A.D., Pliny gives further geographical notices which again allow the construction of an ethnic map. This writer has based his description of Eastern Libya on that of Mela, to whom he added such new details as he had derived from accounts of the Roman military expeditions. The author of the *Historia Naturalis* mentions in Eastern Libya the following tribes :—

1. *Mareotae.*—In the vicinity of Lake Mareotis (= Mariut).[1]
2. *Adyrmachidae.*—Between (1) and the Marmaridae.[1]
3. *Marmaridae.*—Catabathmus Major west almost to Syrtis Major.[2] Really in South-eastern Cyrenaica.[3]
4. *Ararauceles.*—Between (3) and the Syrtis Major.[4]
5. *Nasamones.*—Eastern littoral Syrtis Major.[4]
6. *Hasbitae* (= Asbystae).—Erroneously placed by Pliny after (*i.e.* west of) the Nasamones, with the Macae.[4] Perhaps the reference should be interpreted as meaning that the Asbystae lay north of the Nasamones, the Macae west of them, as is indicated by the other evidence.
7. *Lotophagi.*—Placed by Pliny in the bottom of the Syrtis Major with the Philaenorum Arae as their eastern boundary.[5] Hence, too far to the eastwards.
8. *Macae.*—West of the Nasamones,[6] placed along the western littoral of the Syrtis Major.
9. *Cisippades.*—West side of the Syrtis Major.[7]
10. *Libyphoenices.*—In Byzacium to the Syrtis Major.[8]

[1] Pliny v. 6.

[2] *Ibid. loc. cit.* and v. 5. In the latter place, the Marmaridae are carelessly said to extend all the way to the Syrtis. But from the phrase immediately following, it appears that the Ararauceles and the Nasamones intervened.

[3] Cf. Ptolemy, iv. 5 § 1.

[4] Pliny v. 5. The reading for No. 4 is *Acrauceles*, var. *Acraceles*, *Acrauciles*, but the form given above seems to be the purest, and is preserved as Ἀραραύκηλες, Ἀραυρακίδες by Ptolemy iv. 4 § 6.

[5] Pliny v. 4. *In intimo sinu* [*scil. Syrt. Maior.*] *fuit ora Lotophagon, quos quidam Machroas dixere, ad Philaenorum aras.* (A variant of Machroas is *Alachroas.*) In placing the Machroes (= Machryes) so far to the east, and in confusing them with the Lotophagi, Pliny has committed a double error.

[6] *Ibid.* v. 5.

[7] *Ibid.* v. 4.

[8] *Ibid. loc. cit.* Their extent is there shown by the cities said to lie within their territories. Cf. Livy xxi. 22 on these half-breeds.

[11. *Machryes.*—Confused by Pliny with the Lotophagi as noted above.[1] The notice can be taken only as showing that the Machryes (= Μάχρυες = Μάχλυες) were known in Pliny's day, their true position about Lake Tritonis being made clear from the earlier notice of Herodotus,[2] and the later one of Ptolemy.[3]]

12. *Capsitani.*—Spoken of as in the interior of the Syrtica Regio,[4] and almost certainly to be placed around Capsa (= Kafsah).

The following small communities[5] (Nos. 13-21), some of which lay slightly to the west of Eastern Libya, are mentioned with (12), but are not entered on the map :—

13. *Natabudes.* (Var. *Nattabutes*, *Nathabutes.*)
14. *Musulami.*—The Musulani of Florus[6] = the Musulini of Tacitus.[7]
15. *Sabarbares* (*vide* Map VIII.).
16. *Massyli.*—In the west.
17. *Nicives.*
18. *Vamacures.*
19. *Cinithi.*—About Lake Tritonis.
20. *Musuni* (*vide* Map VIII.).
21. *Marchubi.*

22. *Augilae.*—Considered wrongly by Pliny as an extensive people, whom he erroneously places half-way between Aethiopia and the Syrtis.[8] It may be, however, that the Augilae (*var.* Augylae) had penetrated as far south as the oasis of Kufra, and that it was this which Pliny wished to express.

23. *Psylli.*—Formerly, says Pliny, the Psylli were above (*i.e.* south of) the Garamantes.[8] This extraordinary statement cannot be accepted to mean more than that the Psylli were withdrawn from the coast. The story told by Herodotus of the battle of the Psylli against the south wind[9] appears to have been a native version of the account given by Pliny, to the effect that the Psylli were nearly exterminated by the Nasamones, who then took possession of their territories.[10] The same writer gives indirect testimony of the Psylli's having originally been seated on the littoral, when he says that "they received their name from Psyllus, one of their kings, whose tomb is in existence in the district of the Greater Syrtis."[10] From this evidence the Psylli have been entered on Map VII. in the interior of the Syrtica Regio.

24. *Garamantes.*—Placed by Pliny twelve days' journey from the Augilae,[11] in the interior. Their capital city is mentioned elsewhere as having been Garama,[12] which is doubtless to be identified with Germah ; Talgae and Debris also belonged to them.[12]

25. *Phazanii.*—In a region which he calls Phazania, and locates south of the Syrtis Minor, Pliny places a *natio* or ethnic group called Phazanii, to whom he attributes the towns of Alele, Cillaba, and Cydamus.[12] The last-named town can be identified with Ghadames,[13] which, although it lies to the west of the modern Fezzan, was within the district denominated Phazania by Pliny. This is borne out not only by the evidence of the names,[14] but by the fact that Phazania was

[1] Pliny v. 4 ; *vide supra*, p. 57, *n.* 5.
[2] Herodotus iv. 178.
[3] Ptolemy iv. 3 § 6.
[4] Pliny v. 4.
[5] All mentioned *ibid. loc. cit.*
[6] L. Annaeus Florus, *Hist.* iv. 12.
[7] Tacitus, *Annales* ii. 52, iv. 24 ; cf. C. O. Castiglioni, *Mémoire . . . sur la partie orientale de la Barbarie, etc.*, p. 112.
[8] All mentioned by Pliny v. 4.
[9] Herodotus iv. 173.
[10] Pliny vii. 2. The littoral position of the Psylli may be responsible for the fact that Nonnus, in relating the story of their war against the South Wind, says that the expedition was a naval one (*Dionysiaca*, xiii. 381 *sqq.*).
[11] Pliny v. 4.
[12] *Ibid.* v. 5.
[13] Cf. Procopius, *De aedificiis*, vi. 3 ; cf. V. de Saint Martin, *Le Nord de l'Afrique*, p. 116.
[14] Fezzan فزان was early adopted by Arabic writers, *e.g.* Ibn Ḥaldun, *Kitab el-ʿIbar*, Transl. de Slane, vol. i. pp. 191, 192. Cf. J. M. Hartmann, *Edrisii Africa*, p. 136 *sq.*

primarily a Garamantic country, and as such would, like the modern Fezzan, lie naturally under the Syrtis Major.[1] In the triumph of Cornelius Balbus were exhibited the Garamantic cities of Phazania—Talgae, Debris, and the capital, Garama. In the same triumph were also displayed the five following *nationes*, which are listed in a north-south direction and are not entered on the map :—

26. *Niteris.*
27. *Bubeium.* Cf. the *Limes Bubensis* of the *Notitia Dignitatum.*[2]
28. *Enipi.*
29. *Discera.*
30. *Nannagi.*
31. *Gaetuli.*—The Gaetulians are vaguely placed by Pliny in the interior, north of the Liby-

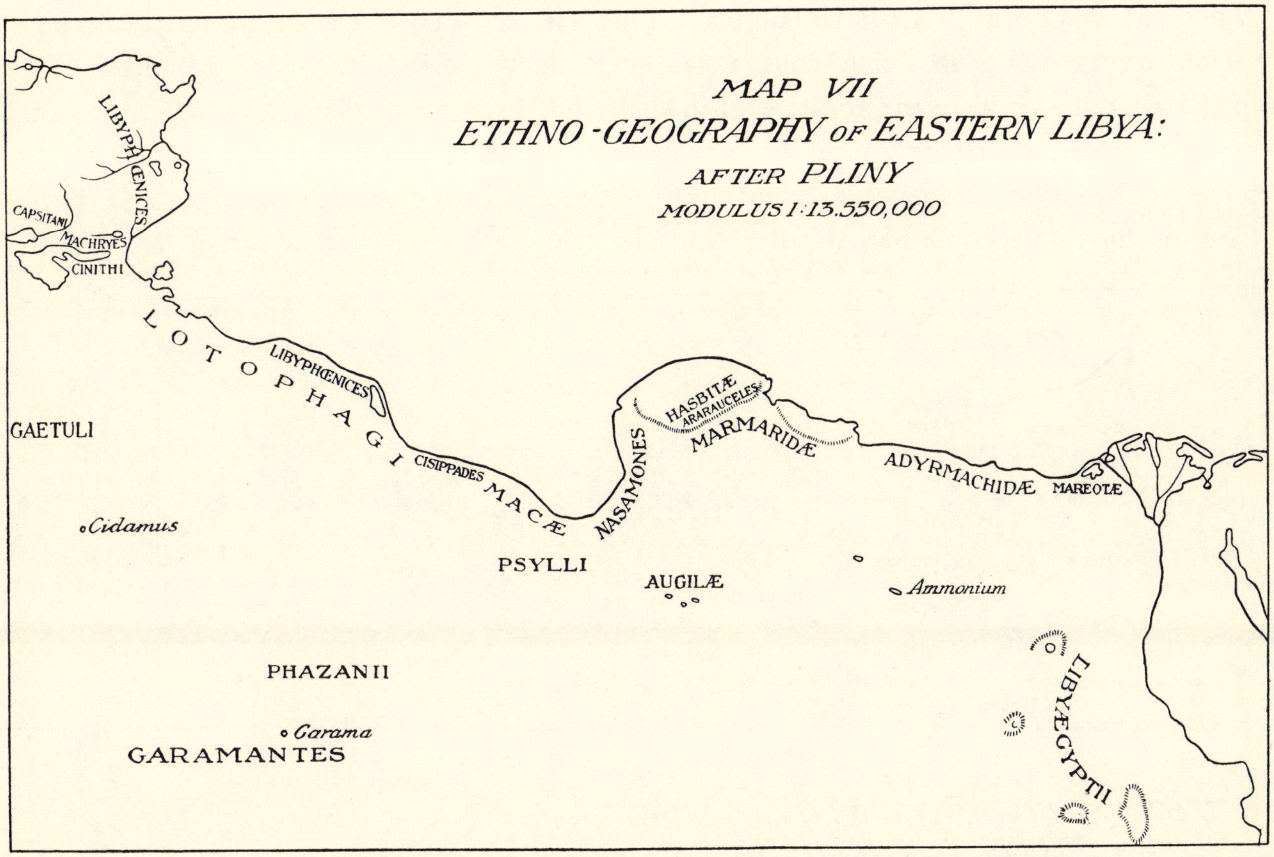

Egyptians,[3] and south (presumably) of the Garamantes. Their true position having been along the north-western confines of the Sahara, and not farther eastwards than the Garamantes, they have not been entered on the map in the position erroneously assigned to them, but at the eastern limits of their territories.

32. *Libyaegypti* (*Libues Aegyptii*).—The Liby-Egyptians lie between the Leucaethiopians and the Gaetuli, in an otherwise unspecified position.[4] On the map they will be seen occupying the Egyptian oases, since they are by Ptolemy placed south of the Nitriotae of the modern Wady Naṭrun.[5]

[1] Cf. Pliny v. 4, xiii. 19 and *passim* in speaking of the Garamantes ; Dionysius, *Perieg.* 216 *sq.* ; Priscian, *Perieg.* 201 *sq.* ; Ptolemy iv. 7 § 10, where the variants are Ἀζανία and Φάζακα, and where, though speaking of the Phazanians vaguely as a people west of the Nile, he notes Garama and other Phazanian towns as Garamantic. Cf. Agathemerus, *Geographiae informatio* ii. 7.

[2] *Notitia dignitatum utriusque imperii*, etc., p. 166. v. Cf. C. O. Castiglioni, *op. cit.* p. 108. *Bubeium* is certainly not to be related to بيان as Castiglioni suggested.

[3] Pliny v. 8.

[4] Cf. Mela i. 4, and Orosius i. 2 § 32.

[5] Ptolemy, iv. 5 § 12.

33. *Leucaethiopes* (*Leucoe Aethiopes*).—The "White Aethiopians" are placed by Pliny[1] south of (32). The location is too vague to be of value geographically, but the name has a distinct and obvious value as anthropological evidence. These Leucaethiopes of Pliny may be the Libyans of the Nubian Nile.

This ends the list of Libyan peoples mentioned by Pliny, and whose relative positions are entered in Map VII.

The following repartition of tribes—that of Ptolemy—demands a word of preface. The Alexandrian writer was, it should be recalled, much more a mathematician than an ethnographer. His tendency is always toward giving astronomically determined locations to the sites and peoples he deals with. With him, even when placing nomadic tribes, it is always an affair of rectangles. This has led often to the commission of really serious errors, and from a map constructed on Ptolemy's data alone it would appear that in his time there were a number of Libyan tribes existing in districts which are sheer desert! It is, therefore, necessary to correct or to confirm his statements, when possible, by other evidence. It may also be remarked that Ptolemy, because he is treating his subject mathematically, tends to deal with small tribes rather than with

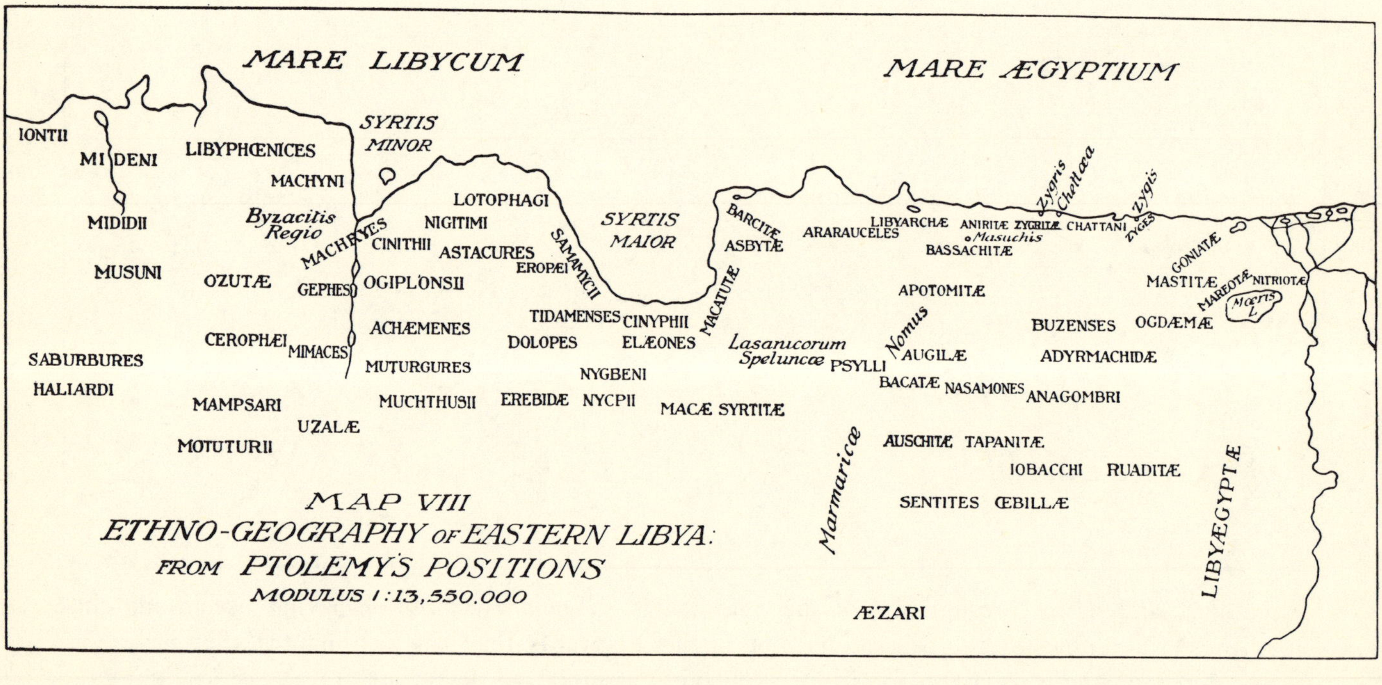

MAP VIII
ETHNO-GEOGRAPHY OF EASTERN LIBYA: FROM PTOLEMY'S POSITIONS
MODULUS 1:13,550.000

larger ethnic groups—*i.e.* his interest being in fixed points, he falls naturally into the habit, when dealing with divisions of a race, of treating them in the smallest possible ethnic groups (cf. Map VIII.). This, while it leads him into exaggerations, has yet its value: from him may be learned, for example, of many tribes in Africa and Asia which are elsewhere unmentioned, and their names are not infrequently of some philological significance. The following are those ethnic units which he mentions as existing in Eastern Libya:—

[1] Pliny v. 8. Ptolemy, iv. 6 § 6, places a group of Leucaethiopes in the west. The "White Aethiopians" are, presumably, the *gentes Libyoaethiopum* of Orosius i. 2 § 88.

1. *Mareotae*, Μαρεῶται.—The population of the modern Mariut.[1] As in the case of (2), (4), (7), (12), (19), and (30), the name is really a locative and not an ethnic. These, and all the other tribes bordering close upon Egypt were undoubtedly much fused with the inhabitants of the Nile Valley.

2. *Nitriotae*, Νιτριῶται.—Inhabitants of the modern Wady Naṭrun, west of the Delta. Placed too far south by Ptolemy, in the northern Fayum.[2]

3. *Libyaegyptii*, Λιβυαιγύπτιοι.—This people—a mixed one as shown by its name—Ptolemy locates west of the Nile in the Middle Egypt.[2] As the only habitable areas in that region are the oases (Ḫargah, Daḫlah, etc.), there can be no doubt but that this descriptive term is an equivalent of, or comprises, the Oasitae, under which designation Ptolemy speaks of the oasis-dwellers. Ptolemy is therefore slightly in error in treating the people which bore both these names as two, instead of as one.

4. *Oasitae*, Ὀασῖται.—The Oasis-dwellers (see (3)).[2]

5. *Goniatae*, Γωνιᾶται.—A little N.W. of the Mareotae. Not otherwise known.[2]

6. *Mastitae*, Μαστῖται.—West of the Mareotae. South of the Goniatae.[3] Not otherwise known.[4]

(*Prosoditae*, Προσοδῖται.—The correct reading should almost certainly be Προσοπῖται, Prosopitae, referring not to a Libyan tribe but to the inhabitants of Prosopis in the Western Delta. Therefore omitted on the maps.)[2]

7. *Ogdaemi*, Ὄγδαιμοι.—South of (6), in the vicinity of Mt. Ogdaemum, Ὄγδαιμον ὄρος. Otherwise not known.[2]

8. *Ruaditae*, Ῥουαδῖται.—Given an impossible position by Ptolemy, west of the Libyaegypti.[2] Not otherwise known.

9. *Adyrmachidae*, Ἀδυρμαχίδαι var. Ἀδυρμαχῖται etc.—This old ethnic group seems still to have existed in the time of Ptolemy, who however places it N.W. of (8) and S.W. of (7) in an utterly uninhabitable region.[2] From previous sources already noted the location of the Adyrmachidae is to be rectified by putting them north of the site allotted them by Ptolemy, almost, but not quite, on the coast. It is probable that the Adyrmachidae included some of the smaller tribes mentioned by Ptolemy, such as (5), (6), (7), (10), and (12).

10. *Anagombri*, Ἀνάγομβροι.—Placed impossibly S. by W. of the Adyrmachidae.[2] Otherwise unknown.

11. *Buzeans*, Βουζεῖς (var. βουτεῖς).—Placed N. by W. of the Adyrmachidae,[2] and so, perhaps, on the coast. If the form of the name as here given is correct, they are otherwise unknown.

12. *Zygeans*, Ζυγεῖς.—On the coast,[2] by the hamlet called Zygis, Ζυγὶς λιμήν, and so correctly located.

13. *Chattani*, Χαττανοί.—Placed by Ptolemy west of (12) on the coast;[2] and correctly, since they are in the vicinity of a small town, Chettaea, Χετταία.

14. *Zygritae*, Ζυγρῖται.—Next the Chattani, and, like them, correctly placed,[2] being in the vicinity of the sea-town of Zygris, Ζυγρὶς κώμη.[5] Cf. No. 12.

15. *Aniritae*, Ἀνειρῖται var. Ἀνειρεῖται.—West of the Zygritae, and on the shore[6] of the Catabathmus Major. Otherwise not known.

[1] Ptolemy iv. 5 §§ 4, 12, mentions the district. For the people, Pliny v. 6.

[2] Ptolemy iv. 5 § 12.

[3] *Ibid. loc. cit.* A tribe of this name also appears in Aethiopia, Ptolemy iv. 7 § 10.

[4] Possibly to be identified with the Μαστηνοί of Philistus, *Frag.* 30 b, in *FHG*.

[5] For Ζυγρὶς κώμη, Ptolemy iv. 5 § 3. An old, but still current, error of identification concerning the Zygritae, Chattani, and Proso(p)itae may here be noted. By G. Unger, *Chronologie des Manetho*, p. 218, these tribes were identified with the *Zakkaro*, *Scharutana*, and *Purista* respectively! These people—in reality the Shekelesh, Sherden and Peleset (Sicels, Sardinians, and Philistines)—Unger believed to have been the Libyans defeated by Rameses III.

[6] Ptolemy iv. 5 § 12. C. Müller, *ad loc.*, suggests as a possibility that the name is a clerical corruption for *Ἀζιρῖται, connecting thus the ethnic with the place-names Ἀζιλίς, Ἀζιρίς, Ἀζαρίς.

16. *Libyarchae*, Λιβυάρχαι.—West of (15), in the Gebel el-ʿAḳabah, and alongshore.[1] Otherwise not known.[2]

17. *Bassachitae*, Βασσαχῖται var. Βασσαχεῖται.—Placed by Ptolemy south of the Aniritae.[3] But C. Müller suggested that as Zygenses, Chattani, and Zygritae were associated with the towns of *Zygis Chettaea*, and *Zygris* respectively, so too the Bassachitae were grouped about the town *Masuchis*, Μασουχίς. The frequency of $\beta = \mu$ equivalences in Greek transcriptions of foreign names renders this at least possible. The frequency of *Mas-* as a Berber ethnic prefix and the resemblance of *Μασσαχῖται to the ($\sqrt{\text{MZ}}$ẓ) names mentioned at the beginning of this chapter raise the possibility to a likelihood.

18. *Apotomitae*, Ἀποτομῖται.—S. by W. of preceding in an uninhabitable region.[3] Otherwise unknown.

19. *Augilae*, Αὐγίλαι.—Placed in nearly the right latitude, but too far to the east,[3] being south of (16) and (18).

20. *Nasamones*, Νασαμῶνες.—Hopelessly misplaced[3] south of (17), and almost due west of (10).

21. *Bacatae*, Βακάται.—Placed south of (19), and almost west of (20).[3] Tribe otherwise unknown, unless the name be a scribal corruption of Βάκαλες.

22. *Auschitae*, Αὐσχῖται var. Αὐχίται.—Misplaced south of (21), south-west of (20).[3]

23. *Tapanitae*, Ταπανῖται.—Adjoining preceding on the east, south of (20).[3] Unknown.

24. *Iobacchi*, Ἰόβακχοι.—Placed impossibly south of (10), and west of (8).[3] Unknown.

25. *Oebillae*, Οἰβίλλαι.—South of (24).[3] Unknown.

26. *Sentites*, Σέντιτες.—Adjoining (25) on the west.[3] Unknown.

27. *Aezari*, Αἴζαροι.—In the far south, below (16), (18), (22), etc.[3] Unknown.

28. *Marmaridae*, Μαρμαρῖδαι.—Not located, but the Marmaric Nome is extended inland to an absurd distance from the sea,[4] southerly from the Gebel el-ʿAḳabah.

29. *Ararauceles*, Ἀραραύκηλες var. Ἀραυρακίδες. (Agroetas has Ἀραυράκη[λι]ν in acc. sing.[5])—This name has already been seen in Pliny's list. Placed almost correctly by Ptolemy,[6] but a little too far south, in south-east Cyrenaica.

30. *Barcitae*, Βαρκῖται var. Βαρκεῖται.—The Libyans about Barca. Rightly placed.[6]

31. *Asbytae*, Ἀσβῦται var. Ἀσβῆται.—The name has been already discussed above, in connection with the tribes in Egyptian times. The variant Ἀσβῆται comes nearest to reproducing the old form *Eṣbet*. Placed by Ptolemy in the south-west instead of in the east of Cyrenaica.[6]

32. *Macatutae*, Μακατοῦται.—Placed in the south-east corner of the Syrtis Major, apparently correctly.[6]

(. . . τὰ σπήλαια τῶν Λασανικῶν var. Λαγανικῶν etc. Ptolemy places these "caves of the Lasanici" well in the interior, in the vicinity of the Psylli, the latter being on the same parallel, farther to the east.[6] It is impossible to say if the Lasanici were a people extant in Ptolemy's day, or what was their true position. In the *Antonine Itinerary* a point Lasamices is found between Semerus and Cyrene, and it has been conjectured that this was the site of the Lasinici,[7] and that they

[1] Ptolemy, *loc. cit.* C. Müller, *ad loc.*, observes, *Libyarchae . . . qui primi post Pentapolim Cyrenaicam commemorantur, ab ipso hoc situ*, Λιβύης ὅτι φαίνεται ἀρχή (*Dionys. Perieg* [*var. lect.*] 214) [in G. Bernhardy, *Geographi Graeci Minores*, vol. i. p. 572] *nuncupari videntur.*

[2] Not to be confused with the Λιβυάρχοντες of the Petrie Papyrus, officers in charge of the affairs of the Libyan Nome, who were bilingual "sheykhs," whose birth fitted them to assume the offices in their districts performed by the Arabarchs in theirs. *Vide* J. P. Mahaffy, *Empire of the Ptolemies*, p. 181, § 116.

[3] Ptolemy, *loc. cit.*, and *vide* C. Müller, *ad loc.*

[4] Ptolemy *loc. cit.*; C. Müller, *Tabulae in Claudii Ptolemaei Geographiam XXXVI.* Tab. XXV.

[5] Agroetas, *Frag.* in *FHG* iv. p. 294.

[6] Ptolemy iv. 4 § 6. Apropos of No. 31, does Philistus (*Frag.* 30 *a* and *b* in *FHG*) intend the Asbystae or Asbytae by the name Ἐλβέστιοι?

[7] *Itiner. Anton.* p. 32 (*Wess.* p. 70, 5); C. Müller, *ad* Ptol. *loc. cit.*

were to be found in what is now the Wady Ḳerayb.[1] The evidence is too slight to allow of anything like certainty on this question.)

33. *Psylli*, Ψύλλοι.—South of (29), east of Augilae, and so out of place.[2]

34. *Macae Syrtitae*, *οἱ* Μάκαι *οἱ* Συρτῖται var. *οἱ* Μακαῖοι Συρτῖται.—South of the south-east corner of the Syrtis Major, too far in the interior.[3]

35. *Cinyphii*, Κινύφιοι ; Κινυφίους in acc. pl.—At the bottom of the Syrtis Major,[3] and so too far to the east. For these people, from their name, belonged to the fertile area about the Cinyps River near Leptis.

36. *Elaeones*, 'Ελαιῶνες.—Below the Cinyphii.[3] This position, that in which later are to be found the *Seli*, leads to the suspicion that the name is rightly *Σελαιῶνες, but of this there is no conclusive proof. It is safer to suppose that the Elaeones were a *part* of the Seli, as were the Macomades.[4]

37. *Nygbeni*, Νυγβηνοί.—S.S.W. of (36).[5] By confusion, a people with another form of the same name are placed in Aethiopia.[6] The Nygbeni are placed immediately north of another people called the Nycpii, Νύκπιοι.[7] That Ptolemy has here registered the same people twice under slightly different names seems quite certain. ΓΒ = ΚΠ, and the -ΗΝ*οι* termination is the Berber plural + the Greek -*οι*. Νύκπιοι is the more Graecized form, as shown both by the introduction of the *π* (unknown in Berber), and by the purely Greek form of the plural in -*οι*.

38. *Nycpii*. (See 37).

39. *Samamycii*, Σαμαμύκιοι var. Σαμαμίκιοι and in acc. plur. Σαμαβυκίους (by $\mu = \beta$).—Along the west Syrtis Major, between the Lotophagi and Cinyphii,[8] and so probably really occupying an intra-Syrtic position. But it may be remarked that the *Notitia dignitatum* placed in the Syrtica Regio the *Mamucensis limes*.[9] Also, at the bottom of the gulf lay the town *Anabucis*.[10] In Berber, *S* becomes easily prefixed to personal names, cf. *Sammon*, سمّون, for *Amon*, in Sîwan legend. Hence, the variant Σαμαβυκ- given above may be related to the town-name, *m* and *n* being universally equivalent in North Africa—[Σ-]*α*Ν*α*Β*υκ*- = *Anabuc*-. As, however, the Elaeones appear to have occupied the scanty space on the west Syrtic littoral in the days of Ptolemy, and as the evidence just cited cannot outweigh that which puts the Samamycii between the Lotophagi and the Cinyphii, they have, with reserve, been given an intra-Syrtic position on the rectified map.

40. *Tidamensii*, Τιδαμήνσιοι var. Οἰδαμήνσιοι, etc.—South of (39).[11] Unknown, unless C. Müller's emendation of *Κιδαμήνσιοι, *i.e.* people of Cidamus or Cidame,[12] be accepted. The plausible Ti- prefix seems against such a correction.

41. *Dolopes*, Δόλοπες var. Δόλωπες.—South of (40).[13] Also far in the interior.[14] Unknown.

42. *Erebidae*, 'Ερεβίδαι.—South of (41)[15] and wrongly so. For this tribe formed part of the Lotophagi,[16] and has been placed accordingly in Map IX.

43. *Eropaei*, 'Εροπαῖοι.—West of (39).[17] Unknown.

44. *Lotophagi*, Λωτοφάγοι.—On the intra-Syrtic coast,[17] and so a little too far to the east.

45. *Nigitimi*, Νιγίτιμοι.—South of (44) between the Syrtes.[17] The name *Nigize Gaetuli* ($z = t$) in the *Tabula Peutingeriana*, suggests that this people are rightly placed in the interior, but that they ought to be put more to the westward.

[1] F. W. and H. W. Beechey, *Expedition to . . . the Northern Coast of Africa*, p. 569. ("Wady Jeráhib.")

[2] Ptolemy, *loc. cit.*

[3] *Ibid.* iv. 3 § 6.

[4] *Tabula Peutingeriana*, *Macomades Selorum*. The name *Macomades* survived in Arabic geographical nomenclature as *Mighmadas*, مغمداس. Cf. H. Fournel, *Les Berbers*, p. 147 *n.* 7.

[5] Ptolemy, *loc. cit.*

[6] *Ibid.* iv. § 7. The Νυγβηνῖται Αἰθίοπες.

[7] *Ibid.* iv. 3 § 6.

[8] *Ibid. loc. cit.*

[9] *Notit. dig.* p. 89. 9. The name survived in the Syrtica Regio as *Ḳaṣr Mamaḳas*—قصر مماقس in J. M. Hartmann, *Edrisii Africa*, p. 305.

[10] *Itiner. Anton.* p. 30 (*Wess.* p. 65, 7).

[11] Ptolemy, *loc. cit.* and C. Müller, *ad loc. cit.*

[12] Pliny v. 5 ; Procopius, *De aedificiis* vi. 3.

[13] Ptolemy, *loc. cit.*

[14] *Ibid.* iv. 6 § 6.

[15] *Ibid.* iv. 3 § 6.

[16] Stephan. Byz. *in verb.* 'Ερεβίδαι calls them . . . *μέρος* Λωτοφάγων, on the authority of Philistus.

[17] Ptolemy, *loc. cit.*

46. *Astacures*, Ἀστάκουρες.—South of (45), west of (39). The position agrees well enough, though a little too far to the north, with that of the *Austuriani* of Ammianus,[1] and perhaps the Astacures are to be identified with that people, who were variously and confusedly known.[2]

47. *Cinithii*, Κινίθιοι var. Κινήθιοι, Κινύθιοι, Κίνθιοι, etc.—South of the eastern shore of the Syrtis Minor, only a little east of what seems to have been their true position.[3] The Cinithii have been already met with among the East Libyan peoples enumerated by Pliny, and they figure in later times as one of the main divisions of the Libyan race.[4]

48. *Ogiplonsii*, Ὀγιπλώνσιοι var. Σιγιπλούσιοι.—Inland from (47) and so, according to Ptolemy, to the south; but perhaps to the west.[5] Unknown.

49. *Achaemeneans*, Ἀχαιμενεῖς var. Ἀχαιμονεῖς.—South of (48).[5] Unknown.

50. *Muturgures*, Μουτούργουρες var. Βουτούργουρες.—South of (49).[5] Unknown.

51. *Muchthusii*, Μουχθούσιοι var. Μουχθουούιοι.—South of (50).[5] Unknown.

52. *Machryes*, Μάχρυες.—In the elbow of the Syrtis Minor,[5] and by both position and the phonetic equivalence of the name, to be identified with the Μάχλυες of Herodotus (λ = ρ),[6] the Μαχλυεῖς, of Nicolaus Damascenus,[7] and the *Machroas* of Pliny.[8]

53. *Gepheans*, Γηφεῖς var. Γυφεῖς.—South of (52).[9] Unknown.

54. *Mimaces*, Μίμακες.—South of (53).[10] Unknown, unless they are to be identified with the Μίμαλκες, ἔθνος Λιβυκόν of Philistus.[11]

55. *Uzalae*, Οὐζάλαι.—South of (54).[12] Unknown.

(*Byzaces.*—Ptolemy mentioning the district called Byzacitis, ἡ Βυζακῖτις χώρα, it is fair to assume that the Byzaces were still to be found in it. He places it with fair accuracy on the north-west of the Syrtis Minor.[12])

56. *Machyni*, Μάχυνοι var. Μαχύνοι, Μόχυνοι.—In the northern part of the Byzacitis *sahel*.[12]

57. *Libyphoenices*, Λιβυφοίνικες.—The mixed Berbers and Semites, who were probably numerous wheresoever the latter had colonies in North Africa, Ptolemy confines to the district where, to be sure, they were to be found in the greatest number—viz. north of Byzacitis, near Carthage.[12]

(The following tribes also appear on Map VIII. in the localities assigned them by Ptolemy.[12]

Iontii, Ἰόντιοι.

Mideni, Μιδηνοί var. Μισηνοί, Μεδηνοί = the Μύνδωνες of Stephan. Byz. *s.v.*

Mididii, *Μιδίδιοι, *correx.* C. Müller.

Musuni, Μούσουνοι = *Musunei*, Iulius Honorius, p. 54.

Saburbures, Σαβούρβουρες; also in interior, Ptol. iv. 6 § 6—Σουβούρπορες.

Haliardi, Ἁλιάρδοι.

Mampsari, Μαμψάροι var. Μάρμαροι.

Motuturii, Μοτουτούριοι var. Ματουτούριοι.

Cerophaei, Κεροφαῖοι.

Ozutae, Ὀζοῦται.

The names of these tribes, as bordering Eastern Libya on the west, are here given without other detail.)

1 Ammianus Marcellinus xxvi. 4. 5, xxviii. 6. 2.

2 *Vide infra* p. 68 and notes. The *Astacures* are also found in Aethiopia (Ἀστάκουροι, Ptolemy v. 6 § 6).

3 Ptolemy iv. 3 § 6.

4 *Chronic. Pasch.* vol. i. p. 59, Ἄφρων ἔθνη καὶ ἀποικίαι εἰσὶ πέντε· Νεβδήνοι, Κνῆθοι, Νουμίδες, Νασαμῶνες, Σαϊοί (for Σακοί). Cf. *ibid.* vol. ii. p. 102, *Afrorum gentes et inhabitationes hae sunt: Lebdeni, Cinti, Numidae, Nasamones, Saci.*

5 Ptolemy, *loc. cit.*

6 Herodotus iv. 178, 180.

7 Nicolaus Damascenus, *Frag.* 136 in *FHG.*

8 Pliny v. 4; *vide supra*, p. 57 *n.* 5. Perhaps = *Mecales* of Corippus, *Johan.* iii. 410 and, *fide* V. de Saint-Martin, *Le Nord de l'Afrique*, p. 55, the modern Berber tribe of the *Maghîlah* مغيلة.

9 Ptolemy, *loc. cit.*

10 Ptolemy *loc. cit.* Also in the interior, *ibid.* iv. 6 § 5.

11 Philistus, *Frag.* 33 in *FHG.*

12 Ptolemy iv. 3 § 6.

The tribes just reviewed make at first sight an imposing array. It has appeared, however, that Ptolemy has in some cases named the same tribe twice (as in the instance of the *Nygbeni* and *Nycpii*), that he has placed almost all of them too far to the south and east, and that in many cases he gives the name of a tribe of which nothing is elsewhere heard. In the rectification of his map, therefore, it is only in the cases of the best-known ethnic groups that it is possible to assert with anything like surety that they occupy their proper

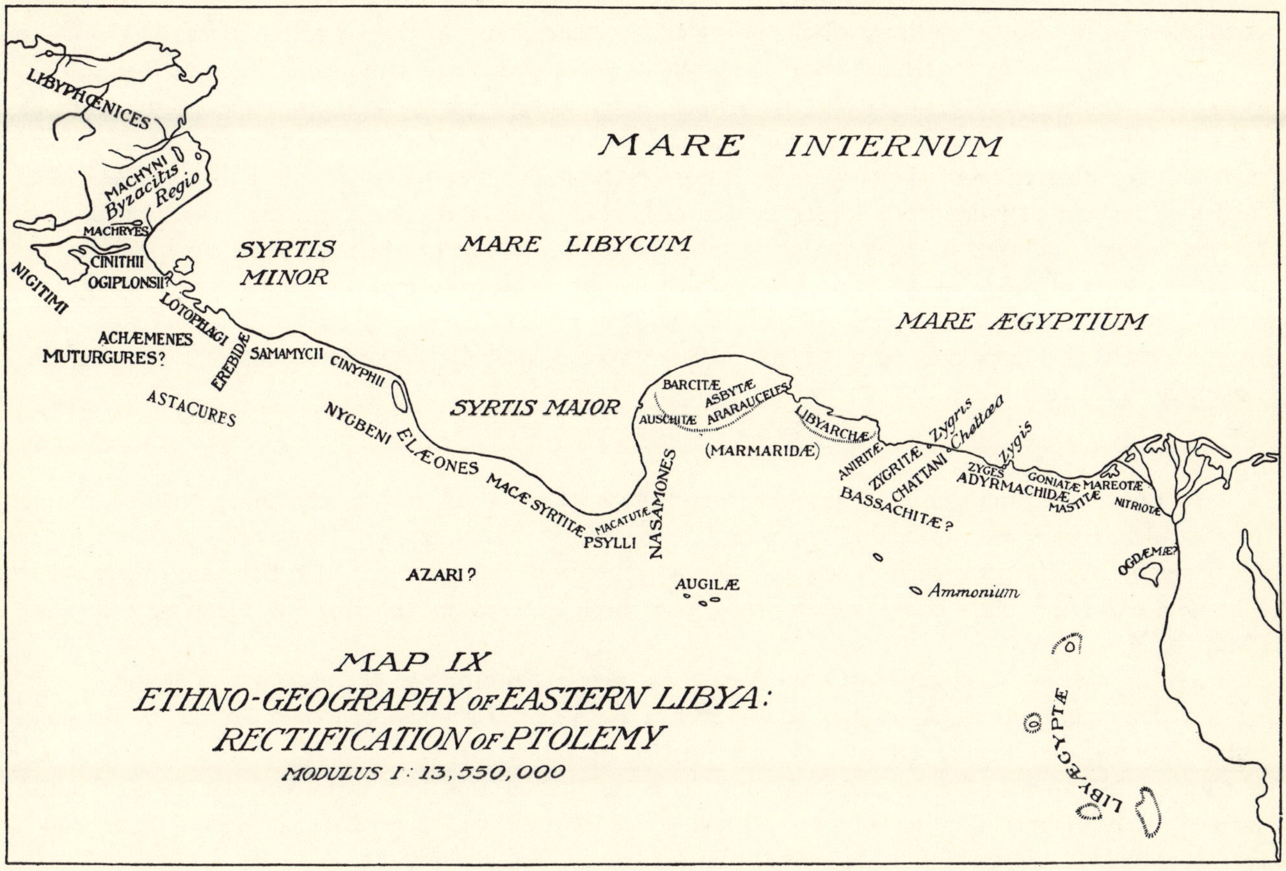

places. Many tribes are omitted on the rectified map (IX.), and almost all have been shifted to accord with other ancient notices or with the necessities of geographical position.

In order to form an idea of the repartition of the East Libyans in late Roman times, shortly before the Arab invasions, it is necessary to draw on a variety of sources. Some of these need to be dealt with cautiously, since they are rooted in a common tradition,[1] as the following parallels plainly show :—

Excerpta Barbari.[2]	*Liber Generationis.*[3]	*Chronicon Anni p. Ch. 334.*[4]	*Origo Humani Generis.*[5]
. . . *Syrta habens gentes tres, Nasamona, Macas, Tautameus*[6] . . .	. . . *Syrtes habens gentes has, Nasomones, Macas, Tautameos* . . .	. . . *Syrthes, Nascimenia, Tautamei* . . .	. . . *Marmaris, Sirtis, Nasamonas, Tautamona* . . .

[1] The relations of the earlier sources, owing to the labours of Detlefsen, d'Avezac, C. Müller, etc., are fairly well established. In the earlier part of this chapter they have been recognized, though not discussed.

[2] *Excerpta Barbari*, p. 61 (= C. Frick, *Chronica minora*, vol. i. p. 202).

[3] In C. Frick, *op. cit.* vol. i. p. 20. [4] In *ibid.* vol. i. p. 88. [5] In *ibid.* vol. i. p. 139.

[6] This form transliterates characteristically the acc. pl. of the lost Greek original *Ταυταμαίους.

Other late sources than these exist, but they are none of them very satisfactory, and it is hard to determine how far they represent the actual ethnography of the period to which they belong, and how far they depend on Pliny and Mela, or on other earlier writers. With this preamble, the following groups may be noted :—

1. *Marmaridae.*[1]—In their old easterly position.

2. *Mazices*, *Mazaces*.[2]—Throughout the interior parts of Eastern Libya ; they bordered on the Austuriani in the west,[3] are heard of as raiding in Cyrenaica,[4] and in the Egyptian oases.[5]

3. *Barcaei.*—The reader has seen that Ptolemy located a small tribe called by him Βαρκῖται or Βαρκεῖται[6] in the vicinity of Barca, from which town this people took their name. One seeks in vain in Herodotus for a native population called after the town Βάρκη, though the historian mentions the district about the city under the term Βαρκαία,[7] and has a gentile adjective, Βαρκαῖος, by which he regularly denotes a Greek citizen of Barca. But in Roman times an ethnic formed on the place-name was used to designate the various remnants of the native population surviving in the neighbourhood of the city—a development which may have been fostered by the fact that throughout its history Barca itself was strongly Libyan in character.[8]

As early as Vergil one hears of the *latique furentes Barcaei*,[9] a phrase echoed long after by Corippus in the line

Barcaei solito curant saevire furore.[10]

In Byzantine times the Barceans were regularly spoken of as a distinct ethnic group. Thus, *Barcaei Mauri Libyae* (var. *Libyes*) in Vibius Sequester.[11] Many writers, however, ignore them, as is conspicuously the case with Synesius. Despite this, and the fact that the Barceans were not a homogeneous tribe, but a conglomerate, they have been entered in the map in the proper locality (Map X).[12]

4. *Nasamones*, *Nesamones*.[13]—Often noticed in their old position in the east Syrtica Regio.[14]

5. *Seli* (*natio Selorum*).—In the south Syrtica Regio.[15] This people would appear to be none other than the old Psylli, returned to their former localities ; ψ, it is hardly necessary to observe, is a sound unknown in Berber language, and it seems that in this late form *Seli*, one is confronted with a fairly correct spelling of this ethnic. The particle SL in tribal names was common—e.g. *Mas-SyL-i*, *Massae-SyL-i*, *Mus-SuL-ani*, *SiL-vacae*, *SiL-cadenit*, etc.

[1] Flavius Vopiscus, *Probus*, 9 ; Corippus, *Johannis*, ii. 138, iv. 1042, 1164, v. 147, 507, 565, 574, 664, vi. 406, vii. 169, 300, 381, 427, 455, 531, 636, 647 ; *Origo humani generis*, *loc. cit.*; Sidonius Apollinaris, *Carm.* v. 338.

[2] Corippus, *Johannis*, i. 549 ; iv. 724, 1020, v. 167, 450, 600, vii. 305 ; Nemesian, *Cyneget.* 261 ; Claudian, *In primo cons. Stilich.* i. 356.

[3] Philostorgius xi. 8.

[4] Ammianus Marcellinus xxvii. 9. 1.

[5] Johannes Moschus, *Vitae Patrum*, x. 112, in *Patrologia Latina*, vol. lxxix. col. 176 *sqq.* ; cf. another notice in the *De vitis patrum*, iii. 199, *ibid.* vol. lxiii. col. 804 ; Evagrius, *Hist. Eccles.* i. 7, etc. In general, cf. Corippus, *Johannis*, *loc. cit.*, *supra n.* 2.

[6] Ptolemy iv. 4 § 6. Steph. Byz. *in verb.* Βάρκη gives the gentile name as Βαρκαιάται. Cf. Oberlin's note in Vibius Sequester, p. 385.

[7] Herodotus iv. 171, Τεύχειρα πόλις τῆς Βαρκαίης.

[8] *Vide infra*, pp. 177 *n.* 4, 230 *n.* 8, 231 *n.* 3.

[9] Vergil, *Aen.* iv. 44.

[10] Corippus, *Johannis*, ii. 123. Cf. *ibid.* iv. 506.

[11] Vibius Sequester, p. 34.

[12] The popularity of the name برقة, Barḳah, in the Arabic authors as a designation for the district of Barcea has perpetuated the name of the region, and thus, indirectly, of the town.

[13] This latter form is found in the *Tabula Peutingeriana*, Seg. vii.

[14] *Chronic. Pasch.* vol. i. p. 59, ii. p. 102 ; Sidonius Apollinaris, *Carm.* v. 338 ; Corippus, *Johannis*, v. 198, 552, 589, 593, 692, vi. 465, 510, vii. 95, 177 ; C. Frick, *Chronica minora*, *loc. cit.*, etc.

[15] Two Syrtic towns of the Seli appear in the *Tabula Peutingeriana*, Seg. vii. The Psylli are mentioned by Sidonius Apollinaris, *loc. cit.*

6. *Macetae*, Μακέται.—This ethnic is but a variant of the earlier *Macae*, Μάκαι, and as there is good evidence of their activity in late Roman times they have been entered on the map (X.) in their

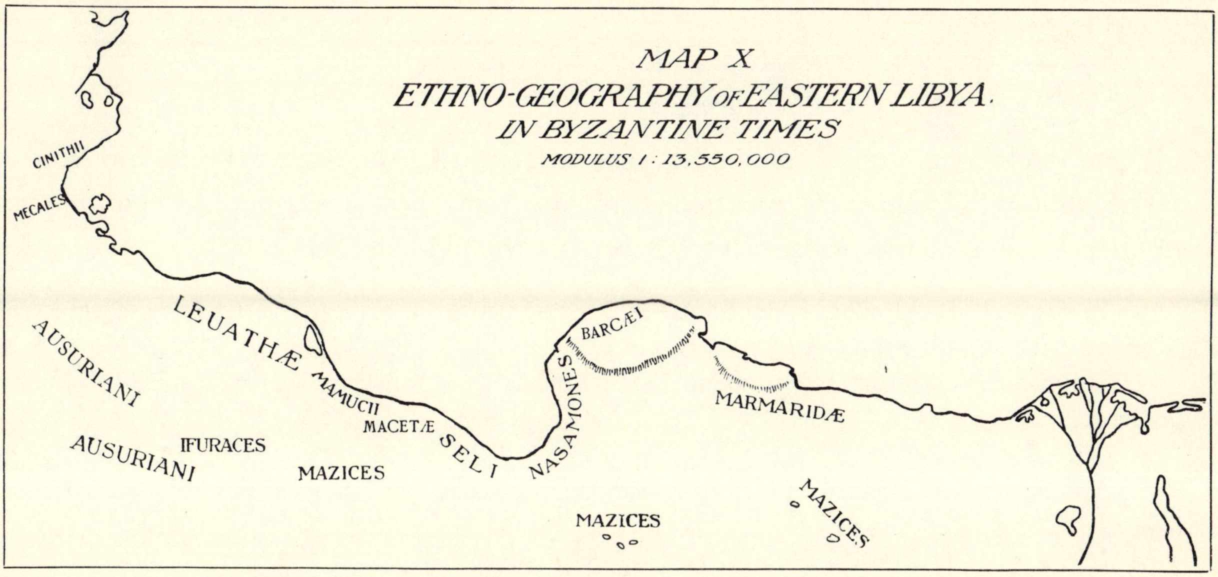

old seat in the western part of the Syrtis Major. The Macetae are mentioned by Synesius[1] as having been associated with the Ausuriani in raids into the Pentapolis. By some modern writers they have been confused with (2), but the identification is very uncertain, despite the geographical proximity of the tribes.

7. *Mamucii*.—A tribe on the west littoral of the Syrtis Major.[2] From the name and the position, one suspects that these people were the Samamycii of Ptolemy.

8. *Leuathae*, Λευάθαι,[3] var. Λεβάνθαι;[4] Λευκάθαι.[5] This name is of interest, since it has been conjectured[6] that, derived of its termination, it presents a form of the old ethnic Λίβυες, for *Λευα-* = *Λεβα-* (by the equivalence, especially in the time of Justinian, of $υ = β$—*e.g.* Βάνδιλοι regularly for *Vandali*). Furthermore, the name and its variants have been held to connect the Leuathae with a tribe which figures prominently in the pages of Corippus[7]—the *Ilaguaten* or *Laguantan* (many variants). For Λευαθ- = *Legath-* (by $u = g$), of which the Berber masculine plural would be **I-legath-en* = *Ilag*(*u*)*aten*. The variant lection Λεβανθ- (= *Leuanth-*) = *Lag*(*u*)*ant-*, a form approached, though probably from some scribal confusion with Gr. λευκός, by the var. Λευκάθαι.

The Leuathae were in Byzantine times spread over a large portion of Tripolitana, as is clear from the Arabic notices of this people under the name لواتة. In Map X., however, they have been entered in the vicinity of Leptis, because there is explicit Byzantine evidence of their having occupied that locality in the time of Justinian.[8]

9. *Ifuraces*.[9]—In the interior of Tripolitana, and from their name and place, to be identified with a fair degree of sureness with the Beni Ifuren of Ibn Ḫaldun and other Arabic writers.

[1] Synesius, *Epist.* 72 *bis.*

[2] *Notitia dignitatum*, p. 89. 9, *Mamucensis limes*. *Vide supra* p. 63 and *n*. 9.

[3] Procopius, *Hist. Arcan.* 5.

[4] Idem, *De bell. Vandal.* ii. 21, 28.

[5] Idem, *De aedific.* vi. 4.

[6] P. Mazzucchelli, *ad* Corippi *Johann.* i. 144 (notes p. 216).

[7] For *Laguantan*, etc. see Corippus, *Johannis*, i. 144, 467, iv. 85, 629, 797, 815, v. 166, vi. 535, vii. 434, 474, 501. For *Illaguaten*, *ibid.*, *var. lect. ad* iv. 797 (*i l a g u a t e n*); *var. lect. ad* v. 166 (*i l l a g u a t e n s i s*); *var. lect. ad* vii. 501 (*l a u g u a t a n*).

[8] Procopius, *De bell. Vandal.* ii. 21 *sqq.*

[9] Corippus, *Johannis*, ii. 113, iv. 641, vii. 490, 648. Cf. McG. de Slane, *Hist. des Berbères*, Appendix i. vol. vi. p. 577.

10. *Ausuriani*, *Αὐσουριανοί,[1] var. Αὐξωριανοί;[2] *Austur*;[3] *Austuriani*;[4] Αὐσοριανοί;[5] a predatory people of the interior of Tripolitana,[6] neighbours of (2) and (9), who in company with the Macetae or the Mazices harried the Pentapolis. The Ausuriani are one of the two native peoples mentioned by Synesius.[7]

11. *Mecales.*—Perhaps the old Μάχλυες, and in their locality.[8]

12. *Cinithii* (*male* Κυῆθοι).—Still extant in late times.[9]

These twelve main bodies of the Libyans in Byzantine times are exhibited in Map X.

The following tribes are mentioned in the later literature, but are not entered in the map because of the unsatisfactory nature of the evidence :—

13. *Tautamaei*, *Ταυταμαῖοι.—Mentioned as a Syrtic people in several related Latin chronicles.[10] The variant *Tautamona* is found in one instance.[11]

14. *Garamantes.*—Presumably in their old position, if not mentioned in a spirit of literary reminiscence.[12]

15. *Gaetuli.*—*Ditto.*[13]

16. *Natabres.*[14]—A Phazanian tribe, presumably located in the vicinity of the "river" Nathabur.[15]

17. *Libyoegyptiae.*[16]—Presumably in the Egyptian oases.

1 Synesius, *Epist.* 119 . . . τὸν Α[ὐ]σ[ο]υριανὸν πόλεμον. . . .

2 Philostorgius, *Hist. Eccles.* xi. 8.

3 Corippus, *Johannis*, ii. 89, 209, 345, iv. 816, vi. 283. May not a variant of **Austures* be seen in the *Astrices* of Corippus (*op. cit.* ii. 75, v. 391, 404, 431, 454, 464)?

4 Ammianus Marcellinus xxvi. 4, 5, xxviii. 6, 2.

5 Priscus Panites, *Frag.* 14 in *FHG.* (iv. p. 98).

6 Position assigned by consensus of evidence and by the explicit statement of Philostorgius, *loc. cit.* . . . Αὐξωριανοὶ μεταξὺ δὲ Λιβύης καὶ Ἄφρων οὗτοι νέμονται κτλ.

7 Whether or not the Ausuriani are to be regarded as the same people as the *Arzuges* of Orosius and others is a *quaestio vexata* on which a word may be said here. The various lections of Ausuriani are given above, and the consensus seems to indicate some such form as *AUS<t>UR as most closely representing the native ethnic. The name **Arzugis* exhibits the variants *Auxugis (*Auxuge* in abl. sing. in Sidonius Apollinaris, *Carm.* v. 338), *Arzucis (*Arzucum* in gen. plur. in Orosius i. 2, § 90, where the best lection is *Arzugum*), and the adjective form *Arzugitanus (*provinciae* . . . *Arzugitanae* in gen. sing. in S. Aurelius, *Concilior. collect.* vol. iv. col. 447, cited by P. Mazzucchelli, note *ad* Corippi *Johan.* ii. 148, p. 232). The consensus here is plainly for some such word as *ARZUG; but the initial AU- of *Auxugis is not quite to be disregarded, because of the frequency of this prefix in Berber names. The difference between G and R as terminations of *Arzug and *Aus<t>ur can be explained readily enough as due to different renderings of an original غ; the equivalence of *Arz-* and *Aus-* offers a more serious, but not insuperable, difficulty. It is not easy to escape the feeling that the two names denote one people, if with the passage already cited from Philostorgius be compared the following: Orosius i. 2, § 90, *Tripolitana provincia, quae et Subventana vel regio Arzugum dicitur, ubi Leptis magna civitas est, quamvis Arzuges per longum Africae limitem generaliter vocentur* . . . (Parallel in *Totius orbis descriptio*, ed. Baudet, p. 72). S. Aurelius, *loc. cit.* [A letter sent in A.D. 419 to all the bishops], *per tractum provinciae Byzacenae et Arzugitanae.* (Hence these districts were continuous, as was noted by Morcelli, *Africa Christiana*, vol. i. p. 84. The "Arzugitan tract" = the *tellus Arzugis* of Corippus, *Johann.* ii. 148.) Coincident location, finally, leads one to suspect that the Ausuriani or Arzuges may be the Ἀστάκουρες of Ptolemy iv. 3 § 6.

8 Corippus iii. 410.

9 *Chronicon paschale*, vol. ii. p. 102.

10 *Excerpta Barbari; Liber generationis; Chronic. an. p. Chr. 334*; *Origo human. gener.*, *loc. cit.*

11 *Origo human. gener.*, *loc. cit.*

12 Aethicus, *ed.* Baudet, p. 72 *bis*; Corippus, *Johannis*, v. 198; Vibius Sequester, p. 35, *Garamantes Mauri Libyae*; Sidonius Apollinaris, *Carm.* v. 337.

13 Sidonius Apollinaris, *loc. cit.*; Vibius Sequester, p. 34, *Gaetuli Afri Libyae*; Corippus, *op. cit.* iv. 1075. It is to be remembered that under the name *Gaetuli*, as under the modern misnomer *Tuareg*, were comprised many desert tribes. Thus, Pliny mentions *Baniurae-Gaetuli* (v. 2) and *Darae-Gaetuli* (v. 1). It may well be that in later times the ethnic names of specific groups supplanted the more general designation.

14 Aethicus, *loc. cit.* var. *Natauros*; Orosius i. 2 § 90, *Nathabres*, var. *Nazabres*, *Natauros*, etc. A Gaetulian tribe (?).

15 Pliny v. 5.

16 Orosius i. 2 § 32.

18. *Libyaethiopes.*[1]—The negroid Libyans of the south.

19. *Magempuri.*[2]—This tribe must have had some importance in the eyes of Vibius Sequester, since they are among the six African peoples he lists. They are otherwise quite unknown.

The names of various other tribes—*e.g.* several in Corippus—I omit altogether, there being no evidence as to whether they inhabited Eastern or Western Libya.

The ethnogeography of Eastern Libya at the time of the first Moḥammadan invasions is complicated by the confusion of the Arabic sources. The Moslem writers are not very explicit, nor do they always discriminate between those indigenous tribes found in the country by the early Moḥammadan conquerors, and those which afterwards came into it from the Moghreb in the train of the Faṭimite invaders of Egypt at the end of the tenth century A.D.[3]

The literary opinion generally current among the Arab writers acknowledged several lines of descent for the various groups of Berbers, each group being referred to an imaginary, and usually eponymous, ancestor. Among these ancestors two—an elder and a younger—by the name of Lua (لوا) figure prominently.[4] The younger Lua was regarded as the father of Zayr, and (through the latter) of numerous Berber tribes known under the general designation of Luatah (لواتة): a name in which it is easy to recognize the Byzantine ethnic Λευάθαι. It is the Luatah who must be regarded as the predominant branch of the Berber stock in Eastern Libya of the seventh century A.D.—the Zenatah and Huarah probably came in on the heels of the Faṭimites about 1000 A.D.

1. *Luatah*, لواتة.—This name (representing, as has just been mentioned, the late Greek Λευάθαι) served the Arab writers as a general designation for all the Berbers of Eastern Libya, much as the cognate Λίβυες had the Greek historians and geographers. Thus, the Luatah appear in the vicinity of Tripoli Town,[5] in Barḳah,[6] and in Egypt.[7]

2. *Zenarah*, زنارة.—A tribe of the Luatah established in Egypt along the western edge of the Delta. They continued there until dislodged by the Mameluks, who drove them into Barḳah,[8] where another group of Zenarah already existed.[9]

[El-Maḳrizî notices the following tribes of Luatah as living in Egypt :—

The *Benu Ballar*, بنو بلار [=the B. Balaîn بنو بالين of Ibn Ḫaldun], who were divided into the sub-tribes of the B. Moḥammad, B. 'Alî, B. Nizar, and B. Thahlan—in the province of Behnasa.

[1] Orosius i. 2 § 88.

[2] Vibius Sequester, p. 36, *Magempuri Libyae*, and Oberlin, *ad loc.* p. 409.

[3] S. Lane-Poole, *History of Egypt in the Middle Ages*, p. 79 *sqq.*, for the Faṭimite incursions.

[4] Ibn Ḫaldun, *Kitab el-'Ibar* (tr. de Slane), vol. i. p. 231 *sq.*

[5] Cf. *Ibid.* (Ar. text), vol. i. p. 115 (=tr. de Slane, vol. i. p. 197 *sq.*).

[6] *Ibid.* vol. i. p. 232. Abu 'l-Maḥasin, *Annales*, p. 85; Ibn 'Abd el-Ḥakam, p. 302; Ibn Abî 'l Dînar, *Kitab el-Munis*, p. 23; el-Idrîsî, *Clim.* iii. § 1; el-Biladurî, *Futuh*, p. 225 . . . "the Luatah Berbers of the country of Barḳah" . . .; Ibn el-Atîr, *Kamil*, iii. 20, where it is stated that the Luatah Berbers extended from Barḳah to Sus; cf. Leo Africanus, *Africae descriptio*, vi. p. 632 = *Description of Africa*, vol. iii. p. 800, where the Luatah are mentioned as extending to the east as far as Egypt.

[7] Leo Africanus, *loc. cit.*; cf. R. Basset, *Le Dialecte de Syouah*, p. 4.

[8] Ibn Ḫaldun, *Kitab el-'Ibar* (tr. de Slane), vol. i. p. 236. According to Ibn Ḫaldun, the Zenatah had been driven to Barḳah from the western Delta.

[9] El-Ya'kubî, *Descriptio Al Mogrebi*, p. 40.

The *Benu Mağdul*, بنو مجدول in the province of Gîzah with part of the B. Thahlan, the Saḳḳarah, B. Abu-Kethîr, and the B. el-Ǵelaṣ.

The *Benu Ḥadîdî*, بنو حديدي the most powerful Berber element in the Ṣa'îd.

The *Benu Ḳaṭufah*, بنو قطوفة comprising the Maghaghah [who by Ibn Ḫaldun were reckoned descendants of the elder, but not of the younger, Luah], and the Waḫîlah.

The *Benu Barkîn*, بنو بركين.

The *Benu Malu*, بنو مالو.

The *Mazurah*, مزورة, comprising the B. Warkan, B. Gheras, B. Gemmaz, B. el-Ḥakem, B. Walid, B. el-Hağğağ, and B. Maḥresah.

The *Benu Yaḥyah*, بنو ياحية.

The *Benu el-Wasuah*, بنو ال واسوة.[1]

The *Benu 'Abdah*, بنوعابدة.

The *Benu Moṣallah*, بنو موصالّة.

The *Benu Moḫtar*, بنو موختر.

The last five tribes, el-Maḳrîzî remarks, were mixed with Zenatah, Huarah, etc., and were located in the province of Manufîah. None of the above tribes[2] have been entered on Map XI. on the authority of el-Maḳrîzî, since their presence in Egypt before the Faṭimite invasion is uncertain, and is significant only as offering an historical parallel to the conditions prevailing in New Empire times.[3]]

3. *Mezatah*, مزاتة.—Mixed Luatah Berbers about Ptolemais in Cyrenaica,[4] and in Wagîlah.[5]

4. *Zenatah*, زناتة.—Mixed Berbers about Ptolemais;[4] perhaps not found in Barḳah until after the Faṭimite invasion.

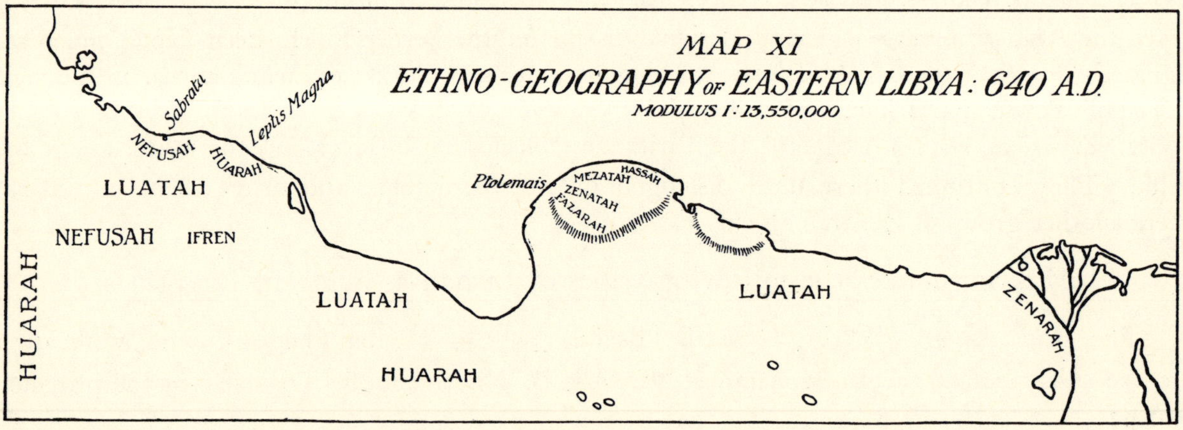

5. *Fezarah*, فزارة.—*Ditto*;[4] *ditto*.

6. *Hassah*, هسّة.—An Arabo-Berber tribe of N.E. Cyrenaica, of uncertain origin.[6]

7. *Huarah*, هوارة; *Huwarah*, هوّارة.—A great division of the "race of Luah," comprising many tribes, the bulk of which were to be found in the west. It is probable that in the seventh century

[1] The B. el-Wasuah = the *Suah*, سوة, of El-Ya'ḳubî (*op. cit.* p. 4), or the *Tîsuah*, تيسوة, of Ibn Ḫaldun, as R. Basset (*op. cit.* p. 4, *n.* 3) has pointed out. These Luatah are those also who, before the fifteenth century A.D., had caused the mediaeval name of the classical Ammonium to change from *Santarîyah*, سنترية, to *Sîwah*, سيوة.

[2] For which see el-Maḳrîzî, *Ueber die in Aegypten eingewanderten arabischen Staemme*, p. 33 *sq.*, x. p. 74 *sq.*

[3] Cf. *infra*, pp. 216, 220, 227. [4] El-Idrîsî, *loc. cit.* [5] R. Basset, *op. cit.* p. 4 *n.* 1. [6] *Vide supra*, p. 47.

A.D. their easterly extension ended in the Gebel Gharyan, though later they were found farther east.[1] A small body of Huarah existed in the vicinity of Leptis Magna (= *Lebdah*, لبدة), and another south of the Syrtis Major.[2]

8. *Ifren*, يفرن ; *Ifuren*, يفورن.—A small division of the people of this name, the bulk of whom were to be found in the west in the vicinity of Tlemsan, was to be found in the eastern part of the Gebel Gharyân.

9. *Nafûsah*, نفوسة.—In the mountains of Tripolitana still called by their name, and still inhabited by their descendants ; also in small numbers on the sea-coast of Sabrata (= *Ṣabrah*, صبرة).[3] This ethnic may be related to that of the more prominent tribe of Africa Minor called *Nefzawah*, نفزاوة.

10. *B. Kazrun*, بنو كزرون.—Near Tripoli Town. A small group not entered on the map.

11. *Maghrawah*, مغراوة.—A group of these Zenatah Berbers, so strongly seated in the west, appears to have existed in the seventh century immediately S.W. of (10).[4] The name has been compared to the ancient Μάχρυες, Μάχλυες, possibly rightly.[5] Not entered in the map.

12. *B. Demmer*, بنو دمّر.—A tribe in the vicinity of the Shott el-Gerîd, comprising the sub-tribes *Zuarah*, زوارة, *Urghmah*, ورغمة and *Urnîd*, ورنيد.[6] Not entered on the map.

A few general deductions may now be made from the maps. It is quite clear that some of the names to be found on them—*e.g.* Mazices, Marmaridae—are ethnic names of a general rather than of a tribal significance, but this does not prevent one's seeing several important points.

In the first place, the Libyans along the seaboard either got pushed back or ceased to exist as significant ethnic units, or became fused with extra-African invaders. This is seen in the decay of the small Cyrenaic tribes, and in the existence of the mixed Libyphoenices.

Secondly, it may be noted that tribes in the less desirable areas tend to show a surprising degree of ethnic stability ; the Nasamones, for example, continued to maintain themselves from the days of Herodotus until Byzantine times—*i.e.* for about a thousand years—within the same area along the East Syrtic littoral. Even the Adyrmachidae, despite their proximity to Egypt, continued to exist until the time of Ptolemy.

Thirdly, in conjunction with this ethnic stability it is found that the names, if not the pure stock, of certain tribes survived for very considerable periods. Thus the Egyptian Esbet appear in classical times as the Asbystae or Asbytae, and the name of the Egyptian Hes possibly survives to-day, after three thousand years, in the name Hassah, borne by a group of Arabo-Berbers of Eastern Cyrenaica.

Fourthly, it is evident that the great general movements of the Eastern Libyans as a whole were anciently in a west-to-easterly direction : the invasion of the Meshwesh was from the west (Map II.), and in the period preceding the Moḥammadan conquests new peoples like the Ausuriani and the Mazices are seen raiding into Cyrenaica and Egypt

[1] E. Mercier, *Histoire de l'établissement des Arabes dans l'Afrique septentrionale*, p. 44, and Map 1.

[2] Ibn el-Aṯîr, *loc. cit.* ; el-Idrîsî, *loc. cit.*

[3] Ibn el-Aṯîr, *loc. cit.* ; Ibn Abî 'l Dînar, *loc. cit.*

[4] E. Mercier, *op. cit.* p. 45 and Map 1 ; Ibn Ḫaldun, *Kitab el-ʿIbar* (Ar. text), vol. i. p. 133, ii. 34 (=tr. de Slane, i. p. 210, iii. p. 228).

[5] But *vide supra*, 64 *n.* 8.

[6] E. Mercier, *op. cit.* p. 47.

from the south and the west. As will be more evident later, it seems as if in ancient times any prolonged political weakening in the Nile Valley was the infallible forerunner of invasions from the west. Even after the Moḥammadan conquest of Africa, the old west-to-easterly movement was repeated in the Faṭimite invasions of Egypt, though this last of a long series of similar movements was counterbalanced by the east-to-west incursion of the Hillal-Ben-Amar and the Soleym-Ben-Manṣur in the eleventh century A.D. The reasons are not far to seek: the Eastern Libyans were not pressed from the Nile, but from the open oasis country to the westward. The actual cause of pressure cannot always be stated; but that, given the opportunity, the Libyan tribesmen should ever have been ready to install themselves in the fertile and easily tenable Nile Valley goes without saying.

CHAPTER III

LANGUAGE AND WRITING

DESPITE the modern prevalence throughout North Africa of Arabic, the language of conquest and religion, there exist by survival from pre-Islamic times a number of dialects of that old indigenous Hamitic speech which is called Berber. The Berber-speaking peoples, as a whole, having never arrived at that stage of civilization in which they would have fixed their tongue in a literary medium, the number of dialects is large. Thus is found, with fundamental similarities of syntax and vocabularies, a great variety among such different branches of Berber as the Zenatah, Shawîah, Tamashek̦, Zenagah, etc., and—a corollary to this instability of the language—it is also to be observed that many loan-words from the Phoenicians, Greeks, Romans, Negroes, and Arabs have crept into Berber speech.

The origin of the language is problematic. Recently there has arisen a fashion of speaking of Berber as a "proto-Semitic" tongue,[1] but it is worth while to recall in this connection that so great a Semiticist as Renan declared that Berber, though having traits of resemblance to the Semitic languages, is profoundly different from them.[2] These differences are the more important, because one of the most striking peculiarities of the Semitic languages is the extraordinary likeness of the various branches to each other, two so remotely separated tongues, for example, as Tigré and Assyrian being more nearly allied than is any branch of Berber with any branch of Semitic. This point must be remembered both in connection with the claims of those who call Berber a "proto-Semitic" language and with a slightly different suggestion, *viz.* that Berber, in common with Bisharîn, Bega, etc., had a remote Arabian origin.[3] The interesting attempts which have been made with a view to connecting Berber with Basque[4] and with Etruscan[5] are not very conclusive, nor have they at all helped toward the settle-

[1] H. Weisgerber, *Les Blancs d'Afrique*, p. 161.

[2] E. Renan, *La Société berbère*; idem, *Histoire des langues sémitiques*, I. ii. p. 81.

[3] A. Erman, *Ägyptische Grammatik*, p. 1, § 1 A.

[4] L. Gèze, *De quelques rapports entre les langues berbère et basque*; G. von der Gabelentz, *Die Verwandschaft des Baskischen mit den Berbersprachen Nord-Afrikas nachgewiesen.*

[5] D. G. Brinton, *The Ethnologic Affinities of the Ancient Etruscans*, *P. Am. Ph. S.*, vol. xxvi.; *On Etruscan and Libyan Names*, *ib.* vol. xxviii. C. de Vaux, *La Langue étrusque, etc.*, Introd. p. xv.; Brinton's theories are there summarily dismissed.

ment of the question of the origins of proto-Berber. Still less convincing is the elaborate essay in which Bertholon has sought to prove that Berber is a fusion of "Illyro-Pelasgic," "Turso-Pelasgic," and "Phrygian" elements cast in a Semitic mould.[1] Like the ethnical origin of the Libyans themselves, that of the language they have spoken since the dawn of history is yet unknown, and all speculation on this head is best set aside until more evidence has accumulated.

In its general character modern Berber is a very simple language. It is consonantal, and words are mainly formed upon triliteral radicals. There is no definite article, properly speaking—the word *ales* (Tamashek̦), for example, signifies equally "a man" or "the man," according to the context[2]—this want being partially supplied by demonstratives. The personal pronoun takes a special form according to whether it is isolated or affixed, and in the latter case serves to denote possession. The verb has but one conjugation, and that of the simplest: the verbal theme, composed of one, two, three, or four radical consonants,[3] at once gives the second person singular masculine of the imperative. Apart from the imperative, there is but one time, serving alike for past, present, and future. A number of particles serve, when prefixed to the verb, to denote whether completed, present, or future action is intended. Thus, in Tamashek̦, the triliteral radicale LKeM means "to follow": *elkem-eع*, "I have followed"; *ad-elkem-eع*, "I shall follow."[4] The persons in the conjugations are regularly marked with prefixes or with suffixes, or with both. Qualificative verbs lose a part of the usual marks of conjugation. The factitive, reciprocal, passive, habitual, etc., senses are imparted to the verb by adding, externally or internally, special elements to the primitive verbal theme, and so producing ten separate verbal forms.

The formation of the feminine in nouns is very simply and regularly accomplished in a manner which serves also to mark a diminutive. The plural is either externally or internally marked, or both. The adjective follows the noun it qualifies, and is subject to the same formative laws. Some particles and most of the numerals have been recently taken over from the Arabic. The construction of phrases is regular; the verb stands at the beginning of the sentence, and is followed by the subject and its complements. In North Africa to-day are some forty Berber dialects to which the above general remarks are applicable, and which, according to their phonesis, are classed as "strong" or "weak."

As already stated, Berber being a language unfixed by literary usage, the difference between the dialects is marked. As the vowel and consonant equivalences they exhibit are important in the study of the significance of ancient names they are here tabulated.

[1] L. Bertholon, *Colons de souche européenne*, part ii.; *Origine et formation de la langue berbère.*

[2] A. Hanoteau, *Grammaire de la langue tamachek̓*, p. 28.

[3] Rarely five or six.

[4] A. Hanoteau, *op. cit.* p. 56 *sqq.*

I. Dentals

Ḍ = D. Cf. aǵellid (Beni Mzab) = agelliḍ (Zuawa), "king"; anebḍu (Zuawa) = anefdu (Ghadames), "summer"; ṯenغiḍ (Zuawa) = tenغid (B. Mzab, Tamasheḳ), "thou hast killed."

Ḍ = Ṭ. Cf. iḍ (Zuawa) = iṭ (Bougie), "night."

D = Ṯ. Cf. adbir (Ghadames) = iṯbir (Zuawa), "pigeon."

D = T. Cf. iudef (B. Menaṣer) = iutef (B. Mzab), "he enters."

T = Ṯ. Cf. tenغid (B. Mzab, Tamasheḳ) = ṯenغiḍ (Zuawa), "thou hast killed"; teffez (Tamasheḳ) = ṯeffez (Zuawa), "to be chewing habitually"; iggat (Tamasheḳ) = ikkaṯ (Zuawa), "he beats continually."

II. Dentals and Palatals

D = G. Cf. aduǵil (Ghadames) = aguǵil (Zuawa), "orphan."

D = Ǵ. Cf. agediḍ (North Tamasheḳ) = agaǵiḍ (South Tamasheḳ), "bird."

Ḏ = G. Cf. aḏmar (Ghadames) = agmar (Shawîah), "horse."

D = Z. Cf. egdem (S. Tamasheḳ) = egzem (Zuawa), "to cut"; tadevvot (Ghadames) = tazabat (Tamasheḳ), "ring."

T = Ṡ. Cf. tasem (Tamasheḳ) = ṣasem (Zuawa), "to be jealous habitually."

T = TŠ. Cf. timimun (S. Tamasheḳ) = tšimimun (S. Tamasheḳ), a place-name.

III. Sibilants

Š = S. Cf. ešek (Ghadames) = isek (Tamasheḳ), "horn."

S = Z = H. Cf. ergeš = ergez (both Tamasheḳ), "to walk"; šund = zund = hund (all Tamasheḳ), "as."

Š = F. Cf. ašulaغ (N. Tamasheḳ) = afulaغ (S. Tamasheḳ), "goat."

IV. Palatals and Sibilants

G = K. Cf. iggat (Tamasheḳ) = ikkat (Zuawa), "he beats continuously."

G = Ǵ. Cf. agenna (Tamasheḳ) = aǵenna (Ghadames), "sky."

K = TŠ. Cf. ufrik (Zuawa) = ufritš (B. Mzab), "sheep."

K = TŠ. Cf. neš (B. Menaṣer) = nek (Zuawa, Tamasheḳ), "I."

G = Š. Cf. agelliḍ (Zuawa) = ašellid (Ghadames), "king."

Ǵ = Š. Cf. amaǵeغ = amašeغ (both Tamasheḳ), "a man of the Imushagh."

غ = Š. Cf. iغed (Zuawa) = ešed (Ghadames), "ashes."

غ = Ḱ. Cf. niغغer = neḱḱer (both Kabyle), "I slay habitually."

Ǧ = Z. Cf. aḳǵun (Zuawa) = aḳzin (B. Menaṣer, Shawîah), "dog."

V. Palatals and Aspirates, etc.

K = Y. Cf. aksum (Zuawa) = aysum (B. Mzab), "flesh."

GG = YY. Cf. aggur (Zuawa) = aiyur (Tamasheḳ), "moon."

ǴǴ = YY. Cf. iǵǵen (B. Mzab, Sîwah) = iyen (Tamasheḳ), "one."

Ǵ = H. Cf. aguǵil (Zuawa) = aguhil (Tamasheḳ), "orphan."

غ = H. Cf. taغaṭ (Tamashek, Kabyle) = tehaṭ (Ghadames), "goat" (fem.).

VI. Labials

B = W. Cf. ṯaburṯ (Zuawa) = tuurt (B. Mzab), "door"; ibboḍ (Zuawa) = iuuṭ (Bougie), "he has come."
B = F. Cf. anebḍu (Zuawa) = anefdu (Ghadames), "summer."
B = V. Cf. tazabat (Tamashek̹) = tadevvot (Ghadames), "ring."
H = V. Cf. ehaḍ (Tamashek̹) = evoḍ (Ghadames), "night."

VII. Liquids

Ḷ = R. Cf. almi = armi (both Kabyle), "as far as."
L = D. Cf. illa (Kabyle) = idda (Marrocan Rîf), "he was"; elli = eldi (both Kabyle), "to open."
N = M (under influence of following labial). Cf. tanfust (B. Mzab) = tamfust (Tamashek̹), "story."

Add

U = G = B (under influence of following *u*). Cf. u urgaz (Bougie) = g urgaz (Illulen) = b urgaz (Zuawa), "of the man."
B = Z (by assimilation). Cf. abzug = azzug (both Zuawa), "moisture."
Metathesis is often found. Cf. aifki (Zuawa) = akafai (Tamashek̹), "milk."

A brief study of the above permutations will convince the reader of the fluid state of the Berber language as a whole, and of the great difficulties attending any attempt at making comparisons between the modern vocabulary and the surviving ancient names. The reader will appreciate also that whereas most of the permutations are well known in Aryan or Semitic languages, some are rather unusual, *e.g.* š = f, l = d.[1]

It is well to begin the consideration of the language of the Eastern Libyans of antiquity with the statement that no textual specimens of their speech exist to-day.[2] It is certain, however, for reasons which follow, that their language was a proto-Berber tongue, which may safely be regarded as the ancestor of the surviving dialects not only of the Gebel Nafusa, of Ghat, and of Ghadames, but also of the sequestered communities farther east, as Wagîlah, Maradah, Sîwah, Garah, and Manshîah el-ʿAguzah in Baḥarîah Oasis. This hypothesis is supported by the following facts.

I. Place-names and Ethnics with T- Affixes in Eastern Libya

In Berber, the feminine is regularly made from the masculine substantive by the prefixing of t- and the suffixing of -t, *e.g. anhil* (masc.), "ostrich," fem. *tanhilt* (Tamashek̹). Diminutives, as already noted, are similarly formed. Words of this sort appear frequently as modern Berber place-names, *e.g.* T-ua-t, T-uggur-t, T-akrif-t, T-idikel-t, etc. The final -t, however, is often lost or sibilated, *e.g. tes* for **test* (Tamashek̹), "cow." Bearing

[1] The latter has its parallel in δάκρυ = *lachryma*.

[2] But note A. Botti, *Manuscrits libyens.* E. Schiaparelli is there said to have found a papyrus containing "Ḳeheḳ war-songs in the Libyan language, transcribed in hieratic." Since 1900 no more has been heard of this remarkable discovery, nor has Dr. Schiaparelli condescended to answer my enquiries concerning it.

this in mind we may recognize Old Berber feminines or diminutives in the following East Libyan names of the Graeco-Roman period.

Places.	Tubactis Talalatus Tabunte Tanabrasta Tabuinatis	Forms with both prefix and suffix.
	Tacape Tarichiae Taucheira Telgae Thuben	Forms which have lost suffix.
Ethnics.	Tapanitae.	Both affixes (?).
	Tidamenses.	Lost or sibilated suffix.

(Stephanus Byzantinus remarks in regard to a number of African ethnics that -ιται, -ιδαι are favourite Libyan terminations.[1])

II. Names made on √MZغ

In the previous chapter it has been shown how widespread among the modern Berbers are the various ethnics having this radical as a base. The ancient occurrence in Eastern Libya of the following names is therefore significant.

Ethnics.	Mazices.	MaZiC-es.
	Maxyes.	MaXY-es (غ = U).
	Masuchii.	MaSuCH-ii (Z = S, غ = χ).
	Bassachitae.	BaSSaCH-itae (M = B, Z = S, غ = χ).
	Mazyes.	MaZY-es (غ = U).
Places.	Masuchis.	MaSuCH-is (Z = S, غ = χ).
	Mazacila.	MaZaC-ila (غ = C).

III. Comparison of the Place-names of Eastern and Western Libya

It has long been well established that the ancient place-names of Africa Minor—such, that is, as were not Punic, Greek, or Roman in their origin—were Berber. If, therefore, a close resemblance between the native names of the west and those of the east existed in classical times, the inference that proto-Berber was the language of Africa from Egypt to the Atlantic becomes much heightened. With this in mind, we may compare the following names :—

In the East.	*In the West.*
Ardan (-is)	Ardal (-is)
(Aus-) ufal	(Gaza-) ufal (-a)
Darnis	Dyrin
Galyba	Cilibba ; (Si[c]-) cilibba

[1] Stephanus Byzantinus, *in verbb.* Αὐτομάλακα, Ἀσπίς, Αἰγίμορος *et alibi* ; cf. idem, *in verbb.* Ἄβοτις, Ἀγκυρῶν *et alibi*, where these endings are spoken of as "Aethiopian" or "Egyptian."

In the East.	*In the West.*
Ger (-as) ; Ger (-eatis)	Ger (-gis)
Lac (-ci)	Lac (-a)
Magru	Macri
Mara (-bina)	Mara (-zana)
Minna	Mina
Musti	Musti
Tamaric (-etum)	Tamaric (-ium)
Thagul (-is)	Thagur (-a)
Tinci (T. Ausari)	Tingi (-s)
Tanabrasta	Tenebreste [1]

A closer analysis proves indisputably a still more intimate connection than that indicated by the above list. Some striking differences are seen—*e.g.* the total absence in the East of place-names compounded with the initial element *Rus*-[2]—but these are due to dialectic variation.

IV. Analysis of various East Libyan Names

If what has thus far been stated be correct—*viz.* that the evidence points to Old Berber as the spoken language of Eastern Libya in classical times—the analysis of the place-names should confirm this thesis. Carelessness and inadequacy of Greek and Latin transcription render this analysis difficult, yet the following words, upon examination, appear to be made on, or to contain, roots[3] which survive to-day in a number of Berber dialects.

Auziqua, *Auzius*, *Ausufal.* The initial element *Auz-* in these names, which belong to stations on the great westerly-easterly Libyan coastal route, is made on the radical $\sqrt{\text{UZ}}$, with the sense "to stop" or "to halt." Cf. اوز (Zenaga), "to halt." Thus, *Ausufal* = "the desert halt," or "the high halt," from $\sqrt{\text{UZ}}$ (*ut supra*) and $\sqrt{\text{FL}}$, as in افل *afel* (Zenaga), "high up," and افل *afel* (subst. masc., Zenaga), "desert." (Cf. Ar. جبل *gebel* = both "mountain" and "desert.")

Azu, "the place of assembly," from $\sqrt{\text{DU}}$ or $\sqrt{\text{ZU}}$, "to march," "to come together," as in اد, *adu* (Zuawa, Warsenis, Bougie, Zenaga, etc.), aorist, يدو *idu* (Tarudant), "to go," "to march"; ازوا *ezua*, aor. ازوا *izua* (B. Mzab, Rîf, Gerba, etc.), "to go"; and ازگا *ezga*, aorist يزگا *izga* (Zenaga), "to come together."

Ausari (in the name *Tinci-* or *Tingi-Ausari*), "old," from $\sqrt{\text{USR}}$, "to be old," as in وسر' *auser* (B. Menaṣer) = اوسر *ausar* (Harakta, Bougie), "to be old." *Tinci*, *Tingi* (cf. *Tingis*) is derivable from $\sqrt{\text{N}ع}$ "to slay," as in تينغ *tin*ع, (Tamashek̦), "slaughter," "killing," from انغ *en*ع (Zuawa, etc.), "to kill," "to slay."[4] The full name *Tinci Ausari*, therefore, would mean "the old place of slaughter," as we might say "Old Waleness." (Cf. *Auser* in the west = "Old Town," as in Arabic عجوزة *'Aguzah.*)

[1] O. Bates, *Place-names in Eastern Libya*, where the above evidence was first presented.

[2] Idem, *North African Place-names prefixed with Rus-*.

[3] For the Berber radicals in the remainder of this chapter, see the following: R. Basset, *Loqmân berbère*, part ii.; Idem, *Étude sur la Zenatia du Mzab, d'Ouargla et de l'Oued Rir'*; E. Masqueray, *Dictionnaire français-touareg*; S. Biarnay, *Le Dialecte berbère d'Ouargla*, pp. 309 *sqq.* Calassanti-Motylinski, *Le Dialecte berbère de R'edamès.* It may be noted that many Berber words of appearance rather formidable are really formed on very simple roots, *e.g.* *tizemmetš* (Tuat), "road," has the biliteral $\sqrt{\text{ZM}}$.

[4] Cf. C. Tissot, *Géographie comparée*, vol. i. p. 516, for an alternative; and C. O. Castiglioni, *Mémoire géographique, etc.*, p. 119, for an impossible explanation.

Darnis (the modern درنة , Dernah), "the mountains," from √DRR, "mountain," as in ادرار *adrar*, pl. يدرارن *idraren* (Tamashek, etc.). The town called Δάρνις lay at the mouth of a deep wady, the high walls of which are very conspicuous behind the modern town. Hence the name, the first R being sacrificed to euphony, as in the transcription Δῦριν, given by Strabo [1] as the native name for the Atlas. Similarly, τὸ Δέρριν ὄρος [2] appears in Marmarica, the word ὄρος being itself confirmatory evidence. (Cf. in the west the name Ῥουσάδειρον [3] = Rhysaddir [4] = Rusadder,[5] where the same root, √DRR, is seen prefixed with the element RUS-.) The same radical, with the same loss of an R, and permutation of N to M, appears in the ethnic Adyrmachidae (Ἀδυρμαχῖδαι) = "mountain men," from √DRR (*ut supra*) and √KK "to come from," "to be," as in اك, *ak*, aorist يكا *ika* (Zuawa), "to come from," "to be," with M prefix, by which nouns of agent, circumstance, and habitude are made from the verbal theme;[6] **mak* = "those who are from." Hence Ἀδυρμαχῖδαι = √DRR + M + √KK, *idraren-*mak* + ῖδαι = *illi ex montibus* = "the mountaineers." (In allusion to the Gebel el-ʿAkabah ?)

Magru (cf. Macri in the west), "the old," or "great," from √MغR, "old," "long established," as in امغار *am*غ*ar* (Shawîa), "chief," (Zuawa), "old"; مغر *ma*غ*ar* (B. Menaṣer), "to grow great"; تموغر *temu*غ*er* (Zuawa), "greatness,"[7] etc. Hence, *Magru* = "the chief place." (Cf. also the ethnic Μάχλυες = Μάχρυες = "the great tribe" ?).

Thagulis (cf. Thagura in the west, and Zagylis in Eastern Libya), "shelter," from √GL, as in تجوليه *ṯuguliah* (Shawîa = Semiticized form), "hut." (Cf. Sudanese تكول or توكل , and Latin *tugurium*.)

Telgae, √LG, "well." Cf. √Lغ, "well," as in اليغ *ali*غ (Wargla) = "well," "shallow well."

Tacape, √KB, "summit."[8] Cf. √KB as in تكابت *takabt* (Shawîa), "mountain-top."

Irasa, √RS, as in ارس *ers*, aorist يرسو *irsu* (B. Menaṣer, B. Mzab, Bougie, etc.), "to descend," "to put down"; يرسا *irsa* (Wargla), "a pitch" for tents (ارس *ers* = "to pitch"). Hence, *Irasa* = "camping-place," "tenting-place."

The above words may be taken as giving fair specimens of the relationships between the ancient place-names of classical Eastern Libya and words in daily use among the modern Berbers. They show, in conjunction with other evidence, that Berber was the pre-Islamic language of Tripolitana, and add force to the remark of St. Augustine, who emphasized the great variety of tribes which were to be seen in North Africa all speaking the same tongue.[9] That Berber, or proto-Berber, was the language of Eastern Libya not only in Greek and Roman but even in pre-historic times will be made clear by the ensuing evidence from the Egyptian sources, which confirms fully the statement of Mela,[10] who says that the Libyans of his day, though Romanized, preserved a language which had been that of their ancestors.

The Libyans at the time of the great invasions of Egypt used certain ethnic names that have already been noted as current in later times. There are, moreover, certain

1 Strabo xvii. p. 825. Cf. Pliny v. 1.
2 C. Tissot, *op. cit.* vol. i. p. 386, *n.* 2.
3 Ptolemy iv. 1 § 3.
4 Pliny, *Hist. Nat.* v. 1.
5 *Itiner. Antonin.* p. 5 (*Wess.* p. 11, 4).
6 *E.g. am-eri*, "friend," from *eri*, "to love"; *am-ahar*, "companion," from *ahar*, "to be associated with" (Tamashek).
7 Cf. Gr. μεγαλ-, Lat. *magn-*.
8 Cf. Lat. *caput-*.
9 S. Augustinus, *De Civitate Dei* xvi. 6, *in Africa barbaras gentes in una lingua plurimas novimus.*
10 Mela i. 8. Cf. Herodotus (ii. 18) who says that the inhabitants of even Marea and Apis spoke a non-Egyptian language.

Libyan elements in archaic Egyptian, and both these facts tend to show that, while the ancient Berbers may never have occupied the Nile Valley, they were at least contiguous to it from a very remote and for a very long period of time. The ethnic names just mentioned are those of the Meshwesh (), the Eṣbet (), the Rebu (), and the Beken (), which in the preceding chapter have been connected with the Mazices (√MZƐ), the Asby(s)tae, the Libyes, and the Bacales respectively. To these ethnics may now be added three personal names borne by leaders in the invasions and a further note on the ethnic RBW.

MŠKN (), personal name, masc. The initial element here, MŠ, is the Old Berber filiative *Mes-*, as seen in such names as *Mas-syli*, *Mas-sasyli*, *Mas-sinissa*, *Mas-iva*, *Mas-tigas*, *Mas-timan*, etc. The second element √KN, is easily recognizable as √GN, "sky," as in يڭّني *igenni* (Zuawa), "cloud," اژّنا *ağenna* (B. Mzab, Rîf, Tuat), "sky," "heaven." The name, therefore, means "son of heaven," and occurs in classical times as *Misagenes*, a name borne in the west by a son of Masinissa.

KPPUR (), personal name, masc. suggests √KBR, the B being a natural equivalent of the Egyptian PP. √KBR as in اكبار *akabbar*, pl. يكبارن, *ikabbaren* (subst. masc., Zuawa), "claws," "talons."[1] Hence, the name would have the force of "the render."

MRY(U) (). The initial element here, MR, is that seen later in the North African names as *Marmaridae*, *Massamarus*, etc. In the Libyan inscriptions of the west it occurs either free, MR,[2] or reduplicated, MR-MR,[3] or in combination as above, MR-W.

RBW (). In regard to this ethnic name, although its persistence in Graecized form has already been commented upon, its survival in one particular place-name is especially curious, and may be here noted. The name is *Leptis*, the earlier form of which was לבכי LBKI = LBU, the U being marked by an equivalent K. The reading לבכי LBKI derived from the legends of the Punic coins of the city,[4] seems not to have been quite forgotten even in Roman times; we have, at least, one inscription giving CIRRA VERNA *LEPCITANA*.[5]

Apart from these and other names connected with the Libyan invasions of Egypt, there exists a piece of isolated evidence afforded by a stela of Intef I.[6] On this stela the king is represented with his hunting dogs, the animals bearing foreign names. These names are transcribed in hieroglyphics, and of the five one is certainly, and another probably, Old Berber. The certain one is ꜣBꜣḲR (), which represents the Berber √BḲR,

[1] J. Halévy, *Études berbères* (*Supplement aux Inscriptions libyques*), suggested that by L = N this name might be connected with the ethnic Cabales. I prefer the explanation given above, and the reading Bakales (Herodotus iv. 171).

[2] *Ibid.* Part i. p. 99, No. 11; p. 188, No. 197.

[3] *Ibid.* p. 140, No. 100.

[4] C. L. Müller, *Numismatique du Nord de l'Afrique*, vol. ii. p. 10. Leptis was a Sidonian foundation (Sallust, *Iugurtha*, 78); but Semitic philology has not satisfactorily explained the name of the town.

[5] L. Renier, *Inscriptions* No. 425. For K = T cf. P. Schröder, *Phönizische Sprache*, p. 115; C. Abel, *Einleitung in ein ägyptisch-semitisch-indoeuropaisches Wurzelwörterbuch*, p. 80 *sqq.*, Nos. 71, 72, 76, 77.

[6] Dynasty XI. R. Basset, *Les Chiens du Roi Antef*, in *Sphinx*, vol. i. 1897, pp. 87 *sqq.*, esp. pp. 89-91. M. Burchardt, *Die altkanaanäische Fremdworte . . . in Ägyptischen*, vol. ii. No. 3. For other literature on this stela (Cairo Museum No. 20512) *vide* G. Maspero, *Études de mythologie et d'archéologie*, *etc.*, vol. iii. p. 331; idem, *RT*, vol. xxi. p. 136. In this last an attempt is made to identify a third name, , TḲRW, as Berber. G. Daressy, *RT*, vol. xi. 1889, *Remarques et notes*, § xviii. pp. 79, 80.

as in ابايكور *abaikur* (Tamashek̦), "greyhound" = ابكور *abekur* (Awelimmiden). From these interesting fragments, however, it is time to turn to a more important consideration—that of the Libyan element in the Egyptian language itself.

It is well recognized that Egyptian, even in the earliest stages at which we know it, contains a proto-Berber element.[1] This Berber element is of a very deep-rooted character. Despite the Semitic nature of the Egyptian verb,[2] even that important part of the language has some features in common with that of the Berber. Both languages, furthermore, have cognate pronominal radicals, and form their plurals and absolute pronouns by the same process;[3] both families form their feminine plurals in a closely related manner;[4] in each *n* is used as a sign of the indirect genitive;[5] and in both, abstracts and collectives are treated as grammatical plurals.[6] Besides connection of this sort, a comparison of the Berber and Egyptian vocabularies shows that the two languages have in common a number of primitive words. No careful comparison of the two vocabularies has yet been instituted; the Marquis de Rochemonteix did not live to publish the one he projected, and the indifference which Egyptologists and Berber scholars have come to feel so largely toward each other's researches has discouraged the comparative studies in which de Rochemonteix made so inspiring a beginning. The citing of the following Egyptian and Berber parallels may therefore be excused:—

Egyptian.			Berber.	
Hieroglyphics.	Primitive Roots.	Values.	Primitive Roots.	Examples.
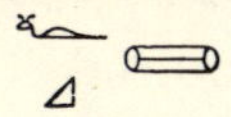	FḲ	"to be rewarded."	FK	افك *offak* (Zenaga), "to give," افك *efk* (Zuawa), "to give."
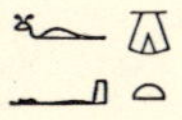	FG(T)	"reward." "pay."		
	MṢ	"to give birth to."	MǦ	امغ *amaǧ* (Zenaga), "to bear," "to give birth to." مجج *Meǵiǵ* (Zenaga), "to be alive." Cf. Old Berber filiative prefix, MES-.

[1] A. Erman, *Ägyptische Grammatik*, p. 1, §§ 1, 1a.
[2] Idem, *Die Flexion des ägyptischen Verbums*, *passim*.
[3] M. de Rochemonteix, *Sur les rapports grammaticaux qui existent entre l'Égyptien et le Berbère*, p. 140.
[4] A. Hanoteau, *Grammaire tamachek*, p. 17; A. Erman, *Ägyptische Grammatik*, p. 55, § 117.
[5] A. Hanoteau, *op. cit.* pp. 26, 27; A. Erman, *op. cit.* pp. 64, 65, §§ 137-139.
[6] A. Hanoteau, *op. cit.* p. 19; A. Erman, *op. cit.* p. 58, § 123.

Egyptian.			Berber.	
Hieroglyphics.	Primitive Roots.	Values.	Primitive Roots.	Examples.
	MṢ(Ḳ)	"to pluck off." "to snatch."	MZ	امزا *ameza* (Dubdu), "to seize," "to take away." Cf. امزا *amza* (War.), "ogre." (Cf. *Ἅρπυιαι, ἁρπάζειν.*)
 var. 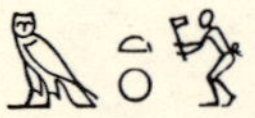	MT	"to die." "death."	MT	امث *emmeṯ* aor. يمث *immeṯ*; (Harakta, Bougie), "to die;" تمتانث *tammettanṯ* (subst. fem.) (B. Mzab, Zenaga), "death." (Cf. Semit.)
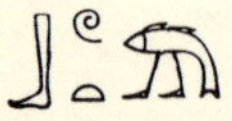 var. 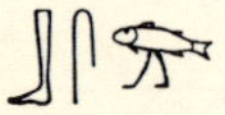	BT BṢ	"to go." "to go into." "to enter."	BD	اباد *ebbad* (Zenaga), "to arrive."
	BŠ	"to be drenched." "to pour out."	BZ(I)	ابزي *ebzi* (B. Menasir), "to be drenched."
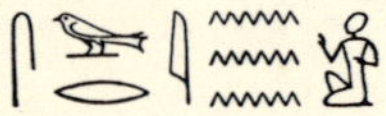	ṢWR	"to drink."	SU	سو *su*, aor. سويغ *sui*غ (B. Mzab, Nafusa, etc.) "to drink."
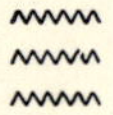	M	"water." "lake."	M	امان *aman*, coll. from ماء* (most dialects), "water." (Cf. Semitic.)
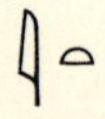 var. 	T T(F)	"father."	T	تي *ti* (Tamasheḳ), "father."
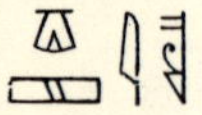	GŠ	"knife." "dagger."	ḲS	ثقوصت *ṯeḳuṣet* (subst. fem.) (Kabyle), "knife."
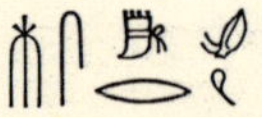	MṢḎR	"ear."	MZغ	امزوغ *amezu*غ (subst. masc.) (Zuawa, Rîf, Harawa, etc.), "ear."

Egyptian.			Berber.	
Hieroglyphics.	Primitive Roots.	Values.	Primitive Roots.	Examples.
 cf. 	MS	"lord;" "master."	MS	مس *mess*, (var.) "master."
	SR	"prince." "chief."	ZR	ازار *ezzar*, aor. يزار *izzar* (B. Menaser), "to be the first," "to precede;" ازار *ezzar* (B. Mzab), "at first," (of time); امزوارو *amzuaru* (Zuawa, Harawa), "preceding," "anterior;" ثزوارا *ṭazuara* (subst. fem.) (Zuawa), "predominance."
	MSS	"belt." "girdle."	BŠŠ	ابشي *abešši* (W. Righ), "belt," "girdle;" بش *bešš*, aor. يبشي *ibešši* (Wargla), "to gird one's self" (with a belt).
	MŠR	"evening."	MDR	ثمديرث *ṭamadirṭ* (subst. fem.) (B. Menaṣer), "evening."
	R	"at;" "to;" "into;" "toward."	R	ار(دار) *ar*-(*dar*) (Shelḥa), "at." (The terminative دار or ذار is emphatic.)
	N	sign. genit.	N	ن *n* (most dialects), sign. genitive.
	R	sign. emphatic.	R	(ذ)ارا (*z*)-*ara* (Zenaga), intensive particle. The ذ is not part of the root.

The common elements in the Berber and Egyptian vocabularies,[1] of which specimens have just been given, and the striking grammatical similarities of the two languages mentioned earlier in this chapter, make it clear that the relationship between the tongues is an intimate one. Just where, geographically, the fusion took place, whether in the upper or lower valley of the Nile, cannot now be determined ; but the evidence points to there having been in Eastern Libya a continuity of language from prehistoric until modern times. Even after so cursory an examination of the facts, one is justified in supposing that the Berber dialects surviving in the east—in Manshîah el-ʿAghuzah, Sîwah, Wagîlah, Maradah, etc.—had their origin not in any mediaeval invasion, but are survivals from the speech of the Eastern Libyans of antiquity. This being so, a careful study of these eastern dialects would be essential to any further attempt to reconstruct the language of the Temeḥu and Teḥenu, the Rebu and the Meshwesh. Unfortunately, material for such investigation has not yet been collected, and is fast disappearing. Basset, with that genius which has placed him in the foremost ranks of Berber philologists, has made a painstaking collection of the Sîwan words and paradigms noted by travellers who visited the oasis before 1890,[2] but much still remains to be done there and in other places.

A brief discussion of the question of writing among the Eastern Libyans may conclude this chapter. The materials for studying the problem are exceedingly scanty, and it may be said at the outset that no Libyan inscriptions comparable to those found in Algeria and Tunisia have yet been reported from Tripolitana or Western Egypt.[3] That exploration will eventually bring such documents to light in these regions seems assured, for an inscription of the usual West Libyan type has been found as far east as Sinai,[4] groups of Libyan letters, inscribed on rocks, have been recorded in Cyrenaica, Marmarica, and the Oases, while at several points on the western border of the Egyptian Delta have been noted traces of inscriptions in what appears to be a local Libyan script.[5] Ever since the discovery in the seventeenth century of the famous bilingual of Thugga,[6] speculation has been rife concerning the origin of the North

[1] And consequently in Berber and Coptic ; not only in onomatopoetic words such as ⲃⲣ̄ⲃⲣ̄, ⲃⲣ̄ⲃⲣⲉⲧ (S.), "to boil" (cf. $\sqrt{\text{BR}}$ (Lat. $\sqrt{\text{FER-}}$) in Berber, as ابر *aber* B. Mzab), but also in old substantives, such as ⲙⲁⲗⲧ (B.) ⲙⲟⲣⲧ (M.), "beard" (cf. $\sqrt{\text{MR(T)}}$ in Berber as تمارت, *tmart* fem. subst. B. Mzab, W. Rîgh, Wargla).

[2] To the words and paradigms therein contained Captain C. V. Stanley and I have added a fairly large number, collected in 1910, which I hope shortly to publish.

[3] V. Reboud, *Recueil d'inscriptions* (pp. 29, 30, 48, and pl. xx. no. 148), gives as Libyan a curious inscription on a bilingual (the alternate text Greek, unpublished) agate from Dernah, first reproduced in a notice by V. de Bourville, *Extrait d'une lettre . . . à Mons. Jomard* (with plate). This inscription, which is a poor rendering, seemingly from an original in the Cypriote syllabary, is certainly not Libyan, although P. Berger, *Histoire de l'écriture*, p. 325, is not alone in having repeated Reboud's error.

[4] J. Halévy, *Études berbères*, p. 100, inscrip. No. 17.

[5] The inscriptions from Gheytah (Vicus Judaeorum) published by W. M. F. Petrie, *Hyksos and Israelite Cities*, p. 60, and Pl. xlviii. ; idem, *Ghizeh and Rifeh*, p. 44, *Addendum to "Hyksos and Israelite Cities,"* are not Libyan. See Appendix II. of this study.

[6] Phoenician and Libyan. Now in the British Museum. Reproduced in Reboud, *op. cit.* pls. xviii., xix., nos. 141, 141 *bis* ; Faidherbe, *Inscriptions numidiques*, pl. i., no. 1 *et alibi.*

African alphabet diversely called "Libyan," "Numidian," "Berber," or "Libyco-Berber," and of its descendant, Tifinagh. Interest in this question has recently been stimulated by the discovery of the early scripts of Crete, and by the indiscretion of those who recklessly have given phonetic values to the owners' marks occurring on early Egyptian pottery, etc. In discussing here the origin of the Libyan alphabet it is not, however, necessary to consider the numerous theories which have recently been woven about it; it is enough to say, in regard to these, that no inscription in Libyan characters has yet been proved older than the fourth century B.C.

The origin of the Libyan alphabet has been variously ascribed to Egyptian,[1] Greek,[2] Vandalic,[3] and Sabaean or Ethiopic[4] sources. These unproved contentions, and that of Littmann, who endeavoured to connect Libyan with the Thamudenean and Safaitic scripts of northern Arabia,[5] may be passed over; and with only slight modifications the statement put forward by Halévy over thirty years ago may still be accepted.[6] Halévy compared the Libyan alphabet with those forms of Phoenician found in North Africa. This comparison resulted in his finding that six out of the thirty Libyan letters had Phoenician prototypes representing the same sounds, as follows:—

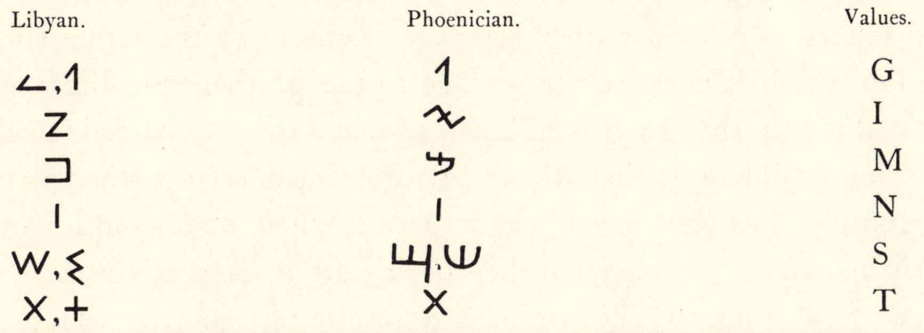

Halévy, beyond this, suggested that the Libyan forms ⊙, ○, and ⊓ might be derived from the respective Phoenician equivalents 9, 9, and Λ. The Punic 7, f, it may be added, has sometimes a form approaching that of the Libyan equivalent X. Even if these latter points be ignored, however, the relationship between the two sets of letters is not easily to be put by, even though the majority of the Libyan letters *without* Phoenician or Punic equivalents forbids the derivation of the Libyan alphabet as a whole from a Semitic source. That the forms noted by Halévy do not resemble their Phoenician phonetic equivalents by mere accident, but because of their derivation, is made yet more certain by the geographical distribution of the Libyan inscriptions. Although they exist outside of Algeria and Tunisia, it is certainly true that those

[1] M. de Saulcy, *Observations sur l'alphabet tifinag*, in the *Journal Asiat.*, 1849, 4th series, vol. xiii. p. 247 *sqq*.

[2] J. W. Harding King, *A Search for the Masked Tawareks*, p. 319 *sqq*.

[3] This is obviously invalidated by the Thugga bilingual. Cf. too Valerius Maximus i. 1. 21, *Ext.* 2, where Masinissa is said to have inscribed some tusks *gentis suae litteris*. But perhaps Punic is here intended.

[4] O. Blau, *Über das numidische Alphabet*.

[5] E. Littmann, *L'Origine de l'alphabet libyen*. This theory, abandoned, I believe, by Littmann himself, is yet held by W. M. Müller.

[6] J. Halévy, *op. cit.* p. 85.

regions are richest in these inscriptions—that is to say, they are commonest in those parts of Africa which were inhabited by sedentary natives living within the Phoenician sphere. The comparative infrequency of their occurrence outside this area is in itself an indication of the connection between Libyan and Phoenician writing. The non-Semitic part of the alphabet is composed mainly of those signs which, from their distribution, might almost be called Mediterranean, and which are seen in the Celtiberian and Turdetan alphabets of the west,[1] in the Cypriote syllabary, and even in Minoan Crete.[2] To ascribe to one people or period the origin of the non-Semitic elements of the Libyan alphabet would be at present extremely rash ; still more rash is the assumption that when these simple figures occur singly or in groups of but two or three on pots, etc., they necessarily represent phonetic values. These facts, and the consideration that many of these signs have been in use in at least one portion of Northern Africa (Lower Egypt) for as long as five thousand years as simple marks of identification, make it reasonable to suppose that at the time Halévy's letters were taken over by the Libyans from the Phoenicians a number of simple marks, of a type widely diffused, were pressed into service to make up the complement of letters necessary to form the alphabet. The same thing seems to have happened in Spain, where borrowed Greek and Phoenician letters were used with "promoted" marks to the same ends. This is at least a supposition which it is easier for science to accept than any theory which would give phonetic values to the Egyptian pot-marks or to the barred pebbles of Mas d'Azil ;[3] and which would assert that all the Mediterranean scripts were derived from one parent system, more or less well defined at a period when man could hardly have felt the need of writing at all. From what has been said it may safely be concluded that the Libyans borrowed from the Phoenicians a few letters and the idea of writing, and that they added to the borrowed letters enough owners' marks to make an alphabet, rude, but suited to their simple needs.

The alphabet thus evolved, as seen on the monuments, consists of thirty letters, which, with their equivalents as determined by Halévy and Letourneux,[4] are given in the following table.

[1] A. Heiss, *Monnaies antiques de l'Espagne*, p. 3 *sqq.* ; D'A. de Jubainville, *Celtes d'Espagne*, in the *Compt. Rend. Acad. des Inscript.*, 1890, p. 219 *sqq.* ; P. Berger, *op. cit.* p. 335 *sqq.* The Turdetan alphabet, as far as preserved, is a primitive one, despite the fact that Strabo assures us (iii. p. 139) that the Turdetani had a written literature.

[2] A. J. Evans, *Scripta Minoa*, vol. i., *e.g.* pp. 39, 89; and hieroglyphic, Nos. 132, 129, 92, and p. 92.

[3] E. Piette, *Les Galets coloriés du Mas d Azil*, in *Anth.* vii. pp. 386 *sqq.*, and *Les Écritures de l'âge glyptique*, in *Anth.* xvi. p. 1 *sqq.* Amongst the supporters of extremely ancient writing it is not surprising to find G. Sergi, *The Mediterranean Race*, p. 296 *et alibi.*

[4] J. Halévy, *op. cit.* p. 78 ; C. Tissot, *op. cit.* vol. i. p. 519. In the equivalents given above I would suggest, among several slight changes, that the absence of the sound P in modern Berber dialects justifies the confining of the value of X̄, ⋈ to ϕ or F.

Libyan.		English.	
Horizontal.	Vertical.	Halévy.[1]	Letourneux.[1]
•	•	A	A
—	I	A	N
I	—	N	Ṣ
O, □	O, □	R	R
⊙, ⊡	⊙ ⊡	B	B
∠	⅂, ⅂, ⌈⌉, ∧, 7, ∨, ∧	G	G
+, X	+, X	T	T
?	T, ⊥	V, U	Ǵ
?	·I·, ÷	ʿA (ع)	Ǵ
≡	III	ʿA (ع)	GH (غ)
?	≡	H	GH (غ)
?	IIII	Ḥ (ح)	H
?	≣	Ḳ (ق)	H
=	II	U	U
II	=	L	L
⊓	[,]	D	D
⊏	⊓	S	S
⊐	⊔	M	M
?	H, ⌶	U, W	F
≻	≻	Ṭ (ط)	T
?	⋊	…	TS
?	⊓⊓	…	TS
⊓⊓	⊔⊔	Z	TH, DH
Z	⸮, ⸮, ⸮, ∿	I	I
⇇ , ⇇	1⅂, 1II	K (ك)	K
⧖, 8	⧖, 8, 8	TS (צ)	Ṯ
⋈	⋈	P, PH, F	P
≷	W, ≷, H	S (ש)	S
⊐	⊔	ʿA (ع)	ʿA
?	C	…	S

Originating in the Punicized regions of Africa Minor, this alphabet became in time disseminated over a large part of indigenous North Africa, the script of the Guanches of Canaria being closely allied to it, and the occurrence of a Libyan inscription, as has been

[1] Of the two systems, that of Halévy is the more accurate. My own system of transliteration will be found in the introduction to the *Sylloge Inscriptionum Libycarum* shortly to be published.

remarked, having been noted as far east as Sinai. It has, moreover, a modern descendant in the *Tifinagh*[1] alphabet, which is still occasionally employed among the Imushagh, a writing of which traces have been found from the Egyptian oases to the Atlas, and from the Mediterranean to Lake Chad. This latter alphabet presents some differences from its prototype, which may be accounted for by the usurpation of characters unfamiliar to the Imushagh by marks of their own; or by abbreviations, such as the regular substitution of · for | or —; by the influence of Arabic; and by the development of double letters (ligatures). The Tifinagh alphabet, as generally employed by the Imushagh, is here set down for comparison with its Libyan prototype.

TIFINAGH (AZGAR AND AHAGGAR).

Name.	Form.	Value.	Name.	Form.	Value.
Taغerit	·	a, i, u	Iel	‖	l
Ieb	◫, ⦶	b	Iem	⊐	m
Iet	+	t	Ien	|	n
Ied	⊓, Λ, ⊔	d	Iek	·:	k
Ieǵ	I	ǵ	Iaḱ	···	ḱ
Iez	⌗	z	Ieغ	⋮	غ
Ieḏ	ⵥ, Ж	ḏ	Ieš	ⵛ	š
Ier	□, ○	r	Iah	⁞	h
Ies	⊡, ⊙	s	Iaḍ	Ǝ	ḍ
Ieg	.I., ·T·	g	Iaḳ	⁙	ḳ
Iegǵ	⋈	gǵ	Iau	:	u, w
Ief	ⵊ,][	f	Iéy	ⵢ	i, y

The double letters are :—

Iebt	+◫	=	◫ and +	=	bt	Ielt	⊢⊣	=	‖ and +	=	tl
Iezt	⌗+	=	⌗ „ +	=	zt	Iemt	+⊐	=	⊐ „ +	=	mt
Iert	⊞	=	□ „ +	=	rt	Ient	†	=	| „ +	=	nt
Iest	+⊡	=	⊡ „ +	=	st	Iešt	+ⵛ	=	ⵛ „ +	=	št
Iegt	·+·	=	·T· „ +	=	gt	Ienk	·†·	=	| „ +	=	nk
Igǵt	+⋈	=	⋈ „ +	=	gǵt						

A comparison of Tifinagh and Libyan shows the following more obvious parallels :—

Tifinagh.	Value.	Libyan.	Value.	Punic.
·	a, i, u	·, —, |	'a	
⦶, ◫	b	⊙, ⊡	b	𐤁
+	t	+, ×	t	×

[1] This name may preserve a memory of the Semitic inspiration of the Libyan writing. For تيفنغ, *tifinaغ*, by the mutation of غ to k, gives a fem. subst. of Φοινικ-. Cf. A. H. Keane, *Africa*, vol. i. p. 77, note 1.

Tifinagh.	Value.	Libyan.	Value.	Punic.
⊓	d	⊓,⊏,⊐	d	9
O,□	r	O,□	r	
∥	l	∥,=	l	
⊐	m	⊐,⊔	m	𐤌
ǀ	n	ǀ,—	n	ǀ
⁝	غ	·ǀ·, ÷ or ǀǀǀ, ≡	غ	
:	u, w	=, ∥	u, w	

Libyan inscriptions are read from below upward, beginning usually with the right-hand column, rarely with the left. Very rarely letters are in horizontal-lines, to be read from right to left, as in the Thugga inscription. The derived Tifinagh may be written to be read →, ↓, ←, ↑, or even in a spiral or circle.

Of such remains of Libyan writing as are known in Eastern Libya it may be said that early in the nineteenth century traces were reported in Marmarica.[1] The following inscription[2] was the first noted :—

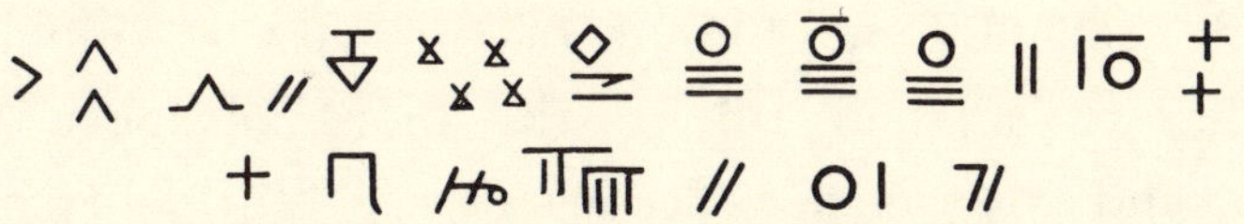

As copied it cannot be read, and the presumption is strong that one has here a number of tribal or personal marks, grouped together by the collector, and so published. Traces of Libyan inscriptions are reported by Hamilton[3] as occurring at Safsaf in Cyrenaica; although it is doubtful if these traces are more than masons' marks, since owners' marks, some of which have the form of Libyan letters, are in use among the modern nomads of Eastern Libya.[4] Signs of this sort were collected from two columns of a ruin at Ḥamed Garushin the Major Syrtis by the British Admiralty Expedition in 1821–1822,[5] together with the names of the tribes to members of which they belonged. Such signs also occur in Western Egypt and in the Egyptian oases.[6]

The following, collected in 1910 from Marmarica, will serve as examples of these signs :—

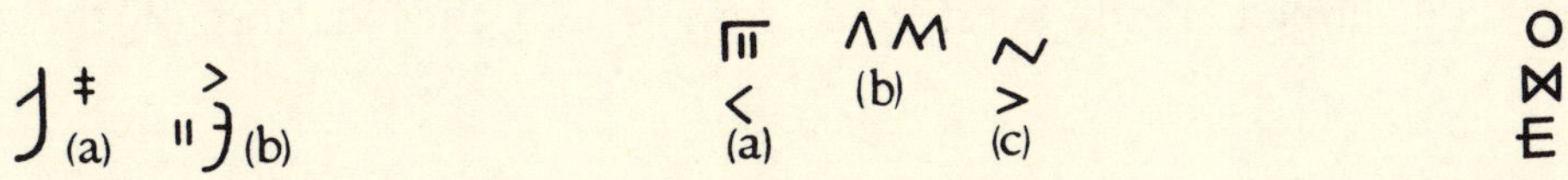

1. Near Marsa Matru. 2. Near Sîdî Baranî. 3. Near Bîr el-Kanays.

[1] J. A. Scholz, *Reise in die Gegend zwischen Alexandrien und Parätonium*, pp. 53, 56, 57; J. R. Pacho. *Voyage dans la Marmarique, etc.*, p. 24.
[2] V. Reboud, *op. cit.* p. 47, and pl. xx. no. 146. After J. H. A. Scholz, *locc. citt.*
[3] J. Hamilton, *Wanderings*, p. 76.
[4] V. de Bourville, *loc. cit.* De Bourville remarks that such signs were especially common among those tribes which have the Berber filiative ايت or ات, instead of the Arabic اولاد or بنى, before their names. They may be seen in Reboud, *op. cit.* pl. xx. no. 147.
[5] F. W. and H. W. Beechey, *Expedition to . . . the Northern Coast of Africa*, p. 161. They had been noted earlier by P. della Cella.
[6] Personal observation in Mariut, about Marsa Matru, and Sîdî Baranî. The scarcity of these marks at Sîwah is extraordinary, but may be due to the poor stone. They do occur.

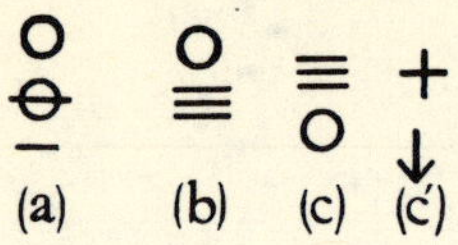

4. Near Bîr el-Kanays.

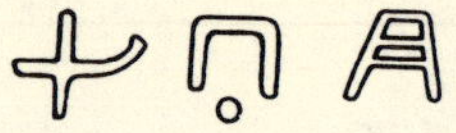

5. Bîr es-Ṣtabl (deep cut in mouth of well).

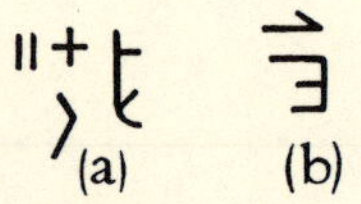

6. Ḥaṭṭîah Gerbah.

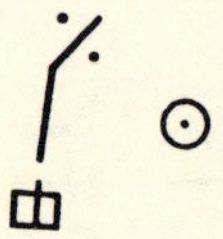

7. Tattooed on hand of an Aulad ʿAlî.

Of these curious signs all to some extent, and (3) and (4) especially, recall either the Libyan or the Tifinagh letters.[1]

Were it not for the meagre traces noted above, so much space need hardly have been devoted to this question of writing. The very scarcity of material, however, although it is safe to predict that it will be increased by exploration, is significant ; it tends to show that in classical times the Eastern Libyans were at a lower stage of culture than were their more sedentary neighbours of the west. Among them the needs of writing were doubtless fewer than among the more advanced natives in Numidia, Byzacium, Zeugitana, and Mauretania Caesariensis. While in the latter areas it was not uncommon to inscribe tombstones with simple epitaphs giving the name of the deceased, in the east, but for the Sinai inscription twice referred to above and due probably to some wandering caravaneer, and but for the Libyan letters signalized by modern travellers as being of general occurrence in Cyrenaica, Marmarica, and the Oases, it might well have been doubted whether in ancient times the Eastern Libyans ever possessed a knowledge of the art of writing.

From earliest times, it may be said by way of summary, there has been a continuity of Berber speech in Eastern Libya, now represented by the disappearing "strong" dialects of Sîwah, Manshîah el-ʿAguzah, Garah, etc. ; the Eastern Libyans can be shown, on linguistic grounds, to have been in contact with the inhabitants of the Nile Valley at a very early period ; and they had at a late period some knowledge of the Libyan script which was developed in the west, and from which the writing of the Imushagh takes its origin.

[1] Some of these signs, it is but fair to state, seem to approximate those of the late North Semitic alphabets rather than the Libyan. Especially is this the case with No. 5.

CHAPTER IV

ECONOMICS

In the discussion of the relation of man to his environment in Eastern Libya at the present time, something has been said of the dependence of the nomadic population on the permanently inhabited centres. The present conditions seem to reflect with fair accuracy those which existed anciently, despite the Herodotean characterization of the whole country as "nomadic."[1] At all events, the degree of nomadism was not, like that prevailing among the Romanies of mediaeval Europe or the Solubbi of modern Arabia, quite unrestricted, for it has been shown in the chapter on ethnogeography that the Libyan tribes had fairly well defined boundaries. The Egyptianized Adyrmachidae,[2] the Hellenized Asbystae[3] and Auschisae,[4] and the Bacales,[5] therefore, could have been nomads only in a limited sense. This is true to an extent even greater of that remarkably stable ethnic group, the Nasamones. These last-named people may be taken as typical; they had their main seat on the Syrtic shore, where they left their herds in summer, while they themselves went up-country to Augila for the date crop.[6] Similarly, the Aulad ʿAlî of western Egypt at the present day leave the coast after sowing their crops in the autumn, and return to their harvest and pasturage in the spring. The Macae, unlike the Nasamones or the Aulad ʿAlî, frequented the littoral during the rains. In winter they lived along-shore, their flocks being confined in pens; but in summer, when there was scarcity of water in the sandy coastal zone, they moved away from the sea into the midlands—presumably into the fertile Gebel Gharyan.[7] The nomadism of the Psylli must have been restricted, since they had permanent wells,[8] and the wanderings of part at least of the "Lotophagi" could not have been very extensive, since they were circumscribed by the confines of a peninsula so small as that of Zuchis.[9] The Machlyes and Auseans both inhabited the region contiguous to Lake Tritonis,[10] where the latter held a yearly festival that began with a procession around the lake.[11]

[1] Herodotus iv. 186 *et alibi*. [2] *Ibid.* iv. 168. [3] *Ibid.* iv. 170.
[4] *Ibid.* iv. 171. [5] *Ibid. loc. cit.* [6] *Ibid.* iv. 172, 182.

[7] Scylax § 109, *παρὰ τὴν Σύρτιν μέχρι τοῦ στόματος τῆς Σύρτιδος παροικοῦντες οἱ Μάκαι χειμάζουσιν ἐπὶ θαλάττῃ τὰ βοσκήματα κλείοντες, τοῦ δὲ θέρους, ὑπεκλειπόντων τῶν ὑδάτων, ἀπελαύνουσι τὰ βοσκήματα εἰς μεσογαίαν ἄνω μεθ' ἑαυτῶν.*

[8] Herodotus iv. 173. [9] *Ibid.* iv. 177. [10] *Ibid.* iv. 180. [11] *Ibid. loc. cit.*

This festival was primarily a tribal one, and not of a general character, as, for example, that of the great Moslem Moled of Ṭanṭah, or that of the Easter Flame at the Holy Sepulchre in Jerusalem. The participants, therefore, like most, if not all, the littoral tribes, were not nomadic in the widest sense of the term. There existed, also, far in the interior, such purely native towns as Garama, Cydamus, Boin, etc., and permanent oasis-settlements in which the indigenes, like those of Sîwah and Wagîlah at the present time, dwelt in houses built of mud and rock-salt.[1] In fine, despite the distinction of Herodotus, who says that to the west of Lake Tritonis live the sedentary agricultural Libyans,[2] it appears that the Eastern Libyans, at least those of the littoral zone,[3] were mostly confined to small areas, and had within their boundaries either permanent centres or regular places of resort according to the seasons. Probably the bulk of the people lived in a state which is to-day paralleled by that of certain Bedawîn in Syria. There, at ʿArak el-Emîr, the Arabs have houses in which, during the winter months, they dwell as cultivators; in the summer they wander about, living in tents, as graziers. The case is a suggestive one, since these Bedawîn were, a generation ago, purely nomadic.[4]

It was in the barren interior, if at all, that tribes anciently existed in a condition completely nomadic. The Gamphasantians are located by Herodotus only in general terms, as being "above the Nasamones" in the south.[5] In those regions tribes probably moved from place to place as do the modern "followers of the rain" in the deserts between the Nile and the Red Sea. *Sine tectis ac sedentibus*, says Mela, speaking of the desert Libyans, *passim vagi habent potius terras quam habitant*.[6] The same writer, in terms which admirably characterize the free nomadic state, says of the up-country Libyans: *Interiores incultius etiam secuntur vagi pecora*, *utque a pabulo ducta sunt ita se ac tuguria sua permovent*, *atque ubi dies deficit ibi noctem agunt*.[7]

The reason for the difference between the nomadic habits of the coast-wise and of the up-country tribes is obvious: where a regular rainfall and suitable soil encouraged agriculture, the Libyan forsook his wandering life to take advantage of these conditions; elsewhere, he perforce remained in a nomadic state.

It is instructive to note the cultural stages which the Eastern Libyans may be seen to have passed through in historic times. In the XIXth to XXth Dynasties they were still capable of relapsing into a semi-migratory state, the impulse which caused the great invasions of that period seeming to have been due to a racial pressure in the Moghreb. A thousand years later, in the times of Herodotus, the migrations have been stilled; limited nomads occupy the arable coastal lands, and the less fortunate

[1] Pliny v. 5, *Domos sale montibus suis exciso, ceu lapide, construunt.* [2] Herodotus iv. 186, 187, 199 *et alibi.*

[3] Even the Gaetulians had their permanent centres, if Vergil's phrase, *Gaetulae urbes* (*Aen.* iv. 42), is to be admitted as evidence.

[4] G. A. Smith, note in *Palestine Exploration Fund Quarterly Statement*, xxxvii. (Oct. 1905), p. 287.

[5] Herodotus iv. 174. *Vide supra*, p. 53. [6] Mela i. 4.

[7] *Ibid.* 1. 8. Yet even a people like the Garamantes seem to have had regular seasonal movements. For they were wont, about the winter solstice, to go into the remoter parts of the interior for the hunting, after which they returned (Lucian, *De dipsadibus*, § 2).

tribes wander vaguely about the interior. Less than a thousand years later, the East Libyans of the littoral had largely settled down as town-dwellers; Marmarica, Cyrenaica, and the Syrtica Regio are dotted with towns bearing native names—Getullu, Auzui, Tinci Ausari, Zygris, etc., etc. But the lean and hungry tribesmen of the desert, now that their northern kinsmen have left their hardy semi-nomadic life to grow soft in sedentary communities, fall in upon them and harry their lands. The Ausurians overrun the Pentapolis, but before they can themselves become sedentary villagers, the Moḥammadan Arabs launch themselves across North Africa and deprive the nomads of those lands in which they could have developed into settled tillers of the soil.

The first economic factor to be considered with regard to the Eastern Libyans after this glance at the general conditions under which they lived is hunting. Wild animals were fairly plentiful along the northern confines of the desert,[1] and the pursuit and capture of game had an origin, of course, much earlier than that of herding cattle, the cultivation of the soil, or the practice of trade by barter. There has already been given a brief outline of the physiography, the Fauna, and the Flora of the country, to which in the present chapter only a few details need be added. The main outlines may be found in the opening chapter of this monograph.

Herodotus remarks[2] that in the regions occupied by the nomads were to be found "antelopes, gazelles, buffaloes, and asses, not of the horned sort, but of a kind that needs not to drink; also oryxes . . . nigh the bigness of an ox; foxes, hyaenas, and porcupines, wild rams, *dictyes*,[3] jackals, panthers, *boryes*,[4] land crocodiles,[5] about the length of three cubits, very like lizards, ostriches, and little snakes, each with a single horn."[6] There was, in fact, a fair variety of game in Eastern Libya, though the stag and the wild boar, the latter of which was known in Africa Minor, were not found.[7]

With these animals inhabiting their country, it is not a matter of surprise to learn that the Libyans used the skins of wild beasts, as well as those of domestic cattle, for clothing,[8] nor to find that, in the XVIIIth Dynasty,[9] the "tribute"—"plunder" would perhaps be a better word—taken by Queen Hatshepsut from the Teḥenu contained "many panther skins of five cubits along the back and four cubits wide."[10] Further-

[1] Herodotus ii. 32, where it is said that "Libya is full of wild beasts" above the littoral zone. Hence this district is characterized by Herodotus as ἡ Λιβύη θηριώδης. From a passage of Lucian (*De dipsadibus*, § 2) it appears that hunting was carried on in the winter even in the far interior. The Greek rhetorician, drawing apparently on a good source, states that the Garamantes "live mainly by the chase." [2] *Ibid.* iv. 192. [3] Δίκτυες, unknown animal.

[4] Βόρυες, unknown animal. [5] The monitor lizards, which occur also in Nubia. [6] *Cerastes horridus* (?).

[7] Herodotus, *loc. cit.* The historian is wrong as regards boars: until a few years ago they existed in the Delta and in the Fayum, and they are credibly reported to be still extant in the reedy shott or the Wady Magharah. Despite Moslem proscription the boar is eaten by the Berbers of the Atlas (A. H. Keane, *Africa*, vol. i. p. 81).

[8] Mela i. 8; Strabo xvii. p. 828; Aelian, *Hist. Anim.* xiv. 16; cf. Hippocrates, *De morbis*, ii. p. 375.

[9] This must be regarded as the earliest evidence on Libyan hunting. L. Heuzey, *Tribu asiatique en expédition*, plates iv. and v., and Maspero, *The Struggle of the Nations*, p. 767, reproduce an archaic Egyptian slate fragment which the latter writer entitles "A Troop of Libyans Hunting." But the figures are Egyptians, wearing the kilt and having curly hair, and using a type of bow seen on one of the Hieraconpolis vases (J. E. Quibell, *Hierakonpolis*, part i. plate xix. fig. 1; cf. *ibid.* part ii. plate xxviii.). The latter representation, on the verso of the smaller Hieraconpolis palette, though non-Libyan, affords an interesting parallel to the Teli-Ṣagha glyph described p. 94.

[10] BAR ii. § 321; cf. W. M. Müller, *Egyptological Researches*, vol. ii. p. 135 and note 2. The same tribute

more, the great use of ostrich plumes among the Libyans as personal ornaments must have necessitated the incessant hunting of the bird, unless it is to be supposed, without other evidence, that the Libyans succeeded in domesticating it.[1]

Only two pieces of testimony, but those of a very interesting sort, have been preserved in regard to the actual methods employed by the Libyans in the chase. The evidence in question exists at Teli-Ṣagha in Fezzan, where the explorer Barth found and copied some pre-historic rock-glyphs, over fifty years ago.[2] One of these drawings, here reproduced in Fig. 5, shows a large animal of some sort apparently walking into a snare or pitfall. Were it not that most desert animals do not drink, but get what moisture they need with their food, it might be thought that the glyph represented an onager or similar beast at water. At all events, Barth's curious explanation that the drawing shows *ein Rind . . . das durch ein Kreis oder Ring springt*[3] is scarcely acceptable.

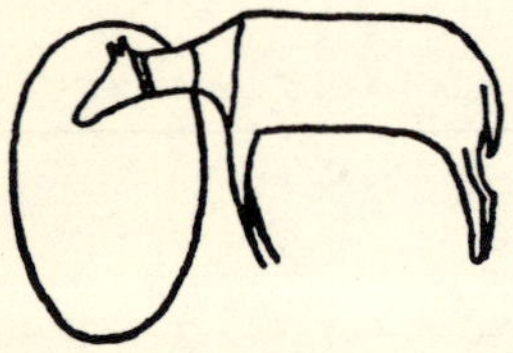

FIG. 5.

A second scene (Fig. 6) is of far greater interest, and capable of definite explanation. It is cut on a block fallen from a cliff-face,[4] measuring about 1·20 m. by 90 cm. Barth was at great pains to relate this monument to Egyptian mythology or to the "Garamantic Apollo," but its real significance is much simpler. In the centre, between the two other figures, is a buffalo. His position, a little higher up than that of the other figures, and his small size, may be meant to indicate, by one of the most universal conventions of primitive art, that he is in the "middle distance" of the scene. From left and right approach the hunters. The one on the left wears a skin, which, as he advances running with his arrow already fitted to the string, blows out behind him. On his head he wears the head of a gazelle with the horns still attached.[5] The other hunter is wearing the skin and mask of what appears to be a doe-gazelle. He holds before him a bow[6] with which he has just shot the quarry, which faces him.

FIG. 6.

contained also "ivory and 700 tusks." This might lead to the supposition that the panther-skins were traded from the south, but the language of the obelisk inscription published by Müller makes this improbable.

[1] The only possible evidence of domestication is the appearance of ostrich eggs among other Libyan tribute in a Tell el-Amarna painting (N. de G. Davies, *The Rock Tombs of El Amarna*, vol. ii. Pl. lx.), but this is not conclusive. (The eggs were probably blown, like those occasionally found in the pre-dynastic Egyptian graves.)

[2] H. Barth, *Reisen und Entdeckungen*, vol. i. p. 210 sqq.

[3] *Ibid.* p. 216 and cut.

[4] *Ibid.* pp. 209-210 for the general position of the glyphs, and the coloured plate facing p. 210. For the scene shown in fig. 6, p. 210 *sqq.*

[5] The horns suggest *Gazella dorcas.*

[6] Or a shield at which the buffalo charges (?).

What Barth, therefore, mistook for a religious representation is in reality a hunting scene. Such pictures are very numerous in primitive art, and the practice of hunting in animal disguise has many parallels.[1]

A third glyph at Teli-Ṣagha (Fig. 7) shows a herd of wild cattle[2] in a naturalistic manner. Despite the scantiness of the evidence, both the nature of it and the conditions under which the Libyans lived assure us that the ancient inhabitants of the country were capable and practised hunters.

Fig. 7.

Passing from the question of hunting to that of the domestication of animals, one enters a field of Libyan economics concerning which more evidence exists. The herds and flocks of the Eastern Libyans—at least of the more nomadic element among them—formed at an early period their principal wealth,[3] and as far back as the Vth Dynasty evidence exists of their having been breeders of cattle. In the *Romance of Sinuhe*, a tale of the XIIth Dynasty, Sesostris, in his campaign against the Libyans, is said to have taken—

Living cattle of the Libyans,
And all cattle without limit.[4]

Merneptah took at one time as many as 1308 head of cattle from the camp of the invading Libyans,[5] and the Papyrus Harris boastfully states that Rameses III. spoiled the Libyans of "cattle in number like hundred-thousands."[6] In classical times, it was generally known that at least part of Eastern Libya was rich in flocks and herds,[7] the earliest Greek notice being found in the *Odyssey*—

καὶ Λιβύην, ἵνα τ' ἄρνες ἄφαρ κεραοὶ τελέθουσιν.
τρὶς γὰρ τίκτει μῆλα τελεσφόρον εἰς ἐνιαυτόν.[8]

The earliest evidence as to Libyan cattle is that afforded by the Vth Dynasty relief showing the Teḥenu suppliant to Sa-hu-re.[9] The four middle registers of that monument contain reliefs of kine with long horns (top), two droves of asses (next to top), and two of goats (bottom two). All these animals are mentioned in the Egyptian notices of the New Empire; goats, for example, formed part of the booty taken by

[1] J. Deniker, *The Races of Man*, p. 189. Cf. the human figure dressed in a jackal's skin and playing a pipe on the smaller Hieraconpolis palette (J. E. Quibell, *op. cit.* part ii. plate xxviii.). It is regrettable that R. Basset, a great scholar, has repeated, in his *Recherches sur la religion des Berbères*, p. 12, Barth's error in regard to this glyph to the extent of seeing Egyptian influence in these drawings.

[2] For the existence of such there is proof in several notices: *e.g.* Aelian, *De natura animalium*, xiv. 11, . . . *καί εἰσιν ὤκιστοι οἵ ἄγριοί τε καὶ ἐλεύθεροι.* . .

[3] Mela i. 8, . . . *solum opimum.* [4] BAR i. § 492. [5] BAR iii. § 589. [6] BAR iv. § 405.

[7] Arrian, *Indica*, *cap. ult.*; idem, *Anabasis*, iii. 28.

[8] Homer, *Odyss.* iv. 85 *sq.* Cf. Dio Chrysostomus, *Orat.* lxiv. *De Fortuna*, vol. ii. p. 333.

[9] L. Borchardt, *Das Grabdenkmal des König S'aꜣḥu-Re*[c], vol. i. figs. 11, 12. The former figure shows the whole relief, the latter a portion of the middle registers.

Merneptah,[1] and appear earlier in the Libyan tribute shown in a XIIth Dynasty tomb-painting at Benî Ḥasan.[2] The Libyan women used goatskins for garments,[3] and these animals are mentioned by at least two Greek writers in connection with Cyrenaica.[4] Oxen were captured from the Libyans by Merneptah[5] and by Rameses III.[6] According to several classical writers, the tribesmen of the interior had a breed of oxen which, on account of their long curved horns, had to graze backwards,[7] although otherwise they were like ordinary cattle, except for the hardness and thickness of their hides.[8] Whether this were the case or not, the Egyptian evidence for the presence of large, long-horned cattle is conclusive, and is not unsupported by other classical testimony.[9]

Sheep, although not specifically mentioned in the Egyptian lists, or seen on the monuments, were numerous in Eastern Libya. Strabo mentions their existence in the interior,[10] and the Homeric passage which testifies to the fitness of the country for sheep-breeding has already been cited. The epithet μηλοτρόφος was applied to Libya by the Delphic oracle,[11] and in Byzantine times sheep were still plentiful in the country.[12]

Asses, which appear in the Sa-hu-re relief, were also taken from the Libyans in the XIXth Dynasty.[13] If they were of the same breed as those found to-day in Umm es-Ṣoghayr and Sîwah Oasis, they were of a very good sort.

The horse was unknown until its introduction from Egypt. The earliest notice of the horse in North Africa occurs in the reign of Merneptah. That Pharaoh captured "horses which bore the fallen Chief of Libya and the children of the Chief of Libya, carried off alive, pairs . . . twelve."[14] But although unknown in early times, the horse became very common throughout Northern Africa, even before the introduction of the camel, which soon followed. In the second Libyan war of Rameses III., 183 horses and asses were taken by the Egyptians,[15] and by classical times the horse had come to be so extensively used as to be employed in the interior and far west.[16] "The breeding of horses," says Strabo, "is most carefully attended to by the kings" (of the interior): "so much so, that the number of colts yearly is calculated at one hundred thousand."[17] Herodotus mentions the horses of the Asbystae,[18]

1 BAR iii. §§ 584, 589.

2 P. E. Newberry, *Beni Hasan*, part i. plate xlvii.

3 Herodotus iv. 189. Cf. *ibid.* iv. 187; Oribasius, *Collect. Medic.* xlv. for the medicinal use of the stale of goats in Libya.

4 Pausanias ii. 26, 29; Synesius, *Epist.* cxlvii. pp. 285-6.

5 BAR iii. § 584.

6 BAR iv. § 111. The list gives 119 (+x) bulls.

7 Herodotus iv. 183. No modern traveller has reported such cattle in Africa. There are, however, several ancient notices of them outside Herodotus. *E.g.* Alexander Mynd. *ap.* Athenaeum v. 20, p. 221 E; Pliny viii. 45; Mela i. 8. It is probable that this story originated from the sight of long-horned cattle grazing backward, the fanciful explanation being a later addition.

8 Cf. F. Hornemann, *Journal of . . . Travels from Cairo to Mourzouk*, p. 127.

9 Synesius, *loc. cit.*; Hermippus *ap.* Athenaeum i. 49. Cows were not eaten, but their milk was probably used, Herodotus iv. 186. The natives of the Upper Senegal, entertaining for their herds that religious sentiment which so frequently develops among a pastoral people, only eat such of their cattle as have died from natural causes. Cf. M. Park, *Travels in the Interior of Africa*, p. 312. Similarly, though a cow-taboo exists among the Nuers of the Baḥr el-Ghazal, great use is made of cattle. Cf. O. Bates, *Sudanese Notes* in *CSJ*, vol. vi. No. 69, p. 135 *sqq*.

10 Strabo xvii. p. 835.

11 *Ap.* Herodotum iv. 155.

12 Synesius, *Epist.* 147, pp. 285-6; *Castast.* p. 301.

13 BAR iii. § 584.

14 BAR iii. § 589.

15 BAR iv. § 111.

16 *E.g.* as among the Pharusii, Strabo xvii. p. 828.

17 Strabo xvii. p. 835.

18 Herodotus iv. 170.

and the extremely high estimation in which Cyrenaic horses were held by the Greeks is proved by the epithets used for the country. Cyrene, or Cyrenaica, receives such titles as *εὔιππος*;[1] *ἱπποτρόφος ἀρίστη*;[2] *ἱπποβότος*;[3] *κάλιππος*.[4] That the classical world recognized the good horsemanship not only of the Theran colonists in Africa, but of the indigenes as well, is amply indicated. The classical reader will recall the

Λίβυες ζυγωτῶν ἁρμάτων ἐπιστάται

of Sophocles,[5] and Lucan's

. . . semper paratus
Inculto Gaetulus equo . . .[6]

The "horses," it should be said, were little more than ponies, but tough, wiry, and fleet.[7] They were often so well schooled as to follow their masters like dogs.[8] They were ridden without saddles,[9] and usually even without bridles, being guided by a light wand.[10] Though in some few cases bridles of rushes were employed,[11] the only trapping which seems to have been in general use was a neck-stall of plaited fibre, *περιτραχήλια ξύλινα*, from which depended a leading-rein.[12]

The importance of the horse, of course, must have declined to some extent after the introduction of the camel—at least in the more desert places. The camel, as has been said, appears for the first time in African history during the Saitic period in Egypt. As early, at the latest, as the fourth century B.C., camels were known in Marmarica, and by Roman times they were common throughout Eastern Libya.[13]

Of other domestic animals it remains only to mention dogs and bees. The former were probably, as at the present time, to be found in every encampment in North Africa. The occurrence of a representation of dogs on a stela of the XIth Dynasty has been mentioned in the preceding chapter, where it was remarked that one, perhaps two, of the animals have their names written in proto-Berber. One of the dogs in question is shown in Fig. 8, and the fact that at the present time animals of his breed are used for coursing small game leaves no reasonable doubt that the "hound" was a hunting dog.

FIG. 8.

1 Pindar, *Pyth.* iv. 2; Callimachus *ap.* Strabonem x. p. 484, xvii. p. 837; Dionysius, *Periegesis*, 213.

2 Dionysius, *Perieg.* 213.
3 Oppian, *Cynegetica*, ii. 263.
4 Nicephorus Blemmyda, p. 407.
5 Sophocles, *Electra*, 702.
6 Lucan, *Pharsalia*, iv. 677 *sq.*
7 Strabo xvii. p. 828.
8 *Ibid. loc. cit.*

9 Strabo xvii. p. 828; Lucan iv. 663 *sq.*—

Et quis nudo residens Massylia dorso
Ora levi flectit frenorum nescia virga.

Cf. *ibid.* iv. 677, *Inculto . . . equo.*

10 Strabo, *loc. cit.*; Lucan, *loc. cit.*; Silius Italicus, *Punica*, i. 215 *sqq.*; Caesar, *De bello Africano*, lxi.; Claudian, *Nilus* 20; idem, *Laus Stilichonis*, i. 249.

11 Strabo *loc. cit.*

12 *Ibid. loc. cit.*; Aelian, *De natura animalium*, xiv. 10.

13 Cf. the early Roman coin of Cyrene showing a camel on the reverse: C. L. Müller, *Numismatique, etc.*, vol. i. p. 154, No. 391; a Roman relief, said to have come from Darfur, but almost certainly from Tripoli, now in Constantinople; Synesius, *Epist.* 130, . . . τοῖς πλείοσιν ἡμῶν τὸ πλουτεῖν ἐν βοσκήμασιν ἦν, ἐν ἀγελαίαις καμήλοις, ἐν ἵπποις φορβάσι

Bees were probably cultivated, at least by the sedentaries, from an early period, if weight is to be attached to the Greek legends of Aristaeus. That the Gyzantes were bee-keepers is expressly stated by Herodotus, who adds that this tribe also prepared an artificial honey.[1]

It may be said in conclusion that while the less civilized portion of the people would be likely to give more heed to their herds, since the sedentaries were less dependent upon them than the nomads, the Eastern Libyans seem in general to have been well supplied with domestic animals, and to have shown intelligence and industry in breeding and raising them.

That such of the Eastern Libyans as were fortunate enough to possess themselves of the more fertile portions of the country should become agriculturalists at an early period was but the natural result of the richness of the soil. The region about the Cinyps was, according to Herodotus, equal to any in the world for the growing of grain, the yields being as great as those of Babylonia.[2] The vicinity of Euhesperis was also good for cereals, one hundredfold being obtained in the best years.[3] Of Cyrenaica Herodotus truly writes that a crop was reaped yearly at successive seasons from the lowest, the middle, and the highest levels respectively.[4]

The earliest notices of Libyan agriculture belong to the XIXth Dynasty. At that time the Pharaoh Merneptah was recorded to have taken "every herb that came forth from their [*scil.* the Libyans'] fields," so that "no field grew to keep alive" the inhabitants.[5] That some of the fields bore cereals is indicated by the statement that "the grain of his [the Libyan chieftain's] supplies was plundered."[6]

In the classical period, the fertile Cyrenaica was almost entirely under Greek or Graeco-Libyan dominion; the Cinyps region was Punic. Something is known, however, of native agriculture outside of these regions. Thus, as has been said, the Nasamones used annually to go up to the coast of Augila for dates; and the inhabitants of Ammonium and the other oases must, almost from the beginning, have been cultivators.[7] Herodotus observed that in northern Phazania the Garamantes covered salty earth with loam, and then sowed it.[8] Grapes were probably grown anciently, as to-day, in various parts of Eastern Libya, as in Marmarica, which attained to an unenviable reputation for the badness of its wine;[9] and in the isle of Cyraunis, where the

κτλ.; Victor Vitensis, *Historia persecutionis*, etc. i.; Procopius, *De bello Vandal.* i. 8. 10 and *passim*; Corippus, *Johannis*, ii. 91 *sqq.*, iv. 597, 995, 1021, 1065, 1133 *sqq.*, v. 83 *sq.*, 194 *sqq.*, vi. 236, 341 *sqq.*; Ammianus Marcellinus xviii. 6. 5 and 6; and *supra*, p. 16 *sq.*

[1] Herodotus iv. 194; Eudoxus Cnidius *ap.* Apollonium Dyscolum, xxxviii.

[2] *Ibid.* iv. 198. Three hundredfold!

[3] *Ibid. loc. cit.*

[4] *Ibid.* iv. 199; cf. J. R. Pacho, *Voyage dans la Marmarique, la Cyrénaïque, etc.*, p. 235 *sq.*; J. Hamilton, *Wanderings*, p. 124.

[5] BAR iii. § 598. In the Athribis Stela; cf. iii. 611 *ad fin.*

[6] BAR iii. § 610.

[7] Cf. Lucan iv. 334, where he says—

. . . qua nudi
Garamantes arant; . . .

and later (ix. 450) places the Garamantes in the oases.

[8] Cf. G. F. Lyon, *Travels*, p. 271, for the preparation of the sandy soil of Fezzan.

[9] Strabo xvii. p. 799.

vine was cultivated together with the olive.[1] The Lotophagi, who so extensively used the fruit of the *Rhamnus zizyphus* (L. = *R. nabeca*, Forsk.), or some such tree, must be regarded as partially agricultural, even if they did not actually plant these trees and cultivate them; since they were so dependent on the lotus fruit for food that Herodotus affirmed that some of them lived upon it exclusively, and that they prepared from it a sort of wine.[2] It is to some such drink, probably, that Mela refers when he speaks of a *succus bacarum* as a Libyan beverage; unless *bacae* is here to be understood as meaning "dates," in which case a mild intoxicant like *lakbî* would be intended.[3]

For the widespread cultivation of the olive in Tripolitana in Graeco-Roman times abundant archaeological evidence exists in the numerous ruined presses of the *torcular* type still to be seen in the country. Herodotus mentions the culture of the olive in the Isle of Cyraunis,[4] and throughout the suitable portions of the African Pentapolis to-day the traveller sees numerous olive-trees, perhaps self-sown from those of a pre-Islamic period.

Of the date-palm something has been said in the chapter on physiography. It remains to add that not only was the fruit used as food by the Libyans, but the fibres served for the making of cords,[5] and a wine called *caryotis* (καρυῶτις) by Pliny, and described as being *capiti inimica*,[6] was prepared from the fruit.

Little as can be gleaned in regard to the present question from classical writers, it suffices to show that the statement of Herodotus to the effect that the nomadic Libyans between Egypt and Tritonis lived on milk and flesh,[7] and his implication that only to the west of the latter place were the indigenes tillers of the soil,[8] are to be taken, even on his own showing, with considerable modification. Probably of old as at the present day, the inhabitants of Eastern Libya who occupied good arable lands were largely agricultural; those with poorer fields sowed them and left them till the time of harvest;[9] while those who could call no arable lands their own wandered about as graziers in the interior.

From a consideration of these questions of the chase, of herding, and of agriculture, one derives some knowledge of the alimentation of the Eastern Libyans—a subject of so much importance both from the economic and the cultural point of view as to warrant its discussion.

At the present time, the principal articles of diet in the interior are various messes of grain, flaps of bread, dates, figs, raisins, and such wild fruits as are edible, onions, tomatoes, cucumbers, melons, etc., and a number of wild plants. For meat, the flesh

[1] Herodotus iv. 195; C. Tissot, *Géographie comparée*, vol. i. p. 302 *sqq*.

[2] Herodotus iv. 177; cf. Strabo xvii. 3. 3; Scylax, § 110, where it is said of the Extra-Syrtic Lotophagi . . . λωτῷ χρῶνται σίτῳ καὶ ποτῷ.

[3] Mela i. 8.

[4] Herodotus iv. 195.

[5] Pliny xiii. 3, *nunc ad funes vitiliumque nexus et capitum levia umbracula finduntur*. Cf. *ibid*. xvi. 24.

[6] Pliny xiii. 4.

[7] Herodotus iv. 186.

[8] *Ibid*. iv. 191.

[9] Like the Aulad ʿAlî to-day. The actual process of sowing was probably mere bush-harrowing, as among the Aulad ʿAlî, or the Western Libyans as mentioned by Strabo xvii. p. 831.

of camels, goats, and sheep is eaten, as is that of the moufflon, antelope, and gazelle when these animals can be procured. Even jerboas and locusts are used for food,[1] though the Imushagh abstain from birds, fish, or the big edible lizards.[2] Oil, butter, fat, and milk are in general use in cooking. Milk is commonly used only after it has curdled, and a dry food is made from it by evaporation. Honey is esteemed as a luxury, and numerous wild plants are used as condiments. The food of the inhabitants of the littoral regions varies little from that of the interior tribes, and is prepared in much the same manner.

The alimentation of the Eastern Libyans of antiquity was, as far as can be judged, little different from that of the modern occupants of their country. Although Procopius states that the Libyans had no bread, but lived upon raw wheat and barley,[3] this is an error which he himself corrects when he mentions a native woman's baking bread, according to the custom of the country, in the ashes,[4] a method often followed to-day. The ancient people made great use of milk as food,[5] certain tribes, particularly those near Aethiopia, even giving it to their sheep.[6] Anciently, as now, a sort of cheese was made from milk.[7] Among vegetable foods, the use of dates, lotus, etc., has already been mentioned, and what Strabo observed in regard to the Numidians, viz. that they were eaters of roots rather than of flesh, was probably applicable to many of the eastern tribes.[8] The consumption of meat was, however, widespread, despite local taboos on certain animals. The natives of the interior, since their wealth was in their flocks, used the flesh of wild animals in preference to that of domestic.[9] The Gyzantes were content to eat Barbary apes;[10] the troglodytes of Phazania, perhaps owing to the scarcity of other game, to eat serpents.[11] The Libyans living along-shore in the Syrtica Regio sought eagerly for such fish as were stranded on their beaches by the tides,[12] and probably the Libyan oysters[13] known to the Graeco-Roman world were also eaten by the tribesmen. The eating of locusts was widespread. Among the Nasamones these insects were "dried in the sun and powdered. This powder," says Herodotus, "they sprinkle on their milk and drink."[14] The same method of preparing this curious food exists in Arabia. The Arabs there mingle the locusts, "brayed small, with their often only liquid diet of sour buttermilk."[15] In Western Africa, the locust powder is boiled with milk, or the insects are—as in many other places—merely boiled.[16] At Murzuk,

[1] H. Duveyrier, *Les Touareg du Nord*, p. 409 *sq.*

[2] *Ibid.* p. 401 *sq.*

[3] Procopius, *De bello Vandalico*, ii. 6.

[4] *Ibid.* ii. 7, . . . οὕτω γὰρ νόμος ἐν Μαυρουσίοις τοὺς ἄρτους ὀπτᾶσθαι.

[5] Herodotus iv. 186; Mela i. 8; cf. Strabo xvii. p. 833.

[6] Strabo xvii. p. 835. The sheep were also given flesh.

[7] *Ibid.* xvii. p. 833.

[8] *Ibid. loc. cit.*

[9] Mela i. 8, *cibus est caro plurimum ferina; nam gregibus quia id solum opimum est, quod potest parcitur.*

[10] Herodotus iv. 194.

[11] Mela i. 8, *Trogodytae . . . aluntur serpentibus.* Lack of game may have accounted for the vegetarianism of the Atarantians (Mela, *loc. cit.*, *Atarantes . . . non vescuntur animalibus*) of the west.

[12] Strabo xvii. p. 835.

[13] Oribasius, *Collect. medic.* ii. 58.

[14] Herodotus iv. 172.

[15] C. M. Doughty, *Wanderings in Arabia*, vol. i. p. 59.

[16] M. Adanson, *A Voyage to Senegal*, p. 161. Among certain Aethiopians, the locusts were powdered with salt and made into cakes (Strabo xvi. p. 772).

in Fezzan, the locust is dried, stripped of its legs and wings, "drawn," and eaten raw. According to an early traveller, it then "has a flavour similar to that of red herrings, but more delicious."[1]

* * *

The main streams of Libyan traffic flowed south and north, rather than east and west. From very early times the Eastern Libyans must have been engaged in caravan commerce, since they were controllers of the routes which, passing through their territories, ran from the Mediterranean southward into the Sudan. The greatest of these routes was, of course, the famous Chad–Tripoli Road, a line of march by which merchandise have been exchanged between north and south for thousands of years. The products of the Sudan have always sought this Ṣaḥaran outlet in preference to the river-ways offered by the Nile, the Niger, or the Senegal;[2] and it was primarily with a view of having factories near the northern terminus of this channel of communication with the interior that the Carthaginians established their *emporia* along the Syrtic littoral.

As early as the XVIIIth Dynasty the Eastern Libyans appear to have been possessed of commodities which they had obtained from the Sudan. Thus, in the "tribute" extracted from the Teḥenu by Queen Hatshepsut, mention is made of "ivory and seven hundred tusks,"[3] which could hardly have been obtained elsewhere than in Darfur, Wadai, or the Chad Region. In classical times the evidence of this ivory trade is explicit, as in the fragment of Hermippus:—

ἡ Λιβύη δ' ἐλέφαντα πολὺν παρέχει κατὰ πρᾶσιν.[4]

It is easily possible, therefore, that the intermediary source of the ivory objects found in excavations in the northern Mediterranean lands, especially in the west, may have been not Egypt but Libya. This applies, for example, to an ivory pendant in the form of a monkey, and to some seals of ivory found at Crete—the probability being here heightened if the conjecture of Evans, who has suggested that silphium may have found its way from Libya to Minoan Crete, be correct.[5]

Another African product which came from Libya to Europe was the ostrich egg, of which examples have from time to time been found in Etruscan tombs.[6]

[1] F. Hornemann, *op. cit.* p. 59. In connection with the custom of eating insects, a disgusting habit of the Adyrmachidae need not be mentioned except by reference (Herodotus iv. 168).

[2] C. Perroud, *De Syrticis emporiis*, p. 143.

[3] BAR ii. § 321. The leopard or panther skins in the same tribute may have been obtained by hunting in Eastern Libya itself; cf. W. M. Müller, *Egyptological Researches*, vol. ii. p. 141 (New Karnak Obelisk, § 6). The existence in ancient times of wild elephants in the Moghreb is doubtful, though Isidorus Hispalensis (*Etymologiae*, xiv. 5, § 12) is explicit on this point—*olim etiam, et elephantis plena fuit* [Mauretania Tingitana] *quos sola nunc India parturit.*

[4] Hermippus Comicus, *Phormophori*, Frag. i. 5. 15, *Poet. Comic. Fragg.*, ed. Bothe.

[5] A. J. Evans, *Scripta Minoa*, vol. i. p. 215 *sq.* As bearing on the connection of Eastern Libya and Crete, a passage of Philostratus, *Vita Apollonii* iv. 34. 3, may be added to what has earlier been said of the proximity of the island to the African main. Apropos of the temple at Lebanaeum, Philostratus comments on the number of Libyans who visited it: πολλοὶ δὲ καὶ Λιβύων ἐς αὐτὸ περαιοῦνται, κτλ. I may remark that in 1909 I saw a lentiscular Minoan crystal intaglio at Marsa Suzah, near which town it was said by its Cretan owner to have been found.

[6] J. Martha, *L'Art étrusque*, p. 106.

These evidences of Libyan commercial activity are, however, of slight importance when compared with the evidence afforded by the Carthaginian factories mentioned as having been established in the Syrtica Regio.[1] These posts, placed along a coast not attractive to a sea-trade and in some parts very barren, could have been founded only with a view mainly to monopolizing and developing the caravan traffic with Libya Interior and Aethiopia. The staple exports of these Punic factories were in all likelihood much the same as those of the mediaeval establishments in Tripolitana. The Venetians had in exchange for their merchandise dried fruits, oil, grain, salt, sheepskins, ox and camel hides, native cloths, grass mats and baskets, horses, saffron, aloes, wool, wax, honey, alum, senna from Fezzan, Syrtic sponges, aromatic gums, skins of wild beasts, gold (both wrought and in dust), ivory, and ostrich feathers.[2] The ancient commerce, in which, since part of the products came from the interior, the Libyans must have played an important rôle, dealt with most of these items, and with yet others. Ivory and hides found their way from fabulous Aethiopia to the coast;[3] the excellent rock-salt of the interior, well known to the classical world,[4] was probably carried to the Punic factories on the coast to be there exported or used in the pickling of fish.[5] From the interior came also several varieties of semi-precious stones in which the Libyans trafficked. The best known of these was the carbuncle. This gem, called *anthrax* by Theophrastus[6] and *carbunculus* by Pliny,[7] was called also, from those who purveyed it to Europe, "the Carthaginian stone,"—ὁ Καρχηδόνιος λίθος.[8] It was brought to the coast from the country of the Garamantes and the Gaetulians,[9] or from the inland territories of the Nasamones. From the Syrtica Regio came the *syrtitis*, a honey-coloured sard (?);[10] while the heliotropes which the Carthaginian merchant exposed for sale in Mediterranean markets had their origin in Aethiopia and Libya Interior.[11] The ebony of Southern Aethiopia of which Herodotus knew,[12] and the rhinoceros horns which Ptolemy mentions in speaking of that vague but sub-Ṣaḥaran region which he called Agisymba,[13] were also probably brought the long way northward by the Libyan caravans. From the littoral zone, moreover, came the famous *thyon* or *citrus* wood, for which the Romans of the Empire paid prices so exorbitant. The best quality was grown in the Oasis of Sîwah, but the wood was found also in Southern Cyrenaica.[14] Finally, from the south came the thin but unending stream

[1] For these *emporia*, C. Perroud, *op. cit. passim*; and the *Carte des Emporia Punica*, *ad finem*.

[2] E. de la Primaudaie, *Le Littoral de la Tripolitaine*, p. 133.

[3] As in the extreme west at the Atlantic port of Cerne. Scylax § 112; cf. C. Perroud, *op. cit.* p. 149.

[4] Herodotus iv. 181, 182, 183 *et alibi*; Pliny xxxi. 7.

[5] C. Perroud, *op. cit.* p. 144.

[6] Theophrastus, *Frag.* ii. 3; cf. L. Marcus, *Histoire des Wandales, etc.*, p. 216; C. Tissot, *Géographie comparée, etc.*, vol. i. p. 269 *sq.*

[7] Pliny xxxvii. 7.

[8] Strabo xvii. pp. 830, 835; cf. Pliny *loc. cit.*

[9] Strabo xvii. p. 835, . . . ἡ δ' ὑπὲρ τῶν Γαιτούλων ἐστὶν ἡ τῶν Γαραμάντων γῆ παράλληλος ἐκείνῃ, ὅθεν οἱ Καρχηδόνιοι κομίζονται λίθοι. Pliny (*loc. cit.*) says that carbuncles were found among the Aethiopians and the Garamantes, and among the hills of the Nasamones. The last named people believed them to be of divine origin, and sought them at the full of the moon,—*nascitur* [*scil.* the carbuncle] *apud Nasamonas in montibus, ut incolae putant, imbre divino. Inveniuntur ad repercussum lunae maxime plenae. . . .*

[10] Pliny xxxvii. 10.

[11] Solinus, p. 138.

[12] Herodotus iii. 14.

[13] Ptolemy i. 8 § 4.

[14] C. Tissot, *op. cit.* vol. i. p. 278 *sqq.*

of slaves to be bought of their captors or first purchasers by the Punic dealers, and by them sold in their own or in foreign markets.[1] Herodotus gives some indication as to the manner in which the supply was kept up. "The Garamantes," he remarks, "have four-horse chariots in which they pursue the Troglodyte Aethiopians, who of all nations whereof any account has reached our ears, are by far the fleetest of foot."[2] The history of the Chad–Tripoli Road, could it be written, would be, from prehistoric to modern times, a continuous record of obscure misery and suffering.

Little direct evidence as to the imports for which the Eastern Libyans bartered the products of their country and of Aethiopia exists. Like all barbarians, they doubtless set such store by the manufactures of civilized countries[3] as greatly to reward those who traded to them.[4] In mediaeval and modern times the Venetians imported into

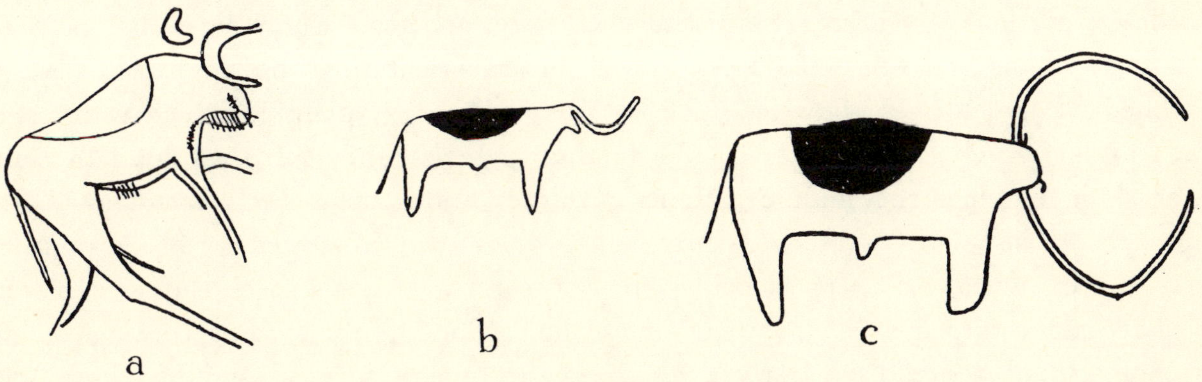

FIG. 9.

Tripolitana glass, corals, silks, and brocades, brasil-wood, wines, iron (in large quantities), helmets and shields, spears and other weapons, lead, tin, copper, and mercury, planks and wood-work.[5] Some of these commodities appear to have been imported in much earlier times. Thus, even on the Atlantic seaboard, Athenian potteries and wine-jars, Phoenician perfumes and glass-ware from Egypt were traded to the Libyans by the Carthaginians.[6] It seems probable also that the Eastern Libyans received their better sorts of cloth from overseas, as well as their weapons of bronze and their vessels of silver.

The means of African transport before the introduction of the camel have already been touched on in the first chapter. Burdens were either imposed directly on the *ḥamlah* oxen or drawn along by them in wains or tumbrils. Saddled oxen are shown in the Barrebi and other petroglyphs of prehistoric date (Fig. 9), while similar rock-drawings at Anai in Fezzan show the ancient caravaneers marching alongside of their

[1] Cf. Terence, *Eunuchus*, Act i. Sc. 2, Act iii. Sc. 2; C. Perroud, *op. cit.* p. 145.

[2] Herodotus iv. 183.

[3] C. Perroud, *op. cit.* p. 149 *sq.* Perroud justly observes: *omnia sane quae in Europa Asiaque fabricata, barbaros sollicitabant.*

[4] Cf. H. Duveyrier, *op. cit.* p. 258, *les bénéfices du commerce saharien sont énormes.*

[5] G. Filiasi, *Sull' antico commercio . . . dei Veneziani*, p. 23; E. de la Primaudaie, *op. cit.* p. 132.

[6] Scylax § 112; cf. C. Perroud, *loc. cit.* The commodities mentioned were exchanged at Cerne for local products.

labouring cattle, which draw behind them clumsy wains.[1] In Asben, the Chad regions, and Kordofan, it may be remarked, porterage by oxen is still in vogue.

In connection with the subject of Ṣaḥaran traffic, it is interesting to recall here Herodotus's famous story of the five Nasamonian youths who adventured from their own country into Nigritia. Although the motive of their journeying was not trade, but a desire to know more of the interior, some idea of the great distances anciently traversed safely to the interior may be gained from the narrative of the historian. Herodotus[2] was told by certain Cyreneans, who had visited the sanctuary of Amon at Sîwah, and there talked with the local chief "Etearchus" (Ἐτέαρχος Ἀμμωνίων βασιλεύς) about the Nile sources, the following story.

Some Nasamones had once come to the court of Etearchus, where they told him that some of the sons of their chiefs had drawn lots for five of their number to explore the desert portions of Libya. Furnished with water and food, the five youths traversed the littoral zone and the "wild-beast tract," and then, entering the uninhabited waste, marched forward toward the west. At last they came to a plain in which were trees, the fruit of which they gathered. While thus engaged, they were captured by some dwarfish men under the middle height. Neither knew the other's language. The captors took the youths across wide marshlands to a town inhabited by black pigmies, who impressed the prisoners as being great sorcerers. After a space the youths were released, and returned safely to their own land. The pigmy town, according to the explorers, stood beside a great river which ran from east to west, and in which were crocodiles. This stream Herodotus believed to be the Nile; but if the statement as to direction be correct, and if the geography of the Ṣaḥaran borderlands has not greatly changed within the (geologically) short time of twenty-five centuries, it appears that conditions were such that five adventurers[3] were able to journey safely from the Syrtic coast to the Upper Niger and back—a state of affairs which prevailed only with limitations in modern times.

The Libyan trader, however, both along the shore and in the hinterland, was even in pre-Islamic times exposed to grave dangers. Caravan-robbing and piracy by wrecking were features of the life of the Eastern Libyans which the student of their economy cannot ignore. It could not have been long after the establishment of the Chad–Mediterranean traffic before the lawless tribes occupying the habitable areas along the caravan lines began to take advantage of their position to pillage the rich bullock-trains which painfully wended their way to or from the Sudan. After the introduction of the camel these raids probably became more frequent, on account, on the one hand, of the increased communication between north and south, and, on the other, of the fact that the robbers could more rapidly move from one point to another, fall upon a *ḳafilah* by surprise, and escape across the desert. By Roman times highway

[1] H. Duveyrier, *op. cit.* pp. 221. There were many oxen suitable for similar work among the Aethiopians; cf. Herodotus iv. 183; for *plaustra*, Silius Italicus, *Punica*, iii. 299; and cf. *infra*, p. 149 *sq.*

[2] Herodotus ii. 32 *sq.*

[3] Of the size of the escort nothing is said.

robbery in the interior had become so prevalent that it was necessary to check it by punitive expeditions on a large scale.

The Libyan chieftains had strongholds in which they stored the superfluous parts of their booty—τὰ πλεονάζοντα ὠφελείας.[1] Diodorus, who supplies this information, adds that the Libyans have neither rulers nor laws—a somewhat exaggerated statement—but live by rapine, suddenly raiding in from the desert—ἐκ τῆς ἐρήμου—to which they as swiftly retreat.[2] So seriously did these forays affect Roman trade with the interior that, as early as the end of Caesar's lifetime, a punitive column was despatched against the Garamantes.[3] Later, in the year 18 B.C., a second and much more important expedition, under the conduct of Cornelius Balbus, penetrated into Phazania, and there subdued many strongholds and tribes of marauders. The account left by Pliny of these difficult operations makes it clear that they were undertaken because of the incessant plundering along the trade-ways.[4] The two remarkable journeys of Septimius Flaccus and of Julius Maternus to Aethiopia,[5] made at a later date,[6] were probably both undertaken to prevent caravan-robbing. The second of these expeditions is of especial interest, since Maternus, who had marched from Leptis Magna to Garama, there joined forces with the chief of the Garamantes against the Aethiopians. As at an earlier date Garama had been one of the towns taken by Balbus,[7] it is clear that since the time of that reprisal the Garamantes had become sensible of the benefits of the regular caravan traffic, and were anxious to keep the roads open, even to the far south.

In the littoral trade the ancient shipmaster had reason to dread not only the ordinary dangers of Syrtic navigation but the wreckers with whom parts of the coast were infested. The Nasamones seem to have been the most active of these "Barbary pirates" of classical antiquity. Their depredations appear to have been confined to wrecking, their shelterless coasts affording more opportunity for this form of piracy than for that practised by the Carian sea-rovers, whose harbours gave them snug shelter, and who preyed on an established commerce instead of on such casual navigators as those who skirted the eastern shores of the Syrtis Major. The Nasamones, however, must have made the best of their limited opportunities, to judge by the "bad eminence" which they achieved, and by the strong measures which were taken against them by the Romans. The

. . . aequoreus Nasamon, invadere fluctu
Audax naufragia et praedes avellare ponto . . .,

of Silius Italicus[8] is so associated in the poet's mind with wrecking that he describes

[1] Diodorus Siculus iii. 49. 3.
[2] *Ibid.* iii. 69. 2.
[3] L. Annaeus Florus iv. 12. The fact only, without details, is there recorded.
[4] Pliny v. 5; F. Borsari, *Geografia etnologica della Tripolitania*, p. 202 *sqq.*; Vergil (*Aeneis*, vi. 794 *sqq.*) is probably referring to the expedition of Balbus in the phrase :—

. . . super Garamantas et Indos
Proferet imperium.

[5] Marinus Tyrius *ap.* Ptolemy i. 8. 5.
[6] Else they would almost certainly have been noticed by Pliny.
[7] Pliny, *loc. cit.*
[8] Silius Italicus iii. 320 *sq.*

even a Nasamonian chief in the Carthaginian service as

Audax in fluctu laceras captare carinas.[1]

An earlier poet had already written

. . . *cum toto commercia mundo*
Naufragi Nasamones habent.[2]

The predatory habits of the Nasamones are further signalized by Quintus Curtius,[3] and the very curious manner in which the tribe is said by Silius to have disposed of its dead[4] is further evidence, quite irrespective of the truth or falsity of the poet's account, that, in Roman opinion, the Nasamones were associated with the sea, and in no creditable manner. Presumably it was in some attempt to regulate affairs in the Syrtic Gulf that two Roman *quaestors* in the time of Domitian lost their lives. For this last outrage a force under the *praetor* of Numidia was despatched against the wreckers. The Nasamones took the camp of the *praetor*, but became so drunk on the wine they found there that the Roman commander, returning, fell upon them and crushed them. Thereafter, it may be supposed, Syrtic trade was on a somewhat better footing, though the barbarians continued to exist, despite Domitian's casual remark to the Senate that "he had forbidden the Nasamones to live."[5]

All Libyan trade was conducted by barter until, perhaps, late classical times. It has been repeatedly stated by a number of writers[6] that the Libyans of the Egyptian invasions had "money," an error which arose from an early mis-translation of an item in the Egyptian lists of spoil. It is needless to remark that no hieroglyphic word for "money" existed at the time of the invasions any more than, among the people of the Mediterranean at that epoch, the thing itself. If any fixed standard of exchange, either in animals or by weight of metal, existed among the Eastern Libyans in early times, no evidence of it remains; although in the dumb-trade carried on by the Carthaginians with the Libyans west of the Pillars of Heracles, commodities were exchanged by the buyer's offering gold for the goods of the seller until a bargain was struck.[7]

There is no evidence that even in full classical times any of the Eastern Libyans had a currency of their own, except in one doubtful instance. This is that of the Macae, to whom have been attributed certain coins in silver and bronze struck after 200 B.C., and bearing in some cases the legend ΛΙΒΥΩΝ on the reverse, together with the letter M or the Phoenician מ.[8] The coins of the Syrtica Regio, however, of which

[1] Silius Italicus i. 409. [2] Lucan ix. 432 *sq.* . [3] Q. Curtius iv. 7. [4] Silius Italicus xiii. 480 *sq.*

[5] Johannes Zonaras, *Annal.* xi. 19 (p. 500); cf. Dionysius, *Periegesis*, 208 *sqq.*:—

κεῖνον δ' αὖ περὶ χῶρον ἐρημωθέντα μέλαθρα
ἀνδρῶν ἀθρήσειας ἀποφθιμένων Νασαμώνων
οὓς Διὸς οὐκ ἀλέγοντας ἀπώλεσεν Αὐσονὶς αἰχμή.

Διός here = Domitian. For the date, Eusebius, *Chronic. ad ann. Abrah.* 2101 = A.D. 86, where the defeats of the Nasamones and the Dacians are mentioned.

[6] Recently by H. Weisgerber, *Les Blancs d'Afrique*, p. 29 and n. 1. The slightest acquaintance with the early history of numismatics should have prevented this error from having ever been perpetrated in the first instance, or repeated later.

[7] Herodotus iv. 196. Gold having had a standard value among the Carthaginians, the Atlantic Libyans with whom they traded must have come to have a rough appreciation of its value.

[8] C. L. Müller, *op. cit.* vol. i. p. 132; B. V. Head, *Historia Numorum*, p. 735.

these are probably a specimen, can hardly be called Libyan, since they owed their origin to the Phoenicians, the Greeks, or the Romans.

In general, if one considers the trade of the Eastern Libyans from an economic point of view, it may be said to have been always of a primitive character. The exports were natural products—either luxuries like ebony, ivory, ostrich plumes, or the skins of wild beasts, or coarse products like hides or salt. The imports were arms and other objects of metal, foreign cloth fabrics, potteries, glass, and all such objects as the Libyans desired but knew not how to make. The effect of such a trade on the natives can be only roughly summarized. Those of the littoral became slightly more advanced than those of the interior, especially as they came into direct contact with foreigners. The caravans to and from the Sudan led to the gradual growth of trade-towns like Cydamus (Ghadames) or Garama (Ghermah), where exchanges could be made and goods left in bond. The Chad–Tripoli road, also, excited the rapacity of the wild tribesmen of the interior, who sought to rifle the passing *ḳafilas*. This in time led to the institution which now exists of paying tolls for protection within a given area; an arrangement by which the various tribes through whose districts the caravans passed derived a surer revenue than that extracted by violence.[1] The trade-routes and the stations which grew up along them must be regarded as civilizing elements in Eastern Libya as elsewhere; but as in modern, so too—and in a greater degree—in ancient times, the European or Asiatic products introduced into Ṣaḥaran Africa affected but little the great body of the people. Where to-day a chief in Kanem has an obsolete musket, one of his predecessors two thousand years ago may have been the proud owner of a cheap Carthaginian corselet. These enviable possessions then, as now, were beyond the reach of common tribesmen. In the trade-towns, a little more sharpness and intelligence, a greater power of combination, and less of the *prisca fides* were probably to be found than in the *gebel*; and in the north, the Libyans of the littoral zone, aping and mingling with the foreign colonists, strengthened their hands with weapons from overseas, but became to a greater extent softened under the influence of foreign luxuries.

[1] Cf. H. Duveyrier, *Les Touareg du Nord*, p. 259.

CHAPTER V

SOCIETY AND GOVERNMENT

To form a just opinion of the sociology and government of the Eastern Libyans, it is best to begin with a consideration of the family. After an examination of the evidence on this question, on marriage, and on the duties and status of women, the problem of government, in its various aspects, can be discussed more profitably.

Although the modern Berber seems indifferent to the marital opportunities sanctioned by Islam, there is no question but that his ancestors were regularly and extensively polygamous. The monumental testimony on this head, as afforded by certain ancient representations of Libyan families,[1] may be set aside in face of the direct, ample, and conclusive testimony of the Egyptian inscriptions and the Greek and Roman writers.

Sallust sensibly remarks that among the Mauri, *i.e.* the native Africans, political marriages were of little value, "since every man has as many wives as he pleases, in proportion to his ability to maintain them; some ten, others more, but the kings most of all. Thus the affection of the husband is divided among a multitude; no one of them becomes a companion to him,[2] but all are equally neglected."[3] This gives force to the answer returned by certain tribesmen to the Byzantine general, Solomon, when he had written to them threatening their hostages. "It is for you," retorted the Libyans, "who cannot have more than one wife, to be concerned with the care of your children; but we, who are able to have, if we wish, fifty wives, are not apprehensive of lacking descendants."[4] This retort is preserved by Procopius, who in the same passage mentions the polygamy of a chieftain called Medisinisas.[5] Strabo states that the Libyans of the interior (where the primitive marriage customs would naturally be best preserved) married numerous wives, and had large families.[6] Mela also, writing of the nomads, observes that each man has several wives at once, and therefore so many children and relatives that the family groups were by no means small ones.[7] Each man of the

[1] Sa-hu-re; Benî Ḥasan; Slunt sculptures.

[2] . . . *nulla pro socia obtinet.* ("*Obtinet*" here absolute as in Livy xxi. 46, . . . *fama obtinet.*)

[3] Sallust, *Iugurtha*, lxxx.

[4] Procopius, *De bello Vandalico*, ii. 11.

[5] *Ibid. loc. cit.*

[6] Strabo xvii. p. 835.

[7] Mela i. 8.

Nasamones, according to Herodotus, had several wives,[1] and further evidence as to Libyan polygamy is derivable from Egyptian sources. The great Karnak inscription of Merneptah says that Meryey, the leader of the Libyans, was accompanied in his campaign by his wife (singular) and his sons;[2] but although only one wife is here mentioned, it is reasonable to infer, if the record is to be taken literally, that the six sons of Meryey were all *men*,[3] and that the chieftain had, or at least had had, other wives, since for one woman among a primitive people to be the mother of six adult males is exceptional in itself, and because it would be yet more extraordinary, supposing she were so in fact, that she should be young enough to accompany her husband on a dangerous and arduous military expedition. The real state of affairs is made clear by a brief item in the Karnak list of prisoners taken by the victorious troops of Merneptah: "Women of the fallen chief of Libya, whom he brought with him . . . 12 Libyan women."[4] Meryey's "wife," therefore, was probably merely the chief lady of the *ḥarîm* in which some of his six sons were born.

In the second Libyan war of Rameses III., as in the earlier invasion under Meryey, the chieftains were accompanied by their women. Kepper, son of Ded, for example, had his "son, wife [sing.], and family"[5] with him in the field. But beside his chief wife he, like Meryey, had also his *ḥarîm*, two references being made to his women in different texts.[6] Three hundred and forty-two wives of chiefs were captured by the Egyptians in this war, together with sixty-five unmarried women and one hundred and fifty-one girls. These latter belonged to the chiefs' families, the male captives of which numbered one hundred and thirty-one boys.[7] These numbers must, of course, include the families of more chiefs than the six who were mentioned in the lists, but must equally have been the families of men of rank; as is indeed distinctly stated with regard to the three hundred and forty-two wives. The twelve hundred and five men taken captive, as well as those slain, appear to have had no women with them in the field.

Further evidence may be gathered from the Serapeum Stela of Harpeson (XXIInd Dynasty), and from the Piankhi Stela (XXIIIrd Dynasty). The former of these documents contains the genealogy of Harpeson, who derived his origin from a family of Libyan settlers in the Egyptian Delta.[8] It is to be noted that in it no husband is recorded as having more than one wife—perhaps because the family, under Egyptian influence, became quasi-monogamous, perhaps because only those women through whom Harpeson descended were deemed worthy of mention. Perhaps each lady mentioned was in her time chief lady of the *ḥarîm*, and no other names were given.

[1] Herodotus iv. 172.

[2] BAR iii. §§ 579, 601 (Athribis Stela); cf. § iii. 595 (Cairo Column), where the presence of women among the invaders is noticed.

[3] BAR iii. § 588; confirmed by Cairo Column, BAR iii. § 601.

[4] BAR iii. 601; cf. BAR iii. § 610 (Israel Stela) . . . "his women were taken before his face."

[5] BAR iv. § 103.

[6] BAR iii. §§ 601, 610.

[7] BAR iv. § 111. The Papyrus Harris, speaking in briefer and more general terms, says merely that Rameses III. took captive the wives and children of the Meshwesh.

[8] BAR iv. § 787. In eleven instances the name of the wife appears with that of her husband.

At any rate, the Piankhi Stela discloses the fact that in addition to their chief ladies, the Libyan dynasts of the Delta had other wives in their *ḥarîms*. Thus the chief lady of Namlot, whose overthrow by the Aethiopian monarch is narrated in the stela of the latter, was the queen Nestent. Visiting the palace of his vanquished enemy, however, Piankhi "caused that there be brought to him the king's wives and king's daughters,"[1] who tried, though with poor success, to amuse the Aethiopian Pharaoh. This may be regarded as summing up what is known of Libyan marriage relations; the people were extensive polygamists, within those *ḥarîms* some one wife occupied a position of pre-eminence much like that of a first wife in a modern Moslem household of the better class.

It is not surprising that the facts, being what they were, should have been grossly misrepresented by monogamous Greeks or Romans who had only a slight acquaintance with African matters. Even modern European travellers have occasionally described this or that form of group-marriage which they have noticed among some primitive people as "irregular promiscuity"; although such a condition does not really exist in the world.[2] Similarly a Roman writer declares that the Garamantes had no marriage institutions;[3] and Herodotus, who has been quoted as testifying to the polygamy of the Nasamones, tells with regard to the latter people much the same story. The Greek historian states that the Nasamones, in their intercourse with their wives, resembled the Massagetae.[4] The marriage customs of the latter people he elsewhere characterizes by saying that although each man is married, he promiscuously enjoys the wives of his fellow tribesmen.[5] This is practically placing at one stroke two peoples in a state which even among the most primitive savages does not exist to-day. Herodotus is here certainly wrong with regard to the Nasamones, and probably also with regard to the Massagetae. Of the Gindanes, Herodotus more credibly states that their women wear on their legs anklets of leather; that each lover a woman has gives her one of these tokens; and that she who can show the most trophies is best esteemed, as she has been sought by the greatest number of men.[6] This story may relate to some such practice of girls obtaining a dowry by prostitution as that in vogue among the Aulad Nayl (Berbers) of the present time. A third charge of promiscuity is brought by Herodotus against the Auseans. He says of that people that they do not marry, but dwell together like gregarious animals; and that their children, when full-grown, are assigned by the tribal assembly to the parents they most resemble.[7] Here, again, arises the initial improbability as to any society's having ever been really promiscuous; and the difficulty, supposing such a state to have existed, of understanding what relationship obtained between the "parents" to whom the children were assigned.

[1] BAR iv. § 849.

[2] J. Deniker, *Races of Man*, p. 231 and notes.

[3] Martianus Capella, *De nuptiis Mercurii, etc.*, iv. (p. 232), *Garamantes vulgo feminis sine matrimonio sociantur.*

[4] Herodotus iv. 172.

[5] *Ibid.* i. 216.

[6] *Ibid.* iv. 176.

[7] *Ibid.* iv. 180; cf. Nicolaus Damascenus, *Frag.* 111 in *FHG*, where much the same story is told of the Liburnians. Λιβύρνιοι should be emended to Λίβυες.

With regard to these errors, which have been too readily credited by certain modern writers, two more points may here be mentioned. The first is the absurdity of supposing that a promiscuous people should have any consciousness of virginity, apart from the physical fact of it. What may be called the moral consciousness of virginity existed, however, among the Eastern Libyans, as in the case of those very Auseans whose marriage customs Herodotus so misunderstood. The Ausean mock-fight, held annually in honour of "Athene," was (*a*) supposed to be performed by virgins, and (*b*) if any participant received hurts from which she died, she was therefore accounted no true maid. Among this people, who felt that an absence of virginity in the person of a participant in a certain religious rite would be punished with death,[1] Herodotus would have his readers believe that there prevailed absolutely unrestricted intercourse between the sexes! The second is that the predominance of *manes*-cultus throughout ancient North Africa testifies to the existence of well-defined ideas of kinship; ideas which could only have existed among a people which fully recognized some form of marriage by which blood-relationships could be easily traced.

Of the marriage customs of the Eastern Libyans but few are known. The Adyrmachidae brought all women about to be married to their king, that he might cohabit with such as were agreeable to him.[2] Among the Augilae it was customary for every bride to prostitute herself on her wedding night to all who paid for the privilege, maugre which, and despite the fact that to have had intercourse with many men on that occasion was deemed a great honour, the woman thereafter remained faithful to her husband.[3] The first of these customs, recalling the *droit de cuissage* of feudal France, may have had its origin in a religious fear of accepting the responsibility of defloration.[4] The second seems allied to the customs of the ancient Gindanes and the modern Aulad Nayl, mentioned above. Even obscurer than these notices is that which states that among the Machlyes, when a girl has several suitors, the men feast with her father or a kinsman, and that thereafter each suitor in turn jests and makes merry before the maiden, who becomes the wife of him who provokes her to laughter![5]

Before leaving this subject, it is necessary to touch briefly on an allied topic: that of the matriarchate. Many modern writers are convinced that this state prevailed in the earliest stages of Libyan society, and it cannot be denied that indications that this was the case are strong, if not conclusive. That sociological condition in which the true head of the family is not the father but the mother has been and yet is widespread in

[1] Cf. the strong sense of virginity among the Atarantians of the Moghreb. Nicolaus Damascenus, *Frag.* 140 in *FHG*.

[2] Herodotus iv. 168.

[3] Mela i. 8.

[4] Defloration before marriage is among some primitive peoples an obligatory act. Among the Bataks and Pelew Islanders it is performed by the parents; among the Bisayas of the Philippines, by the matrons; in Cambodia, by the priests. The Adyrmachid kings, like the Cambodian priests, may have acted as sacred men who could destroy virginity with impunity. Cf. G. A. Wilken, *Volkenkunde van Nederlandsch-Indië*, p. 294; Giraud-Teulon, *Origines du mariage*, p. 33, note; J. Deniker, *op. cit.* p. 230.

[5] Nicolaus Damascenus, *Frag.* 136 in *FHG*. This passage recalls those European folk-tales in which a sad or solemn princess is won by that suitor who makes her laugh. For examples see P. C. Asbjörnsen, *Folk and Faery Tales*, p. 269; J. and W. Grimm, *Household Tales*, vol. i. p. 32. For these references I have to thank my father, Dr. Arlo Bates.

Africa. Thus, the matriarchate is known to have existed in Aethiopia,[1] as in the Meroitic kingdom;[2] and there is no doubt that it flourished in early Egypt.[3] Among many Negritians of the Sudan the matriarchate still persists;[4] among the Berbers of the present time are what appear to be matriarchal survivals. Thus the Imushagh explain their abstention from fish, birds, and edible lizards on the score that these (totemic) animals are "their mothers' brothers," a form of expression emphatically matriarchal.[5] Among the Imushagh, also, the laws of succession, as seen in the case of the Azgar chieftainships, are sometimes based on the matriarchal principle of *partus sequitur ventrem*; a principle not in harmony with the Ḳuran, and therefore probably pre-Islamic in its origin. Those Imushagh whose laws of inheritance have the matriarchal cast call their institution for the transmission of property the law Benî-Ummîah (بنى وممّية), *i.e.* the law *of the Mother's children*, and are themselves said to be Benî-Ummîah Imushagh. According to the Benî-Ummîah all property falls into two divisions: (*a*) that acquired by individual work, and (*b*) that acquired by violence, and called *ehere n butelma*, or "fruits (lit. 'goods') of wrong-doing." On the death of the (male) head of a family, all the property of class (*a*) is divided equally among the children of the deceased, without regard to primogeniture or sex. The property of class (*b*) passes, without division or diminution, *to the eldest son of the eldest sister of the deceased*.[6] This practice existed formerly not only among the northern Imushagh, but also among those known as the Massufa, west of Timbuktu, and was therefore both widespread and of early origin. It is almost certainly a matriarchal survival. In ancient times an Egyptian notice records that, on the defeat of a Libyan chief, one of his brothers, in preference to a son, was installed in his place;[7] a Greek writer records that a number of Libyan tribes had as a common ancestor a "nymph" whom he styles Amphithemis;[8] and a vague story was current in Roman times to the effect that in Libya was a tribe, the Byaei, in which the women were ruled by a woman, the men by a man.[9] The survival, even to a period as late as Graeco-Roman times, of the matriarchate among the less advanced tribes would account for the lengthy and curious relation of Diodorus Siculus concerning the Amazons of North Africa.[10]

[1] Nicolaus Damascenus, *Frag.* 142 in *FHG.*

[2] Cf. Diodorus Siculus i. 33, and the relative prominence given to the *Candacae* as compared to their male consorts in the Meroitic reliefs.

[3] R. I. Fruin, *De Manethone*, etc., p. 20 (*Recensio Africani*), Βινῶθρις . . . ἐφ' οὗ ἐκρίθη τὰς γυναῖκας βασιλείας γέρας ἔχειν. The *Recens. Eusebii* (p. 21) gives . . . Βίοφις . . . ἐκρίθη καὶ τὰς . . . κτλ. Βινῶθρις = Baneteren. Cf. J. H. Breasted, *History of Egypt*, p. 85 *sq.*; W. M. F. Petrie, *History of Egypt*, vol. i. p. 21.

[4] E.-F. Gautier, *Sahara algérien*, p. 138; W. Bosman, *Voyage de Guinée*, p. 197 *sq.* Cf. for Central Africa, P. du Chaillu, *Voyages dans l'Afrique équatoriale*, p. 282.

[5] E.-F. Gautier, *loc. cit.*; H. Duveyrier, *Les Touareg du Nord*, p. 401 *sq.*, noted the taboos, but could get no explanation for them.

[6] H. Duveyrier, *op. cit.* p. 393 *sqq.* The Imushagh who are Benî-Ummîah have an amusing story to account for the origin of this custom. It is well told by Duveyrier, p. 398 *sq.*, but is unfortunately too long to be introduced here.

[7] BAR iii. § 585.

[8] Agroetas, *Frag.* 1 in *FHG.*

[9] Nicolaus Damascenus, *Frag.* 133 in *FHG.*, ἐν Βυαίοις Λίβυσιν ἀνὴρ μὲν ἀνδρῶν βασιλεύει, γυνὴ δὲ γυναικῶν.

[10] Diodorus Siculus iii. 53 *sq.* This evidence has been adduced by D. R. MacIver and A. Wilkin (*Libyan Notes*, p. 4 *sq.*), in connection with the matriarchate, but the other evidence is not presented.

According to this writer, there dwelt in the extreme west of Libya an ἔθνος γυναικοκρατούμενον,[1] an Amazonian race, where the usual status of the sexes was reversed. The "history" of the Amazons, it is needless to say, is pure fiction; the very existence of a nation of fighting women and spinning men is in itself an absurdity; but the length and nature of Diodorus's story point, in conjunction with the evidence cited, and with the fact that both in Berber legend and folk-lore,[2] as well as in authentic history, women figure prominently, to the probability that the matriarchate was at some early period widely established among the primitive North Africans.

The occupations of the Libyan women are of interest from the sociological point of view, but the information on the subject is small. The daily life of the female members of any ancient North African community must, however, have been much what it is at the present time. The women must have prepared and cooked the food, milked the flocks, and, among the more advanced tribes, done the weaving—the last a somewhat laborious process even to this day among the Berbers, who do not, as a rule, employ shuttles. The baskets in which the Libyan women represented in a Benî Ḥasan painting are seen carrying their children on their backs are doubtless the work of their own hands. Of their care for their children but one particular is known—the latter were in most tribes regularly cauterized when four years old with a flock of wool on the top of the head, or about the veins of the temple. "This they do," says Herodotus, "to prevent them from being in their after lives plagued by a flow of rheum from the head; and such, they declare, is the reason why they are so much more healthy than other men."[3] If the child had a fit during the cauterization, the native remedy was to sprinkle it with the stale of a goat.[4] It need hardly be said that firing, both as a curative and as a preventative measure, is at present universally employed, and in some cases with good results, throughout North Africa and the Sudan. Probably most of these operations were in the hands of the women, who would be skilled in simples like the wives of the modern nomads.

The status of women was undoubtedly a good one. It will appear later that they had a real share both in the religious and in the political life of the people, and as represented on the Egyptian monuments they were as well off for personal ornaments as were the men.[5] It is probable that the matriarchate bequeathed to them exceptional privileges, and it is perhaps for this reason that the chiefs' women of the Sa-hu-re reliefs are portrayed as wearing the *penistasche*, a distinctly masculine article of attire which will be described in the section on dress. One of the Medînet Habu tiles also shows a Libyan woman in male dress, in this case the kilt and robe, though from the Slunt sculptures and from a painting at Benî Ḥasan the true feminine dress is known to have been a kirtle belted at the waist. This masquerading in men's garb can have been done

[1] Diodorus Siculus iii. 53. 1. [2] H. Duveyrier, *op. cit.* p. 400 *sq.* [3] Herodotus iv. 187.

[4] *Ibid. loc. cit.*; cf. Oribasius, *Collect. medic.* p. 45, where the Libyans are said to reduce fevers by the drinking of goat's stale, a practice said to have been followed by the Greek physician Evenor.

[5] BAR iii. § 584, for a notice of a woman's gear.

for but one reason, viz. because upon the wife of a chieftain male costume was a badge of dignity. It is in precisely the same spirit that Hatshepsut appears on the monuments of her reign in male attire, and that the queens of Meroë are sometimes sculptured as wearing beards.

After questions of the family, and the status of women, comes naturally that of government. Living in a tribal state, the Eastern Libyans were ruled by chieftains whose powers seem to have ranged from those of the modern Bedawîn sheykh to those invested in some of the great sedentary emîrs of Northern Arabia. The statement of Mela to the effect that the interior tribes lived dispersed in families, without laws, and without undertaking anything in common—*in familias passim et sine lege dispersi nihil in commune consultant*[1]—is but partially true ; it is to be accepted merely as a testimony to the laxness of the social institutions of the people.

The Libyan chieftainship was apparently hereditary within a family ; the general practice seems to have been to bestow it on an individual who had acquired a reputation for justice ;[2] but the holder of the office might be required, if unsatisfactory, to abdicate in favour of a kinsman.[3] This happened in the case of a great chief not of a tribe merely but of a confederacy. As has been said above, the Libyan emîr Meryey, after his defeat at the hands of the Egyptians, was dispossessed, and one of his brothers put in his place.[4]

The chiefs both of tribes and confederacies were assisted in some, if not in all, cases by councils. Rameses III. caused to be brought before him the captive "tens" of his Libyan enemies, these "tens" being councillors.[5] Among the Auseans a council, apparently of all full-grown men, assembled every third month, *i.e.* once in each season of the year.[6] Therefore what seems to have been an ancient usage has to-day its parallel among the Imushagh tribes and confederacies of the Ṣaḥara, *e.g.* in the Berbers comprised in the Azgar Confederation. So distinctive and deep-rooted does the government of the Ṣaḥaran Berbers appear that it is advisable to pause here, and to consider for comparative purposes its principal characteristics as exhibited in the Kel Azgar[7] just mentioned.

The first noteworthy point is that, like all the Imushagh, the Azgar are formed of two elements : (*a*) the aristocratic or noble tribes, *Ihaggaren*, and (*b*) the vassal or servile

[1] Mela i. 8.

[2] The Alitemnii (Ἀλιτέμνιοι Λίβυες = the Ἀλιταμβοί of Ptolemy iv. 6 § 6, a tribe of Libya Interior perhaps to be related to the fleet Troglodytic Aethiopians of Herodotus iv. 183) chose as kings the fleetest among them : to aid him the tribesmen then elected the most just—τὸν δικαιότατον. Nicolaus Damascenus, *Frag.* 138 in *FHG*. Cf. the Alitemnian custom with that of the tall Atlantic Aethiopians, who chose their chiefs for their stature. Scylax § 111.

[3] Pliny, viii. 40, has a curious story of a deposed king of the Garamantes who regained his position with the help of an army of two hundred dogs—a native folk-tale, obviously, suggesting many parallels.

[4] BAR iii. § 586.

[5] BAR iv. § 42. The word  *var.*  may mean either "councillors" or "nobles." Cf. G. Maspero, *Études égyptiennes*, vol. ii. p. 197 *sqq.*; H. Brugsch, *Hieroglyphisch-demotisches Wörterbuch*, *Suppl.*, p. 927 *sq.* That the meaning is here "councillors" is certain for reasons given in BAR, *loc. cit.*, note *c*.

[6] Herodotus iv. 180. The object of the meetings, according to Herodotus, was the assignment of children to parents.

[7] *Kel*, كل = people, *gens*.

tribes, *Imghad*. The latter pay tribute or service in various ways to the former, and lack certain privileges ; in some cases, for instance, an "ignoble" tribe may not own camels, or, in others, bear arms. This division is explicable on the ground that the *Imghad* are the descendants of a conquered people. But it is necessary to state emphatically that though the division into *Ihaggaren* and *Imghad* is so ancient that the Ṣaḥaran Berbers preserve no knowledge of its origin, there is no textual evidence of it in the Egyptian or classical records. The government of the Azgar is a sort of feudal monarchy, tempered by that deep-rooted spirit of communism to be found among all Berber peoples. Each tribe elects from the members of its ruling family its *amghar* (pl. *imgharen*), or chief. These *imgharen* in turn elect from the members of a "royal" family an *amenukal* (pl. *imenukalen*), or "king," to rule with their help and at their pleasure, over the whole confederacy. In the case of misconduct, the *amenukal* is deposed, and in this case, or when he is deceased, the natural heir to the office, who must be confirmed by the *imgharen*, is not the son of the late "king," but rather the son of the late "king's" eldest sister. This form of succession to power or property is the one usual among the aristocratic Imushagh.

The Azgar Confederacy is thus made up : nine noble tribes, six of which are composed of more than one clan, *Ihaggaren*, and thirty-two ignoble tribes, *Imghad*. As a typical noble tribe may be taken the *Imenghassaten*. The *Imenghassaten* are made up of three divisions, the *Inennakaten*, *Tegehe n abbar*, and the *Tegehe n bedden*. A man of the *Inennakaten* calls himself an *Anennakat*, of the *Imenghassaten* (tribe), of the *Azgar* (Confederacy), of the *Ihaggaren Imoshagh* ("noble" or "free" Tuareg). The tribes of the *Imghad* are generally not subdivided.[1]

Certain features of ancient Libyan government are clearly discernible in the constitution of the Azgar Confederacy. It has already been seen that Meryey, like a modern *amenukal*, might be deposed, that he was succeeded, as would happen to-day, not by a son, but by a kinsman on the distaff side, and that there existed anciently, at least among the Auseans, a council such as that which at present appoints the *imgharen*. Yet another parallel exists in the fact that the chieftainships were anciently, as at present, of different grades. The confederated Meshwesh had an *amenukal* who is recorded in the triumph of Rameses III. as : "Chiefs of the Meshwesh . . . . 1 man."[2] But this head-chief had under his command subordinate chiefs, "leaders of the land of Meshwesh,"[3] "his chiefs,"[4] "chieftains of the enemy."[5] Among the Libyan dynasts of the Delta (XXIIIrd Dynasty), the titles of the rulers show a similar variety. The "king" Namlot, a "Great Chief of the Me(shwesh)," is styled "Great Chief of Chiefs," *i.e. amenukal.*[6] Associated with him is another but less important "king," Yewepet,[7] at the head of the Delta Libyans under their "Great Chiefs of Me(shwesh)" and "Chiefs of Me(shwesh)."[8] The monumental sources also point to the Eastern Libyans

[1] A. Hanoteau, *Grammaire de la langue Tamachek*, p. xv. *sqq.*, for the above outline of the Azgar government.
[2] BAR iv. § 111.
[3] BAR iv. § 112.
[4] BAR iv. § 90.
[5] BAR iv. § 111.
[6] BAR iv. §§ 678, 830.
[7] BAR iv. § 830.
[8] BAR iv. §§ 815, 830.

as having been in Egyptian times under chiefs of various grades—there appears to have been a class of Libyan captains wearing but one ostrich-plume; another which wore two.[1]

It was these differences in rank, which have survived to the present day, that led in classical times to the diversity of terms used by Greek and Roman writers in speaking of Libyan chiefs. Mention is made of "kings" (βασιλεῖς,[2] *reges*[3]); of "dynasts" (δυνάσται[4]); "rulers" (. . . τῶν βαρβάρων τοὺς ἄρχοντας . . .[5]); and of "elders" (*primores*[6]). Comprised in a single work, the *Johannis* of Corippus, are a variety of titles. Libyan chiefs are therein designated by the terms *praefectus*, *regens*, *rex*, *princeps*, or *tyrannus*;[7] and in certainly one instance, and probably in many, these rulers were aided or restrained in their conduct of affairs by a council of notables or sheykhs (*proceres*).[8]

Excepting in a general way, the duties and privileges of the Libyan chiefs are obscure. In the Egyptian records they appear as captains in war, or as councillors of the confederacy. In times of peace their authority was in many cases probably but slight, although even then they enjoyed better food and had better gear than the average tribesman. Thus, among the rudest and poorest Libyans, it was only the chiefs who had mats of skins.[9] The sheykhly office had its tokens in regard to which Procopius has an interesting passage. That writer relates that on one occasion the Tripolitan chiefs came to Belisarius, according to their ancient custom, to be confirmed in their positions, and to receive the official insignia—τὰ γνωρίσματα τῆς ἀρχῆς. These marks of office consisted of:—

1. A silver-gilt sceptre (. . . ῥάβδος τε ἀργυρᾶ κατακεχρυσωμένη).
2. A silver-tissue skull cap (πῖλος ἀργυροῦς) with silver fillets.
3. A white robe, fastening at the shoulder with a golden buckle.
4. A white decorated tunic.
5. A pair of gilded sandals.[10]

Older marks of dignity than these were the ostrich-plume or birds' wings;[11] and the long ornamented robe which a consensus of the monumental evidence and a Roman notice[12] show to have been marks of rank. Tattooing also, and the wearing of ceremonial tails, as will appear later, served to distinguish the Libyan rulers from their subjects. As has been pointed out above, the wives of great chiefs were sometimes dignified with masculine attire.

[1] This is paralleled in the case of the negro tributaries seen on the monuments, *e.g.* LD, *Abth.* iii. pl. 117, where the great chief wears two feathers, his followers one each. Cf. W. M. Müller, *Egyptological Researches*, vol. ii. p. 121.

[2] Cf. Eustathius, *ad Dionysii Perieg.* 209, where the Nasamones are said to derive their name ἔκ τινος βασιλεύσαντος; Herodotus iv. 155, 159, 164, 168. Herodotus (iv. 155) says that in the Libyan tongue the word βάττος signifies "a king." Cf. Hesychius, *in verb.*, which cannot, however, be regarded as independent evidence; and Acesander, *De Cyrene*, *Frag.* 5 in *FHG* = *Schol. in Pind. Pyth.* iv. 1, Λίβυες γὰρ βάττους τοὺς βασιλέας λέγουσιν . . . The origin of this much discussed word is unknown.

[3] Pliny viii. 40 . . . *Garamantum regem.*

[4] Diodorus Sic. iii. 49. 3.

[5] Procopius, *De bello Vandal.* ii. 10.

[6] Mela i. 8.

[7] J. Partsch, *Die Berbern, etc.*, p. 15.

[8] Corippus, *Johannis* iv. 333; J. Partsch, *loc. cit.*

[9] Procopius, *op. cit.* ii. 6.

[10] *Ibid.* i. 25.

[11] *Vide infra*, p. 129; cf. Eustathius, *ad Dionysii Perieg.* 209, and Dio Chrysostomus, *Orat.* 71, *De Corporis Cultu*, vol. ii. p. 383 . . . πτερὰ ἔχοντες ἐπὶ ταῖς κεφαλαῖς ὀρθά, ὥσπερ Νασάμωνες . . . Cf. Corippus, *Johannis* iv. 907 *sq.*, where there seems to be a distinction between a warrior of the common sort and a plumed chieftain (. . . *Tiseras de plebe rebelli Mansitalae pinnatus erat* . . .); *ibid.* iv. 972 (*Pinnatum Antifan* . . .), and vii. 543 (. . . *Alacanza* . . . *pinnatus* . . .); and—in reference to the general Nasamonian custom—*ibid.* vi. 510, *Nasamon pinnatus.* . . .

[12] Mela i. 8 . . . *primores sagis veluntur.*

The ancient evidence suggests that the Libyan chieftainship was often, if not regularly, associated with the priesthood. In the Daḫlah Stela, a document of the XXIIIrd Dynasty, recording a dispute in connection with a well among the half-Egyptianized Libyans of the oasis, is mentioned "the son of the chief of the Me(shwesh); chief of a district; prophet of Hathor; . . . prophet of Sutekh; . . . Wayheset."[1] The same Wayheset is more briefly termed in the same inscription the "prophet and chief Wayheset,"[2] or simply "the chief, Wayheset."[3] That something of the sacred character of the priest-king may be manifested in the Adyrmachid *droit de cuissage* has been already pointed out. A more certain indication of the union of sacred and temporal duties in the person of the chief is seen in the account given by Silius Italicus of the warrior-priest Nabis, a Libyan in the army of Hannibal. Nabis is described as an Ammonian chief, splendidly armed, who, feeling himself under the protection of Amon, rides fearlessly through the thick of battle, shouting the name of his god. From his helm depend the sacred fillets of Amon, and his dress, of which an attempt is made to despoil him at his death, is that of a priest.[4] Iernas, a Syrtic prince who figures in the *Johannis* of Corippus,[5] also appears as a fighting chief and as a priest. The leader, around whom the Berbers of the Aures rallied to withstand the Arabs, was the queen-priestess el-Kahinah;[6] and although this and the evidence already cited are insufficient to prove definitely that any sacred offices were regularly attached to the chieftainship, the other instances in which such was the case encourage the belief that the Libyan kings had religious as well as secular duties.

Little is known of the way in which the conduct of the rulers was ordered so as to differentiate it from that of the simple tribesmen. Doubtless many little observances and restraints marked the chief as clearly as did his material insignia. One curious restriction observed by the Numidian chieftains is mentioned by a Roman writer, who says that the native kings were not allowed to be kissed by any of their subjects because by this the dignity of the ruler would have been impaired.[7]

In conclusion of this brief outline of the sociology and government of the Eastern Libyans, it may be said that the ancient institutions probably differed in no vital way from those of the more primitive Berber tribes of the present day. Of course among the sedentary tribes law and order prevailed to a greater extent than among those "people always ready for rapine and rapid incursions, accustomed to live by plunder and bloodshed,"[8] who dwelt in the interior; and it must not be forgotten that, at the time of the invasions, the power of amalgamation among those Libyans who dwelt within striking distance of Egypt showed itself to be of a very formidable nature.

[1] BAR iv. § 726. [2] BAR iv. § 727. [3] BAR iv. § 728. [4] Silius Italicus xv. 672 *sqq.*

[5] Corippus, *Johannis* ii. 109, iv. 667 *sq.*, 1138, *et alibi*; J. Partsch, *op. cit.* p. 15, notices this indication of theocracy, but has not brought other evidence to bear on the question.

[6] From كهن *praesagivit, hariolatus fuit.* Ibn Ḫaldun, *Kitab el ʿIbar*, trans. vol. i. pp. 213, 340; H. Fournel, *Les Berbers*, vol. i. pp. 215, 218.

[7] Valerius Maximus ii. 6. 17: *Ne Numidiae quidem reges vituperandi, qui more gentis suae nulli mortalium osculum ferebant. Quidquid enim in excelso fastigio positum est, humili et trita consuetudine, quo sit venerabilius, vacuum esse convenit.*

[8] Ammianus Marcellinus xviii. 6. 2. Said of the Ausuriani.

CHAPTER VI

DRESS AND ORNAMENTATION

The Eastern Libyans in general appear to have been but scantily clad; and just as in Arabia even the kings of the Nabataeans wore only sandals and a purple loin-cloth,[1] so in North Africa the majority of the inhabitants wore, even in Roman times, so few clothes as to justify the phrases *nudi Garamantes*[2] and *Nasamon nudus*[3] of the poet Lucan. The Byzantine general Solomon, exhorting his troops, emphasized the fact that the Africans were practically naked;[4] and Procopius remarks that the Libyan dress consisted of but one rough tunic which the wearer did not change within the year.[5] Yet such as it was, perhaps because of its very scantiness, to foreign eyes the African costume was distinctive. Herodotus, writing of the Adyrmachidae, observes that whereas they resembled the Egyptians in their manners, they wore the dress of the Libyans.[6]

The simplest cloth garment of the tribesmen, though by no means the commonest, was the kilt, which in Egyptian representations is seen as early as the XVIIIth Dynasty.[7] A modern writer,[8] to be sure, has cited as an early example of the Libyan kilt a proto-dynastic ivory carving, which he adduces as evidence indicating the Libyan origin of the Egyptian waist-cloth; but as the ivory in question represents not a Libyan but an Asiatic[9] this conclusion cannot be accepted. The best representations are those of the faience tiles from Medînet Habu (XXth Dynasty) shown in the Frontispiece. The Libyan loin-cloth, from these representations, appears as a very simple kilt girded above the waist and hanging to a little above the knee. A detail in the Thothmes IV.

[1] Strabo xvi. p. 784.

[2] Lucan iv. 334; cf. Lucian, *De Dipsadibus* § 2, where the Garamantes are described as an agile, *light-clad* tribe of tent-dwellers.

[3] Lucan xi. 429.

[4] Procopius, *De bello Vandalico* ii. 11.

[5] *Ibid.* ii. 6.

[6] Herodotus iv. 168.

[7] Tell el-Amarna tombs.

[8] W. M. F. Petrie, *Royal Tombs*, Part i. p. 23 *sq.* and Pl. xvii. fig. 30 = Pl. XII. Figs. 12, 13.

[9] The ivory, which Petrie, *loc. cit.*, calls a "gaming-reed," bears an Asiatic ethnic in archaic hieroglyphs. For another error of identification, see idem, *Illahun, Kahun, and Gurob*, pl. xix. fig. 43. It is G. Sergi (*Mediterranean Race*, p. 77, fig. 2), however, who has made the grossest of these mistakes—he has reproduced as "Tamahu" Libyan a typical Syrian head.

panel, given in Fig. 31, shows that the kilt, at least when worn with the *penistasche*, was open in front.

The long robe, which first appears in New Empire times, though not worn by the majority of the Libyans, was at least more common than the kilt. From the statement of Mela,[1] and from a consensus of the monumental evidence, it is clear that the long robe was a mark of dignity and rank; and it was as such that long robes, fastened at the shoulders with golden clasps, were given out to the Libyan princes by the Byzantines, when the former received their annual confirmation in office. The Libyan robe is mentioned by Strabo, who describes it as loose and with wide borders;[2] and in late Roman times Mauri of Corippus are mentioned as wearing the coloured *tunica*[3] or the *stragula*.[4] The cut of these robes, as seen in the Egyptian representations, was obviously derived from the skin cloaks which were worn in classical times. The cloth robe was essentially an elongated piece of stuff, cut wider at the top than at the bottom, so as to fold around the shoulders (Fig. 10, Pl. II. Fig. 3, and Pl. III.). The prolonged corners (tabs) of the upper part were often knotted across the chest as would have been the fore-paws in the case of a skin garment.[5] A more elaborate form had a rudimentary sleeve, and was clasped across one shoulder, as seen in the case of the four Libyans in the painting from the tomb of Seti I. (Plate III.).

FIG. 10.

The robes were regularly open from top to bottom, and ungirt,[6] the belt of the sheath or of the kilt being inside. The stuffs of which the robes were made were sometimes ornamented with coloured designs (*Frontis.* and Plate III.),[7] and were further decorated with applied pieces sewn to the garment, generally in the corners (Plate III., *B*, *D*), or at the waist (Plate III., *A*, *B*, *C*, and the cross on the robe of *D*). The robes were regularly bordered, as Strabo remarked, though the Egyptian notices show no border which could be called "wide";[8] in some cases they were fringed (cf. Figs. 11 and 12).

In late times the tunic seems to have been popular among the more civilized Libyans. Two warriors on a monument of late date, now in Constantinople, are seen

1 Mela i. 8 . . . *primores sagis velantur*, etc.

2 Strabo xvii. p. 828.

3 Corippus, *Johannis* ii. 130 *sqq.*, vii. 189 *sqq.*; cf. Procopius, *De bello Vandalico* ii. 6.

4 Corippus, *Johannis* ii. 134, 181. (*Bene emendavit Petschenig ad locc. citt.*)

5 Cf. the Libyan fallen beneath the feet of the Great Chief, in Plate IV.

6 Cf. Silius Italicus ii. 78 *sq.* As, however, the poet is there speaking of the princess Asbyte, he has probably in mind the typical Amazon of classic art.

7 Cf. also the Libyan captive shown in I. Rosellini, *Monumenti*, vol. ii. p. 91 (second throne from the left).

8 A robe bordered with a yellow stripe (fine lines in red and blue) is shown in J. F. Champollion, *Monuments de l'Égypte, etc.*, vol. i. Pl. 17 (the fallen Libyan).

wearing garments of this sort—a kind of sleeveless shirt belted in at the waist (Fig. 13). Two small Libyco-Roman reliefs of Christian times, discovered by Barth at Shabet Umm el-Ḫarab, show in one case two date-gatherers who are wearing tunics with

Fig. 11.

Fig. 12.

sleeves or half-sleeves (Fig. 14), while in another two men of rank (?) are seen sitting in a small boat, enveloped in long cloaks (Fig. 15). These last examples, however, betray too strong a foreign influence to be regarded as good evidence on African costume.

Fig. 13.

The question arises as to whence were derived the stuffs of the Libyan chieftains' robes. Cloth of good quality was not at any time common throughout Eastern Libya, as is proved by the extensive use of skin garments. Parts of the country, it is true, have exported[1] as well as imported[2] cloth fabrics anciently and in mediaeval times; but it is not easy to believe that the flowered and decorated robes worn by the chiefs were made by a people who, to a great extent, used leather for their garments, and who have not, in many localities, come even to this day to employ the shuttle in weaving.[3] If the Egyptian representations may here be trusted in detail, it might be inferred from them that the cloth-stuffs were obtained from the same quarter as that from which the

[1] Vopiscus, *Vita Aureliani* xii.; cf. Solinus xxix. For the dyed cloths of Meninx see the *Notit. Imper. Occident.* lxii.; cf. Pliny, *Hist. Nat.* ix. 36.

[2] Silks and brocades were brought to Tripolitana from Italy in mediaeval times, while woollens were sent back in exchange (E. de la Primaudaie, *Le Littoral de la Tripolitaine*, pp. 129, 132 *sq.*).

[3] Cf. MacIver and Wilkin, *Libyan Notes*, p. 69 *n.*

PLATE III.

TEMEḤU LIBYANS.

Eastern Libyans seem to have received their metal weapons—viz. from the Sherden. In this connection it is interesting to note the similarity between one of the designs seen on the robes, and that incised upon a fragment of Sardinian pottery, as shown

Fig. 14.

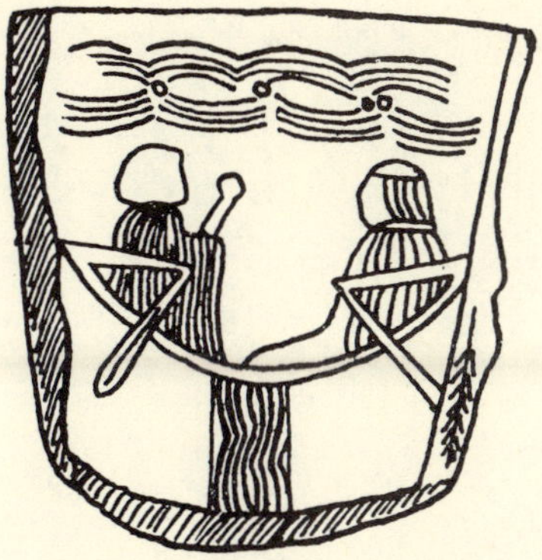

Fig. 15.

in Fig. 16 *a*, *b*. The historical relations between the Sherden and the Libyans, and the geographical proximity of the two peoples, make it at least possible that the former supplied the latter with their better textiles.[1]

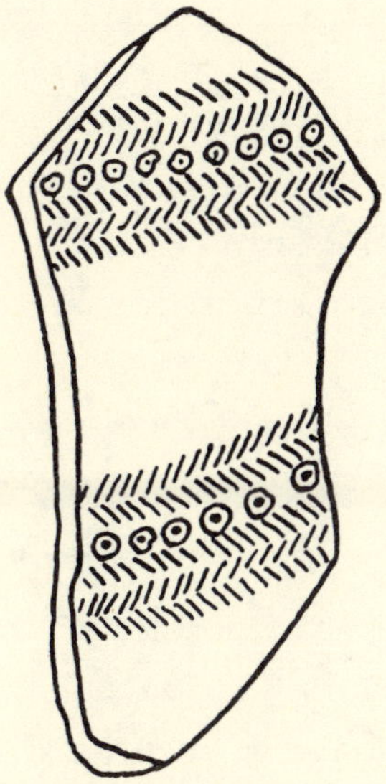

a.

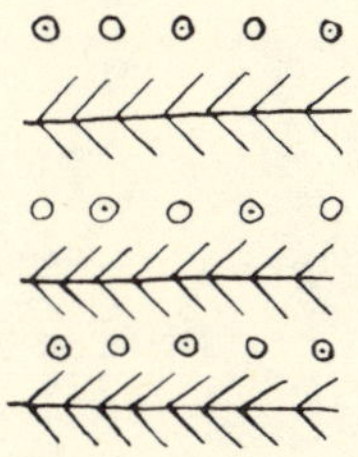

b.

Fig. 16.

Mention has been made above of the resemblance of the long robe to a garment made of the undressed skin of an animal. That skins were largely used for clothing is supported by ample testimony. Strabo remarks of the North Africans in general that "they wear the skins of lions, panthers, and bears, and sleep in them"; and that the Libyan "cloak is a skin . . . which serves also as a breastplate."[2] This last statement recalls the lines of Lucan :—

. . . Afer
Venator, ferrique simul fiducia non est
Vestibus iratos laxis operiri leones.[3]

Mela, having mentioned that the notables wear the *sagum*, adds that the other Libyans of the interior go clad in the skins of wild or domestic animals.[4] The Macae regularly wore goat-skins :—

. . . humerosque tegunt velamine capri
Saetigero.[5]

The same writer describes a typical Marmarid as being clad in skins.[6] Finally,

[1] W. M. Müller, *Egyptological Researches*, vol. ii. p. 126, states his belief in the Libyan origin of the chiefs' robes. He is at least correct in noting that they are non-Egyptian.

[2] Strabo xvii. p. 828.

[3] Lucan iv. 665 *sqq.*; cf. Pliny viii. 16, where a Gaetulian shepherd is said to have stopped a charging lion by casting his cloak over the beast's head.

[4] Mela i. 8; cf. Hippocrates, *De morbis*, vol. ii. p. 375, for domestic, and Aelian, *Hist. Nat.* xiv. 16, for wild, goats' skins.

[5] Silius Italicus iii. 276 *sq.*

[6] *Ibid.* v. 437 *sq.*

it may be mentioned that the Libyan contingent in the army of Xerxes were dressed in leather.[1] The cut of these skin or leather garments doubtless varied ; the undressed skin was probably merely hung from the neck, as among the Bedawîn of Sinai at the present time ;[2] the dressed hides were probably worked up into some sort of shirt or jacket, such as those used among the Imushagh to-day.[3]

The use of robes, kilts, jackets, etc., thus far described in this chapter, while broadly diffused among the ancient North African peoples, cannot be regarded as the most characteristic feature of their dress. The garment which deserves that title is the protective sheath for the generative organs, conveniently known to archaeologists as the *penistasche*, already several times mentioned.

Sheaths of this sort are not peculiar to any one people or period. Similar protections were worn in Minoan Crete,[4] and are used to-day in South Africa.[5] In predynastic and protodynastic Egypt the *penistasche* was known,[6] though it was not, as a recent writer has stated,[7] a national garment in universal use. It has been by some supposed that the word 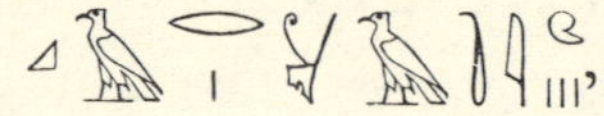, *kꜣ-rꜣ-nꜣ-ty*, found occasionally in New Empire texts, was the Egyptian designation for these sheaths ; but the word really means "foreskin," or "phallus with a foreskin," as Breasted has pointed out.[8]

The earliest instance of the use of the sheath among historic Libyans is found in the Sa-hu-re and Ne-user-re reliefs of the Vth Dynasty. By classical times the *penistasche* seems to have been largely succeeded by some less noticeable form of covering, since the Greek and Roman writers, who would have been impressed by its peculiarity, make no mention of it.

The form of the sheath, as shown in the Ne-user-re reliefs, is given in Fig. 17. Like the archaic Egyptian ones (Fig. 18 *a*, *b*), the protective case depends from a girdle, the manner in which the organ was inserted being clearly seen in the figure. Fig. 19 shows a similar sheath worn by one of the Ne-user-re captives, which differs from the preceding by its being passed up under the belt, instead of falling outside of it. In the New Empire, the *penistasche* is regularly represented as having been passed up under the girdle, as in Figs. 20, 21, 22. Only occasionally in the New Empire

[1] Herodotus vii. 71.

[2] C. M. Doughty, *Wanderings in Arabia*, vol. i. p. 64. The Sinai Bedawîn, according to Doughty, wear "gazelle or other skins hanging from the neck, which," as they will, "they shift round their bodies as the wind blows."

[3] G. F. Lyon, *Travels in Northern Africa*, p. 110. "A leathern kaftan is also much worn, of their [*scil.* the Imushagh] own manufacture, as are leather shirts of the skins of antelopes, very neatly sewed and well prepared." For such a shirt, see *ibid.*, plate facing p. 110.

[4] R. Dussaud, *Les Civilisations préhelléniques, etc.*, fig. 28 ; R. M. Burrows, *The Discoveries in Crete*, plate i. (*frontis.*), A (top register).

[5] Cf. the *michi* of the Kaffirs. See W. M. Müller, *op. cit.* vol. ii. p. 121, note 1.

[6] J. E. Quibell, *Hierakonpolis*, Part i. Plate viii. fig. 1 = Plate X. Fig. 2 ; Plate viii. fig. 3 = Plate VII. sketch, lower register, right = Plate X. Fig. 1. W. M. F. Petrie, *Diospolis Parva*, Plate v. lowest register, B ; Berlin Museum, No. 15084 = A. Erman, *Egyptian Religion*, fig. 4 ; G. A. Reisner, *Archaeol. Survey of Nubia*, vol. i. text, p. 47, fig. 34, grave 7:119 ; *Plates*, Pl. 66 b, 20. Cf. also E. Meyer, *Geschichte des Altertums*, vol. i. part ii. § 167 (p. 50).

[7] G. E. Smith, *The Ancient Egyptians, etc.*, p. 77 *sq.*

[8] Cf. W. M. Müller, *Asien und Europa*, p. 358 *n.* ; J. Capart, *Les Débuts de l'art en Egypte*, p. 55. BAR iii. § 587 note *h* ; iv. § 52.

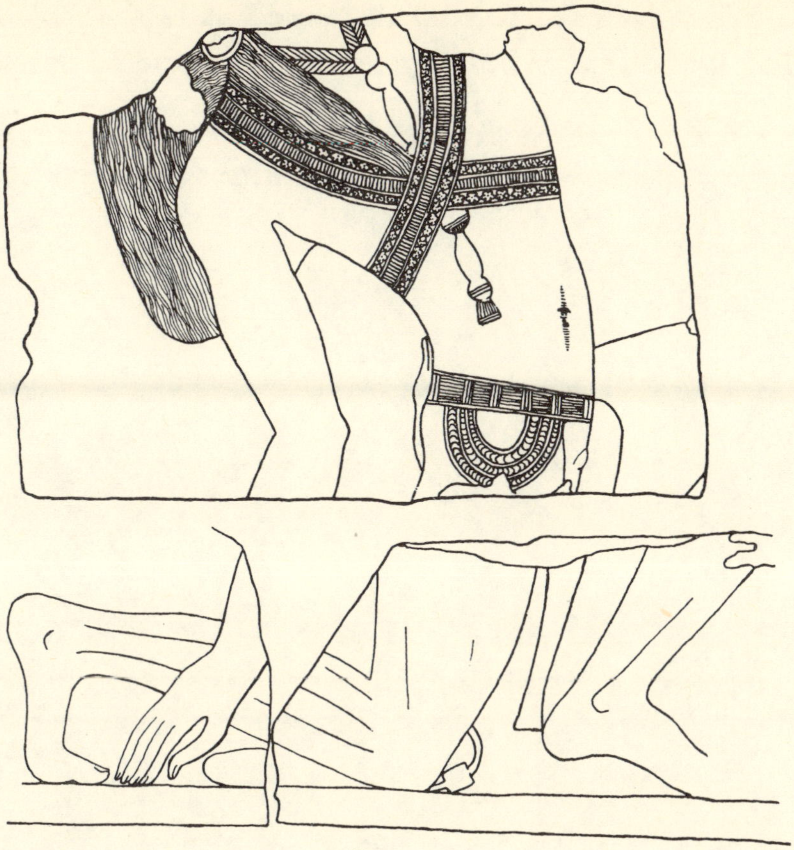

FIG. 17.

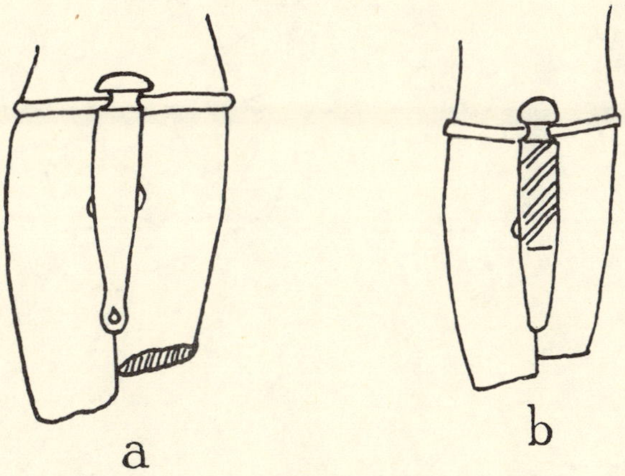

FIG. 18.

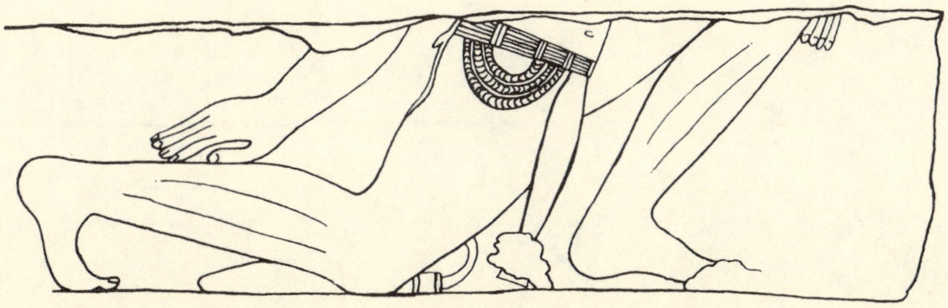

FIG. 19.

are there clear cases in which the sheath falls outside the girdle ; an instance is given in Fig. 23. Often, particularly in the representations of the Meshwesh, the sheaths

FIG. 20.

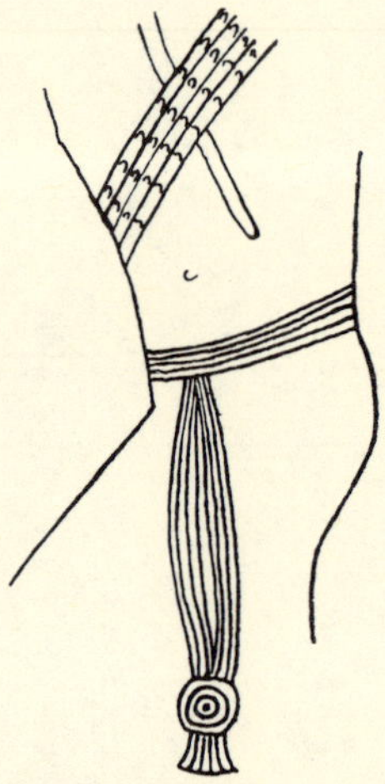

FIG. 21.

carry an ornamental ball[1] near the lower end, giving to them a tasselled appearance, as in Figs. 21, 23, 24. In the last example, the sheath, it may be observed, is

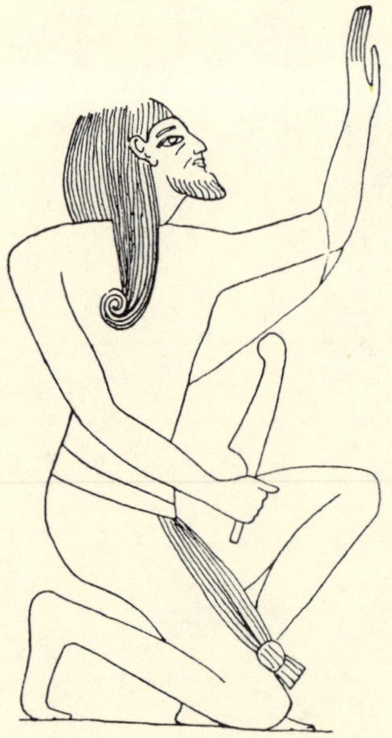

FIG. 22.

FIG. 23.

seemingly supported by a baldric. This, if it is really the case, is a unique instance ; it is more probable that this *penistasche* was held in place by the belt, and appears to

[1] A large bead ?

depend from the baldric merely because of the artist's carelessness. Similarly, from Fig. 23 one might suppose that the loop of the girdle was really part of the *penistasche* which passed down under the belt and was then tucked up under it. That such may occasionally have been the case seems not improbable; but in most instances the loop was independent of the sheath. Thus, in Figs. 21, 22, 24 are seen clear examples of the fastening of the sheath quite without any loop; in Figs. 17 and 19 the loop, from its character, is almost surely a part of the belt;[1] and in Fig. 25 is shown a loop (inverted !) without the *penistasche*.

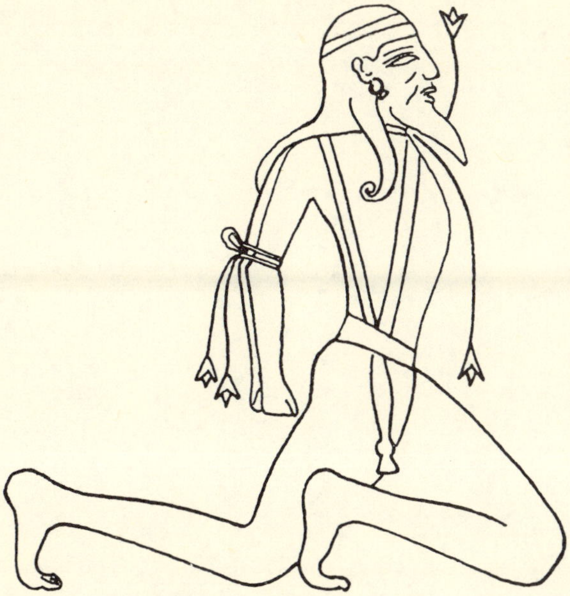

FIG. 24.

Fig. 26 shows with great detail a sheath either Libyan, or very closely resembling the Libyan. This sheath is here reproduced from the fine XIXth Dynasty statue of a Libyan divinity discovered at Karnak and now in the Cairo Museum. In cross-section this *penistasche* is square, and is kept in place by the girdle, which is tied over it with a square knot.

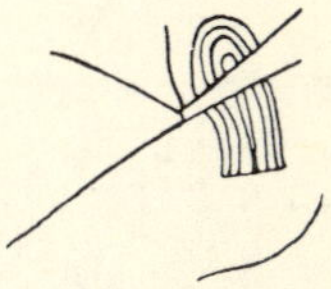

FIG. 25.

The types of *penistasche* shown in the figures seem to have been common to chiefs and tribesmen, and to all Libyans alike. It can only be said that those guards with ornamental ends do not appear until the advent of the Meshwesh in the New Empire, though there is too little evidence extant from an earlier period to make safe an assertion that they did not exist before that event. It is also noteworthy that the younger male children of the Sa-hu-re relief (Plate VII.) do not wear this garment; it was therefore probably a sign of adult manhood.

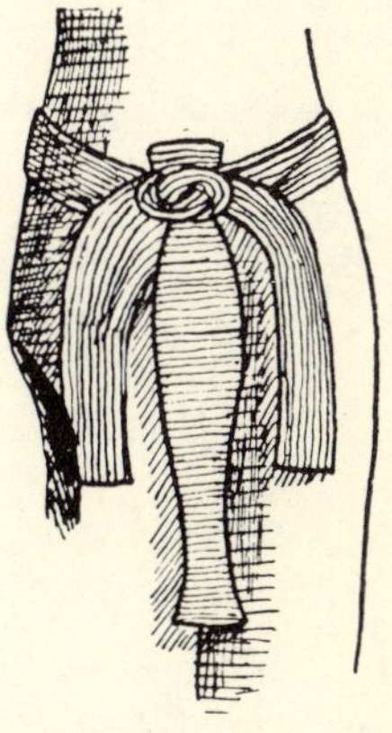

FIG. 26.

The materials of which these curious garments were made are not known. That leather was in some cases used early in Egypt is certain, while in South Africa both grasses and wood are employed. From the forms of the Libyan sheaths it appears that they were occasionally slightly flexible, which suggests that the former two materials, or one of them, were those in use. It is at least certain that the cases were not, as Naville has suggested,[2] made of metal, either in Libya or in Egypt, at any period. In some cases the sheaths were coloured. That shown in Fig. 21 is longitudinally painted red, blue, and white, the ball at the end

[1] Cf. Plate II. Fig. 5, Louvre bronze statuette, where the silver loop is clearly seen to be quite independent of the *penistasche*. The latter in this instance is remarkably small.

[2] E. Naville, *Figurines égyptiennes de l'époque archaïque*, II. in *RT*, xxii. p. 68. Naville speaks of sheaths *d'une matière résistante, telle que du métal, du bois ou du cuir épais*.

being painted with the same colours, in concentric circles.[1] By their exaggerated size and semi-ornamental character, these sheaths, it may be remarked in conclusion, served, like the "chastity aprons" of the Zulu women, not only to protect the parts they covered but to emphasize the sex of the wearer as well.

Belts and girdles were, as has been seen, as common as the sheaths they supported. The phrase of Silius Italicus—

Discinctos inter Libycos populos,[2]

has only a general meaning, signifying "among the loose-robed, or lightly-clad, Libyan peoples." As seen on the Egyptian monuments, the Libyan girdles were like some modern polo-belts, cut broader in the back than in the front. Just how they were fastened is not clear; but from the frequency with which the loops are represented on the left thigh of the wearer, it would seem that in the majority of cases the belt went

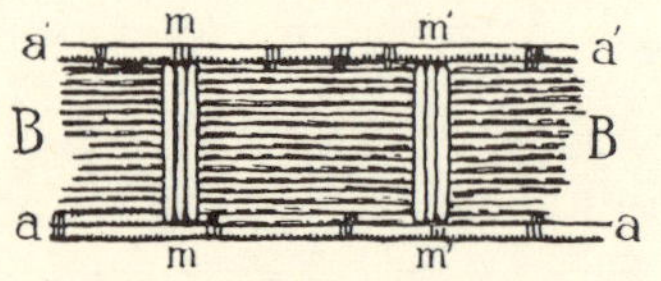

Fig. 27.

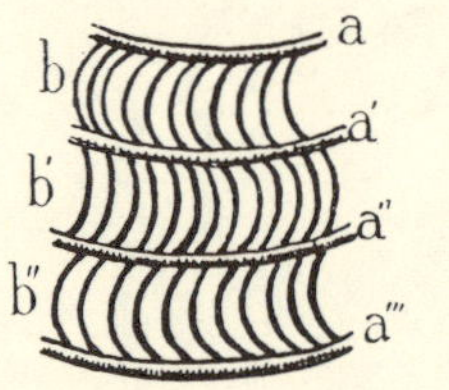

Fig. 28.

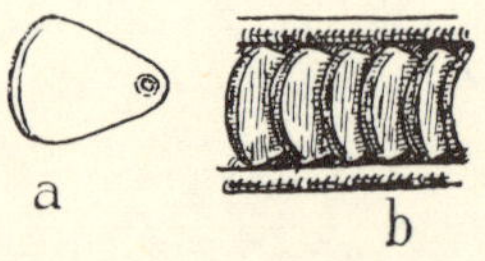

Fig. 29.

more than once around the waist, the end being then pushed down between the body and the girdle, and afterward again brought up and tucked in. It is possible that belt, loop, and sheath were sometimes made in one piece. In this case the sheath would be first adjusted, the length of the girdle would be passed under it after going around the waist, and the loop would then be made as mentioned. The material of the belts was probably usually plain leather,[3] though this was not the case with the ornamental belts worn by chiefs of the Ne-user-re reliefs (Figs. 17 and 19). Here the loop is an ornamental appendage to the belt, which itself was made seemingly of leathern thongs (Fig. 27, *B-B*) laid together, the outside ones (*a-a*, *a′-a′*) being larger than any of the others. At equal distances along this belt, and at right angles to it, were introduced in trios, little bars of shell, ivory, or other material (*m-m*, *m′-m′*). The whole was fastened in front (Fig. 19) with some simple sort of clasp. The loop attached to this belt was apparently of leather, either (like the belt itself) of thongs, or (more probably) of a curved strip on which thongs (Fig. 28, *a-a′*, *a″*, *a‴*) were sewn. The space between the thongs was covered with little scales (*b*, *b′*, *b″*), which were perhaps sectors of shell like those found in a

[1] For examples of coloured sheaths, *vide* J. F. Champollion, *Monuments de l'Égypte*, etc. vol. i. pl. xi. (*penistasche* fluted in black, red-brown, and yellow); Pl. xvii. (red, black, yellow); Pl. xcii. 4 (green and yellow; cf. I. Rosellini, *Monumenti*, vol. i. pl. lxiii. 2).

[2] Silius Italicus ii. 56.

[3] Belts of coloured leather are shown in J. F. Champollion, *op. cit.* vol. i. plate xi., plate xvii., plate xcii. 4; and I. Rosellini, *loc. cit.*

PLATE IV.

KING SETI I. SLAYING THE LIBYANS. DYNASTY XIX.

"C Group" grave in Nubia[1] (Fig. 29, *a*), applied in the manner shown in the sketch (Fig. 29, *b*).

In passing from the question of belts to that of foot-wear, one remarks that, while on the Egyptian monuments even the sheykhs and emîrs of the Libyans almost invariably appear bare-footed, this seems to be due to the indifference of the Egyptian artist. On one of Medînet Habu tiles a chieftain is seen wearing sandals the latchets of which are clearly shown (Fig. 30), and it is recorded of Meryey that in his flight from Memphis he left his "sandals . . . in haste behind him."[2]

Fig. 30.

In the previous chapter has been cited the passage of Procopius with regard to the insignia annually bestowed by the Byzantine government upon the Libyan notables, and the fact that gilt sandals were among the gifts has been noted. Corippus speaks of the native foot-gear as *cruda Maurica*,[3] and no doubt this simple form of protection was widely known. Besides sandals, some of the Libyans had leg-wrappings, like those of the Sardinian peasants of the present day, made either of leather[4] or of woollen.[5]

Fig. 31.

Head-gear was certainly rare among the Eastern Libyans as a whole, despite the intensity of the summer suns. The Libyans of the Egyptian monuments, especially the Meshwesh, wear sometimes head-shawls contained by bandeaux or fillets (cf. Pl. II. Figs. 7, 9), and the skull-cap was not unknown, as is proved by the example worn by the woman of the Medînet Habu tiles (*Frontis.*) and the Libyans of the Thothmes IV. panel (Fig. 31). Perhaps the hats of the type worn by the king in the Arcesilaus vase (the "Silphium-weighing") is African. At all events it is closely paralleled by the hats of some of the modern Imushagh, which are beautifully woven of grasses; and it is not Greek in type. (The hat of Arcesilaus II. is shown in Fig. 32, *a*; a modern North African hat, as worn in the Ṣaḥara, is seen in the same figure, *b*.) Although no classical notices speak of Libyan

[1] G. A. Reisner, *op. cit.* vol. i. *Plates*, Plate 70 b, 13. In this case it must be observed that the shell-sectors were not applied to a surface, but were strung with other beads. Similar plate-beads occur in the Egyptian "Pan-Graves."

[2] BAR iii. § 584.

[3] Corippus, *Johannis* ii. 137.

[4] Strabo xvii. p. 831.

[5] Silius Italicus iii. 280 . . . *Adyrmachidis laevo tegmina crure.*

sun-hats, it appears from a passage in the *Johannis* that in late times head-clouts were worn. These cloths were tied beneath the chin, *nodo suffalta tenaci*.[1]

a b

FIG. 32.

The dress of the Libyan women was as rude as that of the men or even ruder. Herodotus, after stating his belief that the Aegis and dress of the statues of Athena were derived by the Greeks from the Libyans, continues :—

> For, except that the garments of the Libyan women are of leather, and their fringes made of leathern thongs instead of serpents, in all else the dress of both is exactly alike. . . . For the Libyan women wear over their dress[2] goat-skins stript of their hair, fringed at their edges, and coloured with vermilion.[3]

In connection with this passage it may be observed that in some classical representations the fore-tabs of Athena's Aegis depend from her arms in a manner strikingly paralleled in the woman's figure of the Ghadames relief (Fig. 33) ; in other Greek sculptures and vase-paintings the Aegis falls loosely over the back and breast.

FIG. 33.

The evidence of the Ghadames relief, just referred to, also points to the use of a long single (?) robe, the details of which cannot, unfortunately, be made out from the drawing of Duveyrier.

Apart from the data just presented, the Egyptian monuments and the Slunt sculptures give some further information with regard to Libyan feminine attire. In the Slunt sculptures, though the men are shown with-

[1] Corippus, *Johannis* ii. 136, viii. 192. In both passages it is spoken of as a *palla*, here a sort of shawl.

[2] This suggests a cloth undergarment ; cf. Strabo, *loc. cit.*

[3] Herodotus iv. 189. W. R. Smith (*Religion of the Semites*, p. 437) infers that this thonged skin garment was a sacred dress, because Herodotus compares it to the Aegis of Athena. This seems hazardous, since (*a*) Herodotus is half-suggesting a Libyan origin for the Greek goddess because, *inter alia*, the Aegis recalls the dress of the Libyan women, who in general use the fringed girdle (the modern *raḥt*) ; and (*b*) because to-day throughout the Sudan and in Nubia the *roḥt* is a common and purely secular garment. For the colour cf. J. R. Pacho, *Voyage dans la Marmarique, etc.*, p. 59 ; G. F. Lyon, *op. cit.* p. 155 ; cf. *ibid.* p. 139 ; and, as an interesting parallel, the "rams' skins dyed red" which covered the tabernacle in the wilderness (*Exodus* xxvi. 14).

out any discernible sort of dress, the women appear wearing a simple skirt or kirtle which, confined at the waist, falls in simple folds to the feet (Fig. 34). This representation belongs to Roman times, but in the Benî Ḥasan tomb-paintings the same garment is seen worn by Libyan women ; the skirts there shown fall from the waist to the ankles, and are so belted in that a sort of κόλπος or fold is formed in front (Pl. V. Figs. 1 and 3). The bottom of the skirt is either scalloped, or else the wavy line along

Fig. 34. (After Haimann.)

the bottom is intended to show a vertical plaiting. In the Benî Ḥasan paintings, the skirts are coloured red.

*
* *

Since personal ornamentation precedes dress in cultural development, it is not surprising to find that whereas the clothes of the Libyans were of the simplest, they had evolved a number of such decorations as collars, ear-rings, armlets, etc.

The most characteristic Libyan ornaments were the ostrich-plumes, which are almost universally worn by the warriors of the Egyptian monuments. When absent, as sometimes happens, it is for one of three reasons : the artist has sacrificed them to the exigencies of space ; they are made impossible by the difficulty of working in the round ; or the subjects of representation are ordinary tribesmen who have no right to the distinction. For a distinction it was, although, to judge from the Ne-user-re and

Sa-hu-re reliefs, one not known in the Old Empire.[1] A chief, except for the first two reasons noted above, does not appear without the plume after Middle Empire times; but he might appear with but one feather (*e.g.* Pl. II. Fig. 8), even, apparently, when the head of a great confederacy. For in the Merneptah record it is said of Meryey, after his defeat, that "an evil fate removed his plume."[2] The Delta dynasts, also, of the Late New Empire are characterized in the Piankhi stela as "the chiefs who wore the feather."[3] At Umm Beydah, near Aghurmî (Sîwah Oasis), the prince kneeling before Amon wears but a single plume.[4] On the other hand, cases occur in which the wearing of two plumes (Fig. 35, Pl. III., etc.) signifies that the chief so decorated was superior in rank to those who wore but one each. This is paralleled among the Sudanese seen on the Egyptian monuments; the more important of them wear each two feathers, while their followers have but one each.[5] Just how the Libyan

FIG. 35.

FIG. 36.

plumes were fastened in the hair is not clear, but it is probable that they were merely stuck in the root of a side-lock.[6] Among the Sudanese the plumes were often held in place by a bandeau, and so inserted as to have their breadth in a vertical plane, in contradistinction to the Libyan fashion of inserting them with the breadth right and left. (Cf. Fig. 35 with Fig. 36.)

Like most primitive peoples, the Eastern Libyans had ear ornaments, both rings (*e.g.* Pls. I., II., VI.) and studs (cf. Pl. II. 7, 8) being known. Various types of the former, which were worn always in the lobe of the ear, and never, as so frequently

[1] W. H. Müller, *Egyptological Researches*, vol. ii. p. 121 *n.* 2. Müller rightly states that the plume is not a tribal distinction but a personal one. He further suggests that each feather is the token of a slain enemy, as among the Somalis and Gallas. This hardly seems possible if the consensus of the monumental evidence is taken into consideration, though it is quite possible that the plume was the mark of a tried fighting-man. It is worth noting that the wearing of feathers was especially associated, in classical opinion, with the Nasamones. This people, when they travelled abroad, wore wings (πτερά) upright on the head; a usage which is in a manner paralleled by the Amerind use of war-bonnets. *Vide supra*, p. 116, *n.* 11, for the citation from Dio Chrysostomus, *Orat.* lxxii.; *De corporis cultu*, vol. ii. p. 383 (cf. Eustathius *ad Dionys. Perieg.* 209). The wearing of feather head-dresses in the early Mediterranean was not uncommon. Cf. the Peleset (Philistines) of the New Empire monuments, and the heads of Sardus Pater on the Roman coins of Sardinia.

[2] BAR iii. § 610.

[3] BAR iv. § 873.

[4] G. Steindorff, *Durch die Libysche Wüste zur Amonsoase*, fig. 71, p. 95, top register, right.

[5] As in the scene shown LD, vol. iii. pl. 117.

[6] Cf. G. A. Reisner, *Archaeological Survey of Nubia*, vol. i. p. 40, fig. 29 = grave 7:250. This burial (a woman) had a number of ostrich-plumes thrust into the hair.

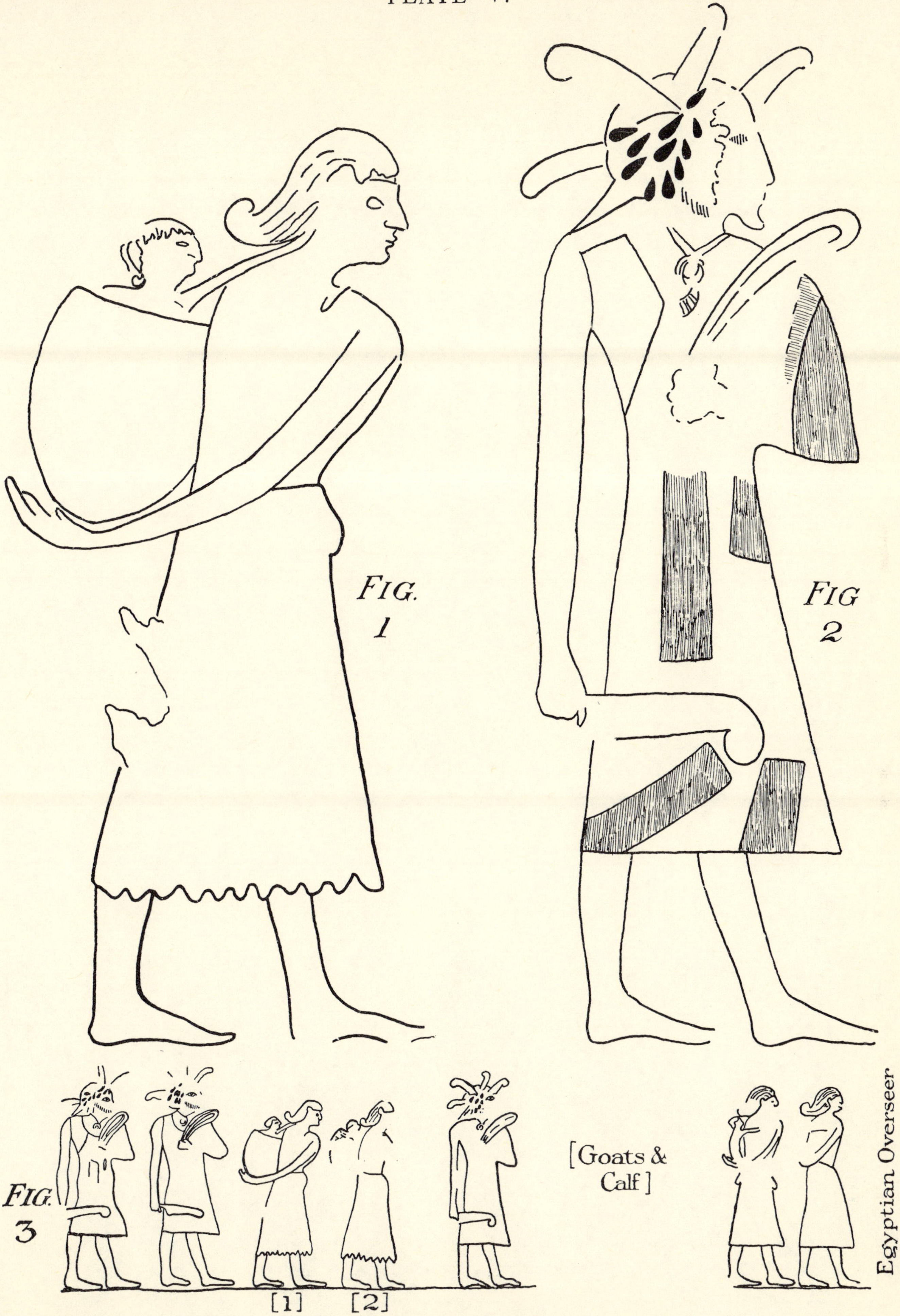

LIBYAN TRIBUTARIES.

happens in modern Nubia, in the upper edge, are here reproduced from the Egyptian monuments in Fig. 37, *b*, *c*, *d*, *e*, *f*, *g*, and *h*. The ear-ring shown in Fig. 37, *a*, is one actually preserved on a cranium which is apparently that of a Libyan;[1] it is of

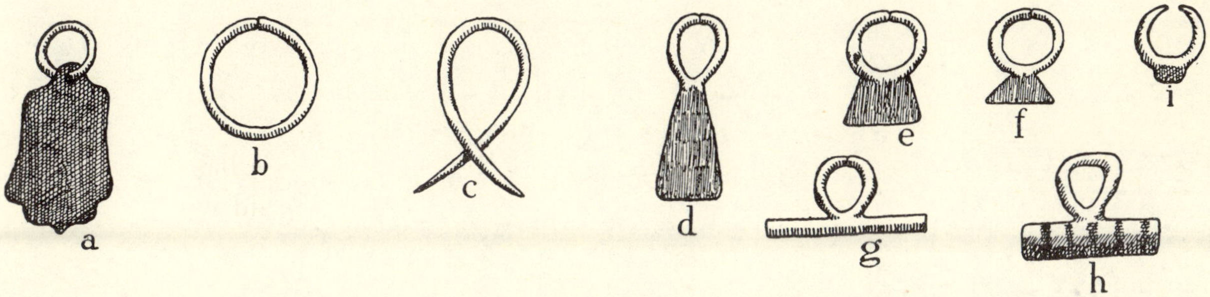

Fig. 37.

copper. The ear-ring shown in Fig. 37, *i*, comes from a proto-Berber grave in the Algerian Ṣaḥara, and is here reproduced because of its analogy to Fig. 37, *e*, *f*. Of the ear-rings seen on the monuments, *b* occurs in the Vth Dynasty and later, while the others are of the New Empire. Fig. 37, *c* appears to have been a simple twist of metal, while *d*, *e*, *f*, *g*, and *h* have little bars or plates attached to the bottom. Fig. 38 shows the ear of a Libyan prince from a relief at Beyt el-Waly. In this case not only is there an ear-ring, but also a plug so inserted as to change the shape of the ear. This is the only clear piece of evidence in regard to the use of ear-studs of this type among the Libyans, but it is probable that, since the fashion was known, it was not uncommon. Small studs are apparently indicated in the examples given, Pl. II. 7, 8.

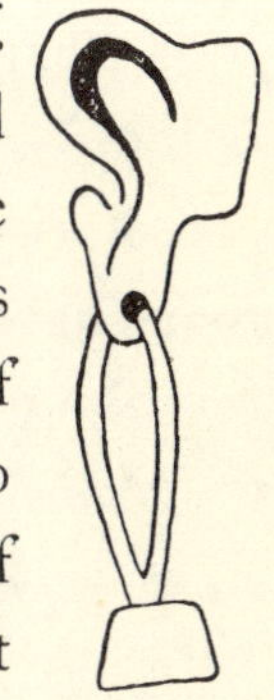

Fig. 38.

Of the necklaces and pendants of the Eastern Libyans, the latter were especially characteristic in design. In the Sa-hu-re relief of the Vth Dynasty both men and women wear collars (Pl. VII.), which appear to have been made up of strings of flat circular beads such as have been found in the proto-Berber graves of the Algerian Ṣaḥara, and of little rosettes (?). In the Medînet Habu tiles, two Libyans are seen wearing necklaces (*Frontis.*), one of which is elaborated with attached beads. The pendants, of which mention has been made above, are seldom represented. The best early examples, from the Abusîr reliefs, show the curious forms given in Fig. 17 and Pl. VII. It is not possible, so unlike are these to Egyptian pectoral ornaments, to say definitely how they were made. They are identical in design with the pectoral ornaments sometimes seen in representations of the Aegean tributaries on the Egyptian monuments, and were probably of spherical or tubular glazed beads. The part that went around the neck seems to have been made of flat shell beads such

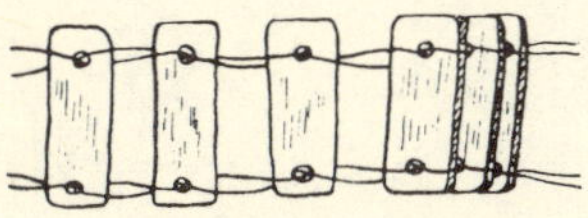

Fig. 39.

[1] W. M. F. Petrie, *Diospolis Parva*, pl. xxv., and there given the cemetery number Y354. No mention of the head, however, appears in the text. A letter from A. C. Mace, who assisted in the work at Diospolis, gives me his opinion that the head is Coptic, because the ear-ring slightly suggests a cross. This slight evidence is overborne, I think, by the side-lock (see Fig. 45); but the case must remain for ever doubtful for lack of proper records.

as those found in the "C Group" graves of Middle Empire Nubia, here represented so as to show the original manner of stringing (Fig. 39). A form of pectoral ornament quite different is shown in Pl. V. 2 : this pendant may have been of nacre or of metal.

Over the pectorals in the Abusîr reliefs pass the crossed bands which were so common a feature of Libyan ornament or dress at all periods.[1] The purpose of the bands was probably to confine a skin cloak,[2] though they are often highly ornamental in character, and are frequently worn by Libyans who are otherwise, except for the *penistasche*, quite nude.

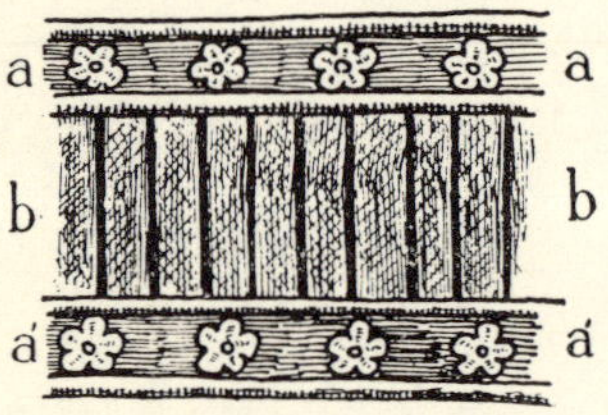

Fig. 40.

The decorative character of the bands is well seen in the Ne-user-re reliefs. The details of these bands are shown in Fig. 40. Two rows of rosettes (*a-a*, *a'-a'*) seem to have been applied to a leather strip at the edges, while the middle zone was overlaid with a series of oblong plate-beads (*b-b*). Along either side of the lines of rosettes run leather (?) cords, as in the belts worn by the same princes. What seem to have been plate-beads may have been such nacre oblongs as are shown in Fig. 39. These beads, already mentioned as belonging to the "Pan-Grave" people of Egypt and the "C Group" of Middle Empire Nubia, would, if applied to a leather strip, give exactly the effect seen in the Libyan band (Fig. 40, *b-b*). Ornamental in character are also the bands worn by the Libyan prince represented in the temple at Beyt el-Waly. The bands are there of leather (?) coloured as seen in Fig. 41. The Egyptian artist seems here to have copied, or at least tried to reproduce, an original pair of Libyan bands, for the colour sequence is non-Egyptian in character.[3]

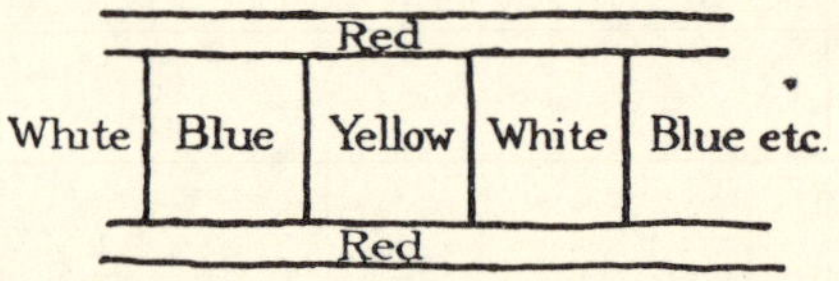

Fig. 41.

Bracelets were apparently not as common among the Libyans as they are among the Imushagh of modern times.[4] It may be, however, that anciently they were more common than one would at first glance suppose, and that they appear to have been unusual only because on the monuments they were drawn in colours which have not survived. Armillae and bracelets are indicated on the arms and wrists of the Libyans of the Abusîr reliefs, and of the Medînet Habu tiles (Pl. VII. and *Frontis.*).

The princes of the Libyans wore, in addition to the usual ornaments, a curious decoration which was employed as a mark of distinction by the Egyptian kings also. This was the animal's tail which depended from the back of the belt (Figs. 42 and 43).

[1] W. M. Müller, *op. cit.* vol. ii. p. 135, states that the cross-bands are not common in Libyan representations. This error must be due to carelessness, since about 70 per cent of the Libyans represented wear these bands.

[2] Cf. F. Deniker, *Races of Man*, fig. 48, p. 172, a Fuegian wearing a primitive mantle of sealskin with crossed bands.

[3] G. Roeder, verbal communication.

[4] They are characteristic of the Ṣaḥaran Berbers, who attach a ceremonial importance to them.

The use of the caudiform appendage is found among numerous primitive peoples,[1] and probably in Egypt and Libya had its origin in a desire to imitate the aspect of totem animals, or from an archaism which preserved the memory of the time when hunting-men wore the skins of animals taken in the chase.[2] The Libyan tail was apparently sometimes weighted, and had an ornamented "head" that passed up under the belt (Figs. 17, 19, 42).

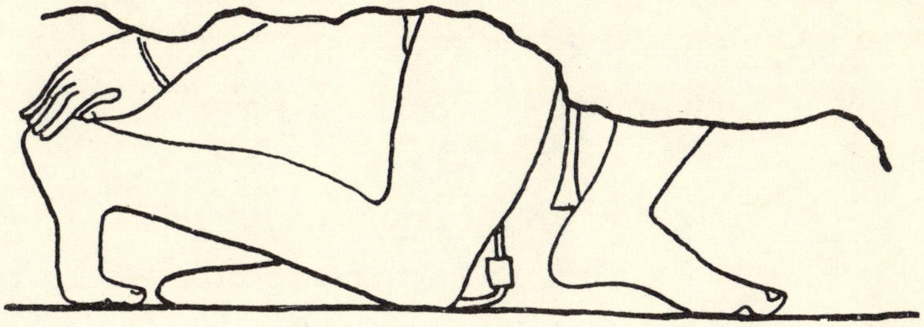

FIG. 42.

The only monumental evidence of the wearing of leg-rings is afforded by the Thothmes IV. panel, Fig. 31, where one figure wears an anklet on the right foot. Herodotus states that the women of the Adyrmachidae wore upon each leg a ring of bronze.[3] With a special significance, as has been noted, the women of the Gindanes wore leathern anklets.[4]

It is to be presumed that the Eastern Libyans, at least during the later periods, made use of those semi-precious stones which were found within their territories, and which they exported through the medium of the Phoenicians and others. No monumental or explicit textual evidence, however, exists in proof of this.

* * *

The Libyans indulged to the full that barbarous foppery in regard to the dressing of the hair which is common to so many primitive people. Strabo, speaking of the Mauritanians, makes a remark which the Egyptian monumental evidence leads one to believe would have been in general as applicable to the Eastern Libyans as to the Western :—

> They [the Maurusii] bestow care to improve their looks by plaiting their hair, trimming their beards, wearing golden ornaments, cleaning their teeth, and by paring their nails ; you would rarely see them touch one another as they walk, lest they should disturb the arrangement of their hair.[5]

The modes of dressing the hair varied among the different tribes, as is clear both from the monuments and from Herodotus. The women of the Adyrmachidae allowed their hair to grow long ;[6] the Macae let the locks "about the crown of their heads grow long, while they clip them close everywhere else," making "their hair resemble a crest" ;[7] the

[1] *E.g.* among the Nagas of Manipur. J. Deniker, *op. cit.*, *Frontis.*

[2] W. M. Müller, *op. cit.* p. 60 *sqq.* and fig. 69. Müller has carefully noted the varieties of these tails in Egypt, but makes, perhaps, too nice distinctions. He asserts that the kings' tails differ when they appear as hunters or as rulers (p. 60, *n.* 2), and believes that the typical Egyptian royal tail was that of a gnu (p. 64).

[3] Herodotus iv. 168.

[4] *Ibid.* iv. 176. For leather armillae, cf. G. A. Reisner, *op. cit.* vol. i. p. 47, fig. 34, grave 7, 119.

[5] Strabo xvii. p. 828.

[6] Herodotus iv. 168.

[7] *Ibid.* iv. 175.

Machlyes and the Auseans "both wear their hair long, but the Machlyes let it grow at the back of the head, while the Auseans have it long in front";[1] the Maxyes "let their hair grow long on the right side of their heads, and shave it close on the left."[2] It is this last-mentioned manner of wearing the hair that is most frequently seen on the Egyptian monuments, which afford the clearest, as well as the earliest, sources on this question.

The earliest of this monumental evidence comes from the Vth Dynasty. The Libyans of that period, as represented in the Abusîr reliefs, wear their hair in a peculiar fashion which is not seen afterwards. The hair, both of men and women (Pl. VII.) hangs below the nape of the neck behind, and the locks falling from just behind the ears hang to the collar-bone. The whole is covered with a head-cloth, which is so turned up over the forehead as to give, at the first hasty glance, the impression that the wearers have over their brows each a small uraeus. The children of the Abusîr reliefs wear their hair short, but similarly covered (Pl. VII.).

The women of later periods have their hair done in fashions different from those of the men. In some cases, as in one of the Benî Ḥasan paintings, the hair was drawn back from the forehead, and curled at the nape of the neck (Pl. V.); or it was simply drawn back in tresses which fell over the shoulders, the head being covered with a small cap (*Frontis.*). In the Ghadames relief, the two female figures wear their hair in an extraordinary fashion, which is not quite clear from the only drawing of the original which we possess. Apparently, part of the hair lay along the nape of the neck, while the rest, passing through a bandeau to which was attached a loose head-cloth, hung bushed out behind (Fig. 33). This head-dress, it may be remarked, may possibly have been not a regular one, but one peculiar to priestesses.

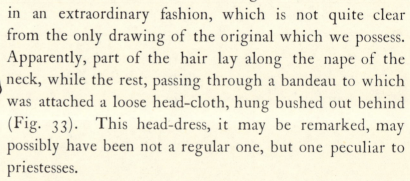

Fig. 43.

The fashions of wearing the hair among the men of the Sa-hu-re reliefs, as has just been said, are not exactly paralleled in the later periods. In one of the Ne-user-re reliefs, however, is seen that dressing of the hair which in the New Empire is usually associated with the Meshwesh.[3] The mass of hair falls behind the shoulders, while a broad unplaited tress hangs from behind the ear and in front of the shoulder, over the pectoral muscles (Fig. 17). This closely resembles the treatment of the hair in the Sa-hu-re reliefs, except that it is not covered, and this mode is seen in the three New Empire types shown in Figs. 22, 24, 43. By far

[1] Herodotus iv. 180. [2] *Ibid.* iv. 191; cf. Macrobius, *Saturnalia* i. 26.
[3] LD iii. 209, where the inscription may be seen accompanying the figure, the head of which is here shown (fig. 24).

PLATE VI.

Fig. 1.

Fig. 2.

SMALL GRANITE HEAD IN CAIRO MUSEUM.

Fig. 3.—RELIEF FROM THE TOMB OF HARMHEB.

the most usual form of hair-dressing among the Eastern Libyans is that of the side-lock, as shown in Pls. I., II., III., IV., etc., or in Figs. 11, 12, 35. This mode is that always associated with the Rebu, and, rightly or wrongly, given by the Egyptian artists to most of the Libyans as well, so that the side-lock has come generally to be recognized by all Egyptologists as a Libyan characteristic. It will be seen from the figures that there are several varieties in this style of wearing the hair. The lock might be a twisted tress (as in Pl. VI. 1, 2), or a plaited braid of several strands (as in *Frontis.* A and Pl. III.), it might hang behind the ear (Fig. 11), or in front of it (cf. Pl. IV.). Also the rest of the hair might be treated in one of several ways. By one method, the front of the hair was brought to the forehead in tresses, while at the back it hung naturally (Pls. I., IV., and Fig. 11); in another the hair was tressed both in front and behind (Pl. VI. 1, 2; *Frontis.*; Pl. VI. 3), in some instances the tresses being frizzed (Pl. III.). A double side-lock on one side of the head (Pl. IV.; cf. Pl. I. Fig. 9, and, for variant, 5) is seen on two chiefs in a relief at Karnak, and in some cases the side-lock was worn on both sides of the head at once (Fig. 4). In connection with this it may be suggested that Libyan captives often appear as wearing but one side-lock on the left or on the right side of the head, according to which profile is shown. Incidentally, the hieroglyph for the "west," *ìment* (Fig. 44), the Libyan land, is seemingly a cap (cf. *Frontis.*), with a plume, and two pendants of unequal length which appear to be side-locks. A parallel is seen among the Imushagh women, who sometimes braid their hair in two side-locks on the right and left of the head.[1] Generally, however, but one side-lock appears to have been worn, the hair on the side of the head opposite to it being trimmed at about the level of the jaw (as in Pl. VI. 1, 2). An actual example of the side-lock is preserved on the Libyan (?) cranium (seen in Fig. 45), which has already been mentioned in this chapter as coming from Diospolis Parva. The tress is there plaited of three strands, exactly as in a small unpublished Libyan head recently (1911) exposed for sale in Cairo.[2]

FIG. 44.

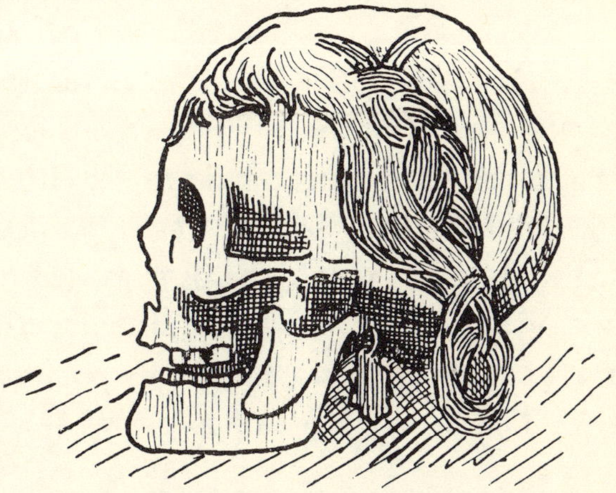

FIG. 45.

A different and very rare style of Libyan hair-dressing remains to be mentioned. It is shown in one of the Benî Ḥasan paintings (Pl. V. 2). The hair is there seen to be confined with some sort of bandeau ornamented with what seem to be shells. It escapes from the fillet and forms a brush behind the neck.

[1] Aymard, *Les Touareg*, p. 96, pl. 14.

[2] Shop of M. Kyticas. Limestone head in round, provenance unknown. Ht. *circa* 12 cm., lower face badly damaged, traces of reddish colour on face.

The occurrence of the side-lock among the modern Imushagh women has been mentioned. Erwin von Bary saw at Ghat three Kel Fadeh men, "two of whom had long, hanging tresses; . . . one even had on each side of the head little braided tufts which gave him an almost feminine air."[1] Occasionally side-locks are worn among the Amazigh of the Maroccan Rîf, while the Fulbé or Fulahs of the Chad-zone sometimes braid the hair in a manner which strikingly recalls the Libyans of the monuments (Fig. 46). Lastly, in the Anglo-Egyptian Sudan the scalp-lock called *gurin*, *gambur*, or *guaga* sometimes recalls the Libyan tresses.

Fig. 46.

The reasons for the differences in hair-dressing among the Libyans cannot be definitely stated. That in some degree they served as tribal marks is clear from Herodotus; but other ideas may also have been associated with the wearing of side-locks. Among the Arabians of the Neğd the men "braid their long, manly side-locks . . . with long hair shed in the midst, and hanging down at either side in braided horns,"[2] simply for reasons of masculine vanity; but the *gurin*,[3] *gambur*, or *guaga* of the Sudan, which is worn by many male children and adults, is supposed to adorn that part of the head which is first presented during birth (it is commonly situated in the right or left occipito-parietal region), the exact locality being carefully recorded by the midwife present at the time.

This lock is allowed to grow:—

> 1. During babyhood as the token of a vow made during pregnancy by the parents that should a boy be granted to them they will not shave the Gambour until they have sacrificed to some saint, Fiki, or the like.
> 2. In the child it is preserved as a convenient handle by which angels may lift him out of harm's way in case of necessity.
> 3. In youth, it may be retained solely as an ornament.
> 4. In later life, again, it may be regrown as a token of a vow on the part of the wearer.
> 5. Some carry it as a safeguard against the heat of the sun.
> 6. While certain Fikis and holy men wear it as a badge of office.[4]

I have quoted the above passage *in extenso*, believing that in this case, as in so many others, modern Sudanese practice may aid in explaining ancient Libyan custom. In connection with the first reason cited above, it may be observed that anciently only men appear with the side-lock, if one excepts the Abusîr women, who wear male attire, and whose hair is dressed in the same way as the men's, though not with a true side-lock. Reason second is probably of Moslem growth. With three should be compared the

[1] E. von Bary, *Dernier Rapport d'un européen sur l'Oase de Ghât*, p. 157; cf. also p. 166.

[2] C. M. Doughty, *Wanderings in Arabia*, vol. i. p. 89; cf. vol. i. p. 185, Zeyd's "Ishmaelite side-locks flying backwards in the wind" as he rode.

[3] This word is probably the Arabic قرن, "horn."

[4] R. G. Anderson, *Medical Practices and Superstitions of Kordofan*, in *Wellcome Research Laboratories*, *Third Report*, p. 311.

PLATE VII.

SUPPLIANT LIBYANS. DYNASTY V.

present practice of the Neǵd Arabs noticed by Doughty, and also the Egyptian "lock of youth" (Fig. 47). This lock is seen in Egyptian sculpture as a mark of infancy, childhood, or youth, and is therefore often given to Ḥer-pu-ḳraṭ (Harpocrates), who is most frequently represented as a child; or to Ḫonsu, a lunar god who at Thebes was also worshipped under the form of a child. Similarly, the lock of youth is seen in Egyptian representations of young princes, etc.[1] It may be that since the association of this side-lock with the idea of youthfulness existed in ancient Egypt, and in some cases prevails to-day with regard to the *gambur* in the Sudan, that a similar association obtained in Eastern Libya.[2] The fourth and fifth reasons given for the wearing of the *gambur* throw no light on the Libyan practice. The side-lock of the ancient Berbers seems to have been regularly worn,[3] and so could not have been "renewed," and it could never have been any protection against the sun. The sixth reason, however, seems to have a Libyan parallel; for as only chiefs are found wearing the double side-lock (Pl. I. Fig. 9), it is fairly certain that that form of the tress was worn as a "badge of office."

FIG. 47.

The Libyans of the Egyptian monuments often appear bearded, in which case the beards are slight and neatly trimmed, recalling the statement of Strabo cited above (Pls. I., II., III., etc.). The words

> . . . *squalentia barba*
> *Ora viris*,[4] . . .

which Silius Italicus uses with regard to the Macae are here in contradiction to the geographer and to the monumental evidence. Slight moustaches were also worn (cf. *Frontis.*; Pl. II. 3; Pl. III., etc.), as is testified by the Egyptian representations.

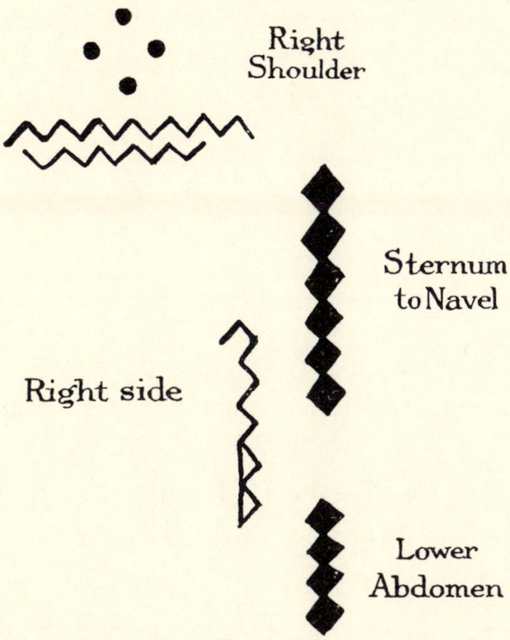

FIG. 48.

* * *

The best early evidence of Libyan tattooing is that afforded by one of the paintings at Tell el-Amarna (Fig. 48), by the XIXth Dynasty representations of Libyan chieftains in the tomb of Seti I. (Pl. III.), and by the glazed tiles of Medînet Habu (*Frontis.*). The Tell el-Amarna captive is a chief, as is shown by his wearing

[1] On the Egyptian and non-Egyptian forms of these tresses cf. W. M. Müller, *Asien und Europa*, p. 298.

[2] According to Lucian (*Navigium*) all Egyptian youths of good birth wore the thick tress until they had reached man hood—a practice which he contrasts with early Attic custom.

[3] Occasional Egyptian representations of Westerners *not* wearing any form of side-lock exist from the time of the Gebeleyn relief to the New Empire. In these cases, however, the people represented wear the Egyptian head-dress of the period, on account of the indifference of the artist.

[4] Silius Italicus iii. 275-6.

two feathers. On his right shoulder is a simple design—a double wavy or serrated line and four dots. On his breast and abdomen are six lozenges in a vertical row, below which, and also vertically placed in a serrated line, are then four more lozenges. This tattooing is a little different in character from that of the other Libyans whose ornamentation is described below. Upon examination of the portraits of the Temeḥu chieftains shown in the tomb of Seti I. (Pl. III.) it will be seen that all four of the Libyan leaders are ornamented with marks of a dark colour on the legs and arms. All have in common an elongated, lozenge-like device above the instep of each foot, the points of each "lozenge" being the ankle-bones. In other respects there is a general resemblance in the style of their tattooing.

In another painting (Fig. 49) a Libyan (Rebu) chief is shown, followed by a sword-bearer, an archer, and a tribesman who bears no arms, and who is, except for a single plume and the *penistasche*, unclad. It is important to note that in this instance only the chief himself, whose decorations are very similar to those of the Temeḥu of the tomb of Seti I., is tattooed.

FIG. 49.

The three coloured faience tiles from Medînet Habu (*Frontis.*) show two bearded Libyan captives who by their rich apparel are clearly chiefs, although, owing to the position they are designed to fill, the artist has had to omit the double plume in order to preserve the isocephaly of the figures in the frieze where they originally belonged. Both chieftains are tattooed, but the only marks on the third figure, a woman, are three horizontal strokes at the navel, here plainly intended to represent the abdominal creases found in many mature women. In adducing these tiles as evidence for tattooing, one must add that not only the marks upon the woman but others seen on the two men are not tattooing at all. Thus in *a* (*Frontis.*) the chief's collar and sandal-ties are represented in the same dark-brown pigment that serves to show his tattooing; the three marks across his right wrist represent a bracelet. In *b* (*Frontis.*) are seen a triple collar, two armillae (left biceps), and a bracelet (left wrist). The other marks are designs tattooed[1] upon the chiefs' bodies.

In regard to these representations, it is first worthy of remark that only the chiefs are tattooed; the followers of the Libyan leader in Fig. 49, and the woman of Medînet Habu, are without ornaments of this sort. This suggests (*a*) that tattooing was in use among the chiefs and not among the tribesmen; and (*b*) that it was employed by the men, and not by the women, of the leaders' families. If this was really the state of affairs it stands in sharp contradistinction to modern practice, as seen, for example, among the Kabyles and certain tribes of Marocco. The men of the former tattoo only for prophylactic reasons; the better sort among them not at all.[2] Among the latter the women

[1] Or painted. The marks are throughout spoken of as "tattooing" for the reasons given below.

[2] H. Weisgerber, *Les Blancs d'Afrique*, p. 68.

habitually practise tattooing,[1] and elsewhere in North Africa tattooing is practised by Berber peoples, and without regard to rank or sex.[2] A parallel to what appears to have been the early Libyan custom is, however, mentioned by Herodotus, who says that among certain Thracian tribes tattooing was esteemed as a mark of noble birth, and that a lack of it was a sign of inferior origin.[3]

The units of design employed in ancient Libyan tattooing are so simple that it is dangerous to try, as has been done,[4] to relate them to extra-African origins. In some cases it is even doubtful whether they may not be due merely to the imagination of the Egyptian artist, and only one or two elements can truly be said to be highly specialized. One of these is the rectangular symbol which has been identified[5] with that of the Saitic goddess Neith, and its occurrence merits careful consideration, both because it has been adduced as evidence in connection with Libyan religion, and further because of the light it throws on the reasons for tattooing among the Libyans. It is seen on one of the chiefs in the form shown in Fig. 50, *a* ; on three in the form *b* (once without the upper antennae-like projections) ; and once as given in *c*. The allied forms *d*, *e*, and *f* also occur.

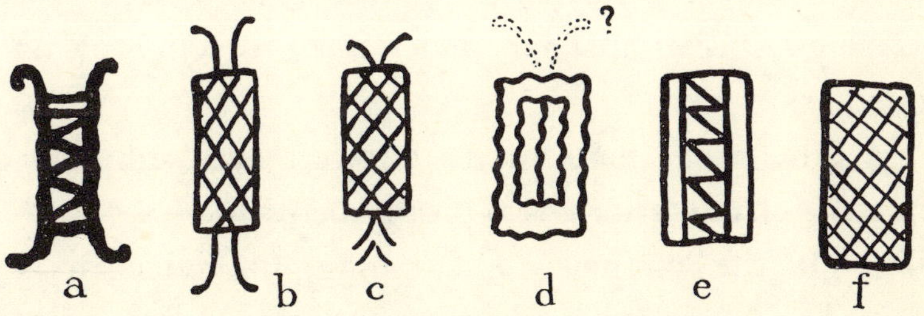

FIG. 50.

There can be no doubt that this highly specialized emblem is a truly Libyan one, despite the ingenious conjecture of Lefébure that the mark is a brand put upon captives who were to be given as servants to the goddess of Sais. For the Egyptian text[6] Léfébure has adduced to support his argument relates only to captives as being branded with the name of a king, and it is hardly credible, even supposing that they were sometimes branded with the name of a deity,[7] that among all the foreign princes represented none should display the name of Amon, the chief divinity of the Egyptians at the time of the Libyan invasions of Seti I., Merneptah, and Rameses III. Furthermore, it would, in this case, be surprising that the symbol of a Delta goddess, and no other, should occur on monuments all coming from near Thebes, the chief seat of Amon, and only on Libyan, to the exclusion of Asiatic, captives.

The fact that there is no proof that the tattoo-marks here discussed were brands applied to captive servants of Neith does not, however, preclude the possibility that the symbol seen on the Libyan prisoners is that of the goddess. The archaic form of the

[1] *Ibid.* p. 172.

[2] H. Bazin, *Études sur le tatouage dans le régence de Tunis.*

[3] Herodotus v. 6 ; cf., for Scythic tattooing, Clearchus of Soli, *Frag.* 8 in *FHG.*

[4] L. Bertholon, *Origines néolithiques et mycéniennes des tatouages des indigènes du nord de l' Afrique.*

[5] First by H. Brugsch, *Religion und Mythologie der alten Ägypter*, p. 340 *sqq.*

[6] In the Papyrus Harris, BAR iv. § 405, the King says : " I have given to them [*sc.* the captives] captains of archers, and chief men of the tribes, branded and made into slaves, impressed with my name ; their wives and their children were made likewise." In note *g*, *ad loc. cit.*, Breasted shows that these captives given to Amon probably served in part as temple neatherds.

[7] Refugees at some sacred asylums in Arabia became ἱερόδουλοι and were tattooed with sacred marks. W. R. Smith, *Religion of the Semites*, p. 148, note.

hieroglyph,[1] as seen in Fig. 51, *a*, is practically identical with the tattoo-mark shown in Fig. 50, *a* ; while Fig. 50, *e*, is like it, save for the lack of the "antennae" at the ends of the rectangle. To the later form of the hieroglyph, Fig. 51, *b* (which came eventually to be written as in *c*), the tattoo-marks in Fig. 50, *b* and *c*, correspond exactly. Fig. 50, *f*, lacks the "antennae." The marks, Fig. 50, *d*, *e*, *f*, may be variants, either accidental or significant, of the hieroglyph , but there can be no reasonable doubt that the marks in Fig. 50, *a*, *b*, and *c*, are the symbol  itself, both in its archaic (Fig. 51, *a*) and New Empire (Fig. 51, *b*, *c*) forms. These identities throw light on the reason of the practice of tattooing among the Libyans. It has been shown that the evidence at present available points to the fact that Libyan tattooing was anciently a prerogative of (male) chieftains, and the common employment of this symbol indicates furthermore that it may have served to show that the wearers were in some special manner under the protection of, or affiliated to, the Libyan-Egyptian goddess.

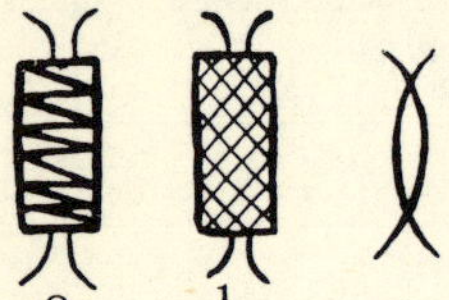

Fig. 51.

The other units of design were very simple ; they are collected in Fig. 52, and may be characterized as typically neolithic.

Of the methods of tattooing, no evidence is preserved ; indeed, what has for convenience been so termed up to this point may have been mere painting. The Gyzantes painted themselves with red all over their bodies ;[2] the Maxyes smeared themselves liberally with red paint.[3] The character of the Libyan designs, however, and the practice in ancient Egypt and in modern North Africa of subcutaneous tattooing, encourage the belief that the skin decorations recorded on the monuments were tattooing in the proper sense.

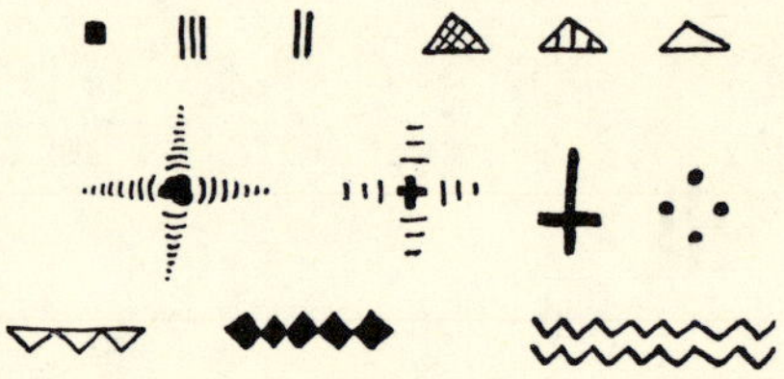
Fig. 52.

* * *

It appears from the Egyptian records that while circumcision was practised by the Sherden and other allies of the Libyans, they were not themselves given to this mutilation.[4] This is in a way confirmed at a later period by the statements of Herodotus. He attributes the origin of the practice to the Egyptians,[5] of whom he remarks that they preferred to be cleanly rather than unmutilated.[6] He does not include the Libyans among those peoples whom he enumerates as observing circumcision, though he correctly says that it was an Egyptian custom, and one which was undoubtedly of very ancient date in Aethiopia.[7] That he is not here, as happens with other Greek writers and once or twice with himself, confusing the Aethiopians

[1] D. Mallet, *Le Culte de Neit à Saïs*, p. 179. The origin of the sign is obscure.
[2] Herodotus iv. 194.
[3] *Ibid.* iv. 191.
[4] BAR iii. § 587 and note *h*, *ad loc. cit.*, § 588, iv. § 53, *et alibi.*
[5] Herodotus ii. 36.
[6] *Ibid.* ii. 37.
[7] *Ibid.* ii. 104.

with the Libyans, is clear not only from the XIXth and XXth Dynasty testimony, but also from that of the Piankhi stela. The Aethiopian Piankhi, having subdued the Delta dynasts, denied them entrance to his presence because they were eaters of an Aethiopian taboo animal—the fish—and, apparently, because they were uncircumcised.[1] Only Namlot was permitted to enter the palace of Piankhi, a favour which was granted him because of his position at the head of the Dynasts; and perhaps because, in conformity with Egyptian usage, he had been "made circumcised."

[1] BAR iv. § 882, note *d*.

CHAPTER VII

MATERIAL CULTURE AND ART

The Use of Metals.—It has been tacitly assumed by many writers that the ancient Libyans of the time of the invasions were in a fairly advanced state of culture because they had arms and utensils of metal. This is a question which needs careful examination, since it has a profound bearing on Libyan civilization, and because it is of deep historical significance.

FIG. 53.

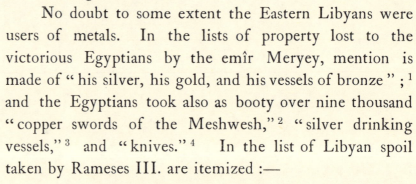

No doubt to some extent the Eastern Libyans were users of metals. In the lists of property lost to the victorious Egyptians by the emîr Meryey, mention is made of "his silver, his gold, and his vessels of bronze";[1] and the Egyptians took also as booty over nine thousand "copper swords of the Meshwesh,"[2] "silver drinking vessels,"[3] and "knives."[4] In the list of Libyan spoil taken by Rameses III. are itemized :—

Swords of five cubits . . .	115 (+x)
Swords of three cubits . . .	124.[5]

These notices receive confirmation from an Egyptian representation of the metal vases of the Libyans (Fig. 53),[6] and from the classical notices of Libyan swords.[7]

It would, however, be wrong to infer from this evidence that the Eastern Libyans were as a whole in a "full metal age." They were, in fact, metal-users only by accident, for their useful metals anciently, as to-day, came to them from without.[8] The metal vases of the princes betray by their forms their foreign origin, and the long swords of the soldiery were

[1] BAR iii. § 584. [2] BAR iii. § 589. [3] BAR, *loc. cit.*

[4] BAR, *loc. cit.* and note *b*. These "knives" have the determinative for copper.

[5] BAR iv. § 111. [6] W. M. Müller, *op. cit.* vol. ii. p. 123 *sqq.*

[7] Hellanicus, *Frag.* 93 in *FHG*; Nicolaus Damascenus, *Frag.* 137 in *FHG*.

[8] I say useful metals, since gold they may have found within or near their territories, *e.g.* as in the Isle of Cyraunis, so reputed for its mineral-pitch (Herodotus iv. 195).

those known in Southern Europe, and employed by the Sherden allies of the North Africans.[1] Between Tunisia and Egypt the scarcity of native metal would in itself be sufficient ground for doubting whether the Eastern Libyans were ever acquainted with the art of working metals. Apart from the haematitic iron in Marmarica,[2] and traces of copper in the Gebel el-ʿAḳabah,[3] no workable metals are found within Eastern Libya. On the western boundary of that area are some deposits of iron,[4] while copper is found in small quantities on the eastern slopes of Atlas.[5] There is no indication that any of these sources was known before Roman times, and the modern inhabitants of the country depend for their metals wholly on the outside world.

An examination of the classical evidence relating to Libyan weapons is especially significant on this head. A warlike people, if amply supplied with copper, bronze, or iron, would certainly have been provided with weapons of metal. Yet this does not seem to have been the case in Greek and Roman times. It is true that, both citing the same source or one the other, Hellanicus and Nicolaus of Damascus speak of Libyan swords,[6] but they are speaking rather of the Punicized Libyans of the west than of the Eastern Libyans proper, of whom Diodorus Siculus, here drawing on a source better than some he uses, remarks that they were armed each with three javelins and a bag of stones, and that they were ignorant of swords, helms, or other arms.[7] The Auseans, it is true, in a religious festival dressed one of the performers in a "Corinthian helmet and a full suit of Greek armour"[8]; not only were these importations, however, but Herodotus declares his ignorance "what arms they used . . . before the Greeks came to their country."[9] It is noteworthy that the arms employed by the Auseans in their religious sham-fights were stones and clubs.[10] For the sake of their clothes and arms the Libyans cut off the stragglers from the Persian army of Aryandes, when it was in retreat from Cyrenaica;[11] while the Libyan contingent in the army of Xerxes was armed with javelins the tips of which had been hardened by fire.[12] The barbed spear, *cateia*, mentioned as a Libyan weapon by Silius Italicus,[13] was not necessarily headed with metal; the same poet, speaking of the Baniurae, says that, lacking iron, they are—

Contenti parca durasse hastilia flamma.[14]

The arms of the Libyans of early Byzantine times, as mentioned by Corippus, were

[1] W. M. Müller, *op. cit.* vol. ii. p. 127, *n.* 2.

[2] Nodules of haematite containing a high percentage of iron, and showing a lustrous silvery fracture, are found in the Libyan desert near Mongar Lebuk. Yuzbashî Nimr ʿAlî, O.C., H.H. Coast Guards, at Ḍabbah, showed me in 1910 a specimen he had collected.

[3] A specimen of the ore was brought by an Arab to Bînbashî L. V. Royle, O.C., H.H. Coast Guards, Marsah Matru, where I saw it in 1910.

[4] H. Duveyrier, *Les Touareg du Nord*, p. 142. Duveyrier pertinently asks *comment l'exploiterait-on sans combustible?*

[5] Tertullian, *Apologia* xii.; Victor Vitensis, *Historia persecutionis*, v. 19; S. Cyprianus, *Epist.* 80; cf. Strabo xvii. p. 830.

[6] Hellanicus, *loc. cit.* The Numidian tribesman has naught save . . . κύλικα καὶ μάχαιραν καὶ ὑδρίαν . . . Nicolaus of Damascus *loc. cit.* Σαρδολίβυες οὐδὲν κέκτηνται σκεῦος ἔξω κύλικος καὶ μαχαίρας.

[7] Diodorus Siculus iii. 69. 4. To make Diodorus's list complete it only is necessary to add only bows.

[8] Herodotus iv. 180. [9] *Ibid. loc. cit.* [10] *Ibid. loc. cit.* [11] *Ibid.* iv. 203. [12] *Ibid.* vii. 71.

[13] Silius Italicus iii. 277. [14] *Ibid.* iii. 303 *sq.* The Baniurae were a Gaetulian tribe of the west, Pliny v. 2.

in some—perhaps in many—cases of metal;[1] but it should be borne in mind that the natives described in the *Johannis* were mainly of the west, and a juster idea of the arms of the Eastern Libyans can be drawn from Procopius.[2] It may be observed that not only is a scarcity of metal apparent from the evidence on arms, but also the vases of gold, silver, or bronze, mentioned in the Egyptian records, do not appear in classical writers, who mention only cups and jars of pottery,[3] or of wood or bark.[4] Whereas, furthermore, the women of the Egyptianized Adyrmachidae had anklets of bronze,[5] their sisters among the Auseans, who were remote from Egypt, had to be content with rings of leather.[6]

Metal, then, was a rarity. The great chieftains had stores of it, the fighting men in contact with Carthage or Egypt succeeded in procuring it. The majority of tribesmen had not enough of it to head their weapons, or to make themselves swords. Descriptions in Silius Italicus of bejewelled and well-armed Libyan chiefs are to be taken as mainly poetic, and as only partially justified by the fact that the leaders of the allies of Carthage would naturally have Carthaginian weapons. It is indeed only as allies of metal-users like the Carthaginians or the Sherden that the Eastern Libyans appear in history as a people advanced beyond a neolithic stage of culture. This point is significant. The island of Sardinia, which was at least partly under the dominion of the Sherden, is rich in metals. The long swords of the Libyan tribesmen were, as has been said, South European in type, and are seen on the Egyptian monuments of the New Empire as the characteristic weapons of the Sherden and Shekelesh mercenaries in the Egyptian service. From this it seems safe to infer that the Sherden sea-rovers associated with the Libyans in their enterprises against Egypt armed their allies. This is of no small significance as indicative of the strength of the bonds between the Northerners and the Africans, and of the character of the great invasions.

*
* *

Arms and Warfare.—What has been said with regard to the use of metals may serve as an introduction to the question of Libyan arms and warfare.

Of offensive weapons the Eastern Libyans do not appear to have despised the humblest, for it was not only in the Ausean sham-fights that they made use of sticks and stones. The latter, as has been remarked, they carried in bags, and threw with great skill,[7] either by hand or from slings.[8] The former were either straight (Fig. 54, *a*) or curved slightly near the end (Fig. 54, *b*, *c*), like a modern camel-stick. If meant for throwing, they were crooked like some of the modern Sudanese *turumbash* (Fig. 54, *c*).

These very primitive weapons were widely employed by the Eastern Libyans, but their weapons *par excellence* were the bow and arrow, and the short javelin. It is the

[1] Corippus, *Johannis*, ii. 115 (*mucrone potens*), 126 (*gladiosque minaces*), 133 (*binaque praevalido . . . hastilia ferro*), 151 (. . . *lancea duplex | iuniperum ferro validam suffigit acuto*), 155 (*mucro fulmineus*), etc.

[2] Procopius, *De bello Vandalico* ii. 11.

[3] Hellanicus, *loc. cit.* Nicolaus Damascus, *loc. cit.* [4] Mela i. 8. [5] Herodotus iv. 168.

[6] *Ibid.* iv. 176. [7] Diodorus Siculus iii. 49. 5. [8] For a Libyan slinger see Pl. V. 2.

bow with which the Libyans are equipped in the great battle scenes of the XIXth and XXth Dynasties. In the Merneptah records Meryey is said to have fallen upon the Temeḥu with his bowmen;[1] and later, in his own flight, to have left behind him his bow, arrows, and quiver.[2] In the booty taken by Merneptah were more than two thousand bows;[3] while bows and quivers, the latter to the number of 2310, were captured by Rameses III.[4] The bows used by the Libyans seem sometimes to have

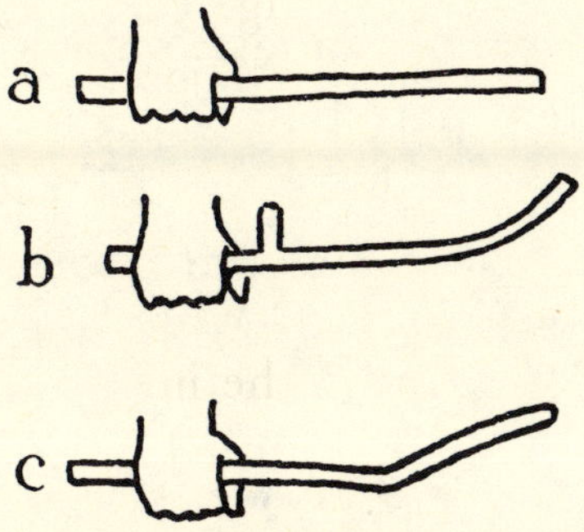

Fig. 54.

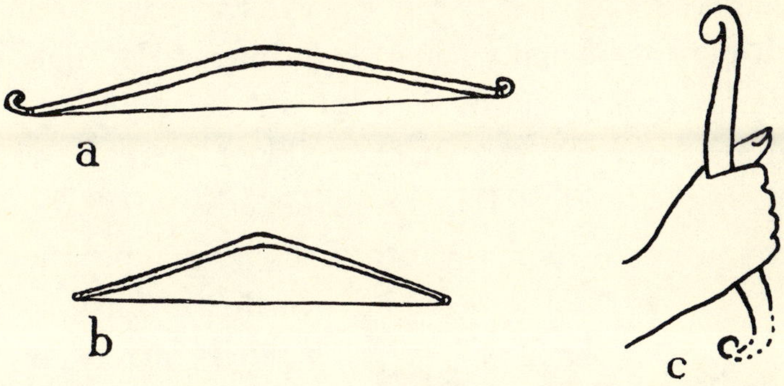

Fig. 55.

been so small as to suggest that they were, as was sometimes the case in Egypt,[5] used for poisoned arrows. As far as can be judged, the shape of the bows (Fig. 55) is rather that of those employed by the Asiatics of the monuments than of those used by the Egyptians or in use in modern Africa.[6] The typical Libyan bow resembled in shape a very obtuse V, having an angle of about 140°. The bows of the chiefs are sometimes shown as having reflexed horns, as in Fig. 55, *a*. In one case (Fig. 55, *c*), the bow itself is so small that it must be regarded as a model,[7] or as having for conventional reasons been made small by the artist.

The forms of the heads of the Libyan arrows were varied. The large number of arrow-heads of flint, carnelian, and similar stones, found in the Ṣaḥara, the Egyptian oases, and the Fayum, makes it probable that these were the points generally employed; while the highly specialized types which these neoliths exhibit, and the fact that even in Egypt some forms of them were in use down into protodynastic times, encourage the belief that they were employed by the less advanced Libyans during the full historic period. A parallel survival may be cited in the case of the Aethiopians, who, even when serving in the army of Xerxes in the fifth century B.C., had arrows headed "not with iron, but with a piece of stone, sharpened to a point, of the kind used in engraving seals."[8] A typical collection of Fayum points

Fig. 56.

[1] BAR iii. § 579; cf. iii. § 609, "the archers threw down their bows."

[2] BAR iii. § 584.

[3] BAR iii. § 601; cf. the unknown item numbering 120,214, mentioned by BAR iii. § 589.

[4] BAR § iv. 111.

[5] G. A. Reisner, *Work of the Expedition of the University of California at Naga ed-Dêr*, in the *Annales*, vol. v. pl. vii., fig. 1.

[6] For which, R. Karutz, *Die afrikanischen Bogen Pfeile und Köcher im Lübecker Museum, etc.*

[7] Cf., however, the "dancing-bows" of the Nuers of the Baḥr ez-Zerraf. These are small mimic bows of purely ceremonial significance. Cf. O. Bates, *Sudanese Notes*, in *CSJ*, vol. vi. No. 69.

[8] Herodotus vii. 69.

is shown in Pl. VIII. 1-31 inclusive; the arrow-head represented in Fig. 56 is one recently found near Gerbah (Sîwah Oasis), and sent to me by my friend Major L. V. Royle. It may be stated with certainty that the Fayum flints are Libyan and not Nilotic, from (*a*) the wide geographical range of many of the types,[1] and (*b*) the preponderance of them in habitable places not in the Nile Valley.

The javelins which, at least after the introduction of the horse, were weapons so characteristically Libyan, seem not to have been common at the time of the invasions. In the list of booty taken by Rameses III., only ninety-two "spears" are listed among the weapons,[2] but by classical times darts, lances, and spears were universally employed throughout North Africa.[3] These weapons were headed much as were the Libyan arrows. In Pl. VIII. 32-40 inclusive are various examples of spear and lance points from the Fayum, the broad, gashing type there shown (32) being especially noteworthy.[4] That spears were sometimes pointed merely by induration of the sharpened end in the fire has been mentioned already.[5]

Fig. 57.

Fig. 58.

The classical writers, in using such terms as *iacula*,[6] *tela*,[7] *spicula*,[8] etc., when speaking of the Libyan javelins, clearly indicate that they were mainly weapons for hurling rather than for stabbing or thrusting. That the javelins were usually carried in pairs appears from Corippus[9] (cf. Fig. 57, *b*), although three was not an unusual number (cf. Fig. 58); and that they may sometimes have been delivered by the aid of a throwing-thong (*amentum*) may be implied by such phrases as—

> . . . *spicula supplex*
> *Iam torquet Garamas* . . .[10]

and

> . . . *tremulum quem torsit missile Mazax*[11]

in the Latin writers. That the barbed spear, known to the Romans as the *cateia*, was used among the Libyans is to be inferred from a line of Silius Italicus.[12]

Besides the weapons mentioned, the Libyans used, to a limited extent and at those times when they were allied to a people more advanced than themselves, the sword. The Egyptians took from the Meshwesh 9111 copper swords,[13] and the swords of five

[1] Cf. E.-F. Gautier, *Sahara algérien*, p. 121 *sqq.* pl. xix. photo. 37; H. Vischer, *Across the Sahara*, Appendix B.

[2] BAR iv. § 111.

[3] Herodotus vii. 71; Strabo xvii. p. 828; Caesar, *De bello Africano* xiv.; Lucan iv. 662; Silius Italicus ii. 89, iii. 277, iii. 303; Diodorus Siculus iii. 49. 4; Claudian, *Laus Stilichonis* i. 249; Procopius, *De bello Vandalico* ii. 11.

[4] (?) The *venabula* of Corippus ii. 11.

[5] The spear of the Temeḥu mercenary shown in I. Rosellini, *Monumenti*, etc., vol. ii. pl. 117, 5, appears to be merely fire-hardened.

[6] Corippus, *Johannis* iv. 513, 551, v. 136.

[7] *Ibid.* ii. 114.

[8] Claudian, *Laus Stilichonis*, i. 345.

[9] Corippus, *Johannis* ii. 133, *bina hastilia*; Procopius, *loc. cit.* Cf. Fig. 57, *b*.

[10] Claudian, *loc. cit.*

[11] Lucan iv. 662.

[12] Silius Italicus iii. 277, speaking of one of the Macae—

> . . . *panda manus est armata cateia.*

[13] BAR iii. § 589.

PLATE VIII.

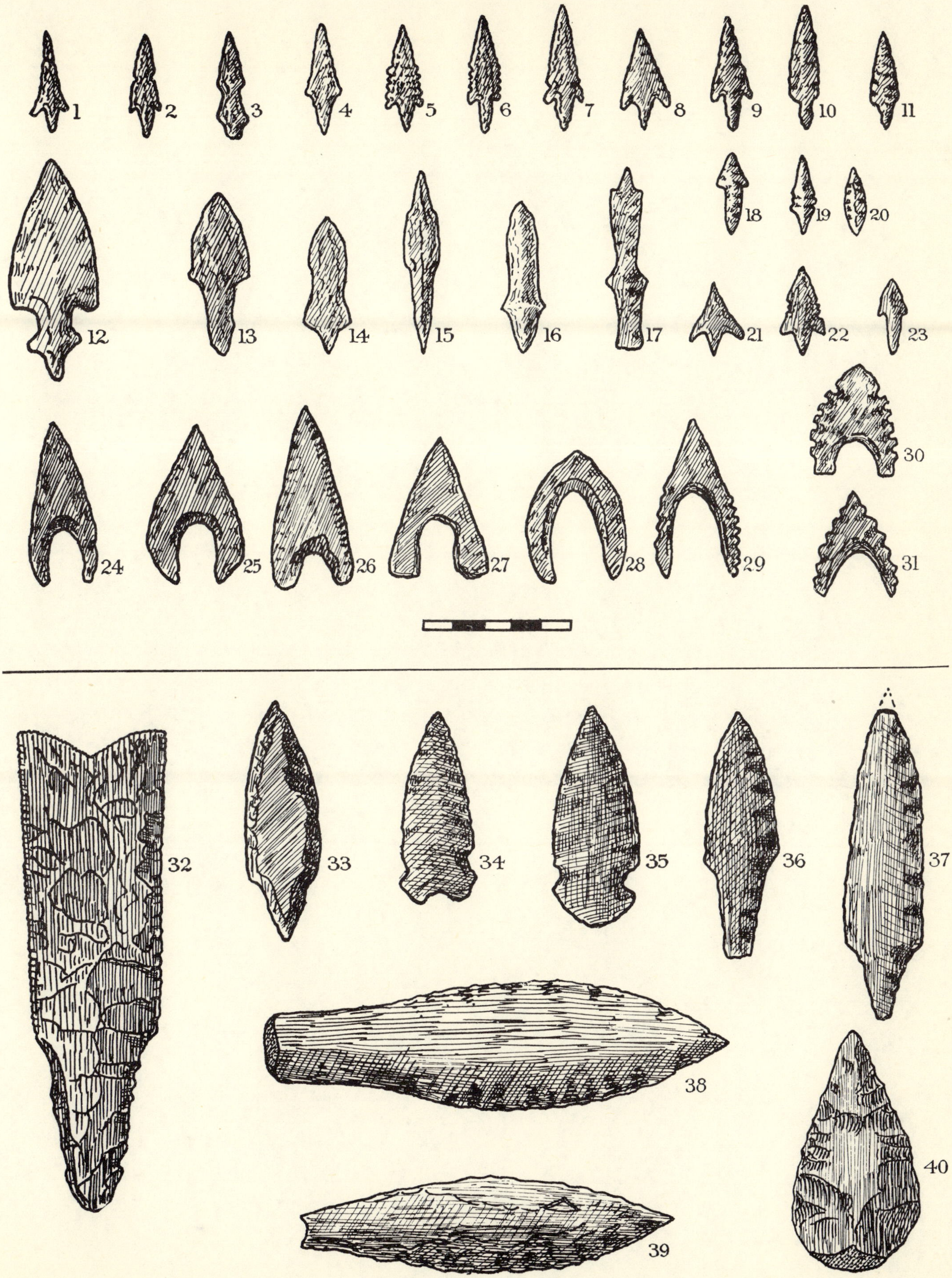

LIBYAN NEOLITHS.

and of three cubits taken by Rameses III. have been mentioned.[1] These powerful weapons were, as has been said, of foreign origin ; an example is shown in Fig. 49.[2] A sword of different type is mentioned by Silius as having been employed by the Adyrmachidae. The Roman poet describes it as *falcatus*,[3] a term which strongly suggests the Egyptian sickle-shaped weapon known as the , *ḥepeš* (Pl. IV. and Fig. 88). If the Adyrmachidae really had a sword of this type, it would be of much archaeological interest, for the *ḥepeš* occupied a curious ceremonial position in Egypt, was an attribute of kings, and had its origin in remote—possibly in neolithic—times.[4] In the classical period the Libyans in contact with the Mediterranean world were in some cases armed with the short sabre, the *machaera*,[5] while in Byzantine times short, small, straight swords,[6] or long knives, were occasionally worn on the upper arm,[7] as with the modern Imushagh

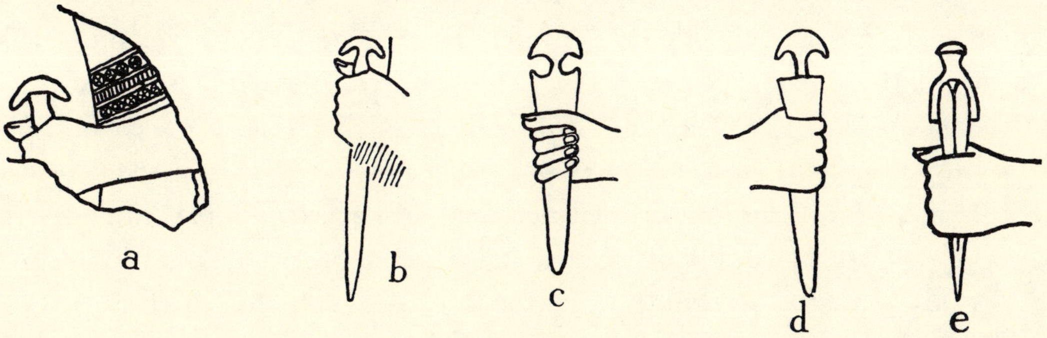

Fig. 59.

and Sudanese. These small swords are to be distinguished from those mentioned in the booty taken by Merneptah.[8] The knives captured by that Pharaoh were presumably such daggers as those shown in the hands of the Libyans as early as in the Ne-user-re reliefs, and as late as the New Empire (Fig. 59). These daggers are hardly distinguishable from Egyptian weapons, and are really Mediterranean. They had sheaths (Fig. 59, *d*), and, as is clear from the type of hilt, were primarily for stabbing.

One more weapon deserves passing mention. A Libyan mercenary in one of the Benî Ḥasan paintings (Fig. 11) carries an axe.[9] The form is the lunate shape so common

1 BAR iv. § 111. Five cubits = 2.63 m. (!) ; three cubits = 1.59 m.

2 Is the modern Imushagh long sword a survival of these old weapons ? For an example see Aymard, *Les Touareg*, *frontis.*

3 Silius Italicus iii. 278 *sqq.*—

> . . . *et falcatus ab arte*
> *Ensis Adyrmachidis.*

4 For an example of this curved sword see I. Rosellini, *Monumenti*, etc., vol. iii. pl. 121, 8.

5 Hellanicus, *loc. cit.* ; Nicolaus Damascenus, *loc. cit.*

6 Corippus, *Johannis* ii. 115, 126, 155.

7 Corippus, *Johannis* ii. 126 *sqq.*—

> . . . *gladiosque minaces*
> *Non solito vinctos lateri, sed circulus ambit*
> *Perstringens modicum, complexus brachia gyro*
> *Vaginasque aptant nudis pendere lacertis ;*

and ii. 155—

> *Mucro fulmineus laevo dependens ab armo.*

8 BAR iii. § 589.

9 I. Rosellini, *op. cit.*, vol. ii. pl. 117, 5, gives another example.

in Egypt, and it is probable that the axe-bearer was armed by those he served. It is, however, to be remarked that Silius twice speaks of Libyans in the Carthaginian army as armed with axes, although in this case the double *bipennis*,[1] and not the lunate form, is specified.

A people in a low state of civilization is better supplied with offensive than with defensive arms. This was well exemplified in the case of the North Africans of antiquity, though it is not necessary to believe that any portion of the inhabitants of the continent were quite so devoid of protection as Herodotus declares the *Gamphasantes to have been.[2] Leather coats were the commonest defence; even the riff-raff in the army of Xerxes wore them.[3] Shields, moreover, were regularly used during the classical period. The common forms were the large round buckler, slightly convex on the outer side, known to the Romans as the *clipeus*;[4] and the *caetra*[5] and the *pelta*.[6] The last two were sometimes slung at the side or between the shoulders of the wearer.[7] The small round shields of the *caetra* type were especially favoured in Africa, as in Spain.[8] They were light, and made of strips or thongs of leather.[9] Examples are seen in the Ṣaḥaran petroglyphs (*e.g.* Fig. 57) in a "Numidian" stela (Fig. 58), and in the Constantinople sculptures (Fig. 13). The last-named instance is of exceptional interest, since the artist has indicated the structure of the shields. The Macae, according to Herodotus, used a shield which must have been of the *caetra* class, made of ostrich-skin.[10]

Fig. 60.

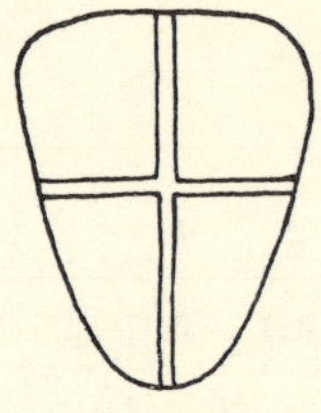

Fig. 61.

A shield roughly resembling the Boeotian type was also known in North Africa; Fig. 60 shows an example, borne by a Libyan wearing a kilt and *penistasche* (?). Another example, somewhat like the body-shield of the Crusaders, is recorded on a petroglyph in Tibesti (Fig. 61). It is ornamented with a cross, perhaps intended to represent colour, since the fact that the Libyans painted their shields is known from Silius.[11]

Helms and body-armour, though occasionally referred to by Roman writers when

[1] Silius Italicus v. 287 *sq.*—

Stabat fulgentem portans in bella bipennem
Cyniphius; . . .

and the "cruel axe" (*saevamque bipennem*) of the Princess Asbyte in ii. 189.

[2] Herodotus iv. 174; followed by Mela i. 8; and by Martianus Capella, *De nuptiis Philologiae*, etc., vi. (p. 232), *Campasantes* [*sic*] *nudi et imbelles externis numquam miscentur.*

[3] Herodotus vii. 71. These jackets probably represented the "armour" of Merneptah records, BAR iii. § 589.

[4] Corippus, *Johannis* ii. 114, 126. The Greek ἀσπίς.

[5] Silius Italicus iii. 278; Corippus, *Johannis* ii. 153. The name *caetra*, *cetra*, is Iberian, and this shield was usually associated with Spain. Cf. Hesychius *in verb.*: καίτρα ὅπλα Ἰβηρικά, and Servius *ad* Vergilii *Aeneidem* vii. 732.

[6] Silius Italicus ii. 80. It may be because this light lunate shield was especially associated in classical art with the Amazons that Silius attributes it here to the Libyan princess Asbyte.

[7] Corippus, *Johannis* ii. 126, 153.

[8] Servius, *loc. cit.*, *scutum loreum quo utuntur Afri et Hispani.*

[9] Isidorus Hispalensis, *Origines* viii. 12, *scutum loreum sine ligno.* Cf. Strabo xvii. p. 828, for shields of elephant-hide.

[10] Herodotus iv. 175.

[11] Silius Italicus iii. 278, *versicolor* . . . *caetra*, in describing an Adyrmachid.

describing Libyan chiefs,[1] do not appear to have been in general use. Diodorus even states explicitly that they were not employed.[2] The warriors of the Constantinople sculptures referred to above wear what might be supposed to be helms, but these may be merely caps, either of cloth or of leather, of the *pileus* type.[3]

As regards equipment, it has already been remarked that the Eastern Libyans, as early as the time of the invasions, made use of quivers. Mention has also been made of the bags in which the slingers or stone-casters carried their ammunition.[4] An important item in Libyan gear was the *kerbah* or water-skin without which it was impossible to travel in the desert. *Ḳerabah* are first noticed in a New Empire record,[5] and in classical times were carried slung under the bellies of horses,[6] a practice which persists to-day.

The booty taken from the Libyans by Rameses III. included nearly one hundred chariots.[7] According to Herodotus, the Greeks derived their knowledge of the *quadriga* from Libya,[8] but this does not, even if correct, in the slightest degree affect the probability that the Libyans themselves drew their knowledge of the chariot from Egypt. By classical times, wheeled vehicles of some sort had become widely diffused over North Africa. They were known to the Asbystae,[9] and to the Zaueces, whose wives drove their husbands' chariots to battle.[10] Even the Garamantes[11] of the interior, and the Pharusii and Nigretes of the far west[12] had cars for travelling or for battle; and the whole Libyan contingent serving with Xerxes was mounted in chariots, just as were the Arabians upon camels—in both cases, that is, the troops served with their usual equipment. It is not therefore strange to find such a phrase as—

Λίβυες ζυγωτῶν ἁρμάτων ἐπιστάται[13]

in Sophocles, nor to learn that Cyrene, εὐάρματος πόλις,[14] was anciently a very celebrated centre for chariotry, although by Roman times the use of chariots in war had declined.

It is not to be imagined that the Libyan chariot, of native make, was the smart vehicle of wood and bronze known in Egypt, Asia, and Greece. Frequently the "chariots" were probably no more than wains. Explicit notices of such exist, as in Silius Italicus, who thus refers to the Gaetulians:—

Nulla domus; plaustris habitant; migrare per arva
Mos atque errantes circumvectare penates.[15]

[1] *E.g.* Silius Italicus i. 415 *et alibi*. Cf., however, the remarks of Pliny x. 1, and Theophrastus, *Hist. Plant.* iv. 41, in regard to ostrich-plumes being worn by the Libyans in their helms. By the Egyptian monumental evidence the use of feathers is confirmed, but that of helms is not.

[2] Diodorus Siculus iii. 49. 4.

[3] Cf. Procopius, *De bello Vandal.* i. 25.

[4] Diodorus Siculus, *loc. cit.*

[5] BAR iii. §§ 609, 610.

[6] Strabo xvii. p. 828.

[7] BAR iv. § 111.

[8] Herodotus iv. 189. The four-horse chariot is at least as early as the Homeric poems—*Iliad* viii. 185, *Odyss.* xiii. 81—and appeared in the Olympic contests in the seventh century, as is attested by Pausanias v. 8. 7.

[9] Whom Herodotus, iv. 170, terms τεθριπποβάται μάλιστα Λιβύων.

[10] Herodotus iv. 193.

[11] *Ibid.* iv. 183.

[12] Strabo, *loc. cit.* The war-chariots are said by Strabo to have been armed with scythes.

[13] Sophocles, *Electra*, 702.

[14] Pindar, *Pyth.* iv. 7.

[15] Silius Italicus iii. 299, 300; cf. Caesar, *De bello Africano* lxxv.; Pliny v. 3.

It is cars of this sort, *robusta plaustra*, and not chariots, which are seen on the rock-glyphs of Northern Tibesti; pictures, if one may judge, of true neolithic wains. Similar carts are to be seen to-day in Kordofan. They are drawn by bullocks, and are made without metal, of tough woods well pegged together and lashed with thongs of green hide. They bear no resemblance to the Libyan war-chariots which are portrayed, only in one doubtful instance, on an Egyptian monument; the type of car there represented is indistinguishable from the Egyptian vehicle, or at least was so rendered by the Egyptian artist.[1]

What has been said of the horses of Eastern Libya may be recalled here in connection with the question of warfare. The North African horses were little more than ponies, but tough and wiry.[2] They first appear in history at the time of the invasions.[3] They were so well trained that they often followed their masters, when the latter went on foot, like dogs;[4] they were ridden without saddles, and often without bridles, being guided by the touch of a light switch.[5] In some few cases bridles of rushes were employed,[6] but they are not heard of among the Eastern Libyans. The one trapping which seems to have been in general use was a neck-stall of palm-fibre or plaited bark, the περιτραχήλια ξύλινα, from which depended a leading-rein.[7] A rude representation of this is seen in the "Numidian" stela, Fig. 58.

In their manner of fighting, the Libyans of the Egyptian period followed a system of tactics very different from that which they practised when, at a later date, they had become a nation of horsemen. The Meshwesh, for example, having overpowered their eastern neighbours, the Teḥenu, forced the latter to join them in their invasion of Egypt. Meryey, the Meshwesh leader, contracted alliances with numbers of Sherden, Sheklesh, Ekwesh, Luka, and Teresh, "taking the best of every warrior and man of war in his country."[8] Thereafter the army of invasion marched upon Egypt, cutting off the detached Egyptian outposts as it neared the Nile Valley.[9] Eventually the army neared the scene of battle, approaching the forces of Merneptah. Before dawn on the day preceding that of the battle, the great chief in person[10] went among the leather tents[11] of his camp, marshalling his men.[12] The next day, the Libyan vanguard[13] was face to face with the Egyptian army, and the battle began. For six hours it raged, the Egyptian archery loosing flight after flight of arrows into the undisciplined but hardy

[1] W. M. Müller, *Egyptological Researches*, vol. ii. p. 121.
[2] Strabo, *loc. cit.* [3] BAR iii. § 589, iv. § 111. [4] Strabo, *loc. cit.*
[5] *Ibid. loc. cit.*; Lucan iv. 663 *sq.*—

Et gens quae nudo residens Massylia dorso
Ora levi flectit frenorum nescia virga.

This passage was, it may be safely assumed, equally applicable for the ruder east. Cf. *ibid.* iv. 658 *sq.*—

. . . semperque paratus
Inculto Gaetulus equo.

[6] Silius Italicus i. 215 *sq.*; Caesar, *De bello Africano*, lxi.; Claudian, *Nilus*, 20; *Laus Stilichonis*, i. 249.
[7] Strabo, *loc. cit.*
[8] BAR iii. § 579. [9] BAR iii. § 580. [10] BAR iii. § 583.
[11] BAR iii. § 589. [12] BAR iii. § 583. [13] BAR iii. § 609. "Their marchers forward."

ranks of the Libyans.[1] Finally the invaders broke and fled, casting aside their bows and water-skins,[2] and leaving over 9000 slain on the field, and as many more taken captive.[3]

Far different from battles and campaigns of this sort, which evince so much military stability—however barbaric—are those of the Libyans of the classical period. In Greek and Roman times, the African was like the Parthian, a light horseman ; swift to attack, yet swifter to retreat, unapproachable by infantry. The native cavalry with which Caesar was forced to engage seldom chose to come to close quarters with an enemy on level ground ; they preferred to lie in ambush with their horses among the wadys, and then suddenly to fall upon their foes.[4] Sometimes, for the sake of greater stability, these horsemen went into action in company with light-armed foot.[5] The mounted African was, as Ammianus said from personal experience, an enemy flanking and sudden, and trusting to secret wiles rather than to regular fighting.[6] Yet these methods of fighting, though not unknown to the Eastern Libyans, were rather those of the Numidians and Mauri of the west.[7] Something of the old stability existed in Tripolitana to a late period, where the natives fought from behind their barrack'd camels,[8] as cavalry use their carbines from behind their horses at the present day.

The existence in parts of Eastern Libya of well-built strongholds leads to the supposition that such tribes as the Auschisae and the Nasamones, within whose territories the occurrence of these forts has been noted, knew how to maintain themselves behind defences. No notices of such actions, however, exist, unless in the case of an Egyptian representation of a fortress which is being stormed by Rameses II. The fortress in question is pictured in the conventional Egyptian manner, and is called Satuna—supposedly a Syrian town. The garrison, curiously enough, is of mixed Asiatics and Libyans—a point well worthy of notice, even if it be admitted that the scene of the action lay not in Libya but in Syria.[9]

In late times, fighting from within a square of barrack'd camels was a favourite mode of sustaining attacks. The men were stationed along the lines, the women and children were placed in the middle of the square.[10] The camels were in some cases partially protected by the men's shields.[11]

In personal courage the ancient Berbers were the equals of their descendants. Like

[1] BAR iii. § 584.
[2] BAR iii. § 609.
[3] BAR iii. § 588 *ad fin.*, and note *a*, *ad loc. cit.*
[4] Caesar, *De bello Africano*, vii.; cf. Diodorus Siculus iii. 49. 3.
[5] *Ibid.* xiv. 69.
[6] Ammianus Marcellinus, *Hist.* xxix. 5, *hostis discursator et repentinus, insidiisque potius clandestinis quam praeliorum stabilitate confidens.*
[7] Cf. Nicolaus Damascenus, *Frag.* 134 in *FHG*, where the proneness of the Massyli to night attacks is emphatically stated.
[8] Procopius, *De bello Vandalico*, i. 8, ii. 11.
[9] W. M. Müller, *op. cit.* p. 175 *sqq.*, and fig. 62. In discussing this fortress, Müller commits two slight errors : he states that the Libyans could not have built such a fortress as Satuna, a statement which the Ghemines fortress and other remains disprove ; and he says that pine-forests, which appear in the Satuna representation, are not known in North Africa, whereas they exist both in Cyrenaica and in the Gebel el-ʿAḳabah.
[10] Procopius, *De bello Vandalico*, ii. 11.
[11] *Ibid.* i. 8.

most barbarians they were subject to panics, as when a handful of Caesar's Gallic horse turned back, by a sudden sally, 2000 native cavalry.[1] Yet under favourable conditions, the North Africans were bold and determined enemies. The revolts of Inarus and of Tacfarinas were in themselves resolute and courageous undertakings, although they failed of their design, and readers of Livy will recall his statement that it was the swords of the Libyan mercenaries that carried the day against Rome at Cannae.[2] Though as a rule poorly and variously armed, the Eastern Libyans, when wholly independent, as in the days of the New Empire, were always numerous and brave enough to be a constant menace to Egypt if they had to a greater degree been possessed of the power of concerted action. In classical times their bravery had remained with them, and they had, through the introduction and dissemination of the horse and the camel, evolved a rude system of tactics which consisted in harassing and wearing out their enemy. Their power of coalescence had not, however, much developed, and their arms, unlike those of other Mediterranean peoples, had not improved. Before the well-disciplined cavalry of Rome, or before the Arabs, close-knit in the initial fervour of Islam, they could not stand. In short, their military history, vaguely as it is known, displays a common characteristic of barbarism—personal bravery, rendered ineffectual through want of subordination, coherence, and stability.

*
* *

Household Gear.—The accoutrements of the Eastern Libyans can have varied so little from those employed by their descendants that it will be pertinent first to give a list of the usual domestic possessions of a modern family of Imushagh, and then one of such household gear as the ancient tribesman is known to have possessed. The following objects are to be found among the modern Berber nomads of the North East :—

Grass mats.
Grass mats for screens.
Woollen rugs, parti-coloured (very rare).
Tanned ox-hides (to eat off of).
Mattress, pillows, covers, beds (all hardly known, except in the families of chiefs. The usual "bed" is the *adeben*, or hollow scooped in the sand).
Leather cushions.
Grass-work baskets.
Leather bags.
Pack-saddles for asses.
Skins for liquids (*ḳerabah*).
Ropes and leather buckets for drawing water.
Gourd noggins.
Pottery jars.
Wooden jars for butter.
Wooden cups for drinking.
Wooden trenchers.
Wooden spoons.
Wooden mortars (with stone pestles).

It is necessary to add, to make the list complete, only a few odds and ends such as firestones, awls, needles, etc.[3]

The ancient household gear of which evidence exists may be itemized thus :—

[1] Caesar, *op. cit.* vi.
[2] Livy, xxii. 47, 48.
[3] For this list, H. Duveyrier, *Les Touareg du Nord*, p. 404 *sqq.*

Chairs. Among the booty taken from Meryey was a "throne";[1] and a camp-chair is shown in the Ghadames relief, Fig. 33. It is to be supposed that furniture of this sort was even more rare anciently than to-day. The same is true of the next item.

Footstool (shown in Ghadames relief).

Metal vases, of gold, silver, or bronze, have been already noticed as despoiled from the Libyan princes. An Egyptian representation of such vases is here reproduced, Fig. 53. By their forms these vases are clearly of Syrian origin, as a comparison with the Asian types on the monuments will show. They are interesting chiefly as testifying to the wealth of the great emîrs, and to their relations with Asiatics.[2]

Vessels of pottery may have been intended in the Egyptian lists, where are mentioned "t·pw-r-vessels," "rhd·t-vessels," and "various vessels,"[3] but the doubt as to the meaning of the first two names leaves the question unsettled. It is, however, certain that the Eastern Libyans had pottery cups and water-jars—the *cylices* and *hydrias* mentioned by Nicolaus of Damascus and Hellanicus in the fragments cited earlier in this chapter. Only in the case of the Garamantes is it probable that pottery was very scarce.

Vessels of Ostrich-shell, however, these people had, making "cups of them; for as there was nothing but sand as material they had no pottery."[4]

Vessels of Wood or Bark are mentioned explicitly by Mela, who says of the Libyans *vasa ligno cortice fingunt*.[5]

Cords would have been made of leather or palm-fibre (حبل ليف). The latter would be well described by the term ξύλινα, an epithet which, as has been noted, Strabo applied to the Libyan headstall. The slings were more probably made of leather. Grass-rope (of *Lygeum spartum*) was also known; a cord thereof bound the grave-clothes of a nomad burial which I excavated in 1910 at Gerbah (near Sîwah).

Water-Skins or *Ḳerabah* have already been noted as part of the Libyan military gear.

Baskets were used, as is attested by one of the Benî Ḥasan paintings, where the Libyan women are seen carrying their children in baskets on their backs (Plate V.).

Skin Mats were known, though Procopius, either describing a poor community or indulging his tendency to exaggerate the barbarism of the tribesmen, says that only the great men among the Moors enjoyed these luxuries.[6]

The Libyans had doubtless many objects of which no notices exist. They must, for instance, have had needles and thread, leather sacks (besides those used for stones in war) and awls for making them, pots for seething flesh, flint and fire-stones, and tools for the working of hides. Those who occupied the northern parts of the Fayum, and were agriculturists, had *metates* on which to grind their grain; these relics of their occupation are yet to be found on their old camp-sites.

*
* *

Music and Dancing.—Libyan music was of the most primitive character. Its simplest form—for from an anthropological point of view this may be considered as "music"—was the ecstatic shouting noticed by Herodotus as characteristic of the Libyans of his day, and which is common all over North Africa at the present time.

[1] BAR iii. § 584. [2] For these vases, W. M. Müller, *op. cit.* ii. p. 123 *sq.* and fig. 46. [3] BAR iii. § 589.
[4] Lucian, *De dipsadibus*, 7. Lucian is here following a source known to Pliny (cf. Lucian, *op. cit.* 3, on a flying scorpion, with Pliny's description of the same marvel, *Hist. Nat.* xi. 25); cf. Pliny, *op. cit.* x. 1.
[5] Mela i. 8. [6] Procopius, *De bello Vandal.* ii. 6.

The Greek historian remarks that, in his opinion, the loud cries uttered in Hellenic sacred rites were derived from Africa "since the Libyan women are greatly given to such cries, and utter them very sweetly."[1] These cries were the modern *zagharît*, heard by all and mentioned by many travellers in Egypt, the Ṣaḥara, and the Barbary States.[2] The *zagharît* is made from the throat, a vibrant quality being given to the prolonged shrill cry by the rapid vibration of the tongue; and it is held to a single pitch.

Besides this crying, with which the modern inhabitants of Eastern Libya signalize any event of importance, the ancient occupants of the country had, of course, their songs. These were in some instances religious. Curtius, for example, mentions that in the worship of Amon at Sîwah the women walked in processions, "singing a certain uncouth hymn in the manner of the country."[3] Just what force lies in the last words may be divined by a consideration of modern Imushagh metrics. Among the Imushagh the metrical unit is, as in French poetics, the syllable, no attention being paid to stress or quantity. The commonest metres are enneasyllabic or decasyllabic, which are sometimes, though rarely, combined in the same poem. In decasyllabic verse, the caesural pause often comes in the middle of a word, which is but one of the very numerous forms of licence to be found in barbaric poetry. Other liberties are the frequent elisions and contractions, the changes of singulars into plurals, of masculines into feminines, or *vice versa*. An Imushagh poem usually, though not invariably, carries the same rhyme, or rather assonance, throughout its length in the final syllables of the lines. This is made easy by the great latitude allowed in rhyme. An assonance such as is contained in the words *denta*, *amserha*, *tegla*, or in the words *tiniri*, *ikki*, is readily accepted. Even consonantal assonance is permitted, *e.g.* *auilan* and *egen*, or *tusid* and *ged*, are regarded as true assonances, it being required in this last case only that the vowels preceding the final consonant should be somewhat alike.[4] Under these circumstances it is not surprising that the Imushagh are facile makers, more especially as they sometimes discard even consonantal assonance and use blank verse. Their poetry is, in general, topical in character, dealing with current events and persons well known to the audiences, and it is allusive in the highest degree. They sing it always in a minor cadence, and often with a long-drawn and quavering tremulo.[5] The primitive qualities of this poetry justify the supposition that the "uncouth hymns in the manner of the country" mentioned by Curtius were composed in much the same mode.

The musical instruments of the Eastern Libyans are known only from the

[1] Herodotus iv. 189.

[2] *E.g.* by G. F. Lyon, *Travels in North Africa, etc.*, p. 52 *sq.*, p. 71 *et alibi*. W. R. Smith, *Religion of the Semites*, p. 431, supposes that the Libyan ὀλολυγή was a cry of ritual lamentation for the sacrificial victim. For this there is no explicit evidence. To-day the *zagharît* is raised on the entry of any notable personage into a camp or village, on the reception of startling news, at deaths and births, etc.

[3] Q. Curtius, *De gestis Alexandri Magni*, iv. 7, . . . *matronae virginesque patrio more inconditum quoddam carmen canentes* . . .

[4] *I.e.*, *-en* and *-in*, *-en* and *-an* are allowed; but not so *-in* and *-an* or *-en* and *-ūn*.

[5] This brief notice of Imushagh poetics is based on the long one by A. Hanoteau, *Essai de grammaire de la langue Tamachek'*, p. 201 *sqq.*, and on notes personally collected.

scantiest evidence. A form of castanets appears to have been used, as seen in the Egyptian representation given in Fig. 62, *a*.

An instrument of a character slightly more developed is the double-headed drum shown in Fig. 62, *b*. In shape it is like a boat's water-breaker, and from the way in which it is corded and crossed it seems perhaps to have been made either of pottery or of staves like a keg. It was headed with skins at both ends, was slung from the shoulders of the drummer by bandolier, and played with the hands as is the modern Sudanese *ḍerbukkah*.

Of the known musical instruments capable of producing notes, one was a simple pipe with a flaring mouth (Fig. 62, *c*), and with an unknown number of stops. This was

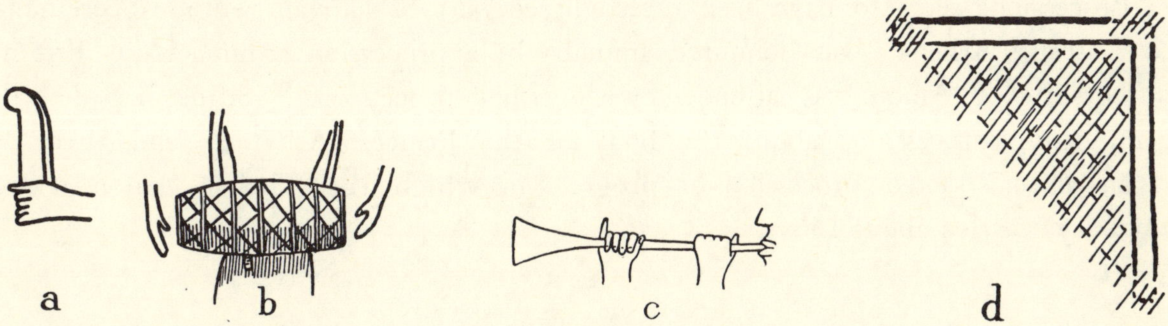

Fig. 62.

probably made of wood, the modern single pipes of the Sîwans and Wagîlans being of that material, or manufactured from the leg-bones of some large bird. Another wind-instrument was the double-pipe, the presence of which among the Libyans is mentioned by Duris Samius.[1]

The most advanced instrument of which we have any ancient evidence was a little harp with a right-angled frame shown in Fig. 62, *d*. This instrument was also used generally in Egypt, along with the more complex forms. All the instruments here enumerated were probably used in concert by the Eastern Libyans on the occasion of their public entertainments, since in an Egyptian relief the castanets, drum, pipe, and harp are all represented as being played in concert.[2]

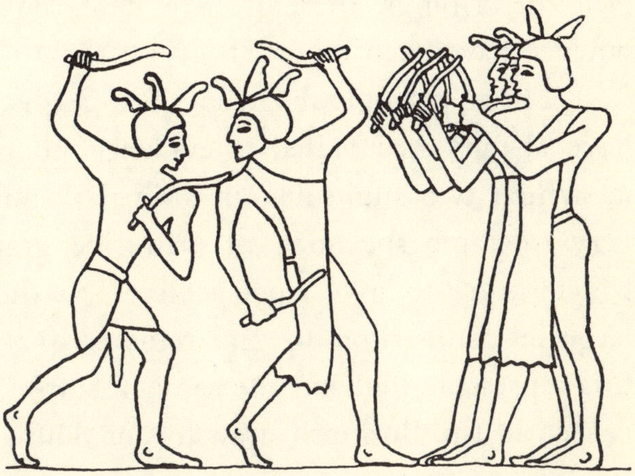

Fig. 63.

The Eastern Libyans had both dances and ceremonial processions. War-dances were practised by the Libyan mercenaries in the Egyptian army at the time of the New Empire (cf. Fig. 63, a war-dance of the Temeḥu auxiliaries). In the scene cited the performers are divided into those who stand

[1] Duris Samius, *Frag.* 34 in *FHG*. Cf. Nonnus, *Dionysiaca*, xxiv. 38, and Euripides, *Hercules furens*, 685 *sq.*, παρά τε χέλυος ἑπτατόνου μολπὰν καὶ Λίβυν αὐλόν ; Hesychius *in verb.* Λίβυς, . . . ὁ ἀπὸ Λιβύης αὐλός.

[2] J. G. Wilkinson, *The Ancient Egyptians*, vol. i. p. 456, and cut no. 224.

clattering time with their sticks and those who are posturing and leaping about; another representation[1] even more strongly recalls the war-dances of many primitive peoples, especially those of numerous American Indian tribes. As a sort of war-dance may also be mentioned the sham-fight of the Ausean virgins mentioned by Herodotus. In connection with dancing, it is remarkable that the Sîwans, on the "birthday" or *moled* of Sheykh Sîdî Suleyman, the patron saint of Sîwah, perform dances of a character totally unlike that of the Arab and Sudanese dances given by them at other times of the year. In the *moled* dances, companies of youths stand in long lines facing each other, and go through various evolutions which recall strangely the "Sir Roger de Coverley" or other English country-dances. Its non-Arabic and non-Sudanese character proves it to be an ancient survival.

Processions seem to have been a recognized part of Libyan religious ceremonies. The Ausean "Athena" was honoured annually by a procession around Lake Tritonis; the worship of Amon was attended with ritual processions; Silius has described the mourning processions about the body of the Princess Asbyte;[2] and there was also an annual sacred procession or progress in which the Theban Amon was for twelve days carried about Libya.[3]

*
* *

Petroglyphs and Sculptures.—Petroglyphs both of ancient and modern date are common in those parts of North Africa where suitable rock exists. In Eastern Libya, the extensive miocene limestone area has discouraged this form of primitive artistic expression, but rock-scribings are nevertheless found in the places suitable for their carving. Much Libyan material undoubtedly exists in the sandstone region of the Nile Valley,[4] but it is not possible to separate it from the similar Egyptian work. No Nilotic scribings, therefore, are here reproduced; it is better to turn at once to Fezzan, whence have been reported several rock-drawings.

Three petroglyphs from Teli-Ṣagha, which were discovered by Heinrich Barth, have already been cited as evidence upon Libyan hunting. The pictograph (Fig. 6) in which two huntsmen in animal disguises approach a buffalo may be regarded as a very tolerable specimen of primitive graphic art. Despite the conventionality which has, in order to give "perspective" to the scene, made the hunters in the foreground so large in comparison to the remoter quarry, there is the same quality of liveliness in this representation, and the same infantile but sincere striving after truthfulness which is seen in the Bushman drawings of South Africa. The block on which this pictograph

[1] Temeḥu mercenaries with their weapons, in I. Rosellini, *Monumenti*, etc., vol. ii. pl. 117, 2.

[2] Silius Italicus ii. 265.

[3] *Vide infra*, p. 190 *n*. 8.

[4] G. Maspero, *Struggle of the Nations*, p. 767, note 4, writes: "I attribute to the Libyans, whether mercenaries or tribes hovering on the Egyptian frontier, the figures cut everywhere on the rocks, which no one up till now has reproduced or studied." This seems to me too sweeping a statement, especially as the remains have not been "reproduced or studied." Most of the glyphs that I have examined are clearly not Libyan but Egyptian.

is scribed measures 1.22 m. by 0.91 m. In Fig. 5, as has been said, a wild animal is seen walking into a pitfall. Here, as in the first example, is seen the anxious fidelity of the artist, as in his endeavour to show all four legs of the animal.[1] The third drawing (Fig. 7) portrays a herd of wild cattle with even more realism. This last picture is on a block of stone measuring 3.89 m. by 1.50 m. and is therefore fairly large. It is noticeable that all three of these glyphs try to present, as is usual in early art, subjects in motion. The technique is good, and in the early Ṣaḥaran manner. The representations are characterized by the large size of the figures, the deep, clean-cut lines, the realistic treatment, and by the picturing of animals which have since become extinct, at least in Libya. This is in contradistinction to the late, or "Libyco-Berber" glyphs of North Africa. These, as a rule, are small, rude, done with a pecked line, and are not at all, or only slightly, patinated.[2]

There have been vague rumours of numerous sculptures to be found between the Chad Road and the Nile, but although these reports are perhaps based upon fact, they must be passed over for lack of definite information. The sculptures actually known in Eastern Libya are few, and are all late. The most interesting exist at Ghîrzah, a point some 70 leagues south of Tripoli town (lat. 31° 10′ N., long. 14° 41′ E.). The reliefs are widely reputed among the modern inhabitants of Tripolitana and Fezzan to be "petrified," an explanation which the sterile Moḥammadan fancy is ever ready to apply to any ancient representations of men or of animals. The ruins of Ghîrzah were first visited by Captain Smyth, R.N., in the early part of the eighteenth century (March 1817). In an abstract from his Journal, sent to Captain Beechey, Captain Smyth thus describes the ruins :—

> The site is mountainous and bare, presenting only dreary masses of lime and sandstone, intersected with the ramifications of the great wadie of Zemzem. And although I had not allowed my imagination to rise at all in proportion to the exhilarating accounts I had heard, I could not but be sorely disappointed on seeing some ill-constructed houses of comparatively modern date, on the break of a rocky hill, and a few tombs at a small distance beyond the ravine. On approaching the latter, I found them of a mixed style, and in very indifferent taste, ornamented with ill-proportioned columns and clumsy capitals. The regular architectural divisions of frieze and cornice being neglected, nearly the whole depth of the entablatures was loaded with absurd representations of warriors, huntsmen, camels, horses, and other animals in low relief, or rather scratched on the freestone of which they were constructed. The pedestals were mostly without a dye [*sic*], and the sides bore a vile imitation of arabesque decoration. The human figures and animals are miserably executed, and are generally small, though they vary in size from about three feet and a half [1.46 m.] to a foot [.30 m.] in height, even on the same tombs, which adds to their ridiculous effect ; whilst some palpable and obtruding indecencies render them disgusting.[3]

[1] In this connection I may be allowed to point out a striking analogy in technique between the now famous paintings of Altamira and the less-known glyphs of Africa Minor. In the paintings, the prehistoric artist has often turned up the hoofs of the bisons, etc., which he has drawn, so that the cleft in the hoof is visible. The same distortion is found in the prehistoric graphic art of North Africa, as in the magnificent ram of Bu ʿAlem, reproduced in Fig. 84.

[2] E.-F. Gautier, *Sahara algérien*, p. 87 *sqq.*, for a short but excellent bibliography and discussion of the differences between the two main classes of Ṣaḥaran glyphs.

[3] F. W. and H. W. Beechey, *Expedition to the Northern Coast of Africa*, pp. 505 *sqq.*, 509.

Despite the disappointment felt by Captain Smyth all but a century ago, it is clear that these ruins are so strongly native in character as to be of great interest. In 1858, a French consular servant in Tripoli obtained fragments of the sculptures through the agency of an Arab. From the brief note that appeared concerning these specimens,[1] one very interesting point is to be gathered. The "sculptures" are described as being mere flat relief, without modelling. They may therefore be regarded as occupying a position half-way between the petroglyphs and true modelled relief. It is probable that they are the work of sedentary Libyans of the Empire, who were inspired by Roman models. Works similar, but with stronger foreign influence, from the ruins at Shabet Um el-Ḫarab, have already been cited in connection with Libyan dress (Figs. 14, 15). Of these sculptures nothing more need be said than that they are essentially provincial Roman.

A relief exists at Slunt, in Southern Cyrenaica, cut on a rock-face in a wady, of six curious figures. The carvings are roughly 1.50 m. high and 2 m. in length, and were discovered by the Italian traveller Haimann. A moulding of the pattern shown in Fig. 64, associated with these sculptures,[2] dates them as of Roman times. The workmanship is very crude, and the figures are badly weathered (Fig. 34). Four of the figures represent adults, two are children, three are females. The upraised hand of the last figure on the right suggests that the monument has been influenced by classical art, and that it is funereal in character. One striking peculiarity of these sculptures is the bigness of the heads of the figures. A little to the left

Fig. 64.

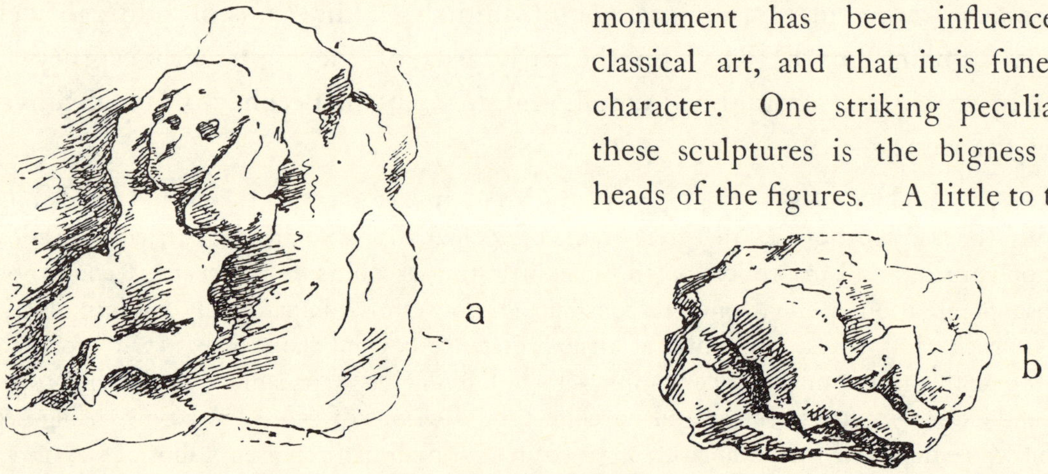

Fig. 65. (After Haimann.)

of this group are a rock-tomb and some confused ruins, among which were found other fragments of sculptures, and, in particular, the two pieces shown in Fig. 65, *a*, *b*. One of these, *a*, is 57 cm. in height, and shows a rude figure, semi-recumbent, with one hand above the head and the other placed against the temple. The other piece, *b*, is battered out of all significance.[3]

A work earlier than the Slunt sculptures was discovered by Duveyrier near

[1] E. du Tour: Note in the *Comptes rendus de l'Acad. des Inscript.*, 1858, p. 152. For a general view of the Ghîrzah ruins, see A. Ghisleri, *Tripolitania e Cirenaica*, p. 77.

[2] A. Ghisleri, *op. cit.* p. 51. A photograph reproduced from J. W. Gregory, *Report of the Commission sent out by the Jewish Territorial Organization, etc.* Plate facing p. 14.

[3] G. Haimann, *Cirenaica*, p. 86 *sqq.*, for the best account of these remains.

Ghadames (Fig. 33), and has been mentioned in the discussion of hair-dressing, etc.[1] The size of this stela and its material are unknown. The scene shows a female figure, facing in profile toward the right, seated on a simple sort of camp-chair, with feet placed on a stool. The woman wears a long robe, and has the hair dressed in a curious fashion. The right arm is extended, and in the raised right hand is a palm-frond or an ostrich-plume, near the end of which is fastened a small triangular object. From the right arm depends a short tab of the robe (?). Behind the seated female figure is another of much less size, but similar to it, apparently an attendant. Before the larger figure is seen half an arched or vaulted structure, toward which the frond or plume mentioned is extended. Beneath this vault was a third figure now unfortunately broken away except for the right forearm and biceps. One of the vertical supports of the canopy may still be seen, as also the edge of the seat (?) of the missing figure.

There can be no doubt that this monument reflects New Empire Egyptian influence. As a whole, the Ghadames relief recalls strongly a class of Egyptian religious sculptures, and this impression receives further support from an examination of the details. Thus the "camp-stool" and the footstool are both of Egyptian form, while the vaulted shelter suggests those Egyptian shrines with arched tops of which one is pictured in the tomb of Rameses V. Though displaying in these details, and in general composition and feeling, strong Egyptian influence, the monument is certified as of local origin by the barbaric dress of the figures. It must be remembered that, in later times, Ghadames (Cydamus) was a town of such consequence that foreign influences made themselves felt there. The significance of the relief is obviously religious; the seated figure and its attendant are going through some form of ceremonial before a god or spirit within the shrine; further than this, however, it would be rash to venture.[2] The work may be provisionally placed within the limits of the Late New Empire.

The material presented above must suffice, until further discoveries in the field, to illustrate Libyan art. Scanty as it is, it is significant. It shows that, whereas the people were fair masters of the neolithic art of rock-scribing, they had not reached a stage at which sculpture in the round was a natural and easy means of expression.

* * *

Architecture.—No truly megalithic monuments have been reported from Libya east of Tunisia. For over fifty years from the time of their discovery, the remains of Roman oil-presses of the *torcular* type were repeatedly asserted to be megaliths,[3] but

[1] H. Duveyrier, *op. cit.* Pl. x. fig. 1, and text, p. 250 *sq.*

[2] C. L. Mélix, *L'Interprétation de quelques inscriptions libyques*, p. 98, has exhibited more zeal than critical power in his comments on this relief.

[3] H. Barth, *Reisen und Entdeckungen*, vol. i. p. 63; E. von Bary, *Über Senam und Tumuli im Küstengebirge von Tripolitanien* in the *Zeitschr. für Ethnologie*, vol. viii. p. 378 *sqq.* Idem, *Senams et tumuli de la chaîne de montagnes de la côte tripolitaine*, in the *Rev. d'Ethnographie*, vol. ii. p. 426 *sqq.*; H. S. Cowper, *Hill of the Graces*, *passim* (mainly a description of these "megaliths"); A. H. Keane, *Africa*, vol. i. p. 138; G. E. Smith, *The Ancient Egyptians, etc.*, *passim* (the thesis of this last publication is based mainly on the wrong assumption that Tripoli abounds in megalithic remains).

their real nature has now become generally recognized.[1] Similarly, traces of cistvaens and alignments reported from Tripolitana as being of great age are all either doubtful,[2] or certainly late.[3]

This is the more noteworthy, as dolmens, menhirs, cistvaens, and cromlechs of primitive style are fairly numerous in Syria. The scarcity of such monuments in Eastern Libya is indeed striking, and is hardly to be accounted for except on ethnological grounds; the rapid diminution of rude stone monuments, as one passes eastward along the North African littoral zone, suggests that in the Moghreb once existed a megalith-building race which was never strongly established in the east. This suspicion tends to become conviction when it is noted that there is, to an extent quite as great as in the east, an absence of true megalithic remains in the Ṣaḥara.[4] In western Europe and in Spain, and in southern Italy (Terra d'Otranto),[5] exist megalithic monuments having distinct affinities with those of north-west Africa. Since in central Italy such monuments are not found, the natural inference seems to be that the megalith builders drifted southward through the Iberian Peninsula, established themselves in the Moghreb, and, by way of Malta and Sicily, even reached southern Italy. The wave that there expended itself in the north appears in the east to have spent its force in Tunisia.

If one attempts to divine what people these megalith builders were, the strong probability appears that they were the Nordic xanthochroids or blonds. That people seems to have come into Africa by way of western Europe, and in the Moghreb, where the rude stone monuments are most numerous, the bulk of the fair Africans is found. This theory, which is fairly well sustained by other facts, and which would attribute the African megaliths to the xanthochroids whom the Berbers have partially assimilated, was first formulated and supported by General Faidherbe,[6] and may still be accepted as essentially true.

In the historic period some of the Eastern Libyans had strongholds, remains of which exist in the vicinity of Bueb Bay (S.W. Cyrenaica). In the precarious lives of the tribesmen it was of great importance that they should have within their area some safe place to which they could resort in time of war, where they could lay up such booty or superfluous goods as came into their hands, and where they could count upon finding a strong band of their fellows. That such centres existed is explicitly stated by two classical writers. "Their leaders," says Diodorus, speaking of the nomadic Libyans, "have

[1] H. M. de Mathuisieulx, *Une Mission scientifique en Tripolitaine* in the *Nouvelles Archives des Missions Scientifiques*, vol. x. p. 272; cf. D. R. MacIver and A. Wilken, *Libyan Notes*, p. 78. The last two writers say explicitly and truly: "many supposed prehistoric monuments of Tripoli are nothing more remarkable than Roman oil-presses."

[2] I have seen ruins of possible cistvaens on Seal Island and near Benghazî. H. Duveyrier, *op. cit.* p. 279 and pl. xv. fig. 3, reports a third from Fezzan. Cf. F. Bernard, *Note au sujet de quelques monuments de pierres brutes relevés chez les Touareg Azgar*; and idem, *Observations archéologiques, etc.* The remains I saw were quite undatable, but by association appeared late, as is certainly the case with Duveyrier's cistvaen, which is of worked slabs.

[3] As in the case of the "alignment" at Messah, for which see H. S. Cowper, *op. cit.* p. 168 *sqq.* and fig. 79 (photographed by H. W. Blundell).

[4] E.-F. Gautier, *Sahara algérien*, p. 61.

[5] P. Pallary, *Instructions pour les recherches préhistoriques, etc.*, p. 35.

[6] L. L. C. Faidherbe, *Recherches anthropologiques sur les tombeaux mégalithiques de Roknia*; idem, *Quelques mots sur l'ethnographie du Nord de l'Afrique, etc.*; idem, *Notices ethnographiques.*

commonly no towns," but "only strongholds near water." In these keeps "they store up the superfluous parts of their booty."[1] This is confirmed by Pliny the Elder, and a stronghold such as those he and Diodorus mentioned is probably meant by the writer of the Stadiasmus[2] when he says that at Eperus,[3] which lay in a desolate part of Syrtis Major, was a native fort.

The literary evidence in regard to these Libyan forts is in itself sufficient to establish the fact of their existence; but, in addition, it fortunately happens that the actual remains of such buildings have been seen in Eastern Libya by modern travellers, and it is possible to gain some idea of their size, plan, and construction.

The ruins of one of these strongholds, of a rude and primitive type, are discernible to-day at Hawah Segal, in south-western Cyrenaica.[4] The remains consist of large, rudely-shaped stones of oblong shape, planted in the earth so as to form a rectangle about 36 by 45 metres. At each corner the stones form small circular bays, about 2 m. in diameter, marking probably—so small is their size—the foundations of circular angle-buttresses meant to give strength to the walls at their points of juncture. In the middle of each of the sides of the fort a pair of larger stones, placed near together, mark the places of the doorways. The rough sketch of Haimann, who discovered this site, is given in Fig. 66.[5] Originally, Hawah Segal was probably a stockade, or a sort of *zarîbah*, the walls being made of mud and brush or small stones.

About a mile from these ruins is a second group, built of fewer, but larger, stones; while to the north lies yet a third, smaller than the other, circular, and enclosing two large cisterns.

The most considerable native remains in Eastern Libya are to be found in the forts built of polygonal masonry in the south-western part of Cyrenaica. At a point just east of Ghemines,[6] in the Syrtis Major, south of Benghazî, "there are," writes Beechey, "several interesting remains of ancient forts, some of which are altogether on a different plan from those [Graeco-Roman ones] which have been already described."[7] The country in the vicinity of these forts and to the north of them is largely "encumbered by blocks of stone, placed upright in long lines, which are crossed at right angles by others, so as to form a labyrinth of inclosures. This peculiarity appears to be occasioned by the nature of the soil, which, although rich and excellent, is covered everywhere with a surface of stone of various thickness, which it is of course necessary to break up and remove, in order to cultivate the soil beneath. To move the blocks, which are taken

[1] Diodorus Siculus iii. 69. 3.

[2] *Stadiasmus Maris Magni*, § 86, . . . φρούριον Βαρβάρων.

[3] On this place, see H. Barth, *Wanderungen*, etc., vol. i. p. 368.

[4] G. Haimann, *Cirenaica* in *Bollet. della Soc. Geogr. Ital.*, 1881, p. 248 *sqq.* and fig. 2 = idem, *Cirenaica*, 2nd ed., Milan, 1886, pp. 58 and cut, 59.

[5] Fig. 66 is reproduced from Haimann's article in the *Bolletino*, fig. 2. In the 2nd edition of the separate publication the same figure is reproduced, but signed "Marzorati," and so retouched as to make the ruins appear more imposing.

[6] H. Barth, *op. cit.*, vol. i. p. 355. Ghemines is there convincingly identified with the ancient Caminos (of the *Itin. Anton.*): (*Chaminos* in the Escurial codex). Barth also notes (*loc. cit.*) the occurrence of groups of these forts at Magrunah, Tel Amun, and Ferashîd, between Ghemines and Benghazî.

[7] F. W. and H. W. Beechey, *Expedition to the Northern Coast of Africa*, p. 244.

up altogether from the ground, would be an endless . . . labor, and they have accordingly been ranged . . . as . . . mentioned, serving at the same time as boundaries to property and as impediments to the approach of an enemy . . . .[1] We discovered that long alleys were occasionally left in different directions, serving as roads. . . . We observed that in the vicinity of the forts the walls were usually placed much closer together, and the inclosures were in consequence smaller than in other parts."[2]

The forts themselves are "built of large unequal-sized stones, put together without

FIG. 66. (After Haimann.)

any cement, and made to fit one into another in the manner which has been called Cyclopian."[3] Broadly speaking, the size of these structures is about 30 to 45 m. in length, by 24 to 30 m. in breadth.[4] "Their form, generally speaking, is square, with the angles rounded off, and some of them are filled up with earth, well beaten down, to within 6 or 8 feet (1.83 m. to 2.44 m.) of the top; the upper part of the wall being left as a parapet to the terrace which is formed of the earth heaped within it. In the centre of the terrace we sometimes found foundations of [later ?] buildings, as if chambers had been erected upon it; the roofs of which, in that case, must have been higher than the outer walls

[1] It is impossible from the description to say whether this is the true explanation. I have seen no such alignments in fertile Marmarica.

[2] F. W. and H. W. Beechey, *Expedition, etc.*, p. 251 *sq.* H. Barth, *op. cit.* p. 353, describes in similar terms this district *ganz bedeckt mit ordnungsmassig in Reihen aufgestellten Steinen.*

[3] F. W. and H. W. Beechey, *op. cit.* p. 244 For "Cyclopian" should probably be substituted the word "polygonal."

[4] H. Barth, *op. cit.* p. 354. The dimensions are there given in feet—100 to 150 by 80 to 100.

which formed the parapet ; and a space seems always to have been left between these central buildings and the parapet, in which the garrison placed themselves when employed in defending the fort. An opening like a window was observed in the parapet of one of the Cyclopian castles of Ghemines, which might have been used for drawing up[1] those who entered the fort, as there was no other mode of entrance whatever."[2]

Near most of these strongholds lies "a small rising ground with one or two wells in it, having the remains of building about it ; they were generally within 50 yards of the fort, by which they were commanded.[3] In some instances we found wells in the trenches surrounding the forts, at others within the outer walls," which enclosed the trenches, though they lay "more frequently without the forts altogether."[4] Tombs, cut in the rocks, occur in the vicinity of some of the forts.

"The castles have, most of them," to quote Beechey further, "been surrounded with a trench, on the outer side of which there is generally a low wall strongly built of large stones. Some of the trenches . . . excavated in the solid rock . . . are of considerable depth and width, and in one instance, occurring between Ghimenez [*sic*] and Benghazi, we observed chambers excavated in the side of the trench, as . . . in that which surrounds the second Pyramid [at Gîzah].[5] . . . The trench of the fort here alluded to is about five and twenty feet in width [about 7.62 m.], and its depth about fifteen [about 4.57 m.] ; the fort itself is an hundred and twenty-five feet in length, and ninety in width [about 38.10 m. by 27.3 m.], of a quadrangular form, and in the centre of each of its [four ?] sides is a quadrangular projection, sloping outward from the top [*i.e.* battering] of twenty feet in length by twelve [6.04 m. by 3.66], which appears to have served both as a tower and a buttress."[6]

It is from these details that the drawings in Figs. 67, 67*a*, 68, etc., have been made. Fig. 67 shows in plan a typical fort of the Ghemines group, the details being derived from the general statements of Barth and Beechey ; Fig. 67*a*, a transverse central cross-section of the same. Fig. 68 represents the stronghold for which Beechey

[1] H. Barth, *loc. cit.*, *Zu Thoren ist natürlich auf diese Weise gar keine Gelegenheit, und man musste die Leute offenbar hinaufwinden, wozu bei einigen sich eine Öffnung oben in der Mauer befindet.*

[2] F. W. and H. W. Beechey, *op. cit.* p. 244 *sq.*

[3] *Ibid.* p. 245. The traces of buildings about the wells "were sometimes very considerable" ; but could testify only to there having been a number of square-built rooms of varying size placed about the wells with some show of regularity, *ibid.* p. 246.

[4] *Ibid.* p. 146.

[5] *I.e.* the chambers were in the outside face of the trench, and not under the fort itself. To judge from their position, the chambers were magazines.

[6] F. W. and H. W. Beechey, *op. cit.* p. 245 *sqq.* It is not said whether the measurements were taken along the top of the walls or along the base ; but in constructing the plan and the sections (Figs. 67, 67*a*, 68, 68*a*), I have assumed the former, since the text says the buttresses sloped "outward from the top," whereas if the measurements were taken below it would be more proper to say they sloped "inward toward the top." On page 246 one reads : "The measurements [of the fort] are here given in the rough, but they will be found in detail by a reference to the ground plan and elevation No. 9 in the plate containing the details of some of the forts." Unhappily, this is one of several of the plates of Beechey's book which were never published then, nor, as was promised (p. 571 note) later, "with others made in Egypt and Nubia." Search for these missing drawings in the British Museum and the Admiralty Archives has proved unavailing. It is greatly to be regretted that Barth, a careful observer for his time, did not record these important remains more particularly than he has done.

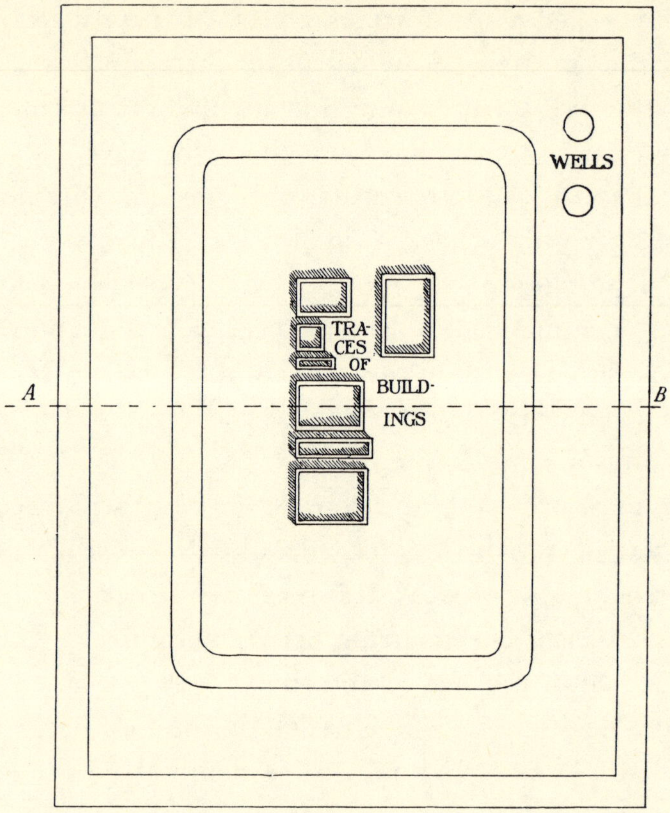

FIG. 67.

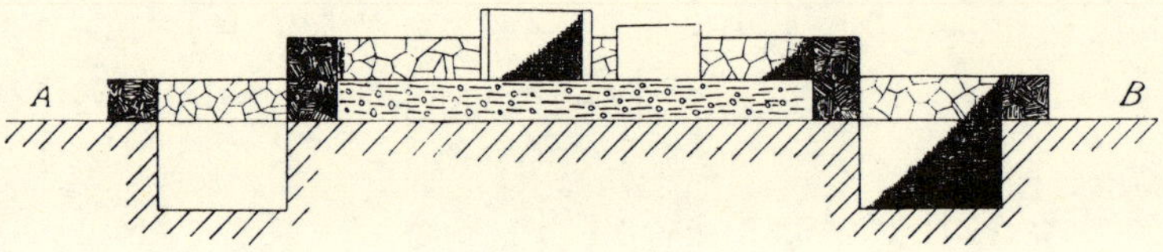

FIG. 67 *a*.

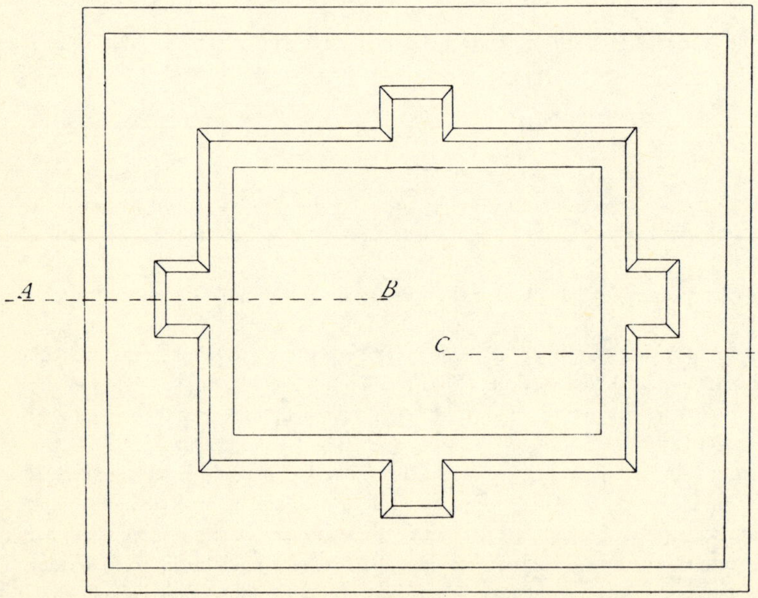

FIG. 68.

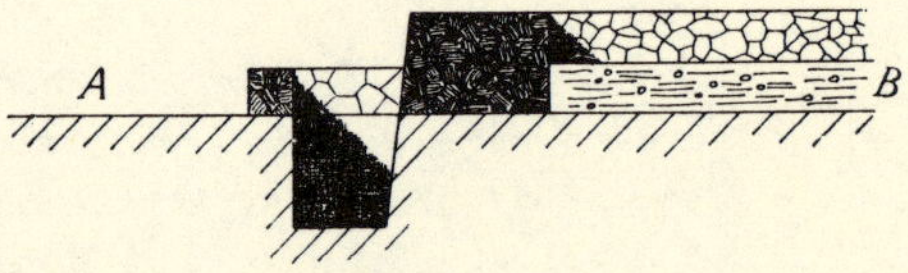

FIG. 68 *a*.

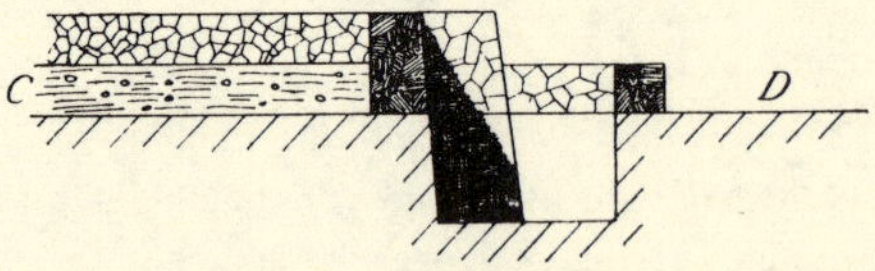

FIG. 68 *b*.

gives his most detailed account. Figs. 68*a*, 68*b*, two sections on the lines A-B and C-D in the plan. A stronghold of the Ghemines type existing at a point[1] between Benghazî and Wagîlah is given in Fig. 69, 69*a*, 69*b*. The details from which the sketches have been constructed are thus given by Hamilton :—

> Henayah is a strong fortress of very early architecture, and by far the most curious construction I had met with in these countries. The squared mass of rock on which the keep is built is not higher than the surrounding ground ; but it is isolated by a dry moat, fourteen feet [4.27 m.] wide and nine [2.74 m.] deep, cut in the living rock. On the square mass, eighty feet [24.38 m.] on every side, left in the centre, rose the walls of the keep, of which only a few feet in height now remain. It is approached by means of a wall, hardly fifteen inches [38 cm.] broad, which is built across the moat on one side. This wall was, perhaps, once the support of a movable bridge. The interior of the rock's base is entirely [?] excavated, forming a centre chamber, now open to the sky, and entered by a flight of steps ; round this chamber are cut a number of vaults, communicating with it, and having small openings, to admit light and air, pierced in the sides. This is, however, only the smallest part of the old stronghold, its size being increased by extensive caves, to the number of twenty-eight, cut in the rock, beyond the moat, into which they all open. In no part of these laborious excavations could I discover any inscription, or evidence of their origin, but judging from the beautiful execution of the whole—from the form of the lamp-niches which are cut in several of the vaults, as well as the general style, resembling what is found in some of the Greek isles—I have no hesitation in ascribing it to a date coeval with the best monuments of Cyrene.[2]

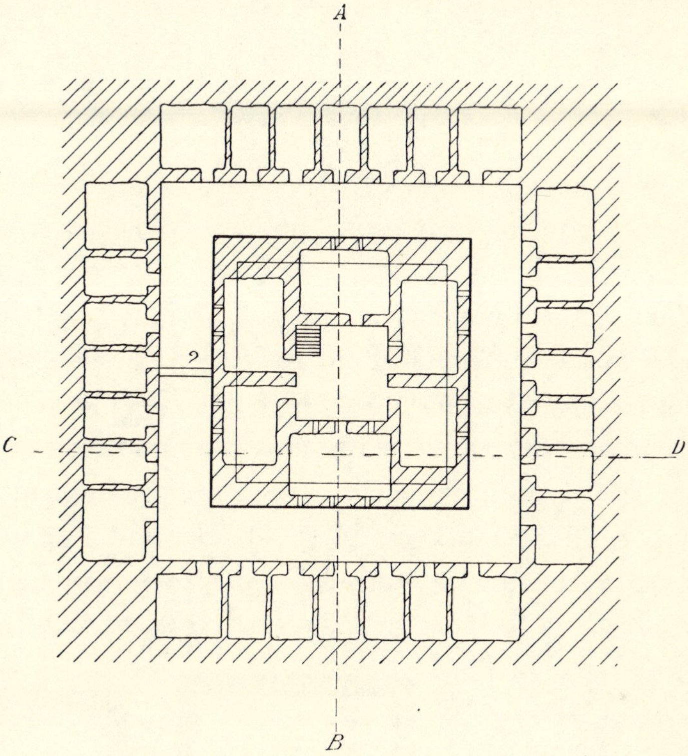

FIG. 69.

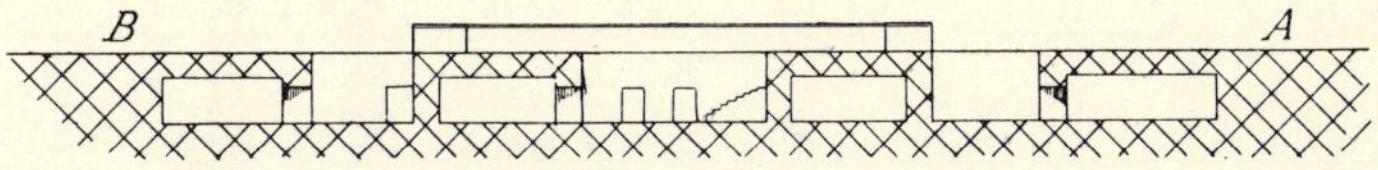

FIG. 69 *a*.

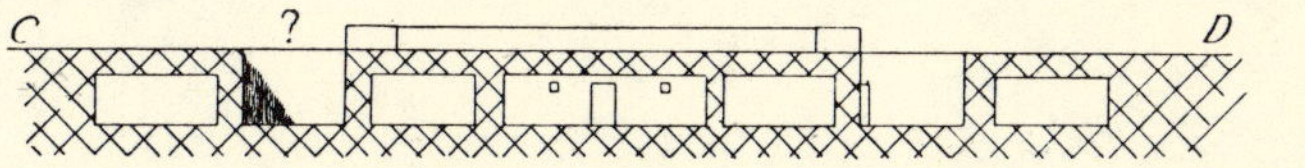

FIG. 69 *b*.

Like the Ghemines group, Henayah commands wells, which contain the last sweet water to be met with before reaching Wagîlah.[3]

There can be no doubt these forts are indigenous, since they are quite different both

[1] About seven miles S.S.W. from Agedabîah.

[2] J. Hamilton, *Wanderings*, p. 175. Needless to say, the plans based on these data are capable of giving only the most general idea of the building. How did the steps run ? What size were the vaults ? What was the width from wall to centre chamber ? etc.

[3] *Ibid*. p. 176.

in plan and structure from the Punic, Greek, or Roman fortifications of Africa, and they are of commonest occurrence in a region where the foreign element was so weak as to be of least importance. Barth supposed that the forts belonged to the Auschisae,[1] since those he saw were on the verge of their old territories ;[2] but it has been shown earlier in this essay that the most stable ethnic group in the eastern portion of the Syrtica Regio was that of the Nasamones, within whose northern frontiers the Ghemines forts lie ; and it is possible that to these tribesmen and not to their less powerful neighbours the strongholds once belonged. At all events, they testify that the builders either possessed no little skill in building stone structures themselves, or that they commanded and directed this skill in others.

In regard to date, it can only be said that by their style they should be fairly early ; and, since they lie within the Mediterranean sphere, they may be provisionally assigned to the great era of polygonal masonry structures, *i.e. circa* the ninth and eighth centuries B.C. They probably are the structures reputed by the Greeks to have been, like similar ones in Sicily, Sardinia, and Italy, the handiwork of Cronus,[3] a possibility which would not in the least interfere with their having served in full historic times as the strongholds mentioned by Diodorus Siculus. The forts of this type, it may be said without reserve, are the most important architectural monuments of indigenous East Libya, and those which call most imperatively for scientific investigation.

In concluding this topic, mention may be made of the fort shown in Figs. 70, 70*a*, 71, 72. This structure has the appearance of being of a late date (presumably

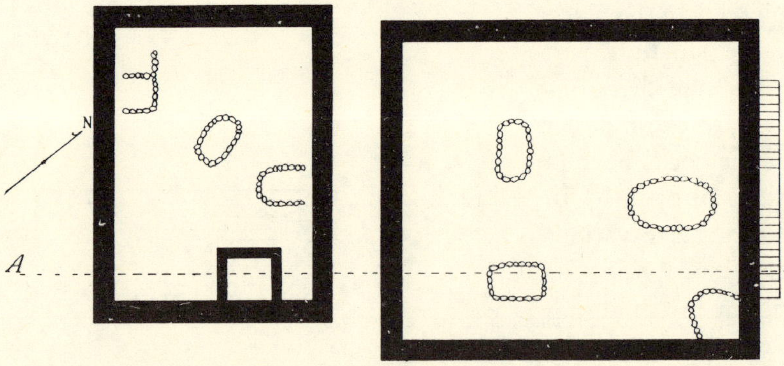

FIG. 70.

FIG. 70*a*.

Roman), but from its having the interior of the enclosures partly filled with earth may be regarded as related in some way to the Ghemines strongholds. It stands in the

[1] H. Barth, *op. cit.* p. 354, *kleine Forts von ganz besondrer nationaler Bauweise . . . die . . . als Werke einer einheimischen Völkerschaft, voll unzweifelhaft der Auschisai . . . darstellen.*

[2] Herodotus iv. 171.

[3] Diodorus Siculus iii. 61. 3 ; cf. Crates in Lydus, *De mensibus* iv. 48.

western part of the Gulf of Bombah, about a mile inland, and consists (Figs. 70, 70*a*) of two rectangular enclosures, a greater (*ca.* 30 by 27 m.) and a less (*ca.* 20 by 25 m.). The latter on its eastern side shows the remains of a smaller enclosure (tower ?) built against

FIG. 71.

the wall; the former, outside the northern wall, has the remains of a double ramp, *ca.* 2 m. wide, leading up from the east and the west to the middle of the

FIG. 72.

wall, and almost to its top (Fig. 72). Within each enclosure are the remains of several Arab grave-circles of small stones. A narrow way, about 3.60 m. wide, separates the two enclosures.[1] The walls, which are ruinous, still stand in places as high as 4 m., and are built of small rudely-shaped stones, laid in courses.

The district in which this fort now stands is one which received slight Roman influence, and is near the site first occupied by the Theran colonists on the Libyan mainland.[2] The plan of the structure, however, leads to the conclusion that one is here confronted with a Libyan building.

The *habitations* of the Eastern Libyans were anciently, as to-day, caves, permanent houses, or movable shelters. In Cyrenaica are a number of inhabited caverns among the hills of Gebel el-Aḫdar, and in the Gebel Gharyan are whole troglodytic communities dwelling in artificial caverns.[3]

The bulk of the Eastern Libyans, however, being semi-nomadic, did not live in stable dwellings, but in tents or booths. The Libyan invaders of Egypt in the XIXth Dynasty had tents of leather,[4] like those still used in Fezzan. That, at a period much later, tents continued to be used, as at the present day, among the Arabs of Tripolitana and western Egypt, is attested by the descriptive term Σκηνῖται applied by Ptolemy[5] to certain of the East Libyans of his time.

Besides tents, another form of movable shelter was in use among the Libyans. This was the *mapalium*[6] of the Roman writers, a portable hut or booth like the *gher* of the Kalmuks of modern Astrakan.[7] Shelters of this sort were used by the Nasamones, whose "dwellings," says Herodotus, "are made of the stems of asphodels and reeds, wattled together."

These booths could be carried about from place to place,[8] and were little more than flimsy screens against sun and wind.[9] Similar structures were used by another Libyan people, farther west, if the name Asphodelides, given to them by Diodorus,[10] may be supposed a descriptive (like the term Σκηνῖται noted above), referring to the use of booths of asphodel-wattling, to the employment of which among the Nasamones Herodotus testifies. Mapalia were used by the Numidians and Mauri in the west,[11] in the interior of Marmarica,[12] and by the African herdsmen generally.[13] In the time of the Punic Wars, the Numidian soldiers had no other shelter in the field than these huts,[14] a circumstance which, because of their inflammability, made it easy for Scipio on one occasion to fire the camp of Syphax.[15] On the outskirts of the Afro-Roman

[1] So in my note-book, and therefore so in the plans; but I confess that my memory recalls and one of the photographs (Fig. 71) seems to show, a slightly greater interval. The visit I made to this site (in 1909) was attended with circumstances which quite precluded the making of such accurate observations as the ruins merited.

[2] H. Barth, *op. cit.* p. 507 and notes. [3] H. Vischer, *Across the Sahara*, p. 38 *sqq.* [4] BAR iii. § 589.

[5] Ptolemy iv. 7 § 10. In southern Fezzan. According to Lucian (*De dipsadibus*, § 2) the Garamantes were tent-dwellers.

[6] Generally found in the plural in a collective sense—*mapalia*, as in Festus, p. 258 (Egger), *Mapalia casae Poenicae appellantur, in quibus quia nihil est secreti, solet solute viventibus obici id vocabulum*, etc. The origin of the name is obscure, but generally supposed to be Punic. A variant is *magalia*. [7] J. Deniker, *Races of Man*, p. 164 and fig. 44.

[8] Herodotus iv. 190. [9] Hellanicus, *Frag.* 93 in *FHG* = Athenaeus, *Deipnos.* xi. p. 462 B.

[10] Diodorus Siculus xx. 57. 5. [11] Sallust, *Iugurtha*, xviii.; Pliny v. 3, xvi. 37.

[12] Mela i. 8. Among the people of Marmarica away from the coast *domicilia sunt quae mapalia appellantur.* Yet farther south the nomads *utque a pabulo ducta sunt, ita se ac tuguria sua permovent.*

[13] Vergil, *Georg.* iii. 339-340; Livy xxix. 31. [14] Livy xxx. 3. [15] *Ibid.* xxx. 5.

towns groups of mapalia were to be found collected, like the Arab or Berber shelters which are pitched outside the modern settlements in North Africa to-day. It was for this reason that the name *mapalia*, *mappalia* came to be used to designate a native quarter. Thus, in an inscription found at Henshîr Mettîsh in Tunisia, a locality is described as FVNDVS VILLAE MAGNAE VARIANI ID EST MAPPALIA SIGA.[1] This name indicates that the Roman town was placed on the site of a native *mapalia* called Siga. At Carthage was a Via Mappaliensis in the time of St. Cyprian Martyr,[2] and as this street was distant from the centre of the town, it probably ran through, and derived its name from, an old native suburb once occupied by booths. A parallel is seen in modern Tripoli Town, where a long street, running south from the Kasbah, passes first among good houses, then among poor and scattered ones, and at last goes through a settlement of wattled huts inhabited by Fezzanî blacks. The modern buildings, as was probably true of those of the Carthaginian street, are slowly encroaching upon the quarter of the booths.

In form the *mapalia* doubtless varied according to the locality, and perhaps even according to the fancy of the individual builders. Some of them looked like inverted boats,[3] and were supported inside by stakes or poles driven into the ground.[4] These could not have varied greatly from the Tripolitan booths mentioned above. Others are described by St. Jerome as resembling ovens: *agrestes quidem casas et furnorum similes, quas Afri appellant mapalia.*[5]

FIG. 73.

This seems to be the type represented in two pastoral mosaics found at el-ʿAlîah in Tunisia.[6] The mosaics show two Nile scenes, but the North African artist has introduced into them pictures of huts which are clearly *mapalia*.[7] The shelters are made of light staves, topped with a wattled cone, which is curiously elongated (Fig. 73).[8] A type somewhat different is that represented in a mosaic of Udnah. In this picture is seen a farm-house, beside which is a low thatched hut with a pent-house roof for the slaves, a style of shelter which there is no reason to think other than native.[9]

Another thatched type[10] is shown on a sarcophagus now in the museum at

[1] J. Toutain, *Nouvelles Observations sur l'inscription d'Henchir Mettich*, pp. 2, 7, 13.

[2] D. Ruinart, *Acta Martyr.* p. 218; C. Tissot, *Géographie comparée*, vol. i. p. 661.

[3] Those of the Numidians. *Vide* Sallust, *Iugurtha* xviii.

[4] Livy xxx. 3.

[5] S. Hieronymus, *In prol. Amos.*

[6] P. Gauckler, in *Compt. Rend. de l'Acad. des Inscript.*, 1898, p. 828 *sqq.*

[7] *Jahrb. d. arch. Instit.* vol. xv., 1900; *Anzeiger*, p. 67, fig. 2, p. 68, fig. 3.

[8] This elongation is exactly paralleled among the Niam Niams to-day; cf. G. Schweinfurth, *Artes Africanae*, pl. 8, figs. 1, 2, 3, 5, especially 5. The purpose of the elongation is to draw off the smoke. *Ibid.* text, in face of pl. xi. This elongated type of hut is seen in a Ptolemaic representation of the Puntite shrine of Min. W. M. F. Petrie, *Athribis*, pl. xx. and text, p. 8.

[9] Daremberg and Saglio, *Dictionnaire*, *in verb.* "Mappalia."

[10] Gsell, *Musée de Philippeville*, p. 32 and pl. ii.; cf. G. P. Campana, *Opere plastiche*, pl. cxiv.

Philippeville (Fig. 74). This little structure has walls of wattle, and a conical roof of thatch.[1] As a whole, the *mapalia* may be considered as divisible into two general classes, within which accident and locality produced many variations: (*a*) the type

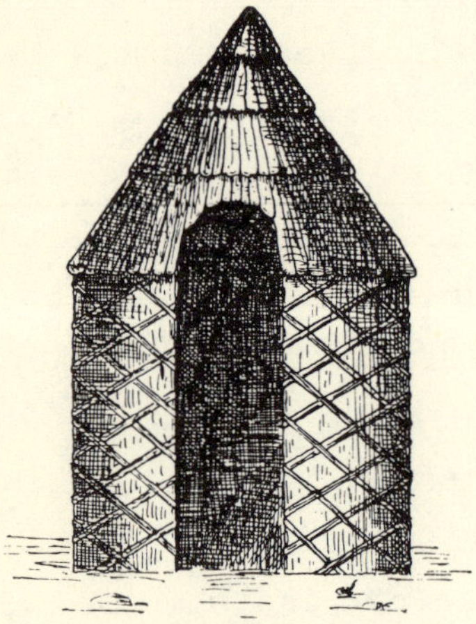

Fig. 74.

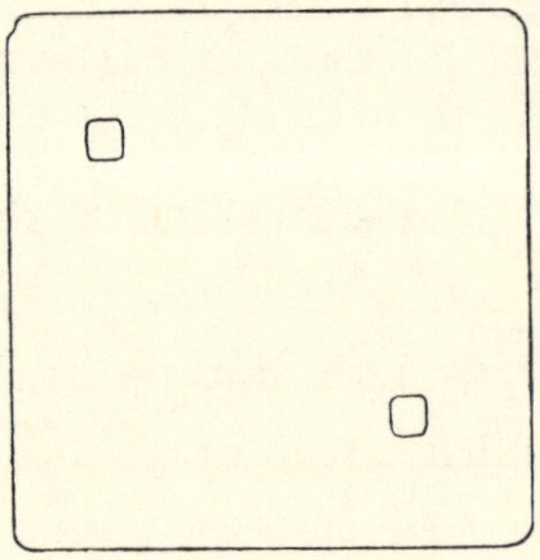

Fig. 75.

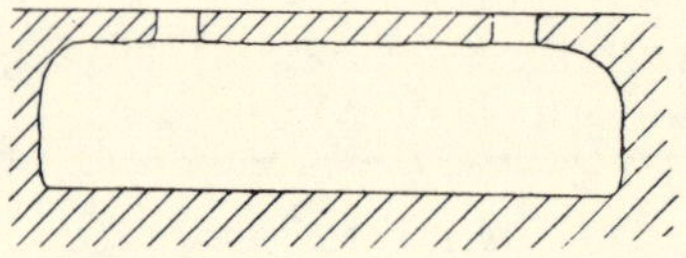

Fig 75*a*.

of which Sallust speaks, and of which the modern Tripolitan booths are examples, and (*b*) the type shown in Figs. 73 and 74. In the first type, an elongated ground-plan is covered by a pent-roof or arched wattling, so as to suggest the shape of a cucumber split lengthwise; in the second, a circular area is enclosed by a wall of paling or wattling, which is capped by a pointed roof. Small portable huts of both sorts are found among the modern Berbers.[2]

Besides dwelling in caves and movable huts or tents, the Eastern Libyans had

Fig. 76.

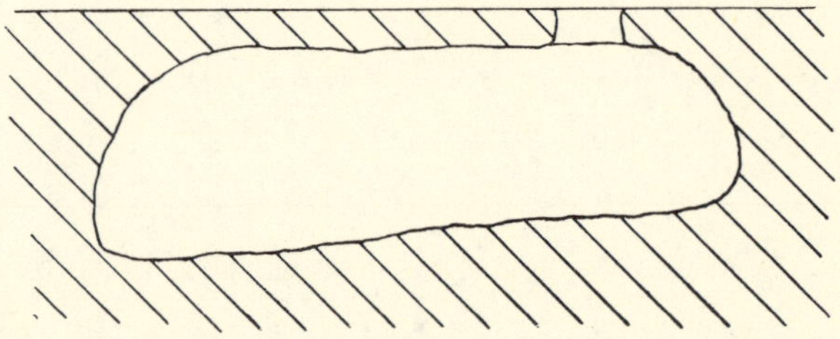

Fig. 76*a*.

permanent houses, at least in the oases. These, Herodotus[3] and Pliny[4] record, were built of salt. This statement is only slightly misleading to-day, for the walls of Sîwan

[1] Probably the top of the door was not cut up into the thatch as shown. The reason why the hut is so represented on the sarcophagus may be simply to allow the sculptor to add to the height of the woman he shows standing in the entrance. In fig. 74, although the female figure is purposely omitted, I have drawn the door as given (incorrectly ?) on the monument. Huts, except for the door, like this *mapalium* are to-day common in Bornu, Borku, and Tibesti. For which *vide* G. Nachtigal, *Sahara und Sudan*, *passim*; and idem in the *Tour du Monde*, No. 14, 1880, pp. 379, 391, 405.

[2] C. Tissot, *op. cit.* vol. i. p. 481; cf. p. 302; O. Meltzer, *Gesch. der Karth.* vol. i. p. 70 *sq.*

[3] Herodotus iv. 185.

[4] Pliny v. 5, said of the Amantes. Cf. *ibid.* xxxi. 7, for similar structures at Gerris in Arabia.

houses, the beams of which are of palm-logs, are constructed of rubble mixed with a hard mud-and-salt plaster.[1]

It remains to say a word in regard to the cisterns and grain-stores of the Eastern Libyans. At a very early period the Libyans must have built wells and cisterns, as opposed to mere water-holes dug in the sand. The Psylli, according to Herodotus,[2] stored their water in tanks; and the great number of wells and cisterns one encounters in passing from Egypt to Tunisia, while largely of Roman construction, had probably in many instances an earlier origin. Grain-stores are often found to-day, but, as with wells, it is seldom possible to say of any one of them that it is Greek, Roman, or Libyan; they are all simply square or bottle-shaped holes cut in the rock, like the modern grain-stores of Malta. That grain-vaults were of frequent occurrence in Libya is known from literary as from monumental sources. "It is the custom of the Africans," says the historian of Caesar's African War, "to place their grain privately in underground vaults, to keep it safe in war-time and to protect it from sudden descents of the enemy."[3] Figs. 75, 75*a*, 76, 76*a*, 77, 77*a* give plan and section of a large cistern in Mariut, a smaller on Seal Island (Gulf of Bombah), and a grain-store at Marsa Suzah (Apollonia) respectively.

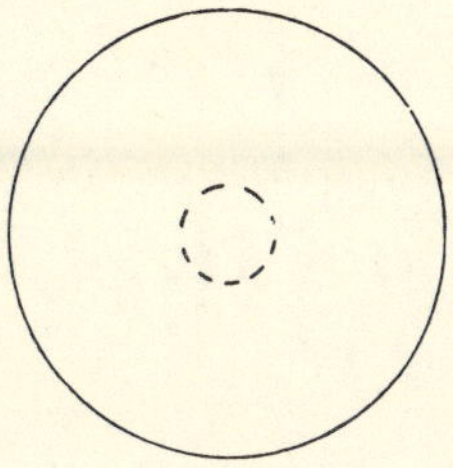

FIG. 77.

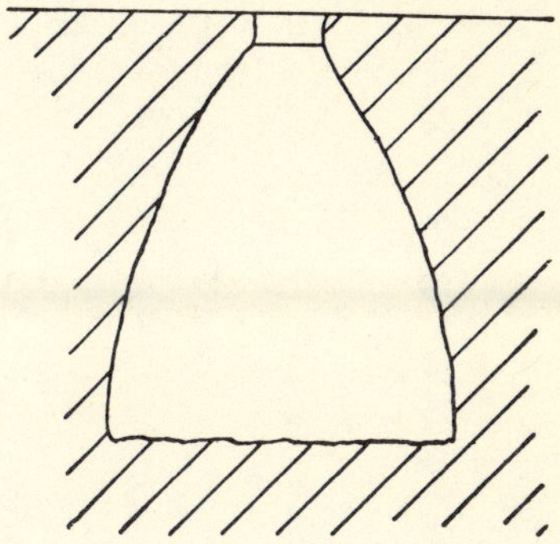

FIG. 77*a*.

[1] G. Steindorf, *Durch die Libysche Wüste zur Amonsoase*, figs. 28, 31, 34, 48, 54, 60, etc., give admirable illustrations of this architecture, which, one may be sure, differs little, if at all, from that of ancient times.

[2] Herodotus iv. 173.

[3] Caesar, *De bello Africano* lxv.

CHAPTER VIII

RELIGION

The extant materials from which may be derived some knowledge of the religion of the Eastern Libyans are in the pages which follow treated by a comparative method which, were there more data, would be unnecessary. It should be further premised that the comparative method employed has forced me to adopt a number of views which have not, hitherto, been advanced elsewhere, and which, therefore, have not the advantage of having been subjected to public criticism. In presenting the evidence, it has been found best to do so under three heads: first, the animistic phases; second, eschatology; third, theology. Detailed consideration of these topics will permit us to conclude with a few remarks of a general nature.

The most primitive religious beliefs of the Eastern Libyans were of the simple animistic sort common to all peoples in an unadvanced stage of development. Very early in their career the world and its phenomena seemed to the savage inhabitant of North Africa pregnant with spiritual forces. Wells, trees, hills, clouds, wind-storms, etc., were each of them the abiding-place of spirits which gave to them their distinctive characters. Long after such beliefs had given place to other and larger conceptions, they themselves yet had a hold upon the popular mind, some of these animistic ideas surviving in Eastern Libya even at the present time. This, for example, is seen in the case of wells. At Sîwah, the people yet believe firmly that the *'ayns* in the oasis are inhabited by spirits which have, under Islamic influence, come to be identified with the Ḳuranic *ginn*. Sometimes these *ginn* emerge from their watery homes in the shape of horses, goats, asses, or other animals. Bathing in Bîr Aḥmed, a well-spring no longer in use for household purposes, is supposed to render women more attractive, and is especially popular with widows and divorced women. Women bathe weekly—generally now on Fridays—in 'Ayn el-Isgawah, 'Ayn el-Baḥarî, and especially in 'Ayn Musa (Tidt mta Musa) that they may be comely. In the last-named well, which is a beautiful pool lined with Roman masonry, and about ten metres across, boys bathe before circumcision; and young women, before their marriage, there bathe themselves carefully, the act being regarded almost as an essential part of the marriage ceremony.[1]

In the face of these modern survivals of primitive superstitions, it is not surprising to find ancient indications of similar beliefs. In classical times the sacred Fountain of the Sun at Ammonium (Sîwah) attracted the notice of a number of writers, who ascribed to it thermal qualities which it probably had, and capricious changes of colour which it almost certainly lacked.[2] In the west, Roman dedications—GENIO FLVMINIS,[3] GENIO FONTIS,[4] etc.—are numerous enough to suggest that, in those parts, native superstition was often attached to streams and springs.[5] Probably the splendid and beautiful fountain at Cyrene, which in Greek times was dedicated to Apollo,[6] had already been an object of reverence before the days of Hellenic colonization.

Stones of remarkable shape or size were, by a people to whom all natural objects were instinct with a mysterious life, considered as having in them what, in modern parlance, we might call "souls." Such a stone is that mentioned by Pliny,[7] on the authority of Mela,[8] as being among the *sacra* at Ammonium. Were a man so bold as to touch it with the hand, there arose straightway a strong sand-wind, violent and harmful. In the west, this animistic conception of stones is yet seen in the case of an aerolith in the *Ḳaṣr* of Tementit in Tuat.[9] If at Sîwah a man stumbles against a stone, and thereafter chance to fall ill, he is thought to have annoyed a *ginnî*, and a ceremony of conciliation to effect the invalid's recovery is gone through at the place of his misadventure.

Besides stones, hills also were revered by the Libyans in classical times. This, naturally, was more particularly the case in the mountainous west[10] than in Eastern Libya, but even in the latter region, hills were sometimes believed to have their informing spirits. In the anonymous Arabic History of Sîwah, one reads of a hill south of Baḥreyn, the ascent of which filled its discoverers with an oppressive and unreasoning terror.[11] A striking analogy is offered by a passage of Pliny in regard to Mt. Atlas: a religious fear, he writes, seizes on the hearts of those who draw near it, especially at the sight of the summit upreared above the clouds, and which seems as if nigh to the very moon.[12] The same feeling of awe at present attaches to the Idînen *massif*

[1] C. V. Stanley, MS. Notes made at Sîwah, 1910; O. Bates, MS. *Journal* at Sîwah, 1910; idem, *Siwan Superstitions*, in *CSJ*, vol. v. no. 55, p. 90 *sq*.

[2] Herodotus iv. 181; Diodorus Siculus xvii. 50; Arrian, *Anabasis* iii. 4; Q. Curtius iv. 7. 31; Pliny ii. 103, v. 5; Mela i. 8; Ovid, *Metamorph.* xv. 309 *sq.*; Lucretius, *De rerum natura*, v. 848; Vibius Sequester, p. 24; Lactantius, *ap. ibid.* (Oberlin's notes); Antigonus Carystius, *Mirabil.* clix.

[3] *CIL.* viii. 9749.

[4] *CIL.* viii. 4291.

[5] Cf. *CIL.* viii. 2662, 2663, 5884.

[6] Cf. Callimachus, *In Apoll.* 88.

[7] Pliny ii. 45.

[8] Mela i. 8.

[9] G. Rohlfs, *Reise durch Marokko*, p. 14; Laquière, *Les Reconnaissances de Géneral Servière*, p. 22 *sq.* with photograph.

[10] R. Basset, *Récherches sur la religion des Berbères*, p. 1 *sqq*.

[11] This MS. is a fragment of a longer work, now lost. The former owner of the book, Sheykh Omar Musellîm, had memorized the parts relating to Sîwah, and at my request dictated those parts to Dr. Ḥasan Effendî Farîd in 1910. Captain Stanley and I thus obtained our copies. The work is of uncertain date, but was said to have been compiled about A.H. 800 = fifteenth century A.D. It certainly, as redacted, has many recent additions.

[12] Pliny v. 1; cf. Maximus Tyrius, *Dissertationes* viii. 7; Martianus Capella, *De nuptiis philologiae*, vi. p. 229 *sq.*, *edit.* Eysennhardt.

north of Ghat, which the Azgar Imushagh (Tuareg) dare not penetrate.[1] Similarly, Mount Udan is regarded with superstitious dread by the local Ihaggaren.[2]

Mention is made above of a sacred stone noticed by Mela and Pliny. The terms in which the former writer speaks of this object are such as to indicate not only an animistic conception of unusual stones, but of the winds as well. The Roman geographer says that at Ammonium there is "a certain stone sacred to the South Wind (*Austro sacra*). When it is touched by the hand, straightway there arises a wind which, hurling the sand about like water, rages as if over waves."[3] In conjunction with other evidence, this passage shows that the Libyans had a belief in the spiritual nature of the south wind—a belief so strongly rooted in the Berber mind that it has endured even until modern times.[4]

Classical readers will readily recall Herodotus's story[5] of the destruction of the Psylli. According to the Greek historian, the tanks in which this people stored their water were made dry by a long continued south wind. The Psylli thereupon determined to go to war with this wind, "so at least," Herodotus cautiously remarks, "the Libyans report." The Psylli marched into the desert, where a great wind arose from the south and overwhelmed them in the sands.[6]

In conjunction with this legend may be noted that of the expedition despatched by Cambyses III. against Ammonium, as related by the same writer. It is only necessary first to remark that such an expedition, directed against a great desert sanctuary, was, according to Herodotean ethics, a thing recklessly impious, doomed from the outset to be visited with divine displeasure. The Persians are said to have left Thebes and to have reached the Great Oasis (Ḫargah) in safety. But thereafter, "naught is to be learned of them, except what the Ammonians, and those who derive their knowledge from them, report." The Persian army never reached Sîwah, nor came again to Egypt, disaster having overtaken them, according to the Ammonian story, at a point midway between Ḫargah and the objective point. "As they were at their midday meal, a wind arose from the south, strong and deadly, bringing with it vast columns of whirling sand, which wholly covered the troops and caused them entirely to disappear—thus, according to the Ammonians," concludes Herodotus, with a complacent sense of impiety avenged, "did it fare with this army."[7]

The former of these stories certainly, and the latter in all probability, is apocryphal. The true story of the Psylli, as will be elsewhere pointed out, appears to be that they were beaten back from the coast by the Nasamones, who seized their lands. As regards the

[1] H. Barth, *Reisen und Entdeckungen, etc.*, vol. i. p. 288 *sqq.*; H. Duveyrier, *Les Touareg du Nord*, p. 416.

[2] H. Duveyrier, *loc. cit.*; M. Benhazera, *Six mois chez les Touaregs du Ahhagar*, p. 60.

[3] Mela, *loc. cit.*

[4] What follows is based on O. Bates, *A Desert God*, in the *CSJ*, vol. iv. no. 51, p. 296 *sq.* I may here take occasion to offer a long-delayed apology for the misprints in that article, which appeared while I was in the desert, out of touch with the posts.

[5] Repeated almost *verbatim* by A. Gellius, *Noctes Atticae* xvi. 11. 3.

[6] Herodotus iv. 173. According to Nonnus (*Dionysiaca*, xiii. 381 *sqq.*) the expedition of the Psylli was made by sea (!), and the ships were sunk by tempests from the south.

[7] Herodotus iii. 25, 26.

expedition of Cambyses, it must be said that a sandstorm which would literally overwhelm an army is a phenomenon outside all modern experience. Such a storm may have occurred, but the likelihood is that, getting bewildered in an ordinary sandstorm, the Persian soldiers became panic-stricken, killed their guides, or were deserted by them, and wandered about until they were overcome by thirst.[1] But whatever the exact historical basis for these tales, the points here to be observed are : (*a*) that in each of the above instances, Herodotus, as so often happens, is repeating a native story ; and (*b*) that in one an affront against the south wind, and in another an impious attempt upon a desert sanctuary, was supposed to have been punished by the offenders being over-whelmed by sandstorms from the south.

A striking parallel exists to the story of Cambyses's army in the anonymous History of Sîwah.[2] According to the Arabic historian, the last pre-Islamic king of Santarîah (Sîwah) despatched against the Moslemîn who had invaded Egypt—again, be it observed, an act which, from the writer's point of view was one of impiety—a great army. The force consisted of "many thousands of men, who after leaving Baḥreyn encountered a very terrible wind two days south of that place, which killed nearly all of them."

Another passage from the same source deserves here to be cited. The historian says that "certain of the Sîwans relate that they visited Baḥreyn, and there found a track going south. . . . This they travelled for two days, and came then to a well-marked road." Following this, they reached a place where "were the statues of four lions, two facing to the north and two facing to the south. And these statues were black. They spied then a *ḥaṭṭîah*, and a dark valley. . . . The Sîwans sought to enter the valley, but a great sand-wind withheld them. They became enfeebled, and returned again to Baḥreyn after much travail."

The primitive idea that the winds were informed with spirits has not died out of Eastern Libya. To this day the *Ḳibly* (قبلي), or South Wind, because of its power and desert origin, is a thing universally dreaded by the caravaneers of North Africa, and is regarded animistically. The dust column whirling along the edge of the cultivation in Egypt is there still spoken of as a *shaytan* (شيطان) or "devil." The Arabs in Egypt regard the *abu zuba'ah* (ابو زوبعة), or whirlwind, animistically,[3] believing that it is caused by the flight of an evil *ginnî*, to defend themselves against which they often cry out "Iron ! Iron !" or "Iron ! thou unlucky !" as the *ginn* are thought to have a great dread of that metal.[4] As late as the middle of last century, a feud which was going on between two Sîwan factions was stopped because there arose a *ḳibly*, which the Lifayah, one of the factions, regarded "as the unfailing signal of some calamity."[5] The Sîwans of to-day believe that the atmosphere is peopled with *ginn*, who, though "good," are irritable and capricious.

[1] Cf. for a modern parallel, S. W. Baker, *The Nile Tributaries of Abyssinia*, London, 1867, p. 12 *sq.*

[2] *Vide supra*, p. 173 *n.* 11.

[3] Dust-spirals were animistically conceived by the mediaeval Arabs, W. R. Smith, *Religion of the Semites*, p. 134 and *n.* 1.

[4] E. W. Lane, *The Thousand and One Nights*, vol. i. *Notes to the Introduction*, p. 34. Cf. idem, *Manners and Customs of the Modern Egyptians*, p. 223.

[5] J. Hamilton, *Wanderings*, p. 253.

Further evidence on this head need not be cited ; enough has already been said to give point to Maternus's remark that part of the inhabitants of Africa, like the Assyrians, gave to the air a sort of domination over the other elements.[1] An animistic view of atmospheric phenomena is one which is shared by many primitive peoples,[2] and the question need not be further dwelt on.

That the rainbow and the mirage were both animistically regarded in Eastern Libya seems proved by the way in which they are still viewed. The former is by some Berber tribes of the west spoken of as the "bride of the rain," or "bride of the sky,"[3] and, like the latter, is regarded as having an informing spirit.

The primitive Libyan, living in a wonder-world of inspired stocks and stones, gave to the heavenly bodies also their share of mysterious life. In later times, the anthropomorphism which grew out of the vague sentiments of the ruder stages of culture, led to the actual worship of the stars,[4] and the doctrine of astral animation is seen surviving in Berber legend to-day.[5] In Roman times the Africans in general were held to be good astrologers : Septimius Severus, who was of African origin, was considered especially adept in this art.[6] This is not extraordinary, when one considers the brilliancy and magnificence of the stars as seen in the desert, or even in Egypt, where a host of animistic beliefs attached at an early time to the "imperishable" stars.[7] The animistic beliefs of the ancient Libyans, in fine, were such as might almost be argued for them *a priori* from a knowledge of their climate and natural environment. In their main outlines they differed but little, in so far as they are known, from those of the Semites of Arabia, or those of the Hamites of East Africa.

It remains, in connection with the more primitive phases of Libyan religion, to say something of taboos, magic, and manes-worship. The Libyan taboos known to-day are but few. The Imushagh abstain, as has been said earlier in this essay, from eating birds, fish, and lizards,[8] on the score that these animals are "their mother's brothers." This reason at once suggests both that these taboos are totemic and matriarchal in their

[1] Firmicus Maternus, *De errore profan. relig.* 3. He adds the later elaboration that the Afri consecrated the air to Juno or to the Maiden Venus. Cf. *CIL* viii. 4635, and, perhaps, viii. 17763.

[2] Cf. Homer, *Odyss. passim* ; J. E. Harrison, *Prolegomena to the Study of Greek Religion*, p. 176 *sqq.* (the Κήρ as Wind-Daemon) ; G. W. Bateman, *Zanzibar Tales*, p. 68 ; R. N. Bain, *Cossack Fairy Tales*, p. 18 *sqq.* In the beautiful Biblical passage in which Elijah has speech with God (1 *Kings* xix. 11) the divine voice is not in the fire, nor in the earthquake, nor in the whirlwind, because the writer of the passage was a protestant against current animistic views of these natural phenomena. The reader is of course familiar with the personifications of Hellenistic art (Boreas, Notus, Zephyrus, etc.), and with the Assyrian wind-daemons portrayed in the reliefs.

[3] R. Basset, *op. cit.* p. 17.

[4] Leo Africanus, *Description of Africa*, vol. i. lib. i. pp. 162, 177. I may here remark that the Libyan habit of reckoning time by nights is not necessarily evidence of lunar observance. The authority for this practice is Nicolaus Damascenus (*Frag. ap. N. Cragium, De Republica Lacedaemoniorum*, etc. p. 562), οἱ Νομάδες τῶν Λιβύων, οὐ ταῖς ἡμέραις, ἀλλὰ ταῖς νυξὶν, αὐτῶν ἀριθμοῦσι τὸν χρόνον. The use of "nights" here is paralleled by the "sleeps" of the Inuit and many modern primitive people.

[5] R. Basset, *op. cit.* p. 15 *sqq.* ; cf. H. Duveyrier, *op. cit.* p. 424 *sqq.*

[6] Spartianus, *Geta*, 2 ; cf. Sidonius Apollinaris, viii. *Epist.* 11 (p. 528) ; Leo Africanus, *op. cit.* p. 177.

[7] A. Erman, *Handbook of Egyptian Religion*, pp. 2, 7, 88, 91. For some classical notices on Egyptian star-cultus, P. E. Jablonski, *Pantheon Aegyptiorum*, Part ii. p. 126 *sqq.* Libyan stellar observance is perhaps to be inferred from a fragment of Lycus Rheginus, who remarks that African cattle, at the rising of Sirius, turn to face it. Lycus Rheginus, *Frag.* 14 in *FHG.*

[8] There are in North Africa several large edible lizards, like the "monitor."

origin. In these senses they have been repeatedly cited by various writers, but it has not been taken into account that these taboos may all of them be of comparatively recent origin among the Berbers. The bird, the fish, and the snake are all great totem-animals in Nigeria; but among the ancient Libyans we find some of the inhabitants of Syrtica Regio who were fish-eaters,[1] as were the Libyan dynasts of the Egyptian Delta,[2] while in the interior of Northern Africa, in Æthiopia Troglodytica, lizards were anciently eaten.[3] The only taboo-animals of the Eastern Libyans, which are known certainly to have been held as such, are the cow and the pig. According to Herodotus, the nomadic Libyans abstained from eating cow's flesh out of respect for "Isis," this taboo obtaining even among the Graecized women of Cyrene.[4] The women of Barca went further, and abstained from the flesh of swine as well.[5]

The dog may also have been a taboo-animal, whose flesh was eaten only for specific reasons. For although the dog's flesh was exposed for sale in North African markets during the Middle Ages,[6] its consumption is still associated with very strongly-marked and widespread superstitions, which seem to descend from a time when the dog was a tabooed animal, which was eaten only on ceremonial occasions. Thus, at Kabes, in the Nefzawah, etc., dogs are eaten; and near Tatahuin, part of the Megabelah tribe partake of dog's flesh "when the date turns yellow, before becoming red," *i.e.* in the autumn. The dogs are slain in an especial manner. The throat is cut, and the animal is then allowed to escape. It runs a short distance and then falls, when it is taken up, singed, and then boiled. The carcase is then drawn, and the head and feet are thrown away.[7] This ceremony is called, according to Bertholon, a "sacrifice," and is one illustration of the formal cynophagy practised to-day in North Africa.[8]

In Tripolitana, dogs, as well as other animals forbidden by the Ḳuran,[9] are eaten as medicines. At Sîwah, dogs are eaten in privacy by syphilitics;[10] people who wish to grow fat eat the flesh of puppies.[11] A modern historian of Carthage has suggested that African cynophagy was connected with the cult of the goddess Tanit:[12] it is more probable, to judge from the extent and nature of the practice as revealed by recent exploration, that it is merely the survival of an ancient indigenous taboo.

A taboo of uncertain origin exists at Sîwah with regard to garlic, which is eaten but one week in the year—in the autumn—with a view to ensuring good health for the ensuing twelvemonth. This custom can be referred only doubtfully to a Berber origin,

[1] Strabo xvii. 835. [2] BAR iv. § 882. [3] Mela i. 8.

[4] The cow-taboo was not universal in Libya. Cf. Herodotus ii. 18.

[5] Herodotus iv. 186. The Libyan character of the Barceans persisted for centuries after the foundation of the city. Cf. Polyaenus, *Strateg.* viii. 47.

[6] El-Moḳaddasî, p. 243; Sheykh et-Tiğanî, *Voyage dans la Régence de Tunis*; el-Bekrî, *Description de l'Afrique septentrionale.* Cf. Justin, *Hist. Phil.* xix. 1.

[7] L. Bertholon, *Essai sur la religion des Libyens*, p. 42 *sq.* This essay contains one or two facts of value, such as this just cited. [8] Idem, *La Cynophagie dans l'Afrique du Nord*, for other instances.

[9] G. F. Lyons, *Narrative of Travels in Northern Africa*, p. 52.

[10] O. Bates, *Siwan Superstitions*, in the *CSJ*, vol. v. No. 55, p. 90.

[11] C. V. Stanley, MS. Notes made at Sîwah, 1910. [12] F. C. Movers, *Die Phönizier*, vi. 405.

because a taboo of the same vegetable exists at Ḫeybar in Arabia,[1] and as both at Sîwah and at Ḫeybar there are many Sudanese blacks, it is perhaps they who are responsible for the custom. Garlic and onions, moreover, held a peculiar position in ancient Egyptian belief,[2] while it is pertinent to add that modern Moslem orthodoxy looks with aversion upon this plant "which renders man's breath disagreeable to the angels."

To come now to the questions of divination and magic, it has been noted that in Roman times the native Africans were reputed to be versed in astrology. Other forms of divination were also in vogue, though information in regard to the details of the processes is unhappily lacking. As in the rest of Africa, and, for the matter of that, as among most of the primitive peoples of the world, the diviner was probably in most cases a woman.[3] Procopius is speaking generally when he says that, among the Mauri, it is the women, and not the men, who prophesy; but that certain of their women, having gone through the prescribed rites, become inspired so that they foretell the future as skilfully as the ancient oracles.[4] In some cases, it is certain that the diviner sought his or her foreknowledge at the grave of an ancestor or other worthy, as is commonly done at the present time. At Augila, according to Mela, only the *manes* of the dead were held to be divinities; the people swore by them, and consulted them as oracles. The grave was visited, the spirit invoked and told what was the wish of the votary, who then slept at the spot and was answered in his dreams.[5] In this the Roman geographer is but restating what had been said by Herodotus, not in regard to the Augilae only, but to all the Nasamones. "For divination," remarks the Greek writer, "they betake themselves to the graves of their own ancestors, and, after praying, lie down to sleep upon their graves: by the dreams that come to them they guide their conduct."[6] This practice exists among too many of the Berber tribes to-day to have been confined to the Nasamones alone. Two cases may be cited. At el-Eṣnam, near Ghadames, women attire themselves in their best garments, and go to certain graves known as those of the *Zabbar*, where they call upon the spirit resident among the graves. This spirit is called *Idebni* (cf. *Adebni*, "a grave"), and he appears in the form of a giant with eyes like those of a camel. He answers such questions as are put to him concerning absent husbands, etc.[7] The consultant, it should be added, must have upon her person no trace of iron or steel. Again, near the Wady Augidit, in the northern Saḥara, is a group of great elliptical tombs. The Azgar woman, when desiring news of an absent husband,

[1] C. M. Doughty, *Wanderings in Arabia*, vol. ii. p. 50.

[2] Pliny says these vegetables were treated as gods by the Egyptians when taking an oath (*Hist. Nat.* xix. 6). Cf. Juvenal, *Sat.* xv. 9. Garlic and onions were tabooed to the Egyptian priests (Plutarch, *De Iside et Osiride*, § 8). Cf. the classical practice of giving garlic as fodder to animals at the summer solstice to ensure their health through the ensuing year. Vegetius, *Mulomedicina* i. 18. 18.

[3] Mythic figures connected with magic and sorcery in Greek legend, it will be recalled, were more usually women than men, as in the cases of Hecate, Selene, Circe, Medea, etc. Cf. E. Doutté, *Magie et religion dans l'Afrique du Nord*, pp. 33 *sq*.

[4] Procopius, *De bello Vandalico*, ii. 8.

[5] Mela i. 8, *Augilae manes tantum deos putant, per eos deiurant, eos oracula consulunt precatique quae volunt, ubi tumulis incubuere, pro responsis ferunt somnia.*

[6] Herodotus iv. 172. Cf. Eustathius *ad* Dionys. *Perieg.* 209.

[7] H. Duveyrier, *Les Touareg du Nord*, p. 415; M. Benhazera, *Six mois chez les Touareg du Ahaggar*, p. 63.

brother, or lover, goes to these graves and sleeps among them. She is thought to be sure to receive visions which will give her the news she seeks.[1] These examples of modern divination at the graves of the dead throw an interesting light on the statements of Herodotus and Mela.

Magic, both "white" and "black," for the practice of which the Moghrebîn are so renowned throughout the Moḥammadan world to-day, was anciently practised. A Libyan custom mentioned by Nicolaus of Damascus affords an instance of sympathetic magic in which a whole tribe participated. Certain Libyans,[2] according to this writer, held annually a festival, which terminated, after the setting of the Pleiades, by the extinguishing of the lights and a promiscuous sexual intercourse.[3] Such a custom is savage, but cannot be described as depraved; for it undoubtedly served a religious purpose, being intended to ensure good crops and harvests.

A form of pledging faith noticed by Herodotus as a Nasamonian custom may here be described, as it is really magical. Each party gave the other to drink from his hand; "and if there is no liquid to be had," adds Herodotus, "they take up dust from the ground and put their tongues to it."[4] The purpose of this ceremony is perhaps to infuse into each party something which is part of the other, and which will help him to keep his pact, and work him ill, without hope of escape, if he violates it.

Magical rain-making was anciently known in Libya,[5] and the Kabyles, the Benî Mzab, and others to-day preserve[6] remembrances of this in the chants they sing in times of drought. In these, Anzar, the rain, figures as a personality :—

Anzar! Anzar!
O God, moisten us even to the root![7]

and

Give us, O God, the water of Anzar!

Magical, too, was the snake-charming for which in classical antiquity the Psylli were famous.[8] The men[9] of this tribe, like the Marsi and the Ophiogenes,[10] were credited with a marvellous power of charming serpents and curing their bites. The same reputation is to-day enjoyed in Egypt by the Rifaʿyah dervishes. The Psylli, like these latter, were thought to cure venomous bites by saliva,[11] though it was believed that the

1 E. von Bary, *Ghât et les Touareg de l'Aïr*, p. 63.

2 Nicolaus calls them Δαψολίβυες, a name not found elsewhere. Ruperti, in his notes on Silius Italicus iii. 261, conjectured that for Δαψο- we should read Θαψο-, and that the Libyans in question lived in the vicinity of Thapsus. I would suggest that the true reading might be Διψολίβυες, applied as a descriptive to Libyans of the poorly watered interior.

3 Nicolaus Damascenus, *Frag.* 135 in *FHG*, Δαψολίβυες ὅταν συναχθῶσι, πάντες ἅμα γαμοῦσιν ἐν μιᾷ ἡμέρᾳ μετὰ δύσιν Πλειάδος, καὶ μετὰ τὴν ἑστίασιν χωρὶς τῶν γυναικῶν κατακειμένων κατασβέσαντες τὸν λύχνον εἰσέρχονται καὶ ὁ τυχὼν ἣν ἂν τύχῃ λαμβάνει. Were these unions permanent? If they were, we have here a primitive form of marriage.

4 Herodotus iv. 172. Cf. for the substitution of dust for water the Moslem use of sand for ceremonial ablutions in the desert. The form of pledge described by Herodotus exists to-day in Algeria, where bride and groom so pledge themselves at marriage. T. Shaw, *Travels in Barbary and the Levant*, vol. i. p. 431.

5 Dio Cassius ix. 9. 6 E. Doutté, *op. cit.* pp. 584-92. 7 Ben Sedira, *Cours de langue kabyle*, p. xcviii. n. 1.

8 [Amometus remarks (*Frag.* 3 in *FHG*) that there was in Libya a city the priests of which charmed crocodiles. This is doubtful evidence on Libyan animal-magic, since Amometus probably refers to the Fayum, where the cult of Socnopaeus, a form of Ṣebek, flourished in Graeco-Roman times. Cf. J. G. Milne, *Egypt under Roman Rule*, p. 129.]

9 The gift was not held by women. Zonaras, *Annales*, x. 31.

10 Crates Pergam. *ap.* Pliny vii. 2, xxviii. 3; Celsus v. 27.

11 Agatharchides *ap.* Pliny vii. 2; Callias, *Frag.* 3 in *FHG* = Aelian, *Nat. anim.* xvi. 28.

persons of the Psylli were in some mysterious way antipathetic to poisonous animals. "In the bodies of these people," writes Pliny, "there was by nature a certain kind of poison which was fatal to serpents, and the odour of which overpowered them with torpor: with them it was a custom to expose children immediately after birth to the fiercest serpents, and in this manner to make proof of the fidelity of their wives,[1] the serpents not being repelled by such children as were illegitimate."[2] Pliny, here as usually the uncritical compiler, has narrated in this account the Greek explanations of the pretended immunity of the Psylli rather than the details of the process by which they were supposed to have effected it. His indication as to the use of saliva, given on the authority of Agatharchides, and confirmed by the historian Callias, suffices to show the magical character of the methods by which the Psylli "charmed" venomous snakes. In classical times, the Psylli were employed as doctors to "charm" snake-bites and scorpion-stings,[3] perhaps the most famous occasion on which their services were requisitioned being one where their powers proved of no avail—for Octavius endeavoured vainly to restore Cleopatra to life by the arts of these serpent-masters.[4] The process by which the Psylli effected such cures as they actually made, and by which they attained their great reputation, is explicitly described by Callias. The bite of the cerastes, he says, is fatal to men and animals unless a man of the Psylli be present to effect a cure. A mild case the Psyllus cured by spitting into the wound; a graver wound he treated by rinsing his mouth in water, which he then gave the patient in a cup to drink; and if, even after this "medicine," the symptoms grew worse, he and the victim stripped and lay close together until, by the peculiar power within him, he had defeated the effects of the poison.[5] In all this one sees clearly an old and respectable piece of tribal magic; later, the charming seems, as not infrequently happens, to have degenerated into a mere catch-penny trade. Pliny speaks of having himself seen "exhibitions" in which the Psylli went through some sorry jugglery with toads (*rubetae*) which the performers irritated by placing on flat vessels heated to redness, after which abominable treatment the bite of the *rubeta*, so Pliny solemnly declares, was deadlier than even that of an asp.[6]

"Black" magic existed in Eastern Libya anciently as to-day. Belief in the evil eye, at present universal in North Africa, is strongly rooted at Sîwah; and as the

[1] Cf. Lucan, *Pharsalia*, ix. 890 *sqq.*; Aelian, *Hist. anim.* i. 57, vi. 33, xvi. 27, 28.

[2] Pliny, *loc. cit.*

[3] Pliny xi. 25. Pliny there makes the weird statement that the Psylli—"who for their own profit have been in the habit of importing the poisons of other lands among us"—tried to introduce a flying scorpion, which, however, could not stand the climate north of Sicily.

[4] Dio Cassius li. 14; Zonaras, *Annales*, x. 31. Psylli also attended the army of Cato on its march across the Syrtica Regio. Lucan ix. 891 *sqq.*; Plutarch, *Cato Minor*, § 56.

[5] Callias, *loc. cit.*; cf. Zonaras, *loc. cit.* Lucan ix. 925; Pliny xxviii. 3.

[6] Pliny xxv. 10. Was the serpent the Psyllic totem? W. R. Smith, *Religion of the Semites*, p. 445, cited [Aristotle] (*Mirab. auscult.* § 149 *sq.*) to the effect that in the Euphrates Valley was a certain small snake fatal to foreigners, but harmless to the natives: whence Smith inferred this snake to have been the local totem. Were this inference correct, a similar one would apply to the Psylli, of whom the same tale is told (Antigonus Carystius, *Mirabil.* xix.), and who were even said to establish the legitimacy of their children by testing their immunity from the poison of asps. But the Psylli were thought to be immune to *all* venomous animals, and these tales strike me as mere idle boasts such as Europeans still encounter in the Levant. Therefore I hesitate to do more than suggest that the totem of the Psylli was a serpent.

manifestations of this superstition there are not identical with those of Egypt, it is fairly safe to assume that the present survivals have descended not only from Arabic, but also from Berber antiquity. It is known, moreover, on the authority of two Greek writers cited by Pliny, that in Africa were "certain families of enchanters (*familias quasdam effascinantium*) who by means of praise (*laudatione*) could cause cattle to perish, trees to wither, and infants to die."[1]

The custom of divination at graves has been spoken of; and the other features of Libyan *manes*-worship may now be considered. In all Africa the cultus of the dead has for ages had a hold extremely strong.[2] In the northern portion of the continent it was developed in Egypt to proportions so enormous as to affect profoundly the whole life of the Nile populations for thousands of years. Among the Berbers it was highly developed ; and traces of it survive from the Red Sea to the Atlantic up to the present time. It will be convenient to consider this phase of Libyan religion under the headings of Burial and Cultus.

Burial.—"The nomadic Libyans," says Herodotus, "with the exception of the Nasamones, bury their dead as do the Greeks."[3] Greek burials were usually diamagnetic—*i.e.* the body lay extended in an E.-W. or W.-E. direction[4]—Athenian custom inclining rather to a position in which the head was toward the west. The Nasamones buried their dead in a sitting posture, a dying man being carefully supported by his friends in the proper position.[5] Further information is supplied by Silius Italicus, whose *De bello Punico* contains a remarkable passage on burial custom, which the pedantic poet must have derived from some rather detailed source. From Silius it is learned that not only did the Nasamones bury their dead as Herodotus relates, but that they also disposed of them in the sea :—

. . . Saevo sepelire profundo
Exanimos mandant Libycis Nasamones in oris.[6]

The same author speaks of the Garamantes as burying their dead in shallow sand-pits :—

. . . reclusa nudos Garamantes harena
Infodiunt.[7]

Burial under mounds was also known : Mela, speaking of Libyan graves, called them *tumuli*,[8] and it is told that the Emperor Probus, having when an officer engaged the Libyan Aradion in single combat, and slain him, caused the soldiers to raise over him a great barrow.[9] Classical readers will readily recall the mention of the barrows of the Philaeni in the east, and the gigantic grave of Antaeus opened by Sertorius in the west.

[1] Isogonus and Nymphodorus *ap.* Pliny vii. 2. Cf. A. Gellius, *Noct. Att.* ix. 4, . . . *in terra Africa familias hominum voce atque lingua effascinantium* . . .

[2] E. B. Tylor, *Primitive Culture*, vol. ii. p. 115.

[3] Herodotus iv. 190, θάπτουσι δὲ τοὺς ἀποθνήσκοντας οἱ νομάδες κατά περ οἱ Ἕλληνες, πλὴν Νασαμώνων.

[4] Cf. Aelian, *Var. hist.* v. 14, vii. 19 ; Plutarch, *Solon*, 10 ; Diogenes Laertius, *Solon*. See too Welcker, *Griechische Götterlehre*, vol. i. p. 404.

[5] Herodotus, *loc. cit.*, οὗτοι δὲ κατημένους θάπτουσι, φυλάσσοντες, ἐπεὰν ἀπιῇ τὴν ψυχήν, ὅκως μιν κατίσουσι μηδὲ ὕπτιος ἀποθανέεται ; Eustathius, *ad* Dionys. *Perieg.* 209, . . . καθημένους δέ, φασί, θάπτουσι [*scil.* οἱ Νασαμῶνες] τοὺς νεκρούς.

[6] Silius Italicus, *De bello Punico*, xiii. 480 *sq.*

[7] *Ibid.* xiii. 479.

[8] Mela i. 8.

[9] Vopiscus, *Probus* 9, . . . *et quia fortissimum ac pertinacissimum virum viderat, sepulchro ingenti honoravit, quod adhuc extat tumulo usque ad ducentos pedes terra elatum per milites, quos otiosos esse numquam est passus.* The raising of this barrow was, however, probably as much a concession to Libyan prejudice, as a task to busy the soldiers, or a memorial to Aradion's valour.

It is to be noted that, while the Libyans practised different forms of interment, they seem all to have used forms of inhumation as opposed to incineration.[1] The modes which are recorded are—(*a*) extended diamagnetic burial, (*b*) sea-burial, (*c*) contracted burial in a sitting posture, and (*d*) burials under a memorial mound.[2]

(*a*) The extended burials which Herodotus noted as usual were probably practised by the Hellenized Libyans best known to the Cyreneans.[3] No sooner are the Nasamones reached than Herodotus notices a different custom, and beyond that people he must, on a point like this, have been ill-informed.

(*b*) The sea-burials of the Nasamones, if they really took place—and there is little reason to doubt it—may have been of fairly late origin, and been due either to the fact that among the Nasamones were the survivals of customs belonging to an invading sea-people, or to a feeling that to the sea from which they obtained so much, the bodies of the dead should be committed.

(*c*) Contracted burials are common to divers primitive peoples. The Winnebagos, for example, buried their dead sitting, as did the Peruvians and the Yumanas of South America.[4] The predynastic Egyptians had the same custom, and in Roman times—an excellent illustration of the fact that the practice had not a chronological, but merely a cultural, significance—the "X-Group" people of Nubia also buried their dead in a contracted position. In Borghu (Benin) "when a man dies a pit is dug . . . and the body is placed in a sitting posture, with the hands and feet tied tightly with a cord, and the head inclining upward."[5] From this it may be seen that the practice of contracted burial is not peculiar to Africa, and that within that continent it is widespread.

There are, of course, different degrees of contraction, and different positions—*e.g.* lying on the side or sitting. Both the postures mentioned were known in Egypt, but it was the sitting one which was in favour with the Libyans. Its employment, or rather

[1] The only case of Libyan incineration for which there is any ancient authority is in Silius Italicus' account (*De bello Punico*, ii. 263 *sqq.*) of the funeral of Asbyte. As that description does not agree with his pedantic but more sober account of burial customs in his xiii. book, nor with the other evidence, and as it is written in a vein picturesque and poetical, it may be dismissed as figmentary.

[2] I do not believe, as by inference from the Balearic custom many appear to, that any form of "dissected burial" was common to the Libyans as a whole. I know only one ancient source for anything of this sort in Africa. Nicolaus of Damascus (*Frag.* 141 in *FHG*) states that the Panebi (Πάνηβοι) Libyans, a tribe of whom even the location is unknown, buried their kings after first cutting off the head of the corpse. The head was gilded and placed ἐν ἱερῷ—among the tribal *sacra*. But the Πάνηβοι Λίβυες may not have been Libyans at all, except by an error of Nicolaus or his copyist. For the practice is explicitly described by Herodotus (iv. 26) as existing among the Issedonians, and by Livy (xxiii. 24) as existing among the Boii of Gaul. May not the Boii have been here confused with the Byaei Libyans?

[3] The numerous rock-cut shaft-graves of the western part of Cyrenaica may have been made under Libyan influence. For these the reader is referred to G. Dennis, *Excavations . . . in the Cyrenaica*, in *Trans. Roy. Soc. Lit.* II. Series, IX. (1870), pp. 147, 153, 161 *sq.* Skeletal remains of horses were found in some of the graves. *Ibid.* p. 163.

[4] E. B. Tylor, *op. cit.* vol. ii. 422 *sqq.*

[5] R. Lander, *Records of Captain Clapperton's Last Expedition to Africa*, vol. ii. p. 139. Cf. H. K. W. Kumm, *From Hausaland to Egypt*, p. 106, where a burial at Joko, in the Shari-Chad Protectorate, is described. In that case the grave was dug in the centre of the deceased's hut. "Fowls were sacrificed, and . . . the body, tied up into a sitting posture, was lowered into the hole, which was then filled with earth and the hut deserted." For similar burials among the Bari, G. Casati, *Ten Years in Equatoria*, vol. i. p. 303, and A. J. M. Jephson, *Emin Pasha and the Rebellion at the Equator*, p. 140. Jephson notes that the sitting corpse has sometimes a hide put over it, and under it.

the care with which the friends of the dying man helped him to conform to it, is significant. Such ritualism with regard to the act of dying points to the strength among the Libyans of their belief in after-life. There is no evidence as yet as to whether their belief favoured a "retribution theory" of the hereafter, the information we possess pointing merely to the existence of a "continuance theory."

(*d*) In the tumulus is an example of the manner in which the burials were marked. Nomadic graves of Roman date examined at Gerbah,[1] near Sîwah, consisted of a rough cist of small flat stones, in which the body, wrapped in coarse cloth, lay extended. Over and about the cist were piled flat stones to a height originally, perhaps, of about 50 cms. At Seal Island, in the Gulf of Bombah, exist a number of enclosures of small stones, generally circular or elliptical in plan. The presence of small offering niches, usually on the S.W. side of these structures, shows them to have been grave enclosures; but it is not possible to say definitely what age is to be assigned to them. Cairns of rectangular ground-plan, with battering sides, exist near Germah, where they were seen by Duveyrier.[2]

Cultus.—As at the present time throughout North Africa and the Sudan, offerings were probably made at graves at the time of interment, and replaced from time to time with fresh ones in the case of a notable personage. The Eastern Libyans had a long memory for their famous dead, as have the modern Arabs for their departed sheykhs. Out of this reverence grew naturally the habit of apotheosizing deceased chieftains, who even in their lifetime were probably credited with spiritual powers which differentiated them from other men. This is seen clearly in the west, as in the case of Juba, whose position is explicitly defined in the curt phrase, *Et Iuba*, *Mauris volentibus*, *deus est.*[3] In Eastern Libya there stood upon the Syrtic shore a tomb which in the time of Pliny was thought to be that of the eponymous chieftain called "Psyllus,"[4] which, one may be sure, was an object of native reverence. The same applies to the famous tomb and altar of the Philaeni at the bottom of the Syrtis Major, though the heroic brothers fabled to have been buried there were, if they ever existed, Carthaginians.[5] In short, the general attitude of the Eastern Libyans toward their dead was markedly religious.

This is confirmed not only to the practice of divination at graves, referred to above, but to the habit of swearing by the dead. Herodotus relates of the Nasamones that among them a man taking an oath "lays his hand upon the tomb of someone considered to have been pre-eminently just and good, and so doing, swears by his name."[6]

[1] Personal observation.

[2] H. Duveyrier, *Les Touareg du Nord*, pl. xv. fig. 2 (facing p. 279).

[3] Minucius Felix, *Octavius*, 23; Lactantius, *De falsa religione*, xv. Cf. *CIL*, viii. 17, 159, and Tertullian, *Apolog.* 24, *unicuique etiam provinciae et civitati suus deus est*, *ut Syriae Astartes*, . . . *ut Mauretaniae reguli sui.* Lactantius, *loc. cit.*, . . . *Romani Caesares suos consecraverunt*, *et Mauri reges suos* . . . ; S. Cyprianus, *De idolorum vanitate*, p. 225, . . . *Mauri vero manifeste reges colunt*, *nec ullo velamento hoc nomen obtexunt.* This cult of princes was perhaps encouraged by Roman apotheosis of Emperors, but its origin in North Africa, as in Egypt, was unquestionably indigenous. R. Basset, *op. cit.* p. 24 *sq.*

[4] Pliny vii. 2.

[5] Sallust, *Iugurtha* lxxv.; Strabo iii. 171; xvii. 836; Valerius Maximus v. 6, *Ext.* 4; Mela i. 7; Pliny v. 4.

[6] Herodotus iv. 172, Mela i. 8, Eustathius *ad* Dionys. *Perieg.* 209. It is, of course, mere rhetorical depreciation which made Procopius (*De bello Vandalico*, ii. 8) declare that the Mauri were ignorant of oaths: . . . ἔστι γὰρ ἐν Μαυρουσίοις οὔτε θείου φόβος οὔτε ἀνθρώπων αἰδώς. μέλει γὰρ αὐτοῖς οὔτε ὅρκων οὔτε ὁμήρων, κτλ.

The custom of swearing at tombs of pious persons is universal in Moḥammadan Africa. In Kordofan, for example, as a recent writer has remarked, tombs "were the favourite spots . . . for the swearing of solemn oaths, and should such an oath prove false, dread consequences were expected."[1] It was just such a sentiment which led to the swearing of oaths at graves among the ancient Libyans; and the practice is proof of the strongest kind of the existence of a belief in a future life.[2]

To pass now from the animistic phases to the more developed aspects of Libyan religion, it will be best to consider first the different divinities with whom we are acquainted under separate forms.

Ash

A Libyan god of this name ( ) is mentioned as early as the Vth Dynasty on the reliefs of King Sa-hu-re.[3] The name also occurs on some jar-sealings of about the same time.[4] From the manner in which he appears in the Sa-hu-re reliefs, it may be conjectured that this god was of some prominence in Eastern Libya at the time of the Old Empire; but nothing further can be said in regard to his nature and functions.

Shaheded

In composition with several personal names found in Late New Empire stelae in the Egyptian Delta, has been noted the element or *šȝḥṯṯ* or *šȝḥdd*. The stelae appear to have commemorated certain Libyan settlers in the Delta, and it has been suspected that the *šȝdd*-names are theophorous. An attempt has even been made to show that Shaheded was a Libyan goddess, but until further evidence has been collected on this point it cannot be regarded as having been satisfactorily established.[5] One need not, however, doubt that the element *šȝḥṯṯ* or *šȝḥdd* is Libyan, for it seems to be preserved in a bilingual Libyco-Latin inscription of the west. The Latin text in question reads SACTVT IHIMIR P VIXIT ANNORVM LXX; the Libyan equivalent of SACTVT reads ṢKTT, which bears an unmistakable resemblance to the hieroglyphic form *šȝḥṯṯ*.[6]

Sinifere

A god of this name is mentioned by Corippus in the *Johannis*[7] as being worshipped by the Eastern Libyans. As far as can be discerned he was a war-god, but only, perhaps, in the sense that he was a tribal god who helped his followers in war as in peace.

[1] R. G. Anderson, *Medical Practices and Superstitions of Kordofan*, p. 292.

[2] R. Neumann, *Nordafrika . . . nach Herodot*, does not exaggerate when he says (p. 139) that this belief *ist bei allen Hamiten Nordafrikas vom Nil bis zu den Kanarien angetroffen worden*. In this connection two late Roman inscriptions at Ghîrzah are noteworthy. These tributes of children to the memory of their parents terminate with the curious wish that the deceased—by their names clearly natives—may revisit their children's descendants and "make them like themselves": VISITENT FILIOS ET NEPOTES MEOS ET TALES FACIENT. Denham, Oudney, and Clapperton, *Travels, etc.*, vol. ii. p. 127 *sqq.* (especially p. 130, note, and p. 131, inscription no. 2).

[3] L. Borchardt, *Das Grabdenkmal des Königs S'aȝḥu-Re'*, vol. i. p. 17.

[4] J. E. Quibell, *Cairo Catal. Archaic Objects*, Plates, p. 8, No. 178, 179; p. 9, No. 200.

[5] A. Wiedemann, *Stelae of Libyan Origin*, p. 227.

[6] For the bilingual inscription, V. Reboud, *Recueil d'inscriptions libyco-berbères*, pl. iv. No. 24, text, p. 36.

[7] Corippus, *Johannis*, iv. 681; J. Partsch, *Die Berbern in der Dichtung des Corippus*, p. 16.

Mastiman

From Corippus one learns of a divinity of this name, who, like Sinifere, appears in the *Johannis*[1] as a war-god,[2] but whose exact nature is obscure. He is thus referred to by Corippus:

> . . . *Maurorum hoc nomine gentes*
> *Taenarium dixere Iovem, cui sanguine multo*
> *Humani generis mactatur victima pesti.*[3]

Partsch, from this gloomy characterisation, was inclined to relate Mastiman to the Dis Severus of an African inscription,[4] and to emend *Taenarium* to *Tartareum*.[5]

The name Mastiman is certainly connected with, and may be the equivalent of, that of a divinity called Autiman in a Latin inscription, where the latter god is associated with Mercurius.[6]

[" Aptuchus " and " Baleus "

A place near Apollonia Ptolemy names Ἀπτούχου ἱερόν.[7] C. Müller conjectured that the reading should be Αὐτούχου, but in Christian Africa there were bishops styled *Abtungensis*, *Aptungensis*, or *Aptuncensis*.[8] This suggests that Ἀπτούχου may be correct, and that in Cyrenaica there may have been a native cult of a god of this name.

Near Cyrene lay a town called Βάλις—ἀπό τινος Βάλεως, οὗ καὶ ἱερὸν ἔχει[9]—otherwise known as Φαλάκρα,[10] Βαλάγραι,[11] or *Balacris*.[12] In these latter forms it is easy to recognize derivatives of the Semitic בַּעַל-קֶרֶן,[13] *baʿal-ḳeren*, recalling the locative epithet *Balcarensis* of the Afro-Punic "Saturnus."[14] Pausanias states that at Balagrae Aesculapius was worshipped under the title of Physician, Ἰατρός;[15] the Tabula Peutingeriana glosses Balacris with the words *Hoc est templum Asclepii.* The inference is that here, under Semitic influence, was established the worship of Baʿal Eshmun, the Baleus of Stephanus, whom classical writers identified with Aesculapius.]

The Sea-Gods

According to Herodotus, the Greeks obtained their knowledge of "Poseidon" "from the Libyans, by whom he has always been honoured, and who were anciently the only people who had a god of that name."[16] This remarkable statement indicates clearly that some sort of a sea-god, of general character, was in fairly high repute among the coastwise Libyans of the fifth century B.C. The cult of "Poseidon" was especially practised about Lake Tritonis.[17] It is impossible to say whether this deity was originally

[1] Corippus, *Johannis* iv. 682, vii. 307.
[2] G. Mercier, *Les Divinités libyques*, p. 1.
[3] Corippus, *Johannis* vii. 307 *sqq*.
[4] *GIL*, viii. 9018.
[5] J. Partsch, *loc. cit.*
[6] *CIL*, viii. 2650.
[7] Ptolemy iv. 4 § 3.
[8] S. A. Morcelli, *Africa Christiana*, vol. i. p. 34 *sqq*.
[9] Stephanus Byz. *in verb.* Βάλις.
[10] Ptolemy iv. 4 § 7. All MSS.
[11] Pausanias ii. 26. 9; cf. Synesius, *Epist.* 104, 131.
[12] *Tab. Peut.* Segm. viii.
[13] קֶרֶן from *קָרַן, primary syllable קר, Gesenius, *Lexicon*, p. 943.
[14] J. Toutain, *De Saturni . . . cultu*, p. 32.
[15] Pausanias, *loc. cit.* Pausanias says the cult at Balagrae was derived from Epidaurus, but notes that goats were offered at the former sanctuary, contrary to usual Greek practice.
[16] Herodotus ii. 80.
[17] *Ibid.* iv. 188. Cf. R. Neumann, *Nordafrika . . . nach Herodot*, pp. 136 *sq*.

a Libyan one, or was a god imported by the Sea-Peoples who were allied with the Libyans in their invasions of Egypt.

The Libyans about Lake Tritonis also venerated a god called "Triton" by Herodotus.[1] In Argonautic legend this divinity is represented as having piloted the storm-driven Jason through the shoals of Lake Tritonis, for the sake of a brazen tripod. The god then "took the tripod," carried it to his own temple, seated himself upon it, and "filled with prophetic fury, delivered to Jason a long prediction," saying that a hundred Greek cities would rise about Lake Tritonis when a descendant of one of the Argonauts should carry off the tripod. "The Libyans of that region," adds Herodotus, "when they heard the words of the prophecy, took away the tripod and hid it."[2] With regard to this legend, it may be remarked that, whereas the Libyan "Poseidon" appears to have been a sea-god of a general nature, "Triton" would seem to have been a local divinity whose activities were confined to a narrower sphere.

Connected with "Triton" was his female counterpart "Tritonis," who bore "Athena," presently to be spoken of at length, to Poseidon.[3]

[" Achor "

An old error, promulgated over two centuries ago, and apparently unchallenged to the present time, would establish a deity of this name in the Libyan pantheon. Selden, in his *De diis Syris*,[4] cites Pliny x. 40 (28) as follows: *Cyreniaci* Achorem *deum* [*invocant*] *muscarum multitudine pestilentiam afferente*, *quae protinus intereunt postquam litatum est illi deo*; and he then refers "Achor" to the place-name "Accaron," and relates the god to Baʿal-Zebub, the *deus Accaronitarum*, etc., as a Θεὸς Μυῖα like the Greek Myiagrus, Zeus Apomyius, Apollo Myoctonus, etc. I am ignorant as to the edition of Pliny used by Seldon, but the texts of Detlefson, Sillig, and Franz, and even that of Erasmus (Basle, 1539), regularly give "Elei" for "Cyreniaci," and "Myiagron" for "Achorum." "Achor" is clearly derived from a corrupt lection of "Myiagron," but how "Elei" became Seldon's "Cyreniaci" I am at a loss to say. The point is only worth noting because "Achor," were this the true lection, would certainly have to be regarded as a non-Greek, and consequently as a Semitic or a Libyan, divinity.]

[" Psaphon "

Maximus Tyrius relates[5] that a certain Libyan named Psaphon, aspiring to divine honours, collected a great number of song-birds which he taught to utter the words "THE GREAT GOD PSAPHON." The birds, having learned their lesson, were set free, and repeated in their native woods the cry they had been taught in captivity. Thereupon the simple Libyans, thinking that the voices were divinely inspired, sacrificed to Psaphon.

It is barely possible that a god of this name really was venerated in some part of

[1] Herodotus iv. 188.

[2] *Ibid.* iv. 179; cf. 178.

[3] *Ibid.* iv. 180. For the Greek conception of Triton, Tritonis, and Athena Tritogenis, *vide* Vater, *Triton und Euphemos*, *passim*; J. Escher, *Triton und seine Bekämpfung durch Herakles*, *passim*.

[4] J. Selden, *De diis Syris*, p. 304.

[5] Maximus Tyrius, *Dissertat.* xix.

North Africa, and that the tale preserved by Maximus is merely a late attempt at explaining the origin of the cultus. Other evidence on this point is, however, lacking.]

The Sun-God

Among the tattoo-marks seen on the Libyans represented on the Egyptian monuments occur some which, as has already been said, had a religious significance. To these are to be added, without lapsing into that extravagance which sees sun-symbols in everything, the cruciform devices shown in Fig. 52, which yet survive among the Berbers. Sun-cultus, to which these emblems seem to be related, was strongly developed among the Libyans in general, Herodotus remarking that all the Libyans sacrificed to Sun and Moon.[1] The manner of sacrifice he thus describes: "The rites which the wandering Libyans use . . . are the following. They begin with the ear of the victim, which they cut off, and throw over their dwellings; this done, they kill the animal by twisting the neck.[2] They sacrifice to sun and moon, but not to any other gods. This worship is common to all the Libyans. The inhabitants of the parts about Lake Tritonis worship in addition Triton, Poseidon, and Athena, especially the last."[3]

This evidence as to the importance of sun-worship in ancient Libya receives confirmation from other sources. In the west have been found numerous non-Mithraic inscriptions bearing the formulae SOLI DEO INVICTO,[4] SOLI DEO AVGVSTO,[5] SOLI INVICTO,[6] or dedicated to sun and moon together.[7] At Ammonium (Sîwah) was a fountain sacred to the sun.[8] A Libyan Helius is mentioned by Diodorus;[9] Ibn Ḫaldun states that in early times the Berbers in general adored the sun;[10] a late writer, who conceived Apollo as primarily a sun-god, mentions that there was an Apollo *Ammonis filius in Libya natus*;[11] Macrobius declares that under the name of *Hammon* the Libyans worshipped the declining sun,[12] etc.

The only name now known for the Libyan sun-god—for that he was only called "Hammon" by confusion will later appear—is that preserved by Çorippus, who mentions him as Gurzil.[13] In the *Johannis* this god appears as a divinity in high favour with the tribesmen. His priest Ierna fights conspicuously in battle,[14] and an image of the god is borne by the Libyans into the fray.[15] He is represented as the offspring of the prophetic[16] god of Sîwah, the ram-horned divinity who, for reasons which will presently be made clear, was widely identified in late times with the Egyptian Amon.

[1] Herodotus iv. 188. He has previously excepted the Atarantes of the west, by saying that they cursed the sun for its wasting heat (iv. 184). Cf. Mela i. 8; Pliny v. 8; Nicolaus Damascenus, *Frag.* 140 in *FHG.*

[2] W. R. Smith, *Religion of the Semites*, p. 431, has misquoted this passage of Herodotus. "The Libyans," he writes, "killed their sacrifices without bloodshed, by throwing them over their huts and then twisting their necks" [!].

[3] Herodotus, *loc. cit.*

[4] *CIL*, viii. 2675.

[5] *CIL*, viii. 4513.

[6] *CIL*, viii. 1329, 1543, 9331, 9629.

[7] *CIL*, viii. 14,688, 14,689.

[8] Herodotus iv. 181; Diodorus Siculus xvii. 50; Arrian, *Anabasis*, iii. 4; Curtius iv. 7. 31; Pliny ii. 103, v. 5, etc.

[9] Diodorus Siculus iii. 57. 4, 5 *et alibi.*

[10] Ibn Ḫaldun, *Kitab el-ʿIbar*, vol. vi. p. 89.

[11] L. Ampelius, *Liber memorialis*, 9 (p. 21); cf. Corippus, *Johannis*, iii. 81 *sqq.*

[12] Macrobius, *Saturnalia*, i. 21. Cf. Martianus Capella, *De nuptiis Philologiae*, ii. p. 44.

[13] Corippus, *op. cit.* ii. 109, 405, iv. 665, 683, 1139 *sqq.*, v. 116, vii. 304, 619; J. Partsch, *loc. cit.*

[14] Corippus, *op. cit.* ii. 109, iv. 631, 1013, 1138, etc.

[15] *Ibid.* iv. 669 *sqq.*, 1139 *sq.* For Semitic parallels see W. R. Smith, *op. cit.* p. 36 *sq.*

[16] *Ibid.* vi. 516, *fatidicus.*

Huic [Gurzil] *referunt gentes pater est quod corniger Ammon*
Bucula torva parens. . . .[1]

His form was that of a bull.[2] The sun as a divine bull is, of course, a natural conception, from the power and splendour of the luminary on the one hand, and the strength and beauty of the animal on the other. A parallel exists in the case of Mnevis of Heliopolis in Egypt, where the sun-bull was held in high honour.[3]

A head which would seem to be that of Gurzil is seen upon the discus of a Roman lamp of the first century A.D. in one of the African museums;[4] a rudely-sculptured head, found at el-Kenayssîah, represents the Amon-Gurzil type, having both the bull's horns of the sun-god and the ram's horns of the god of the Oasis.[5]

The cult of Gurzil seems long to have survived in Eastern Libya. El-Bekrî, writing in the eleventh century A.D., mentions that various tribes in Tripolitana—among others the Huarah—to secure protection for their herds, offered prayers to a stone idol placed upon a hill-top, and named Gurza.[6] The situation of the idol, the purpose of their prayers, and the strong resemblance of names, leave little doubt that this is the Gurzil of Corippus. The name of the god appears in several place-names of classical times, such as the Roman *civitas Gurzensis*,[7] the Gurza of Ptolemy,[8] etc.

Little as is actually known of the sun-god Gurzil, his mythical origin, his general character, and his popularity are easily discernible from the evidence. He was a god whose origin had place in the direct personal nature-worship of early times, and so may be likened to the Greek Helius. His appearance in war was perhaps due to his being regarded as a protector and a dark-dispeller—a god who, like the Apollo with whom he was by some identified, was ἑκηβόλος or ἑκατηβόλος. When he was invoked as the protector of herds, it was as a bull-god, who, naturally, had come to be regarded as the patron of kine.[9]

The Moon-God

The one divinity which, besides the sun, was, according to Herodotus, worshipped by all the Libyans, was the moon.[10] In Berber, the word is a masculine substantive : *aggur*, or *aiyur*. This, as was pointed out by Mercier,[11] suggests the name *Ieru*, which occurs as a divine name, linked with the epithet *augustus*, in an inscription found near Constantine.

[1] Corippus ii. 110 *sq.*

[2] *Ibid.* iv. 666 *sq.*

[3] Ammianus Marcellinus xxii. 245 ; Aelian, *Hist. anim.* xi. 11 ; Macrobius, *Saturnalia*, i. 21 ; Porphyrius *ap.* Eusebius *Praepar. Evang.* iii. 13. For Apis, the Memphite bull-god who was sometimes regarded as a solar deity, see Macrobius, *loc. cit.* and cf. [Lucian], *De astrologia*, § 7.

[4] *Catal. Musée Lavigerie*, vol. ii., Pl. xv. fig. 2, and text, p. 57 and note 1.

[5] L. Carton, *Notes sur les Ruines d'el-Kenissiah*, p. 84, fig. 7, No. 3.

[6] El-Bekrî, *Description de l'Afrique septentrionale*, p. 12.

[7] *CIL*, viii. 69. Cf. *Pagogurzenses* and *Aethogurzenses* in *CIL*, viii. 68 ; cf. Polybius, *Hist.* i. 74.

[8] Ptolemy iv. 3 § 10, Γοῦρζα.

[9] In regard to Gurzil, there may have been some connection between him (in an aspect of the baleful sun) and the baleful south wind which we have already discussed. Cf. the line of Anticleides (*ap.* P. E. Jablonski, *Pantheon Aegyptiorum*, Part i. p. 158) :

Ἥλιος δὲ Νότοιο ἄναξ, ἵεραξ πολύμορφε.

[10] Herodotus iv. 188.

[11] G. Mercier, *Les Divinités libyques*, pp. 12 *sq.*

In connection with Libyan moon-cultus may be noted the North African taboo against pig, already cited from Herodotus,[1] who says in a general manner that none of the Libyans bred swine, and that the women of Barca abstain (not only from cow's flesh, but also) from pork. In Egypt existed a similar taboo, for which is an explanation which might apply to Libya. The Egyptians held swine to be so unclean that "if a man in passing accidentally touch a pig, he instantly hurries to the river, and plunges in with all his clothes on."[2] Yet on days when the moon was at full, swine were offered to the Moon-God, and the sacrificers ate of the flesh, though "at any other time they would not so much as taste it."[3] The Libyan taboo may have had a similar character.

Deus Fatidicus

It is necessary now to discuss a Libyan god whose name is only known through Egyptian, Carthaginian, and Greek identifications: the indigenous Libyan god of the Oasis of Ammonium (Sîwah), who may conveniently be styled the *Deus Fatidicus*.

It has been frequently stated that the Egyptians occupied the Oasis of Sîwah as early as the XVIIIth Dynasty.[4] Of this there is no proof: the earliest remains in the oasis belong to Ptolemaic or late New Empire times; and if the Egyptian occupation be placed as far back as 550 B.C., the archaeological requirements will be amply fulfilled.

When, some time about this date, the Egyptians came permanently to control this oasis, they found there established a cultus of a Libyan god whom they at once identified with Amon,[5] the god who, owing to the political rise of Thebes, his early home, had become the national god of the whole Nile Valley. So firmly established in the popular mind did this identification become, that not only was the *Deus Fatidicus* said to have been of Theban origin,[6] but a number of dragoman-stories were set afloat in late times, which claimed a Libyan origin for the Theban god. Thus, according to one account, Amon was a Libyan herdsman, who brought to Dionysus, when the latter was in Egypt, a large number of cattle. In recognition of this gift, Dionysus gave Amon lands at Thebes, and raised him to the dignity of a god.[7] Another tale of this sort relates that Dionysus (or, as others maintained, Heracles) was on his way to India, and was leading his army through the Libyan wastes; that, being overcome with thirst, the god invoked the aid of his father Zeus, who sent to him a ram (the sacred animal of Amon). Following the ram, he came to a certain spot where the animal pawed with its foot, and a spring gushed forth.[8] Yet another tale relates how, in the region between Carthage and

[1] Herodotus iv. 186.

[2] *Ibid.* ii. 47.

[3] *Ibid.*; cf. Plutarch, *De Iside et Osiride*, § 18. In regard to Libyan Moon cultus, two ancient superstitions deserve notice: (1) the Nasamones searched for carbuncles, which they believed to be of divine origin, when the moon was at its fullest (Pliny xxxvii. 7); and it was believed that the Ammonian salt waxed and waned with the moon (*ibid. loc. cit.*).

[4] Recently by C. Sourdille, *Hérodote et la Religion de l'Égypte*, p. 158.

[5] To avoid over-elaboration, I have used the form "Amon" indifferently for the Theban or the Sîwan god, though it would perhaps be more exact to employ the form "Amon" as a transcript of the Egyptian 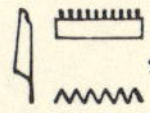, and the form "Ammon" to indicate that a classical source was being used.

[6] Herodotus iv. 181.

[7] Hyginus, *Astronomica*, i. 20.

[8] Servius *ad* Verg. *Aen.* iv. 195. Cf. Hyginus, *loc. cit.*; idem, *Fabul.* 133; Lutatius *ad* Statii *Thebaid.* iii. 476; L. Ampelius, *Liber memorialis*, 2; Tertullian, *De pallio*, 3; Martianus Capella ii. p. 39, *edit. cit.*

Cyrene, some herdsmen found a child seated on the sands, wearing ram's horns, and uttering prophecies. On being taken up, it ceased speaking, but on being again set down, it recommenced.[1] Suddenly it vanished, and the herdsmen, then recognizing its divine nature, there began to honour the god Zeus-Amon.[2] Diodorus Siculus relates vaguely that Amon was a mythical Libyan king;[3] Pausanias,[4] Eustathius,[5] and Macrobius[6] distinctly imply his Libyan origin, while [Lucian], less clearly, does the same.[7]

The stories are of some value, as casting a little light on the nature of the *Deus Fatidicus*. They cannot, however, be seriously regarded as proving anything more than the closeness of the identification between the *Deus Fatidicus* and the Theban Amon in late times. This is the more strongly the case, since from the Egyptian sources can be derived no evidence tending to prove that the Theban and Ammonian gods were one. A custom existed, it is true, of making annually a twelve days' progress in Libya with the image of the Theban Amon and the other Theban gods; but this custom itself was of much the same origin as the above stories, and was not known before late times.[8]

The distinction between the *Deus Fatidicus* and the Theban Amon, despite the identification of the two, can be discerned even in Herodotus. That writer, for example, has different styles for the two gods. The Libyan one he regularly calls "Zeus-Ammon," Ζεὺς Ἄμμων.[9] He suspects that the worshippers of the "Zeus" of the oasis have given their god this name because the Egyptians call Zeus "Amoun."[10] The Egyptian god he regularly terms the "Theban Zeus," Ζεὺς Θηβαιεύς.[11] The Libyan character of "Zeus-Ammon" = *Deus Fatidicus* appears strongly in the story told by Herodotus concerning the inhabitants of Marea and of Apis in the region contiguous to the Egyptian Delta on the west. Those people, counting themselves Libyans, were discontented at the religious impositions forced upon them by the Egyptians. They appealed to the oracle at Ammonium.[12] Again, Cambyses III., while he left the sanctuary of Amon at Thebes in peace, launched against that at Sîwah an expedition which was to enslave the worshippers of "Zeus-Ammon," and "fire the temple where Zeus gave his oracles."[13] As a recent writer[14] has shrewdly observed, this "difference in treatment is significant." Furthermore, if historians are right in supposing that Sîwah was

[1] Cf. the well-known legend of the Libyan Antaeus, who with each fall he took in wrestling gained fresh strength from Mother Earth. Apollodorus ii. v. 11; Hyginus, *Fab.* 31; Pindar, *Isthm.* iv. 52; Lucan iv. 617; Statius, *Thebaid*, vi. 893.

[2] Servius, *loc. cit.*

[3] Diodorus Siculus iii. 68.

[4] Pausanias iv. 23.

[5] Eustathius *ad* Dionys. *Perieg.* 211. Cf. Dionysius, *Perieg.* 211 *sq.*; Nonnus, *Dionysiaca* xiii. 370; Phaestus *ap.* Schol. Pind. *Pyth.* iv. 28; Martianus Capella ii. *edit. cit.* pp. 44, 48.

[6] Macrobius, *Saturnalia*, i. 21.

[7] Hyginus, *Astronomica*, i. 20.

[8] Eustathius *ad* Homer, *Iliad*, i. p. 128; Diodorus Siculus i. 97. Diodorus says of the return of the god—ὡς ἐξ Αἰθιοπίας τοῦ θεοῦ παρόντος. But the geographical requirements, and his own statement that the progress was εἰς τὴν Λιβύην, show that Libya, and not Aethiopia, was meant. Cf. idem, iii. 68. Both Diodorus and Eustathius, *loc. cit.*, have drawn on a common source.

[9] Herodotus i. 46, ii. 18, ii. 32, iii. 25.

[10] *Ibid.* ii. 42, Ἀμοῦν γὰρ Αἰγύπτιοι καλέουσι τὸν Δία. Cf. Plutarch, *De Iside et Osiride*, § 10 (p. 354, Xyland.); Iamblichus, *De mysteriis*, viii. 3, Ἀμῶν; Servius *ad* Verg. *Aen.* iv. 196, . . . *Libyae* [*lege Libyes*], *Isammone arietem appellant.* This last recalls the modern Sîwan ساعون, for Amon (*vide supra*, p. 63).

[11] Herodotus i. 182, ii. 42, 54, iv. 181.

[12] *Ibid.* ii. 18.

[13] *Ibid.* iii. 25.

[14] C. Sourdille, *op. cit.* p. 153.

not occupied by Egyptians before the sixth century B.C., it can hardly be believed that a god *introduced* from Egypt would have attained to such great and such early reputation as the god of Sîwah enjoyed. The "opening up" of the oasis, the dignifying of a barbarous, but strongly supported local cult, by the recognition in its object a form of the Egyptian national god, would explain how the oracle of the *Deus Fatidicus* sprang as suddenly into prominence as it did; but it is absolutely necessary to believe that such a cult existed,[1] or Thebes or Diospolis, and not Ammonium, would have remained the chief seats of the prophetic god. On these grounds it becomes easy to understand how Croesus, in distant Lydia, made trial of the oracle about the time when, or even somewhat before, the Egyptian occupation of Sîwah took place;[2] and how, by the fourth century B.C., no oracle in Africa, not even that of Buto in the Delta, had come into better repute; and why heads of the *Deus Fatidicus* are found so early and in such numbers on the Cyrenaic coins.[3] These arguments, in themselves enough to indicate the originally separate identities of the *Deus Fatidicus* and of the Egyptian Amon, may be supplemented with one more, which is of great weight; the *Deus Fatidicus* was such indeed—essentially a god of prophecy. The immense popularity of the oracle at Sîwah is well known. The trial made by Croesus has just been mentioned; other instances, authentic and fictitious, attest the fame of the desert god. Plutarch states[4] that the god of the oasis foretold the death of Cimon, which took place in B.C. 449; the Athenians kept a special galley at state-charges to convey questions to the Libyan god;[5] around his temple at Ammonium might have been seen a number of columns, surmounted by dolphins, and inscribed ΚΥΡΕΝΑΙΩΝ ΘΕΩΡΩΝ in testimony of the gratitude of his Cyrenaic votaries;[6] there even sprang up in Greece secondary sanctuaries of the god, as at Thebes in Boeotia, where the sculptor Calamis made a statue of the Libyan divinity, which, with an appropriate hymn, was dedicated by the poet Pindar.[7] At Aphytis, where another temple had arisen, Lysander, who had laid siege to the city, withdrew because of a dream-warning from the god, to whose Libyan sanctuary he afterwards made a pilgrimage;[8] and every schoolboy has read some version of Alexander's visit to the desert sanctuary. To go no farther, it may be said that the character of the Libyan god was primarily and essentially that of a seer and a prophet; and herein he essentially and widely differs from the Egyptian divinity with whom he became identified. The Theban Amon was primarily a god of cultivation and of the harvest: later, in his national character as Amon-Re, he was a deity of general scope—a king of gods, a divine protector, a conferrer of national blessings. Although he gave oracles, or rather judgments, in a perfunctory manner, he never

[1] An oasis such as Sîwah must inevitably have been regarded in early times as a spot of peculiar sanctity. Cf. the Semitic conceptions of "Baʿal's land," etc., so strikingly elucidated by W. R. Smith, *Religion of the Semites*, *passim*.

[2] Herodotus i. 46.

[3] C. L. Müller, *Numismatique de l'ancienne Afrique*, vol. i. pp. 101 *sqq*.

[4] Plutarch, *Cimon*, § 18.

[5] Hesychius *in verb.* *τίμια*; cf. Aristophanes, *Aves*, 619, 716; Plutarch, *Nicias*, § 13; Plato, *Leges*, v. pp. 738 c, etc.

[6] Strabo i. p. 49.

[7] Pindar, *Frag.* 36, ed. Bergk.

[8] Plutarch, *Lysander*, §§ 20, 25; Pausanias iii. 18; Nepos, *Lysander*, 3.

FIG. 78*a*.—(Front).

FIG. 78*b*.—(Back)

FIG. 78*c*.—(Right Side).

FIG. 78*d*.—(Left Side).

became reputed as a seer: his functions were quite different from those of the *Deus Fatidicus*, and clearly point to the different origins of the two deities.

In regard to the form of the Libyan god, there has been not a little speculation, chiefly on account of a passage in Curtius which, had he deliberately designed it to engender discussion, could scarcely have been better conceived. *Id quod pro deo colitur*, says Curtius, speaking of this prophetic god of Sîwah, *non eandem effigiem habet, quam vulgo diis artifices accommodaverunt, umbriculo maxime similis est habitus, smaragdis et gemmis coagmentatus*[1] ("that which is revered as a god has not a likeness the same as that which artists have commonly given to divinities: its seeming is most like to an *umbriculum*, studded with emeralds and gems"). The word *umbriculum*, unfortunately, is not found in any other writer, and its meaning is therefore not certainly known. Emendation to *umbraculum* serves only to deepen the mystery; and several editors and writers[2] have, in despair, and against MS. authority, read *umbilico* for *umbriculo*, and supposed that the form of the god was omphalic. That to Greek or Roman eyes it may indeed have seemed so is possible: at present, the important thing to note is that the local aspect was neither anthropomorphic nor zoömorphic; it was of unusual and peculiar form.

This form has been recognized in Egypt by Daressy.[3] Three very peculiar faience statuettes one of which is shown (Fig. 78, *a*, *b*, *c*, *d*), were found some years ago in the excavations by the *Service des Antiquités*[4] at Karnak. These proved to be, by the inscriptions upon them, representations of the god Amon. The god appeared as a lump or mass of curious shape, seated upon an elaborately ornamented throne, the lump or mass itself being lavishly decorated. Daressy called attention to the fact that these strange figures were evidently related to two representations which had been noticed before: the one a relief of Roman times on the temple of Karnak (Fig. 79), the other an etching on a bronze mirror found at Mît Rahînah (Fig. 80).[5] Both these latter show not only the enthroned mass, but show it surmounted by a head of Amon in the Egyptian style, wearing the two feathers. Adopting the conjectural reading *umbilico* in the passage of Curtius cited above, Daressy supposed the enthroned mass to have represented an omphalus. Thus, although he recognized that this form of Amon was non-Egyptian, and wholly

FIG. 79.

[1] Q. Curtius iv. 7. 23.

[2] *E.g.* E. Naville, *Le Dieu de l'oasis de Jupiter Ammon*, in the *C. R. de l'Acad. des Inscr.*; G. Daressy, *Une Nouvelle Forme d'Ammon*, in the *Annales*, ix. 64 *sqq.*

[3] *Op. cit.*

[4] Cairo Museum, Nos. 36,754, 36,755, 38,171.

[5] G. Daressy, *op. cit.* p. 67; Idem, *Une Trouvaille de bronzes à Mit Rahineh*, in the *Annales*, iii. 169 *sqq.*, and pl. ii. fig. 1.

different from the anthropomorphic figures of the Theban Amon, who is regularly represented as a man, sometimes with the head or horns of his sacred animal, the ram, Daressy failed to perceive the real significance of the monuments he was discussing. The enthroned mass represents a body in the sitting posture which Herodotus states to have been that in which the Nasamones buried their dead. Examination of the Karnak figures even shows the cordings of the bale in which the body was wrapped (Fig. 78). The heads with plumes shown in the Karnak relief (Fig. 79) and the Mît Rahînah bronze (Fig. 80) are merely Egyptian attempts at emphasizing the identity of the Libyan *Deus Fatidicus*

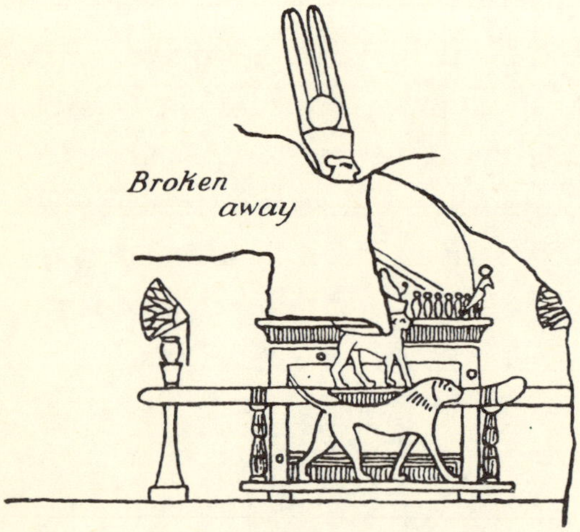

Fig. 80.

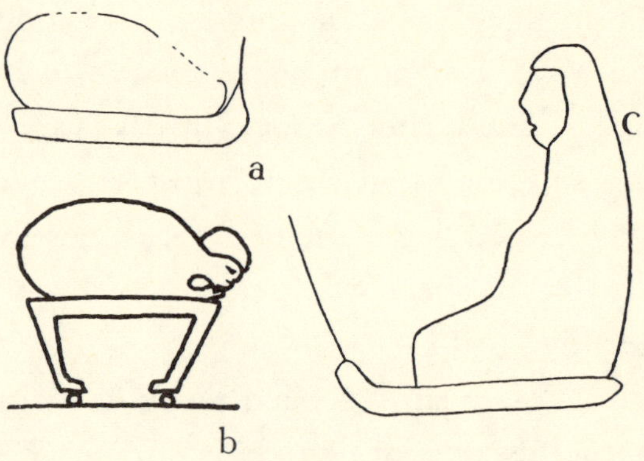

Fig. 81.

with the national god of the Nile. The appearance of these representations as a whole recalls strongly that of the body wrapped in a bull's hide, the , *teknw*, sometimes seen in Egyptian funereal scenes[1] (Fig. 81, *a*, *b*, and especially *c*).

This recognition of the form of Amon, described by Daressy as a body contracted and wrapped for burial, gives the key to the whole situation at Sîwah. The strength of *manes*-worship among the Libyans has been noted, as has the deeply-rooted practice, surviving until present times, of consulting the dead about the future. This accounts for the fact that the god of Ammonium was, first and foremost, a god of prophecy. He was the hypertype of those ancestors or men of renown to whose graves the Libyans resorted to learn the future.

The responses or monitions of the *Deus Fatidicus* were sometimes, as in the case of Lysander, conveyed, as were those of the prophetic dead of Libya, by means of dreams. The formal consultations at Ammonium were, however, delivered in a more imposing manner.[2] The god was borne in a procession through the palm-groves surrounding his temple. Eighty priests bore on their shoulders a barque—this conveyance betrays at once the Egyptian influence of Amon-Re—on which rested the golden shrine of the divinity. The barque was ornamented with numerous silver *paterae* hanging down from

[1] Cf. G. Maspero, in *Mém. de la Mission Française*, V. fasc., iii. pp. 435 *sqq.*; J. J. Tylor, *Wall Drawings . . . of El-Kab, The Tomb of Paheri*, pl. viii. register 7, and text.

[2] For what follows, Q. Curtius iv. 7. 23 *sqq.*; Strabo xvii. p. 814; Diodorus Siculus xvii. 50 *sqq.*

the gunwales—perhaps representing the grave-gear of the dead god—and the image of the god itself was studded, as has been said, with precious stones. A long train of virgins and matrons followed the barque, singing "uncouth hymns in the Libyan tongue," with a view to propitiating the god, and inducing him to return to the consultant a satisfactory answer. The deity was carried in the direction in which he himself willed his bearers to go. This suggests an interesting parallel in modern Egypt, where the attendants at a funeral believe the corpse exerts a mysterious influence on its bearers, directing them as to where they shall go.[1] At Ammonium, after the procession, the god made answer by gestures[2] to the questions put to him. In classical times these responses were interpreted by the priest, who had even the condescension to put the replies into verse, in the manner of the best Greek oracles![3]

The *Deus Fatidicus* was served by both men and women, who were termed by the Greeks *ἱερόδουλοι*. The women took part in the processions of the god; and in Herodotus's story of the Theban origin of the oracle—a story itself patently of Theban origin—it was a woman who was said to have founded the desert sanctuary.[4]

So much, then, concerning the original difference between the *Deus Fatidicus* and the Theban Amon, and for the true nature, in the beginning, of the former. An important and interesting question may now be considered—the sacred animal of the Libyan god. This animal was the ram: a fact which the Egyptians, who held this animal sacred to their national deity,[5] seized on with avidity, as strengthening the bond between the two gods. One might, in fact, be led at first glance to suspect that the ram, as a sacred animal of the *Deus Fatidicus*, had become so by Egyptian means, did not a peculiar body of evidence lead to the conclusion that the ram was one of the important figures among the native Libyan *sacra*. How it became first associated with the god of Ammonium cannot be decided: possibly it was the totem-animal of his worshippers, possibly the *Deus Fatidicus* came to be regarded as a phase of the Ram-god. The wide geographical range of ram-worship in Northern Africa might incline one to the latter view.

The Barbary sheep (*Ovis lervia* and *O. longipes*) was anciently found in Eastern Libya, and its strength and speed, the inaccessibility of its haunts, and its fondness for mountain heights, all tended to make it an animal which, to savage minds, would seem worthy of reverence.

[1] New chiefs were by a certain Hausa tribe thus chosen: A bull was killed as soon as the old chief died. The corpse was wrapped in the hide, placed on a bed, and then carried outdoors. The deceased's kinsmen stood in a ring round his body, while the town-elders thus bespoke the corpse: "O corpse, show us who is to be our chief, that we may live in peace, and that our crops may do well." The bearers then carried the body round the ring, and it would cause them to bump against the man it wished to succeed (A. J. N. Tremearne, *Hausa Superstitions*, p. 104).

[2] Servius *ad* Verg. *Aen.* vi. 68; Strabo *loc. cit.*; Eustathius *ad* Dionys. *Perieg.* 211, *ἱστορεῖται δὲ τὰς μαντείας διὰ συμβόλων ἐν Ἄμμωνος γίνεσθαι, ἤτοι διὰ σχημάτων τινῶν καὶ κατανεύσεων καὶ ἀνανεύσεων.*

[3] [Callisthenes], p. 31, 26. Cf. Silius Italicus, *De bello Punico*, iii. 700 *sqq.*

[4] Herodotus ii. 54. For the *hieroduli* cf. Procopius, *De aedificiis*, vi. 2.

[5] Herodotus ii. 54. Cf. Servius *ad* Verg. *Aen.* iv. 196; Plutarch, *De Iside et Osiride*, § 72; Strabo xvii. p. 559; Clemens Alexandrinus, *Protrept.* p. 25; Proclus, *In Timaeum*, i. p. 30; G. Maspero, *Études de mythologie et d'archéologie égyptienne*, ii. p. 401; C. Sourdille, *op. cit.* p. 155.

At Zenagah, in the Western Ṣaḥara, at a point far removed from Egyptian or other non-Libyan influence, exists a fine and early rock-glyph of a ram, wearing on its head what seems a rayed disc (Fig. 82). The glyph is a full metre in length, and the surface of the rock within the outlines has been carefully and neatly polished. About the neck of the animal is a sort of collar. The rayed disc is surmounted by what appear to be a pair of plumes. The whole is an imposing monument of primitive graphic art, and is

Fig. 82.

Fig. 83.

utterly different in technique from the late "Libyco-Berber" rock-scribings found in all parts of the Ṣaḥara, wheresoever the stone is suitable for them. The Zenagah ram is sculptured on a high face of rock overlooking the palms of the oasis, and, despite its patination, is visible from some distance.[1] Another glyph from the same station shows again the ram, but in this instance the representation is not so good (Fig. 83). The artist has given the animal an attenuated body like that of a greyhound, but the head retains enough character to show what is meant.[2] This glyph measures 82 cms. from head to tail. As in the first instance, the rayed disc is present, and again there appears a collar about the neck. In this case, attached to the collar and worn like a pectoral ornament, is a rudely circular object like a *bulla*. A similar pendant is observed on many popular terra-cottas of Graeco-Roman Egypt[3] which represent the ram of the Libyco-Theban Amon. Besides the Zenagah glyphs, an admirable example exists at Bu ʿAlem in Algeria (Fig. 84). The Bu ʿAlem ram is rendered with

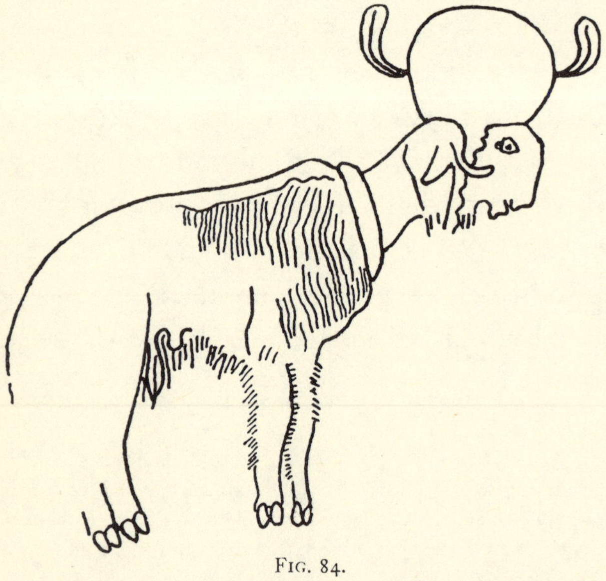

Fig. 84.

[1] E.-F. Gautier, *Sahara algérien*, p. 93 and fig. 14. Gautier well observes at the end of his description, "*On échappe difficilement à la conclusion qu'elle* [the graving] *avait une signification religieuse.*"

[2] *Ibid.* p. 89 and fig. 11.

[3] *E.g.* Berlin Museum, No. 8794. Cf. Cairo Museum, No. 27,053, etc.

great care. Like the other two, it is of generous size, as is regularly the case with the earlier African rock-drawings. About the neck is a collar. The disc on the head has both in front of it and behind it an ostrich plume,[1] and at first sight appears to be tied on by a band passing beneath the animal's throat. When, however, one narrowly examines this supposed band, it appears that it is indicated not by a straight line as a taut band should have been, and as are the parts of the collar. Also the "band" projects a little below the throat. It is therefore justifiable to revise one's first impression, and to think that here, by a curious touch of anthropomorphism, the ram has been dignified with a side-lock such as was worn by the Libyan fighting-men on the Egyptian monuments.

Another representation was found in 1851 at Old Arzeu. This was a head, rudely sculptured, with the nose feebly worked out, and with the eyes, ears, and mouth merely scored. A pair of curved ram's horns were sculptured at the sides.[2] A similar head was not long ago found at Tementit, and identified as a ram's by Basset.[3]

Besides this monumental evidence and the various indirect textual notices, it is explicitly stated by S. Athanasius that the Libyans held the ram sacred.[4] He states that this ram was called "Amen"; but this is probably his own conjecture. El-Bekrî states that until the ninth century A.D. rams were worshipped between Aghmat and Sus.[5]

The sum of this evidence leads to the conclusion that, not only in Egypt, but also in North Africa, the ram was a sacred animal. If one may judge by the rayed discs worn by some of the examples, it would appear that in some localities at least the ram had a solar aspect; but here it is merely necessary to show that he was venerated by the Libyans, and that quite without Egyptian intervention he may therefore have become associated in some manner with the *Deus Fatidicus* of Sîwah.

It was under his Egyptianized form that the cultus of the god of Ammonium became widespread; and this discussion may conclude with a brief account of the later history of this divinity. The oracle of Sîwah declined as rapidly as it had risen, but the worship of the Deus Fatidicus-Amon did not die out until the Christian times.[6] Besides the temples erected to this composite deity outside of Africa, others sprang up in Libya, as at Augila.[7] On the Syrtic littoral was a station called Ἀμούγκλα (var. Ἀμούγκα, Ἀμούνκλα);[8] another called Ἄμμωνος [κώμη],[9] the *Ad Ammonem*[10] or *Ammonis*[11] of the Roman itineraries; yet a third, near the Philaenorum Arae, was known to the Greeks as Ἄμμωνος ἁλοῦς

1 Certainly they seem to be plumes rather than, as has been suggested, *uraei*, else the artist would not have inserted a middle line in each. Cf. for this glyph S. Gsell, *Monuments antiques de l'Algérie*, vol. i. p. 53 and fig. 13.

2 L. A. Berbrugger, *Bibliothèque-Musée d'Alger*, pp. 29 *sq*.

3 E.-F. Gautier, *op. cit.* p. 253.

4 S. Athanasius, *Contra gentes*, 9, col. 20 B.

5 El-Bekrî, *Description de l'Afrique septentrionale*, ed. de Slane, Arab. text, p. 161 = trans. p. 355.

6 The later writers cited *supra et infra*; add Juvenal, *Sat.* vi. 554; Claudian, *De IV. consulatu Honorii*, 144; Ausonius, *Epigr.* 96; and especially Procopius, *De aedificiis*, vi. 2.

7 Procopius, *loc. cit.*

8 Ptolemy iv. 3 § 11.

9 *Ibid. loc. cit.*

10 *Tabula Peutingeriana*, Segm. vii.

11 Cf. C. Müller in Ptol. *Geog.* (notes) i. 2 p. 628 (A), p. 629 (B).

(ἄλσος ?,[1] the Ἄμμωνος πηγαί of the Stadiasmus) ;[2] while a fourth,—ἱερὸν τοῦ Ἄμμωνος—existed near Antipyrgus in Marmarica.[3] At the present time, in the district south of Benghazî, is a place called تل امون, *Tel Amun*, the "hill of Amon," by the natives. From this it appears how popular, after his identification with the national god of Egypt, the god of Sîwah became, even if, before that identification, his cultus was purely local.

The most important of the foreign developments of the *Deus Fatidicus* I have not yet touched ; nor can I now do so more than briefly, for upon the cultus of the Libyco-Egyptian god at Carthage a whole thesis might be written. The divinity whom the Egyptians had assimilated with their 𓇋𓏠𓈖 *imn*, Amon, was adopted into the Carthaginian pantheon under the name of בעל חמן *Baʿal Ḥaman*, the word בעל *Baʿal* being of course nothing more than the title of " owner " or " master ". There is here, it may be remarked, no phonetic difficulty in finding the Egyptian 𓇋 represented by the Punic ח : such dialect equivalence is perfectly possible in Berber phonesis ; and the single מ represents the *m* in 𓏠 and in many of the Greek and Latin transcriptions.[4]

Several thousand Carthaginian votive stelae, constituting at least three-fourths of all those found, are dedicated to the god Ḥaman and to the goddess Tanit.[5] This is the more extraordinary as the state gods of Carthage were the purely Semitic Baalim, Astarte, Eshmun, Melkart, etc., and as, despite the universally theophoric tendency of Semitic personal names, the Punic onomasticon offers few, if any, names in which that of Ḥaman appears. This is explicable on the supposition that Haman was adopted into the Carthaginian pantheon from without ; and that he retained enough of his Libyan character as a god of the dead to deter his votaries from giving to their children his name, which would have such a sinister significance.[6]

That Baʿal Ḥaman was indeed a Carthaginian form of the Libyco-Egyptian god is clear from his form. On his stelae appears sometimes the ram of the *Deus Fatidicus*

[1] Scylax, § 109.

[2] *Stadiasmus Maris Magni*, §§ 82, 83, . . . ἐπὶ Ἀμμωνίου πηγάς. . . . Against the identification of this station with that mentioned by Scylax it may justly be urged that, whereas the latter was apparently near the Philaenorum Arae, the former, according to the *Stadiasmus*, was 305 stades distant from that place. But, on the other hand, Syrtic geography is somewhat vexed, and, if Ἄ. ἄλσος is the correct lection in Scylax, the grove would naturally be dependent on the springs. The Ammonian Springs have been identified with the modern بير الباشر, *Bîr el-bashir*, the name (=*puteus auspicatus*) preserving a memory of the time when the waters were sacred to Amon. Cf. C. Müller, note *ad Stadiasm.* § 82.

[3] *Stadiasmus Maris Magni*, § 38.

[4] Cf. Herodotus ii. 42 ; Iamblichus, *De mysteriis*, 8 ; S. Athanasius, *loc. cit.* Cf. the Hebrew form אמן as in O.T. *Jerem.* xlvi. 25 ; *Ezek.* xxx. 5 ; *Nahum*, iii. 8, and Coptic ⲁⲙⲟⲩⲛ as in O.T. *loc. citt.* (*vers. Copt.*).

[5] Père Delattre, *Les Tombeaux puniques de Carthage*. The typical formula runs as follows (I cite, for want of a better example, one from W. S. W. Vaux, *Inscriptions in the Phoenician Character*, etc., No. 12, plate iv.) :

לרבת לתנת פנבע[ל ר]
לארן לבעל חמן [אש]
נדר חנא בו בד[מל]
קרת בו מגן

"To the lady Tanit, Baʿal-in-face, and to the lord Baʿal-Ḥaman ; that which Ḥanna, son of Bad-Melḳart, son of Magon, consecrated." Cf. *CIS*, i. no. 254 *et alibi*.

[6] The finding of the stelae chiefly in cemeteries to some extent bears this out.

and of Amon, as in Fig. 85. Statuettes of the composite god wearing the ram's horns have been found in Punic cemeteries (Fig. 86). In one instance he lacks the horns,

Fig. 85.

Fig. 86.

Fig. 87.

but bears on his left arm a standing ram (Fig. 87). The figure-heads of the Carthaginian ships often had the form of the ram-headed god. Silius Italicus, in his account of a sea-fight in which a Carthaginian captain, in despair at seeing his ship in flames, stabbed himself and poured a libation of his own blood between the horns of the figure-head, has the words:

. . . dextra inde cruorem
Excipit et large sacra inter cornua fundit.[1]

Similarly, another prays to the Amon-head in the bows of his ship; and Silius, in relating it, remarks parenthetically:

Hammon numen erat Libycae gentile carinae
Cornigeraque sedens spectabat caerula fronte.[2]

Further evidence comes from Sardinia. There, in Punicized sites such as Tharrus, numerous ram's-head amulets of Egyptian style have been found, the importations, certainly, of Carthaginian merchants.[3] Taken in conjunction with the other evidence, this sufficiently proves the identity of Baʿal Ḥaman of Carthage with the Libyco-Egyptian god. How late his worship lasted in Punic Africa is not known, but probably it was extinguished only after the advent of Christianity.

It remains to speak of one special phase of the Libyan *Deus Fatidicus* which has purposely not yet been mentioned, as its discussion is in the nature of an appendix to

[1] Silius Italicus, *De bello Punico*, xiv. 452 *sq.*

[2] *Ibid.* xiv. 440 *sq.*

[3] J. Lieblein, *Notice sur les monuments égyptiens trouvés en Sardaigne*, pp. 13 *sq.* and figs. 22 *sqq.* With these amulets cf. Alexandria Museum, No. 1197/465, and G. A. Reisner, *Amulets* in *Cairo Catal.* Nos. 12,329, 12,330, 12,332, 12,333, 12,336, 12,337, 12,343.

what has now been said. It will be readily conceived that a nomadic people, living in a country largely desert, and constrained to follow the vaguely-defined and waterless trails running between oasis and oasis, would naturally evolve a divinity whose functions were to guide and to protect the traveller—in short, some divinity not wholly unlike the Greek Ζεὺς ξένιος. Even to-day a feeling exists in Africa that the wayfarer enjoys a large share of the attention of Allah. A god of prophecy, a god who advises with foreknowledge, and to whom that which is hidden to men and full of perplexity is clear and patent, is, among a people living in such an environment as that which surrounded the Eastern Libyans, in a fair way to become a god of roads, a divine guide, and the friend of travellers.

Such a development took place in the case of the *Deus Fatidicus*. To one myth which illustrates this phase of his character, reference has already been made—that myth relating how Dionysus (or Heracles), while crossing the desert, being overcome with thirst, invoked the help of "Zeus-Amon" his father, who sent to his aid the ram which pawed a water-hole in the sands.[1] Another story of divine guidance attaches to Alexander's famous visit to the oasis. The Macedonian king, some days after leaving the coast, found himself lost, waterless, and altogether in a strait place. A shower of rain, which partially relieved the thirst of the army, was regarded as due to divine interposition on the part of the god of Sîwah, and the expedition was thereafter guided on its way to the oasis, and on its return thence, by two crows (Aristobulus) or by a pair of serpents (Ptolemy Soter).[2]

In the anonymous Arabic history of Sîwah is told a tale worth citing in this connection. "A certain one of the governours of Egypt," writes the historian, "meted out penalties upon some of his people, but these latter escaped into the desert with a little food. Now after some time, their food being exhausted, they saw a ram, and the ram trotting away into the hills, they followed it, and came to a town with men dwelling in it. The inhabitants paid no taxes and had trees and streams and gardens. The newcomers inquired of the dwellers there concerning their country, and they said that they never had to do with the outside world. And after dwelling there a long while, the fugitives returned to Egypt. Afterwards they sought again for this oasis, but found it not."[3] This interesting story, in which the ram appears as a guide to the lost travellers, may be regarded as one of the latest survivals of the tales, once probably very numerous, of the care bestowed by the prophetic Libyan god of Sîwah upon strayed wanderers in the desert.[4]

[1] Servius, *ad* Verg. *Aen.* iv. 196; Lutatius, *Schol. ad* Luc. *Pharsal.* iv. 672.

[2] Arrian, *Anabasis*, vii. 14. 23; Plutarch, *Alexander*, § 72.

[3] These mysterious desert cities are, in Persia, Arabia, and Africa, the theme of a thousand tales. Readers of the *Arabian Nights* will recall the classic story of the lost city of Iram (Ḳuran, *surah* lxxxix. 6). Perhaps the earliest notice of these hidden cities is in Strabo vii. p. 299, where the geographer cites a Greek critic as censuring many writers for believing such absurdities as "that in Libya there exists a city of Dionysus which no one can find twice."

[4] Such powers of guidance as the *Theban* Amon seems to have had were derived from his neighbour Min of Coptos, patron of the Coptos-Red Sea road. Cf. A. Erman, *Egyptian Religion*, pp. 58 *sq.*

Deus Coelestis

A French scholar, whose works are marked with equal ingenuity and soundness, established the existence among the ancient Libyans of a sky-god of general and vague character, whom it is here convenient to designate simply as *Deus Coelestis*.[1] The oldest conception of the sky among the Eastern Libyans, and one which persisted until the seventh century B.C., was that the firmament was a solid roof above the earth. This idea is shown in the account given by Herodotus, who says that the Libyans who brought the Greek colonists from Aziris to Cyrene praised the latter place by saying that there "the sky leaked"[2]—*i.e.* rainfalls were frequent. This conception of the firmament as solid no more interfered with the evolving of a personal *Deus Coelestis* in Libya than it did in Greece, where similar cosmological views were entertained.[3] Unfortunately, present knowledge of the Libyan sky-god is chiefly derived through a study of the late African "Saturnus,"[4] who was widely[5] venerated in North Africa during the second and third centuries A.D.[6] From such a study, however, the general nature of the Libyan *Deus Coelestis* can be ascertained.

On the votive stelae of "Saturnus" appear not only solar discs, but stars, crescents, etc.—in short, heaven-symbols in general.[7] On some of the stelae, "Saturnus" is represented with Helius-Sol and Selene-Luna;[8] and his Afro-Roman temples were arranged with three *cellae*, that Sun and Moon might flank the Sky-god in the centre.[9] Toutain is therefore justified in his inference that the African "Saturnus" was a divinity *totius caeli et caelestis luminis*.[10] This supposition receives strength from the fact that "Saturnus" was associated with one of those vague nature goddesses of whom Rhea, Cybele, and Ops Regina were examples, and who will be mentioned briefly farther on in this chapter. In short, it seems clear that the more general aspect of "Saturnus" was that of a great sky-father and weather-god, comparable to the Greek conceptions of Ζεὺς ὑέτιος,[11] Z. ἰκμαῖος,[12] Z. ὄμβριος,[13] Z. εὐάνεμος,[14] and Z. οὔριος.[15] The conception of "Saturnus" as a general supreme being, universal and infinite, is elucidated by the dedications made to him as SATVRNO AVGVSTO, S. DOMINO, S. SANCTO, DEO SANCTO, D. MAGNO, or D. INVICTO,[16] and by his confusion with the Roman Jupiter.[17] Among his more

[1] J. Toutain, *De Saturni dei in Africa Romana cultu*. Add R. Cagnat, *Études de mythologie et d'histoire des religions antiques*, pp. 246 *sqq.*; P. Gauckler, *Les Monuments historiques de la Tunisie*, vol. i. pp. 81 *sqq.*, p. 97; idem, in *Nouvelles Archives des Missions Scientifiques*, xv., 1907, pp. 447 *sqq.*; cf. *CIL*, viii. *Supplem.* 12,388 *sqq.*

[2] Herodotus iv. 158, ἄνδρες Ἕλληνες—the Libyans are speaking—ἐνθαῦτα ὑμῖν ἐπιτήδεον οἰκέειν· ἐνθαῦτα γὰρ ὁ οὐρανὸς τέτρηται. The passage does not refer to the fountain. Cf. E. B. Tylor, *op. cit.* vol. ii. pp. 71 *sq.* for similar conceptions of a solid firmament.

[3] For the confusion of the real and personified sky, *vide* E. B. Tylor, *op. cit.* vol. ii. p. 257; Horace, *Od.* i. 1. 25; cf. Clemens Alexandrinus, *Stromat.* v. p. 511; Athenaeus, *Deipnos.* x. p. 430 A; Pausanias ii. 19, etc.

[4] J. Toutain, *op. cit.* pp. 25, 41, 52, 62, 80, 131, 134.

[5] *Ibid.* pp. 22 *sq.*, 31.

[6] *Ibid.* pp. 131, 141 *et alibi.*

[7] *Ibid.* p. 35.

[8] *Ibid.* p. 40.

[9] *Ibid.* p. 96.

[10] *Ibid.* p. 35.

[11] Pausanias i. 19. 8, ix. 39. 4.

[12] Apollonius Rhodius ii. 522 and Schol. *ad loc.*

[13] Plutarch, *Moral.* p. 158 E; Pausanias i. 32. 2.

[14] Pausanias iii. 13. 8.

[15] Aeschylus, *Supplices*, 594.

[16] J. Toutain, *op. cit.* p. 27; occasionally he enjoyed locative titles, *e.g.* SOBARENSIS, etc. *Ibid.* p. 32.

[17] As in *CIL*, viii. 10,624, which bears the dedication IOMSAS = *Iovi Optimo Maximo Saturno Augusto Sacrum.*

specialized aspects, it is not surprising to find this *Deus Coelestis* appearing as a patron of agriculture and, by extension, of flocks. Thus, this deity is called in the late inscriptions FRVGIFER and DEVS FRVGVM;[1] and among his offerings, made largely by native[2] farmers,[3] were first-fruits, grapes, dates, oil, wine, and pine-cones,[4] and in his attributes he resembles the Italian Vertumnus or Silvanus.[5] The Greek heaven-god had a similar phase as Ζεὺς ἐπικάρπιος.[6]

That the weather-god of the African farmer should also have been the guardian of flocks and herds is not unnatural. A weather-god could, if he so willed it, literally "temper the wind to the shorn lamb," and was of almost as much importance to the shepherd as to the cultivator. Bulls, sheep, and oxen,[7] as well as fruits and vegetables, were offered to "Saturnus," who appears occasionally in the Afro-Roman inscriptions as a god of flocks.[8] A god of such broad and such vaguely-defined character was by classical writers not unnaturally sometimes confounded with the Libyan deity who, under his Egyptian name, was best known to the Graeco-Roman world—"Amon" of Sîwah. Hence, Pausanias is found vainly deriving the name "Amon" from an Egyptian word which he gives as ἄμωνι, meaning "to graze" or "a shepherd,"[9] being drawn into this error because he has misapplied the name "Amon" first to the *Deus Fatidicus*, and secondly to the *Deus Coelestis* in the latter's pastoral phase. Tertullian, falling into the same confusion, styles the Libyan *ovium dives* "Amon";[10] and Servius, in the legend cited earlier in this chapter, which tells how "Amon" came as a herdsman to Dionysius in Egypt, may be guilty of the same mistake. These errors are perhaps excusable, since the sacred ram, which has already been noted in association with the *Deus Fatidicus*, is also sometimes associated with "Saturnus."[11]

A comparative study of gods similar in their nature and functions to the Libyan *Deus Coelestis* leads to the belief that it would certainly have been out of the usual course had this divinity lacked his spring and harvest festivals. The rites consecrated to such a god would be, naturally, such as are suggested by the rhythm of animal and vegetable life: the great phenomena, more especially, of procreation, birth and death. The primitive agriculturist is always struck by the phenomena of seasonal changes; to his eyes, European winter, or autumn in North Africa, are periods of dismal sterilization, which he explains as occasioned by the death of a god. There follows,

1 J. Toutain, *op. cit.* p. 30.

2 *Ibid.* pp. 71, 75.

3 *Ibid.* p. 31.

4 *Ibid.* p. 100.

5 *Ibid.* pp. 42, 54; cf. Roscher, *Lexikon*, ii. pp. 1511 *sq.*

6 Plutarch, *Moral.* p. 1048 c.

7 J. Toutain, *op. cit.* p. 106.

8 *CIL*, viii. 2232, 2234, 2236; *Supplem.* 15,075, 17,675, 18,897, etc.

9 Pausanias iv. 23. 5; cf. Eustathius *ad* Dionys. *Perieg.* 212.

10 Tertullian, *De pallio*, 3.

11 Cf. the Thugga stela given in *Nouvelles Archives des Missions Scientifiques*, p. 403; and perhaps, since the horns are lacking to the head of the human figure, the statuette shown here in Fig. 87. In this connection cf. G. Schweinfurth *ap.* J. Ball, *Kharga Oasis*, etc. p. 73. Schweinfurth found a Bulaḳ (Ḫargah) family which cherished as an heirloom a bronze ram, *c.* 10 cms. long, which was esteemed a charm against sterility in women. This may have reference to the *Deus Coelestis* as a god of fertility, or to the *Deus Fatidicus*, as a god of the dead, for the modern Egyptian women often try to touch or walk around corpses to have sons. Recently there was a hideous case of grave-desecration in the Delta in this connection.

after a period, a season of rejuvenation ; the earth becomes again full of life and activity—the primitive mind says : " the god is born again." Once this idea has been evolved, the men who entertain it are not slow to institute *rites of desolation* with which they mourn the death of the god, and *carnivals* whereby they celebrate his re-birth. Whereas the *Deus Coelestis*, in those phases in which he corresponded to the Greek Ζεὺς ὑέτιος, Z. ἰκμαῖος, κτλ., was a god eternal, universal, and unchanging, yet as the *deus frugum*, the *ovium dives*, and the god of the husbandman's year, he could temporarily die. Hence this god, together with Gurzil, the sun-god, is to be credited with having had some share in those carnivals and rites of desolation, traces of which are yet clearly discernible in so many parts of North Africa.[1] Some of these survivals offer striking points of analogy to the carnivals of Southern Europe. The rites of rejuvenation have on the whole survived better than the rites of desolation, man naturally preserving longer his memories of pleasure than his recollections of pain. The ceremonial garlic-eating at Sîwah, however, which is practised annually during one week in October, may have had its origin in a mourning-feast for the temporary death of the *Deus Coelestis*.

Dea Coelestis

The god just discussed appears to have had a partner of much the same nature as himself. Her existence may be inferred from a fragment in Duris Samius, who says that the *tibia* were of Libyan origin, and that they first were used in honour of the Mother of the Gods.[2] In the Roman period this goddess, who appears in Carthaginian times to have been confused with Tanit, appears under the title of *Dea Nutrix*,[3] and as such is not infrequently associated with the *Deus Coelestis*.[4] It would appear that it was this goddess, in her Punicized form, whom Apuleius characterized as *rerum naturae parens*, *elementorum omnium domina*.[5]

The Ausean Goddess

The Auseans, in the district about Lake Tritonis, worshipped a goddess whom Herodotus and others speak of as " Athena." The Auseans had a sanctuary to this divinity,[6] and her cultus is thus described by Herodotus :

> The Ausean maidens keep year by year a feast in honour of Athena, whereat their custom is to draw up in two bodies, and to fight with stones and clubs. They say that these are rites which have come down to them from their fathers, and that they honour with them their native goddess,

[1] E. Doutté, *op. cit.* pp. 496 *sqq.*, 541 *sqq.*

[2] Duris Samius, *Frag.* 34 in *FHG.* = Athenaeus, *Deipn.* xiv. p. 628 B.

[3] *CIL*, viii. 2664 = R. Cagnat, *Catal. du Musée de Lambèse*, pl. iii. fig. 2. Cf. *CIL*, viii. 8245 *sqq.* etc.

[4] Dessau, *Inscript.* 4473 (?) ; *CIL*, viii. *Supplem.* 20,217, 20,592 ; *CIL*, viii. 264, 8245 *sqq.* ; Dessau 4473 ; *CIL*, iii. 314.

[5] Apuleius, *Metamorph.* xi. p. 761, ed. Oudendorp ; cf. S. Ambrosius, *Contra Symmachum.* Cf. J. Toutain, *op. cit.* pp. 50 *sq.*, where she is characterized as *fecundae et genetricis naturae numen.*

[6] Scylax § 110, Ἀθηνᾶς Τριτωνίδος ἱερόν.

who is the same as the Athena of the Greeks. If any of the maidens die of the wounds they receive, the Auseans declare that such are false maidens. Before the fight is suffered to begin, they have another ceremony. One of the virgins, the loveliest of the number, is selected from the rest ; a Corinthian helmet and a complete suit of Greek armour are publicly put upon her, and, thus adorned, she is made to mount into a chariot, and is led around the whole lake in a procession. The Auseans declare that Athena is the daughter of Poseidon and Tritonis ; they say she quarrelled with her father, and applied to Zeus, who consented to accept her as his child, and therefore she became his daughter.[1]

Before commenting on this passage, it may be noted by the way that part of the Syrtes, because of this identification of the native and the Greek goddesses, was regarded by classical writers as peculiarly sacred to Triton and to Pallas. Callimachus, for example, calls Lake Tritonis "Pallantias."[2]

The statements of Herodotus may now be considered in detail.

1. *The Legend.*—From the fact that the goddess is said to have been born of "Poseidon" and "Tritonis," it might be inferred that she was a sea-deity ; but this is not borne out by her association with "Zeus." The explanation, in so far as there is one, would seem to be merely that "Athena" was a goddess of ill-defined dominion, whom it was equally rational to associate with sky-ruler or sea-ruler.

2. *The Annual Feast.*—The annual feast of the goddess suggests that, like the *Deus Coelestis*, she had some association with the seasons. The ceremony, moreover, was one of great importance.[3]

3. *The Ceremonial Arming.*—The selection of the most comely of the virgins of the tribe, and her arming in Greek (*i.e.* the best) war-harness is significant. The maiden, armed and mounted in her car, represented, on the occasion of the festival, the goddess in whose honour the ceremony was performed, and who must, it is clear, have had a warlike aspect.

4. *The Procession.*—The goddess, in the person of the armed maiden, accompanied by the other celebrants, made a circuit of the lake. This procession suggests some form of *lustratio*, whereby the beneficent influences of "Athena" were invoked upon the lands of the tribe. Such a procession is roughly paralleled in the ritual of the Arval Brethren, whose circuit was made with a view to obtaining the protection, chiefly, of the Dea Dia. The circuitous procession ending in a sacrifice was not, in fact, uncommon : in this instance, the conclusion was not a sacrifice, but a ceremonial combat.

5. *The Combat.*—It is the ceremonial sham-fight with which the annual festival concluded that shows most clearly the character of the goddess. One first notes that none but maidens engaged in it, and that those who were accidentally slain were supposed to be *punished* because they were not true maids. This points to the goddess having had a strong virginal aspect. The significance of the combat is not hard to

[1] Herodotus iv. 180 ; cf. Mela i. 7, who adds nothing to this account, except that the annual festival was celebrated on the birthday of the goddess. Cf. R. Neumann, *Afrika . . . nach Herodot*, p. 28 *sq.* and C. Tissot, *De Tritonide lacu*, *passim*, for the geographical setting.

[2] Callimachus *ap.* Pliny v. 4 ; cf. Lucan, *Phars.* ix. 348 *sqq.* etc.

[3] Cf. Herodotus iv. 189.

divine—it was a rain-ceremony in which was acted the strife between drought and rain. The frequency of these drought-and-rain conflicts among primitive peoples,[1] and their survival in North Africa at the present time, lead to the conclusion that the procession of the Ausean goddess was designed to ward off evil and induce blessings on the tribal lands, and the domestic combat with which the ceremony ended was meant to ensure a good rainfall during the ensuing year.

This begets the strong suspicion that the Ausean "Athena" was but a localized phase of the *Dea Coelestis*, the *pollicitatrix pluviarum*, who has already been mentioned as a partner of the Libyan sky-god. From this point of view a very vexed and difficult question may be approached, namely, that of the possible connection of this rain-sender of the Auseans, and the *Dea Coelestis* of the Libyans in general, with a goddess of the western Egyptian Delta. This goddess is Neith of Sais, who has by various modern writers been related to the Ausean "Athena."[2]

Neith[3] was a goddess established in Egypt from archaic times, her name appearing in a royal name, *Meri-Nit*, of the proto-dynastic period.[4] Her chief place of worship was Sais, the sacred name of which city was 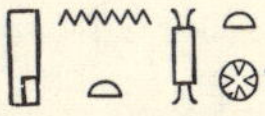, *ḥ-t-nt*, "the Dwelling of Neith,"[5] and where she had an immense temple.[6] Her functions we learn from various sources. On a naophorous statue now in the Vatican she is described as "the mother of the sun, who began to bring forth even before being born."[7] Plutarch says that the shrine of the goddess bore an inscription which he thus translates:

'Εγώ εἰμι πᾶν τὸ γεγονὸς καὶ ὂν καὶ ἐσόμενον, καὶ τὸν ἐμὸν πέπλον οὐδείς πω θνητὸς ἀπεκάλυψεν.[8]

I am all that has been, is, or shall be; no mortal has ever uplifted my garment.

This is confirmed by Proclus:

Αἰγύπτιοι ἱστοροῦσι, ἐν τῷ ἀδύτῳ τῆς θεοῦ, προγεγραμμένον εἶναι τὸ ἐπίγραμμα τοῦτο· τὰ ὄντα καὶ τὰ ἐσόμενα, καὶ τὰ γεγονότα, ἐγώ εἰμι. Τὸν ἐμὸν χιτῶνα οὐδεὶς ἀπεκάλυψεν· ὃν ἐγὼ καρπὸν ἔτεκον, ἥλιος ἐγένετο.[9]

The Egyptians relate that in the inner sanctuary of the goddess this inscription is to be read on the doorway: I am that which is, which shall be, and which has been. None ever uplifted my garment. The fruit which I brought forth was the sun.

[1] Might not the institution of a ceremonial combat of this sort account for the high percentage of fractured fore-arms among the Predynastic Egyptian women? Such an explanation would be at least as probable as that the men so maltreated the women that the arms of the latter were frequently broken. Primitive man does not to this extent mishandle either his women or his other domestic animals.

[2] On this H. Brugsch, *Religion und Mythologie der alt. Ägypt.* p. 342 *sqq.*; A. Wiedemann, *Religion der alt. Ägypt.* p. 77; G. Jequier, in *RT*, xxx., 1908, p. 43; D. Mallet, *Le Culte de Neit à Saïs*, p. 240.

[3] 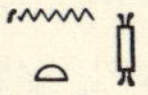 *n-t*; 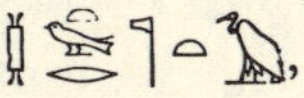, *n-t wr ntr-t mw-t*, "Neith the Great One, the divine mother"; 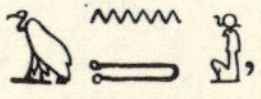, *mw-t nṯ rʿ* "Neith, Mother of the Sun," etc.; D. Mallet, *op. cit.* p. 94. One of the oldest of her symbols is , two crossed arrows on a staff. (The heads of the arrows are not pointed, but have the broad concave cutting-edge, such as is seen in pl. viii. 32.)

[4] C. Sourdille, *op. cit.* p. 180, *n.* 2.

[5] J. de Rougé, *Géographie ancienne de la Basse Égypte*, p. 25.

[6] D. Mallet, *op. cit.* p. 33 *sqq.*; cf. p. 71 *sqq.*

[7] H. Brugsch, *Thesaurus Inscriptionum Aegyptiacarum*, p. 637 i. 8.

[8] Plutarch, *De Iside et Osiride*, § 10 (p. 354, Xyland.).

[9] Proclus, *In Timaeum*, i. 30.

From this it appears that in Neith one is confronted with a great nature-mother of virginal aspect. This virginal aspect led the Greeks to identify her as Athena,[1] but the emphasis laid upon her character as a *genetrix* shows clearly that her primitive rôle must have been one comparable to those of the Mater Deum, Ops Regina, etc. Among other titles, Neith was called , *mḥ-wr-t*, "the cow Meḥurt," and *i h-t mṣ r'*, "the cow which bears the sun."[2] These titles belonged to her as most broadly conceived, *i.e.* as a sky-goddess.

The chief points of similarity between Neith and the Ausean goddess, both of whom Herodotus calls "Athena," may be thus exhibited :—

Saitic "Athena"	Ausean "Athena"
1. Sky-goddess.	1. Sky-goddess.
2. Virgin-mother.	2. Strong virginal aspect.
3. Goddess of vegetation.	3. Rain-sender.
4. Warlike phase, as shown by her nome-symbols : and .	4. Represented at her festival as an armed maiden. Ceremonial sham-fight.
5. Cow-form.	5. Cow-taboo in Eastern Libya. Cows stil sacrificed for rain in North Africa.[3]

These similarities are such that one cannot avoid feeling that, were more material available, they would in all probability be increased in number. They prepare one also for a curious piece of evidence first adduced by H. Brugsch, which was the original cause of the suspicion that the Ausean and Saitic "Athenas" might be local phases of the same goddess. The evidence in question is that afforded by certain tattoo marks seen on Egyptian representations of Libyan captives. Some of these marks are of more than merely ornamental significance, like the sun-emblems already mentioned. Others, as has been said earlier in this monograph, are either identical with, or vary only insignificantly from, the commonest hieroglyphic sign for the Saitic goddess, (early) or (New Empire, late form). These signs have, as tattoo marks, undoubtedly some special meaning : they are not Egyptian brandings, moreover, since they only occur on the Libyan captives, and not on the Asiatics, etc.[4]

A writer who has recently discussed this question has formulated the theory that Neith was originally a goddess of Libyans living in pre-historic Egypt, who with them was forced out of an original position in the south to become firmly established in the north-west.[5] As presented by its propounder, this theory is ingeniously supported ; it lacks, however, archaeological evidence, and not yet has a period arrived where any question of early ethnic shiftings in the Nile Valley can be considered as per-

[1] Herodotus ii. 28, 59, 83, 169, 170, 175 ; Plato, *Timaeus*, p. 474 ; Hesychius *in verb.* Νηῖθη ; Eratosthenes in *Catalog. Regum Aegypt.* xxii., explains the name Νίτωκρις as = Ἀθηνᾶ νικηφόρος, etc. ; cf. Apollodorus, *Frag.* 70 in *FHG* ; cf. Roscher, *Lexikon*, *in verb.* Nit.

[2] D. Mallet, *op. cit.* p. 94.

[3] L. Bertholon, *op. cit.* p. 15. But, as I have said, the cow-taboo was not universal in Eastern Libya ; the inhabitants of Marea and Apis protested against being made by the Egyptians to observe it. Herodotus ii. 18.

[4] These details have been discussed, *supra* p. 139 *sqq.*

[5] G. Jéquier, *op. cit.* p. 43.

fectly safe ground.[1] But from the parallel instituted above between the Libyan and the Egyptian goddesses, from this occurrence of the Neith-symbol as a Libyan tattoo mark, and from the geographical position of Sais, it seems that some connection between the two divinities is highly probable.

General Character of Libyan Religion

If the preceding fragments in regard to the religion of the Eastern Libyans are considered from the point of view of the student of the temper and culture of this people, a few general facts are deducible from them. Briefly, here is seen the religion of a people who, while they had attained to anthropomorphic conceptions of deity, yet held tenaciously to a host of animistic ideas. The religion of the Libyans seems to have been only partially iconic, to have presented many local variations and peculiarities, yet to have been dominated by a few simple and not ignoble ideas which were common to most of the North Africans. Thus, to the prevalent superstitions which regarded seriously various sorts of art-magic and sorcery, was joined the cultus of a number of fairly well-defined gods,[2] and of a few broadly conceived divinities like the *Deus Coelestis*. A belief in the future life also, was deeply ingrained in the people.

In character it does not appear to have had an unusual number of gloomy features, as is so often the case with African religions ; on the contrary, it seems, so far as can be judged, to have been the creation of a race inclined to take a fairly cheerful view both of this life and the next. Naturally, there is no evidence that it contained any but the simplest doctrines, and, in short, it may be best defined as a barbaric religion, half developed from the direct animistic nature-worship of savagery.

If parallels to the religion of the Libyans as it is known be looked for, it is in Egypt that the most striking analogies are to be found. There, for example, the sun was associated, as in Libya, with the bull ; there the belief in the after-life of the dead is strongly developed ; there, as in North Africa, the ram figures prominently as a sacred animal ; and in Neith of Sais has just been remarked a goddess having striking resemblances to a Libyan one. It does not do to build too much on these likenesses, but certainly there seems to have been between the religion of the ancient Egyptians and that of the Libyans a connection closer than existed between that of the latter and that, for example, of the Semites. Just as knit into the Egyptian language is a definite Libyan element, so, too, in all probability exist in Egyptian religion various elements of Libyan origin. These, however, cannot yet be discerned, on account of lack of knowledge in regard to the ancient Libyans.

[1] It is not evidence on this question of Neith and the Ausean goddess that Amasis sent as a gift to Cyrene a statue of Neith (Herodotus ii. 182), for Amasis was especially under the protection of Neith, being called , *iʿḥ-ms-s3-nt*, and Sais was his capital. As for the question of Neith and Tanit, I will only say that I disagree wholly on this subject with L. Bertholon, *op. cit.* p. 8, and *pass.*

[2] Procopius, *De aedificiis*, vi. 2 ; cf. Schol. *in* Apollon. Rhod. iv. 1492, *Cod. Paris.* = Agroetas, *Frag.* 4 in *FHG*, εὐσεβεῖς δὲ οἱ Γαράμαντες, καὶ ναοὶ ἐν αὐτοῖς ἵδρυνται, ὡς ἄλλοι τε καὶ Ἀγροίτας ἱστορεῖ.

In conclusion, the reader is again warned, as at the beginning of this chapter, that a number of the views set forth above are too new to have had the advantage of criticism, and that it is only by the excavation of indigenous sites in North Africa that one can hope eventually to arrive at a more definite knowledge of the subject.

Judaism and Christianity

A few words on Judaism and on Christianity in Eastern Libya may here be added by way of supplement.

In regard to the former, Jewish communities seem to have existed in Eastern Libya from comparatively early times. Thus, a very serious rebellion of the Jews in Cyrenaica took place in 115 A.D., and near Borium, in the Syrtis Major, was a synagogue, the building of which local Hebrew tradition ascribed to Solomon![1] It is a well-known fact that the Berbers get on well with the Jews, and that many have adopted Judaism.[2] This explains how, in the rebellion of 115 A.D., such a large number of insurgents came to be involved; it is almost certain that the war, like its pretext, was religious rather than racial.

Christianity entered North Africa at an early date, and the Christian population, to judge by the archaeological evidence alone, was large and spread over a considerable area.[3] Although pagans existed in the days of Justinian, who "converted" them,[4] in the time of the Arab invasions there were a number of Christianized Berber tribes.[5] It is curious to observe that the Berbers, who are such notoriously heretical Moḥammadans to-day, produced when Christians the heresiarch Arius, and in the western parts of Eastern Libya, under the name of Donatists, committed a thousand savage extravagances.

There is one point which may be mentioned in this connection, since several writers have been slightly in error concerning it. The cross is an element of common occurrence in modern Berber ornamentation, and since the names of some months have in many dialects preserved their Latin forms, and as the word for "angel" exists only slightly modified in Berber, some writers have supposed that the cross[6] in modern Berber tattooing, etc., is a relic of Libyan Christianity. This is an unnecessary supposition, since a shield which, from the size of the cross on it, might have been

[1] Procopius, *loc. cit.* There are a number of Jewish families to-day in Benghazî which claim to have been settled in the country since Roman times. The presence of Jews in the Syrtica Regio in Roman times is attested by the existence of a station called *Scina* [=Χάραξ Ἴσκινα] *locus Iudaeorum Augusti* (*Tab. Peut.* Segm. viii.), the اليهودية, *El-Yahudîah*, of Idrîsî, *Clim.* iii. § 5.

[2] Cf. H. Barth, *Reisen und Entdeckungen*, vol. i. p. 53 *sq.* In the *Jerusalem Talmud*, *Kilaim* viii. and *Sabbath* v., one finds a wire-drawn academic discussion in regard to Libyan proselytes, the question being how long a Libyan family need profess Judaism before being accepted as Jews. The conclusion reached is that the Libyans stand in the same relation to the Jews as do the Egyptians, and that three generations of profession must therefore precede their being received into the fold.

[3] Cf. *ibid.* vol. i. p. 117, the ruined basilica at Shabet Umm el-Ḫarab.

[4] Procopius, *loc. cit.*

[5] Cf. Johannes Abbas, *Chronic.* p. 13; Abu 'l Ḥasan, *Annales regum Mauret.*, ed. Tornberg, pp. 7, 15, 83 (for the west); El-Bekrî, *Description* in *Notices et Extraits*, vol. xii. p. 484; Ibn Ḫaldun, *Kitab el ʿIbar*, Transl. de Slane, vol. i. p. 209 *et alibi.*

[6] For an example, cf. H. Barth, *op. cit.* vol. i. 208, cross on a Targi shield.

a crusader's, exists on a prehistoric rock glyph in Tibesti ;[1] and as the cross is also seen as an ornament in the ancient Egyptian representations of Libyans.[2] Its true origin in North Africa may be referred to the cruciform solar symbols already noticed in this chapter.[3] Christianity, indeed, seems not to have been firmly enough rooted, even in littoral Libya, to have left any deep or lasting survivals. There are no notices of the persistence, in Eastern Libya, of a Christian element that was strong enough, as in Egypt, to withstand the overpowering influence of Moḥammadanism.[4]

[1] G. Nachtigal, *Săhărā und Sudan*, vol. i. p. 308.

[2] Vide *supra*, p. 148.

[3] Cf. the table of solar emblems in J. Déchelette, *Le Culte du soleil aux temps préhistoriques*.

[4] S. A. Morcelli, *Africa Christiana*. The reader is referred to this work for a good general account of African Christianity, written from the Roman Catholic point of view, and based almost exclusively on the literary evidence.

CHAPTER IX

HISTORY [1]

The history of the Eastern Libyans hardly deserves to be dignified by that name, since practically only records of their conflicts with more civilized peoples, made by hostile annalists, survive. Yet in order to understand the life and character of the ancient Berbers, and because of their contact with the important peoples of the Mediterranean, these records are worthy of more study than they have yet received. The history of the Eastern Libyans divides itself into two periods, both because of the two main channels through which our knowledge flows, and because of the different character of their history in earlier and in later times. The first of these periods may be termed the Egyptian period, the second the Graeco-Roman. The first is the epoch extending from the earliest historic times down through the period of the great invasions of Egypt, a period at the close of which the Libyans are dimly discerned in a state of flux, aggressive and unsettled. Our knowledge of this portion of their history is derived almost wholly from Egyptian sources. The second epoch is one of ethnic quiescence, relieved only by the unsuccessful revolts made against foreign dominion in Africa,—an epoch in which the descendants of the invaders are seen as an aggregation of factious and disunited tribes, at various points dispossessed of their territories, and remaining in a state of barbarism—almost of savagery—beyond which the other Mediterranean peoples had advanced. The sources for this period are almost all Greek and Roman. In time, Period I. may be taken as extending from proto-dynastic times to about 1000 B.C., while Period II. may be extended from about 1000 B.C. to the Arab conquest in the seventh century A.D. The date 1000 B.C. is, of course, arbitrary, and must be recognized as such throughout this chapter.

Period I

The first act historically ascribed to the Eastern Libyans is,[2] characteristically, one of combined revolt and superstition. Libyans in Egypt at the beginning of the

[1] The substance of this chapter I have already published in *CSJ*, vol. vi. No. 71 (August 1912).

[2] J. H. Breasted, *History of Egypt*, p. 47, states that King Narmar, at the beginning of the Dynastic Period, put down a Libyan rebellion in the Delta, taking 120,000 captives, 400,000 cattle, etc. This statement was made on the archaeo-

IIIrd Dynasty are reported by Manetho to have rebelled against King Nefer-ka-ra (Nepherocheres), but to have laid down their arms on account of a portentous increase in the size of the moon.[1] The whole episode is quite possibly fictitious, but it is on the other hand conceivable that Manetho has here used an old annalist as his source. It is not, at all events, long after the IIIrd Dynasty that one learns certainly of conflicts between Libya and Egypt, and of friction between the Libyans and the Negroes of the south.

The former are signalized as early as the Vth Dynasty by the reliefs in the Pyramid temples of Ne-user-re[2] and of Sa-hu-re[3] at Abusîr. From these reliefs it is clear that both kings had Libyan victories, and from the position in which the sculptures in the Sa-hu-re temple were placed, it is also apparent that the Libyans defeated by the king dwelt to the south of Memphis, probably in the Fayum. It is worthy of remark that at this early period the Libyan chieftains seem supplied with neatly made personal ornaments as well as, or even better than, at any later period.

In the VIth Dynasty a state of war existed between the Temeḥu Libyans and the Negroes of Yam in the south. A trader-noble of Elephantine, in the time of Pepi II., made four journeys to the Sudan. On the third, as he tells in a record inscribed on his tomb, he encountered a Negro tribe on the march against the Temeḥu. "His Majesty," Harkhuf says in his narrative, "now sent me a third time to Yam. I set forth . . . upon the Uhet road, and I found the chief of Yam going to the land of Temeḥ, to smite Temeḥ as far as the western corners of heaven. I went forth after him to the land of Temeḥ, and I pacified him, until he praised all the gods for the king's sake."[4] That the district of Temeḥ which was to be attacked by the people of Yam was in all likelihood the Libyan bank of the Nile in Nubia has already been pointed out. The incident gives some insight into the state of constant raids and petty wars always flickering along the borders of the Libyan area. It testifies also to the prestige of the Egyptian VIth Dynasty that Harkhuf could travel in safety with a tribe of Negro raiders and pacify the chief of Yam.

This prestige arose partly from the fact that for some time before this the Egyptians had recruited soldiers among the barbarians beyond the First Cataract. In the reign of Pepi I., for example, an officer named Uni got together a number of soldiers in the south, to engage in a campaign with "Asiatic sand-dwellers" (Bedawî) in the north. Besides other recruits, the Negroes of Yam are mentioned, as are also the people of Temeḥ.[5]

In the XIth Dynasty there again were wars between Libya and Egypt. The

logical evidence of the Narmar palette, great mace-heads, ivories, etc., from Hieraconpolis. *Vide* J. E. Quibell, *Hierakonpolis*, pt. i. pl. xi., lower register; xii. fig. 4; xv. figs. 1, 2, 3, 4, 7; xxv., lower register; xxvi. A, top and middle registers; xxvi. B; xxix., etc. I regret to differ from an authority so great as Breasted, but I cannot see how the people over whom Narmar triumphed can be shown to be Libyans. To me they appear to have been Egyptians of the Delta.

[1] Manetho, pp. 22-23.

[2] L. Borchardt, *Das Grabdenkmal des Königs Ne-user-re*, p. 47.

[3] Idem, *Das Grabdenkmal des Königs S'aꜣhu-Reᶜ*, vol. i., *Der Bau*, p. 17 *sq*.

[4] BAR i. § 335.

[5] BAR i. § 311.

first king of the Dynasty, Intef I., had among his hunting-dogs at least one bearing a Libyan name,[1] and that this dog may have been sent to the king as tribute seems easily possible. In the reign of his successor, Mentuhotep I., the Rebu and Teḥenu were defeated by the Egyptians, the victory being commemorated with others in Gebeleyn reliefs.[2] It is not to be supposed that these "wars" were general, or that large forces were engaged. That they were rather in the nature of raids, counter-raids, and petty revolts of the Libyans settled along the Nile seems clear from the summary manner in which they are mentioned by the Egyptian annalists.

Just such a raid is mentioned in the opening of the *Tale of Sinuhe*. The heir to the Egyptian throne, Usertesen (I.), had been sent to the westward by his father, Amenemhat I., to raid the Rebu. Sinuhe says :—

> Behold, his majesty had sent out
> A numerous army against the Libyans ;
> The eldest son was commander thereof,
> The Good God Usertsen.
> Now, just as he was returning, having taken
> Living captives from the Libyans
> And all cattle, without limit, etc.[3]

That this expedition was not merely a literary fiction seems certain from the soberness and detail of the narrative, and from the fact that apparently even until Greek times an echo of it survived. Diodorus relates that as a young man, the prince Usertesen (Sesostris) was sent into Arabia, and then subdued a great part of Libya.[4] It is perhaps in memory of his Libyan victories that the exquisite pectoral of Usertesen I. in the Cairo Museum shows the king as a gryphon trampling the Southerners and the Libyans.

In the thirty-fourth year of the reign of Usertesen, the Libyans had become so impressed with the power of Egypt that it was possible for an officer named Itendidi to visit "the land of the oasis-dwellers"[5] with a company of picked soldiers. The object of his mission is not clear, but since it was both military and peaceful, it may have had as its object merely the further display of Egyptian power. It is notable in the vague notices of these early campaigns that it is the Egyptians, and not, as later, the Libyans who appear to have been on the aggressive. The Libyans seem to have felt a wholesome respect for the power of Egypt all through the XIIth Dynasty. In the time of Usertesen III., an officer of the king brought "for him the good products of Teḥenu by the greatness of his majesty's fame."[6]

Throughout the XVIIIth Dynasty the Libyans were apparently in continuous conflict with the Egyptians. An official of Amenhotep I. mentions that in the king's

[1] BAR i. § 421.
[2] BAR i. § 423 H, and notes *ad loc. cit.*
[3] BAR i. § 492. The tale goes on to say that on his return, Usertesen was met with the news of his father's death.
[4] Diodorus Siculus i. 53.
[5] BAR i. § 527.
[6] BAR i. § 675.

service he captured for him "three hands" of Imukehek "on the north."[1] Thutmose I. records his victory over the Eḳbet;[2] and in a hymn of triumph Amon-Re addresses his successor, Thutmose III., saying:—

> I have come, causing thee to smite the Teḥenu.[3]

Libyan chiefs brought to this king "tribute from the southern and the northern oases,"[4] and Hatshepsut, his powerful consort, received divine assurance that she should "strike among the Teḥenu."[5] Perhaps this prophecy was not recorded until after its fulfilment; at least we know that the Queen levied from the Teḥenu a heavy tribute, which consisted of "ivory and seven hundred tusks," and numerous large skins "of the southern panther."[6] In short, so high was the prestige of Egypt in the reign of Hatshepsut and Thutmose III. that Nehi, the viceroy of Kush, thus commemorated the Egyptian power in the twenty-third year of the king:—

> The countries of Teḥenu do obeisance because of the fame of his majesty, with their tribute upon their backs (*hiatus*) . . . as do the dogs, that there might be given to them the breath of life.[7]

In the middle of the XVIIIth Dynasty, Amenhotep III. conducted a successful war against the Teḥenu, the captives being set to work on an Egyptian fortress.[8] The Libyans within reach of Egypt had seemingly been overawed and reduced to a state of partial subjection to the warlike kings of the early New Empire.

The desultory fighting did not, however, cease with the advent of the XIXth Dynasty. On the contrary, the ethnic pressure from the west, which was presently to culminate in the great invasions, steadily increased. The continuous infiltration of the Libyans into the Egyptian Delta assumed proportions so menacing[9] that, in the second (?) year of the reign of Seti I. that king foresaw that Egypt was likely to be seriously threatened from the west. Before, therefore, setting forth upon his Syrian campaign, he first engaged the Libyans.[10] That the outcome of this brief war was successful we know from the annals of the king, but we are ignorant of its details. During nearly the whole of the second year of his reign, Seti I. seems to have been in the Delta,[11] and he apparently fought at least two pitched battles with the Libyans,[12] commanding in person in both engagements (cf. Plates IV. and IX.). In the end, there came before the Pharaoh the people of "the land of Teḥenu on its knees,"[13] numerous captives were presented to Amon,[14] and the usual "tribute" was obtained from the enemy.[15] Had Seti I., a really able and warlike monarch, followed up his victory and carried the

[1] BAR ii. § 42. [2] BAR ii. § 70. [3] BAR ii. § 660.
[4] BAR ii. §§ 385, 386. The tribute probably contained ivory and ebony. Cf. BAR ii. § 387.
[5] BAR ii. § 225. [6] BAR ii. § 321. [7] BAR ii. § 413.
[8] BAR ii. § 892 and note *c*, *ad loc. cit.* [9] BAR iii. § 121.
[10] Cf. BAR iii. § 135. [11] BAR iii. § 120.
[12] Two general engagements are depicted in the Karnak reliefs of Seti I. *Vide* BAR iii. p. 39, figs. 1, 2, scenes 12 and 13 for relative position of reliefs.
[13] BAR iii. § 147. [14] BAR iii. §§ 134, 135, etc. [15] BAR iii. §§ 137, 138.

Egyptian arms to the westward, instead of turning them to the east, the succeeding course of Libyan and of Egyptian history might have been altered. For had the Libyans, at a time when they had become sensible of a pressure from the west, met in the east with aggression and a crushing defeat instead of with a temporary check, they might in desperation have turned back to the west, might never have come to invade Egypt by force of arms, and might never, as eventually they did by more peaceful methods, have obtained the Egyptian throne. As it was, Seti I. turned to the east, and there fought victoriously. The Libyans, recovering from the check they had received at his hands, were soon able to give trouble to his son and successor, Rameses II. Here again details are lacking, but the record gives various references to the disturbances in the west.[1] Pharaoh is characterized as wasting Teḥenu.[1] Libya falls before his sword.[2] At Beyt el-Waly, the king is shown slaying a Libyan chieftain (Fig. 88), the title of the scene calling the king "lord of the sword, embracing the lands of Teḥenu,"[3] while at Abu Simbel Rameses II. is seen standing on the prostrate body of one Libyan and slaying another with his lance—"the Good God slaying the Nine Bows, crushing the countries of the North."[4]

FIG. 88.

The most important detail in regard to these obscure wars of Rameses II., however, is that here, for the first time, the Sherden, who were so deeply implicated in the Libyan invasions as allies of the Teḥenu, appear in conjunction with them. In the Tanis Stela, the following mutilated but important passage occurs:—

> He [the king] has captured the countries of the West, causing them to be as that which is not . . . [the god] Sutekh on his right, in the battle, King Rameses II. He has ferried over . . . come to him, bearing their tribute; his fear penetrates their hearts. The rebellious-hearted Sherden . . . them; mighty . . . ships of war are in the midst of the sea . . . before them.[5]

This reference to the rebellious Sherden, allies of Libya, and to the war-ships, would indicate a naval battle in connection with the war.[6] The presence of the Sherden allies and their capture are confirmed by another document, the so-called Kadesh Poem, which refers to the Sherden whom "thou [*scil.* the king] hast taken by

[1] BAR iii. § 448. [2] BAR iii. § 448 and note *b*, *ad loc. cit.* [3] BAR iii. § 464. [4] BAR iii. § 457.

[5] BAR iii. § 491. For the first mention of the Sherden in Egyptian documents, cf. BAR iii. p. 136 note *e*, and J. H. Breasted, *History*, p. 424.

[6] BAR iii. § 488.

PLATE IX.

LIBYAN CAPTIVES OF SETI I.

thy might."[1] To the presence of the sea-allies of the Libyans may also be related a sentence in the Aṣwan stela of Rameses II., which says of him that "he plunders the warriors of the sea, the great lake of the north, while they lie sleeping."[2]

In the end, some of the Sherden of "the captivity of his majesty from the victories of his sword,"[3] were enlisted in the army; while he "settled the Teḥenu on the heights, filling strongholds which he built with the captivity of his mighty sword."[4] Yet despite his successes, Rameses II. repeated the mistake of Seti I. his father. The Libyans had before his day been recognized as dangerous neighbours when by themselves; in the time of Rameses II. they should, to a general and a statesman of his sagacity, have seemed the more menacing because of their alliance with the sea-faring Sherden, and they should have been not merely repulsed, but themselves vigorously invaded. Probably the Egyptian king, finding the Sherden ready for mercenary service, calculated that to Sherden allies of Libya, led by hope of plunder, he could always oppose Sherden mercenaries of his own, certain of their pay and incited by the hope of rewards. His interests, moreover, lay largely in Syria, where the political balance could not be disturbed without seriously affecting Egypt.

The Libyan wars of Rameses II. may be justly considered as the prelude to the great invasions which followed. The chronology of the campaigns is somewhat obscure. Petrie is probably right in assigning a Libyan campaign to the first year of the king's reign,[5] the Aṣwan stela above cited being dated in the king's second year. Later in his reign, also, Rameses II. again engaged the Libyans.[6] It is to be remembered, moreover, that this sovereign regularly had Libyan and Sherden soldiers in his army, 4000 such being in a force despatched to the Wady Hammamat.[7]

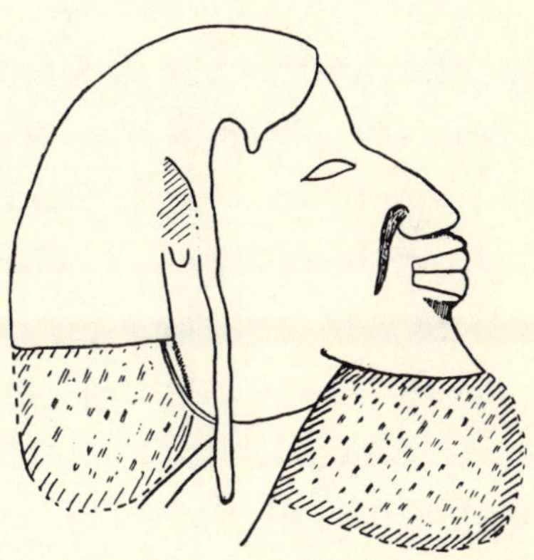

Fig. 89.

The most remarkable series of events in the whole history of the Libyan race must now be considered — the great invasions of Egypt in the XIXth and XXth Dynasties. The causes of these campaigns will be discussed later; at present they will be related in the order in which they occurred, from the Merneptah invasion, which has been characterized by Breasted as "one of the most serious . . . which has ever threatened Egypt."[8] This invasion took place late in March in the year five of the king's reign, when he was sixty-three years old. The Libyans had

[1] *Anastasi Papyrus* ii., v. l. 2. Cf. *ibid. verso* Pl. viii. l. 1 and BAR iii. § 307.

[2] BAR iii. § 479. The same inscription says that the Temeḥu have fallen for fear of the king. The name is spelled Ty-m-ḥ-nw, which leads Breasted to remark, note *c*, *ad loc. cit.*, that "it may be that Teḥenu is meant." Cf. W. M. F. Petrie, *A History of Egypt*, vol. iii. p. 46.

[3] BAR iii. § 307.

[4] BAR iii. § 457.

[5] W. M. F. Petrie, *loc. cit.*

[6] A curious proof of this exists in the Beyt el-Waly temple, where a Syrian prisoner of the king's earlier wars (for which J. H. Breasted, *History*, p. 423 *sqq.*) has been revamped, by the change of hair and beard, into a Libyan (*vide* Fig. 89). I have to thank Dr. G. Roeder of Breslau for calling my attention to this piece of evidence.

[7] J. H. Breasted, *History of Egypt*, p. 449.

[8] BAR iii. §§ 569, 570.

again become menacing. Part of Egypt had become, in the language of a contemporary record, "not cared for; it was forsaken as pasturage for cattle because of the Nine Bows, it was left from the times of the ancestors. All the kings of Upper Egypt rested in the midst of their cities . . . for lack of troops."[1] Libyan marauders "repeatedly penetrated the fields of Egypt to the great river, and spent whole days and months dwelling"[2] in Egypt, where they passed "their time going about the land . . . to seek the necessities of their mouths."[3] The northern oasis and Farafrah—the district of Toyeh—had for some time been cut off from Egypt.[4] This was the state of affairs when the tribesmen of the west formed a powerful coalition against Egypt, and the aged Pharaoh prepared "to protect Heliopolis, city of Atum, to defend the stronghold of Ptah-Tatenen,"[5] and "to protect the people."[6]

The origin of the federation had its place, not among the Teḥenu, the immediate neighbours of Egypt, but among the Libyans farther west. The Rebu, under the command of Meryey, son of Ded, allied themselves with various bodies of Eḳwesh, Teresh, Luka, Sherden, Shekelesh, and "Northerners coming from all lands."[7] With these allies, the Rebu fell upon the Teḥenu, who were probably, from remembrance of the rough handling they had had from Rameses II. and Seti I., disinclined to violent measures. They were not able, however, to stand against the allies, and were forced to join them. The good-will of the Ḫeta (Hittites), then the most powerful rival of Egypt in the north, was secured,[8] and at a time when forage was plentiful and the weather good, the allied forces began the march eastward. The coalition had been formed in the month of March,[9] and in early April news came that the invasion had begun. The Libyan forces were probably marshalled somewhere in Cyrenaica; to oppose them, Merneptah ordered a general muster to be held on the 8th of April—"in . . . Meber, [an unknown locality] the choicest of his bowmen were mustered . . . his chariotry was brought up from every side. . . . He considered not hundreds of thousands in the day of the array. His infantry marched out, those who bear the hand-to-hand fighting arrived, beautiful in appearance, leading bowmen against every land."[10] On the 15th of April the two armies drew near each other in the vicinity of Perire[11] in the

[1] BAR iii. § 577.
[2] BAR iii. § 580.
[3] BAR *loc. cit.* Cf. the retrospect of Merneptah after his victory, BAR iii. § 585, "So this land of Egypt was in their power, in a state of weakness . . . so that their hand could not be repelled." Obviously an exaggeration, but indicative of the real state of affairs.
[4] BAR iii. § 580.
[5] BAR iii. § 576.
[6] BAR iii. § 578.
[7] BAR iii. §§ 574, 579. For the identification of these peoples *vide* H. R. Hall, *Oldest Civilization of Greece*, p. 171 *sqq.*; W. M. Müller, *Asien und Europa*, p. 371 and *passim*. It may be accepted that the Luka = the proto-Lycians; the Shekelesh = the Sicels; the Sherden = the people who, after occupying Sardinia, gave their name to that island. The Ter-esh and Eḳw-esh have been repeatedly identified with the Tyrsi and Achaei. I do not accept all these identifications as conclusively proved, and would further wish to suggest the possibility that the Luka-Lycians, Sherden-Sardinians, and Shekel-Sicels may at the time of the XIXth Dynasty have occupied countries other than those they held in classical times.
[8] BAR iii. §§ 570; 580, and note *h*, *ad loc. cit.*
[9] Cf. W. M. F. Petrie, *op. cit.* vol. iii. p. 108.
[10] BAR iii. § 578.
[11] BAR iii. § 583; cf. § 570.

western Delta.[1] The Libyan vanguard halted, and for a whole day the straggling army of the invaders was massing for the attack.[2] From the numbers of the slain and the captives, it would seem that the invaders numbered from twenty to twenty-five thousand fighting men. It speaks well for the generalship of Merneptah that he held his soldiery in check, and allowed the Libyans to form, rather than to expend his strength in inconclusive skirmishes with advance parties of the enemy. The two armies being assembled in face, the Egyptian infantry and chariotry attacked.[3] When within range the archers of Merneptah began to pour a heavy fire into the Libyan van, their bows being doubtless of a strength superior to that of those of the Libyans. For six hours this fire was kept up, until at length the Libyans were thrown into confusion and began to retreat. Meryey attempted vainly to rally his men, the retreat of the tribesmen became a rout,[4] and the victorious Egyptians pursued them with cavalry as they fled.[5] "Their marchers-forward [their van]," says one of the records, "they left behind them, their feet made no stand, but fled. Their archers threw down their bows, and the heart of their fleet ones was weary with marching. They loosed their water-skins, and threw them to the ground."[6] The pursuit was kept up as far as the Mount of the Horns of the Earth, as the Egyptians called the edge of the plateau on the west of the Delta. The total of the slain was over 9000, and as many more appear to have been made prisoners.[7] Six sons of Meryey, a number of his kinsmen, and other men of rank were killed,[8] while there "were taken before his face"[9] twelve "women of the fallen chief of Libya, whom he had brought with him, being alive."[10] The Libyan camp fell into the hands of the Egyptians, who fired the tents,[11]—"their camp was burned and made a roast."[12] The personal belongings of Meryey were seized, his silver, his gold, his vessels of bronze, the furniture of his wife, his throne, his bows, his arrows, all his works which he had brought from his land, together with his oxen, goats, and asses.[13]

The plunder obtained by the victors was considerable. The following items were listed :—[14]

Weapons of war which were in their hands, carried off as plunder ; copper swords of the Meshwesh	9,111

[1] BAR iii. § 570. The attempt made by Golenischeff, in *Zeitschr. für ägypt. Sprache*, xl. 101 *sq.*, to prove, from a papyrus in his possession, that the meeting took place south of the Fayum, has not met with general acceptance. For one thing the presence of the sea-allies is against this, and, further, the words "western *rwd*" point emphatically to the western margin of the Delta ; for the word *rwd* is a term used only of the Delta. W. M. F. Petrie, *loc. cit.*, is also wrong in placing the battle near Kafr ez-Zayat, for he does so on the strength of an erroneous lection by H. Brugsch, for which the reader is referred to BAR iii. § 579, note *d*, *ad loc. cit.* The exact locality remains unknown.

[2] BAR iii. § 583. [3] BAR *loc. cit.* [4] BAR § 584.

[5] BAR iii. § 584, "Lo, the officers, who were upon the horses of his majesty, set themselves after them." Cf. J. H. Breasted, *A History of Egypt*, p. 468.

[6] BAR iii. § 609. [7] BAR iii. §§ 588, 601 and notes. [8] BAR iii. § 588.

[9] BAR iii. § 610. [10] BAR iii. § 588. [11] BAR iii. § 589.

[12] BAR iii. § 610. [13] BAR iii. § 584.

[14] BAR iii. §§ 589, 601. Both these records, the great Karnak inscription and the Athribis stela, are combined above, but some obscure items, found *locc. citt.*, are here omitted.

(Libyan (?) small arms (?))	120,214
Horses which bore the fallen chief of Libya, and the children of the chief of Libya, carried off alive, pairs	12
Various cattle	1,308
Goats	x
Silver drinking-vessels	x
Tepur-vessels, *rehedet*-vessels, swords, armour, knives [of copper], and various vessels	3,174
Bows [1]	2,000

From the disastrous field Meryey escaped with difficulty, alone or with but few companions.[2] "The wretched fallen chief of Libya," says the Israel stela, "fled by favour of night alone, with no plume upon his head; . . . he had no water in his [water-]skin to keep him alive."[3] In his flight he passed an Egyptian outpost called the Fortress of the West,[4] the commanding officer of which had news of his passage and reported it. The commandant of the Fortress of the West wrote to the court as follows:—

> The fallen Meryey has come, his limbs
> have fled because of his cowardice, and
> he passed by me by favour of night,
> in safety . . . he is fallen, and every
> god is for Egypt. . . . His condition is not known
> whether of death or of life . . . if he lives
> he will not again command, for he is fallen,
> an enemy of his own troops . . . They have
> put another in his place, from among his
> brothers, another who fights him when he sees
> him. All the chiefs are disgusted . . .[5]

The last lines of the above despatch give an interesting glimpse into the position of affairs in Libya after the defeat. Meryey, like many another barbaric leader, found to his cost that his power rested only on his success in arms. The wild tribesmen, angry and indignant at their ill fortune, turned upon their chief and deposed him, just as the fierce Zaporojian Cossacks would have pulled down an unsuccessful hetman. Across the ever-widening gulf of centuries one may still see the unhappy chieftain, a reproach to his people, his ambitions in the dust, allowed to live, in all probability, only because of his princely family. "The face of his brothers was hostile to slay him, one fought another among his leaders. . . . When he arrived in his country, he was the complaint of every one in his land. Ashamed he bowed himself down, an evil fate removed his

[1] This last item, together with the notice of the Libyan archers throwing down their bows in flight (BAR iii. § 609), shows how inaccurate W. M. F. Petrie, *op. cit.* vol. iii. p. 109, is in his account of the battle. "There are no bows stated among the Libyan spoil, and they seem to have relied wholly on hand-to-hand fighting and chariots," says Petrie, and goes on to compare this battle with the "parallel victory" obtained by the exarch Narses over the Franks at Casilinum.

[2] BAR iii. § 584: "Lo, the wretched chief of Libya was in speed to flee by himself."

[3] BAR iii. § 610.

[4] Mentioned later by Rameses III., BAR iii. § 586. Perhaps in the Wady Natrun.

[5] BAR *loc. cit.*

plume. They all spoke against him, the inhabitants of his city : 'He is in the power of the gods, the lords of Memphis ; the lord of Egypt has cursed his name Meryey, the Abomination of Memphis, from son to son of his family, forever.'"[1] The unfortunate chief heard on all sides the praises of his enemy the Pharaoh. Merneptah became "a proverb in Libya ; the youth say to youth, concerning his victories : 'It has not been done to us before since the time of Ra,' say they. Every old man says to his son, 'Alas for Libya !'" The tribesmen "ceased to live in the pleasant fashion of walking in the field ; their going about was stopped in a single day ; . . . their settlements" were "desolated," and they said "concealment is good ; there is safety in a cavern."[2]

In Egypt, on the other hand, intense relief was felt. There was a general national enthusiasm for Merneptah and gratitude to him. No more was there any "uplifting of a shout in the night : 'Stop ! Behold one comes, one comes with the speech of strangers !' . . . The towers are settled again anew," continues the Israel stela ; "as for the one that ploweth his harvest, he shall eat it."

It seems almost as if Merneptah followed up his great victory with punitive expeditions of some sort. At least he appears to have secured a tribute from his enemies,[3] and he is said to have "penetrated the land of Temeḥ."[4] In the Athribis stela, also, Merneptah is mentioned as making the Libyan "camps into wastes of the Red Land, taking . . . every herb that came forth from their fields," so that "no field grew," and "the families of Libya" were scattered "like mice upon the dikes."[5] Whether we are to accept or not as a fact a retributive invasion of Libya does not much matter ; the Egyptians were content with their triumph over the invaders, and the absence of more detailed information shows clearly that, even if bodies of Egyptian troops did harry the neighbouring Libyans, the expeditions were small and not in the nature of a counter invasion vigorous enough to drive the Rebu back upon their western neighbours.

Yet so sure and decisive a repulse would in all likelihood have been effective in preventing the Libyans from making another attempt against Egypt for a long time had not the affairs of the country fallen into confusion on the death of Merneptah. Merneptah's reign was followed by a period during which the power of the empire was weakened by obscure quarrels and the decay of military spirit. The latter is clearly indicated by the manner in which the peaceful occupations of the scribe were exalted in the literature of the day at the expense of the military life,[6] and was one of the main reasons why the Libyans were emboldened again to attempt to enter the Nile Valley by force of arms. Unfortunately for them, the attempt was too long deferred ; when

[1] BAR iii. § 610.

[2] BAR iii. § 611.

[3] Cf. BAR iii. § 591, where mention is made of yearly tribute.

[4] BAR iii. § 608.

[5] Cf. BAR iii. § 598. In the concluding simile I have altered the position of the words. Breasted has "upon the dikes like mice," which is the literal order.

[6] *Anastasi Papyrus* iii. pl. v. 1. 5, pl. vi. 1. 2 ; *Anastasi Papyrus* iv. pl. ix. 1. 4, pl. x. 1. 1 ; G. Maspero, *The Struggle of the Nations*, p. 457 *sq.* ; A. Erman, *Ägypten und ägyptisches Leben*, p. 722 ; idem, *Hieratische Ostraka* in the *Zeitschr. für ägypt. Sprache*, 1880, p. 96 *sq.*

it was put into effect, the XXth Dynasty had been inaugurated under the energetic Setnakht,[1] to whom succeeded a powerful and ambitious ruler, Rameses III. Already the regeneration of the country had begun. The scribes, whose temper suggest so strongly those of their successors in modern Egypt, had had to take again a position secondary to that of the soldiery on whom the welfare of the country depended.

The materials for the Libyan wars of Rameses III. are copious, but unsatisfactory. Of our chief sources, the Medînet Habu inscriptions are so overladen with metaphor and strained imagery,[2] and are so inconsequent, that even a scholar of Breasted's experience is forced to say that his "translation as a whole is exceedingly unsatisfactory to the author";[3] while the account given in the Papyrus Harris, as was long ago recognized, attempts to summarize the first and second wars in a single narrative.[4] Fortunately, however, we are able to trace the main features of both wars, and to see in them an extraordinary parallel to the time of Merneptah.

The first Libyan war of Rameses III. befell in the fifth year of his reign, some two decades after the Merneptah invasion. As in the accounts of that struggle, so here also the narratives show that the invasion was preceded by casual penetration or by raids—"the land had been exposed in continual extremity since the [former] kings";[5] "the Libyans and the Meshwesh were dwelling in Egypt, having plundered the cities of the western shore."[6] Immigration across the western frontier of the Delta had again begun; bands of Libyan robbers wandered among the towns from the vicinity of Memphis to the Mediterranean, or possessed themselves of the fields along the Canopic branch of the Nile.[7] While this tentative advance was being made on the easternmost border of Libya, and while Setnakht and Rameses III. were bringing order out of the chaos in the Nile Valley, in Syria and Asia were happening events which finally resulted in the spurring on of the Libyans to repeat the attempt they had made under Meryey a score of years before. Grave ethnic disturbances in the north were forcing more and more of the older inhabitants to the south. In particular, two peoples appeared, who, while not strong enough to withstand the pressure behind them, were nevertheless both of formidable strength: the Thekel and the Peleset, the latter being the Philistines of the Bible, who had before been settled in Crete. Together with the bands of Denyen, Weshesh, Shekelesh, and Sherden, the Thekel and Peleset had begun to drift toward the south and east. As they moved southward in Syria, the more venturesome of their leaders began to coast along the Delta, and to enter the river-mouths on piratical expeditions. As was natural, they readily fell into the plans of the North African

[1] Manetho begins the XXth Dynasty with Rameses III.; but see J. H. Breasted, *A History of Ancient Egypt*, p. 600 *sqq.*, and BAR i. § 69.

[2] BAR iv. § 21.

[3] BAR iv. § 36.

[4] G. Maspero, *op. cit.* p. 459, note 3; F. Chabas, *Études sur l'antiquité historique*, p. 230 *sqq.*; idem, *Recherches pour servir à l'histoire de la XIX dynastie*, p. 52 *sq.*

[5] BAR iv. § 40; cf. 52, "The land of Temeḥ, Ṣeped, and Meshwesh, who were robbers plundering Egypt every day."

[6] BAR iv. § 405.

[7] BAR iv. §§ 40, 405; J. H. Breasted, *op. cit.* p. 474 *sq.*

leaders to invade and plunder Egypt,[1] and the presence of these new allies gave to the Libyans just that stimulus which was needed to rekindle those ambitions which Merneptah had subdued.

The great chief Meryey, son of Ded, had been set aside after his defeat, and one of his brothers put in his place. In the record of the first invasion under Rameses III., it is stated that the Pharaoh triumphed over Ded, Meshken, Meryey and Wermer, Themer, and every hostile chief "who crossed the border of Egypt from Libya."[2] The occurrence here, so long after the battle of Perire, of the names of Ded and Meryey is certainly remarkable. Either the names are those of the original invaders, returned again after twenty years, or of other chieftains descended from them; or they may have been here inserted by the compiler of the later record, who took them out of the Merneptah account for the greater glorification of Rameses III. The first hypothesis, though supported by Maspero,[3] is hardly possible; for in Merneptah's time Meryey had six grown sons, and if he were then but forty and his father but sixty, it is hardly likely that we should find them again taking the field at the ages of sixty and eighty respectively. The second hypothesis is one which cannot be disproved, but which is much to be suspected from the fact that the only two chieftains named in the Merneptah records should be represented by another pair bearing the same names twenty years afterward. The third possibility, which is the most probable when is considered the easy accessibility of the earlier records to the maker of the later one, is that which Breasted tacitly admits when he supposes that, as given in the notice above cited, the Libyan chiefs are listed in chronological order.[4] If Ded and Meryey are introduced into the Rameses record in a spirit of reminiscence, and if Breasted is right in believing that the names are given in chronological order, the succession of the great chiefs of Libya would be as follows:—

1. Ded.
2. Meshken.
3. Meryey. (Deposed.)
4. Wermer. (Contemporary of Seti II., etc.)
5. Themer. (Leader of Second Invasion.[5])

[1] J. H. Breasted, *op. cit.* p. 477 *sq.*, for these particulars.

[2] BAR iv. § 43.

[3] G. Maspero, *The Struggle of the Nations*, p. 456.

[4] BAR iv. § 43, note *b*, *ad loc. cit.*; J. H. Breasted, *op. cit.* p. 478.

[5] The only certain family relations traceable from the Merneptah records as existing among the chiefs are thus indicated:—

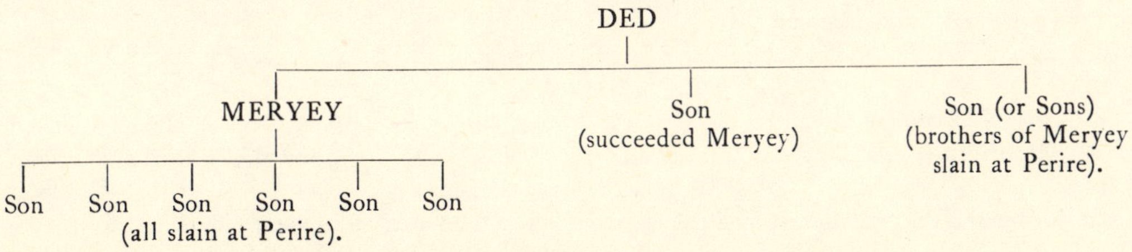

The necessary filiations for Meshken, Wermer, and Themer do not exist.

This debatable ground may be left, however, for the firmer one of the history of the invasions which took place under Rameses III., which may be taken up at the moment of the union of the Thekel and the Peleset with the Libyans against Egypt. As usual, there was a general muster of the tribesmen ; "the land of Temeḥ" came "together in one place in Libya."[1] The assembled Rebu, Meshwesh, and Ṣeped[2] moved eastward to unite with their sea-roving allies, and with those Libyans already settled in the Egyptian Delta, on the friendship of whom they could doubtless count. When joined with the latter, and with the Thekel and Peleset pirates, they could not, to judge from the numbers they eventually lost, have been much under 30,000 strong. Having joined forces, the invaders began to plunder and lay waste the countryside. The pirates, probably with an eye to securing their share of the booty, landed a large part of their crews, and served as "warriors upon land" as well as "in the sea."[3] Those of the allies who remained on shipboard "entered into the river-mouths . . . like wild-fowl creeping into a net."[4] Gradually working their way south along the Canopic arm of the Nile, the Libyans and their allies sacked the towns of the western Delta from Kerben south to Memphis.[5] The resistance had been slight ; the invaders, moreover, had been near to the sea and the coast-road into Libya, and so were in touch with their kinsmen. They became, as is the wont with ill-organized bodies in success, careless and over-confident ; they began "sitting in Egypt,"[6] apparently like so many colonists. Themer and his captains may even have considered their aim as practically accomplished, when, like a thunderbolt, the army of the warlike Pharaoh burst upon them. The defeat was utter, and was attended by a carnage in which over 12,000 of the invaders fell,[7] a large proportion of the slain being the sea-rovers. About 1000 of the allies were made captive.[8] The Egyptian king, personally present at the action, pursued the flying tribesmen in his chariot, accompanied by his mercenary archers and swordsmen.[9] The wretched Thekel and Peleset on the river fared no better than those on shore ; their ships were boarded and carried by the Egyptians—they had indeed "crept into a net." In commemoration of this triumph the site of it was by the royal annalists named Usermare-Meriamon-is-Chastiser-of-Temeḥ.

The captive allies, "with their women and children, like the ten thousand,"[10] were branded with the king's name and put to serve as auxiliary troops,[11] or given to be slaves in the temples.[12] What became of Themer is not known ; but groups

[1] BAR iv. § 40.

[2] BAR iv. § 40 and note *d*, *ad loc.* ; cf. § 52. That the Ṣeped and Eṣbet may be the same tribe has been mentioned in the chapter on ethnogeography.

[3] BAR iv. § 44 ; cf. W. M. Müller, *Asien und Europa*, p. 360, note 4.

[4] BAR *loc. cit.*

[5] BAR iv. § 405. Kerben may have been the site near Abuḳîr known in classical times as Heracletum—the Karbaniti of the records of Assurbanipal. H. Brugsch, *Dictionnaire géographique*, p. 854 *sq.* ; and BAR, note *g*, *loc. cit.*

[6] BAR *loc. cit.*

[7] BAR §§ iv. 52 ; 53, and note *c*.

[8] BAR iv. § 54.

[9] Scenes at Medînet Habu, mentioned by BAR §§ iv. 50, 51. The auxiliaries were Sherden.

[10] BAR iv. § 405.

[11] BAR *loc. cit.*, also iv. § 43, and cf. §§ 402, 403.

[12] Cf. BAR iv. §§ 190, 213, 359 for this giving of captives as temple slaves.

of his "tens," or councillors, were among the prisoners brought before the king.[1] Well might the Pharaoh boast: "I overthrew those who invaded my boundary, prostrated in their place. . . . I laid low the land of Temeḥ. . . . The Meshwesh, they crouch down for fear of me."[2] The broken remnants of the invaders, it is evident, would have been only too glad to rest peaceably in their own lands[3] after this rough handling. Unhappily for them, they were not allowed to do so.

It will be remembered that, in the Merneptah invasion, the Rebu fell upon the Teḥenu, and forced the latter to accompany them against Egypt. Six years after the first victory of Rameses III. a parallel proceeding was put in execution by the Meshwesh. This people, situated to the west of the Rebu, does not appear to have been active in the Libyan-Egyptian wars before the XXth Dynasty. In the Merneptah invasions they are indeed mentioned, and a number of their copper swords have been enumerated among the booty taken from the Libyans. It is in the first Libyan war of Rameses III., however, that the Meshwesh themselves are seen for the first time definitely and in large numbers among the Libyan invaders as allies of the Rebu. After the defeat of the latter, the Meshwesh seem to have been but ill content with the turn of affairs, and to have had a contempt for their eastern neighbours. At all events, they had no scruple in taking advantage of the weakened state of the tribes between them and Egypt. Under Kepper and his son Meshesher, they suddenly fell upon the Rebu and Teḥenu, and overcame them. "The chief of Meshwesh . . . went to one place, his land with him, and invaded the Teḥenu, who were made ashes, spoiled and desolated were their cities, their seed was not."[4] This victory would have been well enough had not the conquerors been spurred on by it to attempt a greater and more difficult venture. Full of confidence from their success, and conscious of their superiority in arms, they readily gave ear to the tales told them by the vanquished Rebu and Teḥenu of the richness and accessibility of the Delta. It may be that the Rebu, anxious to rid themselves of these new masters, deliberately encouraged them to undertake the old quest on which they had themselves failed. The subject Rebu would have argued that either the Meshwesh would succeed in overcoming the Egyptians, in which case Libya would be relieved from this new oppression, and that an old score would be wiped out, or that, in case of defeat, the Meshwesh would lose so heavily that they would be more manageable masters. At all events, there is no doubt that they advised marching against Egypt, advice which the Meshwesh took to their cost, and recalled bitterly afterward, when they said: "Libya has misled us like. . . . We hearkened to their counsels."[5]

[1] BAR iv. § 42, and note *c*, *ad loc. cit.*

[2] BAR iv. § 58.

[3] There is no reason to suppose Rameses carried war into Libya, unless weight is to be attached to the phrase "my flame consumed their towns," attributed by the Medînet Habu inscription to the king. BAR iv. § 54.

[4] BAR iv. § 87. Though the text has "Teḥenu," it is safe to assume that this general term was meant to embrace the Rebu, the immediate neighbours of the Meshwesh on the east.

[5] BAR iv. § 91.

A confederation of the usual sort was formed,[1] five tribes, the Eṣbet, Shai (Shaitep ?), Beḳen, Ḳeyḳesh, and Heṣ, being mentioned[2] as among the allies. It is possible that an understanding of some sort was arrived at with the Amorites of Syria, since the Libyan invasion and the Amorite war of the eleventh year of Rameses III. came close together,[3] and one of the Medînet Habu reliefs shows the Pharaoh leading the king of Amor and the Great Chief of Libya together before Amon.[4] Such an understanding could easily have been brought about through the agency of the Thekel, who were of the allies of the Libyans in the war of the year 5, and who not only fought against Egypt in Syria,[5] but who even had towns there, such as Dor,[6] and plenty of ships.[7]

Be this as it may, the Libyan force began to advance late in the year, fully bent upon occupying the enemy's country, "saying," in the words of the record, "we will settle in Egypt. So spake they with one accord, and they continually entered the boundaries of Egypt,"[8] with a view, doubtless, of marauding and of testing the enemy's strength. The main body of the invaders seems to have met with no serious opposition until it arrived at the stronghold of Hatsho,[9] which they began to invest.[10] This was the moment chosen by Rameses, who with his archery and chariotry suddenly appeared before his fortress to relieve it.[11] The archers marched in the van, supported by heavy infantry that waited before charging until the bowmen had broken the ranks of the enemy.[12] The Meshwesh and other tribesmen found themselves as unable to cope with the Egyptians as had been their predecessors. Pressed by the army and exposed to a galling fire from the fortress, beneath the walls of which they were attacked, they broke and fled, being pursued from Hatsho to the town of Usermare-Meriamon, which was upon the "Mount of the Horns of the Earth." There were made "eight *iters* of butchery among them."[13]

The unfortunate Kepper was taken captive; "he came to salam; . . . he laid down his arms, together with his soldiers. He cried to heaven to beseech his son"[14] for help—vainly, for Meshesher was slain on the field,[15] together with the old chieftain's wife and family.[16] The total number of the slain was 2175.[17] The living captives, 2025 in number, were thus itemized in the account given by the Medînet Habu reliefs:—

[1] BAR iv. § 85. Undoubtedly the Rebu and Teḥenu participated. That only the Meshwesh appear in the Egyptian list of captives is due to the application by the Egyptian scribes of the name of the contingent dominant among the allies, rather than to a defection of the non-Meshwesh allies in the battle of Hatsho.

[2] BAR iv. § 405.

[3] BAR iv. § 133.

[4] BAR iv. § 126. The text with this scene is, "Utterance of the wretched chief of Amor, and the wretched vanquished chief of Libya, 'Breath!'" BAR iv. § 127.

[5] BAR iv. § 64. With the Peleset, etc.

[6] BAR iv. § 565, "Dor, a city of Thekel."

[7] BAR iv. § 588, where eleven Thekel sail are mentioned as lying off Byblus.

[8] BAR iv. § 88.

[9] Some eleven miles from the desert (cf. BAR iv. § 83 and note *b*, *ad loc.*). Cf. the 8 *iters* pursuit from Hatsho to the "Mount of the Horns of the Earth" (BAR iv. § 102). Hatsho was situated by the canal called "The Waters of Re" (cf. BAR iv. § 83 and note *a*, *ad loc.*; § 224 and note *d*, *ad loc.*). For the length of the *iter* see BAR ii. § 965, note *a*, *ad loc.*

[10] Cf. BAR iv. §§ 102, 107.

[11] Cf. BAR iv. § 107. Scene at Medînet Habu.

[12] BAR iv. § 106. Scene at Medînet Habu.

[13] BAR iv. § 102.

[14] BAR iv. § 97.

[15] BAR iv. §§ 90, 100, 103.

[16] BAR iv. § 103.

[17] BAR iv. §§ 106, 111.

PLATE X.

CAPTIVE LIBYANS. DYNASTY XX.

The captivity which the mighty sword of Pharaoh, L.P.H., carried away from the vanquished of the Meshwesh :—

Chiefs of the Meshwesh	1 man.
Chieftains of the . . . enemy	5 men.[1]
Meshwesh	1205 men.
Youths	152
Boys	131
Total	1494
Their wives	342 women.
Maids	65
Girls	151
Total	558[2]
Total of the mighty sword of Pharaoh, as living captives	2052 various persons.

The captured spoil was as follows :—

Cattle, bulls	119 (+ x)
Swords of 5 cubits length	115
Swords of 3 cubits length	124
Bows	603
Chariots	93 (? to 99)
Quivers	2310
Spears	92
Horses of Meshwesh and asses	183[3]

The prisoners were branded with the king's name, and made to serve as auxiliaries ;[4] nearly a thousand were assigned to care for a temple herd grandiosely called "Usermare-Meriamon-L.P.H.-is-the-Conqueror-of-the-Meshwesh-at-the-Waters-of-Re" ;[5] and in commemoration of this victory, which took place in the middle of the twelfth month of the king's eleventh year, Rameses established an annual festival called in the temple calendar "Slaying the Meshwesh."[6]

This was the outcome of the last of the great Libyan militant invasions. The triumph of the king had spread the terror of his name as far as "the Great Bend,"[7] and the Libyans must have been convinced that they could not cope with the Egyptians in war.

As before the invasions, however, the Libyans continued to drift gradually eastward into the Delta, singly, in small groups, or in families, and rose eventually, as will be seen, to hold the supreme power. But before those events, which belong rather to Egyptian than to Libyan history, it is necessary first to consider the cause of all this easterly move-

[1] Were these the chiefs of the five tribes mentioned above ?

[2] BAR iv. § 111. From these data it may be assumed that the invading force was at least 10,000 strong.

[3] BAR *loc. cit.* [4] BAR iv. § 405. [5] BAR iv. § 224. [6] BAR iv. § 145.

[7] BAR iv. § 110. This locality is probably not to be identified with the Catabathmus Major, since both Rebu and Meshwesh lived west of that point. Rather it is the southerly curve of the Cyrenaic coast, entering the Syrtis Major.

ment of the Libyans—a movement of which the great invasions just recorded were simply the most striking manifestations within our historical horizon.

If the Libyan campaign of Seti I. be regarded as the first indication of a general easterly movement of the populations of Eastern Libya, the invasions may be said, broadly, to have occupied the twelfth century B.C. This was an epoch which saw the later and final manifestations of a great ethnic movement in Europe. The southern shifting of the Syrian peoples with whom the Thekel and Peleset were associated has been mentioned already; about 1300 B.C. the Cretan thalassocracy, and, a century later, about 1200 B.C., the late Minoan power itself came to a violent close. Many island and coastwise people, taking refuge in sea-craft which their invaders did not possess, became piratical adventurers like the Peleset. Some of these people, driven from their homes, seized small ports and held them, as the Thekel held the town of Dor. It was a period when, in the Eastern Mediterranean, whole peoples, split up into small groups, were seeking to re-establish themselves in new homes. Such a re-establishment, it may be supposed, resulted in the Carian sea-power of the tenth and ninth centuries B.C. In the west the twelfth century was marked by the introduction of iron into Italy, and about this time the Venetes and Illyrians reached the Adriatic. The Tyrrhenians entered Italy, and pushed before them the Italiot Umbro-Latins. These in turn drove out the Sicels,[1] who, in the Egyptian records already quoted, appear as the Shekelesh. In Spain the firing or abandonment of the sites inhabited in the Bronze Age[2] commemorate the advent of powerful iron-using peoples at this time. In short, all southern Europe and Asia Minor felt the force of the ethnic thrust that pushed the Thracians into the Balkans.[3] The dispossessed heirs of the bronze culture could find a home nowhere if not in Africa, a country eminently habitable, held by a weak neolithic or partially aeneolithic people, and cut off by the sea from the invaders. Large masses of wanderers driven from southern Europe crossed to the opposite continent, particularly, it is reasonable to suppose, in the parts approaching most nearly to Spain and Italy. The landing of a large body of immigrants in the region which is now Marocco, Algeria, and Tunisia, and the presence along the coast of rapacious Sherden, Peleset, Thekel, etc., would naturally produce an ethnic disturbance of some magnitude. This would take the form of an easterly or westerly movement, the desert nature of the interior putting a southerly one practically out of the question; and of the two directions the easterly would be the more likely, as in the west new arrivals were pressing in from the Iberian Peninsula, and as the region east of Tunisia is less mountainous and difficult to traverse than the Atlas belt on the west. Probably a movement from Africa Minor toward Egypt was inaugurated as early as 1300 B.C. It was accelerated by the arrival at various points of detached bodies of sea-peoples, whose arrival was commemorated in later times by legends such as that which said the Maxyes were of Trojan origin.[4] Armed with superior

[1] J. Deniker, *The Races of Man*, p. 315 *sqq.*, 321.

[2] L. Siret, *L'Espagne préhistorique*, p. 73.

[3] J. Deniker, *op. cit.* p. 321.

[4] Herodotus iv. 191.

weapons and more advanced in civilization than the indigenous North Africans, the new arrivals expanded rapidly. An insistent ethnic pressure began to have its effects in the east. Seti I. and Rameses II. felt the force of it in Egypt, and cut off the head of the advancing column. Then the Rebu, pressed on the west, fell on their eastern neighbours and attempted the invasion which was checked by Merneptah. Again a convulsive west-to-east movement—the disastrous invasion in the year 5 of Rameses III.—was blocked by the Egyptians, and again a tribe advancing from the west—the Meshwesh—fell in upon their eastern neighbours, and attempted vainly to establish themselves in Egypt. Such a succession of wars, and the events by which, as will be shown later, it was followed, can be explained only by the facts just outlined; by the arrival of new and powerful ethnic elements in the vicinity of those parts of Africa lying opposite Spain and Italy. The Libyan invasions, it will have been noticed, were accompanied by numbers of women and children,[1] and were animated by a colonizing spirit. They were, briefly, not invasions in the ordinary sense, but waves of a migration which had been set in motion in the west.

The armed migrations terminated with the battle of Hatsho; the impulse which had caused them remained. Under the immediate successors of Rameses III. went on a steady and persistent infiltration of Libyan immigrants into the Delta; under "the weak and inglorious XXIst Dynasty"[2] these families in some cases became powerful. At the beginning of this chapter the first period of Libyan history was set as extending roughly to 1000 B.C., the time by which the invasions or militant migrations had come to an end. It was about this time that the peaceful penetration of the Delta was taking place. In order, however, to understand what was happening at this period, it is necessary to consider some of the later phases of New Empire history in which the obscure immigrants of the eleventh century are seen more clearly in the light of the power they came to attain. For the study of this point there most fortunately remain the records of an immigrant family which may be regarded as typical, the family of the Libyan Buyuwawa.[3]

[1] That more women and children are not mentioned in the Egyptian annals is perhaps due to the fact that their enumeration would not redound especially to the credit of their victors, and perhaps because the majority of the non-combatant Libyans were left in the rear of the militant bodies, awaiting the conclusion of the campaigns.

[2] J. H. Breasted, *op. cit.* p. 527.

[3] The genealogy of the family is contained in the Serapeum stela of Harpeson, BAR iv. § 787 *sqq.* Buyuwawa is there called Teḥen-Buyuwawa. Twenty years ago P. le P. Renouf, *Who were the Libyans?* p. 602, inspired by Oppert, in *Congr. Intern. des Orient.*, Paris, 1873, vol. ii. p. 183 *sqq.*, tried to interpret the name  *thn-bwyw·wꜣ* differently, rendering the word 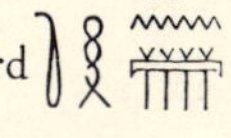 *t ḥ n* as "bright," "shining." He cited 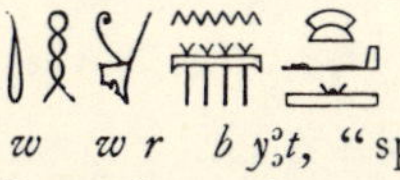 *t ḥ n -ḫꜥ*, λαμπροφανής, from the titulary of Rameses III., and  *t h n ḫ p r w w r b yꜣt*, "splendid of forms, great in marvellous works," from the titulary of Amenhotep III. as parallels. Renouf on these grounds claimed that Teḥen-Buyuwawa, "Radiant" or "Illustrious" Buyuwawa, was a compound name like Λαμπρόπους, or *Longimanus*. Recent scholarship has rejected this explanation, though W. M. F. Petrie, *A History of Egypt*, vol. iii. p. 231 *sq.*, has not only accepted it, but also reissued Oppert's etymologies for the names of this family—*e.g.* *Sheshonk* (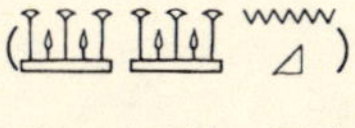) "man of Shushan"; *Nemareth* (thus reading  or ) = *nimr*, Ar. نمر "the leopard"; *Takerat* (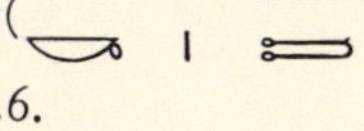) = "perhaps from the Zend, *tighri*, the tiger," etc. *Vide* BAR, *loc. cit.*, and J. H. Breasted, *op. cit.* p. 526.

Early in the XXth Dynasty a Teḥen-Libyan of this name settled in Heracleopolis. His son Musen became priest of the Heracleopolitan temple, and held command of the town's mercenary soldiers. Both these offices became hereditary in the family, which steadily increased in influence, and which became more and more Egyptianized as it advanced in power.

Buyuwawa's great-great-grandson, Sheshonk, "great chief of the Meshwesh," was able, when he found that part of the rich endowment he had provided for the upkeep of his son's mortuary service had been misappropriated, to interest one of the XXIst Dynasty kings in his behalf, and to secure a decision in his favour from the Theban Amon.[1] The grandson of this Sheshonk, who bore the same name, was first a local magnate the extent of whose domains would have warranted his having been rated as a prince. When the XXIst Dynasty had become naturally extinct, or too feeble to continue its nerveless existence, this second Sheshonk removed from Heracleopolis to Bubastis, and in 945 B.C. proclaimed himself Pharaoh.[2]

Thus, in a little more than two centuries after the death of their arch-enemy, Rameses III., the Libyans, having added to their natural hardihood the culture of the civilized Egyptians, became without a struggle rulers of what was still the most powerful empire in the Eastern Mediterranean. The genealogy of the house of Buyuwawa to the accession of Sheshonk I.[3] is as follows; the successors of that king belong rather to Egyptian than to Libyan history :—

1. Buyuwawa.
2. Musen.
3. Nebneshi.
4. Pethut.
5. Sheshonk = Mehetnushet.
6. Namlot = Temsepeh.
7. King Sheshonk I. = Kerome.

The family from which sprang the XXIInd Dynasty kings was a typical one. Evidence exists until late Egyptian times that many Libyan families were established in the Delta, and while their fortunes did not rise as high as those of the house mentioned, they nevertheless produced a number of petty dynasts and princes, such as those seen in the account of the northern revolt suppressed by the Aethiopian Piankhi in the XXIIIrd Dynasty.[4] Such a local magnate appeared at the end of the Egyptian period in the person of Inarus, whose brilliant but unsuccessful revolt against Artaxerxes I. will be mentioned in due course.

[1] BAR iv. § 669 *sqq.*

[2] BAR iv. § 785 *sqq.*

[3] BAR iv. § 787.

[4] BAR iv. § 815 *sqq.*; especially §§ 830, 878.

Period II

The main characteristic of this period is the gradual curtailment of the area occupied by the Eastern Libyans, because of foreign colonization in Africa. To present the scattered notices relating to the Libyans during this period in narrative form is scarcely profitable, the events of which records remain being for the most part isolated and unconnected with each other. All the significant material has therefore been cast in the form of a rough chronicle. In this chronicle are inserted a number of events relating only indirectly to Eastern Libya, yet of enough importance to warrant their being put in. Such items are printed at the right of the page, the facts of East Libyan history being given the full width.

Circa 1175 B.C.

About this time the Egyptian oases were colonized by Rameses III.[1] Ḫargarh became for a time a place of exile for Egyptian criminals.[2]

Circa 935 B.C.

Sheshonk I. sent to Daḫlah, which, from the weakness of the XXIst Dynasty, "had been found to be in a state of rebellion and desolate," a commissioner to restore and maintain order. This commissioner was a priest of Diospolis Parva, a Libyan called Wayheset.[3]

Circa 800 B.C.

About this time Carthage was founded.[4]

763 B.C.

A Libyan, "the great chief of Rebu, great chief of Me[shwesh] Hetihenker," governor of the Western Delta under Sheshonk III.[5]

A Libyan, Weshtehet, serving as master-caravaneer to Sheshonk III.[6]

Circa 700 B.C.

Carthaginian *emporia* established in the Syrtica Regio. By these factories trade with the interior was stimulated, and the career of mercenary service was opened to Eastern Libyans.[7]

Circa 639 B.C.

Greek colonists from Thera occupy Plataea ("Seal Island" in the Gulf of Bombah) in the territory of the Giligamae.[8]

Circa 637 B.C.

Greeks leave Plataea for Aziris on the adjacent main.[9]

1 BAR iv. § 213. 2 BAR iv. § 650 *sqq.* 3 BAR iv. § 726.

4 O. Meltzer, *Geschichte der Karthager*, vol. i. p. 90 *sq.* The factory of Cambe had already been established by the Sidonians.

5 BAR iv. § 784; cf. § 783. 6 BAR *locc. citt.*

7 Cf. C. Perroud, *De Syrticis emporiis*, p. 200.

8 The date is 2 + 6 + 631, since the colonists spent two years on Plataea (Herodotus iv. 157), and six at Aziris before going to Cyrene (Herodotus iv. 158), which they founded in 631 B.C. Plataea = "Seal Island" in the Gulf of Bombah, and not, as many geographers have assumed, Burdah or Bombah Island, which is an uninhabitable rock.

9 Herodotus v. 157.

Circa 631 B.C.

The Greeks leave Aziris at the instigation of the friendly Giligamae, who conduct them to a point within the territories of the Asbystae, where they found Cyrene.[1]

Circa 572 B.C.[2]

The Cyrenaean Greeks are reinforced by fresh colonists. The Asbystae and their chief, Adicran, "being robbed and insulted by the Cyreneans," send messengers to Egypt, and put themselves under the rule of Apries [= Ḥa-ab-ra = Hophra of the Bible], the Egyptian king, who thereupon levies a vast army of Egyptians, and sends it against Cyrene. The inhabitants of that place leave their walls and march out in force to the district of Irasa, where, near the spring called Theste, they engage the Egyptian army and defeat it.[3]

The results of this first conflict between the Greeks and Egyptians, thus brought about by the Libyans, were far-reaching. For Apries was blamed for the defeat, and Amasis (Ahmose II.) revolted and became first co-regent and then sole king.

About this time, or a little before, the Ammonians, who lived under the rule of their own princes,[4] become strongly Egyptianized, if not under direct Egyptian sway. The earliest architectural remains in the oasis belong to this period, and are wholly Egyptian in character. A little later Herodotus described the population as partly Egyptian.[5]

Circa 550 B.C.[6]

The brothers of Arcesilaus II., Perseus, Zacynthus, Aristomedon, and Lycus withdraw from Cyrene with their adherents to Barca, a town in the territory of the Auschisae. This town they are said by Herodotus[7] to have founded, but from its non-Greek name, and the circumstances attaching to the story of the secession, it is almost certain that it was of native origin, ante-dating the arrival of the Greeks, or that the Auschisae had a large share in building it.[8] The brothers fomented a Libyan revolt against Cyrene. Arcesilaus marched against the rebels, who retreat eastward to a place called Leucon. The Libyans there made a stand, and engaged the Cyrenaeans, defeating them so heavily that the Greeks are said to have lost 7000 heavy-armed men.[9]

Circa 525–524 B.C.

Cambyses III. accepts tribute from the Libyans of Marmarica.[10]

[1] Herodotus iv. 158. For the date cf. Theophrastus, *Hist. plant.* vi. 8. 3, as against Solinus xxvii. 44, where the date is given as 597.

[2] For the date $631 - 40 - 16 - x$, x being < 6; for Battus I. ruled in Cyrene forty years, and his successor Arcesilaus I. ruled sixteen (Herodotus iv. 159), $631 - (40 + 16) = 575$ = accession of Battus II. A little time must be allowed for the renewed colonizing activity which led Adicran to call in Apries; hence, as Apries was killed in 569 B.C., the Egyptian expedition must have been between *circa* 573 and 569. But Amasis, after the expedition and before the murder of Apries, ruled with the latter at least two years (W. M. F. Petrie, *History of Egypt*, iii. p. 350 *sq.*), so that the date of the expedition falls within the narrow limits of *circa* 573–571 B.C.

[3] Herodotus iv. 159. Cf. A. Wiedemam, *Geschichte Ägyptens von Psammetich*, i. etc., p. 165.

[4] The names of three of these were copied by G. Steindorff who gives them (in transcription only) in his *Durch die libyschen Wüste zur Amonsoase.* They there appear as "Set-erdaïs, Great Chief of Foreign Lands," son of "Retneb" (same title—p. 118); and as "Un-Amon" (same title) son of "Nefret-ronpet" (p. 121). The "Etearchus" of Herodotus probably belonged to the first half of the fifth century B.C.

[5] Herodotus ii. 32. And, in part, Aethiopian. But by "Aethiopian" Herodotus may here intend Libyan, Greek writers occasionally confusing the two.

[6] *I.e.* some years after the accession of Arcesilaus II. Chalepus.

[7] Herodotus iv. 160.

[8] I have already remarked on the native character of Barca in the preceding chapter (p. 177, note 4), citing Polyaenus, *Strateg.* viii. 47. See too p. 231, note 3.

[9] Herodotus, *loc. cit.*

[10] *Ibid.* iii. 13. The tribute of the Cyreneans was thought insultingly small.

Cambyses III. despatches against Ammonium an army said to have consisted of 50,000 men. The army proceeded from the Nile, *via* Ḫargah. What afterward happened is not clearly known. The army apparently reached Ḫargah in safety, and left for Sîwah. At the latter place it never arrived, local legend reporting that while halting on the road it was overwhelmed by a sandstorm.[1]

Circa 517 B.C.

The Carthaginians and the Macae drive out the Doric Greeks who had established themselves at the mouth of the Cinyps River.[2]

Circa 515 B.C.

Alazir,[3] king of Barca, and his son-in-law, Arcesilaus III., murdered. Pheritime, mother of Arcesilaus, seeks and obtains help from Aryandes, satrap of Egypt. Aryandes besieges Barca, which he takes by treachery, penetrates to Euhesperis, and then returns to Egypt. On the way back the Persians are harassed by the Libyans, who cut off stragglers for the sake of their accoutrements. The captive Barceans are settled in Asia.[4]

Circa 500 B.C.

Ammonium and the Egyptian oases thoroughly subjected to Persia. Darius I. begins his temple at Ḫargah.

480 B.C.

Large Libyan contingent in the army of Xerxes.[5]

460–454 B.C.

Inarus, son of Psammetichus, a Libyan dynast of the Western Delta, revolts from Persia, with the support of the Mareotic Libyans, and perhaps of Cyrene.[6] Aided by the Athenians, who send their fleet from Cyprus, Inarus defeats the Persians in a pitched battle in which he slays Achaemenes, the satrap, with his own hand. He besieges Memphis unsuccessfully, and is forced to withdraw to Papremis. Finally, he is captured and crucified. In accordance with a not uncommon Persian policy, his son, Thanyras, is installed in his stead.[7]

Circa 450 B.C.

The Nasamones fall upon the Psylli, destroy many of them, and force the remainder away from the Syrtic coast.[8]

[1] Herodotus iii. 17, 25, 26; cf. Diodorus Siculus x. 13; Justin i. 9. 3. This expedition may have been directed by Cambyses, who obviously had but a poor knowledge of the desert, against Cyrene as an ultimate objective. Vide *supra*, p. 174 *sq*.

[2] Cf. C. Perroud, *De Syrticis emporiis*, p. 155.

[3] The name Ἀλαζίρ (Herodotus iv. 164), belonging to a king of Barca, is further evidence of the Libyan character of that city. The name is obviously that seen as ΑΛΑΔΔΕΙΡ in an inscription (CIG 5147). A Cyrenaic tile-stamp found at Cyrene by the American Expedition (reproduced in *Bull. Arch. Inst. America*, vol. ii. no. 4, pl. xiv.) seems also to exhibit this name, though no one has chanced to remark it. The stamp as copied is ꓶΛΑ ΙΖ, and the reading suggested is ΑΛΕΖΗ. The spacing calls for one more letter, which permits one to restore the name as ΑΛΕΖΗ(Ρ).

[4] Herodotus iv. 164 *sqq*., 200 *sqq*.

[5] *Ibid*. vii. 184.

[6] Cf. Pindar, *Pyth*. iv. 53-56.

[7] Ctesias, *Frag*. 29 § 32; Thucydides i. 103, 104; Diodorus Siculus xi. 71 *sqq*.; Herodotus iii. 12, vii. 7.

[8] The date must lie between the times of Hecataeus and of Herodotus, since the former calls the Gulf of Kebrît the Psyllic Gulf; and by the time of the latter the Psylli had not only been driven back from the coast, but a legendary account of their removal had sprung up. It is Pliny (*Hist. Nat*. vii. 2) who has preserved the rational record of what took place—*haec gens* [*scil*. the Psylli] *ipsa quidem prope internicione sublata est a Nasamonibus, qui nunc eas tenent sedes*.

413 B.C.

The Spartan Gylippus, on his way westward to the relief of Syracuse, puts into Euesperis from stress of weather, and finds that city besieged by the Libyans. With his aid, the natives are beaten back.[1]

Circa 390 B.C.

The Libyans of Barca make a treaty with Harcoris of Egypt.[2]

Circa 331 B.C.

Alexander of Macedon conquers Egypt and visits Ammonium.

310–307 B.C.

Agathocles of Syracuse levies war on Carthage in Africa, and is partly supported by the discontented Libyans. In 308 B.C. Ophellas marches across the coast-road from Cyrene to join Agathocles, who slays him by treachery.[3]

Circa 277 B.C.

Magas of Cyrene marches from Cyrene against Egypt, and reaches the town of Chi.[4] At that point he learns that the Marmaridae have risen behind him and threaten to cut him off from his base. He withdraws, and puts down the Libyans.[5]

264–241 B.C.

First Punic War. Many African mercenaries in the Carthaginian army.[6] Under Spendius and Mathos, the Libyan, these eventually mutiny.[7]

240–237 B.C.

The mutiny develops into the African war [8] of Carthage.

218 B.C.

The war continues. Scipio invades Africa, where he obtains native support.[9]

149–146 B.C.

Third Punic War ; Carthage destroyed.

111 B.C.

Ptolemy Apion bequeaths Cyrenaica to Rome.

[1] Thucydides vii. 50.

[2] Theopompus, *Frag.* 111 in *FHG.* vol. i. p. 295. C. Müller here reads *βαρβάρους* for the *vulg.* Βαρκαίους.

[3] Diodorus Siculus xx. 3. 3, xvii. 1 ; cf. lv. 4.

[4] Polyaenus, *Strateg.* ii. 28. 2, Χί. In Ptol. iv. 5 § 4, Χεῖ or Χειμώ ; *Stadiasmus Maris Magni*, §§ 5, 6, Χιμώ.

[5] For the date, J. P. Mahaffy, *Empire of the Ptolemies*, p. 124, note 1.

[6] Polybius i. 67. 7.

[7] *Ibid.* i. 69. 6 ; cf. Diodorus Siculus xxv. 5. 2.

[8] Polybius i. 70. 5 *sqq.* ; cf. H. Fournel, *Les Berbers*, vol. i. p. 46, and notes.

[9] Livy xxii. 47.

Circa 87 B.C.

Phaedimus slain by Nicocrates, tyrant of Cyrene, who then marries Aretaphile, widow of Phaedimus. Aretaphile persuades Leander to kill his brother Nicocrates, and Leander succeeds to the tyranny, marrying Aretaphile.

The cruelty of Leander leads Aretaphile to conspire against him with Anabus, chief of a neighbouring tribe. Anabus threatens rebellion, and at a conference with Leander has him strangled.[1]

67 B.C.

Cyrenaica reduced to a Roman province. All the East Libyan littoral under Roman sway.

49 B.C.

Cato marches from Cyrene across the Syrtis.[2]

35 B.C.

Outbreak in Roman Africa.[3]

30 B.C.

Egypt a Roman province.

29 B.C.

Outbreak in Roman Africa.[4]

21 B.C.

Outbreak in Roman Africa.[4]

19 B.C.

Lucius Cornelius Balbus leads a successful punitive force into Phazania (Fezzan) against the marauding Garamantes, of which expedition Pliny gives the following account :—

" . . . beyond the Lesser Syrtis is the region of Phazania ; the nation of Phazanii belonging to which, as well as the cities of Alele and Cilliba, we have subdued by force of arms, as also Cydamus, which lies over against Sabrata. After passing these places a range of mountains extends in a prolonged chain from east to west ; these have received from our people the name of Black Mountains, either from the appearance which they naturally bear of having been exposed to the action of fire, or else because they have been scorched by the sun's rays. Beyond it lies the desert, and then Talgae, a city of the Garamantes, and Debris, . . . Garama, too, that most famous capital of the Garamantes, all of which places have been subdued by the Roman arms. It was on this occasion that Cornelius Balbus was honoured with a triumph. . . . Besides Cydamus and Garama, there were carried in procession the names and models of all the other nations and cities in the following order :[5] Tabudium, a town ; Niteris, a tribe [*natio*] ; the town of Nigligemela,[6] the tribe or town of Bubeium, the tribe Enipi, the town Thuben, the mountain

[1] Plutarch, *De mulier. virtut.* p. 255 *sqq.* ; cf. J. P. Thrige, *Res Cyrenensium*, p. 269 *sqq.*

[2] Plutarch, *Cato Minor*, § 56 ; Lucan, *Pharsalia*, ix. 300 *sqq.*

[3] Dio Cassius, *Hist. Rom.* xlix. 34.

[4] H. Fournel, *op. cit.* p. 49, and note 4, sub-note *d.*

[5] The order is probably that in which the towns were taken, and almost certainly a north to south one. The attempts which have been made to identify these ancient names with those of modern sites in Fezzan are hardly convincing.

[6] *Nigligemela*, though the current form of this name, is not the one preferred by Jahn, who reads *Miglis Gemella.* If this lection is right, one is strongly tempted to see here a Semitic name—مجلس جمل. Cf. in Assyria the Semitic Γαυγάμηλα (Strabo xvi. p. 737).

known as the Black Mountain, Nitibrum, the towns called Rapsa, the tribe Discera, the town Debris, the river Nathabur, the town Thapsagum, the tribe Nannagi, the town Boin, the town Pege, the river Dasibari ; and then the towns in the following order, of Baracum, Buluba, Alasit, Galia, Balla, Maxalla, Zigama, and Mount Gyri, which was preceded by an inscription stating that this was the place where precious stones were produced." [1]

6 B.C.

The Musulini and the Gaetuli defeated in Western Libya by Cornelius Crassus.[2]

A.D. 17.

Revolt of Tacfarinas begins, and lasts till A.D. 24, the scene of war shifting more and more westward.[3]

Circa A.D. 20.

P. Sulpicius Quirinius, proconsul of Creta-et-Cyrene, defeats the Marmaridae and the Garamantes, the latter being, apparently, beaten near their own territory.[4]

A.D. 40–42.

Revolt under Aedemon in the western Atlas, put down by Suetonius Paulinus.[5]

Raids in Numidia.[6]

Circa A.D. 69.

Revolt of Oea and Leptis Magna in the reign of Vespasian. The towns are aided by the Garamantes, who had been in the habit of defending themselves from attack by hiding their water-holes. "Up to the present," writes Pliny, "it has been found impracticable to keep open the road that leads to the country of the Garamantes, as the robber bands of that people have filled up the wells with sand, which wells do not require to be digged to any great depth, if you but have knowledge of the locality." [7]

A.D. 86.

In the reign of Domitian, the Nasamones revolted, slew the Roman quaestors, and took the camp of the praetor Flaccus. Finding a store of wine in the camp, however, they made themselves drunk with it ; the camp was re-taken by Flaccus, and the Nasamones were put to the sword.[8]

Circa A.D. 100.

Christianity begins to be established along the North African coast.

Septimius Flaccus penetrates to Aethiopia at the head of a Roman column.

Julius Maternus, marching from Leptis Magna to Garama, there joins forces with the Garamantes, and proceeds southward against various Aethiopian bands.[9]

1 Pliny v. 5.

2 Dio Cassius, *Hist. Roman.* lv. 26 ; Orosius vi. 21.

3 Tacitus, *Annal.* ii. 52 ; iii. 21 ; etc.

4 L. Annaeus Florus iv. 12, 41 (ii. 31) ; Jornandes, p. 1072 § 64.

5 Pliny v. 1 ; Dio Cassius lx. 1.

6 Dio Cassius, *loc. cit.*

7 Pliny v. 5 ; Tacitus, *Histor.* iv. 50 ; Solinus xxx.

8 Eusebius, *Chronicon*, p. 378 ; Zonaras, *Annales*, xi. 19 (p. 500).

9 Marinus Tyrius *ap.* Ptolemy i. 8 § 4, . . . ἀπὸ Γαράμης ἅμα τῷ βασιλεῖ τῶν Γαραμάντων ἐπερχομένῳ τοῖς Αἰθίοψιν ὁδεύσαντα τὰ πάντα πρὸς μεσημβρίαν μησὶ τέσσαρσι ἀφικέσθαι εἰς τὴν Ἀγίσυμβα, κτλ.

A.D. 115.

Great Judaic uprising in Cyrenaica. Massacre of the Gentiles.[1]

A.D. 117.

Revolts in the Atlas.[2]

A.D. 122.

Hadrian visits Mauretania to re-establish peace.[3]

Between A.D. 138 and 161.

Reign of Antoninus : revolt in the west. The Mauri, driven into the Atlas, sue for peace.[4]

A.D. 170.

Serious revolts in west. The Mauri engage the Romans not only in Africa, but in Spain. They are eventually defeated on both sides of the Straits.[5]

A.D. 180–192.

New outbreaks in the west during reign of Commodus.[6]

A.D. 193.

Septimius Severus becomes Emperor. He was born at Leptis Magna,[7] and was therefore conversant with the local conditions of Eastern Libya. "This prince," says Spartianus, "established the complete security of Tripolis, where he was born, by the defeat of numerous warlike tribes."[8]

A.D. 197.

Agrippinus, bishop of Carthage.[9]

A.D. 200.

Martyrdom of the Scillitani.[10]

Between A.D. 228 and 238.

Mauri repressed in the west by Furius Celsus.[11]

In 238 elevation of Gordianus Pius at Thysdrus.[12]

[1] Eusebius, *Hist. Eccles.* iv. 2. 2 ; Dio Cassius lxviii. 32. 5 ; S. Hieronymus, *Chronicon*, pp. 164, 165, 167 ; Orosius vii. 12 § 6. The extent of this rebellion leads to the conclusion that many Berber converts to Judaism may have been involved in it. According to Orosius, the mortality was so severe as to necessitate a recolonization of the Pentapolis under Hadrian. Jews persisted in the Pentapolis into Christian times, their presence being noticed by Synesius, *Epist.* 137.

[2] Aelius Spartianus, *Hadrianus* 5.

[3] *Ibid.* 12.

[4] Julius Capitolinus, *Antoninus Pius* 5.

[5] Idem, *Marcus Aurelius philosophus* 21.

[6] Aelius Lampridius, *Commodus* 9, 13.

[7] Eutropius, *Breviar. ab urbe condita*, viii. 18 ; Sext. Aurel. Victor, *De Caesaribus* 20 ; idem, *Epitome* 20 ; Aelius Spartianus, *Severus* 1, 18.

[8] Aelius Spartianus, *Severus* 18.

[9] S. A. Morcelli, *Africa Christiana*, vol. ii. p. 44.

[10] D. Ruinart, *Acta martyrum sincera et selecta*, p. 73 *sqq.* ; idem, *Hist. persecut. Vandal.* p. 247 *sq.* ; S. A. Morcelli, *op. cit.* vol. i. p. 50, vol. ii. p. 53.

[11] Lampridius, *Alexander Severus*, 58.

[12] Herodian, *Ab excessu Divi Marci*, vii. 4. 2, v. 3 ; Sext. Aurel. Victor, *De Caesaribus* 26 ; J. Capitolinus, *Maximini duo* 13, 14.

A.D. 253.

Raiding in Numidia.[1]

A.D. 256.

Council of African bishops at Carthage.[2]

A.D. 261.

Raids of Faraxen finally put down by Gargilius.[3]

A.D. 270.

Probus, later Emperor, conducts a successful campaign against the Mármaridae. He marched, according to Vopiscus, "from Libya to Carthage, where he quieted some uprisings. . . . In Africa he fought against a certain Aradion in a duel in which he came off victor."[4]

The Palmyrene generals of Zenobia in Egypt find allies in the Blemmyes, who come north from above the First Cataract and soon overrun the Thebaid.[5]

A.D. 271.

Aurelian breaks the Palmyrene power in Egypt, but the remnants of the forces of Zenobia, together with the rebel Egyptians and the Blemmyes, hold upper Egypt under Firmus.[6]

During this period the Romans have also to engage bands of nomadic robbers who raid from the Libyan desert.[7]

Circa A.D. 292.

Diocletian calls in the Nobatae or Nobadae, a tribe of the western desert, to occupy Nubia, and defend the south Egyptian frontier against the Blemmyes.[8]

In the west, in the Jurjura Mts., breaks out the rebellion of the Quinquegentes, which was eventually crushed by Maximianus.[9]

A.D. 320–325.

Arianism begins to spread.[10]

1 Sanctus Cyprianus, *Epist.* 60 in *Op. Om.* pp. 99, 100. St. Cyprian collected funds for the relief of the plundered Christians of Numidia.

2 Idem, *De haereticis rebaptizandis* (*Op. Om.* p. 329).

3 Inscription from Ṣur el-Ghazlan in T. Shaw, *Travels*, etc., vol. i. p. 95; cf. L. Renier, *Inscriptions romaines de l'Algérie*, p. 25, no. 101; and H. Fournel, *Les Berbers*, vol. i. p. 59.

4 Flavius Vopiscus, *Probus* 9.

5 Zosimus i. 44; Trebellius Pollio, *Claudius II.*; Vopiscus, *Firmus* 2, 3. Cf. D. G. Hogarth, *ap.* W. M. F. Petrie, *Koptos*, p. 34.

6 Vopiscus, *Aurelianus* 32; *Firmus* 5.

7 Zosimus i. 70; Vopiscus, *Probus* 17.

8 Procopius, *De bello Persico* i. 19; cf. J. G. Milne, *History of Egypt under Roman Rule*, p. 86.

9 H. Fournel, *op. cit.* p. 60 and notes; Sext. Aurel. Victor, *De Caesaribus*, 39; Eutropius, *op. cit.* ix. 22; Zonaras, *Annales*, ii. p. 243; Auctor Incertus, *Panegyricus Maximiano et Constantino*, viii. 6.

10 P. Schaff, *History of the Christian Church*, vol. iii. p. 360.

About this time a certain Armatius successfully engaged the Libyan marauders, but died of sickness before achieving any decisive victory.[1]

A.D. 372.

Revolt of Firmus, son of Nubel; Count Theodosius in Africa. Firmus proclaims himself champion of the Donatists, and liberator of Africa. Theodosius crushes the revolt, and is himself rewarded with capital punishment under Gratianus, A.D. 376.[2]

Circa A.D. 390–410.

The Ausuriani or Austuriani, on the borders of Africa and the province of Libya, neighbours of the Mazices,[3] having been for a time quiet, revolted.[4] They ravaged the vicinity of Leptis Magna for three days, and continued to be active even into the reign of Valentinian.[5] About the end of the fourth century they and the Mazices overran the Cyrenaic Pentapolis. The Mazices, during the time of the indolent Strategus Cerealis,[6] actually laid siege to Cyrene itself.[7] The philosopher-bishop Synesius was very active in the defence against these bands, and indeed the Christians of the Pentapolis showed an exemplary degree of bravery in combating their invaders. The clergy of Axomis, near Darnis, having news of a body of marauders who were looting in the wooded valley of Myrtitis, marched forth with their peasant parishioners, and defeated the robbers with slaughter. In that action, the deacon Faustus, at the outset of the conflict, set a good example by felling one of the brigands with a stone, and then seizing his arms.[8] After suffering miserably from bad governors, the Pentapolitans were at length fortunate in having put over them a young and active officer, Anysius, who, with a small force of light horse, hunted down the Ausurian bands, though he lacked strength sufficient to carry war into the enemy's country.

A.D. 428.

Gaiseric, at the head of 80,000 Vandals, crosses into Africa.[9]

A.D. 439.

The Vandals take Carthage.[10] During the Vandalic supremacy in Africa, there were a succession of raids, revolts, and disturbances in the west.[11]

Circa A.D. 445.

Toward the end of the reign of Theodosius II. (d. 450), the Blemmyes are again active in

[1] Priscus Panites, *Frag.* 14 in *FHG.*

[2] H. Fournel, *op. cit.* p. 67 and notes.

[3] Philostorgius, *Eccles. Hist.* xi. 8.

[4] Ammianus Marcellinus xxviii. 6. 2, *paullisper pacati, in geminos turbines revoluti sunt.*

[5] *Ibid.* xxvii. 9. 1.

[6] Cf. Synesius, *Epist.* 74, where the Bishop relates how, in a panic, Cerealis betook himself on ship-board for safety, and thence directed operations against the barbarian harriers. Cerealis' successor, John the Phrygian, was equally worthless (*ibid.* 86, 104), and it was an exception when the Cyreneans found themselves under an honest *praeses* or a *dux* who was better than a robber-chief.

[7] D'Avezac, *L'Afrique, etc.*, p. 136, a condensation of the notices in Synesius.

[8] Synesius, *Epist.* 122.

[9] H. Fournel, *op. cit.* p. 76 *sqq.* and notes.

[10] Procopius, *De bello Vandalico* i. 4.

[11] H. Fournel, *op. cit.* p. 81 *sqq.*

Egypt, and ravage the Oasis Magna. In their retreat, however, they are themselves harried by the Mazices.[1]

A.D. 453.

The general Maximinus, in an expedition against the Blemmyes and Nobatae, takes from them, for the first time, hostages.[2]

A.D. 491.

The Mazices again raid the Pentapolis.[3]

A.D. 518–527.

(Reign of Justin I.) Blemmyes and Mazices plunder Egypt.[4]

A.D. 534.

Fall of the Vandals. The disturbances continue under Byzantine rule.

About this time Justinian forced Christianity on the pagan tribes in the Syrtis and at Augila. He, moreover, repaired many of the old fortresses in Marmarica and Tripolitana, or built new ones.[5]

A.D. 543.

Sergius sent as governor to Tripolitana. According to custom, the chiefs of the Leuathae come with their followers to Leptis Magna to receive from the new governor the usual presents and to go through the form of being re-invested in office. A certain Pudentius, who had had a good deal of experience of the country, recommended to Sergius that only eighty delegates of the tribesmen should be admitted to the town, while the rest of the Libyans, who had come under arms, should remain at some distance from Leptis. Sergius made the delegates fair speeches, and invited them to a banquet, although, according to Procopius, who seeks to excuse what followed, he suspected their good faith. The delegates fell to complaining of certain grievances they had suffered at the hands of the authorities; Sergius made light of their complaints, and gave the signal for retiring. At this moment one of the Leuathae caught the governor by the shoulder, wishing to be heard out; the other Libyans, not without confusion, began to crowd around the pair. At this instant a guardsman drew his sword, and cut down the chief who was detaining Sergius. Uproar ensued; the other delegates were slain on the spot, with the single exception of one who succeeded in escaping. He, when he reached the Libyan camp, inflamed the tribesmen to frenzy with his story. The Leuathae marched on the moment against Leptis, outside of which they met the Byzantine army under Sergius and Pudentius. A fierce hand-to-hand conflict ensued, but the well-armed and disciplined soldiery of Justinian cut the tribesmen to pieces. The Libyan camp was looted, the women and children taken prisoners, and at nightfall Sergius triumphantly re-entered Leptis. Pudentius fell in the battle.[6]

It is not surprising that after such treachery on the part of the Byzantines the Leuathae should embark on a career of rapine and war. Going to Byzacium, where their reassembled forces were

[1] Evagrius, *Hist. Eccles.* i. 7; Coptic *Life of Schnoudi* in the *Mémoires de la Mission Archéologique française*, iv. fol. 53 rect.

[2] J. G. Milne, *op. cit.* p. 100.

[3] D'Avezac, *op. cit.* p. 139.

[4] Coptic *Life of Schnoudi* fol. 47 vers.; Arabic *Life*, p. 380.

[5] Procopius, *De aedificiis* vi. 2 and *passim*.

[6] Procopius, *De bello Vandalico* ii. 21 *sqq*.

joined by the chieftain Antalas, they marched on Carthage. On the road they met the Byzantine general Solomon, and refusing to listen to his overtures, they engaged and defeated him, he himself being taken and slain.[1] The Leuathae then laid siege to Laribus, from which they withdrew on the receipt of a heavy tribute. Sergius, the original cause of these disturbances, was then nominated successor to Solomon, and became speedily an object of hatred to every man under his orders. The Leuathae and Antalas were reinforced from the west by Stozas, with whom they ravaged the country, even taking Hadrumetum.[2] The land became a desert; people fled to Sicily to be safe from the Berbers. It seemed as if Africa was fated to be lost because of the treachery of Sergius, and it was not until Justinian entrusted affairs to Johannes Troglita, an experienced soldier, that matters began to mend.

A general peace of some duration was obtained *circa* 550.[3]

Circa A.D. 580.

Widespread uprisings throughout Africa.[4]

Aristomachus, general of Tiberius II. in Egypt, having defeated the Nubians, turns his arms successfully against the marauding Berbers west of the Nile.[5]

A.D. 616.

In the sixth year of Heraclius the Persians under Chosroes entered and subdued Egypt, and seem to have carried their arms to a point west of the Nile.[6] The statement that they penetrated as far as Carthage, wrecking the shattered Pentapolis on the way, is unfounded.[7]

A.D. 640.

ʿAmr Ibn el-ʿAṣî invades Egypt at the head of an army of Moḥammadan Arabs.

1 Procopius, *loc. cit.*

2 *Ibid.* ii. 23; Theophanes, *Chronogr.* vol. i. p. 325; Count Marcellinus, *Chronicon*, p. 54, col. 1.

3 H. Fournel, *op. cit.* p. 98 *sqq.* The victories of John Troglita form the theme of the *Johannis* of Corippus.

4 Theophanes, *Chronogr.* vol. i. p. 402 *sq.*

5 John of Nikiu, *Chronique*, p. 95. Aristomachus is there said to have subdued the "Mauretanians," but this can only be taken to mean the Libyans west of Egypt.

6 Theophanes, *Chronogr.* p. 252 B, παρέλαβον οἱ Πέρσαι τὴν Αἴγυπτον, καὶ . . . Λιβύην ἕως Αἰθιοπίας . . .; Landolfus Sagax, *Historia miscella*, xx. 5, . . . *totam Aegyptum et Libyam usque ad Aethiopiam*. . . .

7 A number of writers have asserted that the army of Chosroes reached Carthage. They were misled by an erroneous lection of Χαλχηδόνος as Χαρχηδόνος. Even Gibbon committed this mistake (*Decline and Fall*, vol. v. p. 71, and note 76).

A.D. 641.

Having taken Alexandria, ʿAmr marches on Barḳah. He "proceeded at the head of his troops," writes el-Bilad̲urî, "toward the Moghreb, and attacked Barḳah, a city of the Pentapolis. He gave peace to its population, demanding a tribute of 3000 dînars, which they might pay by selling such of their children as they wished to dispose of.[1] . . . ʿAbd Allah Ibn Ṣaliḥ reports on the authority of el-Leyts Ibn Ṣaʿad, who himself reports it from Yezîd Ibn Abî Ḥabîb, that ʿAmr Ibn el-ʿAṣî wrote in the treaty which he gave to the Luatah Berbers, of the country of Barḳah: 'you shall have the right of selling your children and your women to pay off your share of the tribute.'"[2] The inhabitants seem to have collected and remitted this tribute without the unwelcome aid of Arab tax-gatherers.[3] ʿAmr, after subduing Barḳah, sent a light expedition south-westerly into the desert under the command of ʿOḳba Ibn Nafîʿ, who later rose to such eminence as a Moslem general.[4]

A.D. 642–643.[5]

Second expedition of ʿAmr Ibn el-ʿAṣî toward the west. ʿAmr sends in advance ʿOḳba Ibn Nafîʿ toward Barḳah and Zawîlah and the neighbouring districts, which submit. ʿAmr then marches in person and raids Tripoli,[6] which he takes, as well as the mountains of the Nufusa, which were inhabited by Christians.[7] At this time, Arab raids became common in Tripolitana.[8]

A.D. 646.

First great incursion of the Arabs into el-Moghreb.[9]

With this invasion the history of the ancient Libyans may be said to have ended, and that of the modern Berbers to have begun. The long and exhausting succession of wars and raids, the occupations of different parts of Eastern Libya by the Egyptians, the Carthaginians, Greeks, Romans, Vandals, and Byzantines, the introduction of Christianity and of Islamism, all contributed to confuse and to change the ethnology in the northern and eastern zones. In Moḥammadan times the Berbers of Tripolitana and Marmarica tended to become more and more Semiticized, both in speech and in blood. The unruly spirit which the Berbers have always displayed led, as before, to various seditions and uprisings,[10] but with these later struggles of a people that had lost their ethnic purity this study is not concerned. The Arab pressure from the east tended for centuries to push the Berbers of Eastern Libya toward the west, and south toward the desert. So completely Arabized is most of Eastern Libya at the present time that it

1 El-Bilad̲urî, *Liber expugnationis regionum*, p. 224.

2 *Ibid.* p. 225. Ibn el-At̲îr, *Chronicon*, vol. iii. p. 20, states the tribute to have been 13,000 dînars, with which Ibn ʿAbd el-Ḥakam, *Futuh Miṣr.*, vol. i. p. 302, agrees.

3 Ibn ʿAbd el-Ḥakam, *loc. cit.*

4 M. Caudel, *Les Premières Invasions arabes dans l'Afrique du Nord*, p. 43 *sq.*

5 Ibn el-At̲îr, *op. cit.* iii. p. 20; Abu 'l-Maḥasin, *Annales*, p. 85; Ibn ʿAbd el-Ḥakam, *loc. cit.* These writers place the date at 22 A.H. Ibn Abî 'l-Dînar, *Kitab el-Munis*, p. 23, fixes it at 23 A.H. On this divergence see H. Fournel, *op. cit.* p. 18 notes 3 and 4.

6 For the details Ibn el-At̲îr, *op. cit.* iii. p. 20; Ibn ʿAbd el-Hakam, *op. cit.* part i. p. 87.

7 Ibn Abî 'l-Dînar, *loc. cit.*

8 El-Malekî, *Rîad̲ en Nofus*, fol. 2 vers. 1, 9, text cited by M. Caudel, *op. cit.* p. 48, note 3.

9 M. Caudel, *op. cit.* p. 49 *sqq.*

10 Cf. S. Lane-Poole, *History of Egypt in the Middle Ages*, pp. 24, 31 *sq.*, 126, etc.

is a matter for astonishment that in Wagîlah, Sîwah, and Manshîah el-ʿAghuzah (in Farafrah) the old Berber language has persisted, though in the last hundred years Arabic has become more common, and is destined soon completely to supplant the native tongue.

The value of the dry and disjointed chronicle of the affairs of the Eastern Libyans which makes up the greater part of this chapter may not at first be evident, and can be appreciated only by one somewhat familiar with the later history of this people.[1] In ancient times, the history of the Libyans is one of continued protest against foreign dominion, and of failure to amalgamate successfully with their European invaders. With the Carthaginians they certainly mixed to some extent, as is testified by the very name "Libyphoenicians"; with the other colonists there was less fusion. No conspicuous result of these fusions appeared until Arabic times. Then arose the great Berber-Arab dynasties of the Atlas, and eventually the Negro-Berber-Arab Songhay Empire in the south-west. The fierce marauders of the earlier period are seen in later days to have acquired to some extent a quality which, before the advent of the Arabs, they so conspicuously lacked—stability. How much of this characteristic was due to the new faith and how much to Arab fusion it is impossible to say; but when one considers the diversity of religious opinion among Moslemic Berbers and their tendency to heretical views, one is inclined to give a good deal of weight to the second factor. In ancient times great Libyan kingdoms, like that of Juba, had existed in the west; there had been in the east great federations like those which invaded Egypt; but there were no consolidated powers such as those of the Sanhaǵah or Almoravid Dynasties of mediaeval times.[1]

Fierce, predatory, impatient of foreign dominion, and incapable of civilizing themselves, the Libyans seem to have been a race without a mission—unless for the influence, not yet determined, which they may have exerted at an early period in Egypt—until, not without turmoil, they became sufficiently united with the Arabs under el-Islam to give strength and weight to the Moḥammadan dynasties of Africa and Spain.

[1] For which the reader may be referred to H. Fournel, *op. cit.*, with the continuation (vol. ii.) edited by H. de Pierrebourg, or the convenient little synopsis of V. Piquet, *Les Civilisations de l'Afrique du Nord.*

APPENDICES

APPENDIX I

ON THE "C GROUP" PEOPLE OF NUBIA

I HAVE not the intention, nor, until the final reports of the Nubian Archaeological Survey have appeared, the right, to give here a detailed description of the so-called "C Group" or "Middle Nubian" cemeteries excavated by the Khedivial Government between the First Cataract and the Second. What I intend is merely to state my belief as to the ethnological position of the original "C Group" people, by way of an Appendix to what, in the second chapter of the foregoing essay, has been said concerning the southern range of a portion of the Eastern Libyans. For this purpose I shall use the materials published *passim* in the Reports and Bulletins of the Survey, to which, without explicit citation, the reader is referred for the facts adduced in this discussion.

Isolation of "C Group."—The so-called "C Group" cemeteries of Nubia, it was early recognized, were those of a distinctly non-Egyptian people. They extend in time from about the end of the VIth Dynasty to the XVIIIth Dynasty, although the lower date is one to be stated with some reserve. The only people with whom the "C Group" folk are certainly to be connected are those of the so-called "Pan-Graves," a people whose burials occur sporadically in Egypt, as at Hu, Deyr el-Ballas, and Ḫizam. Despite the marked traces of negrism which the majority of the "C Group" exhibit, Dr. Reisner, recognizing the importance of the fact that these traces were most striking in the *later* burials, remarked: "I would like to suggest as a basis for future investigation that the communities which produced" the "C Group" culture "were wandering desert tribes of Nubian origin, living along the edge of the cultivation, much like the Ababdeh in Upper Egypt at the present time, and the Bedawin in Lower Egypt." In the light of the textual evidence presented *supra*, Chapter II., and of certain anthropological and archaeological details which I shall now bring forward, I believe the early suggestion of Dr. Reisner may now be accepted as fact, with the single but important change of substituting "Libyan" for "Nubian."

Physical Character of "C Group."—Since the later "Middle Nubian" crania exhibit negroid traits to a higher degree than do the earlier, it is the former rather than the latter which it is here important to consider. The final anatomical report upon these crania has not appeared; but the reader may appreciate the Mediterranean character of the less negroid skulls from the three here reproduced (Pl. XI.). The aspect of these skulls is ellipsoidal; the occiput tends to flatness; and the frontal eminence to prominence. The bridge of the nose is flattened, but the margins of the nares are usually sharp. The subnasal prognathism of the "C Group" is not of the characteristic negroid type, being, in the words of Dr. G. E. Smith, "an exaggerated form of that prognathism which is so common in the Predynastic Egyptian." Only by exception is the hair woolly or "peppercorn-like"; as a rule it is straight or wavy. The following figures from the observations of Dr. D. E. Derry may here be cited, for although they are taken from subjects between whose lives as much as a thousand years may have intervened, they serve to indicate the general nature of these crania:—

Elements.	Men.		Women.	
	No.	mm.	No.	mm.
Maximum length	123	183.0	132	176.5
Maximum breadth	117	134.0	127	130.3
Height	96	135.0	114	129.3
Cranial base	102	101.8	117	96.4
Facial base	89	99.6	106	96.1
Upper facial height	53	67.2	56	64.5
Nasal index	53	51.5	58	52.7
Cephalic index	41	72.98	42	73.51

I am not in a position to say positively that these figures and the general aspect of the skulls from which they are taken link the "C Group" with such North African crania as those from Rokniah or Biskrah,[1] but will be content merely to recall what has been said in Chapter II. in regard to the appearance of a negroid Libyan type in the Egyptian representations (cf. Figs. 3, 4), and to repeat that, broadly speaking, the "C group" skulls exhibit certain "Mediterranean" aspects. The pilous system of the "Middle Nubian" is, when not negroid, that of the *brun* Berbers.

It is a remarkable fact that the "C Group" crania have an indubitable relationship with those of Predynastic Egypt. As the proto-Berber element in the Egyptian language testifies to the early fusion of the Libyans with the other ethnic elements which made the historic Egyptian race, the affinities between the early "C Group" and Predynastic crania accord well with the theory that the "Middle Nubians" were of Libyan origin.

Archaeology of the Middle Nubians.—It was on archaeological grounds that I first sought to relate the "C Group" to the Eastern Libyans, and I here submit the chief features in their culture which tend to substantiate this theory.[2]

A. The *burials*, as among those Libyans who were least affected by foreign customs, were in a contracted position. The bodies normally lay on the right side with the head to the east. The knees were not drawn up under the chin, but the thighs were at right angles to the spine, the legs being so doubled at the knee that the heels touched the buttocks. The practice of contraction is too widespread to count here as positive evidence; but its absence would be a strong presumption against a Libyan origin.

B. The *earlier graves* are circular or oval, are deep, and are covered with stone slabs. The later graves are rectangular, in consequence, I believe, of the growth of the Negro element, the typical Negro graves of Late New Empire times in the Egyptian Sudan being rectangular. The late "C Group" graves are generally diamagnetic.

Around the graves, by way of superstructure, runs a circular wall of stones, often of considerable diameter. The space enclosed by this was filled with

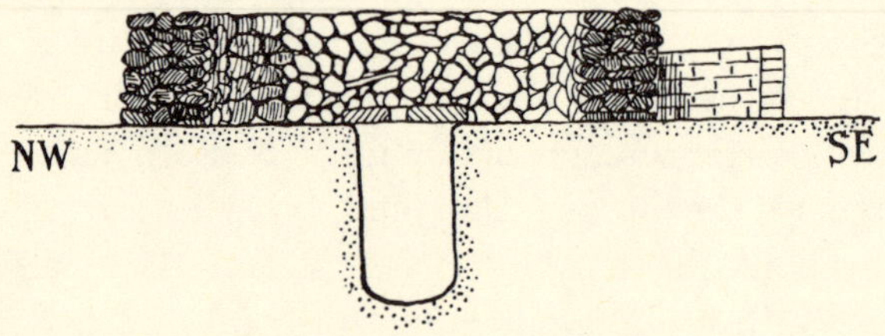

FIG. 90*a*.

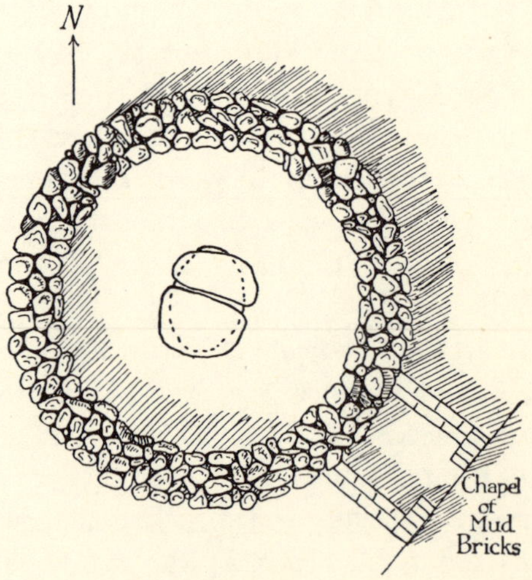

FIG. 90*b*.

[1] Cf. D. R. MacIver and A. Wilken, *Libyan Notes*, pp. 91 and 92 *sqq.*; and pls. xviii., xix.

[2] What immediately follows is an expansion of a letter sent by me to Dr. D. E. Derry, dated "Sebustîah, Syria, 12th August 1910."

PLATE XI.

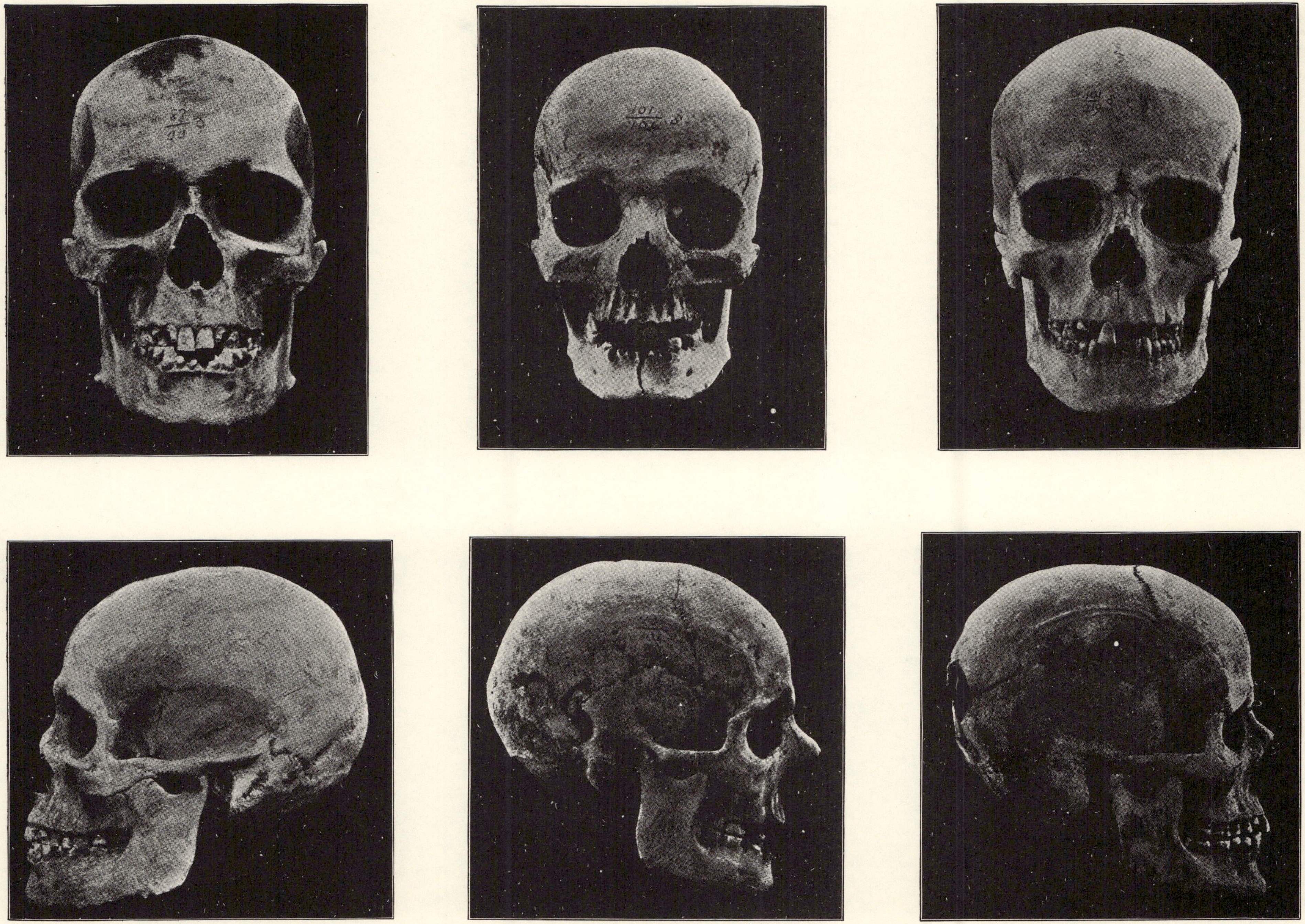

"C-GROUP" CRANIA.

earth or small stones, so as to make a circular cairn under which the pit of the grave lies concealed and protected. Even after the shape of the grave changed from circular to rectangular, the round superstructure persisted. On the east or south-east side of the superstructure was regularly located an offering-chapel of mud-brick, in which was placed the funerary pottery, with the exception of certain types of finely decorated ware, which, probably on account of their superior fabric, were deposited in the actual grave with the personal ornaments and toilet articles. An example of such a " C Group " grave of the early period is shown in Fig. 90 *a*, *b*.

These remarkable graves I would relate to the great and widespread North African circular type —the class known in the Western Sahara as the *reǵem* (pl. *riǵam*).[1] These exhibit a variety of forms, and range in workmanship from the rude cairns of the Sud Oranais, or the circles of " Seal Island," to such finished monuments as the circular tomb of Kubbah (Cyrenaica), the " Tombeau de la Chrétienne," or the tomb of Medrasen—mausolea which are, while African in origin, wholly classical in execution. As an example of this type, I shall cite first a *reǵem* at ʿAyn Sefrah, from the excellent book of E.-F. Gautier, who first recorded it (section in Fig. 91).[2] This circular monument is about 8 m. in diameter and some 2.20 m. high. The cairn or tumulus, with its step-like retaining wall, surrounds and covers a circular grave, 1 m. in diameter, at its centre. The grave is half cut out in the soil and half within the superstructure, the roofing being of slabs raised above the ground-level on others laid flat around the edge of the grave.[3] The burials in these graves are regularly contracted, and the type is one common in the vicinity of Gebel Mekter.[4] External offering-places, differing but slightly from those of the " C Group " superstructures, are not infrequent.

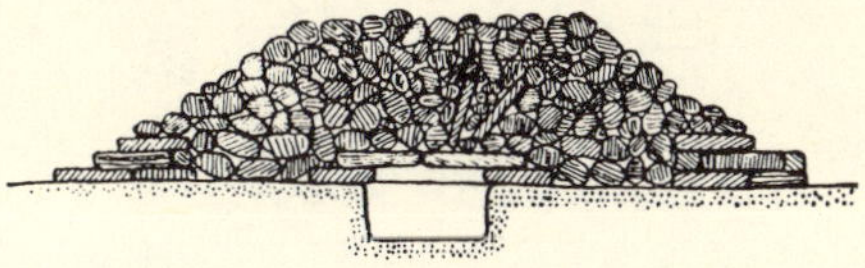

FIG. 91.

It is so far a cry from the Nubian Nile to the Sud Oranais that the instance cited would be of no archaeological value unless it could be shown that the *riǵam* had a continental distribution. This can be done without difficulty, excellent examples of this type of grave-structure existing in eastern Algeria, and even as near to Egypt as at " Seal Island " in the Gulf of Bombah. A plan of one of the east Algerian *riǵam* is seen in Fig. 92. The original is one of many such structures at Ṣenam Msilah. As a rule the circles measure about eight to ten metres in diameter, and are made of natural slabs embedded edgeways in the ground. The circular walls invariably have chapels in them, and these are almost always placed on the south-east. Traces of the filling of the circular enclosures are still discernible in the form of numerous stones lying within them.[5]

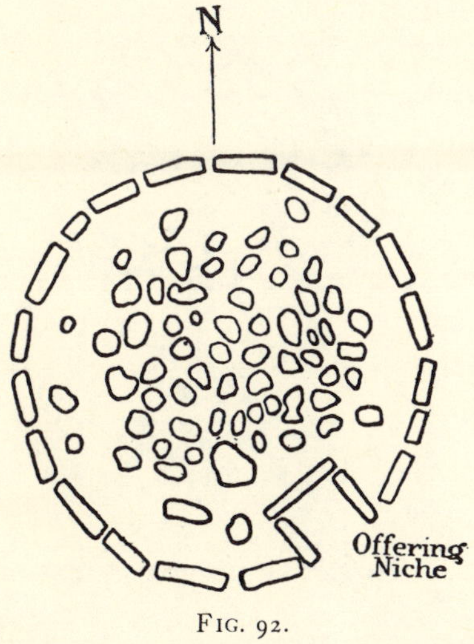

FIG. 92.

The *riǵam* of "Seal Island" are occasionally polycellular, probably because of lack of space and from the desire to save labour in building by the use of the outside of an old wall as part of a new *reǵem*. Both these factors contributed to the development of polycellular tombs ; but numerous examples of the simple circular type are to be found, an example being shown in Fig. 93 *a*, *b*, *c*. Here the stone circle (93, *a*) measures about 9 m. across and about 1.15 m. in height. The wall is built of small stones, and rests, as is regularly the case in these remains, on the granular limestone rock. On the south side, four rude slabs are arranged

[1] رجم *plur.* رجام, *sepulchrum* ; from رجم, *lapidibus iecit.*

[2] E.-F. Gautier, *Sahara algérien*, p. 64 *sqq.* for the date of the *riǵam*.

[3] The slabs over the grave within the superstructure may in the instance shown be the remains of an upper chamber.

[4] E.-F. Gautier, *op. cit.* p. 69.

[5] D. R. MacIver and A. Wilken, *Libyan Notes*, p. 79 *sq.*

so as to make an offering-niche in the bottom of the wall (Fig. 93, *c*, and section *b*). Sometimes the superstructures take an elliptical shape, as in an instance where the major axis of the enclosure measured 8.40 m. and the minor 6.90 m. Again, instead of the four slabs which usually make the top, sides, and back of the niche, this feature may be in the form of a small "chapel" against the tomb, with the walls slightly lower than those of the enclosure.

The heavy rains which annually visit "Seal Island" have in most cases washed away the earth from within the walls, which are themselves generally in a very ruinous condition; but that they once contained earth may be seen from such an example as that shown in Fig. 94. In this case, the smallness of the tomb and the exceptional thickness of the walls have held the earth in place.

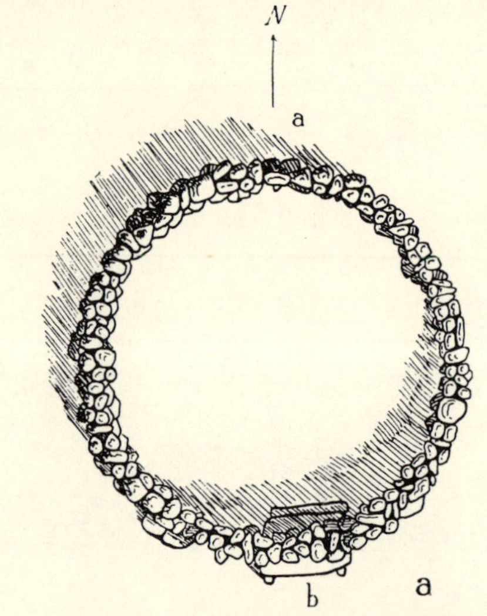

a

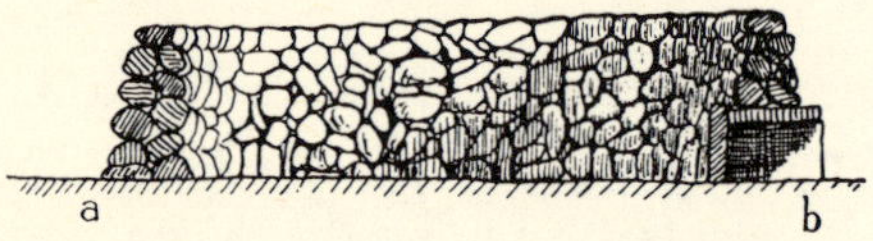

b

c

FIG. 93.

It cannot be denied that the "Seal Island" *rigam* exhibit marked affinities to the "C Group" graves. They are probably late in date, though certainly pre-Islamic; but that, even in Byzantine times, the part of Libya in which they are situated was very slightly affected by foreign influences will be admitted by any one acquainted with Synesius's account of the simplicity of the natives of Marmarica whom he saw while storm-bound on their coast;[1] and there can be no doubt that the "Seal Island" *rigam* are purely Berber monuments reflecting an early and widespread type. The chief differences from the "C Group" which they present are: (*a*) the orientation of the offering niches in most cases toward the south; (*b*) the absence, as far as can be ascertained without excavation,[2] of the grave-pits. The latter difference, I believe to be due to local conditions, as the soil is rarely more than five centimetres deep on the island and the rock is stubborn. As in the "C Group" graves the offerings were mainly outside the superstructure, so at "Seal Island" scarce a shard was found within the circles, although outside them fragments, small and weather-beaten, of coarse brown ware or of cheap Roman pottery were numerous. The small size of some of the tombs—*e.g.* that shown in Fig. 94—testifies to the fact that the Seal Island burials were in some, if not in all cases, contracted.

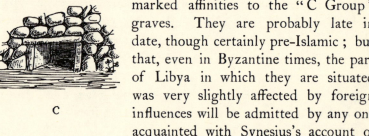

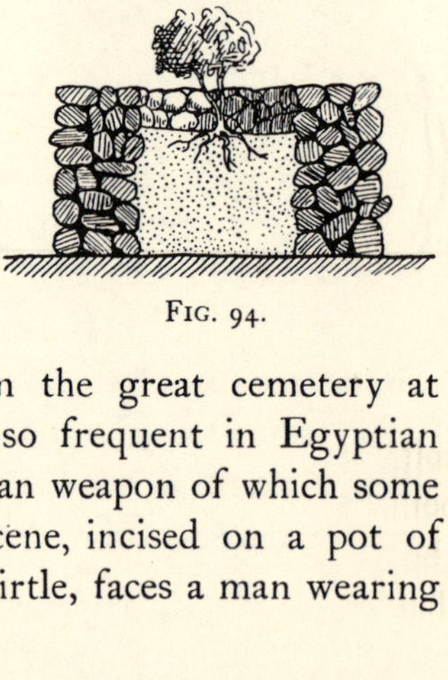

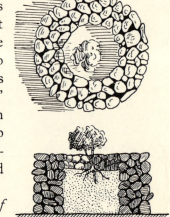

FIG. 94.

C. The "C Group" material affords several *representations of the human figure*, both graphic and plastic. The latter appear to be mostly women, but several of the former represent men. Fig. 95*a* shows two bowmen on a fragment of smoothed, coarse red ware from the great cemetery at Dakkah (Pselchis). The figure on the right is wearing the cross-bands so frequent in Egyptian representations of Libyans, and both are armed with bows, a common Libyan weapon of which some Aethiopians seem to have been ignorant, even in late times. Another scene, incised on a pot of the same ware, is shown in Fig. 95*b*. A steatopygous woman, wearing a kirtle, faces a man wearing

[1] Synesius, *Epist.* xvi.

[2] What is said here of the Seal Island remains, I have extracted from a notebook written during a brief and unsatisfactory visit to the Gulf of Bombah in 1909. I had then no opportunity of making even *sondages*, and have since been unable to revisit the locality.

a sporran-like apron and having in his hair a plume. To the right are traces of a third figure, partially erased by the artist. The complete figures support between them some caduceus-like object; above their heads, at the back of each, is an object recalling the ancient Egyptian or modern African head-rest. The kirtle of the woman agrees with the data concerning Libyan female dress given in Chapter VII.; but that of the man, if, as appears, he is really wearing a "sporran" and not a *penistasche*, is not typical of the Libyans of the monuments. On his head he wears a single plume. It would be impossible to say definitely whether the wearer was in this point conforming to Libyan or to Aethiopian custom, did not other evidence, recently collected in Nubia, prove the former to have been the case. From Amadah comes the XVIIIth Dynasty jar-sealing here represented in Fig. 96. The device stamped on the sealing is one very common in Egyptian graphic art: a victorious ruler standing behind his bound and crouching captive. This sealing is to be related to the "C Group" drawing (Fig. 95 *b*) both by the plume worn by the victor, and by the occurrence, in the field of the stamp, of the same caduceus-like emblem which in the "C Group" drawing the man and the woman support between them.[1] In its turn, the Amadah sealing is identical in period, fabric, and type, with a number of others found at Buhen. But these latter, in place of the "caduceus," have in the field the hieroglyph 𓋀, for 𓋀𓏏𓈖, *imnt*, or 𓋀𓏏𓏏𓈖, *imntt*, "the West"; and the victor grasps in his left hand a bow, which he holds horizontally.[2] The hieroglyph naturally belongs not to the captive, but to the dominant figure in the scene: a point substantiated by the fact that the latter wears a plume. Thus, through the medium of the Amadah sealing, one has a clear connection between plume-wearing "caduceus"-bearer on the "C Group" pot, and the plume-wearing westerner of the Buhen sealings. If it be asked how the latter appears on jar-seals of Egyptian type, found in a site strongly Egyptian in character, the answer is not far to seek: the victor is some Libyco-Nubian dynast[3] in the Egyptian service during the campaigns which from the time of Ahmose I. were conducted south of the First Cataract.

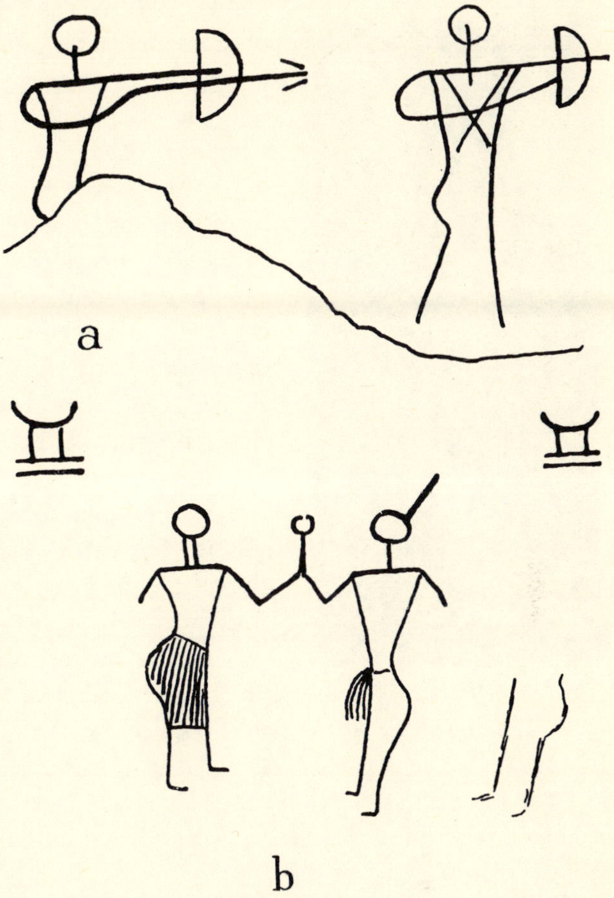

FIG. 95.

FIG. 96.

[1] This emblem recalls curiously an archaic sign (of Min?) noted at Diospolis Parva. W. M. F. Petrie, *Diospolis Parva*, plate v. B 102.

[2] D. R. Maciver and C. L. Wooley, *Buhen*, Text, p. 117, and Plates, pl. 47 (three lowest figures). Maciver and Wooley recognize the common origin of the Buhen and Amadah seals.

[3] The presence of much late "C Group" pottery in the Egyptian fortress of Kubban (Contra-Pselchis) points to the closeness of the relations between the Egyptians in Nubia and the remnants of the old "C Group" population in the XVIIIth Dynasty. If, as I suppose, the "C Group" were southern Temeḥu, this point is important, since it shows the late "C Group" people in the same relation to the Egyptians as that of the Amadah and Buhen dynasts.

Of the plastic figures of the "Middle Nubians," one of the most remarkable is the fragmentary image shown in Fig. 97. The sex is not easily determinable; I incline to believe it intended for a male. It is remarkable as wearing the cross-bands, and the lines of dots descending to the shoulders from the ears may represent side-locks, the plastic portrayal of which the artist felt to be beyond him. (Cf. the rudimentary representation of the arms.)

Fig. 97.

The plastic representations frequently imitate tattooing or painting. For as black galena has been found in the graves, it seems that it was one of these two forms of body decoration, and not cicatrization, that the figurines portray.

The elements observable in "C Group" decorations are shown in Fig. 98. They are so simple as to have only a slight archaeological significance, but they are absolutely the same from a cultural point of view as the Libyan tattoo-marks shown in Fig. 52, and in some cases identical with them.

In concluding this note, I may mention that at Gebel Abu Dîrwah, a few miles inland from Dakkah, are a number of petroglyphs which Mr. C. M. Firth relates to the "C Group" people. Most of these glyphs are of ostriches, giraffes, etc., but one shows a man's profile of distinctly Libyan type.[1]

D. As far as divinable, the *religion* of the "Middle Nubians" offers close analogies to that of the Eastern Libyans. The "C Group" people did not share in the fish taboos of the Aethiopians, for copper fish-hooks have been occasionally found in the graves. As in Libya, the cultus of the dead was strongly developed, and the cow-worship which, owing to Libyan influence, permeated the Western Delta, is paralleled among the "C Group."

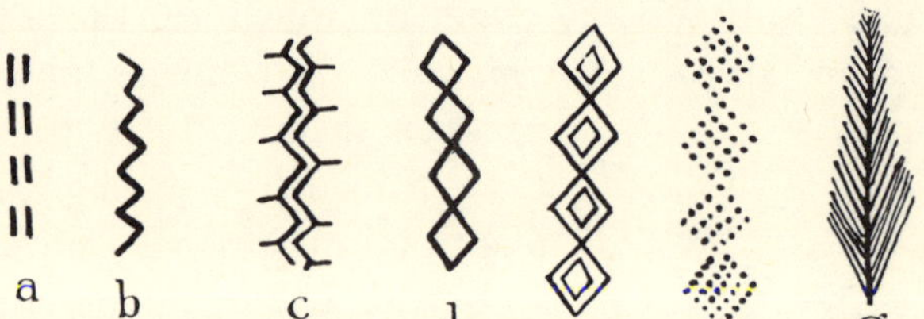

Fig. 98.

Among the circular superstructures in Dakkah cemetery were found a number of sandstone slabs. Those in position were planted upright in the ground. They were carefully, though irregularly, worked; and two had on them representations of cows with their calves. The drawings had incised outlines, were coloured red or black, and both from their position and from their careful execution were unmistakably of religious significance.

E. The *material culture* of the "C Group" agrees well with that of the Eastern Libyans. The presence of copper in the graves is to be accounted for by the geographical position of the people, opposite the river-terminus of a road to the mines of the Eastern Desert.[2] Bone implements, traces of goat-skin and dyed leather, and of loose linen coverings are common. The plate-bead belts of the Abusîr relief seem, as has been mentioned in Chapter VII., to be the peculiarly strung nacre[3] plate-beads so characteristic of the "C Group"; and the two great classes of "Middle Nubian" pottery are, as in both ancient and modern Libya, the cup and the jar. In short, if the Eastern Libyans of the Egyptian period had followed the natural road south from Ḫargah Oasis to the

[1] I regret that I have not a photograph. It is on the west face of the rock described in *Bull. Nub.* v. p. 10, near the middle of the rock-face, about breast-high, and is drawn as though the head were thrown back. It faces south (spectator's right), and shows a slightly aquiline, orthognathous, bearded head.

[2] Cuprous ore occurs, together with slags, etc., both at Kubban (Contra-Pselchis) and at Koshtamnah.

[3] L. Borchardt, *Grabdenkmal des Königs Ne-User-Re*, p. 47, says of these plate-bead girdles: *Der Gurt und sein halbkreisförmiger Anhang scheinen aus Perlen zu bestehen.*

vicinity of Derr, and established themselves on the river as sedentaries, their material culture would not, in any particular that can be named, have varied importantly from that of the early "C Group."

Conclusion

The evidence which would indicate that the "Middle Nubians" were of Libyan origin may thus be summarized from what has been said in this Appendix and in the text:—

1. The great "C Group" cemeteries are on the west bank of the Nile, in a district geographically connected with the Egyptian Oases.	1. The Libyans were first the sole occupants of the oases, and later, as the Libyaegyptians of Ptolemy, the preponderating element. Their southerly position on the Nile is explicitly attested by Strabo, and indirectly by the Harkhuf inscriptions, and by BAR iv. §§ 373, 389, 482.[1]
2. The "C Group" were originally a people with "Mediterranean" crania, though they steadily became more negroid toward New Empire times. They never lost completely their original physical characteristics, and they had striking physical affinities with Predynastic Egyptians.	2. A prognathous, platyrrhinian, thick-lipped type of Libyan is occasionally seen on the Egyptian monuments of the New Empire, *e.g.* Figs. 3, 4, and N. de G. Davies, *Rock Tombs of el Amarna*, part i. plate xxv. and text p. 33.[2] Libyan element in Predynastic Egyptians.
3. "C Group" burials "laxly contracted."	3. Libyan burials contracted in a "sitting posture."
4. Circular superstructures to "C Group" graves. Offering chapels outside.	4. Libyan *reğem*-type throughout North Africa. Seal Island *riğam* with offering places outside circle.
5. "C Group" representations of men with cross-bands. Woman with kirtle from waist. Man wearing feather. Plastic representation of side-lock (?).	5. Libyan cross-bands. (Almost unknown among other Africans represented in Egypt.) Women with kirtles. Libyan plumes. Libyan side-lock.
6. Tattooing or body-painting among "C Group."	6. Libyan tattooing: designs similar to those of "C Group."
7. "C Group" cow-cultus.	7. Libyan cow-cultus.
8. "C Group" material culture: leather garments, bone tools, mats, plate-beads of nacre. (Copper, *ut supra*, from the Egyptian mines east of the Nile.)	8. Libyan material culture: leather garments, mats, plate-beads of nacre (?). (From foreign sources a supply of copper weapons, etc.)
9. Two great "C Group" divisions of pottery: the bowl and the jar. Northern character of "C Group" fabrics, red, polished, black-mouthed ware, as in Cyprus and Predynastic Egypt; negro character of technique: (punctured ornamentation, etc.).	9. Libyan pottery: the "cylix" and the "hydria." Black-topped, polished, red-ware pottery and geometric incised grey or brown ware of Egypt, possibly due to Libyan element in Predynastic Egyptians.

From these parallels I incline to believe that the "Middle Nubians" were originally a body of Libyans, who, while not strong enough to establish themselves, except in small encampments (as at

[1] Add to this, and to what has been said *supra*, Chapter II., the notice for Teḥenu Libyans south of Derr, near Anibis, in H. Brugsch, *Geschichte Ägyptens*, p. 629, citing LD ciii. 229 c, lines 9-10 (= BAR iv. § 482). Cf. also W. M. Müller, *Egyptological Researches*, ii. p. 136.

[2] The negroid head for which J. Capart (*Débuts de l'Art*, p. 250, fig. 179, and p. 256) claims a Libyan origin cannot be here adduced as evidence, since there is no good ground for calling it "Libyan" at all.

Hu, Ḫizam, and Deyr el-Ballas), on the Egyptian Nile, were powerful enough to plant themselves along a stretch of the river between the First and Second Cataracts. For reasons given in the text I believe, furthermore, that it was the Libyan group known as the Temeḥu to which the "C Group" belonged; and that somewhere in the vicinity of Derr lay the region which, by a slight and very natural error, is called the "district of Teḥenut" (*Tyḥnwt*) in the inscriptions of the XXth Dynasty tomb of Penno (*temp.* Rameses IV.).[1] The Egyptians did not always discriminate between the Temeḥu and the Teḥenu, and that a stone[2] named after the former should come from a region occasionally miscalled after the latter is not strange when it is remembered that both names were used almost generically for "Libyan."

[1] BAR iv. § 482.

[2] BAR iv. §§ 373, 389; and *vide supra*, p. 48 *sq*.

APPENDIX II

ON TWO INSCRIPTIONS FROM GHEYTAH

EXCAVATING some third century (A.D.) graves at Gheytah in the Egyptian Delta, Petrie and Duncan discovered two covering-slabs bearing the inscriptions here reproduced in Fig. 99, *a*, *b*. The texts were first published "as archaic Greek, dating from the 6th or 7th century B.C.," but the excavators added that the inscriptions, "though . . . written in Greek characters," were in an unknown language.[1] A year later, in his *Ghizeh and Rifeh*, Petrie stated that the texts were "in the Tifinar character, as used among the Tuareg of Algeria at present."[2] It is because of this statement that they demand notice here.

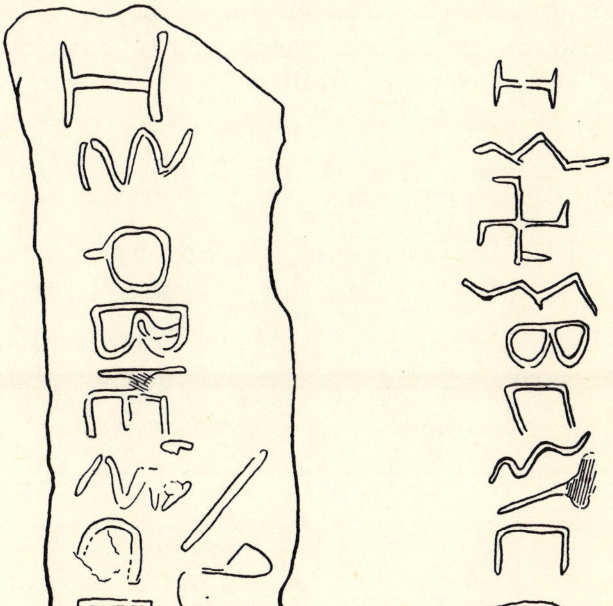

a b

FIG. 99.

No examples of Tifinagh (as opposed to its parent Libyan) are known before mediaeval times; the Gheytah inscriptions contain letters which are not found in either the Libyan or the Tifinagh alphabets; and of the two names which, with difficulty, Petrie transliterates from the texts one, "YSHMYN," he is forced to regard as a corruption of the Semitic יִשְׁמָעֵאל, while the other, "SHNTHY," he can apparently relate to nothing in either the Semitic or Hamitic onomastica. Moreover, Petrie's lection of the first signs in each text as JYR and JYRT respectively, and his seeing in the second instance a T- affix conveying "the sense of becoming or passing into a condition" is no more convincing than his relation of JYR(T) to the Kabyle *geri*, "to remain," the radical of which would be not JYR or GYR, but GR. For these reasons Petrie's second explanation of the inscriptions may be dismissed as as inconclusive as his first.

The fact that Gheytah occupies exactly or very nearly the site of the Roman *Vicus Iudaeorum* suggests the real nature of the inscriptions: they are in a writing very closely allied to Safaitic, Lihyanic, and Thamudenian—Semitic systems which were all in use at the time to which the Gheytah burials are archaeologically assignable. As characteristic examples may be cited the fourth sign

[1] W. M. F. Petrie and J. G. Duncan, *Hyksos and Israelite Cities* (double volume), p. 60 *sq*. In the Plate (xlviii.) showing the inscriptions they are dated seventh century B.C.

[2] Idem, *Ghizeh and Rifeh* (double volume), p. 44, *Addendum to "Hyksos and Israelite Cities."*

from the top in Fig. 99, *a* (= the fifth from the top in 99, *b*), the מ of the Semitic alphabets mentioned; the bottom sign in the short tag (right hand) in 99, *a* = צ; while the second and seventh signs from the top in 99, *a* (= the second, etc., in 99, *b*) is the usual wavy שׁ.[1]

The inscriptions are written vertically, and the tag in 99, *a* indicates that, as here reproduced, they should be read upwards. The initial pairs of signs are common to both texts, as are also the final pairs. The initial element (bottom pair in 99, *a*, left, and in 99, *b*) I would transliterate as ṬB. A natural value for this is found in the Chaldaic טָב, "good" = Hebr. טוֹב, "good"; cf. the Hebr. טוֹב, pret. טבו, "to be good," adj. טוֹב, "good"; καλός, *bonus*, in the sense of *vir bonus*, *honestus*.[2] The terminal element in the texts is also a biliteral, which I would read as ŠZ, ŠḎ, with the force of "cut off" or "departed," by Arab. شَذَّ, *solus separatus fuit, se separavit seorsim mansit.* شَاذٌّ *separatus, solus.* This gives a very acceptable form of mortuary inscription: an honorific, a name, and a verb or verbal adjective denoting death. As for the names, I give my transcription only with reserve. The 卐, *swastika*, in 99, *b*, I regard not as a letter, but as a mere ornament or as a *signum emphaticum.* I tentatively read the name of 99, *a* as ŠT–NMY, perhaps = שֵׁת-نَمَى; שֵׁת pr. n. connected with שֵׁת, "buttocks," and with שָׁת, "columns," etc. (*i.e.* "foundation," "firmness") and so (Gesenius, *in verb.*), "princes," "nobles"; and نَمَى, *increvit, augmentum cepit*, etc. Hence this name would have the force of "*Sedes Incrementarum.*" The tag (bottom, right) is illegible, but may have been, as commonly, a locative. The name in 99, *b*, with similar reserve, I would read as YŠB–MŠ = יֹשֵׁב-מֵשׁ, "dwelling-in-purity"; cf. יֹשֵׁב-בַּשֶּׁבֶת, pr. n., "sitting-in-consessus"; *יָשַׁב, "to sit," "to be seated," "to tarry," and (frequently) "to dwell," "to dwell in," "to inhabit," Hoph. "to be made to dwell," etc.; *מָשַׁע and Arab. مسّع, which by the loss of ع has given the derived مَشَّ, *abstersit*, "to make clean," "to purify"; cf. the pr. n. מִשְׁעָם, Miše'am, apparently = "their-cleansing."

The Gheytah inscriptions, therefore, are not Berber, but Semitic, and may thus be translated:—

Fig. 99, *a*, "The worthy ŠT–NMY; departed" . . .
Fig. 99, *b*, "The worthy YŠB–MŠ; departed."

[1] For the Thamudenian alphabet see J. J. Hess, *Die Entzifferung der tamüdischen Inschriften*, in *RT*, vol. xxxiii. pl. vi.; for the Safaitic, E. Littmann, *Zur Entzifferung der Ṣafâ-Inschriften*, Pl. i.; for Safaitic and Lihyanic, R. Dussaud and F. Macler, *Voyage, etc.*, p. 13.

[2] W. Gesenius, *Hebrew Lexicon*, *in verb.* טָב, *טוֹב. Perhaps these words are both allied to the Arab. طَبَّ, *leniter egit, humanum se praebuit* (G. W. Freytag, *Lexicon*, *in verb*). For טָב in personal names with same force as above, cf. טָבְאֵל, "God-is-good," by Syriasm for טוֹבְאֵל (*Isaiah* vii. 6).

APPENDIX III

TRADITIONAL LIBYAN ORIGINS

SEVERAL notices regarding the origin of the Libyans as a whole, and of separate Libyan tribes, have survived from classical times. These notices are not without interest as exhibiting the mental cast of the proto-Berbers, but to suppose them of any great historical value, as not a few recent writers have done, is to assume that the folk-memory of the North Africans was phenomenally tenacious.

In his *Jugurthine War*, the Roman historian Sallust presents his readers with the following account of the origin of the native Africans :

"Africa," he writes, "was in the beginning peopled by the Gaetulians and Libyans, rude and uncivilized tribes, who subsisted on the flesh of wild animals, or on the herbage of the soil like cattle. They were controlled by neither customs, laws, nor the authority of any ruler ; they roamed about, without fixed habitations, and slept in those shelters to which night drove them. But after Hercules, as the Africans believe, perished in Spain, his army, which was made up of different nations . . . was quickly disbanded. Of its constituent troops, the Medes, Persians, and Armenians, having sailed over into Africa, occupied the parts nearest to the sea [*i.e.* the Mediterranean]. The Persians . . . settled more toward the [Atlantic] ocean,[1] and used the inverted hulls of their vessels as huts, there being no wood in their country, and no chance of getting it, either by purchase or barter, from the Spaniards, because a wide sea and an unfamiliar tongue were barriers to all intercourse. These [Persians] by degrees intermarried with the Gaetulians ; and because, from constantly trying different soils, they were for ever shifting their abodes, they called themselves Numidians [*Numidas*].[2] And to this day the huts of the Numidian peasantry, which they call *mapalia*, are of an oblong shape, with covered roofs, resembling the hulls of ships.

"The Medes and Armenians connected themselves with the Libyans, who dwelt near the African sea ; while the Gaetulians lay more toward the sun, not far from the torrid deserts. And these[3] soon built themselves towns, since, being separated from Spain only by a strait, they opened an intercourse with its inhabitants. The name 'Medes' the Libyans gradually corrupted, changing it, in their barbaric tongue, into *Mauri* [*Mauros pro Medis* !].

"The power of the Persians rapidly grew, and at length their descendants, through excess of

1 *Intra oceanum magis.* Most critics explain *intra oceanum* as denoting the parts lying close to the ocean and bounded by it. There is some confusion in this passage between the names *Persae* and *Pharusii.* The latter were an historic people of the Atlantic seaboard of Africa (cf. Polybius *ap.* Pliny v. 1. 8 ; Strabo ii. p. 131, xvii. pp. 826, 828 ; Ptolemy iv. 6 § 6), whose name readily lent itself to one of those facile etymologies in which the Romans delighted. Thus, in Pliny (v. 8) one finds *Pharusii, quondam Persae* (cf. Mela iii. 10. 3).

2 This popular derivation of *Numidae* from the Greek *νομάζειν*, "to graze," or *νομάς*, "a pastoral wanderer," is questionable. Festus, certainly, is explicit : *Numidas dicimus quos Graeci* Νομάδες, *sive quod id genus hominum pecoribus negotietur, sive quod herbis, ut pecora aluntur* (p. 62 Egger), and Νομάδες as a descriptive of some of the North Africans is clearly intended in several classical passages (*e.g.* οἱ Μαυρούσιοι Νομάδες in Appian, *Bell. civil.* ii. 44). Cf. Oberlin's note in Vibius Sequester, p. 411.

3 *I.e.* the Medes, Armenians, and Libyans.

population, separating themselves from their parents, took possession, under the name Numidians, of those regions bordering on Carthage which are now called Numidia. In time, the two parties, [*i.e.* the early Numidians and the immigrants], each helping the other, reduced the neighbouring tribes, either by force or fear, under their dominion. But those who had spread toward the sea made the greater conquests, for the Libyans are less warlike than the Gaetulians. At last nearly all lower Africa [*Africae pars inferior*, *i.e.* maritime Africa] was occupied by the Numidians; and all the conquered tribes were merged in the nation and name of their conquerors." [1]

The most interesting feature of this detailed relation is that, either by accident or through some vague survival in the folk-memory, it records an ancient invasion from Spain into the Moghreb—an invasion such as really took place in the second millennium B.C. Also of interest, though quite in opposition to the known facts, is the statement that the invaders are said to have been of oriental origin (Persians, Medes, and Armenians). It is not possible to determine whether legend rooted in historical fact, or mere fancy, is responsible for this account of an invasion from Spain; but the oriental nationality of the invaders is more easily explicable.

Among the Moḥammadan Negroes of the Senegal, as among the negroid Berbers of the Rio de Oro and Atlantic Marocco, it is not difficult to find at the present time men wholly free from Arab admixture who assert that they are lineal descendants of Moḥammad (*shurifa* or *ashraf*, شرفا or اشراف "nobles," "nobility," sing. *sherîf* شريف). These false *shurifa* take pride in identifying themselves with the race which has come to have dominion over them, which has imposed upon them its religion, and of which they tacitly acknowledge (while none the less hostile to the Arabs) the superiority. The same eagerness to be thought related to a people at once disliked but admittedly superior is to be seen in the inscriptions of Roman Africa, where purely native names linked with Latin *praenomina* are of common occurrence. In the days of the Carthaginian supremacy in Africa, the same tendency was doubtless at work. The Libyan within the Punic sphere readily sought to aggrandize himself by aping the manners of the Semitic colonists, and by claiming for himself an origin which, like theirs, was oriental. This, I believe, is the reason why the invaders from Spain were said to have been Persians, Medes, and Armenians. Sallust's source was a Libyco-Punic one,—he professes to have derived his information from certain "Punic books said to have belonged to King Hiempsal," [2] the grandson of Masinissa, a source in which the spirit of identification between Africans and Asiatics would have been very pronounced.

The Byzantine historian Procopius has, like Sallust, preserved a story of African origins which reflects this tendency on the part of the Libyans to relate their remote ancestry to Asia Minor. Procopius relates how a certain Jesus (Joshua), the son of Noah, succeeded Moses at the time of the Exodus, and led the Hebrews into Palestine. The littoral of that country was then held by the Girgashites, the Jebusites, and other Phoenician tribes. These, unable to bear the dominion of the new-comers, passed into Egypt; but there being no room for them there, they held on to the westward, and occupied the Moghreb as far as the Straits of Gibraltar. Their flight was commemorated by a Phoenician inscription on two stone columns near a fountain in Numidia. This inscription, in the Greek "translation" of Procopius, runs as follows:

Ἡμεῖς ἐσμεν οἱ φυγόντες ἀπὸ προσώπου Ἰησοῦ τοῦ λῃστοῦ υἱοῦ Ναύη.

"We are those driven forth before the face of Jesus the Robber, the son of Noah." [3]

The Byzantine historian concludes with several remarks on the later history of the exiles, whom he explicitly identifies with the Maurusii.[4]

[1] Sallust, *Iugurtha*, 18. [2] *Ibid.* 17.

[3] J. Selden, *De diis Syris*, p. 18, has translated this inscription into Phoenician, or rather Hebrew!

[4] Procopius, *De bello Vandal.* ii. 10. 2. This story, only slightly condensed, may be found also in Landolfus Sagax, *Historia miscella*, xviii. 12.

Here even more clearly than in the story of Sallust can be seen the Libyan ambition to establish a common origin for both the indigenous North Africans and the Semitic colonists. In a similar vein are a number of tales preserved by Arabic writers,[1] who relate the origin of the Berbers to el-Yemen in Arabia, or to the land of Canaan in Syria. Several writers who maintain that the Berbers originated in the latter region connect their exodus from their first home to their second with the slaying of Goliath by David, and the subsequent victory of the Israelites over the Philistines. Thus, el-Bekrî identifies the Berbers with the vanquished Philistines,[2] and other writers even state that Goliath (جالوت) was the original ancestor of the indigenous North Africans.[3]

* * *

This last point may serve to introduce a topic connected with old ideas as to Libyan origins on which I have not yet touched—the question of eponyms. The above stories seek to explain the origin of the indigenous North Africans as a whole, though they are concerned most intimately with the Western Libyans, who lived within what was once the Punic sphere. A number of theories more purely native in character than those yet cited, and belonging more particularly to the Eastern Libyans, sought to relate the origins of individual tribes to eponymous king-ancestors. Thus, the Marmaridae asserted their race to have sprung from Marmaris, son of Arabs;[4] the Adyrmachidae, Ararauceles, Byzes (or Asbystae ?), Machlyes, and Macae, according to a late arrangement, all descended from the nymph Amphithemis, the mother of Psyllus, the eponymous king-ancestor of the Psylli.[5] The tomb of this Psyllus, according to Pliny, was to be seen on the shores of the Major Syrtis.[6] The Nasamones believed themselves descended from an eponymous Nasamon, *Νασάμων*,[7] whose name the natives pronounced in a manner which differentiated it from the ethnic. Nasamon himself sprang from Garamas, *Γάραμας*, the ancestor of the Garamantes.[8]

The evidence on the old eponymous heroes or kings, though coloured by the classical or Arabic mediums through which it has been transmitted, leaves no room for doubting that the Eastern Libyans, like so many primitive peoples, had numerous tribal ancestors, whose names and deeds probably figured largely in the old folk-lore, and who were venerated as semi-divine founders.

[1] Especially Ibn Ḫaldun, *Kitab el-ʿIbar*, vol. i. pp. 173 *sqq.*

[2] El-Bekrî, *ap. ibid.*, vol. i. p. 177.

[3] *E.g.* Ibn Ḳotaybah, *ap.* Ibn Ḫaldun, *op. cit.* vol. i. p. 175.

[4] Eustathius *ad* Dionys. *Perieg.* 214.

[5] Agroetas, *Frag.* 1 in *FHG*.

[6] Pliny, vii. 2. For Psyllus cf. Nonnus, *Dionysiaca* xiii. 381 *sqq.*

[7] But the older form of the ethnic, as has been said, was Mesamones.

[8] Eustathius *ad* Dionys. *Perieg.* 209; 217. Cf. Isidorus Hispalensis, *Etymol.* IX. ii. 125. The eponymous Garamas in classical legend appears as a son of Apollo: *Garamante rege, Apollinis filio, qui ibi ex suo nomine oppidum condidit* (Lutatius, *Schol. in Lucan. Pharsal.* iv. 334, ed. Oudendorp, p. 290 A).

APPENDIX IV

BIBLICAL NOTICES

I HAVE reserved until now a few words on the Old Testament notices of the Libyans, since they are of interest rather to Biblical scholars than to the student of early North Africa.

When, in frequent conjunction with the Egyptians and the Ethiopeans, appears in the *O.T.* a people called *Lubîm* לוּבִים[1] (once לֻבִּים),[2] there can be no doubt that the reference is to the Libyans—a supposition which is confirmed by the translation Λίβυες in the *Septuagint.*[3] Another, and, as Gesenius suspects, an older, form of the name exists in the *O.T.* as *Lehabîm* לְהָבִים,[4] the Λαάβιειμ (*var.* Λάβειν, Λάβιεμ) of the LXX. Both names are so clearly related to the Egyptian 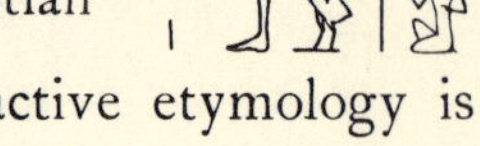 *rb-w*, that it is superfluous to seek another origin for them, although an attractive etymology is suggested by the Arabic لُوبِىٌّ, *regionis aridae incola*, from √לוּב.[5]

No detailed particulars concerning the bearers of these names appear in the Bible. The Lubîm figure vaguely as allies both of Tyre[6] and of Egypt,[7] while the Lehabîm characteristically appear as a "son" of Mizraîm, the "son" of Ham.[8]

[1] 2 *Chron.* xii. 3; xvi. 8; *Nah.* iii. 9. The singular form occurs once doubtfully as לוּב in *Ezek.* xxx. 5.

[2] *Dan.* xi. 43.

[3] The similarity between the early forms of the Semitic ב and ר, and the consequent ease with which they might be mistaken in transcribing a foreign name, have in some cases resulted in the name *Lubîm's* being confounded with that of another people, the *Ludîm*, לוּדִים. Thus in *Jer.* xlvi. 9 certainly, and in *Ezek.* xxvii. 10 perhaps, לוּדִים should be emended to לוּבִים.

[4] Gesenius, *Lexicon. in verb.* (p. 512); *Gen.* x. 13; 1 *Chron.* i. 11. The contexts in which the name *Lehabîm* appears forbid its relation, which some have sought to establish, to the place-name Balah (in southern Judah—*Josh.* xv. 3; xix. 3), deriving לְהָבִים from בַּעֲלָ[ת]ם = בַּלְהָ[ת]ים.

[5] Gesenius, *op. cit.*, p. 524 *in verb.*

[6] *Ezek.* xxvii. 10 reading *Lubîm* for *Ludîm* (*supra*, note 3).

[7] *Dan.* xi. 43; *Ezek.* xxx. 5; etc.

[8] *Gen.* x. 6-13; 1 *Chron.* i. 8-11. Cf. Josephus, *Antiq. Iud.* i. 2. In regard to *Mizraîm* מִצְרַיִם as an ethnic used at a fairly remote period by foreigners for the Egyptians—especially for the Delta—I would, with great reserve, suggest a possible connection between this name and the MZGH names discussed at length earlier in this essay. There is, by Hamitic phonesis, no difficulty in the permutation of غ to the *r* of מִצְרַיִם or the Arabic مِصْر, and the medial sibillant occurs as *s*, *ṣ*, *š*, or *z* almost indifferently. The presence of Libyans using an MZGH name in the early Delta, or even in Sinai, would explain how foreigners came to apply the title generally to the dwellers in the Nile Valley. The greatest difficulty here arises from the existence of the Assyrian word *miṣru*, "border, boundary," and of the (allied?) geographical names *Muṣri* = (1) part of Cappadocia, (2) a place in the Anti-Taurus, and *Muṣur* = Lower Egypt. But if these names are really allied to *muṣri*, may not that word itself have had at first a specific, and later a secondary, general significance? It would be an impertinence if I did not say, in publishing this note, that I have only a reading knowledge of Hebrew, and none of Assyrian.

In regard to the association of the Lubîm with the Tyrians, it is worth while to recall two points which have received attention earlier in this essay. It has been noted that the fortress of Satuna, which was stormed by the Egyptians, held a mixed garrison of Libyans and Asiatics;[1] and that the vases of precious metals represented in an Egyptian relief as forming part of the booty taken from the Libyans are distinctly Syrian in form.[2] This evidence, in conjunction with the vague *O.T.* notices, encourages the belief that the relations between Eastern Libya and the Syrian coast were friendly and fairly intimate.

[1] *Supra*, p. 151.

[2] *Supra*, p. 142 and Fig. 53.

APPENDIX V

THE ANTAEUS-CRATER OF EUPHRONIUS

This well-known masterpiece of fifth-century vase-painting, now in the Louvre, affords an interesting representation of a Libyan, which has not, so far as I am aware, yet been recognized as such. In the scene where Heracles is portrayed as wrestling with his African adversary, the combatants are strongly differentiated. The faces of both (Fig. 100) are shown as orthognathous, but, whereas Heracles is given the usual straight profile common to Greek graphic art in general, and to other Euphronian Greek faces in particular, Antaeus is represented as having a nose well-shaped but slightly aquiline, and strongly marked supra-orbital ridges. The treatment of the hair also differs in the two. That of the Greek hero is short, and ends in a roll of curls at the nape of the neck, and from the ear up and across the forehead. The beard is short and the moustache

Fig. 100.

slight. In the case of the Libyan giant the hair is long and matted, and it projects over the brow in a manner which at once recalls the Egyptian representations. The beard is long and pointed; the moustaches longer and fuller than those of Heracles. As may be seen in Poittier's excellent reproduction (from which I have drawn Fig. 100), the hair of the Libyan is shown as lighter in hue than that of the Greek (which I have left without detail). The lips of Antaeus are realistically parted in the stress of conflict, and the whole is rendered with the care characteristic of a master. In the field is the explanatory name [AN]TAIOΣ.

There can be no question that in this picture Euphronius, without doing violence to current traditions as to what was seemly in his art, has intentionally portrayed Antaeus as rude, grim, and savage. It was inevitable that the Libyan giant should be given a rugged cast of countenance, but the especial type chosen by the artist is the significant matter. From the intercourse between the Libyans and the Cyrenaic Greeks, and between Cyrene and Greece, it is almost a certainty that Libyan sailors were no uncommon sight in the streets and taverns of the Piraeus, even in the fifth century. It is to be recalled, moreover, how early in Greek plastic vase-forms the Athenian potter took his inspiration even from the black Aethiopians of the far south.[1] The possibility that Euphronius may often have seen mingled with the Greek sailors at least stray examples of the African barbarians may, I think, be accepted without reserve.[2] This admitted, what is more natural than to suppose that in conceiving the Libyan giant in this scene he should recall to mind the Berber faces he had encountered in Athens or at the port? Four features seem to bear this out: the projection of the hair over the brow, the marked supra-orbital ridges, the slightly aquiline nose of the Antaeus, and the form of the beard. I would suggest a comparison of this profile with those to be seen in Pl. I. 1, 4, 5; Pl. II. 4, 5, etc. The face as a whole impresses me, after long familiarity with the Egyptian representations, as Berber in character.

[1] A sixth-century instance, of which Dr. G. H. Chase kindly reminded me, is afforded by the Busiris vase in the Oesterreichisches Museum in Vienna, for the bibliography of which see S. Reinach, *Répertoire des vases peints*, vol. i. pp. 169-170. The Antaeus-crater belongs to Euphronius's early period (500–480 B.C.). See H. B. Walters, *History of Ancient Pottery*, vol. i. p. 430 *sq*.

[2] Euphronius's personal fondness for peculiar types is well known, and that the Antaeus-crater is from his own hand is testified by the ἔγραψεν inscription.

BIBLIOGRAPHY

Librorum, qui in conscribendo hocce libro praesto fuerunt . . ., indicem adiiciamus, non vanam eruditionis gloriam captaturi, sed ne lectores ignorent fontes, e quorum auctoritate fides dictorum pendet, neve editionum diversitate forte decipiantur.—J. M. Hartmann, *Edrisii Africa*, p. xiii.

Abel, C.

1. Einleitung in ein ägyptisch-semitisch-indoeuropäisches Wurzelwörterbuch. Leipzig. 1886.
2. Über Wechselbeziehungen der ägyptischen, indoeuropäischen und semitischen Etymologie (I). Leipzig. 1889.
3. Ägyptisch - indoeuropäische Sprachverwandtschaft. 2nd ed. Leipzig. 1903.

Abu 'l-Ḥasan ʿAlî Ibn ʿAbd Allah Ibn Abî Zerʿ el-Fezanî [cited as Abu 'l-Ḥasan].

Annales regum Mauretaniae a condito Idrisidarum imperio ad annum fugae DCCXXVI. Ed. Tornberg. Upsala. 1843–46.

Abu 'l-Maḥasin Gamal ed-Dîn Ibn Taghrî-Bardî [cited as Abu 'l-Maḥasin].

Annales. Ed. Juynboll. Leyden. 1852–61.

Acesander.

Fragmenta in *FHG*, vol. ii.

Adamantius.

Physiognomonicon. Ed. Franz in *Script. Physiog. Vet.* Altenburg. 1780.

Adanson, M.

A Voyage to Senegal. London. 1759.

[Admiralty, British.]

1. Chart No. 664-449 : Mediterranean Sea.
2. Chart No. 1031-241 : Benghazi to Derna.
3. Chart No. 1030-245 : Bombah.
4. Chart No. 1029-244 : Derna to Ras Bulau.

Aelianus, Claudius.

1. De animalium natura. Ed. Hercher. Leipzig. 1864.
2. Varia Historia. Ed. Hercher. Leipzig. 1866.

Aeschylus.

Tragoediae. Ed. Weil. Leipzig. 1907.

Aethicus [Cosmographus].

1. Cosmographia. Ed. Riese in *Geogr. Lat. Min.*
2. Cosmographie d'Éthicus. Ed. Baudet. Paris. 1843.

Aethicus Ister. *See* Avezac-Macaya, M. A. P. d'.

Agathemerus.

Geographiae informatio. In *Geogr. Graec. Min.*

Agroetas.

Fragmenta in *FHG*, vol. iv.

Alexander Myndensis.

Frag. ap. Athenaeum, Deipnos. v. 20.

Alexander Polyhistor.

Frag. ap. Steph. Byz. in verb. Λιβύη.

Ambrosius [Sanctus].

Opera omnia. Ed. Migne. Paris. 1845.

Amometus.

Fragmenta in *FHG*, vol. ii.

Ampelius, L.

Liber memorialis. Ed. Salmasius. Amsterdam. 1660.

Anderson, R. G.

Medical practices and superstitions amongst the people of Kordofan. In *Wellcome Research Laboratories III. Report.* London. 1908.

Annales = Annales de Service des Antiquités (Egypt).

Anonymous.

1. Tarîḫ Waḥ es-Sîwah ; History of Sîwah. [Arabic account from a fifteenth-century source obtained at Sîwah by C. V. Stanley and O. Bates in 1910.]
2. History of the war between the United States and Tripoli, etc. Salem. 1806.
3. [Review of E. Huntingdon's theories on climatic oscillation in the] *GJ*, vol. xxxvi., No. 6, p. 732.

Anonymus.

1. Expositio totius mundi et gentium. In *Geogr. Lat. Min.*
2. Chronicon paschale. Ed. Dindorf in *Corp. Script. Hist. Byz.* vol. ix. Bonn. 1832.

See Auctor Incertus ; Excerpta Barbari ; Geographus [Anonymus] Ravennas.

Anth. = *L'Anthropologie* (Paris).

Anticleides.

Fragmenta. Ed. Müller. Paris. 1846.

Antigonus Carystius.

Historiarum memorabilium collectanea. Ed. Meursius. Leyden. 1619.

Apollodorus.

Bibliotheca. Ed. Hercher. Berlin. 1874.

Apollonius Dyscolus.
Historiae commentitiae liber. Ed. Meursius. Leyden. 1620.
Apollonius Rhodius.
Argonautica. Ed. Seaton. Oxford. 1909.
Apuleius.
Opera omnia. Ed. 2, Hildebrand. Leipzig. 1842.
Aristophanes.
Comoediae. Ed. Hall and Geldart. Oxford. 1900.
Arrianus, Flavius.
1. Anabasis Alexandri. Ed. Roos. Leipzig. 1907.
2. Indica. Ed. Dübner. Paris. 1846.
Asbjörnsen, P. C.
Folk and fairy-tales. Trans. H. L. Braekstad. New York. 1883.
Ascherson, P.
Drias e sylphium. In *L' Esploratore*, vol. vi. p. 1 *sqq*.
Athanasius [Sanctus].
Opera omnia. Ed. Migne. Paris. 1857.
Athenaeus.
Deipnosophistae. Ed. Kaibel. Leipzig. 1887 *sqq*.
Auctor Incertus.
Panegyricus Maximiano et Constantino. Ed. Jaeger in *Panegyrici Veteres*. Nuremberg. 1779.
Augustinus [Sanctus].
Opera omnia. Ed. Migne. Paris. 1841 *sq*.
Ausonius, D. Magnus.
Opuscula. Ed. Schenkl. Berlin. 1883.
Avezac-Macaya, M. A. P. d'.
1. Afrique. Esquisse générale de l'Afrique et l'Afrique ancienne, etc. Paris. 1844.
2. Éthicus et les ouvrages cosmographiques intitulé de ce nom, etc. Paris. 1852. (Acad. des Inscript. *Mémoires*, vol. ii.)
Aymard [Captain].
Les Toureg. Paris. 1911.
Ayra, G.
Tripoli e il suo clima. Turin. 1896.

Babelon, E. C. F.
Le Cabinet des antiques à la Bibliothèque nationale. Paris. 1887.
BAGS = *Bulletin of the American Geographical Society*.
Bain, R. N.
Cossack Fairy Tales. London. 1894.
Baker, S. W.
The Nile Tributaries of Abyssinia. London. 1867.
Ball, J.
1. Kharga Oasis: its topography and geology. Cairo. 1900.
2. Topographical and geological results of a reconnaissance survey of Jebel Garra and the Oasis of Kurkur. Cairo. 1902.
Ball, J., and Beadnell, H. J. L.
Baharia Oasis: its topography and geology. Cairo. 1903.
BAR = Breasted, J. H. Ancient Records, *q.v.*
Barbarus Incertus.
Excerpta Barbari. *See* Scaliger, J. J., *Thesaurus temporum*.
Barth, H.
1. Wanderungen durch die Küstenländer des Mittelmeeres (I). Berlin. 1849.
2. Reisen und Entdeckungen in Nord- und Central-Afrika (I). Gotha. 1859 *sq*.
Bary, E. von.
1. Le Dernier Rapport d'un Européen sur Ghât et les Touareg de l'Air. Paris. 1898.
2. Über Senam und Tumuli im Küstengebirge von Tripolitanien. In the *Zeitschr. f. Ethnologie*, vol. viii. p. 378 *sqq*.
3. Senams et tumuli de la chaîne de montagnes de la côte tripolitaine. In the *Rev. d'Ethnog.*, vol. ii. p. 426 *sqq*. 1883.
Basset, R.
1. Le Dialecte de Syouah. Paris. 1890.
2. Loqmân berbère. Paris. 1890.
3. Étude sur la Zenatia du Mzab, de Ouargla et de l'Oued Rir'. Paris. 1892.
4. Études sur les dialectes berbères. Paris. 1894.
5. Les Chiens du Roi Antef. In *Sphinx*, vol. i. 1897.
6. Recherches sur la religion des Berbères. Paris. 1910.
Bateman, G. W.
Zanzibar Tales. Chicago. 1901.
Bates, O.
1. A Desert God. In *CSJ*, vol. iv. No. 51.
2. Siwan Superstitions. In *CSJ*, vol. v. No. 55.
3. Umm es-Shiatta and Umm Ghurbi. In *CSJ*, vol. v. No. 56.
4. Dr. G. Elliot Smith and the Egyptian Race. In *CSJ*, vol. vi. No. 68.
5. On certain North African place-names prefixed with *Rus-*. In *CSJ*, vol. vi. No. 69.
6. Sudanese Notes. In *CSJ*, vol. vi. No. 69.
7. On some place-names in Eastern Libya. In *PSBA*, Nov. 13, 1912.
Baux, A.
La Poterie des Nuraghes, etc. In the *Rev. Archéol. III. Series*, vol. v. 1885.
Bazin, H.
Études sur le tatouage dans la régence de Tunis. In *Anth.*, vol. vi. No. 571.
Beadnell, H. J. L.
1. Farafra Oasis: its topography and geography. Cairo. 1901.
2. Dakhla Oasis: its topography and geology. Cairo. 1901.
3. Mr. Huntington on climatic oscillations in Kharga Oasis. In *GJ*, vol. xxxvi. No. 1, p. 108 *sq*.
See Ball, J.
Beechey, F. W. and H. W.
Proceedings of the expedition to explore the Northern Coast of Africa from Tripoli eastward, etc. London. 1828.
el-Bekrî, Abu ʿUbeyd ʿAbd Allah Ibn ʿAbd el-ʿAzîz Abî Musʿab [cited as el-Bekrî].
1. Das geographische Wörterbuch, etc. Ed. Wüstenfeld, Göttingen. 1876–77.
2. Description de l'Afrique septentrionale. Ed. de Slane, Algiers. 1857.

Benédite, G.
Un Guerrier libyen, etc. In *Mém. de l'Acad. des Inscript.* v., 1902 (*Fondation Piot*, ix.), p. 123 *sq.*

Benhazera, M.
Six mois chez les Touareg du Ahaggar. Algiers. 1908.

Berbrugger, L. A.
Bibliothèque-Musée d'Alger. Algiers. 1860.

Berger, P.
Histoire de l'écriture dans l'antiquité. Paris. 1891.

Bernard, F. C. E.
1. Note au sujet de quelques monuments de pierres brutes relevés chez les Touareg Azgar. Paris. 1885.
2. Observations archéologiques, etc. In the *Rev. d' Ethnog.*, 1886, vol. v.

Bertholon, L.
1. La Cynophagie dans l'Afrique du Nord. Tunis. 1896, vol. v.
2. Origines néolithiques et mycéniennes des tatouages des indigènes du Nord de l'Afrique. (Extr. from *Arch. d' Anthrop. criminelle*, vol. iii. No. 130.) Lyons. 1904.
3. Les Premiers Colons de souche européenne dans l'Afrique du Nord. (Part ii.) Origines et formation de la langue berbère. Paris. 1907.
4. Essai sur la religion des Libyens. Tunis. 1909.

Biarnay, S.
Étude sur le dialecte berbère de Ouargla. Paris. 1908.

Bible.
Biblia Hebraica. Ed. Bible Society of London. 1906.

el-Biladurî, Aḥmed Ibn Yaḥya Ibn Gabîr [cited as el-Biladurî].
Liber expugnationis regionum. Ed. de Goeje. Leyden. 1866.

Bissuel, P. H.
Les Touareg de l'Ouest. Algiers. 1888.

Blau, E. O. F. H.
Ueber das numidische Alphabet. In *Zeitschr. d. Deutsch. Morgenl. Gesell.* v. p. 330. 1851.

Bochart, S.
Geographia Sacra, seu Phaleg et Canaan. In *Opera omnia*, vol. i. Ed. 4. Leyden and Utrecht. 1712.

Borchardt, L.
1. Das Grabdenkmal des Königs Ne-user-reʿ. Leipzig. 1907.
2. Das Grabdenkmal des Königs Sáʾḥu-reʿ. Leipzig. 1910.

Borsari, F.
Geografia etnologica e storica della Tripolitania. Turin, etc. 1888.

Bosman, W.
Voyage de Guinée. Utrecht. 1705.

Botti, A.
Manuscrits libyens . . . dans le Musée de Turin. (Extract from *Bull. de l'Inst. Égyptien.*) Cairo. 1900.

Bourville, V. De.
Extrait d'une lettre . . . à Mons. Joumard, etc. In *Bull. de la Soc. Géogr.* vol. x. (1849) p. 172 *sq.*

Breasted, J. H.
1. Ancient Records of Egypt. Chicago. 1906 *sqq.*
2. A History of Egypt, etc. Ed. 2. New York. 1911.

Brinton, D. G.
1. The ethnological affinities of the ancient Etruscans. In *P. Am. Ph. S.*, vol. xxvi. p. 506. 1889.
2. On Etruscan and Libyan names. In *P. Am. Ph. S.*, vol. xxviii. p. 39. 1890.

Broca, P.
Les Peuples blonds et les monuments mégalithiques dans l'Afrique septentrionale. In *Rev. d' Anthrop.* vol. v. p. 393. 1876.

Brown, R. *See* Pory, J.

Browne, W. H.
Travels in Africa, Egypt, and Syria. London. 1806.

Brugsch, H. C.
1. Die Geographie des alten Ägyptens. Leipzig. 1852.
2. Hieroglyphisch-demotisches Wörterbuch. Leipzig. 1880.
3. Thesaurus Inscriptionum Aegyptiacarum. Leipzig. 1883 *sqq.*
4. Religion und Mythologie der alten Ägypter. Leipzig. 1885.

Bull. Arch. Inst. Am. = *Bulletin of the Archaeological Institute of America.*

Bull. Nub. = Archaeological Survey of Nubia: *Bulletins.* Cairo. 1908 *sqq.*

Burchardt, M.
Die altkanaanäischen Fremdworte und Eigennamen im Ägyptischen. Leipzig. 1909 *sq.*

Burrows, R. M.
The Discoveries in Crete. London. 1907.

Caesar, C. I.
Commentarii. Ed. Hoffmann. Vienna. 1888.

Cagnat, R.
1. Musée de Lambèse. Paris. 1895.
2. Études de mythologie et d'histoire des religions antiques. Paris. 1909.

CSJ = *Cairo Scientific Journal.*

Calassanti-Motylinski, G. A. de.
Le Dialecte berbère de R'edamès. Paris. 1904.

Callias Syracusanus.
Fragmenta in *FHG*, vol. ii.

Callimachus.
Hymni et Epigrammata. Ed. 3 Wilamowitz-Möllendorf. Berlin. 1907.

[Callisthenes].
Frag. in Arrianus, *ed. cit. supra.*

Campana, G. P.
Antiche Opere in plastica, discoperte, raccolte, e dichiarate. Rome. 1852.

Capart, J.
Les Débuts de l'art en Égypte. Bruxelles. 1904.

Capella, Martianus.
De nuptiis Philologiae, etc. Ed. Eyssenhardt. Leipzig. 1866.

Capitolinus, Iulius.
1. Antoninus Pius. In *Script. Hist. August.*
2. Maximi duo. In *Script. Hist. August.*

Carton, L. B. C.
Notes sur les ruines d'el-Kenissiah. In *Bull. Soc. Arch. ae Sousse*. 1907.

Casati, G.
Ten Years in Equatoria, etc. London. 1891.

Cassiodorus [Florus], Magnus Aurelius.
Opera omnia. Ed. Garet. Venice. 1729.

Castiglioni, C. O.
Mémoire géographique et numismatique sur la partie orientale de la Barbarie, etc. Milan. 1826.

[Castorius]. *See* Tabula Peutingeriana.

Catal. Musée Lavigerie. *See* Delattre, A. L.

Caudel, M.
Les Premières Invasions arabes dans l'Afrique du Nord. Paris. 1900.

Celsus, A. Cornelius.
De artibus quae extant. Ed. Milligan. Edinburgh. 1831.

Chabas, F.
Études sur l'antiquité historique. Paris, etc. 1873.

Chaillu, P. B. du.
Voyages et aventures dans l'Afrique équatoriale. Paris. 1863.

Champollion, J. F.
Monuments de l'Égypte et de la Nubie d'après les dessins exécutés sur les lieux. Paris. 1835 *sqq*.

Chronicon ann. p. Christ. 334. In Frick, C., *Chronica Minora*.

Chronicon Paschale. *See* Anonymus, 2.

Chrysostomus, Dio.
Orationes. Ed. Reiske. Leipzig. 1784.

CIG = *Corpus Inscriptionum Graecarum*, etc. Ed. Boeckh. Berlin. 1828 *sqq*.

CIL = *Corpus Inscriptionum Latinarum*, etc. Berlin. 1863 *sqq*.

CIS = *Corpus Inscriptionum Semiticarum*. Paris. 1881 *sqq*.

Clapperton, H. *See* Denham, D.

Claudianus, Claudius.
Opera quae extant. Ed. Bipont. 1784.

Clearchus of Soli.
Fragmenta in *FHG*, vol. ii.

Clemens, T. Flavius, Alexandrinus.
Opera quae extant. Ed. Potter. Oxford. 1715.

Collignon, R., and Deniker, F.
Les Maures du Sénégal. In *Anth.* vol. vii. p. 257. (1896.)

Corippus, Flavius Cresconius.
Iohannis, seu De bellis Libycis. Ed. Bekker in *Corp. Script. Hist. Byz.* Bonn. 1836.

Cosson, E. St. C.
1. Descriptio plantarum novarum in itinere Cyrenaico a G. Rehlfs detectarum. In *Bull. Soc. Botan. Fran.* vol. xix. (1872) p. 80 *sqq*.
2. Plantae in Cyrenaica et agro Tripolitano notae. In *Bull. Soc. Bot. Fran.* vol. xxii. (1875) p. 45 *sqq*.

Cowper, H. S.
The Hill of the Graces. London. 1897.

Cragius, N.
De republica Lacedaemoniorum. Heraclidae Pontici de politiis libellus. Ex Nicolai Damasceni Universali Historia, etc. Leyden. 1670.

CSJ = *Cairo Scientific Journal*.

Ctesias, Cnidius.
Ctesii Cnidii Fragmenta. Ed. Müller-Didot. Paris.

Curtius, Q. Rufus.
De rebus gestis Alexandri Magni. Ed. Van der Aa. Leyden. 1696.

Cyprianus, Thascius Caecilius [Sanctus].
Opera. Ed. Maran. Paris. 1726.

Daremberg, C. V. and Saglio, E.
Dictionnaire des antiquités grecques et romaines, etc. Paris. 1877 *sqq*.

Daressy, G.
1. Révision des textes de la stèle de Chalouf. In *RT*, xi. 1889.
2. Une Trouvaille de bronzes à Mit Rahineh. In the *Annales*, iii. 1902.
3. Une Nouvelle Forme d'Ammon. In the *Annales*, ix. 1908.
4. Statues de divinités. In the *Cairo Catalogue*. Cairo. 1906.
5. Plaquettes émaillées de Medinet Habou. In the *Annales*, xi. (1911.)

Davies, N. de G.
The Rock Tombs of el-Amarna. London. 1903 *sqq*.

Déchelette, J.
Le Culte du soleil aux temps préhistoriques. Paris. 1909.

Delattre, A. L. [Père].
1. Les Tombeaux puniques de Carthage. Lyon. 1890.
2. Catalogue du Musée Lavigerie. Paris. 1900.

Denham, D., Oudney [Doctor], and Clapperton, H.
Narrative of travels and discoveries in Northern and Central Africa, etc. 2nd ed. London. 1826.

Deniker, J.
The Races of Man. London. 1900.
See Collignon, R.

Dennis, G.
On recent excavations in the Greek cemeteries of the Cyrenaica. In *Transac. Roy. Soc. Lit.* ii. Series, vol. ix. 1870.

Desjardins, A. E. E.
La Table de Peutinger, d'après l'original conservé à Vienne, etc. Paris. 1869 *sqq*.

Dessau, H.
Inscriptiones Latinae selectae. Berlin. 1892 *sqq*.

Detlefsen, D.
Die Geographie Afrikas bei Plinius und Mela und ihre Quellen. Berlin. 1908.
See Plinius, C. Secundus.

Dietrich, K. von.
Byzantinische Quellen zur Länder- und Völkerkunde. Leipzig. 1912.

Dio Cassius Cocceianus.
Historiae Romanae quae supersunt. Ed. Sturtz. Leipzig. 1824.

Diodorus Siculus.
Bibliotheca historica. Ed. Wesseling. Amsterdam. 1746.

Diogenes Laërtius.
Vitae philosophorum. Ed. Cobet. Paris. 1850.

Dionysius [Periegetes].
Periegesis. In *Geogr. Gr. Min.* vol. ii.

Doughty, C. M.
Wanderings in Arabia. [Abridged from *Idem.* Travels in Arabia Deserta, Cambridge, 1888, by R. Garnet.] London. 1908.

Doutté, E.
Magie et religion dans l'Afrique du Nord. Algiers. 1910.

Dümichen, J.
Die Oasen der libyschen Wüste. Strassburg. 1877.

Duncan, P. *See* Petrie, W. M. F.

Duprat, P.
Essai historique sur les races anciennes et modernes de l'Afrique Septentrionale, etc. Paris. 1845.

Duris Samius.
Fragmenta in *FHG*, vol. ii.

Dussaud, R.
Les Civilisations préhelléniques, etc. Paris. 1910.

Dussaud, R., and Macler, F.
Voyage archéologique au Safâ et dans le Djebel ed-Drûz. Paris. 1901.

Duveyrier, H.
Les Touareg du Nord. Paris. 1864.

Egyptian Government [Survey Dept.].
1. [Map] District of Mersa Matru ; 1 : 25,000. Cairo. 1904.
2. [Map] District of Ras allem Rum ; 1 : 25,000. Cairo. 1904.
3. Meteorological Report for the year 1908. Cairo. 1910.
4. Almanac [Statistics, etc.]. Cairo. 1911.

Eratosthenes.
Fragmenta. Ed. Berger. Leipzig. 1880.

Erman, A.
1. Die Pluralbildung des Aegyptischen. Leipzig. 1878.
2. Die Flexion des ägyptischen Verbums. In the *Sitzungsber. der Berliner Akad.* for 1900.
3. Ägyptische Grammatik. 2nd ed. Berlin. 1902.
4. Handbook of Egyptian Religion [translated by A. S. Griffith]. London. 1907.
5. Ägyptisches Glossar. Berlin. 1904.

Escher, J.
Triton und seine Bekämpfung durch Herakles. Leipzig. 1890.

Eudoxus Cnidius.
Frag. ap. Apollonium Dyscolum, q.v.

Euripides.
Fabulae. Ed. Murray. Oxford. [1902 *sqq.*]

Eusebius.
1. Chronicon. Ed. Mai. Milan. 1818.
2. Praeparatio Evangelica. Ed. Viger. Paris. 1628.

Eustathius.
1. Scholia in Homeri Iliad. et Odyss. Ed. Stallbaum. Leipzig. 1825 *sqq.*
2. Scholia in Dionysii Periegesin. In *Geogr. Graec. Min.*

Eutropius.
Breviarium ab urbe condita, etc. Ed. Droysen. Berlin. 1879.

Evagrius Scholasticus.
Historiae ecclesiasticae libri sex. Ed. Migne. Paris. 1860.

Evans, A. J.
Scripta Minoa (I). Oxford. 1909.

Excerpta Barbari. In Scaliger, J. J., *Thesaurus temporum.*

Exiga *dit* Kayser. *See* en-Naṣîr, Moḥammad Abu Ras Aḥmed.

Faidherbe, L. L. C.
1. Recherches anthropologiques sur les tombeaux mégalithiques de Roknia. Bône. 1868.
2. Quelques mots sur l'ethnographie du Nord de l'Afrique et sur les tombeaux mégalithiques de cette contrée. In the *Bull. de l'Acad. de Hippon.* 1868.
3. Collection . . . des inscriptions Numidiques. Lille. 1870.
4. Notices ethnographiques, etc. Paris. 1871.
5. Instructions sur l'anthropologie de l'Algérie. In the *Bull. de la Soc. d'Anthr.*, 2nd Series, viii. p. 603 *sqq.* Paris. 1873.

Festus, S. Pompeius.
Fragmenta. Ed. Egger. Paris. 1838.

FHG = *Fragmenta Historicorum Graecorum.* Ed. Müller. Paris. 1841 *sqq.*

Filiasi, G.
Sull' antico commercio, arte, e marina dei Veneziani. Padua. 1811.

Finsch, O., and Hartlaub, G.
Die Vögel Ost-Afrikas [=von der Decken's Reisen in Ost-Afrika, Bd. iv]. Leipzig, etc. 1870.

Flamand, G.- B.- M.
1. Note sur les inscriptions et dessins rupestres de la Gara des Chorfa du district de l'Aoulef. [Extr. from *Bull. de Géogr. histor. et descript.* iii. (1903).] Paris. 1904.
2. De l'introduction du chameau dans l'Afrique du Nord. Paris. 1906.

Florus, L. Annaeus.
Epitome. Ed. Jahn. Leipzig. 1852.

Foucauld, C. de.
Reconnaissance au Maroc. Paris. 1888.

Fournel, M. J. H.
Les Berbers (I). Paris. 1875.

Freytag, G. W.
Lexicon Arabico-Latinum ex opere suo maiore . . . excerptum. Halle. 1837.

Frick, C. [Edit.]
Chronica minora. Leipzig. 1892 *sqq.*

Fruin, R. F.
De Manethone Sebennyta librorumque ab eo scriptorum reliquiis. Leyden. [1848.]

Furlong, C. W.
Gateway to the Sahara. New York. 1900.

Gabelentz, G. von der.
Die Verwandtschaft des Baskischen mit den Berbersprachen Nord-Africas nachgewiesen. Brunswick. 1894.

Gauckler, P.
1. Note in the *Compte rendu de l'Acad. des Inscript.* 1898, p. 828 *sqq.*
2. Les Monuments historiques de la Tunisie. Paris. 1898 *sq.*
3. Rapport sur des inscriptions latines découvertes en Tunisie de 1900 à 1905. In *Nouv. Arch. des Missions Scient.* Tom. xv. fasc. 4. 1907.

Gautier, E.-F.
Sahara algérien [*Missions au Sahara*, I]. Paris. 1908.

Gellius, A.
Noctes Atticae. Ed. Hertz. Berlin. 1883 *sqq.*

Geographus [Anonymus] Ravennas.
Ravennatis Anonymi cosmographia et Guidonis geographica ex libris MSS. Ed. Pinder and Parthey. Berlin. 1860.

Georgius Cyprius.
Descriptio orbis Romani. Ed. Gelzer. Leipzig. 1890.

Gerhard, E.
Griechische und etruskische Trinkschalen des . . . Museums zu Berlin. Berlin. 1840.

Gesenius, F. H. W.
A Hebrew and English lexicon, etc. 3rd ed. Robinson. Boston. 1849.

Gèze, L.
De quelques rapports entre les langues berbère et basque. Toulouse. 1883.

Ghisleri, A.
Tripolitania e Cirenaica dal Mediterraneo al Sahara. Milan, etc. 1912.

Gibbon, E.
History of the Decline and Fall of the Roman Empire. Ed. Bury. London. 1896 *sqq.*

Geogr. Gr. Min. = *Geographi Graeci Minores.* Ed. Müller. Paris. 1855 *sqq.*

Geogr. Lat. Min. = *Geographi Latini Minores.* Ed. Riese. Heilbronn. 1878.

Giraud-Teulon, A.
Origines du mariage et de la famille. Geneva. 1884.

GJ = *The Geographical Journal.* [London.]

Golenischeff.
Offener Brief an Herrn Professor G. Steindorff. In *Zeit. f. ägypt. Spr.* xl. (1902) p. 101 *sqq.*

Gorringe, H.
A cruise along the northern coast of Africa. In *JAGNY*, vol. xiii. p. 54 *sqq.*

Greenhow, R.
History and present condition of Tripoli, etc. Richmond (Va.). 1835.

Gregory, J. W.
Report on the work of the commission sent out by the Jewish Territorial Organization . . . etc. London. 1909.

Grimm, W. and J. Household Tales. Trans. M. Hunt. London. 1884.

Gsell, S.
1. Musée de Philippeville. Paris. 1898.
2. Monuments antiques de l'Algérie. 2nd ed. Paris. 1903.

Haimann, G.
1. Cirenaica. In *Bollet. della Soc. Geogr. Ital.* 1881.
2. Cirenaica. Milan. 1886.

Halévy, J.
Études berbères. [Extr. from the *Journ. Asiat.* 7th Series, vols. iii. and iv.] Paris. 1874.

Hall, H. R. H.
The oldest Civilization of Greece. London. 1901.

Hamilton, J.
Wanderings in North Africa. London. 1856.

Hamy, E. T. *See* Quatrefages, J. L. A. de—de Bréau.

Hanoteau, L. A.
1. Essai de grammaire kabyle. Paris. [1858.]
2. Essai de grammaire de la langue tamachek̓. Paris. 1860.

Hanoteau, L. A., and Letourneux, A.
La Kabylie. Paris. 1872–73.

Harrison, J. E.
Prolegomena to the study of Greek religion. 2nd ed. Cambridge. 1908.

Hartlaub, G. *See* Finsch, O.

Hartmann, J. M.
Edrisii Africa. 2nd ed. Göttingen. 1796.

Ḥasan Ibn Moḥammad el-Wezaz el-Fasî. *See* Leo Africanus.

Hawes, C. H. and H. B.
Crete the forerunner of Greece. London, etc. 1909.

Head, B. V.
Historia numorum. Oxford. 1887.

Hecataeus.
Fragmenta, in *FHG*, vol. i.

Heiss, A.
Description . . . des monnaies antiques de l'Espagne. Paris. 1870.

Hellanicus.
Fragmenta, in *FHG*, vol. i.

Heraclides Ponticus. *See* Cragius, N.

Hermippus [Comicus].
Fragmenta in *Poetarum comicorum Graecorum fragmenta.* Ed. Bothe. Paris. 1855.

Herodianus.
Ab excessu Divi Marci libri octo. Ed. Bekker. Leipzig. 1855.

Herodotus.
1. The History of Herodotus. Tr. and annot. G. and H. Rawlinson and J. G. Wilkinson. New York. 1859.
2. ΗΡΟΔΟΤΟΥ ΙΣΤΟΡΙΩΝ Δ, Ε, Ζ. Herodotus: the fourth, fifth, and sixth books. Ed. and annot. Macan. London. 1895. [App. xii. vol. ii. p. 260 *sqq.* *The Libyan Logi.*]
3. Historiae. Ed. Hude. Oxford. 1908.

Hesiodus.
Carmina. Ed. Rzach. Leipzig. 1902.

Hess, J. J.
Die Entzifferung der thamûdischen Inschriften. In *RT*, vol. xxxiii. p. 156 *sqq.*

Hesychius Alexandrinus.
Lexicon. Ed. Alberti and Ruhnken. Leyden. 1746 *sqq.*

Heuzey, L.
Tribu asiatique en expédition. In the *Rev. Archéol.* Sér. iii. tome xv. (1890) pp. 145, 334.
Hieronymus [Sanctus].
1. Opera omnia. Ed. Martianay. Paris. 1693 *sqq.*
2. Chronicorum libri duo. Ed. Schoene. Berlin. 1866.
Hildebrand, G.
Cyrenaïka [*sic*] als Gebiet künftiger Besiedelung. Bonn. 1904.
Hippocrates.
De morbis. Ed. Kühn. Leipzig. 1826.
Hirtius, A. *See* Caesar, C. I.
Historia miscella. *See* Landolfus Sagax.
Hohler, T. B.
Report on the Oasis of Siva. [With an appendix (B) by G. Maspero on the wells of Marmarica.] Cairo. 1900.
Homerus.
1. Ilias. Ed. Dindorf and Hentze. Leipzig. 1904.
2. Odyssea. Ed. Dindorf and Hentze. Leipzig. 1904.
Honorius, Julius.
Cosmographia. In Riese, *Geogr. Lat. Min.* 21.
Horatius, Q. Flaccus.
Eclogae cum scholiis veteribus, etc. Ed. Gesner and Zeune. Leipzig. 1815.
Hornemann, F.
Journal of . . . travels from Cairo to Mourzouk, etc. London. 1802.
Huntington, E.
The Kharga Oasis and past climatic changes. In *BAGS.* Sept., 1910.
Hyginus, G. Julius.
1. Fabulae. Ed. Schmidt. Jena. 1872.
2. Astronomica. Ed. Bunte. Leipzig. 1875.

Jablonski, P. E.
Pantheon Aegyptiorum. Frankfurt. 1750, 1752.
JAGNY=Journal of the American Geographical Society of New York.
Iamblichus.
De mysteriis liber. Ed. Gale. Oxford. 1678.
Ibn ʿAbd el-Ḥakam, Abu ’l-Ḳasim ʿAbd er-Raḥman [cited as Ibn Abd el-Ḥakam]. Futuḥ Misr.
Ibn Abî Dînar er-Ru’aynî el-Ḳayruanî [cited as Ibn Abî ’l Dînar].
Ibn el-Aṯîr. *See* ’Izz ed-Dîn Ibn el-Aṯîr.
Ibn Ḫaldun, Abu Zayd ʿAbd er-Raḥman [cited as Ibn Ḫaldun].
Kitab el-ʿIbar. Bulak. A.H. 1284. *See* de Slane, W. MacG.
Ibn Ḥauḳal, Abu ’l-Ḳasim [cited as Ibn Ḥauḳal].
Viae et regna. Descriptio ditionis Moslemicae, etc. Ed. de Goeje. Leyden. 1873.
Ibn Ḫordadbah, Abu ’l-Ḳasim ʿUbayd Allah Ibn ʿAbd Allah [cited as Ibn Ḫordadbah].
Liber viarum et regnorum. Ed. Leyden. 1889.
el-Idrîsî, Abu ʿAbd Allah Moḥammad Ibn Moḥammad Ibn ʿAbd Allah es-Sherîf [cited as el-Idrîsî].
Description de l’Afrique et de l’Espagne. Ed. Dozy and de Goeje. Leyden. 1866.
Jephson, A. J. M.
Emin Pasha and the rebellion at the Equator. London. 1890.
Jequier, G.
Notes et remarques. In *RT*, vol. xxx. (1908).
Joannes Laurentius [Lydus]. *See* [Lydus], Joannes Laurentius.
Johannis Biclarensis [Abbas].
Chronicon. Ed. Migne. Paris. 1849. (In *Patrol. Curs. Complet.* lxxii. p. 863 *sqq.*)
John [Bishop] of Nikiu.
Chronique. Ed. Zotenberg. Paris. 1883.
Jornandes.
Romana et Getica. Ed. Mommsen. Berlin. 1882.
Josephus, Flavius.
Opera. Ed. Bekker. Leipzig. 1855–56.
Isidorus Hispalensis [Sanctus].
Opera omnia. Ed. Migne. Paris. 1850.
Itinerarium Antonini.
Ed. Parthey and Pinder. Berlin. 1848.
ʿIzz ed-Dîn Ibn el-Aṯîr [cited as Ibn el-Aṯîr].
Chronicon quod perfectissimum (el-Kamil) inscribitur. Ed. Tornberg. Leyden. 1851–76.
Jubainville, H. d’A. de.
Notice sur les Celtes d’Espagne. In *Compte Rendu de l’Acad. des Inscript.* sér. iv. vol. xviii. (1890) p. 219 *sqq.*
Junioris Philosophi Orbis descriptio. In *Geogr. Graeci Min.* vol. ii.
Justinus.
Historiae Philippicae libri xliv. Ed. Frotscher. Leipzig. 1827 *sqq.*
Juvenalis, D. Junius.
Satyrarum libri v. Ed. Hermann. Leipzig. 1865.

Karutz, P.
Die afrikanischen Bogen Pfeile und Köcher im Lübecker Museum, etc. Lübeck. 1900.
Keane, A. H.
Africa (I). 2nd ed. London. 1907.
King, W. J. Harding.
A search for the masked Tawareks. London. 1903.
Kumm, H. K. W.
From Hausaland to Egypt. London. 1910.
el-Ḳuran.
Corani textus arabicus, etc. 3rd ed. Flügel. Leipzig. 1869.

Lactantius, L. Coelius—Firmianus.
Opera quae extant. Ed. Gallaeus. Leyden. 1660.
Lampridius, Aelius.
Commodus. Alexander Severus. In *Script. Hist. August.*
Lander, R.
Records of Captain Clapperton’s last expedition to Africa. London. 1830.

Landolfus Sagax.
Historia miscella. Ed. Eyssenhardt. Berlin. 1869.
Lane, E. W.
1. The Thousand and One Nights. London. 1839 *sqq.*
2. Manners and Customs of the Modern Egyptians. 5th ed. London. 1860.
Lane-Poole, S.
History of Egypt in the Middle Ages. London.
Langhans, P.
Wandkarte von Afrika (1 : 7,500,000). Gotha. 1909.
Laquière.
Les Reconnaissances de général Servière. Paris. n.d.
LD = R. Lepsius, Denkmäler, *q.v.*
Leo Africanus (Ḥasan Ibn Moḥammad el-Wezaz el-Fasî).
1. Africae descriptio. Leyden. 1632.
2. *See* Pory, J.
Lepsius, R.
Denkmäler aus Ägypten und Äthiopien, nach den Zeichnungen der von S. M. Friederich Wilhelm IV. nach diesen Ländern gesendeten und in den Jahren 1842–45 ausgeführten wissenschaftlichen Expedition (cited as LD). Berlin. 1849 *sqq.*
Letourneux, A. *See* Hanoteau, L. A.
Liber generationis. In Frick, C., *Chronica minora.*
Lieblein, J. D. C.
Notice sur les monuments égyptiens trouvés en Sardaigne. In the *Forhandliger i Videnskabs-Selskabet i Christiania*, No. viii. (1879).
Littmann, E.
1. Zur Entzifferung der Safâ-Inschriften. Leipzig. 1901.
2. L'Origine de l'alphabet libyen. In the *Journ. Asiat.* sér. x. tome iv. p. 423 *sqq.* 1904.
Livi, R.
Antropometria militare (I). Rome. 1896.
Livius, T.
Rerum Romanorum ab urbe condita libri. Ed. Alschefski. Berlin. 1841 *sqq.*
Lucanus, M. Annaeus.
Pharsalia . . . cum scholiaste hucusque inedito, etc. Ed. Oudendorp. Leyden. 1728.
Lucianus.
1. De dipsadibus. In *Opera*, vol. iii. Ed. Jacobitz. Leipzig. 1887.
2. Navigium. In *Opera*, vol. viii., *ed. cit.*
[Lucianus.]
De astrologia. In *Opera*, vol. ii., *ed. cit.*
Lucretius Carus, T.
De rerum natura. Ed. Bernays. Leipzig. 1857.
Lutatius.
Scholia in Lucan. Pharsal. *See* Lucanus, M. Annaeus.
[Lydus.], Joannes Laurentius.
Opera quae extant. Ed. Bekker. Bonn. 1837.
Lyon, G. F.
Narrative of travels in Northern Africa. London. 1821.

Macan, R. W. *See* Herodotus (2).
MacIver, D. R., and Wilkin, A.
Libyan Notes. London. 1901.
MacIver, D. R., and Woolley.
1. Areika. Philadelphia. 1909.
2. Buhen. Philadelphia. 1912.
Macler, F. *See* Dussaud, R.
Macrobius.
Saturnalia, etc. Ed. 2. Eyssenhardt. Leipzig. 1893.
Mahaffy, J. P.
The Empire of the Ptolemies. London. 1901.
el-Maḳdîsî. *See* el-Moḳaddasî, Abu ʿAbd Allah.
el-Maḳrîzî, Taḳî ed-Dîn Abu 'l-ʿAbbas Aḥmed [cited as el-Maḳrîzî]. Ueber die in Aegypten eingewanderten arabischen Staemme. Ed. Wüstenfeld. Göttingen. 1847.
el-Malekî.
Riaḏ en-Nofus.
Mallet, D.
Le Culte de Neit à Saïs. Paris. 1888.
Mandoul, J.
De Synesio Ptolemensi episcopo et Pentapoleos defensore. Paris. 1899.
Manetho. *See* Fruin, R. J.
Marcellinus, Ammianus.
Rerum gestarum libri quae supersunt. Ed. Gardthausen. Leipzig. 1874.
Marcellinus [Comes].
Chronicon. Ed. Scaliger, J. J., in *Thesaur. Temp.*
Marcianus Heracleensis.
Periplus Maris Externi. In *Geogr. Graeci Min.*
Marcus, L.
Histoire des Wandales. Paris. 1836.
Marinus Tyrius.
Fragmenta ap. Ptolem. Geogr.
Martha, J.
L'Art étrusque. Paris. 1889.
Martin, S.
1. Aufsatz über das silphium. In the *Monde Pharmaceutique*, Paris, Sept. 20, 1874.
2. Note sur le prétendu silphium Cyrenaicum. In the *Bullet. génér. thérap. méd. chirurg.* Paris, vol. xci. 1876, p. 23 *sq.*
Maspero, G.
1. Études égyptiennes. Paris. 1879 *sqq.*
2. Le Nom d'un des chiens d'Antouf. In *RT*, xxi. (1899) p. 136.
3. Études de mythologie et d'archéologie égyptienne. Paris. 1893 *sqq.*
4. Le Tombeau de Montouhikhopshouf. Le Tombeau de Nakhti. In the *Mém. de la mission archéol. française*, v. fasc. 3. Paris. 1894.
5. The Passing of the Empires. New York. 1900.
6. The Struggle of the Nations. New York. 1900.
7. The Dawn of Civilization. New York. 1901.
Masqueray, E.
1. Dictionnaire français-touareg. (Dialecte des Taïtoq.) Paris. 1893.
2. Observations grammaticales sur la grammaire touareg et textes de la tamahaq des Taïtoq. Paris. 1896 *sq.*
3. Le Djebel Chechar. In the *Revue Africaine*, 1878.

Maternus, I. Firmicus.
De errore profanarum religionum, etc. In the *Varior.* ed. Minucius Felix. Leyden. 1709.
Matheseos libri viii. Ed. princ. Venice. 1497.
Mathuisieulx, H. M. de.
Rapport sur une mission scientifique en Tripolitaine. Paris. 1904.
Maximus Tyrius.
Dissertationes. Ed. Reiske. Leipzig. 1774 *sq.*
Mehlis, C.
Die Berberfrage. Braunschweig. 1909.
Meinhof, C.
Die Sprachen der Hamiten. Hamburg. 1912.
Mela, Pomponius.
De chorographia. [De situ orbis.] Ed. Frick. Leipzig. 1880.
Mélix, C. L.
L'Interprétation de quelques inscriptions libyques. [Reprinted from *Bullet. de l'Acad. d'Hippone*, 1891–92, No. 25.] Bône. 1892.
Meltzer, O.
Geschichte der Karthager. Berlin. 1879 *sqq.*
Mercier, E.
Histoire de l'établissement des Arabes dans l'Afrique septentrionale. Constantine. [1875.]
Mercier, G.
Les Divinités libyques. In the *Recueil des notices de la Soc. Arch. de Const.* xxxiv. (1900) p. 177 *sqq.*
Meyer, E.
Geschichte des Altertums. 2nd ed. Berlin, etc. 1909.
Miller, C.
Die Weltkarte des Castorius genannt die peutinger'sche Tafel. Einleitender Text. . . . Ravensburg. 1887.
Milne, J. G.
A History of Egypt under Roman rule. London. 1898. Vol. v. of W. M. F. Petrie, No. 5.
Minucius Felix, M.
Octavius. Ed. Ernesti. Langsall. 1760.
el-Moḳaddasî [or el-Maḳdîsî], Abu ʿAbd Allah [cited as el-Moḳaddasî].
Descriptio imperii Moslemici. Ed. de Goeje. Leyden. 1876.
Mommsen, T.
Römische Geschichte. Ed. 7. Berlin. 1881–85.
Morcelli, S. A.
Africa Christiana. Brescia. 1816 *sq.*
Moschus, Joannes.
Pratum spirituale [Λειμωνάριον]. Ed. Migne. Paris. 1850.
Motylinski, A. de C. *See* Calassanti-Motylinski, A. de.
Movers, F. C.
Die Phönizier. Bonn. 1841–56.
Muenter, F. C. C. H.
Religion der Katharger. Copenhagen. 1816.
Müller, C.
1. Tabulae in geographos Graecos minores. Paris. 1855. Part of *Geogr. Graeci Min.*
2. Tabulae in Claudii Ptolemaei geographiam xxxvi. Paris. 1901.
3. *See* Ptolemaeus, Claudius.
4. See *FHG.*
5. See *Geogr. Graeci Min.*
Müller, C. L.
Numismatique de l'ancienne Afrique. Copenhagen. 1860–74.
Müller, W. M.
1. Anmerkungen zum Siegeshymnus des Merneptaḥ. In the *RT*, xx. (1898) p. 31 *sq.*
2. Asien und Europa nach altägyptischen Denkmälern. Leipzig. 1893.
3. Egyptological Researches (II). Washington. 1910.

Nachtigal, G.
Săhără und Sûdân. Berlin. 1879.
Nardin, E.
Maroc-Algérie-Tunisie. Carte politique et physique. 1 : 2,700,000. Paris. n.d.
en-Naṣîr, Maḥommad Abu Ras Aḥmed.
Description de l'Isle de Djerba. Trans. Exiga *dit* Kayser. Tunis. 1884.
Naville, E.
1. Figurines égyptiennes de l'époque archaïque. In *RT*, xxi. (1899) p. 212 *sqq.* ; xxii. (1900) p. 65 *sqq.*
2. Le Dieu de l'oasis de Jupiter Ammon. In the *Compte Rendu de l'Acad. des Inscript.* 1906, p. 25 *sqq.*
Nemesianus, M. Aurelius Olympius.
Cynegetica. Ed. Haupt. Leipzig. 1838.
Nepos, Cornelius.
De viris illustribus. Ed. Gitlbauer. Freiburg. 1883.
Neumann, R.
1. Afrika westlich vom Nil nach Herodot. Halle. [1892.]
2. Nordafrika (mit Ausschluss des Nilgebiets) nach Herodot. Leipzig. 1892.
Newberry, P. E.
Beni Hasan. London. 1893 *sqq.*
Nicephorus Blemmyda.
Geographia synoptica. In *Geographi Graeci Minores.* Ed. Bernhardy. Leipzig. 1828. (Vol. i. p. 404 *sqq.*) [Also in *Geogr. Graeci Min.* vol. ii.]
Nicephorus Callistus Xanthopulus.
Historia ecclesiastica. Ed. Migne. Paris. 1865.
Nicolaus Damascenus.
1. *Fragmenta*, in *FHG*, vol. iii.
2. *See* Cragius, N.
Nonnus of Panopolis.
Dionysiaca. Ed. Marcellus. Paris. 1856.
Notitia dignitatum et administrationum omnium tam civilium quam militarium in partibus orientis, etc. Ed. Böcking. Bonn. 1839–53.

Obsequens, I.
Quae supersunt ex libro de prodigiis. Ed. Oudendorp. Leyden. 1720.
Oppianus.
Cynegetica. Ed. Boudreaux. Paris. 1908.
Oribasius.
Collecta medicinalia, etc. Ed. Bussemaker and Daremberg. Paris. 1851 *sqq.*
Origo humani generis. In Frick, C., *Chronica minora.*

Orosius.
Historiarum adversus paganos libri vii. Ed. Zangemeister. Vienna. 1882.
Oudney [Doctor]. *See* Denham, D.
Ovidius, P. Naso.
Opera omnia. Ed. Burmann. Amsterdam. 1727.

Pacho, J. R.
Relation d'un voyage dans la Marmarique, etc. Paris. 1827.
Pallary, P.
Instructions pour les recherches préhistoriques dans le nord-ouest de l'Afrique. Algiers. 1909.
P.Am.Ph.S. = *Proceedings of the American Philosophical Society.* (Philadelphia.)
Park, M.
Travels in the interior of Africa. Ed. J. M. Dent & Co. London. [1907.]
Parthey, G. F. C.
Der Orakel und die Oase des Ammon. Berlin. 1852.
Partsch, J.
Die Berbern in der Dichtung des Corippus. Breslau. 1896. Extract from *Satura Viadrina.*
Pausanias.
Descriptio Graeciae. Ed. Spiro. Leipzig. 1903.
Perrot, G. and Chipiez, C.
Histoire de l'art, etc. Paris. 1882 *sqq.*
Perroud, C.
De Syrticis emporiis. Paris. 1881.
Petrie, W. M. F.
1. Racial photographs from the Egyptian monuments. London. n.d.
2. Royal Tombs, etc. London. 1900 *sq.*
3. Illahun, Kahun, and Gurob. London. 1891.
4. Diospolis Parva. London. 1901.
5. A History of Egypt. London. 1894 *sqq.*
6. Athribis. London. 1908.
7. Koptos. London. 1896.
Petrie, W. M. F., and Duncan, J. G.
Hyksos and Israelite cities. [Double volume: *Egypt. Res. Acct.*] London. 1906.
Petrie, W. M. F. and others.
Gizeh and Rifeh. London. 1907.
Petronius [Arbiter], T.
Satirae. Ed. 3. Buecheler. Berlin. 1882.
Philistus.
Fragmenta in *FHG*, vol. i.
Philostorgius [Cappadox].
Historia ecclesiastica. Ed. Migne. Paris. 1858.
Philostratus [Senior].
Philostratorum quae supersunt omnia. Ed. Olearius. Leipzig. 1709.
Piette, E.
1. Les Galets coloriés du Mas d'Azil. In *Anth.* vii. (1896) p. 386 *sqq.*
2. Les Écritures de l'âge glyptique. In *Anth.* xvi. (1905) p. 1 *sqq.*
Pindarus.
Carmina. Ed. Schroeder. Leipzig. 1900.
Piquet, V.
Les Civilisations de l'Afrique du Nord. Paris. 1909.
Plato.
Opera. Ed. Stallbaum. Leipzig. 1821–25.
Plinius, C. Secundus [Senior].
Naturalis historiae libri xxxvii. Ed. Janus. Leipzig. 1870 *sq.*
Plutarchus.
1. Vitae parallelae. Ed. Sintenis. Leipzig. 1879 *sqq.*
2. Über Isis und Osiris. Ed. G. Parthey. Berlin. 1850.
Poinssot, L.
In *Nouvelles Archives*, xiii. (1906) p. 155 *sqq.*
Poittier, E.
Vases antiques du Louvre (II). Paris. 1901.
Polemon.
Physiognomonicon. Ed. Franz in *Script. Physiog. Vet.* Altenburg. 1780.
Pollio, Trebellius.
Claudius. In *Script. Hist. August.*
Polyaenus.
Strategematon. Ed. Melber. Leipzig. 1887.
Polybius.
Historiae. Ed. Büttner-Wobst and Dindorf. Leipzig. 1866 *sqq.*
Porcher, E. A. *See* Smith, R. M.
Pory, J.
The history and description of Africa . . . by . . . Leo Africanus, done into English, etc. Ed. Brown, R. London. 1896.
See Leo Africanus.
Primaudaie, E. de la.
Le Littoral de la Tripolitaine. Paris. n.d.
Priscianus.
Periegesis. Ed. Krehl. Leipzig. 1819–20.
Priscus Panites.
Fragmenta in *FHG*, vol. iv.
Proclus.
In Timaeum Platonis. Ed. Diehl. Leipzig. 1903 *sqq.*
Procopius.
Opera. Ed. Dindorf. Bonn. 1833 *sqq.*
Provotelle, P.
Étude sur la Tamazir't ou Zénatia de Qalaât. es-Sened. Paris. 1911.
PSBA = *Proceedings of the Society of Biblical Archaeology* (London).
Ptolemaeus, Claudius.
Geographia. Ed. Müller. Paris. 1883–1901.

Quatrefages, J. L. A. de—de Bréau (and Hamy, E. T.).
Histoire générale des races humaines. Paris. 1887–89.
Quibell, J. E.
1. Hierakonpolis. London. 1900 (I); 1902 (II).
2. Archaic objects. [In *Cairo Cat.*] Cairo. 1904–5.

Rainaud, A.
Quid de natura et fructibus Cyrenaicae Pentapoli antiqua monumenta . . . nobis tradiderint. Paris. 1894.

Ravenna, Anonymous of. *See* Geographus [Anonymus] Ravennas.
Rawlinson, G. and H. *See* Herodotus (1).
Reboud, V.
Recueil d'inscriptions libyco-berbères. [Extr. from the *Mém. de la Soc. Franç. de Numis. et d'Arch.*] Paris. 1870.
Reclus, E.
Nouvelle Géographie universelle [vols. x., xi.]: L'Afrique septentrionale. Paris. 1885–86.
Regny, P. V. de.
Libya Italica. Terreni ed acque, vita e coltura, etc. Milan. 1913.
Reinach, S.
Répertoire des vases peints grecs et étrusques. Paris. 1899 *sqq.*
See Tissot, C.
Reisner, G. A.
1. Work of the expedition of the University of California at Naga ed-Dêr. In the *Annales*, v. 1904. p. 105 *sqq.*
2. Amulets. [In *Cairo Cat.*] Cairo. 1907.
3. The Archaeological Survey of Nubia (I). Cairo. 1910.
Renan, J. E.
1. Histoire des langues sémitiques (I). Ed. 4. Paris. 1863.
2. La Société berbère. In the *Rev. des Deux Mondes.* 1873. Période ii., tome 107, p. 138 *sqq.*
Renier, C. A. L.
Inscriptions romaines de l'Algérie, etc. Paris. 1855–86.
Renouf, P. le P.
Who were the Libyans? In *PSBA*, vol. xiii. (1891) p. 599 *sqq.*
Ridgeway, W.
The Origin and Influence of the Thoroughbred Horse. Cambridge. 1905.
Rochemonteix, M. de.
Essai sur les rapports grammaticaux qui existent entre l'Égyptien et le Berbère. [In edit. collect. works by G. Maspero, *Biblioth. Egyptolog.* tome iii.] Paris. 1894.
Rohlfs, F. G.
1. Reise durch Marokko, etc. Bremen. 1868.
2. Das Silphium. In Österreich. Monatsschr. f. d. Orient (Vienna), vol. xvii. (1891) p. 23 *sq.*
Roscher, W. H.
Ausführliches Lexikon der griechischen und römischen Mythologie. Leipzig. 1884 *sqq.*
Rosellini, I.
I monumenti dell' Egitto e della Nubia, etc. Pisa. 1832 *sqq.*
Rossberg, W.
Quaestiones de rebus Cyrenarum provinciae Romanae. Frankenberg. N. d.
Rougé, J. de.
Géographie ancienne de la Basse Égypte. Paris. 1891.
RT = Recueil de travaux relatifs à la philologie et à l'archéologie égyptiennes et assyriennes pour servir de bulletin à la mission française du Caire. Paris. 1870 *sqq.*
Ruinart, T.
Acta martyrum, etc. Ed. Paris. 1802–3.

Sainte-Marie, E. de.
Mission à Carthage. Paris. 1884.
Saint Martin, L. V. de.
Le Nord de l'Afrique dans l'antiquité, etc. Paris. 1863.
Sallustius, C. Crispus.
Jugurtha. Ed. Kritz. Leipzig. 1834.
Sarasin, P. *See* Vischer, H.
Saulcy, M. de.
Observations sur l'alphabet tifinag. In the *Journ. Asiat.* iv. ser., vol. xiii. (1849) p. 247 *sqq.*
Scaliger, J. J.
Thesaurus temporum. 2nd ed. Amsterdam. 1658.
Schaff, P.
History of the Christian church. New York. 1886–1910.
Schirmer, H.
De nomine et genere populorum qui Berberi vulgo dicuntur. Paris. 1892.
Schneider, W.
Die Religion der afrikanischen Naturvölker. Münster i. W. 1891.
Scholz, J. M. A.
Reise in die Gegend zwischen Alexandrien und Parätonium. Leipzig. 1822.
Schröder, P.
Die phönizische Sprache, etc. Halle. 1869.
Schweinfurth, G.
Artes Africanae. Leipzig, etc. 1875.
Scriptores Historiae Augustae. Ed. Peter. Leipzig. 1884.
Scylax.
Periplus. In *Geog. Graec. Min.* vol. i.
Sedira, Belkassem Ben.
Cours de langue kabyle. Algiers. 1887.
Selden, J.
De diis Syris syntagmata II. Ed. Beyer. Leipzig. 1672.
Sergi, G.
1. The Mediterranean race. London. 1901.
2. Africa: antropologia della stirpe camitica. Turin. 1897.
Servius.
Commentar. in Vergilii carmina. Ed. Thilo and Hagen. Leipzig. 1878–1902.
Sethe, K. H.
Das ägyptische Verbum im Altägyptischen, Neuägyptischen und Koptischen. Leipzig. 1899–1902.
Seton-Karr, H. W.
Fayoom flint implements. In *Annales*, v. (1904) p. 145 *sqq.*
Shaw, T.
Travels, or observations, relating to several parts of Barbary and the Levant. 3rd ed. Edinburgh. 1808.
Shelley, G. E.
Handbook to the birds of Egypt. London. 1872.
Sidonius, C. Sollius Modestus Apollinaris.
Opera. Ed. Savaron. Paris. 1609.

Silius Italicus, C.
De bello Punico. Ed. Ruperti and Lemaire. Paris. 1823.
Siret, L.
L'Espagne préhistorique. Paris, 1893.
de Slane, W. MacG.
Histoire des Berbères . . . par Ibn-Khaldoun. Algiers. 1852–56.
(*See* Ibn Ḫaldun, Abu Zayd ʿAbd er-Raḥman.)
Smith, G. A.
Note in *Palestine Exploration Fund Quarterly Statement*, xxxvii. (Oct. 1905) p. 282 *sqq*.
Smith, G. E.
The Ancient Egyptians and their Influence upon the Civilization of Europe. London. 1911.
Smith, R. M., and Porcher, E. A.
History of the recent discoveries at Cyrene, etc. London. 1864.
Smith, W. R.
Religion of the Semites. 3rd ed. London. 1907.
Solinus, C. I.
Collectanea rerum memorabilium. Ed. Mommsen. Berlin. 1895.
Sophocles.
Tragoediae. Ed. Jebb. Cambridge. 1897.
Sourdille, C.
Hérodote et la religion de l'Égypte. Paris. 1910.
Spartianus, Aelius.
Hadrianus. In *Script. Hist. August.*
Septimius Severus. In *Script. Hist. August.*
Geta. In *Script. Hist. August.*
Stadiasmus Maris Magni. In *Geogr. Graec. Min.* vol. i.
Statius, P. Papinius.
Opera quae extant. Ed. Dübner. Paris. 1838–45.
Steindorff, G.
Durch die libysche Wüste zur Amonsoase. Bielefeld, etc. 1904.
Stephanus Byzantinus.
Ethnica. Ed. Westermann. Leipzig. 1839.
Strabo.
1. Rerum geographicarum libri xvii. Ed. Casaubon. Paris. 1620.
2. Strabonis geographica. Ed. Müller and Dübner. Paris. 1853–58.
Suetonius, C. Tranquillus.
De XII. Caesaribus. Variorum ed. Utrecht. 1708.
Synesius.
Opera. Ed. Migne. Paris. 1859.

Tabula Peutingeriana. *See* (1) E. Desjardins; (2) C. Miller.
Tacitus, C. Cornelius.
Opera. Ed. Oberlin. Leipzig. 1801.
Talmud, The Jerusalem. Ed. Žitomir. 1866.
Terentius Afer, Publius.
Comoediae. Ed. Dziatzko. Leipzig. 1884.
Tertullianus, Q. Septimus Florens.
Opera omnia. Ed. Semler. Halle. 1770–76.
Theophanes.
Chronographia. Ed. Classen. Bonn. 1839.
Theophrastus.
1. De lapidibus. Ed. Meursius. Leyden.
2. Historia plantarum. Ed. Wimmer. Leipzig. 1854.
Theopompus.
Fragmenta, in *FHG*, vol. i.
Thrige, J. P.
Res Cyrenensium. Copenhagen. 1828.
Thucydides.
Historiae. Ed. Jones. Oxford. [1909 *sq.*]
et-Tiĝanî. [Sheykh.]
Voyage dans la régence du Tunis. Trans. Rousseau. 1853.
Tissot, C. J.
1. De Tritonide lacu. Dijon. 1863.
2. Sur les monuments mégalithiques et les populations blondes du Maroc. In *Rev. d'Anth.* v. 3 (1876).
Tissot, C. J., and Reinach, S.
Géographie comparée de la province romaine d'Afrique. Paris. 1884–88.
Totius orbis descriptio. In Aethicus. Ed. Baudet.
Tour, E. du.
Note in *Compte Rendu de l'Acad. des Inscr.*, 1858, p. 152 *sq.*
Toutain, J.
1. De Saturni dei in Africa Romana cultu. Paris. 1894.
2. Nouvelles Observations sur l'inscription d'Henchir Mettich. In *Nouvelle Rev. Hist. de Droit franç. et étrang.* vol. xxiii. (1899).
Tremearne, A. J. N.
Hausa Superstitions and Customs, *etc.* London. 1913.
TSGS = Topographical Section, General Staff (British Army).
1. Map No. 1539–7. Tripoli. 1 : 1,000,000.
2. Map No. 1539–14. Sella. 1 : 1,000,000.
3. Map No. 1539–15. Aujila. 1 : 1,000,000.
4. Map No. 1539–8. Ben-Ghazi. 1 : 1,000,000.
Tylor, E. B.
Primitive Culture. 4th ed. London. 1903.
Tylor, J. J.
Wall drawings . . . of el-Kab: the tomb of Paheri. London. 1895.

Valerius Maximus.
Exemplorum memorabilium libri ix. Ed. Var. Leyden. 1670.
Vater, F.
Triton und Euphemos. Kasan. 1849.
Vaux, C. de.
La Langue étrusque: sa place parmi les langues. Paris. 1911.
Vaux, W. S. W.
Inscriptions in the Phoenician character now deposited in the British Museum, London. 1863.
Vegetius Renatus, P.
Ars veterinaria sive mulomedicina. Ed. Schneider. Leipzig. 1794 *sq.* [In *Script. Rei Rusticae* iv.]
Vergilius Maro, Publius.
Opera. Ed. Heyne. Leipzig, etc. 1830–41.
Vibius Sequester.
De fluminibus, fontibus, etc. Ed. Oberlin. Strassburg a. R. 1778.

Victor, S. Aurelius.
De Caesaribus. Ed. Picklmayr. Leipzig. 1911.
Victor Vitensis.
Historia persecutionis Africanae provinciae. Ed. Petschenig. Vienna. 1881.
Vischer, H.
Across the Sahara from Tripoli to Bornu [With appendix (II) by P. Sarasin on the neolithic axes, etc., found on the march]. London. 1910.
Viviani, D.
Florae Libycae specimen, etc. Genoa. 1824.
Vopiscus, Flavius.
Aurelianus. In *Script. Hist. August.*
Probus. In *Script. Hist. August.*

Unger, G. F.
Chronologie des Manetho. Berlin. 1867.

Walters, H. B.
History of ancient Pottery. London. 1905.
Weisgerber, H.
Les Blancs d'Afrique. Paris. 1910.
Welcker, F. G.
Griechische Götterlehre. Göttingen. 1857–63.
Wiedemann, A.
1. Geschichte Aegyptens von Psammetich I. bis auf Alexander den Grossen. Leipzig. 1880.
2. Stelae of Libyan origin. In *PSBA*, xi. (1889), p. 227.
3. Religion der alten Ägypter. Münster i. W. 1890.
Wilken, G. A.
Handleiding voor de vergelijkende volkenkunde van Nederlandsch-Indië. Leyden. 1893.
Wilkinson, J. G.
Manners and customs of the ancient Egyptians. Ed. S. Birch. London. 1878.
See Herodotus (1).
Woenig, F.
Die Pflanzen im alten Aegypten. Leipzig. 1886.
Wolff, J. G.
De principibus reipublicae Carthaginiensis magistratibus. Bonn. 1857.
Woolley, C. L. *See* MacIver, D. R.

el-Yaḳubî, Aḥmed Ibn Abî Ya'ḳub Ibn Waḏih el-Katib [cited as el-Ya'ḳubî].
Descriptio Al Magribi. Ed. de Goeje. Leyden. 1860.

Zeitschrift für ägyptische Sprache.
Zonaras, Ioannes.
Annales. Ed. Pinder and Büttner-Wobst. Bonn. 1841–97.
Zosimus.
Historiae. Ed. Mendelssohn. Leipzig. 1887.

PHILOLOGICAL INDEX

*
* *

᾿Αδυρμαχῖδαι, 79
ΑΛΑΔΔΕΙΡ, 231 *n.* 3
ΑΛΑΖΗ(Ρ), 231 *n.* 3
᾿Αλαζίρ, 231 *n.* 3
᾿Αμούγκα, ᾿Αμούγλα, ᾿Αμούνκλα, 197
᾿Αμοῦν, 190 *n.* 10
[ΑΝ]ΤΑΙΟΣ, 260
᾿Απτούχου ἱερόν, 185
῞Αρπυιαι, ἁρπάζειν, 82
᾿Ασβέται, 47
᾿Ασβύται, 47
ΑΥΣ-ι-Γ-Δ-αι, 52 *n.* 5
*Αὐσουρίανοι, 68
ΑΥΣ-Χ-ιΣ-αι, 52 *n.* 5
ΑΥΣ-Χ-ιΤ-αι, 52 *n.* 5
Αὐτούχου, 185

B permuting to M, 62, 63
Βάκαλες, 48
Βαλάγραι, 185
Βάλις, 185
Βάνδιλοι = Vandali, 67
Βόρυες, 93 *n.* 4
Βάττος, 116 *n.* 2
Βυζ-, 54
Βύζαντες, 55

Γ permuting to B, 54, 55
*Γαμφάσαντες, 53
Γαυγάμηλα, 233 *n.* 6
ΓΒ = ΚΠ, 63
Γυζ- and Ζυγ-, 52 *n.* 3
Γυζ-, Ζυγ- and Βυζ-, 54
Γύζαντες, 55

δάκρυ = lachryma, 76 *n.* 1
Δάρνις, 79
τὸ Δέρριν ὄρος, 79
δίκτυες, 93 *n.* 3
Δῦριν, 79

Ζαβυ- for Βυζα-, 53 *n.* 2
Ζύγαντες, 55

-ιδαι, 77
ἴστε = ἴδ-τε, 47
-ιται, 77

*Κιδαμήνσιοι, 63

λ = ρ, 64
Λάβειν, Λάβιειμ, Λάβιεμ, 258
Λεβανθ- (= Leuanth-) = Lag(u)ant-, 67
Λευα- = Λεβα-, 67
Λευαθ- = Legath-, 67
Λιβυάρχαι, 62 *n.* 1
Λίβυες, 46, 258
Λιβύη, xix *n.* 1
M permuting to B, 62, 63
Μάζικες, 42 *n.* 9
*Μασσαχῖται, 60
Μάχλυες, 79
Μάχμες for Μάχλυες, 52 *n.* 19; cf. 53 *n.* 1
Μάχρυες, 79
μεγαλ-, 79 *n.* 7
μέσος ψάμμος, 52 *n.* 8
*Μιαίδιοι, 64

νομάζειν and Numidae, 255 *n.* 2

Π not known in Berber, 63

Ρουσάδειρον, 79

Σαϊοί for Σακοί, 64 *n.* 3
Σ-]αΝαΒυΚ- = Anabuc-, 63
*Σελαιῶνες, 63

*Ταυταμαίους, 65 *n.* 6

Φαλάκρα, 185

Ψ unknown in Berber, 66

*
* *

א, ا

اباد, 82
ابايكور, 81
ابر, 84 *n.* 1
ابري, 82
ابشي, 83
ات, 89 *n.* 4
ادرار, 79
دو, 78
ار(دار), 83
ارس, 79
ازار, 83
ازگا, 78
ازوا, 78
اژنا, 80
اشراف, 256
افلك, 81
افل, 78
اك, 79
اكبار, 80
اليغ, 79
امان, 82
امت, 82
امزا, 82
امزوارو, 83
امزوغ, 82
امژ, 81
امغار, 79
אמון, 198 *n.* 4
انع, 78
اوذ, 78
اوسر, 78
اولاد, 89 *n.* 4
ايت, 89 *n.* 4

ב, ب

בד-מלקרת, 184 *n.* 4
برقة, 66 *n.* 12
بريس, 12 *n.* 3
הַלְהָ[תִ]ים, 258 *n.* 4
בַּעַל, 198
בַּעַל-חַמָּן, 198 *n.* 5
בַּעַל-קֶרֶן, 185
בַּעְלָ[תִ]ם, 258 *n.* 4
بنو بركين, 70
بنو بلار, 69
بنو بلاين, 69
بنو حديدي, 70
بنو دصّر, 71
بنو عابدة, 70
بنو قطوفة, 70
بنو كزرون, 71
بنو مجدول, 70
بنو مالو, 70
بنو موختر, 70
بنو موصالّة, 70
بنو الواسة, 70
بنو ياحية, 70
بني, 89 *n.* 4
بير الباشر, 198 *n.* 2

ת, ت

تكابت, 79
تل امون, 198
تكول, 79
تمارت, 84 *n.* 1
تمتانت, 82
تمتانت, 82
تموغر, 79

* * *

, 147

, 47, 80

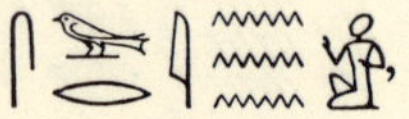, 82

, 83

, 48 *n.* 5

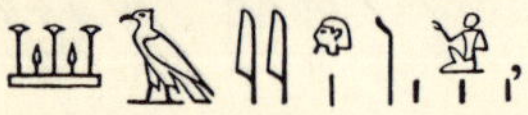, 47

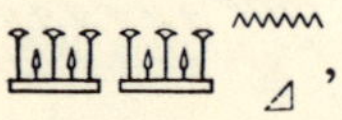, 227 *n.* 3

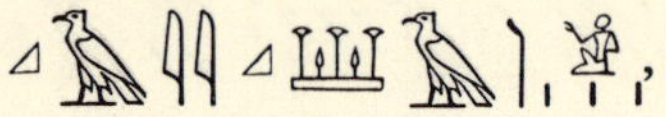, 47

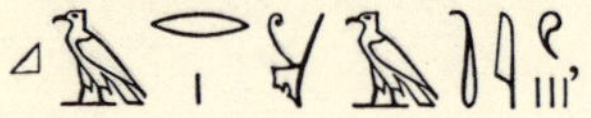, 122

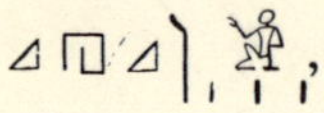, 47

, 80

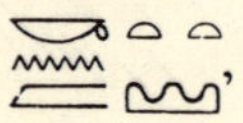, 48 *n.* 5

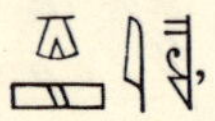, 82

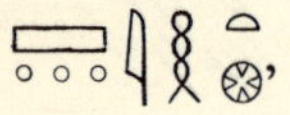, 48 *n.* 5

, 82

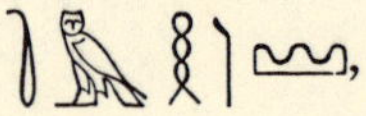, 46

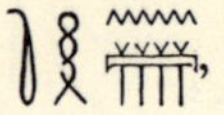, 227 *n.* 3

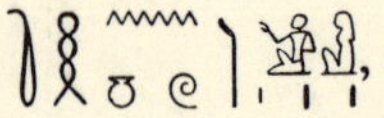, 46

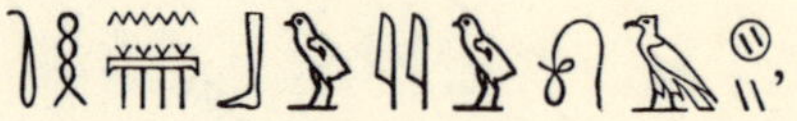, 227 *n.* 3

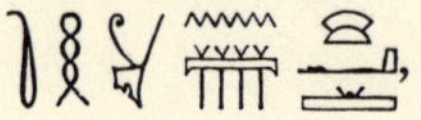, 227 *n.* 3

, 227 *n.* 3

, 80 *n.* 6

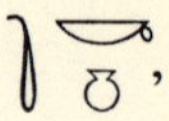, 194

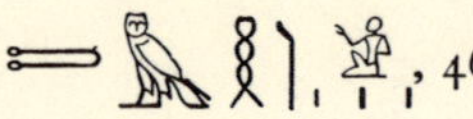, 46

, 46

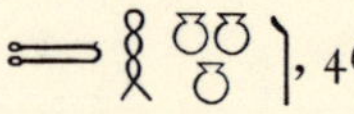, 46

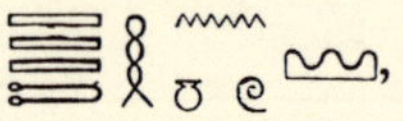, 46

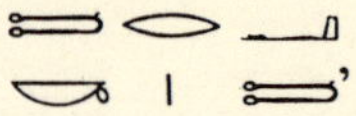, 227 *n.* 3

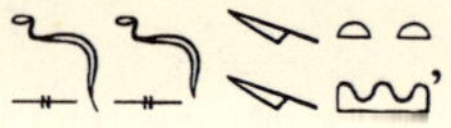, 48 *n.* 5

GENERAL INDEX

Ababdah of Upper Egypt, 245
'Abd Allah Ibn Ṣaliḥ, quoted, 240
Abel, C., cited, 80 *n.* 5
Abuḳîr, 222 *n.* 5
Abu 'l Ḥasan, cited, 208 *n.* 5
Abu 'l Maḥasîn, 69, 240
Abu Naym, 14, 30
Abu Simbel reliefs, 211, 214, 250
Abusîr reliefs, 131, 132, 134
Abu'Ungar, oasis of, 11 ; ruins at, 32, 32 *n.* 1
Abu Zuba'ah, 175
Abyssinia, absence of blonds in, 41
Abyssinians, 45
Acacia, 27
Accaron, 186
Acesander, quoted, 116 *n.* 2
Achaei, 216 *n.* 7
Achaemenes the Satrap, slain by Inarus, 231
"Achor," 186
Adamantius, quoted, 44 *n.* 1
Adanson, M., cited, 100
Adeben, 152
Adicran, chief of Asbystae, 230
Adjectives, in Berber, 74
Admiralty, British, Charts, 2 *nn.* 1 and 2, 4 *nn.* 1 and 3
Adyrmachidae, 101 *n.* 1 ; claimed descent from Amphithemis, 257 ; curved swords of, 147 ; dress of, 118 ; hair of, 133 ; leg-rings worn by women, 133, 144 ; marriage customs of, 111 ; nomadism of, 91 ; placed by Herodotus, 51 ; by Pliny, 57 ; by Ptolemy, 61, 64 ; by Scylax, 54 ; ethnic stability of, 71
Aedemon, revolt of, 234
Aegis of Athena, 128
Aelian, cited, 93, 97, 121 *n.* 4, 179 *n.* 10, 180 *nn.* 1 and 6, 181, 188 ; quoted, 95 *n.* 2
Aerolith, at Tementit, 173
Aeschylus, cited, 201
Aesculapius, cult of, at Balagrae, 185
Aethicus, cited, 42, 69 ; quoted, 42 *n.* 9
Aethiopia, circumcision in, 140 ; confused with Libya by Diodorus, 190 *n.* 8 ; fish-taboo in, 141 ; ivory and hides from, 102 ; matriarchate in, 112 ; Nygbeni in, 63
Aethiopian troglodytes, 103
Aethiopians, confused with Libyans by Herodotus, 230 *n.* 5 ; arrows of, 145 ; black and woolly-haired, 51 ; dispute with Libyans, 49 ; early representations of, on Greek vases, 261 ; eat locusts, 100 *n.* 16 ; some ignorant of bows, 248
Aethiopians, Atlantic, choice of kings among, 114 *n.* 2
"Aethiopians, White," 60. *See* Leucaethiopes
Aethiopic origin of Libyan writing not proved, 85
Aezari, placed by Ptolemy, 62
Africa, open to dispossessed Europeans, 226 ; outbreaks in Roman, 233 ; Sallust's account of the peopling of, 255 *sq.*
Africa Minor, defined, xxi ; ethnic shift toward Egypt from, 226
Africa, North, ram revered in, 197
Africa, North-western, megaliths in, 160
Africa, South, Bushman drawings of, 156
African, *see* Berber, Imushagh, Libyan, Nomad
Agatharchides, 179
Agathemerus, cited, 59 *n.* 1
Agathocles, levies war on Carthage, 232 ; slays Ophellas, 232
Aghlebites, 34 *n.* 1
Aghmat, rams worshipped between Sus and, 177
Aghurmî, town of, 10
Agisymba, region of, 102
Agriculture, Libyan, 98 *sq.*
Agrippinus, bishop of Carthage, 235
Agroetas, cited, 54 *n.* 2, 62, 112, 257 ; quoted, 207 *n.* 2
'*Agul*, 26
Ahmose I., Nubian campaigns of, 249
Ahmose II., rise of, 230. *See* Amasis
Aïr, Territory of, 15, 30
'Aḳabah es-Sollum = Catabathmus Major, 55
"Akel Amarig," 42 *n.* 4
Alachroas. *See* Machryes
Alasit, 234
Alazir, murdered, 231
Alele, 58, 233
Alexander in desert, 200 ; visits Ammonium, 191, 232
Alexandria, taken by 'Amr Ibn el-'Aṣî, 240
Algeria, *rigam* of, 247 ; ram-glyph at Bu 'Alem in, 196 *sq.*
El-'Alîah, mosaics at, 169
Alimentation of Eastern Libyans, 99 *sq.*
Alitemnii, choice of rulers, 114 *n.* 2
Alphabet, Libyan, distribution of, 84, 87 *sq.* ; origin of, 85 ; table of, 87
Alphabet, Tifinagh, table of, 88
Altars of the Philaeni, 55. *See* Philaenorum Arae
Altimira cave, paintings of, 157 *n.* 1
Amadah, jar-sealing from, 249
Amasis, 230 *n.* 2 ; sends Neith statue to Cyrene, 207 *n.* 1
Amazigh, side-locks worn by, 136
Amazons, 112 *sq.* ; lunate shields of, 148 *n.* 6
Ambrosius, St., cited, 203 *n.* 5
Amenhotep I., 212 *sq.* ; sends Usertesen (I.) to Libya, 212
Amenhotep III. conquers Teḥenu, 213
Amentum, use of in Eastern Libya, 146
Amenukal, 115
American army, march of, from Alexandria to Bombah, 14
Amghar, 115
Ammianus on Libyan cavalry, 151
Ammonians, placed by Herodotus, 54 ; subject to Egypt, 23
Ammonium, Cyrenaic votive columns at, 191 ; Egyptian ascendancy in, 230 ; expedition sent against, by Cambyses III., 174 ; forms of responses at, 195 ; inhabitants agriculturists, 98 ; Libyan *sacra* at, 173 ; native princes of, 230 *n.* 4 ; subject to Persia, 231 ; visited by Alexander, 232. *See* Sîwah
Amometus, 179 *n.* 8
"Amon," use of this form, 189 *n.* 5
Amon, captives presented to, 213 ; grove of, 198 *n.* 2 ; myths of the Sîwan, 189 *sq.* ; presented with captive kings by Rameses III., 224 ; priest of, in army of Hannibal, 117 ; processions in cultus of, 156 ; sites anciently named for, 197 *sq.* ; songs used in worship of, 154 ; the father of "Apollo," 187 ; worship of at Memphis, 188 *n.* 3
Amon, Theban, 191 ; annual progress of in Libya, 109 ; distinguished from *Deus Fatidicus*, 190 *sq.* ; Sheshonk and, 228
Amon-Gurzil type, 188
Amon-Re, 191 ; bark of, 194 ; hymn of triumph to, 213
Amor, king of, led captive by Rameses III., 224
Amorites, Egyptian war with, 224
Ampelius, L., cited, 189 *n.* 8 ; quoted, 187
Amphithemis, Libyan tribes claimed descent from, 257 ; mother of Psyllus, 257 ; nymph-ancestress, 112
Amr Ibn el-'Aṣî invades Egypt, 239 ; marches on Barca, 240 ; second expedition of, 240 ; makes treaty with Berbers, 240
Amulets, ram's head, 199
Anabucis, 63
Anabus, conspires with Aretaphile, 233 ; strangled, 233
Anagombri, placed by Ptolemy, 61
Anai glyphs, 103
Anastasi Papyrus, cited, 215 *n.* 1, 219
Anderson, R. G., cited, 136 ; quoted, 184
Andes, absence of blonds in, 41

THE END

Printed by R. & R. Clark, Limited, *Edinburgh.*